A New Entrepreneurial Dynamic

21st Century Startups and Small Businesses
Version 1.0

Greg Autry

A New Entrepreneurial Dynamic: 21st Century Startups and Small Businesses
Version 1.0

Greg Autry

Published by:

FlatWorld
292 Newbury Street
Suite #282
Boston, MA 02115-2832

Gen: 202201121749

Brief Contents

About the Author
Acknowledgments
Dedication
Preface
Foreword Entrepreneurs and the New Entrepreneurial Dynamic, by Randy Komisar
Chapter 1 The Entrepreneur in Context
Chapter 2 The New Entrepreneurial Dynamic
Chapter 3 Strategy: Capturing and Maintaining Competitive Advantage
Chapter 4 Opportunity Recognition
Chapter 5 Feasibility Analysis and Opportunity Evaluation
Chapter 6 Team Building and Leadership
Chapter 7 Funding
Chapter 8 Launching
Chapter 9 Brand Building
Chapter 10 Marketing
Chapter 11 Selling
Chapter 12 Operations
Chapter 13 Accounting
Chapter 14 Managing Cash Flow and Finance
Chapter 15 The Business Environment and Government
Chapter 16 Exiting and Harvest
Appendix A Final Thoughts
Index

Contents

About the Author 1

Acknowledgments 3

Dedication 5

Preface 7

Foreword Entrepreneurs and the New Entrepreneurial Dynamic, by Randy Komisar 11

Chapter 1 The Entrepreneur in Context 15

1.1 Let's Start Small 16

It's Small, but Is It a Small Business? 16

Corporate Intrapreneurship 17

The Rapid Growth Startup 18

The Main Street Entrepreneur 19

The Organic-Growth Small Businesses 19

The Buyable Startup 20

The Lifestyle Business 20

The Social Entrepreneur and Nonprofits 21

1.2 The New Entrepreneurial Dynamic—Fusion Firms, Shifters, and More 22

Fusion Firms and Shifters 22

Franchises 22

Online Stores, Apps, and the Virtual Businesses 24

1.3 Who Are the Entrepreneurs? Are You One? 25

Entrepreneurial Talent—Born or Learned? 26

Risk and Coping with the Unknown 26

The Serial Entrepreneur 27

An Ever-Changing Economy and Today's Nontraditional Entrepreneurs 29

1.4 Challenges 32

Survival 32

Who's the Boss? 34

Getting Stuck 35

Where to Start: Make a Bucket List 36

It's Not Always About You 37

Stay Healthy 38

1.5 Case Study: Tiantian, Kai, and Hip Hot Restaurant: Entrepreneurs Learn and Adapt 39

1.6 Endnotes 40

Chapter 2 The New Entrepreneurial Dynamic 41
2.1 The Stormy Seas of Commerce 42
Business Plans 42
What Is the New Entrepreneurial Dynamic? 43
Planning Depends on Forecasting 44
And Yet, There Is a Time for Everything 48
Added Monetary Value Makes an Organization a Business 48
Customers Are Required, Everything Else Is Optional 49
2.2 Uncertainty Is the New Normal 50
Risk and Reward 51
Embracing Open Innovation 52
Globalization 54
2.3 Networking Starts Before Your Business Does 55
Building a Team 55
Total Commitment, Burn Your Boat 56
Let's Go! 56
2.4 Case Study: Pivoting Pet Adoption with *Adoptimize* 58
2.5 Endnotes 60
Chapter 3 Strategy: Capturing and Maintaining Competitive Advantage 61
3.1 Being Strategic 62
Strategy, a Serious Game 62
Market Disruption 64
Objectives, Strategies, and Tactics 66
Overcoming Barriers to Entry 67
The Two Basic Strategies: Price and Differentiation 69
Let's Get Small 69
Tactics 70
3.2 Sustainable Competitive Advantage 71
Dynamic Advantage 71
Innovation Strategy 72
Operational Effectiveness Strategy 72
What Exactly Is a Market? 73
3.3 The Economic Basis of Business Strategy 75
The Supply Curve 76
What About Profits? 82
Where's the Strategy? 83
Start at the Top 85
3.4 Strategy Analysis Toolkit 87
Porter's Five Forces 87
SWOT Analysis 92
3.5 Strategic Fit 96
Sync to Market Conditions 97
Trends Matter 97
3.6 Case Study: Overcoming Barriers to Entry via Strategic Partnerships 98
3.7 Endnotes 100

Chapter 4 Opportunity Recognition 101
4.1 Searching for Ideas 102
Choosing a Destination 102
Yes, There Are Two Paths You Can Go By! 104
Customer Pain and Delight 105
4.2 The Entrepreneur as Innovator and Disrupter 107
Creative Destruction 107
Disruptive Innovation 108
Imitation and Second Mover Advantage 109
Last Mover Advantage 110
Serendipity 111
Managing Chance 112
4.3 1 + 1 = New 113
When Preparation Meets Opportunity 113
Networking with Creators 114
Open Innovation 116
External Acquisitions 117
4.4 Saving an Opportunity—Improving Existing Products or Target Markets 118
Adaptation 118
Scouring the Global Supply Chain 119
4.5 *De Novo* Industries: The Challenges of Paving a New Road 121
De Novo Industries 121
TNBT, Riding Trends While Avoiding Fads 122
Quick Opportunity Screening 123
Experience and the Power of Naivety 123
Geographic Opportunity 125
Is Buying a Franchise or Licensing for Me? 125
4.6 Case Study: Fred Ross Takes the Entrepreneurial Plunge with Deckside Pool Service 128
4.7 Endnotes 132
Chapter 5 Feasibility Analysis and Opportunity Evaluation 133
5.1 Feasibility Analysis 134
Vetting 134
Your Market and Industry 136
The Value Chain 137
Value Mismatch 139
Technical Feasibility 140
Resource Feasibility 140
Commercialization and Scale Feasibility 141
5.2 Opportunity Valuation 142
Talking to Customers 143
Customer Development 144
Beta Testing and the Minimum Viable Product 146
Safety and Environmental Concerns 147
5.3 Financial Feasibility 148

Capital Investment 149
Pricing, Margins, Affordability, and Demographics 150
5.4 Difficult Distribution Channels 152
Access Barriers 152
5.5 Does the Idea Really Fit the Entrepreneur? 154
Business-Entrepreneur Fit 155
Business Model Transformation: When Your First Idea Isn't Quite the Thing 155
5.6 Case Study: 121C, Inc.—The Skateboard MVP 157
5.7 Endnotes 158
Chapter 6 Team Building and Leadership 159
6.1 How to Entrepreneur 159
Learning Leadership Skills 160
Leadership Styles 161
The Elite Network 162
Building the Right Team 163
6.2 The Organizational Chart 165
Structure 165
Traditional Positions and Titles 167
Designing the Dynamic Team 168
6.3 Slicing the Pie and Valuing Startup Inputs 169
The Equity Split 170
Dynamic Equity Adjustment 172
Whose Intellectual Property Is It? 173
6.4 Evolving Roles as Your Business Matures 174
The Challenges of Growth 174
Culture Change and Inertia 175
Recruiting 176
Building an Ethnically Diverse or Global Team 179
Avoiding Troublesome Hires and CYA 182
Dispute Resolution 185
Layoffs Versus Sharing the Pain 185
Termination 186
Departures 186
6.5 Case Study: Brian Fitzgerald and Future Point 187
6.6 Endnotes 190
Chapter 7 Funding 191
7.1 Source of Capital 191
Early Capital 192
Determining Startup Funding Requirements 194
Personal Credit and Savings 195
The Three Fs 196
Angels 197
Venture Capitalists 199
Other Sources of Equity Capital 204

Classes of Stock 204
Crowdfunding 204
Other Prepayment Financing Schemes 207
7.2 Debt Financing—Loans 208
Small Business Bank Loans and Government Programs 208
Home Loan 209
Selecting a Bank 210
Establishing Your Business Credit 213
7.3 Case Study: Embedded Ventures 215
7.4 Endnotes 218
Chapter 8 Launching 219
8.1 Reducing Launch Risk 219
Smart Entrepreneurs Don't Seek Risk, They Manage It 220
Still Other Forms 228
Spinoffs, Distractions, and Focus 231
8.2 Getting Going 232
Leaving Your Comfy Day Job 232
Preventing a Lawsuit 234
Avoiding Disaster 234
Good Communications 235
Solid Written Agreements 236
Insurance 237
Facilities 239
8.3 Case Study: An Entrepreneurial Marketing Misfit Finds His Niche 242
8.4 Endnotes 246
Chapter 9 Brand Building 247
9.1 Product Branding 248
Perception Management 248
Defining Your Brand 249
Managing the Brand 252
Trademarks, Brandmarks, Copyright 263
9.2 Your Brand in the New Entrepreneurial Dynamic 264
Building Your Brand 265
Cashing In on Your Brand 266
9.3 Case Study: Wahoo's Tacos 269
9.4 Endnotes 270
Chapter 10 Marketing 271
10.1 Beyond Brands 272
Marketing Versus Advertising Versus Selling 272
Satisficing and Differentiating 273
Advertising Campaigns 275
The Technology Adoption Life Cycle 276
10.2 Marketing Strategies 280

Riding Your Brand Power 281
Radio and TV 281
Managing the News 283
Trade Shows 285
Social Media 287
Internet Ads 289
Traditional Print Ads 294
Marketing Integrity 296
10.3 Case Study: Building One Hot Brand 299
10.4 Endnotes 301

Chapter 11 Selling 303
11.1 The Context of Selling 304
The Process of Selling 304
People Buy Stuff from People 304
Sales and Business Development 305
Marketing and Ads Fill the Sales Funnel 306
Integrated Marketing 307
11.2 The Sales Process 308
Working the Funnel 309
Additional Important Sales Topics 316
Corporate Sales 318
11.3 Customer Loyalty and Maintenance 323
Keeping Your New Customer Is Job 1 323
Customer Relationship Management 326
11.4 Organizing Sales 328
Sales Compensation 328
Outsourcing Sales 331
11.5 Case Study: Unboxing the Sales Process with unboXt 335
11.6 Endnotes 337

Chapter 12 Operations 339
12.1 Execution and Resources 340
Execution Is Everything 340
Measuring What You Manage 340
Facilities (or Not) 345
Manufacturing 349
Service and Retailing 357
12.2 Managing Growth 360
Planning to Grow Dynamically 361
Inventory Management and Cash Flow 362
The Challenge with Staffing 364
12.3 Globalized Operations 366
The Global Imperative 366
Managing across Space and Time 368

12.4 Case Study: Shifting Operations at Nikki's Kitchen 371
12.5 Endnotes 374

Chapter 13 Accounting 375
13.1 Managerial Accounting 376
Basic Accounting Skills 376
13.2 Financial Accounting 380
Income Statements 380
Cash Versus Accrual Accounting 382
Amortization and Depreciation 386
Balance Sheets 387
Cash Flow Statements 388
International Accounting Standards 392
Finding and Selecting Accounting Professionals 393
13.3 Accounting Systems 395
Software 395
Online Solutions 396
13.4 Case Study: When Things Go Bad, Very Bad: An Accounting Nightmare 397
13.5 Endnotes 400

Chapter 14 Managing Cash Flow and Finance 401
14.1 Cash Flow 402
Analyzing Data 402
Bankruptcy and the Return of the Living Dead 406
Renting and Leasing 408
14.2 Finance 410
Collateral for Loans 410
A Cautionary Word on Debt 412
14.3 Case Study: Betting It All: An Unorthodox Cash Flow Gamble by Your Author 414
14.4 Endnotes 416

Chapter 15 The Business Environment and Government 417
15.1 The Business Environment 418
Factors of the Business Environment 418
The Biggest Environmental Influence Is Government 421
Regulations and Taxes 423
Lawsuits 427
15.2 The Macroeconomic Environment 428
Keynesian Economics 429
The Business Cycle and Your Business 433
Global Secular Trends 436
15.3 Cultural Environment 441
The Culture of Doing Business 441
Globalization 442
Dynamic Culture 443

Government and Culture 445
15.4 Technical Environment 446
15.5 Government as a Customer or a Vendor 448
The Inside Track 449
Governmental Competitors 450
15.6 International Trade 451
15.7 Case Study: A Young Entrepreneur Learns about Taxes the Hard Way 456
15.8 Endnotes 460
Chapter 16 Exiting and Harvest 461
16.1 The End of the Road 462
Should You Stay or Should You Go Now? 462
Capturing the Value You've Created 464
Valuation: What Is It Worth? 471
16.2 The Self-Sustaining Business 473
The Milking Strategy 474
Inheritance Strategies and Tax Considerations 474
16.3 The Sale 475
Diligence 476
Part Way In/Part Way Out 477
Payment Structures 477
Exit Strategy Starts at Day One 478
16.4 Case Study: Selling Trojan Storage 479
16.5 Endnotes 481
Appendix A Final Thoughts 483
Index 485

About the Author

Greg Autry

Greg Autry (PhD University of California, Irvine) is Clinical Professor of Space Leadership, Policy, and Business at Thunderbird School of Global Management, Visiting Professor in the Institute for Security Science and Technology at Imperial College London, and affiliate professor with the Interplanetary Initiative at Arizona State University where he leads the world's first degree-program in the business of space. He also serves as the Chair of the Safety Working Group on the Commercial Space Transportation Advisory Committee (COMSTAC) within the U.S. Federal Aviation Administration (FAA); a former advisor to Relativity Space, a startup rocket manufacturer; a board member of Interstellar Lab; and Vice President for Space Development at the National Space Society. Greg previously served as White House Liaison with NASA and was Presidential Nominee for Chief Financial Officer of NASA. Prior to joining Thunderbird School of Global Management, Greg was Assistant Professor of Clinical Entrepreneurship in Marshall School of Business at the University of Southern California.

Greg is a serial entrepreneur who co-founded HAL Labs, a game developer that coded an Apple version of Pac-Man while he was still a high-school student. That software was subsequently purchased by Atari. Greg also co-founded Dr. Micro, a PC services firm sold to CompuCom System; Wired Images, an ecommerce content creator; Network Corps, a developer of healthcare enterprise applications for Kaiser Permanente; and Elevated Materials, an upcycler of aerospace carbon fiber scrap.

Acknowledgments

I would like to acknowledge the contributions of the following individuals:

- Dr. Laura Huang, Harvard, who contributed to the initial planning of this text
- Dr. Kaye Schoonhoven, UC Irvine, for her mentoring and work that inspired the title
- Dr. Peter Navarro, UC Irvine, for invaluable lessons in authorship and life
- Emily Carney, for editorial assistance early on
- Susan Holden Martin, MBA, J.D. for editing, support, and encouragement in getting through the last, very challenging months of the project
- My wife, Susan Autry, for her immense patience with this project
- Dr. Helena Yli-Renko, for being the world's most supportive boss during the development of this book
- Cassidy Masters and Lani Faualo for assistance developing test and homework items
- Everyone at NASA Headquarters for making the process interesting
- Dean Sanjeev Khagram for daring to dream big!
- The team at FlatWorld, for being willing to do something different with a textbook

I would also like to thank to the following individuals who reviewed the text and whose contributions were invaluable in shaping the final product:

- Stephanie Kloos Donoghue, Pace University, Lubin School of Business
- Francis Green, Penn State University
- Martin Luytjes, Florida International University
- Johnie L. Reed, MPOD, M.Ed., AFC®, Assistant Professor, Business Administration, Cuyahoga Community College
- Joseph N Scarbaci, Raritan Valley Community College
- Joy Turnheim Smith, ECSU
- Leann Mischel, PhD. Coastal Carolina University
- Jeffrey Muldoon, Emporia State University

Dedication

Dedicated to the business partners who shared my journey through the entrepreneurial school of hard knocks: Tom DeLellis, Brian Fitzgerald, Tony Tribelli, David Verespey, Dan Haste, John Thompson, Brian Bishop, Ryan Olliges, Paul Olliges, and Adrian Stern.

Preface

You'll likely notice that *A New Entrepreneurial Dynamic* (NED) is a very different textbook. I started this writing adventure because I couldn't find just the right book for my own students of entrepreneurship at the University of Southern California. Most texts were intolerably expensive, longer than necessary, inaccessible, and often boring. I'm not alone in that evaluation. Many of my colleagues, leading professors of entrepreneurship, have abandoned those texts in favor of a self-assembled collection of articles and case studies. While that sort of bricolage-based approach is affordable, personal, and accessible, it cannot provide business students with the organized and complete toolkit they will require in the arena of the marketplace. So, I've written a textbook!

I made the conscious decision to keep NED more personal and more engaging. I hope you'll sense that I've enjoyed my own entrepreneurial journey as well as my career in management research and instruction. It's been a heck of a ride for a first-generation college student who dropped out on his first attempt. I want you to share my enthusiasm for just how awesome entrepreneurship can be. Many of the businesspeople I use as examples or detail in the case studies are founders that I've had the pleasure to observe directly or work with during my dual careers as a startup founder and as an academic. As a very young entrepreneur in the early personal computer game business, I had the good fortune to spend time with Apple cofounders Steve Wozniak and Steve Jobs. I also encountered many brilliant, engaging, and dangerously disruptive individuals who are less famous but no less amazing.

As a researcher and leading expert on commercial spaceflight entrepreneurship, I've been similarly blessed to personally engage with Richard Branson, Elon Musk, and Jeff Bezos. This resulted in the president appointing me to leadership roles at NASA—an amazing experience that made the six-year-old in me very happy. Looking back on it, I could have made better choices at several junctures, and those experiences inform the lessons in this book. But personally, I enjoyed the journey so much that I probably wouldn't change my own path.

NED offers recommendations for managing your personal life as well as your business because I have learned that in reality, they are inseparable for the entrepreneur. I once founded a business so that I could leave my corporate job in order to finish college and spend time at home with my newly adopted son. That business grew, lasted for nearly twenty years, and made millions.

Textbooks that leave that out and silo every aspect of a business into neatly divided and separately manageable activities are excellent at preparing students for exams. However, those students are unlikely to survive contact with the marketplace. So, NED contains the wisdom of academic researchers, the insights of real businesspeople, and my own learning moments.

The textbook author, as an 18-year-old entrepreneur, stands at the right.

Source: Greg Autry

The author and his wife outside Mission Control at Kennedy Space Center, 2017

Source: Greg Autry

The author with his son at his college graduation.

Source: Greg Autry

At some points in the text, I break the fourth wall and address the reader directly. That's unheard of in the tradition-bound world of textbook publishing, but I felt it was exactly what was needed to bring the reality of entrepreneurship to the classroom setting. I'd like to thank the editors at FlatWorld for being daring enough to embrace all this and for providing you with a complete, affordable, and innovative textbook. I hope you enjoy your quarter, semester, or self-study journey through the *New Entrepreneurial Dynamic*.

Greg Autry, Southern California, 2021

Supplements

A New Entrepreneurial Dynamic: 21st Century Startups and Small Businesses is accompanied by a robust supplements program that augments and enriches both the teaching and student learning experiences. I wrote all supplements to ensure both accuracy and full alignment with the book's narrative. Faculty should contact their FlatWorld sales representative or FlatWorld support at support@flatworld.com for more information or to obtain access to the supplements upon adoption.

Sample Syllabi

Sample syllabi based on either 16-week or 10-week terms provide useful templates that help new adopters transition from their current course textbook to *A New Entrepreneurial Dynamic: 21st Century Startups and Small Businesses*. Faculty can download the syllabi from the FlatWorld website or they can be obtained by contacting your local FlatWorld representative or FlatWorld support (support@flatworld.com).

Instructor's Manual

The instructor's manual (IM) includes learning objectives, an outline, key takeaways, interactive activities, and key terms with definitions for each chapter.

PowerPoint Slides

PowerPoint lecture slides provide a concise but thorough outline for each chapter and include relevant tables, figures, and images from the text to enliven lectures and stimulate class discussions. These PowerPoint slides also include a list of Learning Objectives by chapter. Instructors can use the slides as composed to support lectures or customize and build upon them to suit their particular teaching needs.

Test Item File

The Test Item File (TIF) includes more than fifty questions per chapter in multiple-choice, completion, true/false, and essay-question formats. All answers are provided, including possible responses to the essay questions. The items have been written specifically to reinforce the major topics covered in each chapter and to align with FlatWorld Homework and in-text quiz items. The Test Item File questions are also available in pre-formatted form for easy export into popular learning management systems such as Canvas or Blackboard.

Test Generator—Powered by Cognero

FlatWorld is pleased to provide a computer-generated test program powered by the leading assessment provider, Cognero, to assist instructors with selecting, randomizing, formatting, loading online, or printing exams. Please contact your local FlatWorld representative or FlatWorld support (support@flatworld.com) for more information or to request the program.

FlatWorld Homework

Accompanying FlatWorld Homework for this text is provided in an easy-to-use interface. Multiple choice, fill-in-the-blank, matching, and other question types are available for use and are all auto-gradable. Students who utilize the homework questions should see their performance improve on examinations that are given using the Test Item File questions provided to adopters via Word documents or LMS packages.

Online Quizzes

Quiz questions for student self-evaluation are available by section and by chapter in the online version of this text. Students can use the quizzes to test themselves on their comprehension as they move through the different sections of the text or once they have completed a chapter.

Foreword: Entrepreneurs and the New Entrepreneurial Dynamic, by Randy Komisar

A century ago it was believed that great entrepreneurs were born, that the entrepreneurial process itself was intuitive, mysterious . . . unknowable. There was surely some deep, primeval force lurking deep inside Thomas Edison that compelled him to forge General Electric, a force of nature that could no more be captured or duplicated than could the mysterious electrical fluid that lit the night sky on dark and stormy nights.

At the same time, the lowly shopkeeper was born to his job, exactly as the plowman or aristocrat was born to his. Economists saw the *bourgeoisie* (small business owners) as a class or a condition, not as a choice. While the great entrepreneurs like Edison, Carnegie, and Ford were awe-inspiring figures surrounded by cults of personality, the status of a small businessperson was seen as an unearned inheritance and perhaps as an unenviable burden. The shopkeeper was tied to his shop and the ironsmith to his forge. His employees were generally his children or *indentured servants*. While self-employment provided sustenance, it lacked security and social standing. Small businesses offered neither mobility nor the opportunity for personal growth. Small business ownership was a dead end.

In the mid-twentieth century, the advent of scientific management radically shifted the business landscape. Modern techniques and tools were developed that drove efficiencies in the large, multinational corporations that dominated that period. Smart young college graduates lined up to join conglomerate firms like IBM, Honeywell, and ITT, which made everything from typewriters to military weaponry.

It was assumed that the modern management principles that drove these behemoths could be miniaturized and applied to any new firm with similar success. It was the heyday of Peter Drucker, and the precision engineering of businesses, large and small, was all the rage. Grand old businesses deemed inefficient were snapped up by *corporate raiders* in *leveraged buyouts* and hacked into shape by legions of pinstriped MBAs and CPAs with little regard to their noncapital stakeholders. Small businesses would launch with a carefully organized fifteen-chapter *business plan* that commenced with an irresistibly compelling executive summary and culminated in a set of five-year cash flow projections. Growth was always the objective, and the new business would then move forward with the stately conviction of the planets in their Newtonian orbits.

Entrepreneurs need only apply The Plan to a given product or service idea, and eager investors would pave the road under their feet with dollars to drive marketing and scale the enterprise quickly, seizing the all-powerful *first-mover advantage*. Customers, unable to resist the brilliance of The Plan, would line up to hand over their paychecks, fulfilling the certainty of those cash flow projections. The business globe had been mapped, reason had replaced faith, and all the forces in the management universe were now encompassed within The Plan.

Armed with this knowledge, would-be entrepreneurs obtained MBAs, abandoned their safe corporate and government jobs, and raced to apply The Plan to countless ideas, both new and old. Big box stores and standardized service organizations rolled across a national and global landscape formerly occupied by the small shopkeepers and regional chains. Hamburger stands, coffee shops, and pet stores became standardized, predictable, global profit-generating mega-chains. Housekeeping services, exterminators, and tax preparation firms were similarly commoditized and globalized. Shopkeepers became shift managers, and entrepreneurship seemed limited to the graduates of prestigious business schools backed by a tightly connected group of venture capitalists. Small business was still a dead end.

As the last century came to a close, the internet presented the perfect opportunity to demonstrate the power of The Plan to conquer new territory. The very model of the modern major entrepreneur blessed with a prestigious university pedigree generated her magnificent business plan for a massive online drugstore, grocery delivery service, or internet pet store. Venture capitalists, captivated by the perfect elevator pitch, funded these new enterprises with tens of millions of dollars. Spiffy corporate headquarters were built. Coffee bars, beanbag chairs, and ping-pong tables were installed, and hundreds of really smart young people were hired. Everything in the internet world moved forward according to The Plan. The website went up, the firm captured the first-mover advantage, and its initial public offering (IPO) secured hundreds of millions of dollars more. Success was clearly inevitable....

Oddly, the customers failed to follow The Plan. It turned out a lot of customers weren't really ready for an internet pet store or at least not the one described in The Plan. Lacking any alternative plan or even a mental process for developing or approving an alternate plan, those great and wonderful internet giants went down in glorious flames. The time had come to find a New Entrepreneurial Dynamic.

I've been lucky enough to work at a lot of great places, learn from a lot of amazing people, and take part in some amazing things. I've been a corporate lawyer, an entrepreneur, a venture capitalist, and even a concert promoter. I was at Apple in the early days, launched a spin-off and sold it back, worked for George Lucas' game company, and have been the "virtual CEO" of several cool startups like TiVo and WebTV. I am now proud to be at one of Silicon Valley's most successful and most diverse venture capital groups, where I've funded and mentored incredible firms like RPX and Nest. I've also taken the time to travel broadly and to seek out people whose lives and viewpoints are very different from my own.

What I've gained from all those experiences are a few very simple but very important lessons. Among these is the fact that we generally don't control our circumstances; we only control ourselves. A lot of things in life and business are left to chance. To manage that risk, we've got to manage ourselves holistically and enjoy the process. Business and life are inseparable, and we must surf the waves we catch and learn to enjoy them.

I feel the time is right to challenge a fundamental assumption of small businesses: that they must scale into big businesses or die. The imperative to scale is not even taught in business schools today; it is assumed. But why? I think the answer is simple: Capital likes to scale, and our current market culture is driven by the needs of capital—not the desires of customers, workers, or their communities. The relentless drive of capital to scale has had negative implications for the types of jobs that satisfy human beings. And we only have to revisit the leveraged buyout days of the go-go 1980s to remember the devastating impact on communities of blindly maximizing returns.

Small businesses are not all destined to be big businesses. But if they support their constituents—their workers, their customers, and their communities—then they have the means of success at whatever their appropriate scale is. Being conscious from the inception of why you are starting a business and what success means to you is core to being a great small business owner.

I assert that being an entrepreneur is not limited to starting businesses; it's a philosophy of life. It's about finding a purpose that makes your success important. Teaching entrepreneurship is not only about creating businesses, it's a way of seeing the world, a world that is half full of wonderful opportunities and experiences. The biggest risk of all is not failing; it is not trying and, therefore, not experiencing and learning.

The book you are about to spend your semester or quarter with approaches small business with that mindset. *A New Entrepreneurial Dynamic* covers the mundane technical skills every business owner needs to keep the gears of profit turning, while recognizing that those profits are a very necessary resource but not the goal of entrepreneurial life. In the pursuit of real goals, the author brings you insights from inspired entrepreneurs, both great and small. Greg Autry understands that all businesses are not created equal, and each must identify, understand, and leverage its unique advantages and deal with its particular shortcomings. He will show you how well-run small businesses can act smarter and move faster than their bigger competitors.

Understanding all this can make owning your own small business more lucrative and a lot more fun than joining the ranks of a big corporation or even a well-funded startup. Importantly, your author also recognizes the noneconomic contributions that small shops and artisanal manufacturers bring to our lives, communities, and culture. In this century, being a small business owner of the right sort can be very cool. Enjoy the journey.

—Randy Komisar

Randy Komisar with Stacyann Walker and Carlie Carpio, two of the author's former students from the University of Southern California. The trio are holding a carbon fiber skateboard from another student startup.

Source: Randy Komisar

Randy Komisar is a partner at Kleiner Perkins Caulfield and Byers. Randy holds a BA in economics from Brown University and a JD from Harvard Law School. Some of his career highlights include serving as senior counsel at Apple Computer, CEO of Lucas Arts, and founding Claris Corporation. He is the author of The Monk and the Riddle *and* Getting to Plan B *(with John Mullins) and teaches entrepreneurship at Stanford University.*

CHAPTER 1
The Entrepreneur in Context

Two roads diverged in a wood, and I—
I took the one less traveled by,
And that has made all the difference.
—*Robert Frost*

Almost every business starts small; a few will grow very large.

Source: Shutterstock, Inc.

This book is about entrepreneurs, and by extension businesses that are usually small—those that will remain small, those that will grow, and the rare few that will scale rapidly into huge corporations. We all think we know what "small business" means. The media is full of stories about the growth of small business, the job creation power of small business, the significance of small business in our economy, the political interests of small business owners, and more. Still, "What is a small business?" turns out to be a curiously difficult question to answer. To the average person, the definition of small business remains limited to "I know it when I see it." When you press further, things begin to break down.

1.1 Let's Start Small

Learning Objectives

1. Understand that startup companies nearly always start as small businesses but diverge from that point based on the entrepreneur's intent and opportunities.
2. Recognize that it is not as easy to tell what a "small business" is as we may think.
3. Learn the different types of startups and their characteristics.
4. Understand that that many entrepreneurs have goals beyond just growth or profits.

It's Small, but Is It a Small Business?

Each Starbucks location appears to be a small business. Is it?

Source: Thinglass/Shutterstock.com

How does this business differ from a Starbucks location?

Source: Gina Power/Shutterstock.com

nonprofit

An organization, very like a business, that does not generate returns for its investors. It may run on donations as well as revenue, but all profits are returned to its mission.

Consider that a Starbucks Coffee store may contain only a handful of employees and a handful of customers and perhaps do only a few thousand dollars of business per day. That sounds like a small business, but the unseen weight of another 20,000 or more corporate branded locations tells us, "This is *not* a small business." However, even though the similar shop owned by the nice lady across the street is very much a small business. Okay, that is simple enough, but let's try a trickier one: Is a single McDonald's franchise owned by a local family a small business, even if it must look and operate identically to the thousands of locations owned by the McDonald's corporation?

A new software firm with five team members and no profits clearly seems to be a small business. But what if that same startup attracts millions of dollars in venture financing in hopes it can be sold to Google for some tens of millions, anticipating that Google will shut the operation down just to get the team and technology? An exclusive, privately owned jewelry store in Tokyo grosses more than $30 million a year with less than a dozen full-time staff. Is it small? What about a factory with 150 employees that grosses $5 million a year? Think about a little **nonprofit** organization that funds its social advocacy by selling T-shirts. It's small, but is it a "business"? Is a 5,000-acre family-run California almond farm a "small business"? Would you answer differently if you knew that the land was valued at $25,000 per acre?

The U.S. **Small Business Administration** (SBA) has the unenviable task of officially defining a small business for qualification in its business assistance programs. The SBA has created the Table of Small Business Size Standards, which allows a small business to have as many as 1,500 employees and revenue up to $38 million per year, depending on the industry.[1] Using these criteria, the SBA tallied that the United States had some 28 million small businesses as of 2012. The majority of these are "nonemployer" firms, with only the entrepreneur at work.[2]

Small Business Administration

A U.S. government agency that provides support services for small businesses, including loan assistance and guarantees.

Taking a closer look at an SBA table shows that a casket manufacturer is small if it has an "average employment" of fewer than 500 employees. That may be sensible, but consider that as soon as the very same firm hires employee number 501, it's somehow an entirely different beast and disqualified from a number of beneficial government programs and opportunities. Similarly, a liquor store can gross up to $7.5 million and still be small, but after it sells one additional case of beer, it is transformed in the eyes of the government into a large business.

The European Commission (EC) defines Small and Medium-Sized Enterprises (SMEs) as having fewer than 250 employees and €50 million in revenue ($60 million) and less than €43 million ($51 million) in net assets. According to the EC's 2014 report, Europe has 21 million SSMEs, and they constitute a full 99.8 percent of European firms. The vast majority of these (92.4 percent) are what the EC terms "micro-enterprises," with fewer than ten employees.

While the SBA or EC defines the legal criteria for small businesses in their economies, these are arbitrary and inflexible definitions. In fact, they are pretty much useless for our purposes. Measurements of employees and revenues deal only with the outward manifestations of the business and neglect the essence of a small business. They also fail to understand that there are several different types of small businesses.

Consider the Chinese giant panda. At birth, a giant panda is about 3 inches long and weighs in at 1/900 the mass of its mother. Would biologists categorize this baby as a separate "small animal" species until it grows past a certain point and then reclassify it as a "large animal"? Of course not! A baby panda cannot survive on its own without the protection of its massive parent. It is an infant large animal, not a small animal. Similarly, any useful categorization of businesses must be more nuanced and contextually aware than "small" and "large" allow for.

In the end, the New Entrepreneurial Dynamic suggests that a small business is better recognized by the nature of its business model than by its size. This text will discuss **business model** in more detail, but for now consider a business model to be the way in which a business is run, creates value for its customers, and captures profits from that activity. You will find the business model described in this book fits firms whose nature does not *require* them to scale rapidly, whose top management knows all the employees, and whose owners are likely to be involved in both strategic decision-making and daily operations. Adopting a Cinderella approach to our question, I define "small business" as an organization that fits the tools offered you in this book!

business model

A description of how a business operates with an emphasis on how it engages customers, produces its product, makes a profit, and generates returns on investment.

Corporate Intrapreneurship

Imagine that the Coca-Cola Company decides to enter the hot new beverage category of "artichoke water" by launching a startup company. In its first quarter, that new venture might have only fifty employees and a few million dollars in revenue. Like our baby panda, such an organization would be well supported by its parent and designed from the outset to be large-scale. Its mandate would be to grow very large in the first year or two. Failing to grow large, it would be shut down. While the SBA rules would call this firm "small," such a corporate spin-off would not be a small business by our definition. Some tools in this book that are applicable to such corporate *intrapreneurship*, but that will not be our focus.

The Rapid Growth Startup

angel investor

An investor or small group that funds early-phase startup businesses with the capital they need for early growth, usually in the range of hundreds of thousands of dollars. Most large startups start with angel investment.

venture capitalist

A sophisticated investor who makes large investments in startups with the hope of occasionally finding a big hit. Venture capitalists typically look for firms with potential markets measured in billions of dollars and make investments of $5 million and more.

Similarly, many new firms are tiny at birth but are designed to become very large, very quickly, and they will perish if they fail to grow. Entrepreneur, educator, and author Steve Blank calls these businesses "Scalable Startups." These firms often follow the Silicon Valley startup model, which depends on several rounds of **angel** and/or **venture capital** investment to fund rapid growth. One of the unique things about these firms is that they start out with an "exit strategy," a plan for investors to get their money back. Typical exit strategies include either selling the firm to a larger competitor or collecting billions of dollars in a Wall Street initial public offering (IPO).

Google (Alphabet) is the archetype for a rapid growth startup. It was not small for long.

Source: Uladzik Kryhin/Shutterstock.com

While the best-known rapid-growth firms are high-tech companies like Apple, Google, and Facebook, the category also includes the more mundane retail field. So-called "big box" stores such as Best Buy and Home Depot and restaurants such as Starbucks and Outback have leveraged a scalable design and venture funding to quickly proliferate across the national and global landscape. The arrival of these well-crafted and well-funded ventures often results in the demise of the local main street businesses. This process of displacement has been so successful that during the first decade of this century, it has rendered the shopping districts of many cities around the world eerily identical.

The excitement of the Rapid Growth Startup has allowed them to dominate coverage of entrepreneurship in the financial press and has also made them the primary focus of business school courses and textbooks on the topic. Steve Blank remarked, "When I started teaching, I thought all entrepreneurs and startups did what I did for twenty-one years—aim for billion-dollar markets and keep at it until you achieved liquidity or ran out of money."

However, Rapid Growth Startups represent an infinitesimal percentage of global startups, and while the rocket-ride approach to business is exciting, the vast majority of these firms fail very quickly. In fact, venture capitalist funds generally anticipate about a one-in-ten hit rate from the small subset of companies they actually fund. The Rapid Growth Startup is a very unique animal and requires a unique set of tools to mature.[3]

The Main Street Entrepreneur

The main street firm is the quintessential small business. We find the main street firm in every city, in every country. It's your neighborhood donut store, malasada stand, or dim sum joint. It's the landscaping company with one truck or the Amish furniture manufacturer. An individual, a family, or a couple of partners typically owns the main street firm. Although it may have bank loans and credit cards, as well as real estate, equipment, and inventory financing, the main street firm rarely has outside investors.

A classic American "Main Street" lined with small businesses.

Source: © Shutterstock, Inc.

The goals of the main street firm are usually to maximize returns to the operators rather than fund growth. They are typically one-location firms that have become fixtures in their communities. The main street business is often given short shrift in textbooks of entrepreneurship but will be a major focus of this text.

The Organic-Growth Small Businesses

This does not mean a small business must follow the Buyable Startup or the Silicon Valley model in order to grow. An **organic growth** business is *a small business that can operate successfully while being small and reinvest its profits to fund growth.* These businesses may seek expansion funded primarily by their own profits. Small factories may add capacity; retail stores may grow to include a handful of locations, usually in a particular region. Avoiding outside investors, the organic growth model allows the founding entrepreneur to maintain full control of his operation as well as retain

organic growth

Growing a firm with money from its own profit stream.

all the profits from his endeavor. I believe this is a preferable strategy for most entrepreneurs, and I will be focusing on it throughout the book.

The Buyable Startup

What Steve Blank has called the "Buyable Startup" is a smaller scale variant of the Rapid Growth Startup. It's a business that puts out the "For Sale" sign even before the "Open for Business" one. The purpose of a buyable business is to develop or demonstrate a particular technology, product, or service and sell the firm to a larger company for millions (rather than billions) of dollars as quickly as possible. This less ambitious model is much more likely to succeed. The Buyable Startup offers entrepreneurs who love the launching process a great way to relive that and to cash out again and again.

While applicable to nearly any industry, the buyable startup has recently become a very popular model for software service and mobile app firms. These firms typically begin to generate revenues extremely quickly and may even be profitable. The best of them are capable of being self-sustaining, removing any obvious pressure for the founders to reach a deal that would be exploited by potential buyers.

A resort business can support a personally rewarding lifestyle for an entrepreneur.

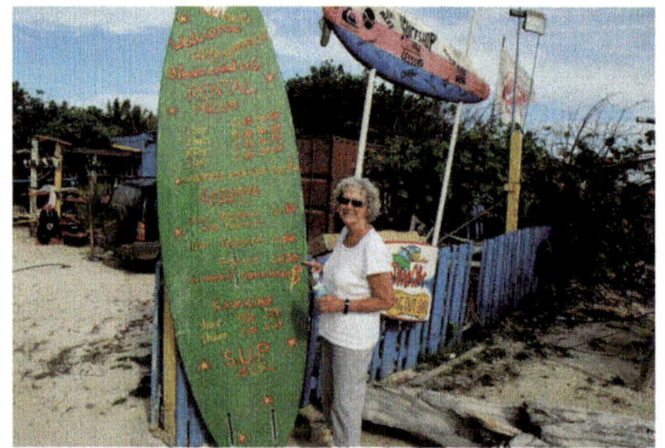

Source: Greg Autry

lifestyle business

A business designed to support the lifestyle of the entrepreneur.

The Lifestyle Business

At the far end of the business spectrum from the corporate spin-off and the Silicon Valley model startup, we encounter the **lifestyle business**. A lifestyle business is a firm whose primary mission is not to achieve growth, but rather to enable the desired lifestyle of the founder/owner. While this must include some reasonable amount of income, other considerations override the pursuit of profits and scaling. These considerations include allowing the entrepreneur to work in the geography of her choice (perhaps by being entirely mobile), providing scheduling flexibility that enables her to attend to other interests, or even simply being in an industry she finds attractive. Examples of lifestyle businesses include the following:

- A scuba shop in Hawaii allows an amateur marine naturalist to combine her work with her love for the sea. While not generating a great deal of profit and having little growth potential, this entrepreneur has secured her opportunity to "get wet" every day and spend time with people who share her passion for diving.
- A small resort composed of a dozen rental cabins near Aspen, Colorado, permits a mountain enthusiast to hit the slopes on his snowboard several days a week during the winter and fly-fish for trout in the summer.
- A college student runs an online specialty store that processes transactions while connecting his customers to fulfillment centers run by other firms. The entrepreneur carefully selects products and organizes the sales site, but partner firms handle the fulfillment, shipping, and returns. He never touches the products. The arrangement allows him to study in the winter and backpack around the world while working from his laptop and mobile devices.

In the mid-1990s, the author of this book established a "virtualized" software development firm that had no physical offices or full-time employees. The firm provided me with reliable income and enabled my pursuit of other personal interests, including traveling, completing my PhD, conducting academic research, writing, and advocacy.

The Social Entrepreneur and Nonprofits

Social entrepreneurship is a growing field of businesses that pursue growth and profits in support of a broader social mission, usually in an area of specific interest to the firm's founder. A familiar example of social entrepreneurship, found on the shelves in any American grocery store, is the Newman's Own brand of packaged food products. Actor Paul Newman and his neighbor, A. E. Hotchner, founded the firm in 1982 with their now-classic salad dressing recipe. Over the course of three decades, the firm's profits have fueled an expansion into more than 100 products, including pasta sauce, lemonade, frozen foods, and even pet food. At the same time, the firm has been able to divert in excess of $400 million to charities, including the SeriousFun Children's Network, a summer camp program for children with serious illnesses.

Actor Paul Newman and his neighbor founded a business that would leverage Newman's fame to support charities.

Source: ZikG/Shutterstock.com

Like Paul Newman, many social entrepreneurs launch businesses that compete directly in traditional markets and simply redistribute a portion of their profits to charity. Such firms may gain free media exposure or be able to charge *premium pricing* by appealing to the public's sense of charity.

Other firms actually fulfill their social mission through the nature of their operations by working in a more environmentally sustainable fashion or educating the public. Goodwill Industries fulfills its mission by hiring disadvantaged and disabled employees. Elon Musk founded his firm, SpaceX, a rapidly growing commercial space launch company, to perform a social good of epic proportions—moving human beings to Mars. This is a feat he considers essential to protecting humanity from an inevitable extinction event such as the impact of an asteroid or nuclear war. A nonprofit, like Goodwill, does not return funds to shareholders. Other forms of social entrepreneurship, like SpaceX, may be very profitable for their investors while fulfilling their social mission.

As we have seen, the wide variety of small businesses take very different forms and have different objectives. This means that not every piece of advice, every textbook lesson, or every great recommendation from the pages of *Inc.* magazine will apply to every startup. Understand which path you have chosen, and as you read this book (and others) chose what applies best to your own entrepreneurial journey. That is the New Entrepreneurial Dynamic.

Key Takeaways

- A potential entrepreneur has many different choices when launching a new business.
- There are many types of startups and small businesses.
- A startup can be a tool for achieving objectives beyond making money.
- A business could be the best way to enable your lifestyle choice.
- A business could be the best way for you to make a difference in the world.
- Since not all startups are the same, not all lessons will apply to every startup.

1.2 The New Entrepreneurial Dynamic—Fusion Firms, Shifters, and More

Learning Objectives

1. Understand that some businesses don't fit into one category. They may combine models or change models.
2. Recognize the opportunities and risks that franchising and multi-level marketing may offer.
3. Understand why online and virtual businesses are increasingly attractive for new entrepreneurs.

While these categories of small business do seem nice and tidy, they are still somewhat arbitrary constructs, and it may be difficult to force many real-world businesses into them. A New Entrepreneurial Dynamic acknowledges that the barriers between categories are really quite permeable. As soon as you draw lines between two items, as in establishing the difference between horses and donkeys, somebody will certainly present you with a mule—a mating between the two that produces a pack animal celebrated for its strength and versatility.

Fusion Firms and Shifters

fusion firms

A firm that combines more than one basic type of firm into its model.

A number of small businesses may be a lot like that mule: working in two or more categories simultaneously and stronger for it. There's no reason the social entrepreneur might not choose a business that also enables his or her lifestyle choice. Imagine an environmentalist working to save the orangutans of Sumatra establishing a business that allows her to live close to the hairy primates she adores. An entrepreneurial couple living above their main street corner shop may feel greeting familiar customers each morning *is the optimal lifestyle*. A social entrepreneur could even plan to rapidly grow his business with an investment from a socially conscious venture fund. I label such hybrid companies **fusion firms**.

shifters

A firm that moves from one type of firm to another. For instance, a firm started as a lifestyle project could find a product with huge potential and shift into a scalable startup mode.

Similarly, a business can certainly *shift* from one category to another. At one time, McDonald's was truly a small business of hamburger stands owned by Richard and Maurice McDonald of San Bernardino, California. The two brothers developed standardized production and service processes that revolutionized the fast-food industry. It was a great little organic growth business that eventually reached eight restaurants along with a scattering of franchises the brothers had sold to local entrepreneurs. It took an exceptionally ambitious outsider, Ray Kroc, to see the *massive scalability* in the McDonald's model. Kroc bought out the brothers and took their little hamburger chain to the next level, creating the publicly traded global icon we know today. Firms that change their plans so radically as to shift entirely into another category, I label **shifters**.

Franchises

Speaking of franchising, it can be a fantastic way for someone with the entrepreneurial spirit to get started without having to invent and commercialize a new product, service, or build a business model. A franchisor supplies proven products, professional marketing materials, and a complete operational system. The right to use these items, along with assistance, training, and documentation, are offered in exchange for upfront fees and recurring royalties on the business.

In the very best of franchises, the products are solid, the business model is well-designed and tested, and the franchising company is dedicated to ensuring only successful candidates take on their brand. With such firms, the likelihood of success is very high when the entrepreneurs do their part. A 2012 SBA report showed that a number of major franchises had no **loan defaults** for the previous decade! Not one of the forty-four SBA-backed Wendy's franchisors failed to repay their SBA loans in that year. Tim Horton's Donuts, Planet Fitness, Harley Davidson dealers, and another forty-seven different franchise opportunities also had perfect SBA records.

loan defaults

The failure of a firm to meet its payment obligations on a loan.

A franchise can be an attractive option for entrepreneurs without specific inspiration.

Source: QualityHD/Shutterstock.com

However, things are not always so pretty, and many entrepreneurs who pursue franchises do fail. The SBA reported that 94 percent (16/17) of the Wings-N-Things locations the government agency had backed had failed, and that more than $2 million in taxpayer-backed loans were **charged off**. Other firms with higher than 75 percent failure rates included Athlete's Foot shoe stores, Executive Tans salons, and Blockbuster Video outlets. Why do you think the failure rate for the giant video rental chain was so high?

charged off

A loan that a lender has given up on collecting.

Being prepared for change is a key element of the New Entrepreneurial Dynamic. In the franchise model, the franchisor designs your product and your business model. The entrepreneur buying a franchise is entirely dependent on this mother corporation to fit *the market*. Being very large and geographically diversified, franchise businesses don't change rapidly. Part of their attraction to the consumer is a proven model with the promise of stability, and they are less likely to experiment or to pivot when their environment changes. Therefore, franchisees must research the market they are getting into and perform their own **due diligence** on the business model they are buying into.

due diligence

The research work that investors do about a firm and its potential in order to ensure they are making a wise investment.

This startup period also provides an opportunity to realize that while getting into the "next big thing" might seem most attractive, timeless products are much less risky. As technology and consumer tastes evolve, the demand for products and services can shift, sometimes very suddenly. The movie rental business that drove Blockbuster's popularity early on rapidly collapsed in the face of competitors like Netflix and Apple's iTunes, which could provide in-home downloads and live streaming of movies on demand. This shift was entirely predictable and had already played out in the music business, wiping out chains like The Warehouse and Tower Records. While fashionable trends toward healthier eating may impact their relative popularity, hamburgers and donuts are unlikely to disappear from the market in our lifetimes.

Online Stores, Apps, and the Virtual Businesses

logistics

The actual work involved in managing the resources (usually physical) in your business operations. Shipping, storing, processing, and delivering.

startup costs

The money needed to get the business off the ground and usually designed to help it reach the point where it is stable.

barriers to entry

The obstacles that prevent new businesses from entering a market. High capitalization, specialized equipment, certifications, or licensing are examples.

There was a time when an entrepreneur planning to sell goods to the public had to spend a great deal of money to secure and improve an attractive retail location and even more to stock it with goods. The shop owner also had to hire employees to handle customer interactions and the **logistics** of receiving and delivering the product. Those locations and employees had to be paid for regardless of the sales volume the store experienced, creating significant financial risk. These **startup costs** established serious **barriers to entry** for entrepreneurs in the retail world.

The arrival of the internet and the globalization of business over the last decade has changed all that. The coronavirus pandemic of 2020 accelerated this trend. Even big firms are virtualizing. Apple can sell you an iPhone from its website and will ship the phone directly to you from its manufacturer, Hon Hai Precision Industry Co. (Foxconn) in Shenzhen, China. Apple doesn't ever touch its product but collects the significant portion of the profits! This model is so successful that despite trailing Android phones in sales, the iconic Cupertino, California, company has been able to grab the vast majority of profits in the smartphone industry. (Apple took 20 percent of sales but 93 percent of profits according to a 2015 report.)[4]

Millions of apps can be found on the Google Play and Apple iOS App Stores.

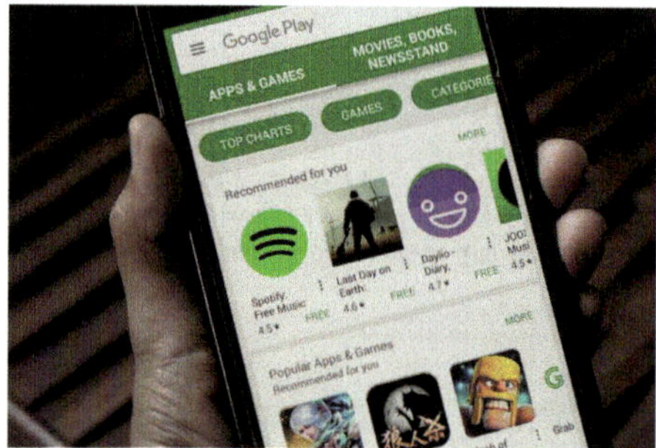

Source: Creative Caliph/Shutterstock.com

Any small businessperson can enjoy a similarly lean sales and distribution model selling products on the internet. Amazon, eBay, and a plethora of smaller firms will host your online store, and many vendors will drop-ship the products to your customer. In fact, with Amazon's Associates Program, you can even create a special interest site that directs people to Amazon's own store and collect a royalty check from Amazon. On the Apple App Store or Google Play, home software developers can upload their games, utilities, and other apps and just sit back waiting for their payments to roll in—minus a royalty to Apple or Google, that is. The barriers to entry are nearly nonexistent, which seems really attractive. Do you think there might be a problem with that?

It turns out that nearly everyone and their brother wants to play in the virtual online business world, and that creates a lot of competition for the would-be entrepreneur. With literally millions of online stores and apps out there, getting in front of your customer in the online world is hard. It usually takes a lot of money, just like leasing the best corner in town or a spot in the shopping mall did for the old-style retailers. A small businessperson working in this field has to be clever and nimble to compete with better-funded entrants.

Key Takeaways

- Don't limit your entrepreneurial opportunities to any one business model.
- Consider taking advantages of other firms' business models via franchising.
- If you do consider paying for a business model, you must perform your due diligence to understand what you are paying for and what you will really get.
- Never underestimate the opportunities technology offers virtualized businesses, but realize that nearly everyone else is thinking the same way.

1.3 Who Are the Entrepreneurs? Are You One?

Learning Objectives

1. Understand that many factors contribute to entrepreneurial success, including talent, predisposition, and education.
2. Recognize that the entrepreneur assumes the risk of the business operation and that managing risk is fundamental to entrepreneurship.
3. Differentiate between perceived risk and actual risk.
4. Understand the difference between serial and parallel entrepreneurs.
5. Understand how necessity creates entrepreneurs.
6. Recognize that entrepreneurship can be a path to comfortable wealth.

There are known knowns. These are things we know that we know. There are known unknowns. That is to say, there are things that we know we don't know. But there are also unknown unknowns. There are things we don't know we don't know.

—*Donald Rumsfeld*

Entrepreneurial Talent—Born or Learned?

Photo from the Homestead High Yearbook of Steve Jobs at age 14 in 1969.

Source: https://commons.wikimedia.org/wiki/File:Steve_Jobs_in_1969_Pegasus.jpg

Steve Jobs is probably the very model of the New Entrepreneurial Dynamic. Jobs founded Apple Computer with engineer Steve "Woz" Wozniak in 1976. Although Woz did the design work, it was Jobs' vision that defined the personal computer as a product and shaped the personal computer industry. When Apple ran into trouble in the late 90s, Jobs returned to rescue the company by entirely reinventing it. In his second term at the helm, he changed the world again with amazing products like the iPhone and iPad. In doing so, he built Apple into the world's most valuable company and brand. In his spare time, Jobs had purchased Pixar, an obscure computer animation firm, from *Star Wars* director George Lucas. Jobs nurtured that seed as it grew into a beloved global phenomenon, producing megahit family films like *Toy Story* and *Finding Nemo*. In 2006, he became the first modern entrepreneur to earn over a billion dollars in two distinct industries when he sold his film company to Disney.

Steve Jobs was born to Joanne Schieble, an unwed student at the University of Wisconsin and was raised by his adopted parents, Paul and Clara Jobs. By all accounts, his birth parents were both very bright, and his biological father, Abdulfattah Jandali, even earned a PhD. Jobs, however, gave the credit for his success to his working-class adoptive family, stating, "Paul and Clara are 100 percent my parents."

There has been a long-running debate about whether some people are simply born to be entrepreneurs. Two factors should be considered. One factor is *entrepreneurial talent*—are some people naturally more adept at running a startup just as certain children are clearly more talented at music or sports? The other factor is *entrepreneurial predisposition*—are some people more determined than others to launch new ventures?

This two-dimensional view of entrepreneurship is very important because both aptitude and determination are required elements of success in any endeavor. Entrepreneurship then might be similar to the world of professional baseball where there will always be a small number of highly successful individuals possessing both the talent and determination to win in the major leagues as well as a large group of frustrated minor leaguers whose love of the game exceeds their abilities on the field.

The flip side of this question is, "Can people learn to be entrepreneurs?" I believe they can! Jobs credited his dedication to quality work to lessons learned from his adopted father. I believe that most people with a desire to pursue their own business will find success and joy. You won't all be the next Steve Jobs, but you should be able to make a good living in small business and enjoy your work as well. With a little luck, you might even become moderately wealthy. The purpose of this book is to help you find your entrepreneurial happy place.

Risk and Coping with the Unknown

One particular trait that academic scholars have spent a lot of time looking at is the entrepreneur's ability to deal with risks and cope with things unknown. Some people may not have the tolerance for perceived risk or perceived ambiguity necessary to enjoy the entrepreneurial experience. Being in business for themselves gives them ulcers and migraines!

Note that I use the phrases *perceived* risk and *perceived* ambiguity—that's important. It isn't clear whether it is riskier to be a small business owner or part of a large and *seemingly* stable institution. While entrepreneurs are often seen as gamblers, throwing caution to the wind and diving headfirst into waters of unknown depth, in reality, nothing could be further from the truth.

The manager in a large corporation, using other people's money, is much more likely to make a quick and ill-informed decision because the financial consequence does not directly impact her. Losses accrue to the owners of the firm, not the employees. Corporations must, therefore, employ complex processes (project approval and review procedures) and motivational tools (bonuses and performance evaluations) to align the interests of the managers who run the business with those of the stockholders who own it. Entrepreneurs face no such problem of **agency**. With their very own livelihoods in their hands, business owners are among the world's most practical and cautious decision-makers. They may take risks, but they tend to be well-chosen risks.

agency
The capacity for self-directed action that often results in a conflict of interests between the personal motivations of an individual and those of his employer.

However, business risks are frighteningly visible to the entrepreneur. The entrepreneur can view the scope of her entire business. Seeing the declining sales in her stores or the slow payments from major clients, she cannot help but anticipate the consequences to her income. The superior information that the entrepreneur has about the state of her own business actually adds to the sense of uncertainty she experiences. Lacking the false sense of security created by the processes of a large firm, the entrepreneur is more aware that there are "unknown unknowns" lurking out there.

The big company manager whose check has always arrived automatically and dependably may never suspect that he is about to lose his health benefits, be laid off, or that the corporate pension fund he has been paying into has been raided to cover a departing CEO's enormous bonus. Upper management doesn't like bad news getting out to investors or undermining employee morale and will hide it as long as possible. A corporate manager may be unable to see clearly beyond the horizon of his own unit or store. If that is doing well, he could be entirely clueless about a much larger disaster brewing at headquarters until he reads a story about his company's mounting woes on some investment blog or in a news story.

I have found that a quiet self-confidence marks many successful entrepreneurs. The New Entrepreneurial Dynamic suggests that entrepreneurs who honestly match their aspirations to their abilities and accept that there are things beyond their control will be successful and at peace with themselves.

The Serial Entrepreneur

Many entrepreneurs find they are particularly adept at launching a business or perhaps enjoy the startup process more than they enjoy daily management. The **serial entrepreneur** founds one new firm after another, typically selling their previous firm first. Serial entrepreneurs are most often found in the rapid-growth startup or buyable startup. Still, many main street business owners have had one or two ventures before settling into their current business. Steve Jobs was a serial entrepreneur.

serial entrepreneur
An individual who launches many businesses, one after another.

A rare breed of entrepreneur, the **parallel entrepreneur** manages to run more than one successful business at a time. Steve Jobs was also a parallel entrepreneur, running both Pixar and Apple. Elon Musk is today's quintessential serial plus parallel entrepreneur (see "Interview with Elon Musk—The Quintessential Serial and Parallel Entrepreneur"). In 1995 he founded Zip2, a web-based city guide for newspapers, and sold it for $307 million to Compaq Computer. After that, he founded X.com, an electronic payment service that, through mergers, eventually became PayPal and was sold to eBay in 2002 for $1.5 billion. Musk is now CEO of Tesla Motors, the first successful new American auto company in the last ninety years, as well SpaceX, the world's leading private commercial space launch provider. In his spare time, he also serves as chairman of Solar City, the second-largest solar installer in the United States.

parallel entrepreneur
An individual who launches many businesses at the same time.

On a more typical scale, a retail shop owner may find that he also has the time to run an online store or perhaps get involved in helping his children launch a startup. Just as some workers may need more than one job to pay the bills, some micro-entrepreneurs may need more than one business to keep ahead during difficult economic times. A donut shop owner may be selling real estate in the afternoon.

Interview with Elon Musk—The Quintessential Serial and Parallel Entrepreneur

Elon Musk

Source: Courtesy Elon Musk

Elon Musk and his brother Kimbal launched Zip2, a web software company, in 1995. This was a small business developing an internet "city guide" for the newspaper publishing industry. Musk had much grander aspirations in mind. He obtained contracts with the *New York Times* and the *Chicago Tribune*. Compaq later acquired his company for $307 million in cash and $34 million in stock options. Musk received 7 percent or $22 million from the sale. Musk then went on to found X.com, which was rolled into the hugely successful internet payment service, PayPal. He was the largest PayPal shareholder when that firm was sold to eBay for $1.5 billion. In 2002, he founded Space Exploration Technologies (SpaceX), the leading commercial space launch services company. Musk also serves as the CEO and chief product architect of the innovative electric carmaker, Tesla Motors. In his "spare time," he is the chairman of SolarCity, America's second-largest installer of solar panel power systems. I had a conversation with Elon Musk in his cubicle at the Hawthorne, California headquarters of SpaceX.

Prof. Autry: Entrepreneurship is thought to be laden with failure. Why do you think so many have failed where you have succeeded?

Elon: Well, I believe those who do not succeed have perhaps faced, perhaps, a situation where they weren't able to gather a sufficient critical mass of talent or they ran out of money or they had an approach where success was not one of the possible outcomes—or all three.

Prof. Autry: What about the role of perseverance? You have a reputation for perseverance—do you feel that that is a big factor?

Elon: Yes. Sure, part of perseverance is changing strategy, knowing to change strategy when you need to.

Prof. Autry: Along those lines, you're often seen as this idea-driven inventor, but looking at Tesla and SpaceX, it's also clear that you're tenacious and brilliant at execution. Which do you think is more important?

Elon: I have far more ideas than I can execute on. I do think ideas are much easier than execution. If you want to try and bring something useful to a broad audience, it's a very difficult execution. It's one thing to make a prototype that is extremely expensive and unreliable and handmade by a group of engineers—that is easy. To try to make that whole thing so that average people can afford it in high volume, and it's reliable and passes all the regulatory requirements, is super hard.

Prof. Autry: So how do you know if you have an idea worth pursuing?

Elon: I'm just trying to solve problems that I think are important for the future. That's really all. I mean, I like working on things that are on the edge of technology because I find that intrinsically fulfilling. It's exciting; it's new. I like the creative process of coming up with new products and technology.

Prof. Autry: Is this something that you have always known about yourself, or something that you realized over time?

Elon: It was partly in college. Mostly I didn't go to class. I found the data rate of a lecture was too slow. It was much faster to read the book. And I'd also hang out with students and sort of exchange information without realizing that I was learning.

Prof. Autry: And so what does that mean for prospective entrepreneurs and the ability to "learn" entrepreneurship through examples?

Elon: There is a lot of reasoning by analogy, or general sort of copying what others do, that occurs. It is a far easier thing to do than to come up with something by first-principle reasoning—which is tremendously arduous, and you basically would not be able to get through your day. You should use heuristics and analogies and copying, in general, to get through your day. You don't need to reinvent how to use a knife and fork or drive a car. There's like no point in doing that. But if you are trying to come up with something new where the result could be counter-intuitive, that doesn't work . . . you can't copy if you're trying to design something new.

An Ever-Changing Economy and Today's Nontraditional Entrepreneurs

As the global economy has evolved over the last two decades, multinational corporations have significantly redistributed their production and services to take advantage of cheaper labor, more attractive regulatory environments, and lower tax rates. They have also invested significantly in automation and information systems that increase efficiencies and reduce employee headcount. Millions of working people in the **developed world** have found their job **offshored** or **automated** out of existence in recent years. Worse than simply losing a particular job, they have found that this tectonic shift in the business world has completely derailed their career. There is no domestic demand for their skills, and they have few choices beyond working one or more low-paying retail jobs.

developed world

Countries with sophisticated economies and high standards of living such as the United States, Japan, and Germany.

offshoring

The practice of moving production, usually manufacturing or software development, to another country with a cheaper labor rate.

automated

A process done by technology such as robots.

The situation is no better for many young people entering the workforce, a matter that should concern our readers. While more high school graduates are pursuing college degrees than ever before, the value of that degree is in question. A 2014 study by the Federal Reserve Bank of New York reports that half of recent U.S. college graduates are either unemployed (6 percent) or working in jobs that do not require their college degree (44 percent)—often a financial burden they are still carrying. More importantly, about a fifth of recent graduates are working in "low wage jobs" (under 25,000 per year with few benefits), and another fifth are working part time.[5] A report in the same year from the Economic Policy Institute notes that nearly 70 percent of recent graduates do not have employer-covered health insurance. Finally, it appears that despite some improvement in the overall state of the economy, most of these negative trends are continuing.

Necessity being the mother of invention, many people in both of these groups have turned to entrepreneurship, perhaps more out of a sense of desperation than of inclination. Unable to find suitable employment in the corporate market, they are creating jobs for themselves by establishing businesses. This chart (Figure 1.1) from the U.S. SBA highlights that trend by showing the relative growth of non-employer (single person) enterprises over the previous decade. Fewer and fewer people are establishing small businesses that create jobs for others, while more and more are working for themselves.

part-time entrepreneurship

Running a business as a sideline while working a full-time job.

direct sales

When a business sells its products directly to the consumer rather than through intermediaries such as distributors or retailers, often through the internet.

Some employed people are finding their traditional jobs offer little growth or inadequate salaries and take on **part-time entrepreneurship**. An office worker might have a small business representing a **direct sales** product like Avon or Cookie Lee jewelry. An elementary school teacher might spend the summers working another job or provide tutoring services for money in the evenings after school.

In many ways, being some sort of entrepreneur is the "new normal" in America. As the chart of New Business Foundings in the United States shows, unemployment driven by the 2020 pandemic resulted in a huge number of involuntary entrepreneurs founding businesses.

FIGURE 1.1 New Business Foundings in the United States
High-propensity applications are likely to be employers; others reflect self-employment.

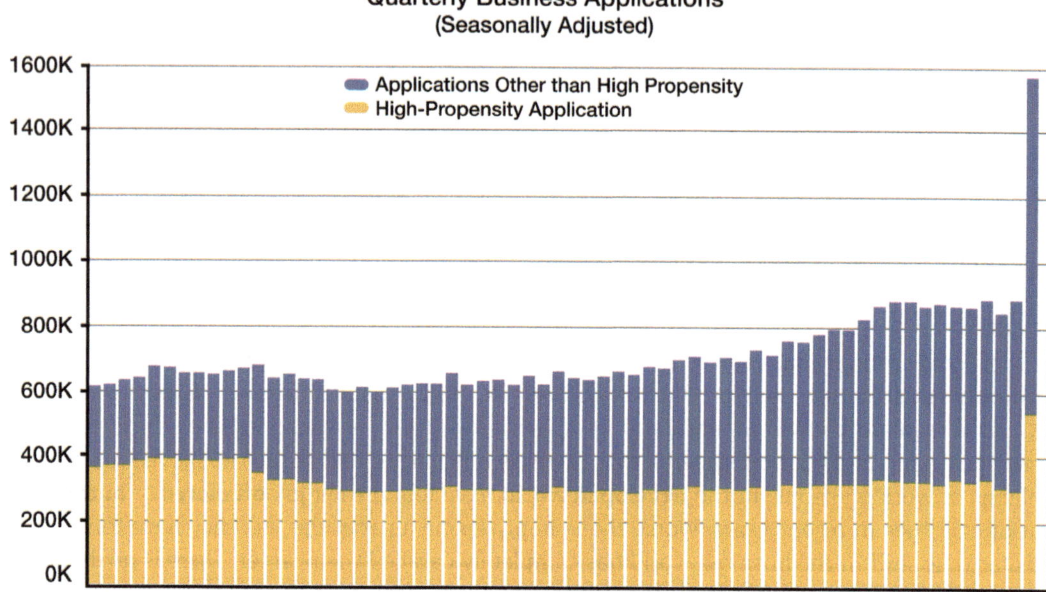

Source: United States Census Bureau, https://www.census.gov/econ/bfs/index.html

Opportunities

Owning a small business can be financially rewarding; many aspiring entrepreneurs view it as the ticket to wealth, and the data support that. The richer you are, the more likely you are to be a business owner. A 2014 U.S. Federal Reserve study reports that families with incomes in the top 10 percent are significantly more likely to own a private business (see Figure 1.2) than their middle- and lower-income peers. Americans with incomes above the average were more than twice as likely to be business owners!

FIGURE 1.2 Families That Own a Business Are Wealthier

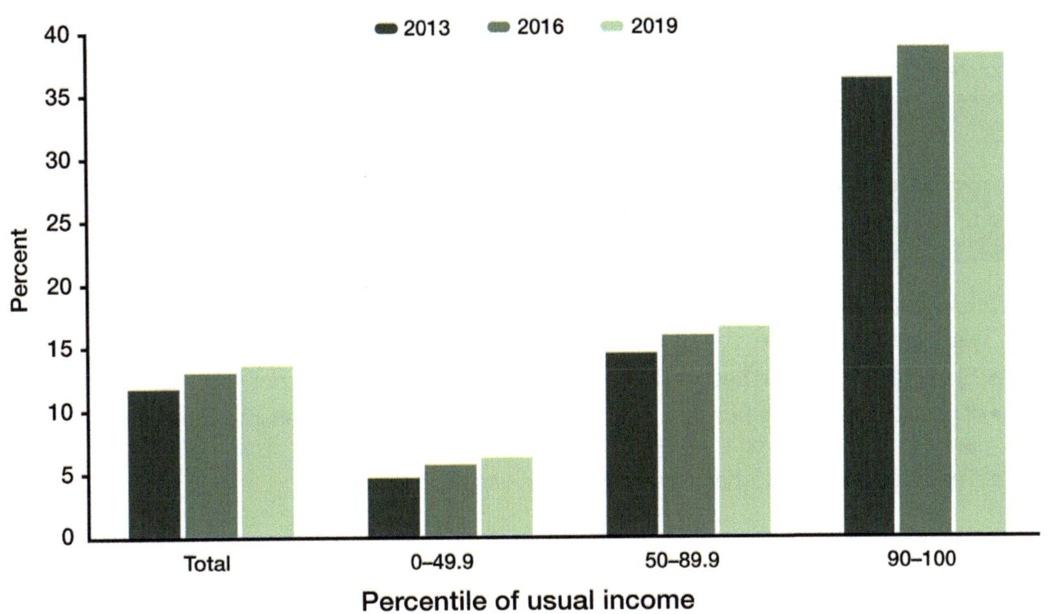

Source: U.S. Federal Reserve Consumer Finance Survey https://www.federalreserve.gov/publications/files/scf20.pdf

Across the globe, the opportunities for entrepreneurs are encouraging. Founding a business is also one of the best ways to climb the economic and social ladder in the developing world. In most of Asia, Africa, and Latin America, business owners enjoy significantly higher standards of living than those who are working for others. Nowhere is this more evident than in China, where the career choice for ambitious young people is stark; either spend your life working the notorious politics required to climb the ladder in a large **state owned enterprise** (SOE) or opt for independence and hopefully fortune in a private business. According to Zhibin Li, chairman of the China Association of Small and Medium Enterprises, there are now more than 35 million registered private businesses in China, and 90 percent of these are SME (small and medium-sized enterprises).

state owned enterprise

A business primarily owned or controlled by a government—the United States Postal Service, for example.

Yorba Linda, California

Entrance to Yorba Linda Main Street.

Source: Barbara Kalbfleisch/Shutterstock.com

In 2007, the residents of Yorba Linda, California, woke up to the headline, "Yorba Linda Is Richest U.S. City."[6] Taking a drive through the sleepy Orange County town whose motto is "Land of Gracious Living," you'*Orange County Register*, Les Fujimoto, a Yorba Linda real estate agent, remarked, "You go to Newport, and there's cars that cost $350,000 running up and down the streets. You don't see that in Yorba Linda."

Yorba Linda's source of understated wealth was in great part due to the large number of small businesspeople who chose to live there. A city official commented to me, "We've got a lot of folks who own contracting firms, insurance agencies, computer service companies, and small manufacturers. Their business may be in other cities, but they are bringing home six and seven figures. These are millionaires, not billionaires, but we've got a lot of them."

Key Takeaways

- Some people are natural entrepreneurs, but almost anyone can learn to run their own business well.
- Entrepreneurship may seem riskier than a traditional job, but that is not necessarily the case.
- If you succeed in one business, you may be just as likely to succeed in another either at the same time or when you've exited the first one.
- The global market is dynamic, and entrepreneurs must be as well.

1.4 Challenges

Learning Objectives

1. Understand the reality of business failures.
2. Understand that most business startups do fairly well.
3. Learn about opportunity cost and the sunk cost fallacy.
4. Understand that your entrepreneurship must support your broader plans, life goals, and family.

> What [President Obama] misunderstands is that nine out of ten businesses fail.
>
> —*Senator Rand Paul (R-Ky), Jan 26, 2014*

Survival

The first challenge in business is simply surviving. You've surely heard someone authoritatively pronounce, "Nine out of ten businesses fail!" as the United States senator does in the quote above. This is a scary "fact" that nearly everyone accepts, and many intelligent people repeat. However, as with the popular advice that you should drink eight glasses of water a day,[7] it has no scientific basis whatsoever, and Senator Paul's comment is just misleading. The truth is that ten out of ten businesses fail, eventually! Nothing lasts forever, and as famed economist John Maynard Keynes quipped, "In the long run, we are all dead." What is more interesting to know is how long our businesses are *likely* to live. The chart entitled "Business Survival over Time" shows business failure rates in the United States based on their number of years in existence. You can see that about half of U.S. businesses still exist five years after their founding, and more than a third are still around after a decade.

While a 50 percent five-year survival rate is still a daunting statistic for entrepreneurs who view their glass as half empty, the reality of business survival is more encouraging. Firstly, not all firms meet their end in bankruptcy. They may disappear for more cheerful reasons, including that the firm is acquired for a big windfall. They may also shut down simply because a successful entrepreneur retired or passed away at a comfortable old age or moved on to pursue an even more exciting new venture or career.

If you develop products that fit your market, adapt to change, execute well, and work very hard, it is likely your business will provide you with sustenance and satisfaction for many years. I encourage prospective entrepreneurs to view their glasses as more than half full!

FIGURE 1.3 Survival Rates of Establishments, by Year Started and Number of Years Since Starting, 1994–2015

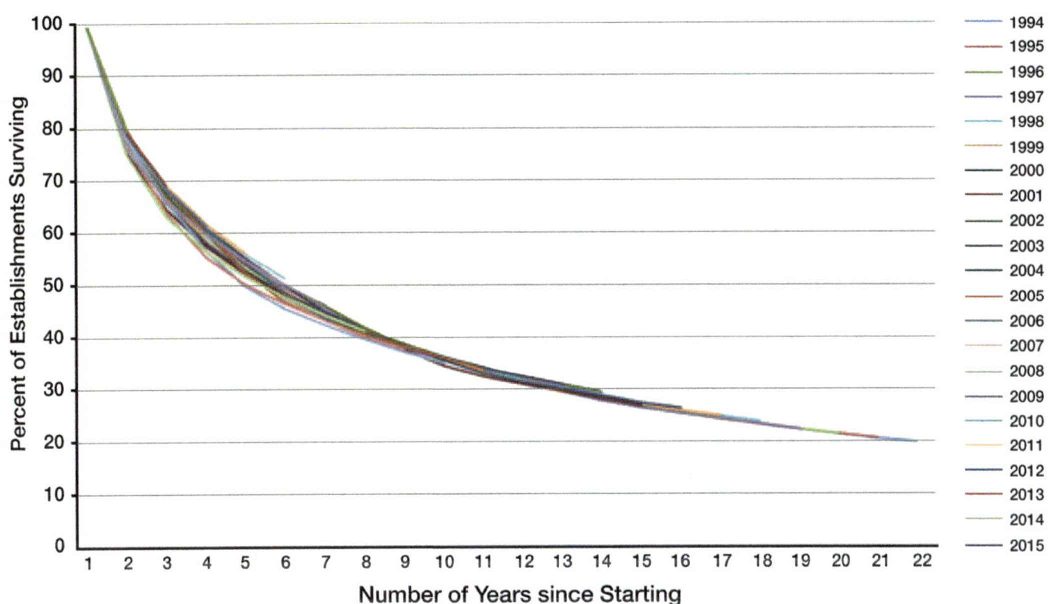

Source: U.S. Bureau of Labor Statistics

How Long Can a Firm Live? Interview with Brian O'Shaughnessy (Revere Copper)

Front entrance to the Revere Copper office in Rome, NY.

Source: Revere Copper

Brian O'Shaughnessy owns America's oldest manufacturing company! The iconic American patriot, Paul Revere, established Revere Copper in 1801, and his firm rolled the copper to sheath the hull of the U.S.S. Constitution ("Old Ironsides"). A hostile takeover of Revere's parent company resulted in spinning off three of its four business units, leaving the core business founded by Revere. The corporate raiders then hired O'Shaughnessy, who soon realized that they were preparing to lay off its employees and liquidate the firm's valuable copper holdings. O'Shaughnessy borrowed money and bought the investors out, returning Revere to a family-run company.

Prof. Autry: What do you believe are the most important factors in firm survival?

O'Shaughnessy: You have to stick to your knitting and know what your strengths are and play to those. You also have to be brutally honest about your weaknesses. We don't do things on the spur of the moment. Based on our guiding principles, we can do them quickly, but we don't do them spur of the moment. You must be team-based and practice what you preach.

Prof. Autry: Give us an insight into the importance of teamwork.

O'Shaughnessy: The people at Revere feel it is very important to keep this company going. They respect its heritage, and I'd given them 30 percent of the ownership, so they participate in the good times and understand how in the bad times, we must all work together.

Prof. Autry: What does "brutal honesty" mean in business?

O'Shaughnessy: Let me give you an example. One day in a meeting, I said something unfortunate about our CFO that did not reflect well on him. Greg sat back, and then he said to me, "F-you, Brian!" The team was shocked, but my response to that was, "You're right. I shouldn't have said that, and I apologize." That told other members of the team they could challenge me, and that's important. I don't want any "yes men" on the team.

Prof. Autry: When has your survival been threatened?

O'Shaughnessy: A South Korean family-owned firm purchased a lot of Canadian equipment and set up operations in the U.S. I understand they spent up to $500 million, which is way more than us. In order to recoup that kind of money, they really needed to dominate the market. They needed to put Revere Copper out of business. They have not succeeded, and part of that is the dedication our team has to keeping this American company going.

Prof. Autry: How is being an iconic American firm important to you, and what does that have to do with anyone else's business?

O'Shaughnessy: That's what's special about our firm, its national heritage. That has kept it alive and part of the reason I took the chance to keep it going. I think every company has really got to know what is important about their firm. It's got to have a reason more important than just making money for the owners, and the employees have to buy into that.

Leaders create and maintain a culture that unites everyone as part of a team with a mission to succeed. My son added a line to our mission statement to enshrine that: "Our future will consider equally our employees and shareholders, our customers and our country." You know, a lot of Korean and German companies have that sense of country, and that has worked great for them and for their nations.

Prof. Autry: What do you think kills small companies?

O'Shaughnessy: A lot of privately held firms fail because of the generational shifts. The heirs are not well-suited to run the firm; they have a sense of entitlement or are pressured by others to gut it for cash.

Prof. Autry: How can a small business avoid that?

O'Shaughnessy: We had three sons. When they were growing up, we encouraged them to go outside and make it on their own and then come back if they wanted to. I told them, "You are going to come into Revere at a level that reflects the knowledge and ability you've demonstrated elsewhere." You should not expect to just be bumped up to the top, and there might be better people above you. They must feel they are competing.

Who's the Boss?

Many aspiring entrepreneurs envision the establishment of a small business as a liberating experience that will free them from the tyranny of an unreasonable boss or a repressive bureaucracy.

Often, they are surprised to find that rather than reporting to one person or a single organization, they suddenly have a plethora of "bosses" in the form of demanding customers, employees, vendors, bankers, and governmental regulators. Each of these constituents has a surprising amount of leverage over the freedom of action of a small business owner. Worse, each of them has a separate agenda with little or no respect for the demands of the others or the bandwidth of the entrepreneur.

The customer of your specialty bakery simply doesn't care if your baker goes out on six months of state-mandated maternity leave or that a city health inspector has delayed approval on the installation of the new oven you need to deliver the customer's muffins. She wants the muffins when she needs them. Similarly, the employee and the inspector are more concerned about their own schedules than about your customer's needs, and you have absolutely no authority to force them to act; they hold all the power. If you can't deliver the muffins, you won't get paid, and you will miss the lease payments on the uninstalled oven. Guess what? Your lender doesn't want to hear your excuses, and the government still wants its taxes! You lay awake at night wondering if the bank or the IRS might foreclose or attach your home, and if your wife leaves you, who will get the kids since you have no home and . . . suddenly living with your old boss doesn't sound so bad after all.

Take a deep breath and relax. Small business management is a challenge, and entrepreneurs will encounter trying times similar to the scenario outlined above. The key to success in business in the New Entrepreneurial Dynamic is finding the right balance of planning, preparation, and adaptability. Several positive things could have been done to mitigate the frightening bakery scenario. Our entrepreneur should have planned to keep enough reserve cash on hand to avoid losing his bakery over one order of muffins. He should have developed friendly relations with other local bakers that could have helped him fill the order while his oven was down. He should have invested the time in advance to establish positive relationships with local political leaders who could intervene with the inspector. Seeing the problem unfolding, he might have approached his pregnant baker to see if she had colleagues willing to temporarily fill her position when she went on leave. He might also have reached out to temporary employment agencies. He should have contacted his creditors in advance to explain the possibility he might need to delay payments. In the coming chapters, I will help you develop a prepared and adaptable business and become a confident and cool entrepreneur.

Getting Stuck

> You got to know when to hold 'em, know when to fold 'em, know when to walk away, know when to run.
>
> —*Kenny Rogers*

sunk cost fallacy

A misguided focus on investments that have been previously made into a project, rather than on the project's immediate potential for success. Sunk costs often compel entrepreneurs to keep working on doomed efforts and investors to "put good money after bad."

The only thing worse than watching the business of your dreams die might be finding yourself stuck inside an unfulfilling venture that won't die. Watching entrepreneurs stay with struggling firms that are always on the edge of disaster is one of the saddest spectacles I have observed. Admitting that you're not going anywhere and that all your work on an enterprise might have been for naught is very difficult for entrepreneurs who see their firms as their "babies." Even worse, the more time, money, and resources an owner has invested in trying to keep his business going, the more pressure he feels to justify that investment by continuing to support it! The truth is that his remaining cash and labor might be much better spent on another venture. The bad logic behind this insidious trap is known as the **sunk cost fallacy**.

You might not want to stick with the struggling business for two main reasons. One of the best ways to avoid this snare is to solicit constructive criticism from credible outsiders who view your situation more objectively. Seek out individuals whom you know to be informed and frank. Avoid listening to either the "doomsayers" whose glass is always half empty and the "cheerleaders" who will tell you to stick with your dream no matter how dire the situation looks. In the end, the decision to cut loose from a business must be your own choice, but it easier to do when you have good mentors and advisers.

opportunity cost

The value of something that must be sacrificed in exchange for pursuing a venture. If you choose to work full-time on your startup, your opportunity costs include the money you might have earned in a regular job.

There are two main reasons that you may not want to stick with the struggling business. One is the economic **opportunity cost** generated when declining other lucrative prospects. The other is the emotional toll such a struggle takes and the damage it may cause to those around you. When your time and energy are consumed in a stressful enterprise, you are probably not enjoying life to its fullest, and you may very well be making life miserable for your spouse, family, and friends. Striking a balance between your work and your social life is a challenge for all workers in today's competitive environment, and it can be particularly difficult for the small business owner. It is critical that you establish a sense of where you want that balance to be so that you can plan for and manage a business that meets your goals.

Where to Start: Make a Bucket List

bucket list

The list of achievements one would like to accomplish in their life.

One of the tasks I often assign to aspiring entrepreneurs is to prepare a ***bucket list*** of things they'd like to achieve in life. Do you plan to travel the world? Do you want to make a million dollars for its own sake? Do you want to continue your education and get a master's degree? Do you want to make a significant contribution to some social, religious, political, or environmental cause? If so, then make sure your business commitments can support these long-term personal goals.

A public bucket list, Hot Springs, NC

Source: CREATISTA/Shutterstock.com

In fact, the income and flexibility that a successful small business can produce make entrepreneurship the ideal career path for many highly aspirational individuals to achieve their non-business dreams. Bill Gates has leveraged his entrepreneurial success into a second career working on philanthropic causes with his wife, Melinda. "Business" is by far the most common occupation listed by members of the U.S. House of Representatives. In the 113th U.S. Congress, 187 members self-identified as businesspeople, significantly more than the 156 who identified as lawyers.

It's Not Always About You

As you establish your personal goals, you'll find out they include and depend on a lot of other people. Your next step is to consider the needs of those important individuals in your life. I don't mean to suggest that you must abandon your own dreams to keep others happy, but you should avoid profiting at the expense of people you love. Too often, I have sat down with successful entrepreneurs to look back at their amazing careers and found them dwelling over the trail of broken relationships they've inadvertently left in their wake. Their single-minded focus on their business has emptied their lives while filling their bank accounts. Finding a business model that doesn't alienate your spouse, children, friends, and community can be just as important as finding one that is profitable. Again, balance is the key to success. When all these things are aligned, businesses run more smoothly and entrepreneurial lives are happier, more rewarding, and often more financially successful.

Stay Healthy

Staying healthy is job 1 for entrepreneurs.

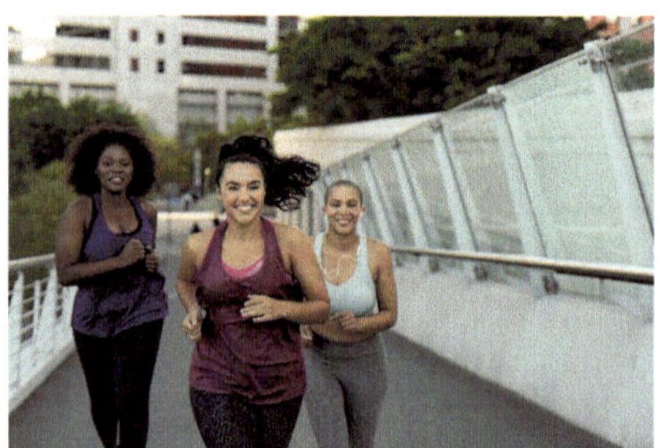

Source: © Shutterstock, Inc.

Entrepreneurship is not just about your business, and it's not just about your obligations to others. Sustained success requires a sharp mind. Research shows that your physical health is a significant determinant in maintaining mental fitness. Diet and exercise are the two most important factors you can control. Finding the time and energy for working out while working hard is a challenge. Demanding schedules and stress can erode your sleep. The convenience of fast food and the easy refuges of other poor lifestyle choices may present a constant challenge to the will power of the busy business owner. Often starting or running your own business may seem incompatible with a healthy lifestyle.

What is most important for the entrepreneur to understand is that as the boss, all of these choices are actually within his or her control. Making time to keep your most important asset—yourself—working well is just as important as closing the next big deal, shipping the next order, or finding the next employee. You've got to make it happen. While I'm not going to offer you any detailed health prescriptive—you and your health care providers know what those are—I can say from experience and research that regular exercise, good sleep, and a balanced diet are all positive factors in entrepreneurial performance. Being tired and overweight and smoking or drinking too much are likely to slow you down and perhaps land you in a hospital bed, which, even in today's connected world, is not the optimal place from which to run a business.

NED Theme: The Six Types of Startups . . . and the Fusion Firm as the Seventh Type

1. Lifestyle Startups: "Your job is your passion."
2. Small-Business Startups: "Your own gig."
3. Scalable Startups: "A focus on growth."
4. Buyable Startups: "Being the perfect target to be bought."
5. Social Startups (as a nonprofit, for-profit, or hybrid): "Doing good; making a difference."
6. Large-Company Startups: "Continuous innovation."

And . . . the Fusion Startup:

Remember that entrepreneurship is dynamic. There is no reason why you cannot start with one type of startup and then shift to another type . . . or even shift back again. Goals will change and your business will evolve. The New Entrepreneurial Dynamic encourages startups that combine, or evolve to be, many of these types of startups at once.

Key Takeaways

- Don't believe the story that most businesses fail.
- Learn that your time is your most valuable asset and don't invest it in efforts that aren't going to return sufficient value.
- Identify your personal life goals and integrate them into your startup planning.
- Know that other people depend on you, and your entrepreneurial choices may impact the lives of many others.
- Keeping physically fit must be job 1 for a successful entrepreneur.

1.5 Case Study: Tiantian, Kai, and Hip Hot Restaurant: Entrepreneurs Learn and Adapt

Tiantian, a student from Chengdu, China, recently graduated from the Marshall School of Business at the University of Southern California. Tiantian has two great passions in life—cooking and entrepreneurship. Cooking is something she has always loved. She loves experimenting with new ingredients and trying out new combinations. When she first met her boyfriend, Kai, and discovered that he was a picky eater, Tiantian saw it as a welcome challenge. Night after night, she would use Kai as her taster to create meals that would meet the approval of even the most discerning palates. Entrepreneurship, on the other hand, was a passion that was appointed to her. Like many other first-generation Chinese immigrants, she held her father's opinion in extremely high regard—and he always told Tiantian that going into business for herself was the only way to avoid getting taken advantage of by others.

Business owner Tiantian Qiu takes an order during Chinese New Year in her newly opened restaurant.

Source: Greg Autry

Not surprisingly, she decided to start a business of her own soon after graduation. Given her love for cooking, starting her own restaurant was her natural choice. In fact, it was the only choice. "I knew I needed to go into business for myself. That was the only way. And the only thing I've ever known is cooking . . . cooking authentic Chinese food."

Tiantian, with a little financial assistance from her father, began to search for locations for her restaurant within the greater Los Angeles' growing Chinese district. While the assistance from her father began as a small amount of capital, it very quickly skyrocketed. As she noted, "My father told me, if you go to a casino and bet $50, you have the potential to win perhaps $100. If you go to a casino with $1, then the luckiest you'll get is walking away with $2." That was how her father justified the large infusion of cash, which totaled in the hundreds of thousands of dollars.

Kai joined his girlfriend in the endeavor as a business partner. They settled on cuisine that catered to the local population—authentic Chengdu cuisine with a Szechuan flair that would leave not only the tongue tingling with spice, but also the body. They would name their restaurant Hip Hot. They also settled on a location on Monterey Park's Atlantic Boulevard in the fashionable nouveau center of LA's Chinese diaspora. It's a location that young, hip Asian trendsetters would frequent and where there was a dense population of other restaurants sharing her mission of providing an authentic Chinese eating experience. In fact, a dumpling house had previously occupied the real estate Hip Hot would be taking over. After steadily decreasing sales, the dumpling house folded, and the location became available.

One reason they gave for the possible decline of the dumpling house was the typical clientele that would frequent restaurants in the area. These patrons would often leave sharp-tongued comments on Yelp if the food was not authentic—something Tiantian saw as a challenge. As Tiantian has adamantly stated, "That would be a loss of my pride—to have people saying my food was not authentic. That would be shameful."

They did consider an alternate location at one point—close to a large college campus where there was a large population of students who craved authentic Chinese cuisine. Demand for this cuisine was almost entirely unmet in this area, but as Tiantian remarked: "We just couldn't find a place to rent. The rent was almost double what we are paying now."

As they began to start their restaurant, Tiantian and Kai realized the immensity of the endeavor they had embarked upon. There were a number of issues that they faced.

First, they realized that they just did not understand the business culture of the United States. The bureaucracy around building permits, paperwork, local government regulations, and legal and tax issues began to worry them. The more they were overwhelmed, the more they relied on the Chinese community to assist them. Soon they found that it was most reassuring to rely on a Chinese contractor for construction work, a Chinese lawyer that her father knew through a friend, and a Chinese accountant who could speak with them entirely in Chinese to explain tax regulations.

Yet, after a brief period of relief from working with people culturally familiar to them, Tiantian and Kai began to feel unsettled and realized that they were getting taken advantage of on a number of accounts. Legal discussions that were initially "very straightforward and not a problem," soon became an expensive task that they had to pay serious money for. A shipping container of authentic porcelain dishware that was supposed to cost only $5,000 to ship became delayed and only deliverable upon an extra payment of $3,000. The same shipping container arrived with 40 percent of the dishware broken, and Tiantian and Kai had no recourse for getting any money back.

Another issue that perhaps compounded their situation was the realization that they were being taken advantage of because people saw them as being young and in their early twenties—and hence not serious about entrepreneurship. They were repeatedly asked if they were "just doing this for fun" with Tiantian's father's money.

Tiantian and Kai began to do more themselves. When they were told that it would cost $500 to paint a wall, they decided to do it themselves. But as they took on more, there were also disastrous repercussions. When they were told that it would cost $4,000 to install video cameras, Kai took this task on himself, and it resulted in a fall from the second story of the building that left him hospitalized. He lost his sense of smell entirely and only partially regained his sense of taste six months after the accident.

Despite these setbacks, Tiantian and Kai held steady with a "learn by doing" attitude. Echoing the famous NASA maxim, Kai maintains, "Failure is not an option."

As they prepare for their grand opening, they plan on doing a number of things to promote their restaurant while holding steadfast to the Chinese way of doing things. They plan on having a day where all meals are free for those who are a part of Tiantian's WeChat network (a popular Chinese social communication app similar to WhatsApp). They are also determined to stay true to the Chengdu taste and not cater too much to Western taste buds. Tiantian and Kai place great importance on these sorts of ideas as they remain fearful of being blasted on Chinese social media. "That is also success," Tiantian remarks of gaining positive WeChat comments.

With the stress over needing to achieve success in multiple ways—profitability from the standpoint of her father's investment and authenticity from the standpoint of the community—it is no wonder that Tiantian is nervously excited about opening day.

Endnotes

1. You can find this table on the SBA website: https://www.sba.gov/content/small-business-size-standards.
2. https://www.sba.gov/sites/default/files/FAQ_March_2014_0.pdf
3. Rapid growth will be discussed later in this book, but if you are launching such an ambitious startup, there are a number of additional books that are recommended, including *Launching New Ventures* by Kathleen Allen, and *The Startup Owner's Manual* by Steve Blank and Bob Dorf.
4. http://fortune.com/2015/02/09/canaccord-apple-took-home-93-of-mobile-profits-last-quarter/
5. http://www.newyorkfed.org/research/current_issues/ci20-1.pdf
6. *Orange County Register* (http://www.ocregister.com/articles/linda-11551-yorba-newport.html).
7. http://psychcentral.com/blog/archives/2010/12/08/the-myth-behind-drinking-8-glasses-of-water-a-day/

CHAPTER 2
The New Entrepreneurial Dynamic

> No business plan survives first contact with customers.
>
> —*Steve Blank*[1]

The future is unpredictable.

Source: © Shutterstock, Inc.

business plan

A written plan that outlines business goals, methods to achieve them, and a projected timeline.

Traditional textbooks of entrepreneurship presume that startup founders can not only see into the future but that they can act on that knowledge in advance, eliminating ambiguity and reducing risk. These books focus most of their chapters on the **business plan**, funding sources, pitches, and other activities that go *before* doing business. This curriculum has produced legions of well-trained entrepreneurs armed with special-purpose business tools, carefully selected to overcome predefined obstacles, and who believe they are setting out with a road map to success! Seemingly, nothing is left to chance. . . .

However, the real world will swiftly show them that *chance remains the most important variable in any business model, regardless of the level of preparation*. It won't be long until the confidence of these well-trained entrepreneurs is shattered by completely unexpected challenges for which they find no suitable tools in their kits. At that point, they realize that their textbooks contained very little information on how to actually conduct business in a constantly changing real world.

2.1 The Stormy Seas of Commerce

Learning Objectives

1. Understand why traditional business plans are inappropriate for most startups.
2. Recognize that businesses exist in a dynamic environment and must adapt rapidly to survive and prosper.
3. Understand that planning depends on having accurate information about the future.
4. Appreciate the value of developing business capabilities to cope with both expected and unexpected events.
5. Realize that what makes an organization a business is its search for profits.
6. Understand that customers are the one thing every business must have.

Business Plans

The New Entrepreneurial Dynamic is all about change and adaptation. In their excellent book, *Getting to Plan B*, Stanford Professor John Mullins and famed venture capitalist Randy Komisar tell us:

Every aspiring entrepreneur has a Plan A. And virtually all of these individuals believe, like [PayPal founder Max] Levchin, that Plan A will work. They can probably even imagine how they'll look on the cover of Fortune, or the comments they'll give when asked, "How did you create the world's best business?" Unfortunately, they are usually wrong.[2]

Mullins and Komisar have seen a *lot* of plans, many of them well laid and some well funded. They have also seen that in almost every case, *the plan fails*. Occasionally, however, *the startup succeeds*. When the startup succeeds, it is usually because the entrepreneurs themselves refused to follow their own dubious plans into failure. Mullins and Komisar respect those entrepreneurs who "lick their wounds, get back on their feet, and morph their newly found insights into great businesses."

In fact, most entrepreneurs simply launch blindly into the stormy seas of commerce in search of opportunities without any formal plan. Natural entrepreneurs often resent the energy, money, and time spent producing written business plans and are intuitively skeptical of their relevance in the real world. Their startups are faster, nimbler, and far more tolerant of ambiguity than the ones featured in the textbooks.

Recently, management researchers analyzing the value of planning have found that these entrepreneurs are not misguided. Lange et al. (2007)[3] conclude that "new ventures launched with formal written business plans do not subsequently outperform ones launched without them." Chwolka and Raith (2012)[4] note that "the majority of ex-post successful entrepreneurs may not have a business plan."

For example, Steve Wozniak and Steve Jobs had no business plan when they launched Apple in 1977. The entrepreneurial duo just went for it, guided by instinct and a lot of real-world feedback from potential customers. Their Apple II quickly became the most successful home computer of its time.

Five years later, a more mature Apple produced a business plan for their Macintosh and LISA computers, developed in a closed, secretive process. The Macintosh was going to be launched in 1982 at $1,000, with an even cheaper "Very Low Cost" (VLC) computer to follow. Mac and VLC would grab market share on price, introduce users to the graphical computing of the 1980s, and convince professionals to move up to the more expensive LISA system.

This plan turned out to be significantly disconnected from reality. The cost estimates were off by more than 100 percent, and competing on prices was not an option. The Mac was actually introduced in 1984 at $2,500 and its price *increased* with new versions. VLC never saw the light of day, and LISA was discontinued. Apple suffered a significant reputational and financial blow from this misdirect. However, the firm quickly **pivoted** out of the plan, redeployed the best of its ideas, and went on to eventually become the world's most valuable firm.

pivot
A significant change in a firm's business strategy.

FIGURE 2.1 Product Price and Timeline Page from the 1981 Apple Business Plan
Essentially all the products, prices, and time estimates shown here were wrong.

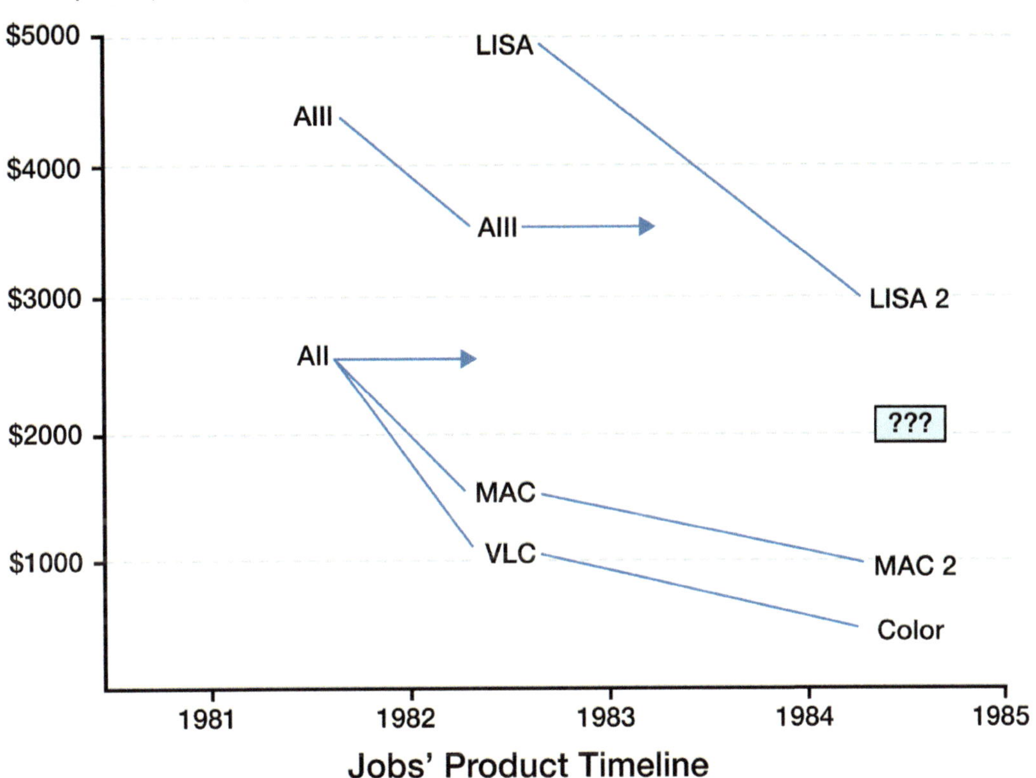

Source: The Computer Museum https://www.computerhistory.org/collections/catalog/102712692

Like Christopher Columbus, entrepreneurial explorers may not reach the goal they were aiming for, but they remain confident they will find treasures along the way. They mitigate risk not by planning every little detail in advance but by surrounding themselves with flexible people and building a versatile rather than a specialized toolkit.

What Is the New Entrepreneurial Dynamic?

After years of research and decades of working as and with entrepreneurs, I have come to believe that a rigidly formal business plan actually robs startups of their primary source of competitive advantage against their larger, entrenched competitors. That competitive advantage is *the flexi-*

bility required to learn from failure and to swiftly adapt to environmental changes. This insight establishes the basis for the New Entrepreneurial Dynamic, with *dynamic* being the key word.

Dynamic adaptability is the most important single aspect of the successful entrepreneur. Consequently, I am thrilled to see that venture capitalists, popular press pundits, and even business schools are labeling the traditional approach to teaching and planning as passé for *startups and small businesses*. Entrepreneur and educator Steve Blank has written:

> *Today, after half a century of practice, we know unequivocally that the traditional MBA curriculum for running large companies like IBM, GM, and Boeing does not work in startups. In fact, it's toxic.*[5]

Toxic! That's a pretty strong word, but Blank should know. He's been involved in launching eight startups, has taught entrepreneurship at the University of California at Berkeley, New York University, and Stanford, and written some great books on the startup process. The New Entrepreneurial Dynamic concurs with Blank; startups and all forms of small business are not simply scaled-down models of the multinational corporations that our traditional educational business education curriculum has been designed to serve. The core of this curriculum is a formal strategic planning process and supporting toolkit that has worked very well for large organizations, with vast resources, in refining their competitive advantages in existing industries or entering other established markets.

That doesn't suggest that business planning itself lacks value or that business plans must *always* be ignored. The *process of planning* can be a valuable experience of entrepreneurial self-discovery (see Ike the Planner sidebar). Carefully imagining how one or more future business scenarios might play out and planning for how to best execute on that particular reality can be a very valuable exercise. What is critical in this exercise is understanding that any one of these scenarios is *only a single possibility among a multitude of alternative futures*. Modern academic research backs up this approach. Chwolka and Raith (2012) conclude that the value of planning lies in "evaluating alternative actions and being able to improve strategies."

Planning Depends on Forecasting

To be useful, a plan must assume that you know what you are planning for, and it is here that the single biggest weakness of the traditional business plan emerges. As with forecasting the weather, the economy, or any other complex system, there are countless points of possible divergence from any particular path.

Consider Figure 2.2, which illustrates a very simple progression of market events for a hypothetical snack food company. At the current time, the baseline market state is at time zero, designated T_0. The past is T–1, and there is only one possible event shown between there and now because we know exactly what did happen in the previous event. T+1 is the immediate future, and our firm faces two possible anticipated events, things we suspect may shape the future market. This event might be future consumers preferring chocolate or hazelnut.

Such a simple divergence can be anticipated, and each contingency could be planned for in advance. Planning for both might require a larger product development group (two teams working on flavored snacks) or establishing an e-commerce site just in case. This sort of planning is very doable, though it will increase costs and necessitate keeping a bit more cash on reserve or slightly reducing profits for a more significant reduction in risk. It's a management choice over contingencies.

FIGURE 2.2 The Chain of Market Events

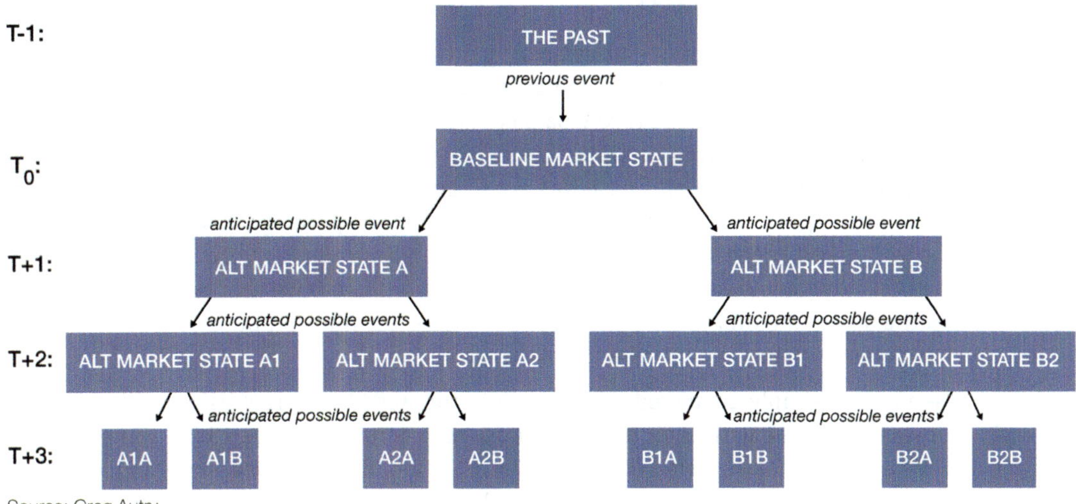

Source: Greg Autry

Contingency planning begins to unravel when you realize how many such events there are in the firm's future. Looking ahead to T+2, we face one more set of possibilities. Perhaps this is a coming government regulation that mandates a healthier rather than tastier ingredient. We now have four possible scenarios. We can plan for the development of two separate supplier relations for different ingredients (e.g., healthy versus tasty). We now have to prepare for chocolate healthy, chocolate tasty, hazelnut healthy, and hazelnut tasty. That's four possible realities.

contingency planning

The process of planning in advance for more than one possible outcome or set of circumstances.

If we face another two-choice decision at T+3, say the development of a possible new online distribution channel, we now have eight possible scenarios to plan for and to fund contingency operations. That's expensive! Worse, decisions aren't always binary; there may be three, four, or more possible directions. Most businesses would face many dozen possible scenarios in a few years. Many of them would be similar, but many would be different enough to require changes in plans.

Further, each point of divergence also has a probability of events going one way or the other. You could bet on the favorites to reduce the need for planning! If the odds of event A occurring the way you planned are 70 percent, and the odds of event B going your way are 70 percent, then you may feel pretty confident, right? Sadly, however, the odds of each event occurring must be multiplied (0.7 × 0.7 or 70 percent of 70 percent). Now the chances of your getting to your point C are already down to less than half (42 percent)!

The longer the time frame covered, the less likely the plan will match any future environmental reality. Imagine if there were 100 discreet points of possible critical divergence. Even if each of these had a 95 percent probability of going your way, it's still very unlikely you'll get to your predicted scenario. The multiplication of all these probabilities makes it very improbable that your business plan is designed for the future in which you will find your company operating. In fact, even being assured of these odds presumes you at least know in advance where all the possible points of market divergence are. That's impossible—you can barely see the most immediate ones. Some *unexpected* chance occurrences *will* eventually render *any* long-term plan dangerously out of sync with reality. You can't make contingency plans for events you don't even see coming. The history of business is littered with the corpses of great firms that failed to see a significant **market disruption** coming.

market disruption

A circumstance where markets stop operating in the normally accepted way. Market disruptions often result in value loss for incumbent firms and investors and create an opportunity for new entrants.

The computer industry is the perfect laboratory in which to view this process because it has continued to evolve quickly over several decades. In the mid-1970s, a handful of innovative young firms centered around Boston were riding high. Firms like Digital Equipment Corporation (DEC), Data General, and Wang Laboratories had successfully disrupted the dominance of the mainframe computer companies led by IBM. They had leveraged newly developed integrated circuit technology to create a new class of smaller, cheaper computers. The PDP-8, Nova Eclipse, and other "minicomputers" quickly became the systems of choice for manufacturing and engineering firms. The new firms viewed their mainframe predecessors as dinosaurs. The entrepreneurs who founded

DEC, Ken Olsen and Harlan Anderson, were rightly hailed as geniuses of innovation and planning. Their venture capital team was headed by a professor from the Harvard Business School.

Sadly, these newly minted captains of industry paid no attention to a group of hobbyists in California who were building "homebrew" computers based on the even newer microprocessor technology. These hobbyists included Steve Wozniak and Steve Jobs, whom we met earlier founding Apple. DEC and the other minicomputer firms executed on traditional business plans. An unexpected disruption from the West Coast was not in any of the plans, and consequently, it did not exist for their management. They were unwilling to significantly change their plans in the face of a changing reality, and as the saying goes, "reality bites." In less than ten years, every last one of the minicomputer firms was swept away by the personal computer wave that emerged from Silicon Valley. In the face of an unpredicted disruptive challenge, the minicomputer firms had proven to be even less dynamic than their mainframe predecessors.

Ken Olsen at first simply dismissed the personal computer (PC) market as nonexistent; then he insisted it was out of line with their new VAX superminicomputer strategy. Why compete with themselves? When DEC finally entered the PC market, they found themselves far behind and playing a hopeless game of catch-up *with their old rival IBM*, which had wisely pivoted their strategy to embrace the PC.

empirical evidence

Knowledge derived from direct observation of the actual world.

Olsen and the other minicomputer entrepreneurs weren't any less brilliant than Steve Jobs or Bill Gates. Ironically, the primary difference was they had completed college, whereas their PC competitors had dismissed school as irrelevant and dropped out. The minicomputer moguls were *victims of their superior education*. Their engineering and business school training had taught them to design everything up front, and their investors expected them to execute according to a plan. Apple and Microsoft simply dove into the market, determined only to meet customer needs. Sadly, many schools and texts on entrepreneurship continued to teach the business plan approach long after the **empirical evidence** had demonstrated its failure in actual practice.

The third generation of computer firms embraced the foundations of the NED, and that is why many of them are still going strong. Companies like Apple and Microsoft intuitively replaced traditional business planning with rapid and iterative product development. They are *dynamically redefining themselves to fit the actual realities of the market*. Apple has repeatedly attempted to disrupt itself, fearlessly introducing new product lines even when they threatened the firm's most significant revenue sources; witness the Macintosh displacing the more expensive LISA and the early cash-cow Apple II and more recently, the iPad eating into the sales of the popular MacBook notebooks.

The complexity of a market environment, the speed at which that environment changes, and the precision of your data on how it is changing will determine how far ahead you can reasonably look into the behavior of any particular system. For weather predictions, anything beyond a week or two is highly speculative. In economic forecasting, usefulness is measured in months. In the rapidly evolving technology business climate, any business plan that looks beyond a year is probably not worth the trouble. There is a very good reason why one of today's leading journals on the tech business is called *Fast Company*!

Ike the Planner

Eisenhower led the most complex logistical planning operation in history.

Source: https://commons.wikimedia.org/wiki/File:Dwight_D._Eisenhower_as_General_of_the_Army_crop.jpg

Before he became president of the United States in 1950, Dwight D. Eisenhower was a general in the U.S. Army. During WWII, he served as chief of the War Plans Division and was eventually appointed allied supreme commander, directing all the forces of Free Europe against Hitler. Ike, as he was affectionately known, oversaw the planning of the most complex military action in history, the amphibious invasion of Normandy, France, on June 6, 1944, code-named "Operation Overlord." This immense effort was the most important step in liberating Europe from Nazi occupation and restoring freedom to many millions of Europeans.

The D-Day beach landings at Normandy involved more than 150,000 soldiers from several nations acting in unison. Despite years of study and planning by the most talented military minds from America and Britain, the soldiers who fought the battle that day universally describe it as completely chaotic. Not surprisingly, the real-world actions of the defending German soldiers pretty much failed to match those dreamed up by the generals back in London. The film *Saving Private Ryan* accurately displays the changing landscape in which officers quickly ditched their plans and were forced to improvise tactics merely to keep their troops alive during the first hour of battle. To most of them, D-Day looked like a disaster in progress. Nonetheless, the information the allied commanders had collected and the preparations that Ike and his staff provided for the officers worked well enough for the invasion to gain its foothold. The Allies held the beaches, and the war in Europe was over within a year. Millions were saved from the brutal oppression and genocidal activities of the Nazi regime. Considering this and other lessons from his career, Eisenhower famously remarked, "I have always found that plans are useless, but planning is indispensable."

And Yet, There Is a Time for Everything

disrupt

The act or strategy of a small business to enter an established market, and successfully challenge the well-established incumbent business model.

All that said, I believe that the traditional business plan does have a place in some markets. It is entirely appropriate for "me too" businesses entering relatively static environments. For instance, if you were planning to open a chain of conventional donut shops in Canada, we'd instantly point out that the national champion, Tim Hortons, truly owns that territory. We'd strongly advise you to develop a more innovative strategy with which to **disrupt** the Canadian breakfast foods market. However, if you were determined to simply do one better than Hortons, you had better plan very well indeed. A detailed business plan and a whole lot of financial backing would be minimal prerequisites for such an uphill, head-on assault against a powerful and entrenched competitor.

Tim Hortons is the most successful fast-food chain in Canada.

Source: https://commons.wikimedia.org/wiki/File:Tim_Hortons,_Tottenham.jpg

The traditional business plan is also an extremely useful prop for presentation to your most conservative constituents, such as your bankers or your parents! These folks *want* you to tell them that every aspect of your business is completely predictable and totally under control, even if, in their hearts, they know that can't really be true. These folks sleep better at night believing in the plan.

In this chapter, we will review several alternative approaches to planning that better reflect today's dynamic business environment. These solutions focus on establishing a team, a business model, and a culture that are dynamic. The New Entrepreneurial Dynamic calls for a powerful, diverse core team, united in a common mission; a virtualized structure; and decision-making close to the point of customer contact. These firms need a culture that supports individuals stepping beyond their assigned roles, and that even celebrates their valiant failures. In lieu of a business plan, what the twenty-first century small business requires, are systems to provide real-time data collection and analysis in support of rapid market hypothesis testing and decision-making.

The life expectancy of a business model has become shorter and shorter, and firms that survive often have to change theirs regularly. Consider the world when Coca-Cola opened its doors. The market opportunity for a new class of "soft drinks" was clear. The business model was smart but fixed: produce a quality product, develop a leading brand, and deliver the product at a profit through regional bottlers to soda counters and stores. This model worked flawlessly for more than a century and developed into a global phenomenon that seemed as if it would never end. Today, however, trends in fashionable beverages from energy drinks to organic coconut water come and go at a torrid pace, and traditional soda sales are in a sharp decline. To survive the last decade, the venerable Coca-Cola corporation has had to constantly reinvent itself. Similar situations face nearly every institutional firm from McDonald's to General Motors.

Today's business mantra is "change or die." Entrepreneurs must prosper in an environment defined by mobile devices, constant interruptions, fast fashion, and an entire generation with incredibly short attention spans. This is a world where Facebook reports back to advertisers which percentage of their viewers stuck with an ad video for *10 seconds or more*, and sadly, 25 percent is a good result for that paltry level of consumer engagement.

Added Monetary Value Makes an Organization a Business

It may seem obvious that a business is an organization, but not all organizations are businesses. Consider the Red Cross. Is it a business? The Red Cross is clearly well organized. Further, it is an organization with a powerful and instantly recognizable brand. It handles millions of dollars and has thousands of employees. People around the world have benefited from the value its services provide. So, is it a business?

The Red Cross is a charity. A charity is a particular type of nonprofit enterprise we discussed in Chapter 1. The important difference is found in the way that a charity's services are essentially disconnected from its revenue. A charity collects donations to provide services to people who usually pay nothing. It has benefactors, and it has beneficiaries, but it doesn't have customers. It is not a business.

Red Cross workers distribute supplies to Syrian refugees.

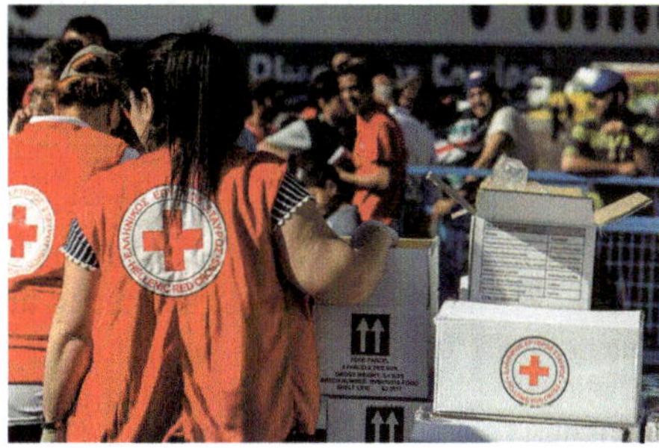

Source: Richard Panasevich/Shutterstock.com

All businesses have customers. Customers are the people who pay money for a product or service, and they define a business. Better serving the changing needs of customers effectively maximizes the value they receive and will pay for. Understanding that your customers' perception of value changes, sometimes in predictable ways and sometimes in unpredictable ways or ways that may even render your product irrelevant, is part of the New Entrepreneurial Dynamic.

Businesses have owners or shareholders whose goal is usually to obtain the returns on their investment. They put their hard-earned money into the enterprise in hopes of getting more money out of it.

However, this is not to say that a firm's owners may not have a greater vision or social mission. They may even reinvest their returns into the business so it can further those larger goals. There are some nonprofit enterprises whose entire purpose is to deliver their product or service to the customer who needs it and not to capture the value it has created. This is very different from the old-school philanthropy model, where profitable firms or successful entrepreneurs would assuage their sense of guilt by making large donations to charities or running internal corporate fundraisers.

Having a popular social mission can add value to customers and actually increase a firm's revenues. These are the best of the social enterprises that we mentioned in Chapter 1. Newman's Own can charge more for a comparable bottle of spaghetti sauce than its competitors because customers want to be part of the mission. Recognizing that doing good can be a firm's core value and an important source of strategic advantage rather than an afterthought is part of the NED.

Would you consider a blogger or a YouTuber a business? If these individuals have revenue (money from ads), the state would consider their activity to be a business for tax purposes, but are they really running "organizations?" A blogger or YouTuber's organization is the audience they build into an online community. It is the size and engagement of this community that allows them to capture value by selling ads. It is as if they have turned customers into workers. You can think of traditional radio and television in the same way. There are many ways to compose an organization and even more ways to create value.

Customers Are Required, Everything Else Is Optional

In 2013, Snapchat, the photo-sharing app, received an investment that valued the firm at over half a billion dollars. The firm had no revenue and no revenue model. Does that make any sense? Would you rather own Snapchat or a profitable dairy farm? A subcategory of the Rapid Growth Startup, the *Silicon Valley Startup* emphasizes growth over profits to the point that even sales are optional. California's venture capital moguls believe that just about any MBA student can type up a tight business plan and structure a profitable-looking model. Still, if they cannot drive enough customers into that model, the firm's impact will be completely irrelevant. For them, the first step is always a myopic focus on market share and brand. Once that has been established, the profits can be extracted from the brand's loyal followers.

While the Silicon Valley Startup seems obsessive, and it is, the lesson should not be lost on any small businessperson. No matter how much market research you do, if your product sells, it sells; if it does not sell, you must fix it. Customers are required; everything else in a business is optional.

data analytics

The formal analysis of data sets to draw conclusions relevant to decision making. Data analytics is particularly important in the marketing of products.

customer discovery

A process of interviewing and surveying customers about their needs. Customer discovery is critical to the process of developing products and services.

Customers are also the greatest source of insight for your company. Listening carefully to what the customer wants is a whole lot easier than trying to sell them something they really don't need. Find out how your product or service idea can best fit into the lives of real consumers or the operations of real businesses. Get out and ask real people how they are currently dealing with the problem you think you may have solved. Don't bias them with your ideas; just listen. As your product develops, continue this process to refine it. Get feedback, use surveys, make your shoe fit the customer's foot as perfectly as possible before you make it. This customer-focused trend has resulted in an explosion in **data analytics**. Google AdWords and other tools are designed to provide insights from customer behavior that will improve your product and its positioning in the market. This process of **customer discovery** is integral to the New Entrepreneurial Dynamic.

Key Takeaways

- Your business will always exist in a business environment filled with unexpected events that cannot be planned for.
- You must build up dynamic capabilities that allow you to adapt and prosper under any circumstances.
- Planning is valuable, not because it produces a plan you can follow to the letter, but because it forces you to think about the future environment and your capabilities.
- A startup can be a type of organization other than a business.
- Finding and keeping customers is the most essential element of any business.

2.2 Uncertainty Is the New Normal

Learning Objectives

1. Appreciate the trade-off between risk and reward in a startup.
2. Understand the power of innovation.
3. Recognize the power of disruption.
4. Appreciate the significance of the impact of globalization on businesses and the economy they exist in.

Risk and Reward

One of the most important lessons in finance is that there is a correlation between risk and reward. Investors expect higher rates of return for risky investments and will accept lower rates for safe ones. As I write this, the average savings **certificate of deposit** (CD) account at a bank is paying about 1 percent interest, and many government bonds are paying real negative rates (less than the rate of inflation). This record-low interest rate situation has been a global phenomenon for more than a decade. What does this tell you about the concern that investors are showing over risk?

certificate of deposit

A bank instrument that pays a higher rate of interest in exchange for a guarantee by a depositor that funds will not be withdrawn for a specified period of time.

If investors weren't so eager to buy up these CDs and bonds, banks and governments would have to offer them higher rates. Low interest rates suggest that global investors have become quite **risk averse** on average. Stagnant growth in developed economies, insecurity in the developing world, financial crisis, and terrorism have tempered their moods. On the other hand, funding a startup is clearly a risky endeavor. Do you suspect that funding for startups and small businesses has become more difficult to find during the same period?

Bank deposits are guaranteed by the FDIC.[6]

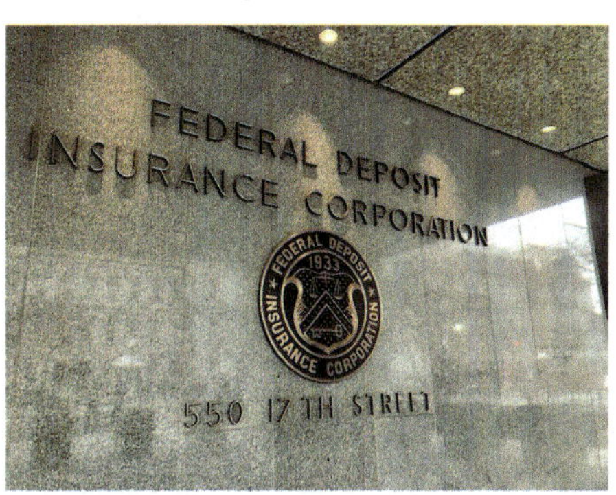

Source: DCStockPhotography/Shutterstock.com

Surprisingly, growth in the founding and funding of new businesses remained strong during much of this period. Global uncertainty has been good for entrepreneurs. On the high end, the so-called "Unicorn" startups like Uber and Snapchat were able to secure huge investments at high valuations. In the small business world, foundings also soared. The growth in small business launches has been driven by this low interest rate environment as well as the factors we will cover in Chapter 16, such as unemployment and low wage growth. Investors with even a moderate tolerance for risk were appalled at the idea of tying their money up in CDs or bonds that would be whittled away by inflation, and they were increasingly attracted to the startup scene. Firms big and small benefited from this. Can you think of other ways small business has benefited from low interest rates?

risk averse

The state of being overly concerned with taking chances. A risk-averse individual or firm is unlikely to invest in new concepts or technologies for fear of missing out.

When rates are low, a small business can afford to borrow money for expansion. They build, grow, and hire, and their suppliers do the same. This business growth to low interest rates relationship is the primary reason that the government historically lowers rates during a recession.

Uncertainty offers another great benefit for entrepreneurs: change in the economic and business environment. Dynamic small businesses are simply better equipped to adapt to change compared to their larger competitors. Consequently, uncertain environments favor entrepreneurs over large corporations. In fact, in the most chaotic environments—countries torn by civil war, for instance—small businesses are often the only game in town as large competitors flee from uncertainty.

While this uncertainty is not for the faint of heart, entrepreneurs who are willing to tolerate sleepless nights and an ulcer or two will enjoy plenty of thrills and perhaps some great rewards. Business in a dynamic environment is a lot like a poker tournament: You must manage and exploit risk. Intelligently deciding when to bet heavily, when to hold, and when to fold will give the entrepreneur a statistical edge; the rest depends on fate. While our careers depend on educating entrepreneurs, there really are opportunities so valuable that it makes sense to drop out of college and invest all of your money in a small business. That plan worked for Bill Gates, Steve Jobs, and many others, right? You shouldn't be surprised to know that the same choice has had disastrous consequences for many entrepreneurs that you'll never hear about. Like everything else, these life choices come down to risk management. The NED is about playing uncertainty to your advantage.

Embracing Open Innovation

STEM

Science, Technology, Engineering, and Mathematics. These disciplines are highly correlated with innovation and economic development.

It is commonly accepted that innovation is the lifeblood of technology companies. Google believes profits and success come from letting the problem-solvers think outside the box. In order to drive innovation as a startup, Google at first hired *only* engineers. The quintessential internet firm still aims to have more than half of its employees be scientists or engineers. Google wants these **STEM** majors working in management and other nontechnical areas because they are trained to think as experimenters and problem solvers, not as "rule followers." Many of Silicon Valley's technologists believe that innovation gets bogged down when people trained in rote thinking obtain positions of power. They, very rightly, fear that professionals educated in rule-following—accountants, MBAs, and lawyers—bring dangerously narrow, risk-averse perspectives into startups. As these "business professionals" take over, they increasingly define what can't be done, or shouldn't be attempted, reducing the firm's exposure to innovation and closing off the possibilities. Does innovation matter to your small business?

disruption

A sudden dislocation that results in major shifts to a market. Consumer choices, dominant vendors, distribution channels, and pricing models may all change. Often caused by innovation in processes or technology.

In today's fast-moving, technology-driven world, even the simplest small businesses find themselves victims of **disruption**. Before 2010, a New York City cab driver, holding one of that town's precious taxi medallions, was ensured of a comfortable, independent living. Similarly, the owners of a quaint New England bed and breakfast were confident that their time-tested business model guaranteed a lifetime of enjoyable self-employment. By 2013, these small business operators found themselves in fights for their livelihoods with unexpected opponents: Uber and Airbnb, amateur operators backed by the technology, capital, and marketing prowess of Silicon Valley startups. Whether you own a dry cleaner or a donut store, you can bet that there is a group of brilliant young people in San Francisco, Bangalore, or Shanghai planning the downfall of your industry and powerful investors with billions of dollars are ready to back their all-out assault on your small business. If you don't want to be a victim, you've got to be one step ahead of that innovation game or ready to join it. The New Entrepreneurial Dynamic demands constant innovation, even in the simplest company. As a small business, how might you inspire or even enshrine innovation in your company culture?

Ridesharing disrupted the taxi business during the 2010s.

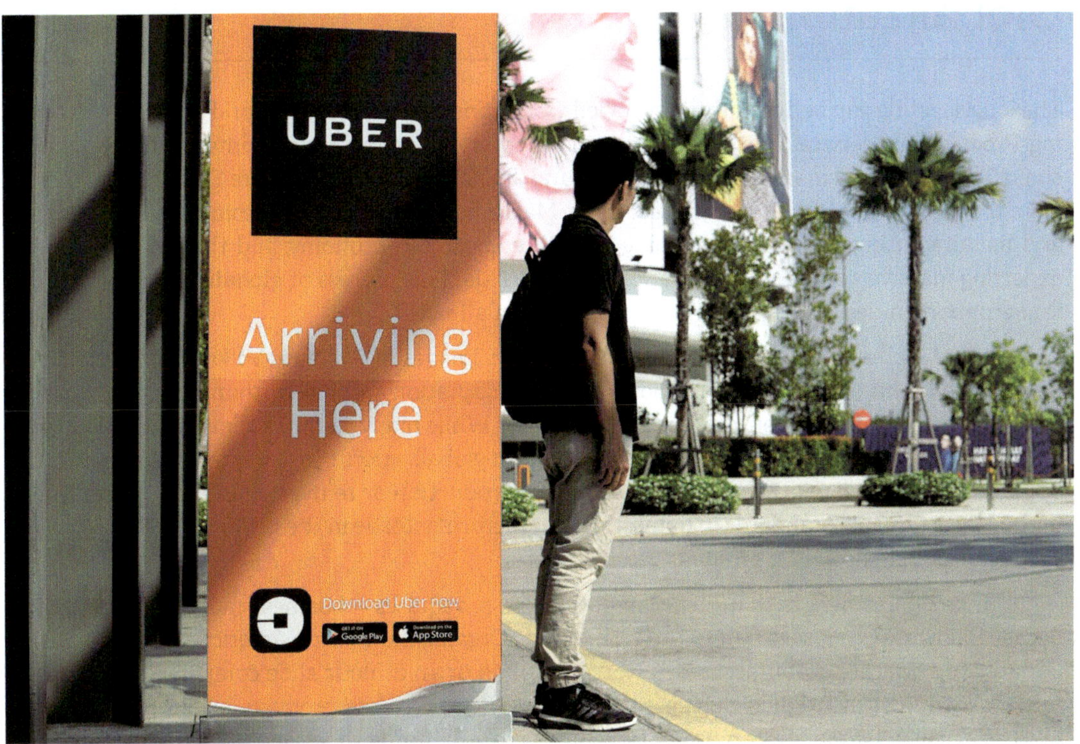

Source: TY Lim/Shutterstock.com

One great way to inspire endless innovation is by using a **moonshot**, an organizational goal that is both audacious and inspiring. It needs to be an objective you can't achieve quickly, perhaps ever, but which will drive your employees to do great things. The **spinoffs**, unexpected products and technologies that are generated in these efforts can drive companies to new heights. Elon Musk has famously used this technique with his startup, SpaceX. From its day of founding in 2002, the firm's stated goal was to get human beings to Mars, a task that the most powerful governments were still very far from achieving. For years, the little firm struggled with launch failures and with finances, but its "Occupy Mars" goal drove the SpaceX team to work insane hours and achieve amazing things. They eventually mastered the technique of space launches and established a growing and profitable space launch services business, lofting payloads for NASA, the U.S. military, and global commercial firms. Along the way, the SpaceX team was compelled to develop more efficient engine designs, to perfect scalable rocket manufacturing, and to revolutionize the economics of space travel by developing reusable orbital boosters. The Red Planet remains their goal. Can any small business achieve this?

moonshot

A majorly ambitious effort or program designed to achieve a particularly audacious goal.

spinoff

A product or service that is developed as the fortunate outcome of an investment in another development project. A spinoff is often the serendipitous application of some technology developed in order to move the primary project forward.

I believe the moonshot can be applied to any firm or market. Simple businesses like McDonald's and Starbucks started as tiny, local entities in highly competitive, mature markets. When they launched, nobody would have expected anyone to become a billionaire flipping hamburgers or serving coffee. In each case, it took a visionary (Ray Kroc and Howard Schulz, respectively) with the audacious goal of covering the world with their outlets and to differentiate themselves from their competitors. To achieve this scalability, the little firms were forced to innovate. They designed new products, new procedures, developed world-class efficiencies, and perfected the art of customer satisfaction. If they had aspired simply to be the biggest hamburger chain in Southern California or have the most coffee houses in Seattle, they might not have succeeded at all. Your little firm can do the same, and if, perchance, you don't conquer the global market, you will most likely have a more profitable, competitive, and manageable small business.

Globalization

globalization

An ongoing process of internationalization of markets characterized by increased cross-border travel and trade and reduced barriers to these activities. Globalization has disrupted markets around the world.

offshoring

The process of moving manufacturing from the domestic market to another country to capture higher profits via lower wages and less onerous worker safety and environmental regulations.

The longstanding gap between the "developed world" and the "developing world" is rapidly narrowing. Products and services are produced around the world in an increasingly interconnected supply chain. The traditional manufacturing/agricultural divide that used to separate Europe and America from the rest of the world has vanished. India, Malaysia, and Turkey are becoming hubs of service and manufacturing. China is developing a mature consumer economy, and the United States is exporting massive amounts of grain and poultry to Asia. This process of **globalization** brings with it new opportunities as well as challenges for firms of all sizes.

While the phrase "global business" brings to mind images of Walmart, Volkswagen, or IBM, we believe smaller firms always have the advantages of adaptation and speed. Changing environments are good environments for entrepreneurs who adapt. While many traditional manufacturing firms in America and Europe have suffered very badly from globalization, those who either exploited the opportunities of lowered costs by **offshoring** their production or reinvested in their commitment to the highest quality standards in domestic manufacturing (Made in the USA or Made in Germany products, for instance) have profited.

The key point here is that environmental change requires a business model change. In the decade following China's entry into the World Trade Organization, 57,000 American factories closed. For a wood furniture manufacturer in North Carolina or an athletic shoe company in Massachusetts, following their original business plan when cheap Chinese products began to flood their market was just like walking off a cliff. New Balance, the running shoe company, adapted by simultaneously offshoring its low-end products and by refocusing its U.S. production on high-end customized footwear. The economics of globalization have also changed the makeup of entire markets, driving income up but often increasing inequality. In the United States, wealth rapidly increased for a select few, while more and more Americans found themselves with declining real incomes. The Gini coefficient, a measure of inequality, has shot up in recent years. A figure of zero represents pure income equality (all incomes are equal), and 1 represents total inequality (one person holds all income). As of 2018, the U.S. reached 0.49, up from 0.43 in 1992.[7] By 2015, the American middle class had become a minority for the first time since the Great Depression. Small businesses with products aimed at high-income buyers have flourished. So have those aimed at the poorest consumers. Consequently, we've seen a boom in luxury boutique clothing stores, as well as corner payday check-cashing firms. The trend in much of Europe has been similar. Understanding economic trends is part of the New Entrepreneurial Dynamic.

Meanwhile, a growing middle class in China has created opportunities for entrepreneurs in Shanghai and Beijing to duplicate many of the traditional Western small business models. Chinese are now drinking wine, buying pet supplies, and looking for distracting entertainment, and small businesses are popping up everywhere to serve these trends. The boom in Chinese "escape rooms" is a perfect example of this trend. Still, the Gini coefficient is relatively high in China (0.468 vs. 0.328 in the United Kingdom in 2018) due primarily to newly wealthy Chinese entrepreneurs and well-connected government figures advancing much more rapidly than the working class.

supply chain

The network of suppliers and subsuppliers (your suppliers' suppliers) that provide the inputs your firm requires to produce its product or provide its service.

Offshoring creates some important inherent challenges. A firm that offshores suffers from increased shipping costs and a time lag of several weeks. It also faces challenges of oversight and communications that can result in quality issues. Receiving a big shipment of incorrect or flawed products in October has spoiled many a firm's entire holiday season and even put a few of them out of business. Many American manufacturers are now bringing much of their production, or at least final assembly, closer to home. They are reshoring to the U.S. or seeking suppliers in lower-cost Latin American countries like the Dominican Republic. Similarly, many European producers have located production in Turkey. Small firms that help these manufacturers improve their **supply chain** are involved in this process all along the way.

Zara made Amancio Ortega one of the world's richest men. Ortega saw the weakness in globalization and was able to exploit it with his own integrated manufacturing and retailing solution. He mastered the art of "Fast Fashion," getting cheap trendy clothes from local producers into his stores before his rivals could ramp up their Asian production. By the time the competing products arrived in Europe, Zara had moved on to the next hot thing. Consumers chose Zara to stay ahead of the fashion curve. Recognizing that one firm's problem almost always creates an opportunity for another firm is key to the NED.

The largest factory in the world produces many products for Apple in Foxconn City, Shenzhen, China.

Source: Greg Autry

Picture a small American producer of specialty iced teas. It's a simple operation: brew fine teas, infuse them with high-quality natural flavors, bottle them, and ship them to customers around the world. Such a business could find its tea supply chain interrupted by an unexpected breakdown in a Chinese-Taiwan trade deal. The global collapse of honeybee colonies may drive its sweetener costs up. It may find market demand drops due to instability in Greece that lowers the purchasing power of all Euro consumers. Its sales might rise due to unexpected consumer trends in India.

Key Takeaways

- You must evaluate every opportunity in light of the risk it entails.
- Innovation is critical to every business in the twenty-first century.
- All businesses are being disrupted by technology; be the disruptor, not the victim.
- Every business in the world now exists in a global market.

2.3 Networking Starts Before Your Business Does

Learning Objectives

1. Understand that every business that plans to grow is about a team, not just an entrepreneur.
2. Making a firm commitment to your endeavor is critical for its success.
3. Understand the power of video technology in pitching your firm.

Building a Team

Building a business usually requires building a team, and building a successful business requires building a great team. Without a qualified team, your ship is sunk before it leaves port because, in the end, execution is all-important. If you must outsource labor or find talent elsewhere, you need to prioritize doing it right. A haphazard launch with the wrong people or partners will surely lead to failure. Category Five Boat Shoes CEO, Jason Shuman, was perfect for the job but found that his buddy's cofounders were actually liabilities and they kept the company from getting funding and securing the best connections.

Finding the right people and partners isn't as simple as gathering students in a project team for your entrepreneurship class. You'll need to network a lot to find people with the right mix of attributes, experience, and education. When you find them, you can't simply invite them to hop on. You'll find that great people have a lot of other options—job offers or their own startup ideas. You'll have to nurture the relationship and demonstrate your own capabilities and value while doing it. To do that, you must interact with these people regularly. Networks such as LinkedIn, Facebook, etc. are good for keeping track of and connecting to these useful people, but you need to make it more personal than that. Even if you don't need them today, once you've got a valuable connection, take them to lunch or coffee, or talk on the phone every few months at the least.

Total Commitment, Burn Your Boat

Painting in the Naval History Museum, Mexico City.

Source: Alejandro Linares Garcia. Source: https://commons.wikimedia.org/wiki/File:ScuttleFleetNHMDF.JPG

In 1519, the Spanish Conquistador Hernán Cortés and his 500 men faced a seemingly impossible task: conquering an unknown continent with a population of millions ruled by the powerful Aztec empire. Shortly after landing on the Yucatan peninsula, the small Spanish force was confronted by intimidating masses of Mesoamerican warriors. The conquistadors were confused by unknown customs and terrified by acts of human sacrifice and the ritual cannibalism the Aztecs demanded. Several of Cortés's troops planned to mutiny and flee via the sea. Cortés hung the leaders and forced the rest to recommit by destroying all the ships that could carry them back to Spain. With nowhere to go but forward, the small band of conquerors outmatched the Aztecs in ruthlessness and brought Mexico under Spanish rule in just two years.

Many entrepreneurs like to play it safe and approach their business as a side-job. They play with it and hope it takes off, but meanwhile, they keep their day-job to pay bills and fund their little experiment. This safe route leads to complacency. If you quit your day job, you *will* find a way to pay the bills from your startup, and your business will be much more likely to succeed. You will have more time to dedicate to the success of your startup, and more importantly, you will feel tremendous pressure to succeed. While embracing flexibility, the New Entrepreneurial Dynamic also requires commitment.

Let's Go!

You've got the idea now. Today's small businesses need to be constantly in touch with their changing environment. They must constantly adapt as that environment evolves, and they may occasionally need to pivot to entirely new models. Dynamic entrepreneurs must embrace new trends and technologies. The remainder of this textbook will take you through the mechanics of launching and running a real-world business in the context of the New Entrepreneurial Dynamic.

Video Pitches Are the New Executive Summary

The New Entrepreneurial Dynamic embraces technological progress. We live in the age of video, and if a picture is worth a thousand words, a video must be worth a million! The pitch video is the centerpiece of crowdfunding on sites like Kickstarter, and it is rapidly becoming the best bet for reaching investors. In a world of 280-character tweets, few of us look forward to reading long documents, and nobody is more tuned into the fast pace and technology of content delivery than today's investors. Sending a printed and bound business plan to a Silicon Valley venture capitalist immersed in today's interconnected media makes no sense. Every startup should have a solid pitch video in its arsenal.

Video rules because ultimately, investment decisions are likely based on your team and understanding what your product or service does. No compilation of phrases and charts can convey that the way a video can. If your team is tangible on the video, your product is doing its thing.

Video pitches need not be elaborate productions. They should be short, sincere, and well executed, but anything is usually better than nothing. The New Entrepreneurial Dynamic embraces the latest technology and media.

 **What is Snapchat?**

Snapchat founder Evan Spiegel explains his vision for a new social media app.

View in the online reader

Google a video entitled "What is Snapchat?" and watch that Internet phenomenon's founder, Evan Spiegel, pitch his vision. While the video isn't a masterpiece of production quality (you will do better), it is sincere and explains the service in four minutes. Spiegel reveals himself as both innovative and passionate about his project, as well as showing why Snapchat is so cohesive with regular communication. Apparently, it worked, but we'd recommend you spend a few bucks on a videographer and editor. Recruit some cinema or video production students from your local university if you can. They love to add projects like this to their resumes.

Key Takeaways

- Building a team needs to be in your plan; great entrepreneurs do not succeed on their own.
- Never approach a business half commited.
- Use the latest tools to run and represent your business.

2.4 Case Study: Pivoting Pet Adoption with *Adoptimize*

The Adoptimize app.

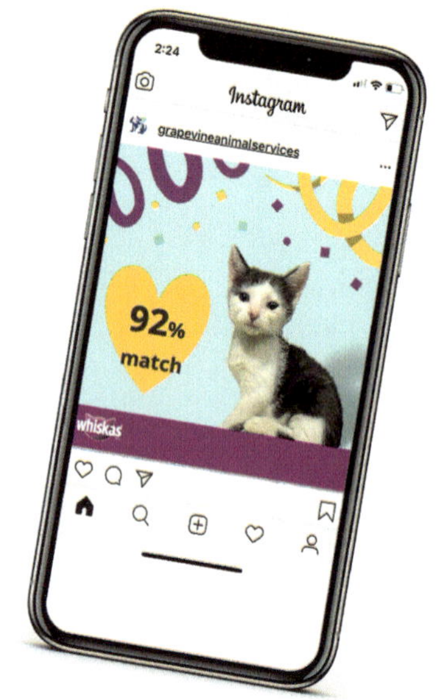

Source: Jessica Schleder

As a student in an MBA entrepreneurship class at the University of Southern California, Jessica Schleder needed an entrepreneurial project idea. Her expertise was in marketing and digital media. She had produced major campaigns for large firms like Nestlé, Universal, Sony, and 20th Century Fox. While each of these seemed exciting at the time, she realized that "Helping Bart Simpson pitch Butterfinger candy bars just didn't add a lot of meaning to my life." At the encouragement of her professor, she began to look for an intersection where her passions might meet a real market need. Where could she simultaneously create value for a consumer or organization as well as for herself? Was there a customer with a pain point that she shared?

Jessica's mind quickly settled on the plight of shelter pets, an issue about which she had long been passionate. According to the American Society for the Prevention of Cruelty to Animals (ASPCA), nearly 6.5 million companion animals end up in U.S. pet shelters annually. Only about 10 percent of these lost pets make it back to their owners. ASPCA reports that 1.5 million of them are euthanized each year. A lot of pet lovers are disturbed by these figures, and many of them donate to no-kill shelters or put in volunteer time with their local shelters. However, Jessica wanted to do something bigger—something scalable that would have an impact beyond the money or time she could personally contribute to this problem. She began to think of ways to improve the odds for animals seeking adoptive families.

Jessica's first thoughts revolved around the match-making process. One of the problems in the animal adoption world occurred when prospective pet parents fell in love with an animal that wasn't really behaviorally appropriate for their circumstances. Breeds were misidentified by intake workers, and so many animals were mixed breed that determining activity level based on description was hard. Shelters didn't have the capability to post a video showing the orphaned animal "in action," but Jessica reasoned that an AI algorithm could analyze an animal's motion and categorize its activity level to help fit it to prospective adoptive families and their homes.

Jessica named her startup "Adoptimize," recruited a programmer, and began to work on the concept. Working with faculty mentors, she refined the business pitch and entered USC's premier business competition, the New Venture Seed Competition. Adoptimize took second place and a $15,000 check.

Real-world testing quickly made it clear that the behavior of dogs and cats at a shelter wasn't representative of their actual personalities in a normal home environment. The aspiring pet match entrepreneur recalls that "I noticed that a very active dog might become frightened and meek after being dragged into the holding area and a normally calm animal might completely freak out."

Shelter photo of a dog.

Source: Jessica Schleder

Jessica began to look for a related problem she could pivot her effort toward and settled on the idea of improving photographs. Scrolling through thousands of ads for shelter pets, she immediately noticed that most of them looked like bad prison mug shots. The animals were posed awkwardly and looked uncomfortable. Often the animal was actually chained into position so the shelter worker could take the photo. The backgrounds were usually dreadful cement cells with stained floors and walls. Jessica remarked, "The overall impression from these photos was that animal shelters didn't even care about the animals—and this is so far from the truth."

Looking through her videos, Jessica noticed that there were almost always moments when the animal was moving, vibrant, and happy. She thought, "What if we could use AI to identify those happy moments and grab the best frame to present the animal?" In that case, the shelter worker could just let the dog or cat loose and shoot a minute or so of video and let the software find a great shot. A good shot would be one with the eyes facing the camera, tail held high, ears perky, etc. She set her coder to work.

Adoptomized photo of a dog.

Source: Jessica Schleder

Jessica confided, "The first attempt was pretty hilarious!" Wanting to ensure that the animal's eyes were always centered in the frame, the programmer used an existing library of code that was designed to identify human eyeballs in photos. The whites of the human eye are always visible, surrounding the darker iris. Animal eyes are usually all iris, with no white showing. The software was looking for a dark spot surrounded by a lighter circle and consistently selected photos focused on the animal's anus. "We turned the algorithm on and it spit out all these perfectly framed pictures of dog butts!" she laughed.

The programmer was able to resolve that issue, but the backgrounds were still an issue. Jessica developed a standardized pet studio with a camera, lighting, and a white cloth backdrop and looked for a site to test her system in the field. The Amarillo, Texas, animal shelter was her first break. Amarillo was far from convenient to her base in Los Angeles and not the most exciting place to work, but Jessica dug in. She quickly discovered that her setup was going to have trouble in the real world. A white background worked great for darker animals but was problematic for the lighter subjects. Worse, the critters that Jessica was trying to help find their "forever home" simply showed no respect for her studio. "I think it was the third dog I tried that peed on the background cloth, and every one that followed after that had to leave their own signature." The cloth was quickly unusable. Being a persistent problem solver, she switched to vinyl and considered offering different color backgrounds. She spent a lot of money and rolled the solution out to five shelters across the country.

The whole process ended up being a lot of work for understaffed shelters plus a 30-second video took too much time when shelters were intaking 100 dogs a day. The expenses of buying a studio with a standardized digital camera reduced their ability to pay for Adoptimize's software services. On top of that, some dogs didn't even need a video because they sat and looked at the camera. "I realized that we had way overengineered that solution," Jessica recalled.

Once again, Jessica looked for a pivot. Why not just remove the background in the software? On top of that, every shelter worker had a very capable camera in their phone; why not leverage that investment? In its third iteration, Adoptimize let shelter workers shoot pictures with their phones and upload them to the processing website where the software identified the animal, stripped out the background, and replaced it with a cheerful solid color. This was faster and cheaper for the shelter, leaving more funds to pay for the startup's software services.

Jessica also pivoted her economic model. Rather than trying to get payment from shelters that always seemed to be just scraping by, she reached out to commercial pet product suppliers for sponsorship. Adoptimize photos could include the sponsoring company's logo, and these sponsors would also be able to send special offers to the new pet parents. Connecting these firms with adoption was good marketing, and connecting them with new customers could directly drive sales. It was a real win/win, and Jessica quickly signed up some sponsors.

This new Adoptimize system was easy, effective, and paid for by someone else. What's not to love for the shelters? Jessica found out that even a free and useful system can run into opposition. She shared, "I've discovered that shelters have occasional volunteer photographers who do really nice shots of a few of the animals, and they don't like being displaced. Often these individuals are significant donors and volunteers that the shelters don't wish to offend." She contemplated how to deal with this latest challenge, "It's always something. I'll figure it out."

Endnotes

1. Blank, S. G., & Dorf, B. (2012). *The startup owner's manual: The step-by-step guide for building a great company* (1st ed.). Pescadero, CA: K & S Ranch; 53.
2. Mullins, J. W., & Komisar, R. (2010). *Getting to plan B: Breaking through to a better business model*. Boston, MA: Harvard Business Press.
3. Lange, J. E., Mollov, A., Pearlmutter, M., Singh, S., Bygrave, W.D. (2007). Pre-startup formal business plans and post-startup performance: A study of 116 new ventures. *Venture Capital 9*, 237–256.
4. Chwolka, Anne, and Matthias G. Raith. (2012). "The value of business planning before start-up—A decision-theoretical perspective." *Journal of Business Venturing 27.3:* (2012), 385–399.
5. Blank, S., and Dorf, B. (2012) *The start-up owner's manual*. K&S Ranch, Inc. p. xii
6. The FDIC standard insurance amount is $250,000 per depositor, per insured bank, for each account ownership category. https://www.fdic.gov/resources/deposit-insurance/#:~:text=Deposit insurance is one of,for each account ownership category
7. https://www.statista.com/statistics/219643/gini-coefficient-for-us-individuals-families-and-households/

CHAPTER 3

Strategy: Capturing and Maintaining Competitive Advantage

> To win by strategy is no less the role of a general than to win by arms.
>
> —*Gaius Julius Caesar*

Your business strategy forms the brain of your business model.

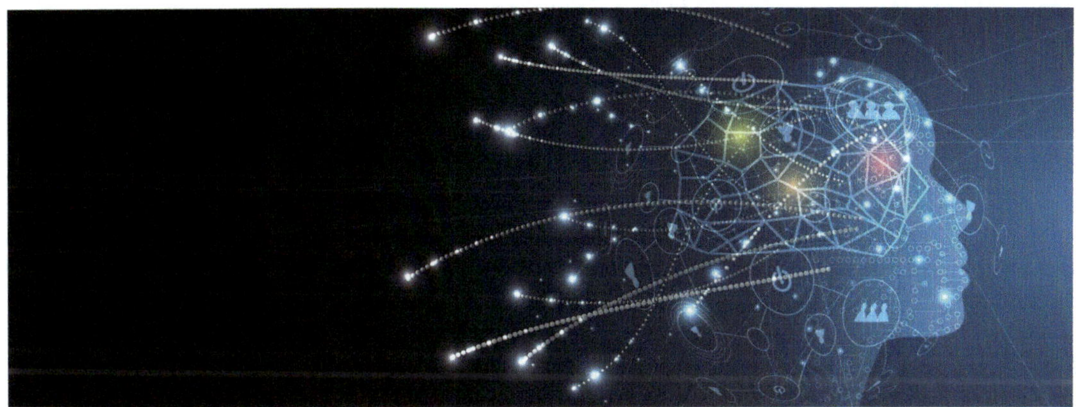

Source: © Shutterstock, Inc.

A business **strategy** forms the brain of your business model. A strategy is a planned method that an organization uses to achieve a specific objective over time. It is the art of analyzing a position and planning for moves that, within the rules of the game and considering the capabilities of the competitors, will result in strategic advantage. **Strategic management** is the discipline that coordinates all the other areas of a business to advantage. A startup without a strategy is adrift, and its outcomes are random at best. A business with a well-conceived strategy that fits its environment and its competition and executes that strategy well will not fail. This chapter will introduce you to the fundamentals of strategic theory with powerful examples from firms you probably know well, as well as some surprising analogies from historic military strategy and even gaming. It will also reveal how small businesses can obtain an advantage over their larger rivals.

strategy

The art of analyzing a position and planning for moves that, within the rules of the game and considering the capabilities of the competitors, will result in strategic advantage.

strategic management

The discipline that coordinates all the other areas of management to advantage.

3.1 Being Strategic

Learning Objectives

1. Embrace the power of disruption in entrepreneurial success.
2. Understand the central role of strategy in business competition.
3. Understand the relationship of objectives, strategies, and tactics.
4. Appreciate the lessons that military and sports strategy offer to business leaders.
5. Understand that a successful business must have either a price advantage or a significant differentiator.
6. Recognize the strategic advantages that startups and smaller businesses possess.
7. Remember that tactics support strategy.

Strategy, a Serious Game

Chess, a popular game of strategy, originated in India.

Source: © Shutterstock, Inc.

Strategic thinking is fundamentally the same in sports, warfare, and business. At the most abstract level, these are all "games." Each of these endeavors features a competitive battle between opponents who are simultaneously attempting to achieve some goal while also defending their own position. For a baseball coach, the goal is to get more runs than the opponent. For an army general, a reasonable goal might be to capture the enemy's capitol. For an entrepreneur launching a food services business, the goal might be to capture the downtown catering market. Lacking a clear goal or objective, there can be no effective strategy. You've got to know where you want to go in order to develop the process and plan required to get there. Organizations led by generals, coaches, or CEOs who are unable to identify and clearly communicate objectives to their teams invariably flounder and fail.

Classic games of skill like chess and Go (Weiqi, 圍棋) are commonly identified as good strategic training grounds for businesspeople. They have clearly defined rules and are challenging mental exercises in strategy. While this is true, both of these games lack one of the most important elements in determining business success. Can you think of what that is?

Screenshot from the Inc.com website.

NEWSLETTERS SUBSCRIBE

You have **3 free stories** left this month. **Upgrade for unlimited access** or **login** now.

STRATEGY

Winning Business Lessons From Chess Grand Masters "Finding the most direct route from point A to point B, eliminating as many steps and diversions as possible, will fuel your performance."

BY JOSH LINKNER, ENTREPRENEUR, AUTHOR, VC, JAZZ GUITARIST @JOSHLINKNER

Source: https://www.inc.com/josh-linkner/a-winning-secret-from-chess-grand-masters.html

The element I'm referring to is luck, the influence of random external events that change the environment in which competition occurs. The only thing that can surprise you in chess and Go is your opponent's moves, which are all foreseeable possibilities. These games lack any element of luck. Consequently, strategies designed for these games are like the old school business plans that presume the entrepreneur can follow a predetermined set of directions. The New Entrepreneurial Dynamic emphasizes that the business environment is influenced by random events, and therefore chess and Go are actually of limited value in preparing for business competition.

On the other hand, popular games of chance, like craps, blackjack, or Monopoly, have so much luck in them that there is little to be learned from them at all. There are fairly straightforward statistical strategies anyone can master in a few hours that will nearly maximize your results in these games (though most players put their money on the table without learning these). Can you think of a popular game that balances the planning of chess with the statistical analysis of blackjack?

The most popular game that balances strategy and luck would be poker. Competitive poker requires players to compete in an environment they have little control over. Each hand is, for the most part, determined by the randomly dealt cards. However, players can analyze their own strengths, estimate their opponents' resources, and then maximize the chances of a winning outcome based on both mathematical skills (knowledge of statistics) and psychological tactics. As Kenny Rogers' famous song, "The Gambler," reminds us, in poker, "Every hand's a winner, and every hand's a loser." Strategy is what makes a weak hand a potential winner and differentiates poker tournament champions from rank amateurs. Another game that balances luck and strategy is the popular board game, Catan.

Poker offers a combination of luck, strategy, and psychology that is similar to business competition.

Source: Iurii Osadchi/ Shutterstock.com

Massively multiplayer online games (MMO/MMOG), such as Blizzard's *World of Warcraft*, offer complex environments that combine luck with strategic and tactical challenges. They are often statistically analyzable and may even include rudimentary marketplaces subject to microeconomic forces we will be exploring in this chapter.

BlizzCon 2019 banners outside of the Anaheim Convention Center.

Source: Natalia Leen/Shutterstock.com

Given the nature of human history, it's probably no surprise that many of the greatest minds have been dedicated to planning warfare and destruction. It is not uncommon for business leaders to study *The Art of War* by Chinese military strategist Sun Tzu and the writings of the Prussian General Carl von Clausewitz. They may also be familiar with battles, from the German flanking of the French Maginot Line in 1940 to the American blunders at Tora Bora in 2001.[1]

You may not think about it, but like all games, the strategic options in warfare are constrained by rules. These aren't just the ones in the Geneva Convention, an international treaty that restricts the use of weapons like poison gas and defines the treatment of prisoners of war. Generals and admirals are also restricted by geographic realities, the technology of their time, the laws of physics, and even the political realities in which their rulers operate. Rules define what options strategists can choose from. Chess players can't knock over the board, poker players can't peek at the face-down cards, and American generals cannot use nuclear weapons to solve their problems in foreign wars. Business rules are determined by economic forces and by local and national laws.

At higher levels, the mathematical discipline of **game theory** is useful in simulating all of these competitive fields. Game theory is the science of identifying algorithms for maximizing optimal decision-making in strategic settings. Economist Oskar Morgenstern and mathematicians John von Neumann and John Nash developed this science in the 1940s. The **Nash Equilibrium**[2] is a particularly famous example that defines circumstances where once all players have defined a strategy, no player can improve his situation by making a change. It is useful in analyzing military standoffs as well as oligopolies in business. An **oligopoly** is a situation in which a small number of firms dominate a stable market. The smartphone business is an oligopoly currently under a Nash Equilibrium; neither Apple nor Google (Alphabet) can do much strategically to change the balance in the iOS vs. Android market shares. A two-member oligopoly is referred to as a **duopoly**.

game theory

A branch of math theory which models the optimal decision-making of players in a competition.

Nash Equilibrium

A model in game theory in which each player reaches an optimal strategy from which they will not deviate after considering the opponents' choices. In business this results in stable oligopolies.

oligopoly

A situation in which a small number of firms dominate a stable market.

duopoly

A market dominated by two firms.

Market Disruption

Consider the luxury auto industry, dominated for several decades by major firms BMW, Audi, Mercedes, and Lexus, with minor players like Jaguar and Cadillac. In 2012, the Tesla Model S burst out of nowhere to completely disrupt this equilibrium. The nine-year-old California firm had suddenly become the first successful U.S. car company to emerge since Chrysler was launched in 1925. Over the next three years, the Model S captured an astounding number of accolades, including 2013 Motor Trend Car of the Year, *Automobile* magazine's 2013 Car of the Year, and *Time* magazine's Best Inventions of 2012. In 2015, *Car and Driver* even dubbed it "The Car of the Century."

After exhaustive testing, *Consumer Reports* gave the Tesla Model S its best rating in history, chose it as "Best Overall Vehicle" two years running, and described the car as "so revolutionary and advanced, it's like a car from another planet." The Tesla even topped the U.S. National Transportation Safety Board testing regime by scoring perfectly in every category and subcategory, earning the highest rating ever. Most importantly, the car sold well. Tesla cars proliferated across California and then the nation. By 2013, the Model S was outselling similarly configured sedans from Lexus, BMW, Mercedes, Audi, and Porsche. In fact, sales were primarily constrained only by the firm's ability to deliver cars fast enough. Tesla buyers were placing deposits and waiting for several months to get their cars. In 2014, Tesla began taking deposits for its SUV, the Model X, and quickly presold more than 20,000 cars, sight unseen. The surprising fact was that all of Tesla's cars were *electric vehicles*, a category previously restricted to unattractive, low-performance cars sold in low volumes. How did this happen? Was it luck or simply great execution?

There are key moments in business history when the dominant players of a **mature industry** suddenly find themselves challenged by an unexpected upstart that enters their market from out of the blue with a new technical approach. We call this process **market disruption**. In the early 2000s, the music industry found its traditional distribution of products through retail record stores upended by a digital music revolution dominated by Apple's iPod plus iTunes ecosystem.

Planning to cause market disruption is possibly the most powerful strategy a business can employ. In the case of disruption, the objective (or goal) is to capture **market share** from **entrenched competitors**. Apple's iconic leader, Steve Jobs, was the all-time master of market disruption.

mature industry

An industry where the dominant design (technical standards), firm positions, and market shares have been established. Where little change has been seen recently.

market disruption

A fundamental shift or change to a market that results in the appearance of new firms and the elimination of incumbents that fail to adapt.

market share

The percentage of a particular market or product segment held by one firm or product.

entrenched competitors

Incumbent firms that have a strong market position; difficult to assail.

skunkworks

A development facility intentionally isolated from the public and other divisions of a firm. Typically working on the most leading-edge technologies.

Steve Jobs, Master Disruptor

The iPad was one of many dominant products Steve Jobs brought to market.

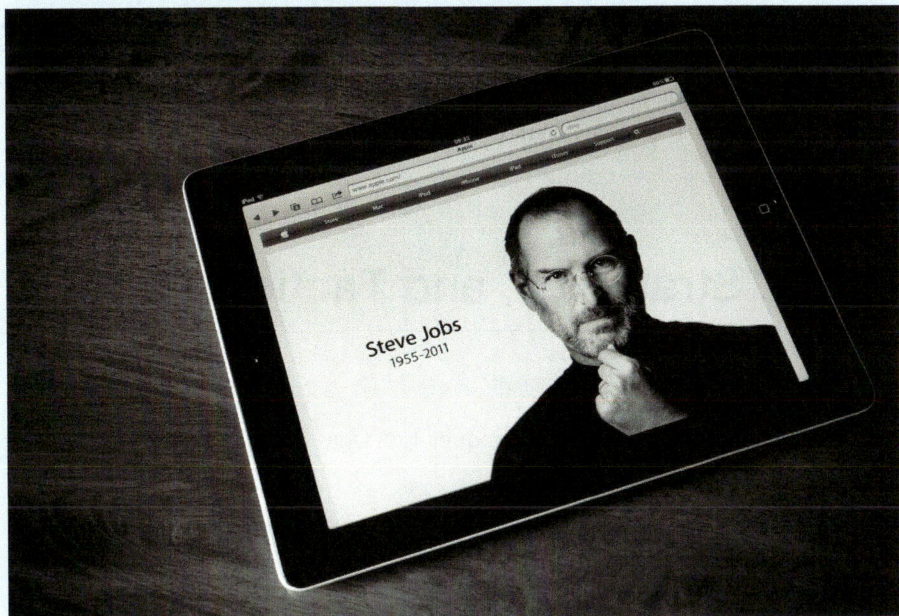

Source: Bloomicon/Shutterstock.com

Steve Jobs disrupted more markets than any entrepreneur since Thomas Edison. Jobs was the adopted child of a working-class family in California's Silicon Valley, an area famously filled with engineers, inventors, and entrepreneurs. With his partner, Steven "Woz" Wozniak, Jobs formed Apple Computer in 1976. With $1,300 scraped together from the sale of a Volkswagen van and an HP calculator, the duo set out to take on IBM and the powerful mainframe and minicomputer firms that dominated computing. Four years later, the firm's IPO made history, creating 300 new millionaires. When the dust cleared, a new industry (the personal computer) had been born, and a new entrepreneurial paradigm (the Silicon Valley college dropout startup) had become enshrined in business culture.

Jobs' next trick was to disrupt Apple itself by recruiting a group of engineers to work on a **skunkworks** project that was not entirely endorsed by Apple's executives, in a building that was topped with a Jolly Roger (pirate) flag. The result was the Macintosh computer that was introduced in early 1984 and still defines how all personal computers operate to this day.

Jobs' lack of respect for rules and his famously abrasive personality turned out to be too much for a maturing company that was seeking to ingratiate itself with conservative corporate institutions. Shortly after the launch of Macintosh, Apple's board of directors chased him from the company that he'd founded. Insulted, but undaunted, Jobs pursued a new computer firm, NeXT, and in his spare time, he funded and then purchased Pixar Animation Studios from director George Lucas. Pixar was formed to develop hardware and software tools to assist movie makers with special effects. However, Jobs saw more in Pixar than its technology and led the company in its development into the world's leading animation studio, knocking out hit films like *Toy Story*, *Monsters Inc.*, and *Finding Nemo*. The amazing, three-dimensional renderings of these computer-animated films obliterated the traditional hand-drawn films that were the mainstay of companies like Disney. In 2006, Disney purchased Pixar for $7.4 billion, and Jobs ended up as Disney's largest shareholder.

By the late 1990s, Apple Computer was a company adrift and in financial trouble. The firm had been cranking out slight improvements to the Macintosh computer for a decade but had not executed any disruptive innovation since Steve Jobs' departure. Market share was down, and industry observers were predicting the firm's collapse. In 1997, Jobs returned and took the helm at Apple with a powerful intent. He quickly overthrew everything from product development to distribution and began looking for disruption opportunities. In 2001, Apple introduced the iPod and, in 2003, its iTunes music store. This powerful combination of player and convenient content distribution destroyed the CD player business, dominated by Japanese firms like Sony, and retail music stores like Tower Records and Wherehouse Music that had been present in America's malls and shopping centers for decades.

Jobs topped his iPod success in 2007 with the introduction of the iPhone, a device that decimated cellphone giants Nokia, Blackberry (RIM), and Motorola and completely upended the relationship between hardware suppliers and network providers (ATT, Verizon, etc.). Once again, he had essentially defined exactly how a ubiquitous consumer device would function and how an entire industry would be run. The iPad followed shortly after that, defining the dominant design for the tablet computer market. In the process, he captured immense profits and drove Apple to be the world's most profitable firm and the most admired brand on Earth.

Objectives, Strategies, and Tactics

> All men can see these tactics whereby I conquer, but what none can see is the strategy out of which victory is evolved.
>
> —*Sun Tzu*

While it's clear to most students that strategy involves planning to outwit an opponent, it is not always obvious how strategy integrates with other aspects of entrepreneurship to produce superior results. Figure 3.1 helps you visualize how strategy is part of a process that begins with setting a goal or objective.

FIGURE 3.1 Strategic Execution

Source: Greg Autry

Objectives or goals shape your strategy. Strategy defines which tactics to apply. Tactics drive execution. Excellent execution of the proper tactics at the right time produce great business results.

Overcoming Barriers to Entry

You've also got to know what obstacles might be obstructing the path toward your objective. Almost all industries have obstacles that make it difficult for new firms to get established. We call these barriers to entry. These barriers are represented in Figure 3.1 by the bar that blocks the objective arrow. You'll notice that the strategy arrow passes through the barrier. Strategic planning is the solution to overcoming barriers to entry.

When Elon Musk and the Tesla founders decided to enter the automobile market, they did not find the road ahead smoothly paved for a new electric car company. It turns out that the process of manufacturing a car and getting it tested, approved for sale, and distributed to consumers is very difficult. One very simple example of a barrier to entry was encountered by Tesla when they discovered that many parts suppliers were not eager to work with a small new startup. Wanting to get all the best parts, the company sought out the top supplier for hundreds of simple components like sun visors and mirrors. Very often, they discovered that the existing suppliers were unwilling to accommodate them in a timely manner. It is possible these suppliers just didn't want to bother with a small firm that they felt wasn't very likely to succeed, or it may be that out of loyalty to their big clients, they intentionally refused to service new competitors. Either way, the big firms had established barriers to entry that throttled Tesla's supply chain.

Tesla saw similar barriers to entry on the distribution side, where the big auto firms had thousands of car dealers running sales lots across the country staffed with hundreds of thousands of salespeople, finance managers, and service staff. Creating such a network would require years of work and billions in capital. Convincing independent dealers to take a chance by filling their lots with a radical new car would be a real challenge. Getting them to sell a car that was designed to last longer and required much less of their high-cost repair services was going to be even harder. The dealerships' hold on access to car buyers represented another barrier to entry.

Good strategy can guide your organization around the barriers to entry that keep you from achieving your objectives. A classic example of such a strategy is the Persian victory over the Spartans in 480 BCE at the Battle of Thermopylae. The Persian emperor, Xerxes, sailed to Greece and deposited the most massive army in history on a wide coastal plain. Access to the cities beyond was blocked by a chain of mountains very near the seashore, with a pass just 300 feet wide permitting travel. Before the Persians could move their forces through this narrow point, the Greeks dispatched a contingent of about 7,000 soldiers to block the Persian advance. The Greeks, led by the Spartan general Leonidas, held the pass for two days, using themselves and their shields as an extremely effective barrier to entry.

flanking maneuver

A strategy or avoiding direct confrontation with an (often superior) enemy by going around the end of its lines and attacking from the side or rear.

outflanked

To be a victim of a flanking maneuver when an opponent goes around your defenses to attack your vulnerable side.

Xerxes was frustrated by his inability to move forward and was facing a real disaster unless he quickly captured significant Greek food stores and farms to feed his enormous army. Recognizing that the Persians would pay dearly for access, a Greek traitor alerted Xerxes to the existence of a trail through the hills that could circumvent Leonidas' forces. Such a strategy of going around the side of a barrier to entry is called a **flanking maneuver**. Leonidas dispatched most of his army to fight the Persians on the trail and continued to hold the pass with a few hundred men. The Persians overwhelmed the Greeks on the mountain trail and **outflanked** Leonidas. The general and his 300 Spartans then famously stepped out onto the plain in front of the million Persian soldiers and fought to the death.[3] The three-day delay weakened the Persian army as well as Xerxes' resolve, and the Greeks were eventually able to drive the invaders out of their peninsula.

FIGURE 3.2 The Battle of Thermopylae, 480 BCE.

Maps courtesy of the Department of History, United States Military Academy.

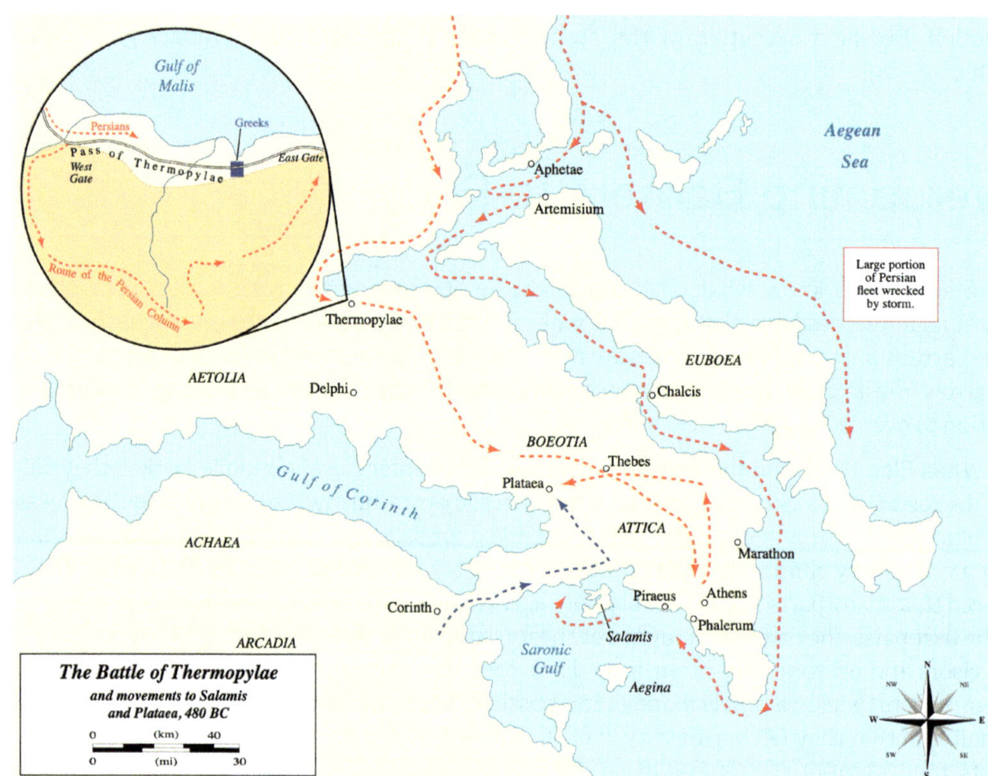

Source: https://commons.wikimedia.org/wiki/File:Battle_of_Thermopylae_and_movements_to_Salamis_and_Plataea_map-it.svg#/media/File:Battle_of_Thermopylae_and_movements_to_Salamis_and_Plataea_map-en.svg

vertical integration

The purchase of suppliers and or customers to create a firm that encompasses more of its value chain. A fully vertically integrated firm would take in raw material and sell products directly to end-users.

In a similar move, Tesla Motors similarly decided to drive around market barriers erected by Toyota, Ford, and the other big auto firms. First, Elon solved his firm's supply frustrations through **vertical integration**, a strategy of building many of your own parts, which was famously executed by Henry Ford with his Model T and Model A production. To get around the car dealers, Tesla marketed directly to consumers via the internet, positive word of mouth, and small but stylish showrooms located inside malls. It turned out, not surprisingly, that American car buyers weren't in love with the whole car dealership sales and service experience in the first place, and they flocked to buy the Model S. Musk had outflanked the giants of Detroit and Kyoto.

However, the story doesn't end here as the major car manufacturers and their dealers quickly responded by trying to assert that it was illegal for Tesla not to sell through dealers. Several U.S. states passed dealership-backed laws blocking Tesla's direct sales model. Manipulating the government in order to establish legal barriers to entry is a timeless counterstrategy and is a topic covered in detail in a later chapter of this text.[4]

The Two Basic Strategies: Price and Differentiation

Harvard Business School professor Michael Porter is considered by many to be the academic godfather of business strategy. His famous book, *Competitive Advantage*, details the ways businesses position themselves for success in markets. One of Porter's major insights is that when distilled to their core, business strategies come down to one of two things: either they depend on offering a lower price, or they provide unique features customers are willing to pay extra for. Lower pricing may be secured through exclusive access to raw materials or unique efficiencies in the logistics of production, distribution, or sales. Lacking either a price advantage or **differentiation** from their competitors, a firm is doomed to be another "also-ran" or "knock-off" from the customer's perspective. Such a firm is unlikely to secure or hold a significant position in their market. Why should customers choose them or stick with them?

differentiation

The way in which a firm is able to distinguish its products (positively) from its competitor's offerings.

Walmart stores are the poster child for effective pricing strategies. Almost every factor at Walmart, from store displays to advertising, is done with little money or attention, and it shows. Nobody shops at Walmart for the ambiance, but everyone expects to get a great price. In order to deliver that low price to its shoppers, the Benton, Arkansas-based retailer is always focused on reducing costs. The firm famously pressures its vendors and logistical suppliers to lower their prices. Walmart can be so tough on its suppliers that a common joke among entrepreneurs is: "What is the quickest path to failure for a small business?" The answer? "A big order from Walmart."

Differentiation is based on better performance, perceived product quality, superior service, or positive brand associations. Think about Apple here. Apple buyers readily pay significantly more for their laptops, phones, and tablets than they would for similar products from competing companies such as Korea's Samsung or China's Lenovo Group. They pay this higher rate because they perceive that Apple's products are designed and built better than their competitors and because they wish to be associated with a brand that reflects their values and lifestyle.

Let's Get Small

We've now seen some pretty big examples, but strategic thinking, disruption, and flanking are strategies utilized by small business entrepreneurs every day. Imagine that you've decided to open a small coffeehouse but, not surprisingly, there are Starbucks locations on nearly every corner in town. Starbucks has a great product, they're well known and trusted, and they've got amazing corporate resources in marketing, planning, etc. Is there any way you can differentiate yourself and succeed?

You must follow another of Sun Tzu's admonitions, "If you know your enemies and know yourself, you will not be imperiled in a hundred battles . . . if you do not know your enemies nor yourself, you will be imperiled in every single battle." When you understand your capabilities and those of your competitors, you can develop a strategy that turns their advantages into weaknesses.

In the case of startup versus Starbucks, you can always compete on price. Starbucks is not cheap, and with their corporate headquarters setting prices, demanding fancy outlets, and bragging of a commitment to relatively higher wages, individual locations are vulnerable to a price play in markets where consumers are really price conscious. Consider locating near a community college campus, where students enjoy the coffeehouse experience but are counting their pennies for textbooks. By choosing a noncorner location, a slightly less glamorous storefront, finding your furnishings, and paying your student workers a bit less, you can cut the cost of fancy coffees without cutting the quality.

You can also differentiate by playing up your "indie" position versus "corporate" Starbucks. Students appreciate the rebel attitude—if they get the product and service they want. To be clear, this won't be the easiest thing you've ever done. Your execution must be perfect, particularly on-site design and style. Customers can smell the difference between shabby chic and just plain shabby: One is cool; the other is sad. Make sure you get good style advice and test it with potential customers in advance. Also, make 100 percent sure your store is packed with happy coffee campers on launch. That means promo coupons, giveaways, and bribing friends and family to hang out and talk up the place.

Tactics

tactics

The individual actions used to implement a strategy.

Once you've established a strategy designed to reach your major objective, you will send your forces forward to conquer the market! However, in doing so, they will quickly encounter more immediate obstacles. Maneuvers designed to overcome those short-term challenges are **tactics**. Tactics support the execution of strategy.

Patton was a tactical genius.

Source: Tupungato/Shutterstock.com

A great tactician is prepared to make quick adjustments in the field and keeps a mental playbook of tactics on hand to outwit the enemy. Looking back to the Second World War again, Major General George S. Patton Jr. was the master of armored vehicle tactics and author of a handbook on desert warfare tactics. Among his tactical insights was the simple instruction that tanks should adopt staggered formations and must never form a line in any direction because he learned that a line is most efficiently strafed with machine-gun fire from aircraft. In general, startups and small businesses have the tactical advantage because they can shift tactics quicker when they learn.

Many business tactics are similarly straightforward and seemingly obvious after the fact. A common tactic we are exposed to every day is the retail pricing gimmick whereby a package of chips is offered at $2.98 rather than $3.00 because it turns out that even math majors are psychologically inclined to truncate digits. While we rationally know better, when we see 2.98, our subconscious brain simply rejects dealing with the complexity of 2.98 and takes a bad short cut directly to "2." Another retail tactic is to position more profitable items on shelves that are easiest to see and reach, placing the least expensive stuff on those lower shelves where you'll have to bend over to get it. Advertising tactics include the time-honored tradition of featuring attractive people, sometimes placing them in inappropriately suggestive poses to manipulate our instinctive impulses to look at such things.

Key Takeaways

- Disruption is inevitable; find strategic opportunity when it occurs.
- Objectives (goals) drive strategy, which drives tactics, which require execution.
- Barriers to entry can often be avoided with innovative approaches.
- If you want to be a major competitor, you must either find a way to be less expensive (price) or provide unique (differentiation) value to your clients.
- Being small can be an advantage in itself.
- Even the most brilliant strategies cannot succeed unless supported by smart tactics.

3.2 Sustainable Competitive Advantage

Learning Objectives

1. Understand the value of competitive advantages and the higher value of a sustainable competitive advantage.
2. Understand the strategy of constant innovation.
3. Recognize that operational effectiveness is an advantage.
4. Understand clearly what defines a market.

The strategies for holding a position are as critical as those involved in taking it. To dominate a market, what a firm truly needs is a **sustainable competitive advantage**. A **competitive advantage** is a factor that provides a firm with a position of market power to generate profits. A sustainable one is a factor that a firm can maintain in the face of attacks from its competitors over time. When investing in a strategy to gain advantage, you must consider how durable that advantage is likely to be.

sustainable competitive advantage

An advantage that is not transitory and can clearly be maintained by the firm for some time in the future as in patented intellectual property that cannot be duplicated.

competitive advantage

A unique value proposition, market position, technology, or other resource that gives one firm the ability to outcompete another in the market.

Imagine you own a local solar installation company. You know there are some new, ultra-efficient panels coming out that customers will prefer over all the existing options. You could sign up as one of many dealers and go head-to-head with your local competitors to sell this hot new product. Everybody would do well for a while and capture higher profits from eager new customers who insist on the newest thing. However, once the easy customers were sold, you'd have to start discounting to keep or gain market share among the remaining customer pool. Your competitors would naturally follow suit, and the profits would soon evaporate from that business. What could you do to avoid this scenario?

What if you approached the ultra-efficient panels manufacturer in advance and offered to commit to a high number of their panels up front and to heavily promote their product above all others—or even abandon selling competing panels? Perhaps you could ask them for an exclusive distribution contract, where no other firm in your area could sell these panels, for some period of time—say five years. The longer you can negotiate such an agreement, the more sustainable your competitive advantage would be.

Dynamic Advantage

As an entrepreneur, you can't always hold a competitive advantage just because you'd like to. As noted in the solar panel example above, exclusive contracts have **terms**, and when they end, so does your advantage. If you tie your fortune to a single producer for a long period of time, then you have become dependent on another firm maintaining your competitive advantage. That's out of your control, and if your supplier loses its edge, it may take your business down. A twenty-first-century business must strategize by both planning ahead and being willing to swiftly deviate from the plan.

terms

Details and/or the length of time of an agreement.

When Apple was designing the iPod, they realized the key to "1,000 songs in your pocket" would be the super small hard drive in their first-generation device. When they found that Toshiba Corporation of Japan was developing such a hard drive, Apple negotiated to purchase *all* of Toshiba's micro drives production for the first 18 months. This strategy prevented anyone from "knocking off" Apple's design, and *the iPod had no real competitors for more than two years*. Jobs saw the benefit from this strategic move as sustainable just long enough for him to make two more moves.

A first-generation iPod.

Source: marleyPug/Shutterstock.com

Jobs' first follow-up move was to establish an "ecosystem" that made iPod users dependent on the device and the convenient iTunes software that organized their Mp3 songs on their computer into playlists. Users who switched to another Mp3 player would have to give up this software and recreate all their playlists. We call the trouble of changing from one platform to another a **switching cost**. When users face high switching costs to leave your product, you've established a barrier for your competitors.

Jobs' second move was to use Apple's market dominance as a lever to negotiate deals with the major music labels to distribute their songs on its new iTunes store, which launched in 2003. iPod owners could now buy digital songs conveniently and legally, but the music they had paid for was copy-protected with a system called Digital Rights Management (DRM) that the record labels wanted in place to prevent users from sharing music files freely. DRM songs from the iTunes store came in a format that was not easily transferable to non-Apple Mp3 players. If you bought another device, you'd lose your investment in music.

switching cost

Costs incurred by a customer when changing to a competing product or service. Typically, the time consumed with learning a new procedure.

The music library issue was a very tangible switching cost that worked, and the barrier to entry it established was unsurmountable. The vast majority of users stuck with Apple and ignored offerings from Sony, Microsoft, and others. No matter how inexpensive Microsoft eventually made their Zune player, your song library was probably worth more than any hardware savings, and you just weren't going to buy one. No amount of marketing could overcome that barrier to entry.

Ironically, it was the music companies that had wanted the copy protection on songs, and Jobs saw the benefit for Apple. However, Jobs was never a fan of the inconvenience of protected media. In 2009, long after Apple's competitors had invested in developing and deploying their own DRM schemes, Jobs convinced the labels to remove iTunes' protection and promoted several song sharing techniques, providing Apple with another source of advantage. Great strategists in the New Entrepreneurial Dynamic are always at least one step ahead of their competitors, often several.

Innovation Strategy

innovation strategy

A strategy based on the development of new technologies or processes that will provide a competitive advantage.

Apple's strategy is an **innovation strategy**. Constantly developing new sources of competitive advantage can allow your firm to deliver either the lower price or differentiation and sometimes both. Of course, "constantly innovating" is easier said than done. Doing it right requires a combination of foresight, genius, and daring. This involves the entrepreneur having vision, being inspirational enough to recruit the best team members, and having the stomach to step outside the bounds of the proven orthodoxy. It's a tough thing for a small firm to do, but that makes it a very powerful strategy if you're in a market dominated by small firms.

Operational Effectiveness Strategy

operational effectiveness

The ability of a firm to execute well.

Some companies just do what they do very well. As a customer, it is a pleasure to do business with them. You are sure things will go well, and if they don't, the problem will be promptly corrected. Southwest Airlines, Costco, and Disneyland are all examples of businesses that embrace **operational effectiveness**. Operational effectiveness is one of the most straightforward strategies for a small firm to capture. Establishing a culture of excellence within your organization is the key to this advantage. Everyone must be focused on delivering the very best product or service at all times.

Many industries that are dominated by small firms are notorious for inconsistent customer service. They lack the processes, human resources, and inventory to deliver products and services in a dependable matter. Breaking that mold can be powerful. It does happen. In the late 1980s, Howard Schultz was convinced that he could change the way coffee was consumed in America. At that time, you went to a "coffee shop," and it was a low-end, full-service restaurant that offered one type of mediocre coffee for cheap, usually something like 50 cents a cup. The coffee might be stale, it might be cold, it might be weak—you never knew, and the unsympathetic waitress usually didn't care. Schultz purchased a little six-shop coffee shop chain in Seattle to execute his strategy. By offering a consistently good product and a pleasurable in-store experience, he transformed coffee from a price-driven commodity into a differentiated, high-margin product and made a fortune. Today Starbucks has more than 20,000 locations around the world.

What Exactly Is a Market?

You probably think you know what a **market** is, right? Well, if you thought it was a place where you went to buy groceries, your definition is only partially correct. Technically a market is a place where goods or services are sold for cash or bartered, but *it need not be a physical place!* Think of the online auction site eBay. It's a huge market or multiple markets for many different categories of goods. While the London, New York, and Shanghai Stock Exchanges have physical locations, most of their transactions happen somewhere in cyberspace with buyers in offices and homes around the world. Using smartphones or even watches, people buy and sell billions of dollars in goods and equities while riding on the train or sitting on the beach.

market

An environment, real or virtual, where buyers and sellers can negotiate and exchange of products and services or money.

For your small business, your market might be defined by the type of good or service you sell, but your customer base could be national or even global. Consider a student in Taiwan who has a store on Amazon.com selling collectible Hello Kitty merchandise. Her customers might be in Japan, Europe, or Africa.

Your market might also be restricted to a more limited geography for practical reasons. Suppose you're running a residential construction business. In that case, you probably keep most of your jobs within 50 miles or so for a number of reasons, including controlling the time and expense of travel to sites, maintaining a network of local customer references, or maintaining a network of local contract workers.

Rental bicycles parked in front of a London café.

Source: Thinglass/Shutterstock.com

A café in the gentrified Soho district of West London is likely to consider their market as defined by the other cafés within a half dozen blocks or so. Clients may come into the area by car or tube, but they probably came to shop, not to eat at your café. They will select a place to eat while they are there. So, it's really the local competitors that define the scope of the market.

In strategizing, it's always important to understand and demarcate your market as clearly as possible. In particular, you need to define the market, so you know who your competitors are. This doesn't mean you can't intentionally expand the scope of your market definition or go after entirely different markets; you just want to make sure you understand the territory and its inhabitants before you land your forces.

Existing Versus New Markets

de alio markets

An existing market.

de novo markets

A new or emerging market.

There are existing markets, or **de alio markets**, where people and firms have been doing business for some time. New markets, or **de novo markets**, are usually centered around a change in technology, culture, or law. Can you guess which type of market is more attractive to a startup?

New markets lack powerful incumbents and are often not heavily regulated (because the government hasn't noticed them or figured them out yet). This means they are likely to have lower barriers to entry and are easier for very small businesses to get a start in on the cheap. Steve Wozniak and Steve Jobs entered the personal computer business in 1976 with a few hundred dollars. Can you think of any problems with entering new markets?

Existing markets are proven quantities; people understand how they work, their characteristics, and who the opponents are. Planning an assault on an existing market may take capital and other resources, but the objectives are clear. With new markets, nobody quite knows how they work, the characteristics, who the customers are, who the opponents are, or what it will cost to conquer them. When personal computer firms first started advertising, they often pictured the computer situated in the kitchen as a tool for storing recipes.

1970s "Videophone."

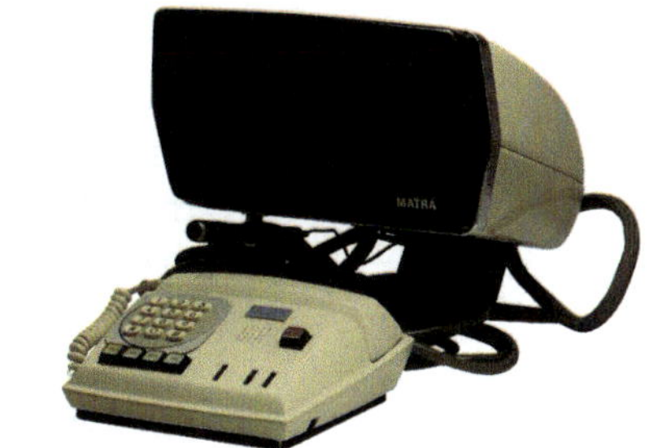

Source: https://commons.wikimedia.org/wiki/File:Videophone_IMG_1107-white.jpg

New markets are risky. Often, it is not even clear they will turn out to be sustainable industries. In the mid-1970s, many people believed that there would be a booming market in wired video telephones that sat on your desk. AT&T actually launched a service, but nobody cared. Banks, for one, distrust new markets and loathe lending funds for industries they don't understand. New markets demand risk-tolerant investors, such as venture capitalists, and they will insist on taking significant equity positions in your firm. Entering a new market is often called a blue ocean strategy, whereas entering an existing market, especially a highly competitive one, is a red ocean (think blood and sharks) strategy.

Key Takeaways

- If you want to be a top-level competitor, you must find a competitive advantage(s).
- Today's dynamic environment demands that entrepreneurs constantly seek new advantages.
- Doing your work better than the competition can be a significant advantage.
- Being clear about which market(s) you choose to compete in is essential to success.
- Consider the advantages and disadvantages of entering established versus new markets.

3.3 The Economic Basis of Business Strategy

Learning Objectives

1. Learn or review the basics of microeconomics.
2. Learn to price strategically within the supply and demand of your market.
3. Understand the relationship between sales prices and quantities sold to profits.
4. Understand the power of discriminatory pricing.
5. Appreciate the power of capturing the high end of markets.

Business strategy is a game about capturing profits from markets. The principles of **microeconomics** define many of the rules of the game. You've likely had an economics course in high school or college, but now is a good time to review a few basic concepts starting with supply and demand.

microeconomics

The study of the forces of supply and demand within a particular market.

The Supply Curve

Imagine you own a bakery that supplies cakes to catering businesses. Do you want to get more or less money for your cakes? This is not a trick question. You want more, and so do your competitors, the other bakers. If prices are high, you'll bake more cakes! It will be worth staying late, investing in extra ovens, whatever. When prices are low, you'll be inclined to provide fewer cakes, and so will your competitors.

FIGURE 3.3 Supply Curve

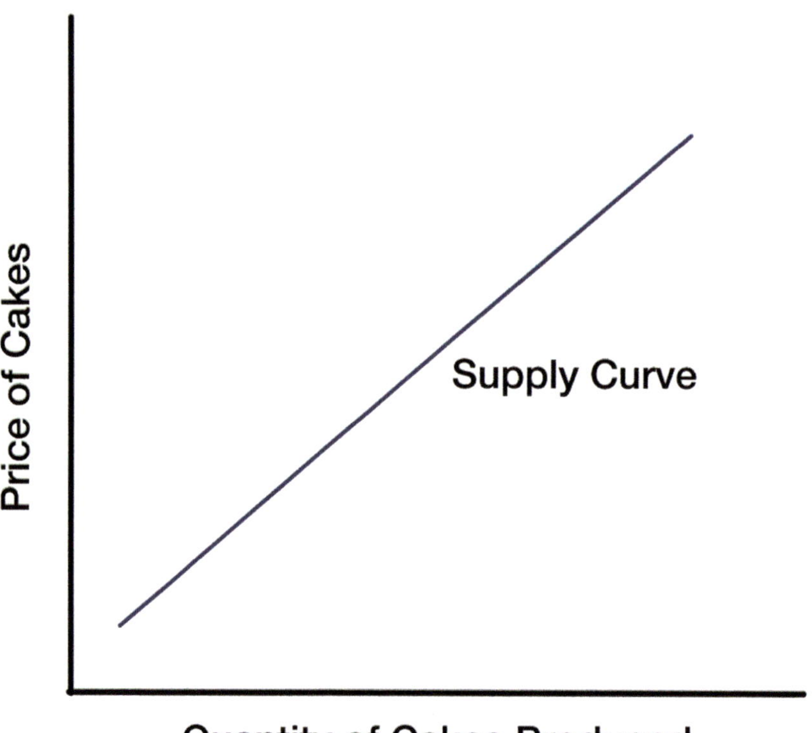

Source: Greg Autry

supply curve

A curve showing the quantity supplied by producers for a given product or service at each price point.

If we took each possible price level for a cupcake and calculated how many cakes all the suppliers in your market would provide, we could represent this as a mathematical function. Such a function is graphically depicted in Figure 3.3, which depicts a **supply curve** for cakes. The vertical axis shows the price of each point, and the horizontal axis shows the quantity produced. The supply curve slopes upward as prices and quantity supplied increase together. In reality, the shape of the curve would not be a perfectly straight 45° line, but it would surely slope upward.

The Demand Curve

demand curve

A curve showing the quantity demanded by consumers for a given product or service at each price point.

Now imagine you're the caterer who buys cakes. Do you want to pay more or less for cakes? Again, it's not a trick question. You want to pay less. If cakes are cheap (presuming quality doesn't suffer), you'll buy more cakes. If cakes are expensive, you'll substitute pies, ice cream, or something else. Graphically, this looks like Figure 3.4, which depicts a **demand curve** for cakes. The demand curve slopes downward as prices and the quantity demanded move inversely. Again, we've used a hypothetically straight line.

FIGURE 3.4 Demand Curve

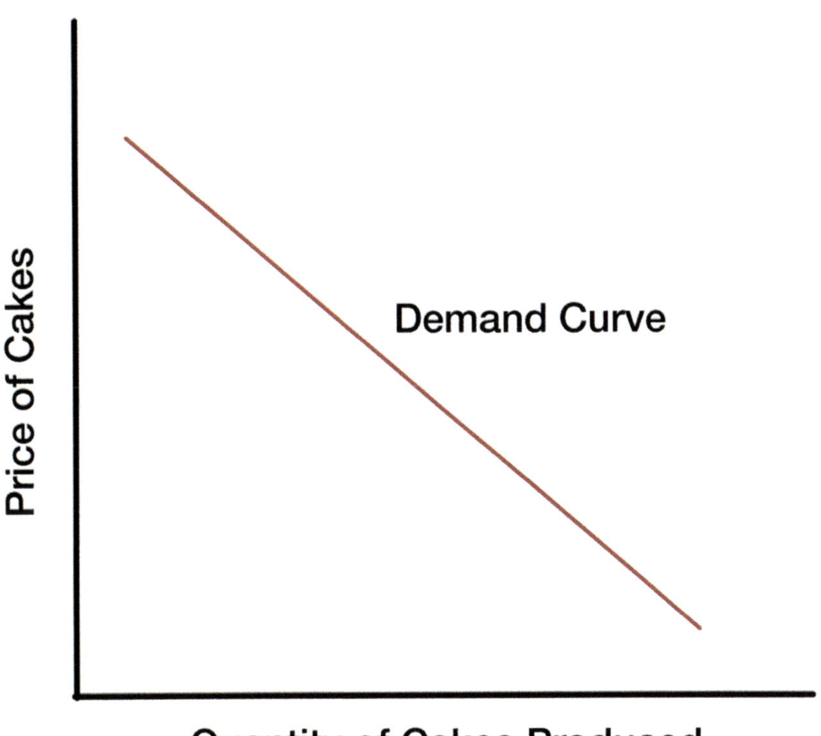

Source: Greg Autry

Supply, Demand, and Market Equilibrium

Now we bring supply and demand together. A supplier wants higher prices, and a buyer wants lower prices. It is this interchange of these motivations that establishes a **market price** and a **market quantity**. Figure 3.5 shows us how the supply and demand curves work together to determine this market price and quantity.

market price

The price of a commoditized product or service as determined by market forces of supply and demand.

market quantity

The quantity of a commoditized product or service produced as determined by market forces of supply and demand.

FIGURE 3.5 Supply & Demand Curves + Equilibrium

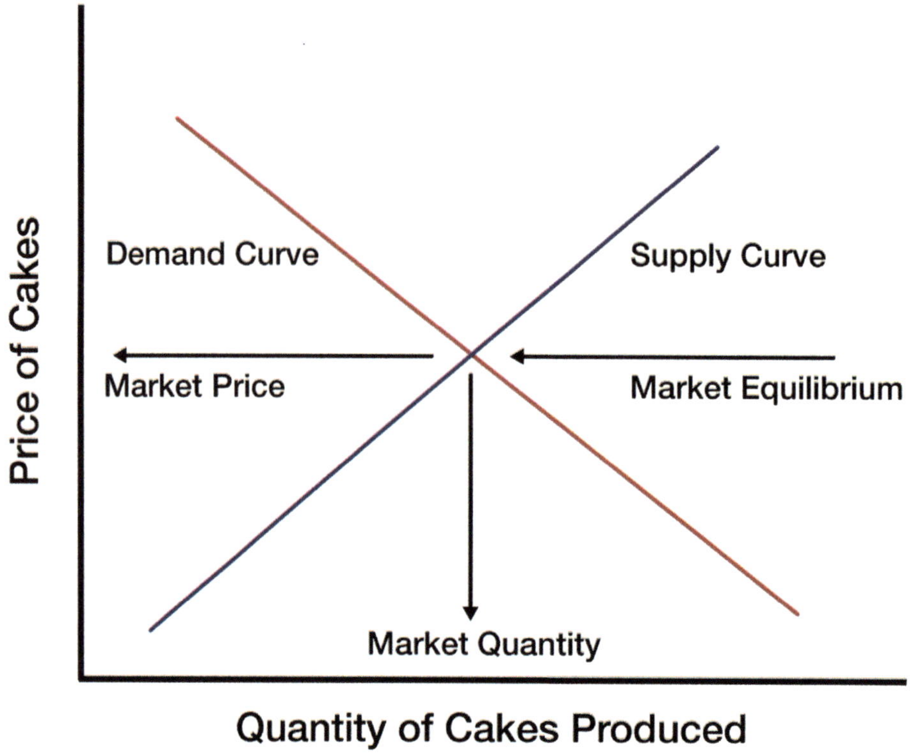

Source: Greg Autry

market equilibrium

The point at which the supply of products from producers and the quantity demanded by consumers are equal.

efficient market

A market in which market forces easily produce equilibrium. Also, in the equities or bond markets, a market in which current prices accurately reflect future earnings from those investments.

logistical complexities

The difficulties in the coordination of transporting and storing material goods or delivering services.

The point at which the curves intersect—where the suppliers' desires and those of the buyer meet—is called **market equilibrium** (or just *equilibrium*). The number of cakes produced and the average price of cakes sold can be found by looking at where this point maps to on each axis. If you follow the straight arrow to the vertical axis on the left, you can determine how many cakes will be sold. If you follow the straight arrow down to the horizontal axis, you can determine how many cakes will be produced. In a theoretical model, the quantity produced and the quantity consumed are always equal, and the consumer can afford the pricing. We call this an **efficient market** because there is no waste of money or product. In the real world, there are **logistical complexities**, timing problems, and human error, so it's just pretty close to efficient.

Price Elasticity

As I noted earlier, the demand curve is not actually a straight line. Its shape varies by product, and that has important implications for strategy. **Price elasticity** is the cause. Consider that some items, like gasoline and basic foodstuffs, are products people must have, regardless of price, and the quantity demanded doesn't vary a lot regardless of price. How often do you see gasoline on sale? We call these sorts of goods **inelastic goods** because their demand is less flexible than other goods.

price elasticity

The ratio in which a price change impacts demand for that product or service.

inelastic goods

A product where price changes have a limited impact on demand, which consumers find so necessary that they generally continue to buy it regardless of price increases.

FIGURE 3.6 Elasticity of Demand

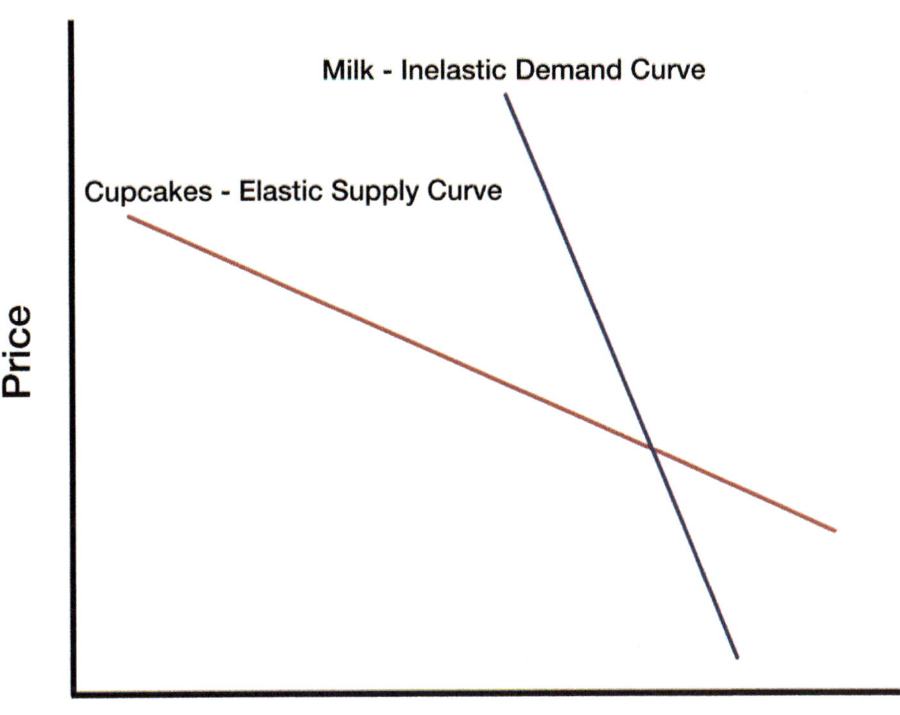

Source: Greg Autry

This inelasticity does not mean that one vendor can simply raise prices. Consumers will choose the lowest price, which is why nearby gas stations are almost always priced within a few cents of each other. They will lower prices when their costs drop to gain a few customers, and that will force their neighbor to do the same. It's the overall market relationship that we are looking at here. When the market price rises or drops, inelastic products see little change in the quantity demanded.

Other items like cameras or boats are non-necessities that people will avoid buying when prices are high and leap at when they are on special. These products are **elastic goods**. Figure 3.6 shows the relationship between an elastic and non-elastic demand curve.

elastic goods

A product where price changes have a significant impact on demand, in which consumers easily stop purchasing or choose substitutes when prices increase.

You'll notice that the milk demand curve is steeper. Its slope indicates that each change in price has less impact on the quantity of milk sold. Milk is, therefore, more inelastic. The demand curve for cupcakes, on the other hand, is shallow. Its slope indicates that even a small change in price will significantly impact the quantity sold. Cupcakes are, therefore, more elastic. What do you think the demand elasticity of cigarettes would be? Why?

Capturing All the Revenue Under the Demand Curve

Consider the demand curve pictured in Figure 3.7. Every point along that curve represents a possible transaction, a point at which a buyer and seller could agree on a price. Notice that the curve doesn't actually touch the horizontal axis because there are few products where a seller can or will agree to a zero price, and if they did, demand might (theoretically) be infinite. The curve realistically ends at the point where, regardless of economies of scale, the seller's cost equals the price of the good or service. Anything below that would be operating at a loss, and you can't make up losses in volume.

FIGURE 3.7 Quantity Determined by the Demand Curve at Price $50

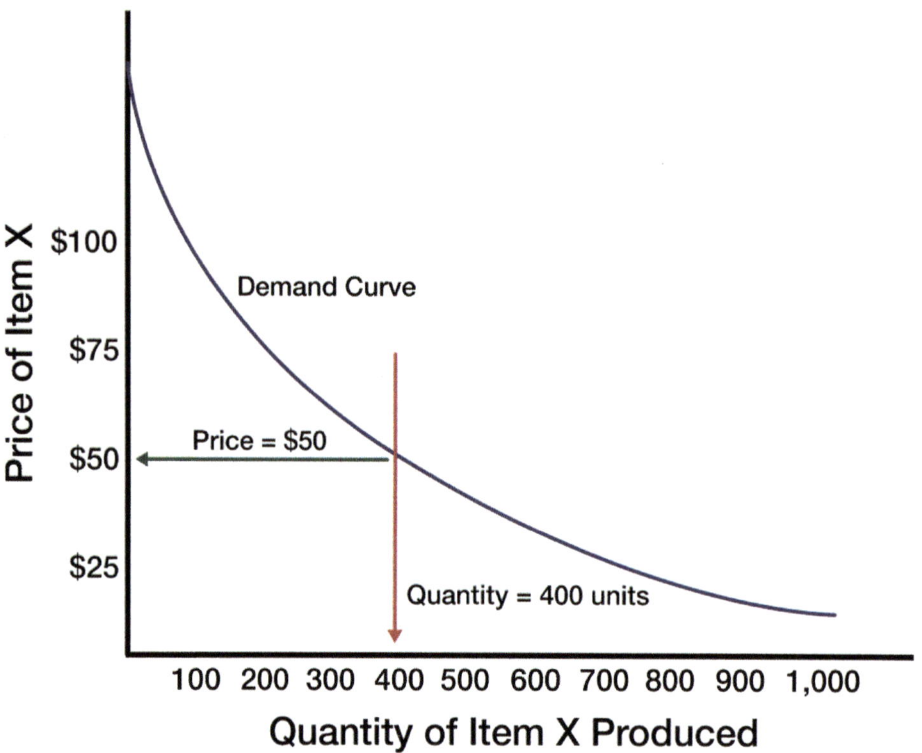

Source: Greg Autry

revenue

All the money generated by a firm by the sale of products or in payment for services rendered.

The area under the demand curve represents all the consumer sales available in the market. At each point, we can calculate the price and multiply it by the quantity sold at that point and get the **revenue**, or total monetary value of our sales.

$$\text{EQ 1: Revenue} = \text{Price} \times \text{Quantity Sold}$$

Working our way down the curve, we'd get the maximum possible revenue of the entire market. Doing that with a nonlinear function involves calculus, and that's not a requirement of this text, so we're going to pass (phew!). What we are going to do is look at a few specific price points on the curve.

FIGURE 3.8 Quantity Determined by the Demand Curve at Price $100

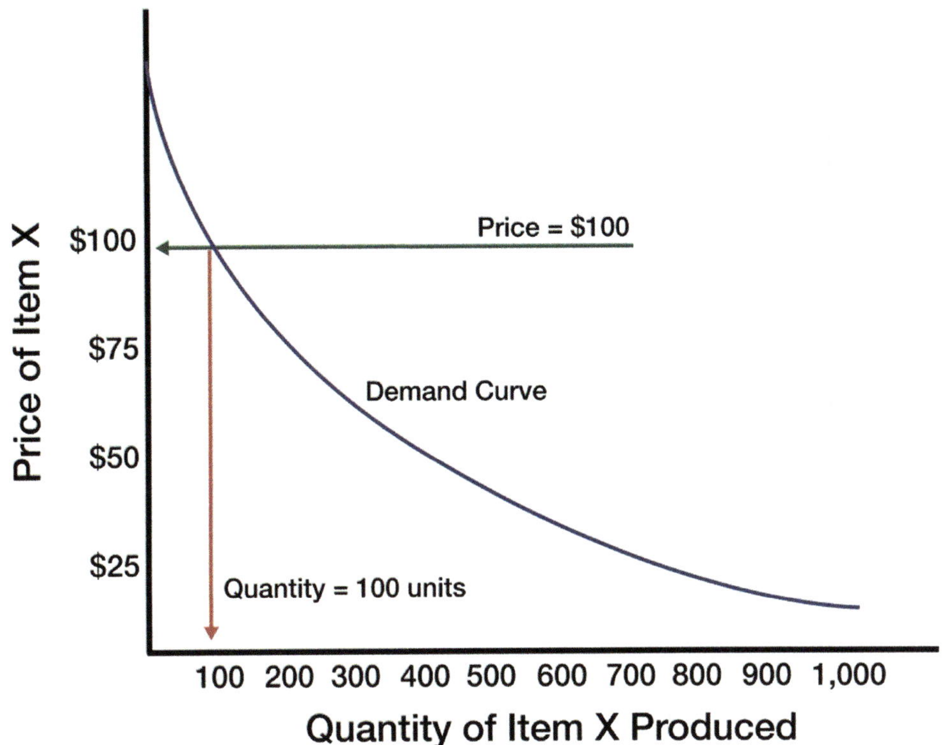

Source: Greg Autry

If you're the purveyor of Item X, and you price Item X at $50, you can see that the curve tells you that you will sell 400 units of Item X. How much money is that? Your revenue will equal the price ($50) times the volume (400 units), or $20,000. All 400 buyers in your market who were willing to pay $50 *or more* bought your product. Did you maximize your revenue? No! Why? You did not capture all the revenue because there were buyers willing to pay more than $50! However, if you'd priced at $100, as in Figure 3.8, you can see you would have gotten much fewer sales.

In fact, at $100, you only sell 100 units. What is your revenue then? It's $100/unit x 100 units = $10,000. Not as good. Does that mean you should price at $50? What about going lower? Figure 3.9 shows the outcome at $25.

FIGURE 3.9 Quantity Determined by the Demand Curve at Price $25

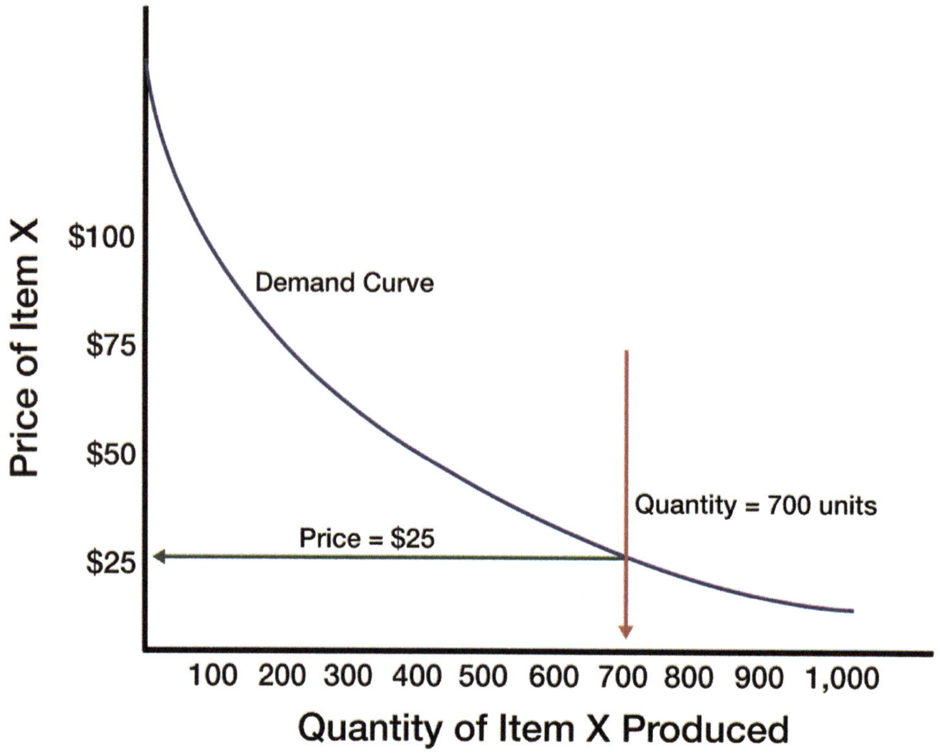

Source: Greg Autry

You will see that if you offer Item X at $25, you'll have 700 eager buyers! Lower price means lots more buyers. Great! Let's run to Walmart (high volume, low prices)! But wait! How does that work out revenue-wise? It turns out that $25/unit x 700 units = just $17,500. We'd make more revenue ($20,000) with fewer customers at $50/unit. Sometimes less really is more! So, if your objective is to maximize revenues, you'll price Item X at $50.

What About Profits?

Now, it turns out that running a business isn't really about maximizing revenue. You don't get to keep revenue. It's about maximizing your profits, the money you have left after your costs are subtracted. We will cover that in more detail in the chapters on accounting and finance. For now, here's the simplified version below.

$$\text{EQ 2: Profit} = \text{Revenue} - \text{Costs}$$

Let's say that each Item X costs you $20 to make (no matter how many you produce). If you make 100 units, your costs are $20/unit x 100 units = $2,000. Since we already know that your revenue at 100 units was $10,000 ($100/unit x 100 units) your profit must be $10,000 - $2,000 = $8,000. What are your profits at each pricing level?

$$\$100\text{ Price, }100\text{ units} = \$10,000\text{ revenue} - (\$20/\text{unit} \times 100) = \$8,000\text{ profit}$$

$$\$50\text{ Price, }400\text{ units} = \$20,000\text{ revenue} - (\$20/\text{unit} \times 400) = \$12,000\text{ profit}$$

$$\$25\text{ Price, }700\text{ units} = \$17,500\text{ revenue} - (\$20/\text{unit} \times 700) = \$3,500\text{ profit}$$

So, again, in this case, maximizing profits would suggest that you go with the $50 price. The $100 pricing yields a nice $8,000, and in this case, the Walmart strategy yields much less.

It is not always the case that profits maximize at the same point as revenues. Let's imagine a scenario where you get price breaks at different quantities from your suppliers. Your costs are $36 for 100 units, $34 for 200 or more units, and just $22 for 500 or more units. Manufacturing in quantity might be the way to go here, right? Let's see.

$$\textbf{\$100 Price, 100 units} = \textbf{\$10,000 revenue} - (\textbf{\$36/unit} \times \textbf{100}) = \textbf{\$6,400 profit}$$

$$\textbf{\$50 Price, 400 units} = \textbf{\$20,000 revenue} - (\textbf{\$34/unit} \times \textbf{400}) = \textbf{\$6,400 profit}$$

$$\textbf{\$25 Price, 700 units} = \textbf{\$17,500 revenue} - (\textbf{\$22/unit} \times \textbf{700}) = \textbf{\$2,100 profit}$$

Wow. The low-price leader is still the low-profit loser, and both the $100 price and $50 price yield the same profit! What would you do? Go with $50 again and sell 400 units? The tactical choice is to go with the $100 price and do a lot less work and make the same amount of profit selling 100 units.

But how do you determine the demand curve for my market? Well, you can survey a group of potential customers and say, "What is the most you'd pay for my product?" With an adequate number of respondents, you can approximate a curve. Otherwise, you can do this exercise less precisely in your head, then validate it by adjusting your actual prices up and down a bit (if that is possible in your business).

Where's the Strategy?

It's great to understand pricing (and we will cover that more in Chapter 10), but is that strategic? Not really. It's a tactical move that every business owner should consider. Here is the real strategic objective: Try to capture *all* the profits (or revenue) under the demand curve! Look again at Figure 3.7, with the $50 price. In that case, we are maximizing revenue and profits (if we have a fixed $20 cost), but we aren't really getting the money out of all the rich folk who are willing to pay $100 or more, right? How can we get some people to pay more and still offer the product to others for less?

Businesses do this all the time, and it is called **discriminatory pricing**. Though it may not be entirely "fair," it's not illegal since the discrimination is based on income rather than legally protected classes like race, religion, or disability.

discriminatory pricing

A pricing model designed to maximize sales revenue by charging more to those willing to pay more and less to those who will not.

Geographic Pricing Strategy

Harrods is a popular high-end department store.

Source: Wei Huang/Shutterstock.com

At the most basic level, discriminatory pricing is seen when fancy stores in nice neighborhoods charge more for the same stuff than stores in less affluent areas. If you're in London, check out the price of a Nike brand shoe at Harrods in Knightsbridge, and then run down to some discount sports shop in Soho and see how much the same shoe costs. You'll find the same effect in Los Angeles (Rodeo Drive versus Sports Authority), Shanghai (Shanghai Times Square versus Super Brand Mall Pudong), and any other major city.

Model Pricing Strategy

One way to achieve this in the same location is to create an artificial distinction between products. When Apple introduced the Apple Watch, it started at about $350 for an aluminum-case "Sport" version. Apple also had a more expensive stainless-steel version starting at about $600 and a crazy expensive solid gold "Edition" for $10,000. You can even spend $7,000 on a fancy band for it—seriously. The actual watch electronics were the same in all versions. With around a half-ounce of gold in the watch case, the added cost for the Edition was surely less than $1,000. Still, the added price to the affluent consumer was a whopping $9,000 to $16,000, making the profit margins pretty insane. There weren't a lot of people willing to shell out that much, but Apple set out to capture them.

Time Pricing Strategy

Another way to do this is to vary your price over time. You've seen this as well. When a new product comes out, it is introduced at $100 and all those who can't wait pay that high price. Then when that market segment is tapped, the vendor lowers the price to capture a larger market segment.

Apple is also famous for this pricing strategy. Each year, last year's model is discounted so it is within the reach of a large group of people, and a new model is trotted out at a very high price. You can bet that about 12 months from now, you'll be able to buy that version for about 30% less if you're willing not to be the coolest smartphone user on campus. The time pricing strategy suggests you can lower prices to capture different segments of the market. Can you also move up?

Start at the Top

Military strategists have long understood that it is critical to occupy the high ground first. Assailing a competitor entrenched on the top of the hill from a position at the bottom is an extraordinarily difficult and dangerous task, even if you have a numerically or qualitatively superior force. During the U.S. Civil War, one of America's most brilliant generals famously ignored this maxim at the battle of Gettysburg. On July 3, 1863, Robert E. Lee directed General George Pickett to lead three divisions of Confederate troops in a futile uphill assault against a fortified Union position atop a hill, ironically named "Cemetery Ridge." The attempt was a complete disaster. The casualty rate for the Southern attackers was more than 50 percent, the Confederate troops were demoralized, and Lee's reputation as an unbeatable strategist was destroyed. Some historians credit this single poor gamble with sealing the fate of the South and preserving the Union.

This high-ground rule applies to business as well. From a commanding position in the high end of the market, you can more easily move into the higher-volume, lower-end market. Moving from the low-end to the high-end market is rarely successful. Making it work requires enormous expense, perseverance, and time. Should you start at the bottom of the demand curve and then move your price up? No, that won't work because when you set a price, everyone above that point will be able to buy your product at the lower price and will do so. If you start low, you'll have engaged most of your buyers at that price. There's also another issue that arises in setting prices. When you set the price high on a quality product, it becomes an **aspirational good**, something people want even if they cannot afford it. When the price later drops, you'll already have eager buyers lined up. The exact opposite effect can occur when you try to move a product up the pricing scale. The original low price will have tarnished the image of the product. It will be perceived as an overpriced, low-end good.

aspirational good

A product that a company priced above a customer's ability to pay, but which they wish to have.

High-ground strategy applies not just to individual products but your entire brand image and how customers perceive your firm (we will explore this more in Chapter 9 and Chapter 10). Consider fast-food branding. In 1973, Andrew Cherng and his father, Master Chef Ming-Tsai Cherng, opened an award-winning Chinese restaurant in Pasadena, California, and later expanded to five Panda Inn locations. In 1983, they opened a "Panda Express" store in the food court of the nearby Glendale Galleria. The high-quality reputation of the firm's restaurants supported the new fast-food concept, and it was a big success. The chain now owns more than 1,700 Chinese fast-food outlets worldwide. Most customers have probably never heard of the Panda Inn, but it only heightens their appreciation of the Panda Express experience. Could McDonald's open a high-end, sit-down restaurant chain? Probably not. McDonald's entered the market at the bottom of the demand curve, with low prices and high volume. They do an amazing job in that space, but the firm has experienced resistance in repeated attempts to move into more upscale sandwiches, and the public would simply laugh at a $22 McDonald's meal.

Market Entry Point Strategies: The Model S and the Leaf

The Nissan Leaf was an early low-end entry in the electric car market.

Source: Massimo Parisi/Shutterstock.com

Nissan introduced its all-electric Leaf vehicle in 2010. The Leaf was priced at $33,000 in the United States. It was eligible for $7,500 in federal tax credits as well as state subsidies ($2,500 in California) that could cut as much as 30 percent off the purchase price. This is an affordable car, clearly targeted at the broad base of the demand curve, and by all accounts, it's been a hit with the environmental and cost-conscious buyer. The Leaf dominated the U.S. sales statistics for electric cars. The vehicle was also designed to appeal to the environmentally conscious consumer with a utilitarian design that would never be described as "sexy."

A Tesla Model S.

Source: Des-Green/Shutterstock.com

In 2012, Tesla Motors began to ship its Model S. The Model S pricing started at $70,000 in the U.S., but most Model S cars were configured at well over $100,000. The Model S was eligible for the same subsidies as the Leaf, but they were proportionately much less significant—typically being worth less than 10 percent off the purchase price. The vehicle was clearly aimed at the top of the demand curve. The design of the Model S was powerful and sexy. Like the Leaf, the Model S was an instant hit, and by mid-2015, it was outselling the Leaf by a small margin.

Strategically the Tesla position was enviable. The firm enjoys gross margins that are twice the automobile industry average (22 percent versus 11 percent). The Model S has received countless accolades (noted earlier), and many drivers who cannot afford the Model S clearly aspire to own a Tesla. It was reasonable to presume they would gladly snap up a Tesla that was priced similarly to the Leaf. With that demand already in place, Elon Musk announced that the company would be introducing the Model 3 in 2016 at an estimated price of $35,000. The Model 3 swiftly became the world's best selling electric car.

Is there any demand for a $100,000 luxury Leaf? Probably not. Despite its positive reviews and thousands of satisfied owners, the Leaf's reputation as a utilitarian, everyman's car will not help it at all with the affluent buyer looking to distinguish themselves. It will require significant branding or building a whole new brand to make that leap into the high end. It's almost always better to start at the top.

Key Takeaways

- The laws of microeconomics—not your costs or desires—determine market pricing for your products.
- You can use strategic pricing to capture more profits from a market over time.
- Selling more units is not always the right strategy; often selling fewer units at a higher price is both easier and more profitable.
- Finding ways to charge more to those who can pay more is critical to maximizing profits.
- It is most effective to establish a reputation as the best before making more affordable products.

3.4 Strategy Analysis Toolkit

Learning Objectives

1. Learn a variety of strategy tools and where to apply them.
2. Learn to apply Porter's Five Forces model to analyze market attractiveness.
3. Learn to use SWOT analysis to understand your firm's strategic position.

Strategic analysis comes with a plethora of models. Here are a couple of the more popular ones to use with your small business.

Porter's Five Forces

Michael Porter's **Five Forces model** is probably the most famous of all strategy tools. The model is designed to determine whether a particular market is attractive to enter. Though Porter developed it for large corporations to consider their diversification options, it's a great instrument for the likely small business owner as well. Figure 3.10 depicts the model.

Five Forces model

An analysis tool developed by Michael Porter of the Harvard Business School that determines the attractiveness of a market.

FIGURE 3.10 Porter's Five Forces Model

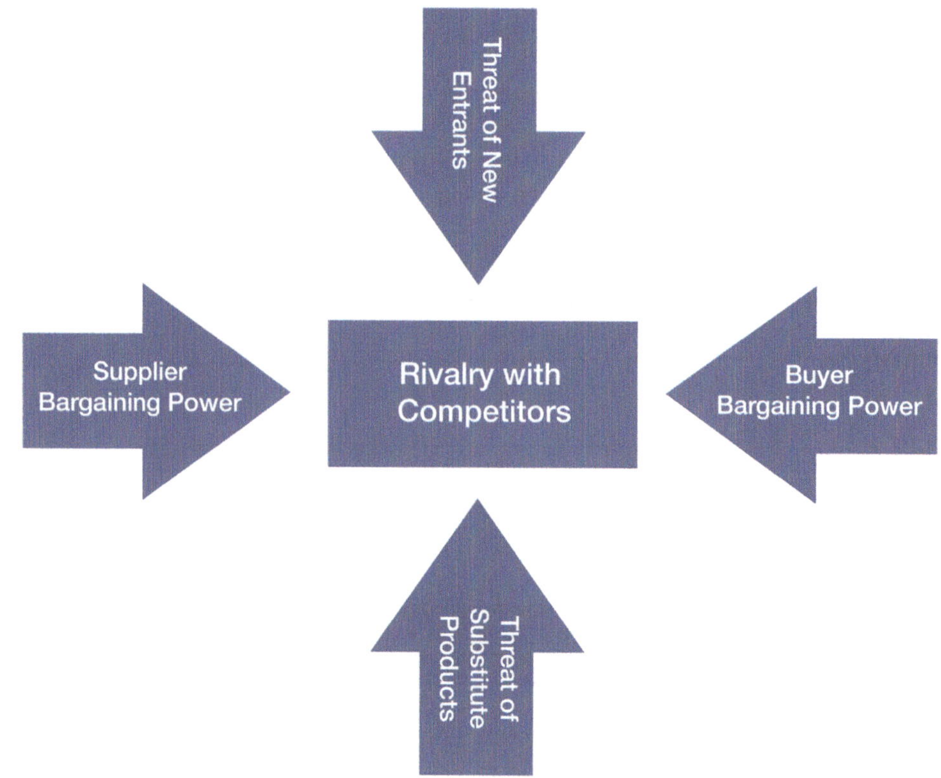

Source: Greg Autry

The methodology of Porter's model is to determine whether a market should offer the opportunity to generate significant profits for your firm by looking at the "power" of each of the five forces.

Rivalry

Rivalry with Competitors

The intensity of infighting among competitors in a particular market.

In the center of the model, you will find **Rivalry with Competitors**. This is a measure of the intensity of competition within the market. Markets with low rivalry are preferred. Some markets are brutally competitive, while others are more passive. Convenience food companies (cereal, sodas, snacks) often go after each other in ads and even pay supermarkets for guaranteed shelf space as a tactic to block rivals. At first, you might think all businesses fight tooth and nail like this, but that is not always the case. There are markets where the competitors are relatively congenial with each other.

industry culture

The particular social characteristic of one market as compared to another.

In the healthcare field, general practitioners and family doctors rarely advertise and essentially never bad-mouth their competition. Why do you think that is? The first reason is **industry culture**. Medical doctors generally view their profession as a sacred trust with humanity, above the fray of commercial endeavor. While they are happy to make a lot of money and drive nice cars, they generally disdain the idea of fighting for market share openly. Every industry is a community with a culture. The participants generally know each other, were trained together, and often have worked together in the past. For family doctors, this means medical school and membership in professional organizations such as the American Medical Association (AMA). They've even taken the Hippocratic Oath, which holds to them obligations to their patients and to the society of physicians. The oath specifically states that prosperity comes only from fulfilling these obligations. To aggressively market their services to patients and undermine the practice of a fellow physician would be a breach of this sacred trust.

A second reason is demand. Doctors who cure illness cannot generate more demand no matter how much they advertise. People are either ill, or they are not. To try to convince the healthy that they are sick would also be a violation of their Hippocratic Oath.[5]

A third reason is supply. When every vendor in a market has plenty of customers, there is no need to fight over market share, but when there are many more vendors in a market than required to supply customers, things usually get ugly. The AMA attempts to regulate this competitive pressure by specifically limiting the number of degrees awarded in the United States.[6] The family doctor market has low rivalry. Can you think of other industries where there is little rivalry? How about somewhere rivalry is very intense?

Porter suggests that in most cases, the worst competition occurs when there are a "handful" (five or so) major competitors in a market. The theory is that when there are two or three big competitors, they are able to reach a point of stability where they each have a nice half or third of the market, and they don't want to risk their own position by provoking a fight. Also, when there are dozens, nobody can gain a large market share. In the five or six competitor range, there is always an **underdog** firm eager to make a leap at the throat of the market leader.

underdog

The competitor deemed least likely to win by participants.

In general, it is preferable to avoid markets with intense rivalry because the cost of marketing to stay competitive drains profits and resources from your firm, and the risk of being upended by an aggressive competitor is higher. For the small businessperson, such markets often suggest late nights, stress at work and at home, ulcers, and perhaps an early heart attack. Stay away from these if you don't love a fight.

Threat of New Entrants

At the top of the model, you will find the **Threat of New Entrants.** This is a measure of the likelihood of new competitors entering the market. Do you recall from our earlier reading in this chapter what prevents new entrants from entering your market? It is barriers to entry. If complex regulations, high capital investment requirements, or intellectual property restrictions such as patents or **trade secrets** protect your market, then the threat of new entrants is low, and you needn't worry so much about this factor. Such a market is more attractive *if you can get into it in the first place.* You want to enter a market with the highest barriers to entry that you are capable of scaling, and then there will be fewer climbers coming in after you!

Threat of New Entrants

The likelihood of new firms entering the market to compete, constrained by barriers to entry.

trade secrets

Information (usually technical) kept secret by a firm and protected by law from industrial espionage.

The cupcake store business has virtually no barriers to entry. Baking is an art that goes back hundreds of years with much public sharing of recipes and techniques. There are few real "secrets" to protect. The cost of setting up a shop with mixers, pans, and ovens is not trivial, but it's within reach of most serious entrepreneurs. The regulatory environment in food services does include some paperwork and inspections, but it's something many, many people have expertise in managing. Consequently, the threat of new entrants is high in the cupcake store market, and it is not attractive from this perspective.[7]

On the other hand, the family doctor business has high barriers to entry, including the serious requirement of obtaining a medical degree, board certification, insurance, and expensive special equipment. The threat of new entrants is low, rendering this business attractive.

Threat of Substitute Products

At the bottom of the model, you will find the **Threat of Substitute Products** (or services). This is a measure of the likelihood of someone choosing a *different type* of product or service to meet their needs.

Threat of Substitute Products

The likelihood of customers switching to an alternative solution to their needs.

A market where the product is unique or indispensable has few or no substitutes and is more attractive. A market where your product is easily displaced or replaced by something else that can do the job has many substitutes and is not very attractive. For example, suppose you own a used car dealership. In that case, you generally consider your competitors to be other car dealers your customers might choose, right? Well, for your customer there are more options than are dreamt of in your market; they could buy a motorcycle or bike, or take public transport! Your cupcake shop has the same problem as sugary dessert substitutes abound. Ice cream, snow cone, yogurt, and candy shops are all considerations for your potential clients with a sweet tooth. Again, a cupcake shop does not appear attractive when viewed from the model.

Let's think of a market where there are few substitutes. How about a swimming pool service? If you are a customer and you own a pool, you can't exactly hire a gardener or a plumber to clean it and adjust the pH level. The only practical substitute is to do it yourself. So, overall, the threat of substitutes is low, and the swimming pool services business is pretty attractive from the perspective of this force.

Buyer Bargaining Power

Buyer Bargaining Power

The ability of your customers to negotiate price and terms with your firm. Often a measure of their dependence upon your product.

state-owned enterprise (SOE)

A business that is owned entirely or substantially by the government. Common in socialist and communist countries. The U.S. Postal Service is a state-owned enterprise.

customer loyalty program

A marketing program that involves rewarding repeat customers as an incentive to ensure their return, such as airline frequent-flyer programs or promo codes or membership cards providing a discount or extra service.

On the left of the model, you will find **Buyer Bargaining Power**. This force measures the amount of *leverage* that your buyers hold over your business. Are you really dependent on your buyers' satisfaction and cooperation, or do they basically have to put up with you? Well, if you happen to run a monopoly like a **state-owned enterprise (SOE)**, say a national telephone system or municipal bus service, your customers just have no choice.

Being a monopoly is not very likely for most small businesses, but you could own an exclusive dealership for some popular product or service in your area. For instance, Harley Davidson isn't going to authorize two motorcycle dealerships side-by-side. Like all smart franchisers, they keep their locations far enough apart that buyers are compelled to go to a particular location. Having such a dealership means buyers have low power and that the business is attractive from the perspective of this force.

Again, the cupcake buyer can easily go someplace else. One way to reduce this is to establish a switching cost by instituting a **customer loyalty program**. Perhaps you give out a punch card, and for every six cupcakes purchased, your customers get one for free! Somebody with four punches on their card is less likely to stray across the avenue because they would rather earn that free cupcake from you. On the other hand, a cupcake shop has hundreds or thousands of customers, and that reduces the power of any one particular buyer. A business where there are many customers who are not organized has low buyer power and is attractive. If you have few customers or the customers are organized into some sort of buying coalition, it can make life more difficult.

Some small business owners may subcontract work for only a single customer. Consider a machinist who takes early retirement from Boeing aircraft and then sets up shop as a subcontractor making parts for his old firm. He understands their needs and processes perfectly, and Boeing can avoid the capital investment of equipment and the overhead involved with hiring unionized employees. This is a very common situation. Although this makes for a very easy to manage business, buyer power is extremely high in this situation. Boeing must be kept happy, or all is lost. Such a business is very unattractive from the perspective of this force.

Cupcakes on display.

Source: © Shutterstock, Inc.

Supplier Bargaining Power

On the right of the model, you will find **Supplier Bargaining Power**. This force measures the **leverage** that suppliers have over your business! The lower this force, the more attractive your market, and it operates very much like buyer power. In this case, you want lots of suppliers who operate independently and compete for your business—you want your suppliers to be in an industry with intense rivalry. What you don't want is to be dependent on a single, critical supplier or a coalition of suppliers who operate together in a **cartel** to control prices or constrain supplies.

If you're in the cupcake business, you're going to love this force. You've got thousands of firms that can supply you with flour, sugar, sprinkles, etc. You can buy ovens and pans from many sources. It's all good from a supplier perspective. Supplier power is low, and the cupcake store business is attractive from the perspective of this force.

On the other hand, if you own that Harley Davidson dealership, you've probably got one supplier of product—motorcycles and Harley licensed swag—and they've got serious power over you. Supplier power is very high, and from the perspective of this force, having a franchise operation is unattractive. However, to be fair, it is clearly in the franchisor's interest that all their franchisees succeed. So, they are not likely to put the screws to your operation.

A worse situation would be if you were in a nonexclusive relationship for a key component of your business from a single company that did not need you as a customer. Imagine you're starting up a firm manufacturing carbon fiber paddles for stand-up paddleboards (SUP), and you engineered your entire production and marketing around a very high-performance material that is only available from a single supplier. The firm that makes this stuff normally sells in large quantities to huge aerospace companies. The volume of business you do is entirely inconsequential. If they encounter a temporary shortage of material, it isn't going to be Lockheed or Airbus they cut off first; it's the small businesses like yours. It is also possible they could decide dealing with their small customers isn't worth the overhead and shut you down. That's a very unattractive business from the perspective of this force.

Supplier Bargaining Power

The ability of your suppliers to negotiate prices and terms with your firm. Often a measure of your dependence upon them.

leverage

The ability of one group to compel another to take a particular action they otherwise might not choose to do.

cartel

A group of suppliers or buyers organized together to obtain leverage over their vendors or customers. OPEC, for example, has often been able to keep oil prices higher than the market would normally bear by limiting competitive production.

The Sum of All Forces

The point of any model is to use it to reach a solution. Always complete the Porter Analysis and determine whether the market as a whole is attractive. An attractive market typically yields a business higher profits for a longer time. What we want to know, when balancing all of these individual forces, is how things will pan out. Let's review a couple of our examples with a quick analysis and summation.

Cupcake Store

Rivalry = Medium to High. Not Attractive. Probably too many competitors all fighting for market share.

Threat of New Entrants = Very High. Not Attractive. It's very easy to get into this business.

Threat of Substitutes = Very High. Not Attractive. Ice cream, yogurt, candy, etc.

Buyer Power = Medium. Moderate. Buyers have many choices, but you have many potential buyers as well, and they have no organized power.

Supplier Power = Low. Attractive. You have many suppliers, and they have no leverage over you. The only exception might be the landlord if you desire to locate in a particular spot.

Conclusion: Not Attractive. Three of the five forces are not attractive, and only one is rated attractive, driving profitability in this business down. Don't enter this market unless you are truly determined.

Family Doctor

Rivalry = Low. Attractive. Competitors don't fight much.

Threat of New Entrants = Low to Medium. Moderate. It's relatively hard to get into this business due to significant education and capital requirements—however, the threat of new entrants has been more of a problem recently.

Threat of Substitutes = Low. Attractive. Religion and new age alternative medicine aside, there aren't any scientifically viable choices for most of the services a medical doctor provides.

Buyer Power = Low to Medium. Attractive. Buyers have many choices, but you have many potential buyers as well, and they have no organized power. More importantly, they don't tend to shop around once they make a choice.

Supplier Power = Medium. Moderate. You have many suppliers of equipment and services, and they have no leverage over you. The exceptions are malpractice insurance, board certification, governmental licensing, and payments from government health plans. The pressure to reduce payments from government health plans and increasing paperwork complexity has resulted in lower collections for private doctors in the United States and has put significant pressure on the business lately, reducing profits.

Conclusion: Attractive. Three of the forces are attractive, and none are rated not attractive, thus keeping profitability in this business up. This is a good market if you can afford the cost of entry-education. The increasing supplier pressure from the federal government is a serious concern for family MDs however.

Always complete the Porter Analysis by determining if the market is attractive or not. That is the purpose of the exercise.

SWOT Analysis

> This above all: to thine own self be true.
> —*Shakespeare*

SWOT Analysis

An analysis tool used to determine the fit of a firm to its market by evaluating the firm's strengths and weakness in relationship to the opportunities and threats in the market.

While Porter's Five Forces is a tool for analyzing the attractiveness of a particular market for any organization, **SWOT Analysis** is used to determine your firm's suitability to compete in a particular market. In general, it makes sense to work through the Porter model on your target market(s) and then conduct a SWOT analysis informed by your Five Forces conclusions to see if your firm is likely to succeed. It's a very simple and useful exercise to repeat regularly as your organization and the environment evolve over time.

What Is SWOT?

FIGURE 3.11 SWOT Analysis

SWOT is a popular tool for analyzing a firm's competitive potential in a market.

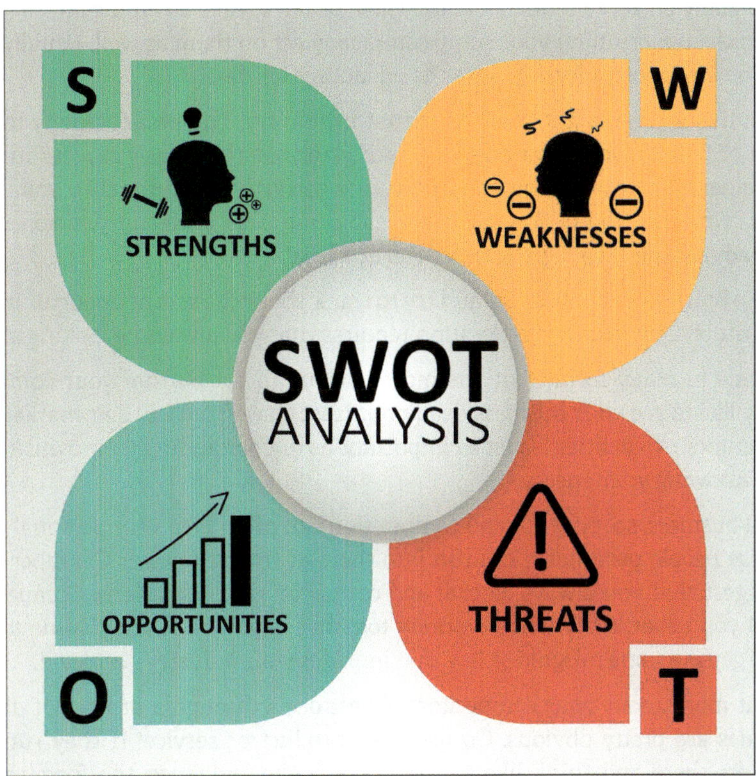

Source: © Shutterstock, Inc.

SWOT is an acronym for **S**trengths, **W**eaknesses, **O**pportunities, and **T**hreats. The first two items are an internal analysis of your business's capabilities, and the second two are external factors that determine your fit for this market. In all cases, the quote[8] above should guide you. Be brutally honest about yourself, your team, your resources, and the challenges you face. To do otherwise is to do yourself a great disservice and to lead others on a foolish mission that may put them into harm's way, at least financially.

Internal Control—Strengths and Weaknesses

What does your organization do well, and what are you not really good at? Notice that I said, "not really good at" rather than using the kinder phrase "could do better at." This is no time to worry about people's feelings.

Start your analysis by making a list of your strengths. First, list the *unique* resources your firm has. These are things that no other firm in your market has. Do you have a lease on the very best location in town? Do you have a strong personal relationship with the decision-maker at the largest customer in your market? Do you own a patent or exclusive right to some material? It's okay if you don't have any unique resources; few businesses do.

Next, list things that make your firm better than average. Is your alumni network really helpful? Are you a master of the social media universe? Is the chef at your restaurant one of the best in town? Do you have a lock on an amazing location?

Finally, list your weaknesses—things that you do not do well or areas in which you need improvement.

External Control—Opportunities and Threats

opportunity

A chance to do something good, such as providing a product or service to solve a problem that customers will pay well for.

first-mover advantage

A theoretical advantage held by the first firm to enter the market. Often from consumer awareness or association of the firm with the product or service.

second-mover advantage

The advantage a firm gains entering a market after the market leader. The ability to learn from the success and mistakes of the first mover.

An **opportunity** is a moment in time when a situation exists that would allow you to do something positive. Opportunities require both recognition and action. They are rarely lucky events that just fall in your lap. Many entrepreneurs fail to see them or fail to take advantage of them. Opportunities are rarely exclusive, meaning your competitors may act on them as well. Usually, the first firm to *execute well* on an opportunity will seize the advantage it offers.

To be clear, this winner is not always the first firm to *try*. The first company to try gains the elusive concept of **first-mover advantage**, but as often as not, these early movers still fail. The failure of your competitor to execute on an opportunity correctly will bring it to your attention and educate you on what not to do! You can then leap on it. This powerful position is known as a **second-mover advantage**. (See "Opportunity Fail at Xerox".)

Make a list of current opportunities and try to think about the sort of opportunities that might emerge in the future. Opportunity recognition requires that you always be looking ahead!

Threats come in many forms, but the most obvious threat is from your competitors. They would probably like to see your business dead or at least chased out of their market. Understanding your competitors' capabilities is just as important as understanding your own. Remember Sun Tzu's advice on knowing your enemy.

For a small business, scoping out the competition can often be a very personal task. You may even know these people personally. You run into them at trade shows or Chamber of Commerce meetings. I suggest that you always be civil and cordial on these occasions. Competitors are also colleagues, and you never know when working together might be of great value to you in some endeavor—like getting some misguided law that impedes your industry corrected.

Finding out more about your competitors is best done through a process of discovery. Most of the techniques are pretty obvious. Go use their product or service! If they run a competing restaurant, go eat there and think like a critic. How is the ambiance, the food, the service, the value? Discover what they do well and where their weaknesses are located. Test the business under nonoptimal conditions, when it's busy or the weather is bad. Challenge them with more difficult logistical tasks. If it's an online store, try returning something. If it's a plumbing service, call them in the middle of the night and see if you can reach anyone. Most companies do their jobs pretty well in normal conditions; it's under adversity that operational excellence and vulnerabilities really show.

U.S. Navy SEALS

Source: © Shutterstock, Inc.

Don't trust only your own evaluations. You have particular likes and dislikes that, try as you might, cannot be dislodged. So, ask other people you trust to give you their candid opinions. Look at their online reviews and see what their customers praise or criticize. Are these valid comments or just bogus reviews from their parents and friends? Are the negatives real info for you or just the snarking of internet trolls and personal enemies?

Confidence is a great strength of entrepreneurs, but it can also be a major weakness. Sometimes confidence extends to bluster, and the entrepreneur is simply unable to see their own shortcomings or those of their team. Don't let your ego get in your way. There are tasks that a particular group of people will never perform well, and no amount of training is going to fix that. A U.S. Navy SEAL Team is composed of some of the fittest, bravest, smartest, best-educated, well-trained, and most resourceful folks you'll ever find. If you want to rescue hostages or take out a terrorist hiding in some remote and hidden lair, I highly recommend them. However, that doesn't mean the SEAL team is going to win on *America's Best Dance Crew* or capture the World Cup next year. Michelle Wie could easily whip any SEAL in eighteen holes of golf. You and your firm have weaknesses too.

Golfer Michelle Wie

Source: Mai Groves/Shutterstock.com

market capitalization

The total worth of a firm's stock. Its share price multiplied by the number of shares outstanding.

Opportunity Fail at Xerox

Xerox Alto computer.

Source: https://commons.wikimedia.org/wiki/File:Xerox_Alto_mit_Rechner.JPG

A classic example of opportunity recognition and execution failure occurred in Palo Alto, California, in the early 1970s. At the time, the Xerox corporation was one of the world's premier multinational firms. They had introduced the modern photocopy process in 1959 and quickly rose to prominence and wealth. Many people considered it the most successful product ever developed (before the iPhone), and "Xerox" became a common American verb synonymous with "copy." Understanding that their fundamental patents on "xerography" would expire and that there was a "paperless office of the future," Xerox developed a strategic plan.

Xerox's strategy was to invest heavily into research and development of modern office automation tools. It was a smart move. The focus of this effort was a famous research and development facility called Xerox PARC (Palo Alto Research Center) in California's Silicon Valley. The PARC team was led by the visionary computer engineer, Bob Taylor, and the team was filled with computer geniuses destined to be future tech luminaries and entrepreneurs. Taylor's team immediately saw that the fundamental problem with the computers of the day was the difficulty in supporting and using them. The room-sized and cabinet-sized beasties of the day required dedicated support teams. The cryptic instructions these computers used compelled potential computer users to get days of specialized training even for a simple task, like writing a letter. The arrival of the integrated circuit would allow them to build a "personal computer station," and modern programming techniques (object-oriented programming) would enable them to create a graphical user interface

(GUI). This was an amazing opportunity to capture first-mover advantage in a new era of computing and take out IBM, DEC, and the other firms that dominated the computing landscape of the 1970s.

The Alto computer system that the PARC engineers developed was way ahead of its day. Nearly fifteen years before these things became standard on computers, the Alto had a mouse, windowing software, movable documents with a variety of fonts, a local area network (LAN), and a laser printer. In fact, the Alto was so advanced that the corporate management at Xerox "just didn't get it" and did not immediately commercialize the system.

Not only did Xerox completely fail to exploit its opportunity to own the global computer industry, it compounded the problem by demonstrating the product to Apple Computer's Steve Jobs and his development team! Apple ironically "Xeroxed" the features of the Alto and developed a failed computer called Lisa, which in turn inspired their wildly successful Macintosh. Microsoft imitated Apple's success to create its popular Windows operating system. As of this writing, Apple is now the world's most valuable company with a **market capitalization** of $620 billion. Microsoft is number five at $335 billion. Xerox isn't ranked on any lists, and the market values it at just $10.5 billion.

Xerox failed to execute on the most significant opportunity in business history. They had also failed to see that tiny Apple and Microsoft were actually their competitors. The rest, of course, is history. Basically, all computers, phones, and tablets are reflections of the vision of Bob Taylor's team. Unfortunately for the shareholders who funded the incredible research and development at PARC, it wasn't Xerox history.

Key Takeaways

- There are a variety of tools you can use to analyze your strategic environment.
- Understanding the reality of your market is critical to success.
- Being honest about your organization's capabilities is empowering.
- Never let overconfidence lead you into danger.

3.5 Strategic Fit

Learning Objectives

1. Understand that strategy must fit the circumstance.
2. Understand that the strategy must be appropriate to the entrepreneur.
3. Learn to spot and exploit trends.

Eddie would go.

—*Mark Foo, surfer*

Sync to Market Conditions

Being in sync with its environment is crucial to the long-term success of any endeavor. Besides competitors, your startup will have a host of environmental conditions to consider, including the health of your local economy, the strength of your customer base, and the **regulatory and tax climate.** A successful strategy must consider and work within the realities of that environment. You probably shouldn't launch a luxury product in a depressed neighborhood, nor push a low-price service in a wealthy one. You don't want to be peddling umbrellas in Phoenix, Arizona, which gets just 8 inches (20 centimeters) of rain a year, or sell swimwear in Helsinki, Finland, where the average temp in July is just 62°F (17°C). As with Darwin's theory, the better your business model fits the environment, the more likely your firm will survive.

regulatory and tax climate

From the point of view of a firm, the level of intrusion and cost generated by regulations in a given region and the level of the taxes they are subject to.

Sync to the Entrepreneur

A business strategy must also fit the entrepreneur herself. The business must work in a way that will not continually produce conflict with your personal life. If the physical demands of production, the hours required, the commute time, or any of a hundred other factors create stress, it will impact the organization. While we often encounter the stereotype of an entrepreneur worked to the bone, burning the midnight oil, and sacrificing their personal life for their company, that model is unsustainable. Startups are hard work, but in the long run, a healthy, happy leader is essential to the success of any organization.

Trends Matter

Don't just take a snapshot of your situation; look at where it's going. What are the vectors and the trends in your business and your market? Opportunities and threats are constantly emerging. Twenty-first-century markets are particularly dynamic. Technology and fashion appear to be changing at a rapidly increasing rate. The business strategist finds himself on a treadmill keeping up with the changing environment.

Where is technology taking your market? Are you possibly working in the next doomed industry? Did you ever hear of a one-hour photo lab (a place to develop old school film photos onto paper prints)? That was a significant growth industry for young entrepreneurs a generation ago, but today it is gone. You've probably seen DVD and Blu-ray disks at yard sales. Before internet bandwidth allowed streaming movies at home, there were thousands of DVD rental stores across the U.S. and DVD rental kiosks in every grocery store. It's amazing how many entrepreneurs, big and small, went down with that ship. No amount of strategic brilliance or excellent execution can save a business in an extinct market. Never bet into a losing hand; move on when the market moves on.

Your strengths and weaknesses will change as your business matures, and your team changes with losses, additions, and maturity. Is your restaurant filled with older folks? That's swell in the short term because they are probably loyal repeat customers, but you need to bring in a continual flow of new clients because, sadly, the old ones are not going to last forever.

However, the most fundamental lesson of the New Entrepreneurial Dynamic is that *change is opportunity*. Embrace change because your small business has an amazing advantage over your large competitors: You can plan strategy and execute on tactics quicker than your large competitors. Speed is the sustainable competitive advantage intrinsic to startups and small businesses; use it!

The Young Entrepreneur and the Sea

A surfer waits for one last wave.

Source: © Shutterstock, Inc.

The entrepreneur walks along the California shoreline. Kicking the sand and watching the sea, she considers the power of waves. She is eager and prepared to harness the power of the next tech wave. She plans to control that power, to define the new market, and then ride out all of her competitors.

A crusty old surfer hauls out of the sea in front of her. He throws his long but thinning blond hair over a mahogany tanned shoulder and pauses on his way to the showers to exchange the obligatory greeting. Annoyed by this distraction but polite, the entrepreneur asks the requisite question, "How was it?"

As though sensing her thoughts, the surfer remarks cryptically, "You can't shape the waves; you can only shape your board."

The entrepreneur considers this and asks, "Is there nothing more you can do to keep from wasting your day?"

The surfer chuckles and adds, "You should look at the surf report and choose the best beach. Then keep your eye on the swell and be patient enough to wait for the right wave. Then you just have to paddle like hell and make the best out of the ride you find yourself on top of."

That is the essence of strategy and execution in harmony with the dynamic environment.

Key Takeaways

- You can't force the market to accept a business model it doesn't want.
- You won't succeed at a business you can't run well.
- When the market changes, change with it or get out.
- As always, change is opportunity, and startups are best at it.

3.6 Case Study: Overcoming Barriers to Entry via Strategic Partnerships

King Health Systems is a large Health Maintenance Organization (HMO) headquartered in California. The King Health system comprises of dozens of hospitals and hundreds of clinics equipped with pharmacies, labs, and radiology centers. The organization directly employs thousands of providers (medical doctors, nurse practitioners, and physician assistants) as well as clinical staff, pharmacists, and technicians. It also has an extensive internal information technology (IT) group that manages one of the largest and most sophisticated corporate enterprise networks in the world. King's IT domain incorporates large data centers, dedicated wide area networks (WANs), local area networks (LANs), and Wi-Fi networks connecting thousands of desktop computers, laptops, and mobile devices. This infrastructure supports an area of software products, from off-the-shelf items such as Microsoft Office to customized diagnostic tools and clinical information systems.

e-Rx is a startup producing an electronic prescription authorization system that replaces traditional paper scripts. e-Rx identified King Health as the best target for their solution because of their integrated clinical and pharmacy system and sophisticated IT infrastructure. The e-Rx team chose an upcoming medical technologies conference as the best venue to connect with King employees and start a sales process. At the conference, e-Rx's business development executive, Steve Biden, captured the attention of a King Health Pharmacy operations manager, Sami Jones. Biden intrigued Jones with the potential of his firm's products. Biden quickly realized she was a visionary, willing to look into new ideas and see their potential. She also had the respect and charisma to advocate for major projects within the King organization.

Jones offered the e-Rx sales team a foot in the door at King, but Biden and his team faced an uphill battle because they were unknown to the higher-up decision-makers. e-Rx also lacked referenceable clients; their system had never been installed anywhere. Convincing King's administrators, doctors, and pharmacists to take a chance on an unproven system from an unproven vendor would be a real challenge. Getting the IT department to grant security access to the data centers and logins to develop interfaces for existing databases would be a sales job in itself. These groups were likely to say, "Go try this out with some minor league clinic and show us how that went."

There was really no way for e-Rx to prove themselves by putting their system into a smaller client organization as a minimum viable product, or MVP. The nature of the e-Rx solution required an extensive, integrated health system that controlled its own pharmacies and possessed a sophisticated IT infrastructure. More importantly, e-Rx's strategy was to quickly establish themselves as the leader in the emerging electronic prescription management market and get venture funding to back that. The team was sure that a big client would bring them the big investors needed to establish their firm as a fixture in the booming electronic health industry. This was a classic "chicken and egg" problem for a small firm going after a very large client.

Sami Jones understood the sales dilemma that e-Rx faced and was sensitive to their plight. Jones conceived a strategy for getting through the barriers to entry that e-Rx faced. She introduced Steve Biden to Gary Rogers. Rogers owned Network Labs, a systems integrator that had, for many years, provided network installation and support services for King Health. Network Labs would be perfectly suited to set up the servers, support the networking requirements, and train users. Even more importantly, they were an established and respected vendor within King's environment. If Network Labs joined e-Rx in the sales effort and promised to be on-hand to support the installation, deployment, and training, King's decision-makers would have a much higher degree of confidence.

Biden was attracted to the idea, but he did find the suggestion somewhat presumptuous. He recalls, "Our customer was reworking our corporate strategy to get us over barriers to entry her own firm had established." He was also hesitant to partner up with a company and individuals he had never met before. Biden notes, "I wasn't sure what Network Labs was going to be like, but I figured we were going to have to find out, so I accepted the meeting, and it turned out to be the best strategic partnership we ever made."

The e-Rx and Network Labs teams shared the "startup mentality," and the two groups quickly bonded. Gary Rogers was particularly impressed with Robyn Ross, the software genius behind e-Rx. Ross had developed the entire solution singlehandedly, in just a few months. She was not only able to build the SQL database on the backend but also built a slick and easy to use web-based frontend and swiftly coded custom interfaces to multiple mainframe databases that were unique to King.

The sales cycle for the e-Rx system took many months. The combined e-Rx and Network Labs solution had to address many concerns as well as the efforts of saboteurs within King Health, who wanted to develop internal solutions they could direct. In the end, a very lucrative deal was struck. e-RX received $300,000 in advance payments for customization and deployment as well as a monthly software licensing fee of $48,000. The e-Rx team was able to bring in Silicon Valley investors who appointed a new president with extensive corporate experience to run the firm. The e-RX implementation and training requirements allowed Network Labs to significantly expand the size of their team within King Health.

A few years later, King Health expressed a need for a clinical messaging system of similar configuration and scope to the e-Rx system. They requested proposals on the new system from e-Rx and HAL, a huge international computer and consulting firm. e-Rx's new president, installed by the investing group, had sidelined Biden and the founding team and replaced them with a traditional group of experienced experts. These old healthcare pros produced a complex and expensive proposal for King that was indistinguishable from the HAL solution.

This proposal worried Gary Rogers over at Network Labs. Rogers believed that advocates within King had intentionally set up the proposal competition in e-Rx's favor, expecting the startup to provide another nimble, cost-effective solution that would have looked very attractive compared to a pricey and cumbersome HAL bid. He tried to warn the new e-Rx leadership that they were going down the wrong path with King Health, but the new e-Rx president wouldn't even meet with him.

King ended up with two big, complex, and expensive proposals, and they didn't want either. The e-Rx founders and sales team were extremely frustrated with their new management, but they also believed they were tied to e-Rx by their stock options. Rogers was frustrated too. He wanted the implementation work to go to Network Labs and knew HAL would rely on its own army of engineers to do that. Rogers decided the right strategy at this time was to jettison the burdensome part of the e-Rx partnership and capture the portion that added value. He went to Ross, the original e-Rx developer, and proposed offering King an unsolicited proposal from Network Labs with software by Ross.

Endnotes

1. This often involves acknowledging the strategic genius of very disagreeable tyrants from Napoleon to Bin Laden, while recognizing the inhumane goals to which they applied it.
2. Nash, John F. "Equilibrium points in n-person games." Proceedings of the *National Academy of Sciences 36(1),* 48–49.
3. The very same location was used as a defensive position during the Second World War (1941) by Allied forces opposing the Nazi invasion of Greece. In this case, the German mechanized forces could not use the mountain trail and the British were able to delay them long enough to evacuate thousands of New Zealand and Australia soilders to Crete.
4. At the time of this writing the Tesla versus state dealers battle was still raging, but our money is on the entrepreneur.
5. Some noncritical specialties such as cosmetic surgery are a clear exception. People don't need liposuction, botox treatments, or breast augmentation to save their lives, and doctors in these fields need to generate demand and advertise very aggressively.
6. As of late this has not been entirely effective in the United States, and family doctor incomes have been under pressure. This has been due to degrees awarded to U.S. doctors from offshore schools and the immigration of foreign medical doctors into the U.S.
7. That isn't to say you can't succeed there if you are passionate. Just be aware you will face constant competition in addition to dealing with the possibility that such shops are a passing fad.
8. Laertes final advice to his departing son, Polonius, in the play *Hamlet*.

CHAPTER 4
Opportunity Recognition

> Eureka!
>
> —*Archimedes*

Finding your opportunity.

Source: © Shutterstock, Inc.

Do you already know what your next, or perhaps your first, entrepreneurial endeavor will be? The very first step in any project requires identifying the destination. In business, that means knowing what business you are going to enter.

4.1 Searching for Ideas

Learning Objectives

1. Understand some founders come to entrepreneurship with a clear business idea, while others chose entrepreneurship seeking an opportunity.
2. Understand the approaches of exploration and exploitation.
3. Understand that adding value is what makes an idea an opportunity.
4. Recognize how customer pain points create business opportunities.
5. See that delighting people is of huge value.

Choosing a Destination

severance package

Extra monies provided by a company to an employee who is leaving, typically during a layoff.

seed capital

The initial money used to fund a new venture.

hang a shingle

Traditional English businesses would hang a painted shingle outside the door indicating the type of business inside: pub, barber, bookseller, etc.

What is your business "idea"? This question is a "no brainer" for the thousands of small business owners who find themselves taking over the operations of an existing firm, either through careful planning or a lucky break. They may inherit the family construction business, buy out their boss at a specialty aluminum foundry, or purchase their favorite corner pub with a corporate **severance package**. Many skilled craftspeople and professionals know exactly which business they are going into. If they have the **seed capital**, they can move directly into business after completing their education or apprenticeship, or transition fairly easily from working for another firm. A baker, electrician, or lawyer often feels they need only **hang a shingle** to be in business. So, this chapter might not be so important to them, though this book will make it clear that there is a lot more to finding success in business than opening your door and waiting for customers to arrive!

A skilled tradesperson with tools can hang a shingle and go into business.

Source: James Kirkikis/Shutterstock.com

Another big group of entrepreneurs is made up of creative workers: particularly artists and engineers. Artists are eager to generate new ideas because they are inclined and trained to look at the world differently. Engineers are educated to define problems and produce solutions. However, creative workers often freeze up when forced to *choose* between an abundance of great ideas. Some entrepreneurs fail simply because they're unable to restrain themselves from pursuing every idea they encounter. These may be their own ideas, those proposed by friends, or ones they encounter in the world or read about online. As has been noted by Thomas Edison and Elon Musk, ideas are abundant. Getting them done and done right is nearly impossible. Time, money, and other resources have limits, and each new idea you take on reduces the value you can add to the previous ones.

Chapter 5, on **feasibility analysis**, will help solve the dilemma of selecting the idea with the best potential to be a successful business. However, I understand that not everyone is burdened with Elon Musk's or Thomas Edison's problem of having too many world-changing business ideas clogging up their heads. Many otherwise entrepreneurial-minded people have trouble launching their own ventures simply because they cannot find a clear reason to start one. Business students often say things like, "I really want to be independent and run my own company, but I don't know what it should be," or "I want to be part of a startup, but I don't have a great idea of my own." How might such an aspiring entrepreneur search for ideas? If you're one of those ambitious souls who want to be their own boss or just start something new, but you aren't sure in exactly what area, this chapter is designed to help you stir up a lot of ideas for further analysis.

feasibility analysis

Take the time to review the aspects of your business plan to see if it is achievable.

Yes, There Are Two Paths You Can Go By!

innovation

The process engineers or artists pursue to create something new. See also *creative destruction*; *disruption innovation theory*; *exploration*.

exploration

Searching for new business ides. See also *innovation*.

exploitation

The process of creating new products from the modification of existing and proven products.

slack

The resources, such as time, money, or facilities, that an organization does not require for its immediate operations and can therefore be allocated to the development of new products or services.

risk tolerance

The ability to face unknown outcomes without stress.

Innovation is the process that artists or engineers follow to create something new. There are two basic paths to innovation: **exploration** or **exploitation**.

Exploration involves searching for new ideas, experimentation, and failure. Some new ideas already exist, just not within your organization, and part of exploring is hunting for them. Most small businesses involve some degree of exploration of this sort. They require the entrepreneur to discover a customer need and fill that need by finding a solution. Sometimes that solution involves developing a whole new product category.

Exploitation offers an easier path for product development, available to businesses that already exist and have working products. Rather than creating or finding a new product category via exploration, exploitation depends on incrementally modifying existing products or applying them to new markets. Product production or service delivery is usually relatively straightforward because this has been done before. Customers are typically able to understand and eager to embrace incrementally improved products.

Management scholars have spent a great deal of time looking at the appropriate allocation of resources between exploration and exploitation. Professor James March of Stanford noted in a seminal 1991 paper that the development of new products within organizations is restricted by the limited resources of employee time, money, and facilities. Most firms are focused on the process of producing and delivering their goods to the customer. Additional resources, not used in that process and available to pursue something new, are known as organizational **slack**. Balancing between the potential bigger payoffs from a breakthrough versus the more assured outcomes from an incremental product depends on the available slack and the **risk tolerance** of the management team.

Doing innovation via exploration may involve the invention of an entirely new class of electronic products or an inspired new fashion line unlike anything else on the market. It's not an incremental improvement or surface-level change to something that already exists. This sort of opportunity is much riskier. There are two fundamental types of innovation risk: development risk and market risk. Firstly, because a truly new product often requires the development of new technologies or processes to deliver it, it may actually turn out to be impossible to do what you propose to do, at least at any reasonable cost.

There are two fundamental paths to finding a business opportunity

Source: © Shutterstock, Inc.

Apple's early attempt to develop a personal digital assistant (what we now think of as a smartphone, minus the phone part) was a classic example of innovative vision overreaching technical capabilities of the day. The Apple Newton MessagePad was released in 1993 and promised to give users a portable computer in their pocket to manage dates and contacts, take notes, and run other "apps" using a touch screen with handwriting recognition. The computing power of the day made the device the size of a brick, gave it a short battery life, and resulted in notoriously humorous blunders on the part of its recognition system. Though most everyone loved the idea, nobody loved the product, and it was a total failure. Today the vision of the Newton can be found in any Apple or Android smartphone.

This innovative touch screen tablet, called the Apple Newton MesagePad, was a failure in the market.

Source: Christopher W., https://commons.wikimedia.org/wiki/File:Apple_Newton_2100.jpg

Secondly, innovation is difficult because you have to convince customers to try something new. This may involve changing their routines or even their sense of identity, and a great deal of customer education may be required.

For example, despite the environmental benefits and higher performance, electric vehicles initially faced great resistance from those accustomed to, and often in love with, specific types of gasoline-burning automobiles. People were perplexed about the idea of charging. They kept imagining that a huge network of chargers would be required on every corner—much like gas stations, but larger—and the whole process would be time-intensive. It took a while for them to discover that for daily commuters, the process of charging a car overnight at home or in a work parking lot actually saved time over visiting gas stations. Others simply weren't ready to give up their Jeep or Mercedes because they saw themselves as a "Jeep person" or "Mercedes driver." Being seen in a Nissan Leaf or a Tesla would be disruptive to a major expression of their personal identity. Chapter 5 will investigate ways to minimize the risks associated with exploration-based innovation.

Customer Pain and Delight

No, we aren't talking about anything odd; today's hot button opportunity generation methodology is the search of customer **pain points**. By pain points, I mean the things that really annoy your potential customers. Most people will pay good money to get rid of an annoyance and a lot of money if the annoyance is a serious threat to their livelihood. If there is a technology or process available to solve it, an entrepreneur will find it. As Dean Kamen, inventor of the Segway, mobile insulin pump, freestyle soda machine, and many other things describes it, "Every once in a while, a new technology, an old problem, and a big idea turn into an innovation."

pain points

Circumstances that produce great discomfort or simply mild annoyance for potential customers.

Pain points can be massive, shared problems like global warming or problems that are incredibly important to individuals like heart disease. They can be even relatively trivial matters like uncomfortable travel pillows. A simple small business pain point might be the lack of a good breakfast cafe along a particularly busy urban block. The observant entrepreneur who sees this situation leaving thousands of morning commuters under-caffeinated and hungry on their way to work could find a living in that.

Rush hour commuter traffic presents a massive, shared problem that offers many opportunities for businesses that can alleviate this pain.

Source: © Shutterstock, Inc.

Thankfully, business is not always focused on pain! Entrepreneurs can also succeed by creating joy where it did not previously exist. Think about Disneyland. Billed as "The Happiest Place on Earth," this mind-bogglingly successful amusement park in Anaheim, California, brightens 50,000 lives every day. Nobody *needs* a Disneyland, Disney World, Tokyo Disney Resort, Disney Cruise line, or animated princess films, but the company that created these things runs a massive global business based entirely on creating joy. We call that value **customer delight**.

College-educated entrepreneurs love business school jargon like "pain points" and "customer delight." However, be careful about letting authoritative language elevate something extremely trivial into the realm of serious discussion. Buzz words like these are often used to deceive entrepreneurs and investors into solving problems that are very abstract. A solution can only become a business if the customer is convinced that it adds enough **net value** (total value after purchase and associated costs are deducted) to her life. Net value will be discussed further in Chapter 5, but keep in mind that as an entrepreneur, you are looking for relatively serious pain points or very significant delights.

In economic theory, the process of either stopping pain or creating joy increases a consumer's **utility**. However, people are not the robots most economists would like to study. Human behavior results in many economically **suboptimal choices**. Consider that people willingly buy tobacco products, even though the net utility over time is rendered negative by a significant increase in the risk of developing several fatal health conditions. Tobacco consumers may also wish for insurance when they are diagnosed with lung cancer but aren't always willing to pay for solving tomorrow's problems. Alleviating *immediate* pain and providing *instant* satisfaction is an easier sell than addressing long-term problems.

Remember our global warming pain point? A big problem, but if you solved it, who would you bill? Would they pay? Beyond being able to fix a pain point, Chapter 5 will investigate whether you can get someone to pay for it.

customer delight

The value added when a product or service brings joy to the purchaser.

net value

The total value of a solution after purchase and associated costs are deducted. See also *net utility*.

utility

The total satisfaction derived by a consumer from a product or a service. See also *net value*.

suboptimal choices

An economic decision that does not produce the final best financial result. A choice that does not optimize net value or consumer utility.

Key Takeaways

- A systematic approach to search can be very effective.
- Some ideas may be new discoveries, but most will likely be improvements to or new applications of existing ideas.
- Recognize that some great ideas may not be technically possible, yet.
- Always assume the customer's perspective when looking for opportunities and imagine their pain points or potential sources of delight.

4.2 The Entrepreneur as Innovator and Disrupter

Learning Objectives

1. Understand market disruption.
2. Recognize the danger of being overconfident with your own success.
3. Accept that changes in consumer demands and technologies are inevitable.
4. Understand that second mover advantage is easier to recognize than a new idea.
5. Understand last mover advantage.
6. Appreciate that chance can be encouraged.

Creative Destruction

Peter Thiel, a famed technology entrepreneur and venture capitalist, writes in his book *Zero to One* that the hardest thing to do is to create something entirely new. He contends that taking the world from "zero to one" in a novel category is orders of magnitude more difficult than developing one, five, or even a dozen new versions of an existing technology. Imitation is always simpler and less risky, and this makes it attractive to the vast majority of business founders, but this approach usually offers a smaller potential upside.

When something brand new succeeds, it very often displaces an existing inferior solution to the customer's pain or steals the payments being made for customer delight. These new products disrupt the existing markets and drive entire industries out of business. Economists refer to this process as **creative destruction**, a phrase coined by the Austrian economist Joseph Schumpeter (1942).[1] Today, creative destruction has become a key component of economic theory, economic policy, and business strategy.

creative destruction

A phrase coined by Austrian economist Joseph Schumpeter (1942) to describe the process by which an innovative product or technology supplants an existing product or technology, thereby disrupting a market. See also *disruption innovation theory*.

The mass-produced automobile destroyed a transportation industry built around horses.

Source: © Shutterstock, Inc.

tyranny of success

The inability of mature organizations to adopt disruptive solutions that threaten existing successful businesses.

A classic example of Schumpeterian creative destruction was Henry Ford's Model T automobile, which decimated the business of carriage makers, horse breeders, stables, feedlots, and veterinarians. More recently, Apple similarly destroyed Nokia's "feature phone" mobile business with its innovative touchscreen iPhone. DVD and BluRay discs disrupted the market for video cassette tapes in the 1990s and 2000s only to be annihilated by video-on-demand services like Netflix in the 2010s. In most of these cases, it is worth noting that the process of creative destruction took many years, and the designs of the new products were plainly visible long before they gained significant market share. The incumbent firms, dependent on the old paradigm (e.g., Nokia, Blockbuster), had plenty of time to exploit the new designs (copy) or explore (invent) for even better solutions. Despite having a dominant position and vast resources, they failed to execute because they were too comfortable with what they had been doing so well. This syndrome is known as the **tyranny of success**.

Disruptive Innovation

disruption theory

Clay Christensen of Harvard Business School identified disruption innovation as "a process by which a product or service takes root initially in simple applications at the bottom of a market and then relentlessly moves upmarket, eventually displacing established competitors."

Creative destruction manifests itself in entrepreneurship scholarship in the study of disruptive innovation. **Disruption theory**[2] was made famous by Harvard's Clayton Christensen in several articles and his seminal book, *The Innovator's Dilemma*.[3] Christensen describes disruptive innovation as "a process by which a product or service takes root initially in simple applications at the bottom of a market and then relentlessly moves up-market, eventually displacing established competitors."

There is no secret formula for disruption. Invention ultimately comes from looking at inefficiencies in the modern world and figuring out interesting solutions to overcome them. Walter Lawrence Gill, a young inventor in the early twentieth century, noted that cars and airplanes needed specialized starter batteries. Early internal combustion engine vehicles required a manual crank or prop-push to start. Electric starters were plagued by the fact that wet batteries would spill dangerous sulfuric acid when tipped or jostled. At the time, there was no textbook to tell Gill how to identify such an opportunity or how to exploit it. With a pair of eyes and a mind open to possibilities, Gill developed a specialized battery and later a nonspill cap to solve these problems. He had his first factory up and running when he was just nineteen years old.[4] Gill later sold his firm to Teledyne, which makes his products to this day.

Christensen is very aware of the tyranny of success and has pointed out that when technical innovation disrupts a market, it may ultimately put its own creator out of business! A classic example of this was Kodak corporation's pioneering work bringing digital cameras to market. Although they developed the technology that made the modern digital and phone cameras possible, they completely failed to gain traction in that market while these same devices destroyed their traditional film business. In Chapter 3 of this text, you read the story of Xerox corporation's Palo Alto Research Center (PARC). The computing technologies developed there eroded Xerox's copier business and helped reduce a former global giant to an also-ran in the business technology world.

If your plan is technological disruption and taking on big incumbents, you're probably not going to be a small business for long. You're likely running a rapid-growth startup. You'll need money and resources from outside to maintain momentum. I will discuss fundraising requirements in a future chapter. However, do you think disruption happens at the small business level? Are there small incumbent firms that fail to adapt to new circumstances in a way that other small entrepreneurs can take advantage of?

A traditional Hawaiian appetizer, poke, diced raw fish, became a global food fad in the 2010s.

Source: © Shutterstock, Inc.

If you'd been watching small street-front restaurants in Los Angeles, California, over the last twenty years, you would have seen a large number of ice cream stores replaced by frozen yogurt or "froyo" shops, including popular franchise chains like Penguins and Pinkberry. Did the dominant ice cream chains like Dairy Queen and Baskin-Robbins make the transition with consumer tastes? How hard would that have been to see or to execute on? No, the tyranny of success doomed them to stick with their model and perhaps adding one or two flavors of yogurt to no avail. Not that it would have mattered because just a few years later you would have seen many of these froyo shops replaced by juice bars—think Jamba Juice or Nekter. Next came cupcake shops and then poke (a popular Hawaiian dish of diced raw fish). Consumer businesses subject to fashion changes are like this. Sticking with the old product is unlikely to succeed, but changing your business every five years is really expensive too. Can you think of how you could best profit on such a process of continual disruption?

Imitation and Second Mover Advantage

For a businessperson, pursuing the well-worn path of proven success is not the worst thing. In fact, it may be the best thing! Not everyone is meant to or needs to change the world. The New Entrepreneurial Dynamic is not just about being a driver of change, because few people do that; it is mostly about recognizing when the environment has changed and adapting to it. Most businesses, big or small, ride the waves; they do not create them. Many great firms have captured the majority of profits from a sector after watching an innovator struggle in a market and then moving in to do the job.

Apple wasn't the first maker of a smartphone. A company called Palm struggled for years to establish that market. The screen on the Palm Treo was too small; the physical keyboard took up half the phone, and the requirement to use a stylus was awkward. RIM's Blackberry essentially copied these features and failings but added encryption and strong corporate marketing. Consumer adoption of smartphones remained sporadic until Apple "got it right" with the iPhone's large, all-glass screen and visual voice mail system. That is the second mover advantage we learned about in Chapter 3.

For a small business entrepreneur, the same rules apply. Imagine that you observe that a newly established Thai cuisine fast-food restaurant near your school is doing moderately well. However, you conclude that the *Thai Pad* has made a poor economic choice by locating in a low-income urban neighborhood. Students are flocking to the place, but the locals have neither the income nor the inclination to test exotic foods. You carefully note that this business has done well with its menu, food preparation, presentation, and process, and then you open a similar place across town in an upscale neighborhood. While your new *Bangkok Plates* restaurant is also situated next to a large campus with hungry students, it will capture a lot more value from wealthier local customers who can afford to be more adventuresome in their dining habits. You may simply enjoy your small business until you retire, or you might try to build that into a national chain, à la *Panda Express*.

But what if Thai food loses its consumer appeal? Remember our question ending the last section, on how to profit from continuous disruption in LA's fad-driven street-front restaurant scene? One way to ride the waves is to time the market and "flip" businesses.

Any experienced SoCal surfer studies the surf before entering the ocean. It is critical to understand the size, timing, and duration of the swells for a good ride and to remain safe. The same is true of fad-driven business. Wait for the swell of the next big fad to emerge and then open a business. Observation would show that LA food fads peak after three to five years. Don't ever be the first poke joint, be the second mover. When the frenzy reaches a peak, along with your revenues, sell your business for the highest value before the wave inevitably crashes. Then, move on to the next fad and repeat the process!

What other businessperson, besides the restaurant owner, must pay attention to these waves? How about the landlord? The food and restaurant equipment suppliers?

Last Mover Advantage

last mover advantage

Business concept identified by Peter Thiel in which an innovative product or service is developed with the mature market in mind.

In *Zero to One*, Peter Thiel suggests that the secret of long-term success is to "study the end game first." If you can foresee what the mature market for an innovation will look like, can you aim for a dominant position that lasts for years? That is where the real value of future cash flows is found. Thiel calls this **last mover advantage**. Can you think of any examples?

Thiel is famously the first outsider to invest in Facebook. Did Facebook launch the social media frenzy? Actually, a product called Myspace launched first and was the biggest social media site in the world until 2009. Meanwhile, Facebook lingered quietly in the college market. In fact, until 2006, you couldn't use Facebook without having an ".edu" email account.

Perhaps the greatest example of a last mover is Microsoft Windows. At the time it was launched in 1985, Windows was seen as an obvious copy of Apple's Lisa (1981) and Macintosh (1984) operating systems. Less well known is that Apple was the second mover, having borrowed all the fundamentals from a 1970s-computer development project at Xerox. In any case, the last mover, Microsoft, has ruled the business desktop for more than thirty years and captured the vast majority of the profits in the market for graphical user interface operating systems.

Microsoft used last mover advantage to capture a leading position in the graphical computer operating system market.

Source: Wei Huang/Shutterstock.com

This isn't to suggest that even in a proven market you should produce a traditional business plan and sit back while it is executed. The New Entrepreneurial Dynamic still applies. Adaptability will be required every step of the way. Facebook, founded by and for college students, faces the problem of having an aging demographic. While the firm still captures the lion's share of social media advertising profits, all those students graduated a long time ago, and many young people don't want to be on a social media platform with their parents or grandparents. The company has responded by buying and integrating Instagram into its highly profitable advertising machine.

Serendipity

Many great business opportunities, big and small, arrive entirely by chance. Sometimes people are not looking for a business opportunity at all, and something great just "falls into their lap."

I call this lucky process of the right entrepreneur accidentally encountering the right idea **serendipity**. And by "right," I don't mean just someone who likes the idea, but an entrepreneur who has the skills and resources to execute on it as well. You stumble across a cool 3D display and decide the world needs a 3D smartphone, but could you make one or turn that into a business? Unless you're also an engineer or know where to find one, you won't be able to produce even a prototype, and at that point, you'll still also need access to a lot of funding. Do you know anyone with an extra $100 million to invest in a new phone startup? If not, you can try to get some meetings with venture capitalists on California's famed Sand Hill Road, but you might be better off setting your sights lower.

serendipity
An unanticipated intersection of circumstances that results in a positive outcome.

A great historical example of serendipity is the microwave oven, a convenience in every kitchen, and one that many undergrads keep in their dorm room today. Any idea where it came from? It was a product discovered entirely by accident! Percy Lebaron Spencer was orphaned at an early age, dropped out of grammar school, and became a self-taught engineer. After working in a mill and serving in the Navy, he found work at the Raytheon Corporation working on radar systems. While developing a new, mass-producible magnetron, Spencer noticed that the candy bar in his pocket had completely melted. He began testing microwave radiation on other foods, including popcorn. Pleased with the results, the inventor developed a contained metal cooking box and installed the first one in his boss's kitchen. In 1945, Raytheon filed for a patent on the microwave oven, which it named the "Radar Range." This serendipitous spin-off of an aerospace firm into consumer products is an example of corporate *intrapreneurship*, which I discussed in Chapter 1.

This ubiquitous home appliance came from an accidental discovery in a defense lab.

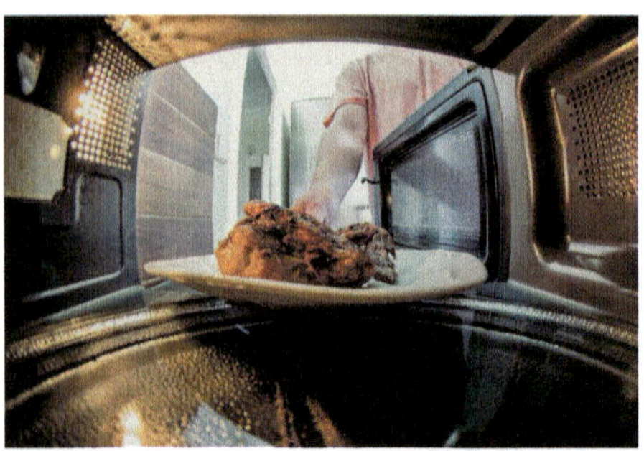

Source: © Shutterstock, Inc.

While the microwave is an amazing creation by someone who wasn't planning to launch a new product, most lucky entrepreneurs are actively engaged in an opportunity **search process** but find something other than what they thought they were looking for. They succeeded because they were not **myopic** in their searching; they kept their eyes and minds open for the unexpected.

search process

A systematic procedure for looking for new things.

myopic

An unhealthy, short-sighted focus on one thing that prevents the viewer from seeing other things that are equally or more important.

Canadian entrepreneur Stewart Butterfield has experienced this process of accidental discovery twice. In the early 2000s, Butterfield's team at Ludicorp was launching a game called "Game Neverending," and although that product never gained much traction, it did include a unique feature that allowed you to upload your own images and share them. The image sharing function turned out to be more attractive than the game and resulted in the popular social image program Flickr, which Butterfield sold to Yahoo for more than $20 million.[5]

In 2009, the serial entrepreneur then moved back to the game development process with more experience and money. His new firm, Tiny Speck, worked on an online massively multiplayer game product named "Glitch." Having had a lot of experience with the complexities of software development, which involved a lot of communications and sharing of files over multiple systems, Butterfield and his team set about creating an internal tool to manage the flow of all this information between the development teams and made it mobile and searchable in a single app they called "Searchable Log of All Conversation and Knowledge." Glitch failed to gain traction for a variety of reasons, including being dependent on Flash, a web technology that fell out of favor about the same time the game was launched. Tiny Speck, which had raised tens of millions in venture capital, concluded that their communications information management tool might be more valuable and opened S.L.A.C.K., later reduced to just "Slack," up to the world with huge success. In 2018, it had 8 million users and 3 million paid accounts, and according to Crunchbase, it was raising additional funds at a $7 billion valuation. Butterfield's first business "failure" made him a multi-millionaire; his second blunder made him a billionaire.[6]

Managing Chance

So, if serendipity is essentially just chance, could your company manage chance like any other resource and use it to increase your likelihood of finding the right opportunity? Do you recall our discussion of the significance of chance in Chapter 2?

Big pharmaceutical companies utilize a process of controlled serendipity for the development of a majority of their drugs. These companies have a database with millions of various chemicals, and they fairly randomly select batches of them to test for properties that might cure diseases they have identified as having high-value market potential. Tens of thousands of compounds are tested for one chemical that proceeds to product development. Many simulations, animal tests, and human trials are conducted before you find it behind the counter at your local pharmacy. It's a very expensive way to do business—and one of the reasons healthcare is so costly—but their customers literally have the highest pain points and will pay a great deal to get relief or perhaps even to live. Can a small business entrepreneur utilize this sort of exposure to chance to find their product?

Many small business owners conduct similar "random path searches," by essentially leaving themselves open to discovery. They may spend years looking for the right path out of an unfulfilling corporate job. They may investigate franchises, consider opportunities to join a friend in an existing business, work with their spouse to refurbish and "flip" homes, or consider pursuing their favorite hobby as a business. While you may not stumble upon a miraculous business model entirely by accident, very often your startup will seemingly find you. Travel and keep yourself open to networking introductions, random encounters, and odd conversations with strangers. Most important, keep your ears and your mind wide open.

Key Takeaways

- Be prepared to take advantage when incumbents become overconfident.
- Look for good ideas executed poorly, where you can do better.
- Be open to serendipity when it comes.

4.3 1 + 1 = New

Learning Objectives

1. Recognize the possible combination of existing products into new solutions.
2. Recognize that you must understand what your core competency is.
3. Understand the power of networking.
4. Understand that the addition of business acumen to technical or artistic endeavors can create a powerful combination.
5. Appreciate the power of the open innovation concept.
6. Understand you can simply acquire an entrepreneurial activity.

When Preparation Meets Opportunity

Occasionally, a new product emerges from the fruitful combination of two existing ones. In 1906, St. Louis, Missouri, hosted the World's Fair. In addition to exhibits of technology and culture from across the globe, the event featured a variety of vendors offering all sorts of new foods and products. During one particularly hot summer day, an ice cream vendor at the fair was doing a brisk business. Next door, the waffle vendor was struggling with a slow day. Eventually, the ice cream seller ran out of paper cups and could not sell any more ice cream, despite having plenty of product and solid demand. The waffle vendor had time to observe this dilemma and, being a natural entrepreneur, curled his waffles into cones and sold them to the ice cream vendor as a new-fangled ice cream holder. Out of this collaborative innovation, a truly iconic new product category, the ice cream cone, was born. Customers have been delighted ever since!

Sweet treats sell because they delight customers.

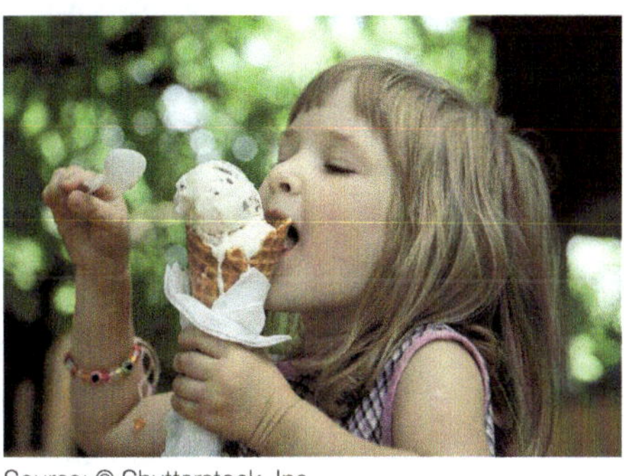

Source: © Shutterstock, Inc.

I'm not really sure who first said, "Luck is when preparation meets opportunity,"[7] but like any good scout, an entrepreneur must always be prepared to seize and execute on the right idea or chance to launch an enterprise. Carry a tablet, notepad, or smartphone to keep notes. Have your business cards, your phone contact entry, and your social media profile up to date and ready to share. Interact with your peers and even your competitors on a regular basis.

Networking with Creators

Do you like meeting new and interesting people? If you are a business student or an aspiring entrepreneur, locating the scientists, artists, engineers, or craftspeople required to make your dreams real can be both fun and challenging. You will not have an opportunity if you can't gather the resources required to make it work. While I dig into the meat of evaluating available resources in Chapter 5, as I indicated back in Chapter 2, under the New Entrepreneurial Dynamic, "Networking Starts Before Your Business Does." Finding an opportunity and the people to help make it real are best approached as an integrated process because making the fit later will be both more difficult and less perfect.

Consider the classic American story of entrepreneurship, the founding of Apple. Steve Jobs and Steve "Woz" Wozniak were introduced by a mutual friend, Bill Fernandez, who recognized their love of technology and of pranking. From almost the very start, the Jobs-Woz relationship was business focused. Fernandez and Woz had been working to build a hobby computer, and Jobs almost instantly saw the business potential. Jobs did not have the engineering skills to build the machine, but in Woz, he found both the product and the person who could do it. Fernandez became Apple's first employee and very wealthy—networking pays!

gig economy

A market environment in which individuals and organizations contract with independent workers for short-term engagement.

In today's **gig economy**, many business students have come to view engineers and artists as commodities they can purchase on a market. Using a growing variety of online services like fiverr.com and freelancer.com, you can find engineers and artists who will work cheaply. This process has always existed, and before the internet, it depended on personal networking. In 1971, Phil Knight, an accounting professor at Portland State University, was rebranding his running shoe company under the new name, "Nike." Knight recruited a student named Carolyn Davidson to create a logo that conveyed fluid motion and paid her $35 for the now iconic "Swoosh."[8]

The iconic Swoosh logo was commissioned for $35.

Source: TY Lim/Shutterstock.com

Phil Knight obviously got some exceptional value, but when you hire people as commodities to develop your product, expect to get a commodity-class product. That may be what you need to get by in the marketplace, provided your website or logo or promotional photo is not a **core competency** of your business. By this, I mean that it is not a **mission-critical component** of your business or the secret sauce that generates your profits.

core competency

A specific ability that your organization does particularly well and by which you create value for your customers.

mission-critical component

An element of a business (software, device, personnel, etc.) that is crucial to its success.

However, if you've got an amazing idea for rocking the business world, you probably won't want to share your super disruptive technology or process with some online stranger. An exceptional product or service requires more than a great idea; you must have the very best in execution as well. If you want to build a brand that will last, your company will need at least a core of dedicated, long-term team members. The software development and graphic artist A-Team is not sitting around on fiverr.com waiting to bid on your work.

Recruiting the best people requires that you treat them and the positions you wish to fill with the greatest respect! There is a tech recruiting blog on Tumblr entitled "Whartonite seeks code monkey."[9] While the operators may have chosen the name as a tongue-in-cheek attempt at humor, it reflects a real and unhealthy attitude in some business schools. Referring to your future business partner or key employee as a "code monkey" is no way to attract a quality candidate.

If you're an artist or an engineer looking to **commercialize** your work, this situation may be exactly reversed. Many creative visionaries view businesspeople as exploitive profit mongers who step on inventors and creative employees in order to accumulate wealth for themselves. This distorted stereotype is constantly reinforced in our media. Sadly, this sort of Scrooge McDuck caricature is particularly prevalent in films and TV aimed at young people, which perpetuates a cynical, anti-social view of business. If you're a creative sort and want the resources to work on your dreams, demonizing the people who know how to acquire and manage those resources is self-defeating.

commercialize

To undertake a process of transforming an invention or artwork into a for-profit business model.

Overcoming this fundamental disconnect requires viewing everyone who contributes to your opportunity as a stakeholder. All your stakeholders deserve to be viewed and treated with respect. Conduct your search with this attitude, and good people and great results will follow.

Finding the best people for the long haul will come via an exhaustive search and personal networking. A great place to start is local colleges. The placement offices of colleges are always looking for internships and jobs for their graduates. If you're looking for engineers or a marketing expert, pick a school that excels in those areas.

As a small business owner, you may find it really hard to recruit the top candidates. Multinational corporations and prestigious consulting firms are going to be throwing money at all the *summa cum laude* grads. Don't worry, that's okay. Not everyone on the A-Team is necessarily an A-student. Actually, students who fit the organized and rigorous academic world may not fit very well into the chaos that is a startup. Steve Jobs and many other business geniuses dropped out of college after finding that an academic one-size-fits-all approach to evaluating and advancing talent did not comport with their outside-the-box thinking. Did you know that Bill Gates left Harvard University to take a job writing software and answering the help desk phone at a tiny computer startup operating out of a strip mall in Albuquerque, New Mexico?

FIGURE 4.1 Altair Computer Manual
Page from the Altair 8800 Computer Manual, Circa 1975

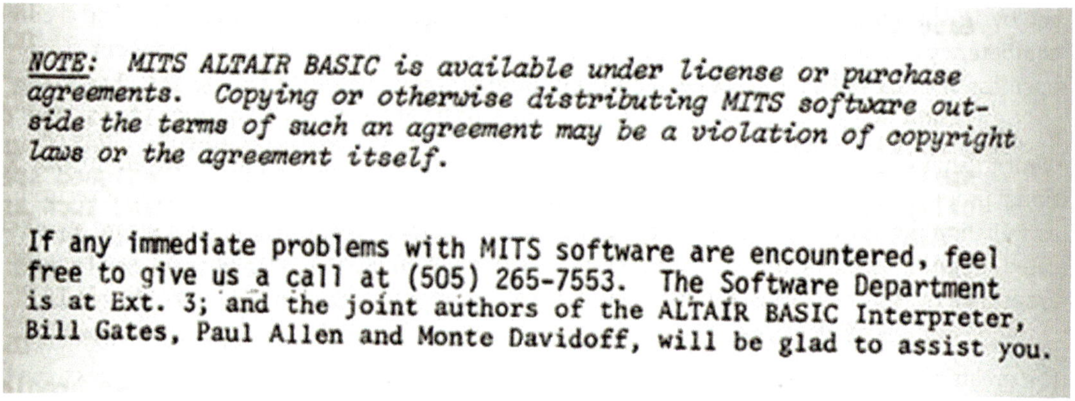

NOTE: MITS ALTAIR BASIC is available under license or purchase agreements. Copying or otherwise distributing MITS software outside the terms of such an agreement may be a violation of copyright laws or the agreement itself.

If any immediate problems with MITS software are encountered, feel free to give us a call at (505) 265-7553. The Software Department is at Ext. 3; and the joint authors of the ALTAIR BASIC Interpreter, Bill Gates, Paul Allen and Monte Davidoff, will be glad to assist you.

Source: Library of Greg Autry

Open Innovation

open innovation

A process of collaborative development of technology across organizations based on rules of shared ownership.

pecuniary

Having to do with money.

Open innovation is a business discovery and development concept popularized by Henry Chesbrough at the University of California at Berkeley's Haas School of Business.[10] Open innovation integrates development components from internal and external sources. Under open innovation, the transfer of knowledge between organizations may be **pecuniary** or nonpecuniary, meaning the user of the information may or may not be required to pay the developer. Some individuals and firms offer their ideas and work for free, and others ask you to pay if you use their work.

It offers a particularly attractive paradigm for the small business entrepreneur or startup on a budget because it outsources expensive research and development to a broad community of developers. Utilizing outside resources eliminates the time and capital investment required to build a dedicated development team and helps provide diversity (often international) to a small team.

Small businesses also benefit from the fact that large corporations are engaging in the open innovation approach for their own development projects. They do this in order to tap the vitality of the New Entrepreneurial Dynamic, since they are coming to understand that their corporate cultures and recruiting processes serve to weed out the sort of radical thinkers that drive innovation. Online communities collaborating with universities, crowdsourcing information, and participating in competitions like hackathons are some of the most productive ways for entrepreneurs to engage in open innovation.

Operating in the open innovation model, you will also share your developments. You may even develop an additional revenue stream profiting from them. Do you think that could also be a problem?

enlightened self-interest

The understanding that some sacrifice for the communal good is in your own best interest. A state of constructive competition and cooperation differentiated from "greed."

Recall our concept of sustainable competitive advantage in Chapter 3 and how that was often based on intellectual property resources that were either protected by patents and copyrights or hidden by trade secrets. While open innovation makes development a lot more affordable and is arguably good for a broader community, it makes it very difficult for any organization to obtain the competitive advantage needed to claim higher profits. Some have argued that open innovation may slow progress because it reduced economic motivations to develop new knowledge. Advocates of open innovation suggest it is a form of **enlightened self-interest**. In defining this concept, Alexis de Tocqueville wrote of Americans that "enlightened regard for themselves constantly prompts them to assist each other and inclines them willingly to sacrifice a portion of their time and property to the welfare of the state."[11]

Under the New Entrepreneurial Dynamic, you are free to choose between open and closed or some hybrid. Think carefully about whether open innovation is right for your startup. Do the high costs of development threaten the launch of your business? Is most of the value you will add to be found in your execution rather than in the ideas? If so, open may be the way to go. On the other hand, if you come to your business with amazing, proprietary concepts, you should consider closed.

External Acquisitions

In *Zero to One,* Peter Thiel recalled that during a debate over how their nascent PayPal startup might compete with Elon Musk's firm X.com, "One of our engineers actually designed a bomb." While the idea of literally blasting their problems away was certainly not pursued, *Fast Company* reports that several of PayPal's founders pursued the dubious hobby of homemade pyrotechnics while they were in high school.[12] While most innovators don't try to kill their competitors, they are often the sort of folks who will not score well on the personality exams or background checks that large established corporations require of new employees. Corporations often try to maintain an arms-length relationship with radical thinkers who would not fit into their corporate culture via contracting and research collaboration.

Ambitious small businesses can leverage this corporate timidity to support their own development efforts with a cash infusion from these collaborations with large firms. The Mojave, California, startup XCOR Aerospace supported the development of their Lynx spacecraft by consulting on engine design with aerospace giant United Launch Alliance (ULA). A large satellite launch provider, ULA focused on the military market that XCOR did not view as a potential competitor in its target market of suborbital space tourism.

The original XCOR aerospace hangar in Mojave, California.

Source: Greg Autry

acquisition

Taking control of a company by purchasing it outright or by acquiring a majority of the company's stock. Instead of investing funds in in-house development, established companies often buy startups to obtain an existing innovation or technology.

Very often, a larger firm would rather just buy an existing business than develop a similar product. When Facebook wanted to get into the social photo-sharing trend, it could have added features to its core product or developed a specialized app, but instead, it simply bought Instagram for nearly a billion dollars of cash and shares. This sort of **acquisition** happens on a smaller scale every day. Who knows? The owners of Panda Express might conclude that the best way to get into the Thai cuisine business is to purchase your little Bangkok Plates chain for several million!

Key Takeaways

- Look for ways to combine existing products into new opportunities.
- Always be networking.
- Follow open innovation developments.
- Consider buying a startup or eventually being bought out.

4.4 Saving an Opportunity—Improving Existing Products or Target Markets

Learning Objectives

1. Understand that opportunity identification can be a continuing process.
2. Understand the business opportunities the global supply chain offers.
3. Realize you can travel virtually through online global marketplaces.
4. Be aware that tariffs and trade restrictions may interfere with your import/export-based opportunities.

Adaptation

Sometimes your first idea doesn't quite turn out to be a real opportunity. You could abandon the whole enterprise, or you could look around and perhaps discover that your *real* opportunity involves a change to the product or to your target market. Chapter 5 will discuss how these mistakes might be avoided in the first place, but it is important to consider how an existing effort could be applied to a slightly different opportunity.

Imagine that you've produced a skateboard design you love. It's exactly the sort of longboard you like. It turns and feels just the way that is most comfortable for you. You've built it out with your favorite trucks and wheels. The deck's finish has a deep wood-grain varnish that you adore. But it turns out that the market is not as in love with your creation as you had hoped. The longboard appeals to a limited market; it's expensive to make and more expensive to ship. Your customers keep praising the style and the finish but tell you they'd like a smaller board, similar to the Penny brand boards, that fit easily into school lockers. A lot of them also tell you that they don't love your choice in wheels and want to build their own "complete" skateboard. You have two choices at this point. You can stick with your vision and probably not have a business, or you can adapt to the needs of the market. Making a smaller deck and selling it without trucks and wheels will be cheaper and easier to ship. If that change in product design results in increased sales and margins, you may have a business! Listening to your customers is the key.

Also, maybe it is not the product but the **distribution channel**. Maybe going directly to your consumer base with your new skateboard is not the ideal strategy. Your **B2C** (business to consumer) model failed because reaching a sufficient number of new skaters required a lot of social media advertising that was prohibitively expensive, costing you more to get each sale than you earned. Perhaps you are better off selling to skate shops rather than skaters. In that **B2B** (business to business) model, you may only need to reach a few dozen stores in order to access thousands of end customers. Once you've built brand awareness and skaters are looking for you, then selling direct will be profitable. Opportunity identification may be a continuing process.

distribution channel

The way in which your product reaches consumers, such as retail stores, online sales, or multilevel marketing.

B2C

Business to consumer. A financial exchange between a business and an end user of that business's service or product.

B2B

Business to business. A financial exchange between two businesses, for example, between the manufacturer of a component part and the manufacturer of the finished product.

Scouring the Global Supply Chain

Another simple way to get a business going is to locate and import a foreign product that you believe would be popular or price competitive in your home market. Keep your eyes open when you're on vacation. Consider the business of importing Mexican soda into the United States. For years, U.S. soda companies like Coca-Cola saved money by substituting high-fructose corn syrup for cane sugar (sucrose) in their soda recipes.[13] Many consumers believe that the high-fructose substitution spoiled the taste of the product, and some are concerned that it may even contribute to systemic health issues.[14]

A bottle of Mexican Coca-Cola relabeled for sale in the U.S.

Source: Greg Autry

Long ago, American tourists in Mexico discovered that not only did Mexicans still enjoy the original Coke formula (with sugar) but that it also still came in the distinctive glass bottle that kept it icy cold. Some enterprising entrepreneur realized he could sell the product to his American friends for a high price and began trucking cases of it across the border into California. The relabeled Spanish language bottles are now commonly available across the United States and sell for as much as $3 a bottle—several times their price in Tijuana.

If you're not up for traveling in hopes of finding a serendipitous idea, you could conduct an online search. Travel blogs are full of people sharing discoveries of awesome local foods, cool crafts, and amazing conveniences from around the world. Those amazing African chili recipes, Peruvian finger puppets, and space-age Japanese toilets could find an enthusiastic market in the U.S.

Alibaba and Friends

There are also online global marketplaces where you can source millions of products, many of them at astoundingly low prices. Alibaba.com, one of the world's largest online commerce sites, uses the tagline "Global trade starts here," though, in truth, almost all of its products come from China. You can find almost anything on Alibaba, in large quantities, and at very competitive prices. Cruising Alibaba can be fun and profitable for aspiring entrepreneurs. A search for the phrase "phone case" found 18,062 results, of which 17,995 came from mainland China. There are cases made of all sorts of materials, including leather, wood, plastic, and metal. They are available in every color of the rainbow and with custom printed logos or photos as well. Almost all of them are offered wholesale for less than $2, and *some of them are priced at just three to five cents apiece*! Imagine the profit margin per unit that the little kiosk in your mall is enjoying. They may be selling you a ten-cent phone case for $19.95!

Case for iPhones on Alibaba.com

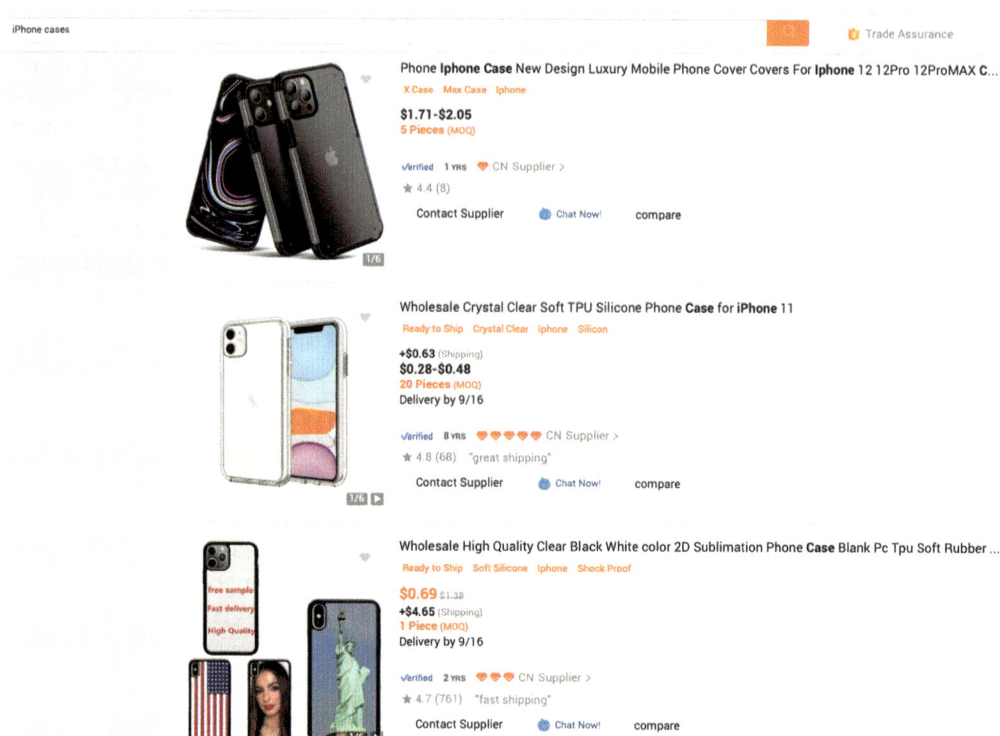

Source: Alibaba.com

There are challenges with using importation as a competitive advantage. Remember that any of your competitors can and will get the same pricing from Alibaba or other online markets. Distinguishing yourself with these commodity products is very difficult. Alibaba vendors are also notorious for offering counterfeit brand name products—so don't assume the Disney or Ralph Lauren labeled items are genuine or even legal in your market. If the European Union Customs officials impound a container of bogus Gucci handbags you paid for in advance, you'll probably never get your money back. There are also delays, logistical problems, and communications challenges associated with receiving products from halfway around the world. Quality control problems can also be common, and resolving them with a vendor who is distant and doesn't speak your language can be a challenge as well.

Finally, it is important to note that trade regulations are constantly changing and subject to domestic political trends as well as geopolitics. Tariffs and trade restrictions, which were generally falling during the first part of this century, have been returning. This has been particularly true in the case of Chinese imports to the U.S., where tariffs have increased and, in some cases, products have been banned. China has banned U.S. social media products like Twitter and Facebook in its markets for many years. In 2020 the American government responded to this and other security concerns with attempts to block China's popular WeChat and TikTok apps.

Key Takeaways

- You may not correctly identify your real opportunity at first. Adapt.
- Consider how importing products into a new market may offer a simple opportunity.
- Use online marketplaces.
- Avoid being dependent on a source or export market that may suffer from trade disruptions.

4.5 *De Novo* Industries: The Challenges of Paving a New Road

Learning Objectives

1. Understand the opportunity de novo industries offer.
2. Realize that big players in new markets are establishing a new supply chain full of opportunities.
3. Understand that being an outsider to an industry can bring a powerful perspective.
4. Understand the value of franchising and the different models of franchising.

De Novo Industries

You may recall that in Chapter 3 it was stated, "There are existing markets, places where people and firms have been doing business for some time, and then there are new markets, usually centered around a change in technology, culture, or law." Sometimes such changes allow a completely new or *de novo* industry. When these shifts occur, the fast-moving entrepreneur can join a new population of business leaders embarking on enterprises that have never been done before. Think about smartphones enabling app businesses, the focus on healthy eating driving new types of restaurants, and marijuana legalization creating an entirely new legal value chain to be filled (for better or worse).

In 2004, Richard Branson stood on the runway of a small airport in the California desert to announce he was starting the world's first dedicated space tourism business, Virgin Galactic. He was going to send anyone to space, at least anyone with $200,000 to spare! At about the same time, Elon Musk decided to parlay his PayPal winnings into Space Exploration Technologies, or SpaceX, a firm that would achieve its goal of putting humans on Mars by taking on international state-owned entities in the commercial space launch business.

Ryan Olliges and his skateboard.

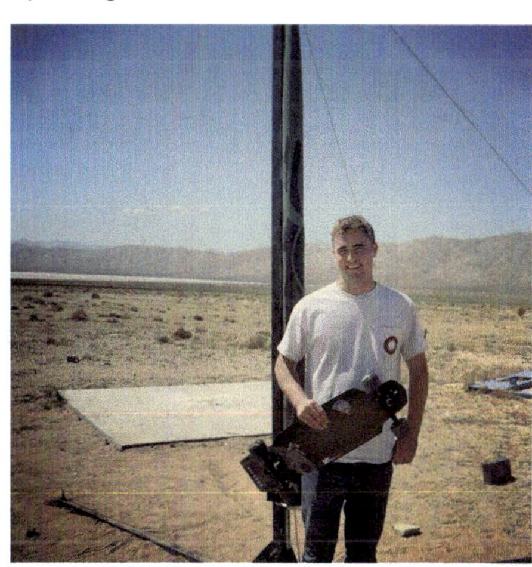
Source: Greg Autry

While Branson and Musk are rock star entrepreneurs whose businesses are known around the world, what you don't see is the hundreds of startups and small businesses that have joined them in an industry known as New Space. Nongovernmental space programs have diverse supply chain needs that include a plethora of components, software systems, space suit manufacturing, and private astronaut training.

Ryan Olliges, an aerospace engineering major at the University of Southern California, discovered that rocket production produced a significant amount of carbon fiber scrap. Ryan collected material from the USC Rocket Propulsion Lab and designed a custom machine to cure it into skateboard decks. He took his prototype skateboard to a business school professor familiar with the New Space industry. Together they launched 121C, a business that collects and upcycles scrap material into skateboards and other consumer products. The firm had two successful crowdfunding campaigns and raised over half a million in private capital. There could also be a small business opportunity for you in space or perhaps closer to Earth. Keep your eyes open.

TNBT, Riding Trends While Avoiding Fads

Prospective entrepreneurs and investors are often eager to talk about The Next Big Thing colloquially known as "TNBT." The result is they tend to find themselves caught up in fads. We noted this trend earlier in food choice with the frozen yogurt to poke trend. However, lasting new industries do emerge as well. In the 1980s, it was the personal computer. In the 1990s, it was the internet. In the 2000s, it was smartphones. In the 2010s, the commercial spaceflight industry boomed.

green tech

Technology developed to be environmentally friendly or to mitigate environmental harm. See also *greenwashing*.

Today, **green tech** is an important topic. Environmental awareness among consumers, driven by new data and increased political attention to climate change, drove a strong interest in environmentally friendly products. It has been very fashionable to be a green tech startup or to invest in one. Large corporations and small businesses have worked to burnish their environmental credibility as well. For a while, it seemed that everyone was pushing recycling, alternative energy, carbon capture, and electric cars. Green tech investment boomed in the United States and Europe. Even Chinese state-owned enterprises, long criticized as major polluters, have gotten into the game by announcing a number of ambitious environmental initiatives. Is it wise for a small business entrepreneur to leap into this green frenzy?

greenwashing

Creating the deceptive appearance of a product or service being environmentally sound for economic gain or positive public image. See also *green tech*.

The answer depends on the strategy. Increasing its environmental credibility in recycling and sustainability could boost any firm's reputation and attract new customers. As long as the effort is not prohibitively expensive, it could hardly hurt. Consequently, companies big and small have launched green initiatives. It quickly became difficult to distinguish between genuine environmental programs and token efforts at **greenwashing**—an insincere process of making a company or product look more environmentally conscious than it actually is.

Going "all in" on a new green startup offered a much less certain path than greenwashing. Many new green firms collapsed in ignominy after burning through millions in investment capital. The photovoltaic solar cell manufacturer Solyndra became the poster child for what many believe is a green tech bubble. The high-flying environmental firm had collected hundreds of millions in venture funding and received a $535 million U.S. federal loan guarantee in 2009. Astoundingly, under pressure from cheaper imports, the company managed to go bankrupt in just two short years.

However, it's important not to let a few high-profile disasters taint your view of an opportunity. Not every green tech effort failed. While people's attention comes and goes, global and local environmental concerns are very real, and they will not solve themselves. Real business opportunities abound in this sector. The secret to success is to do something serious that someone can and will pay for. In order to prosper and to last, your business proposition must add immediate value for your customers and have a positive environmental impact in the long run. If your product costs more, offers lower performance, and is less attractive, consumers will quickly tire of paying for only the "feel good" factor and return to their old ways.

Elon Musk understood this very well when his firm, Tesla, designed the Model S. He built an electric car that boasted "zero emissions" but was also very competitive among its peers. The Tesla Model S was priced similarly to high-end sedans from BMW and Mercedes and did not have the "quirky" look that branded many other environmentally conscious vehicles. Most reviewers agreed that Musk's electric car design was gorgeous and offered safety, speed, and technology features that completely outdistanced its rivals. The new car captured the highest rating ever given by *Consumer Reports* and the highest safety rating ever issued by the U.S. National Transportation Safety Board (NTSB). It was not only the highest performing large sedan but also the world's quickest car, capable of embarrassing even Lamborghinis and Ferraris.[15] Not surprisingly, Tesla's biggest challenge became keeping up with orders. Feeling good about going green was only icing on the cupcake for Tesla owners.

You can find similar success with a small business. Kaemerz Dotiwala was an executive in a petroleum firm. During a cyclical downturn in the oil business, he recognized an opportunity to collect and recycle used oil. In 2003, Dotiwala founded Q Environmental, which does just this, as well as selling environmentally friendly products that automobile oil change companies can use. In 2004, he received an SBA loan to expand his business.[16] Because Dotiwala's business makes economic sense for its customers as well as being environmentally friendly, he's likely to do well. He has even secured a contract with the city of Houston to help them convert the cost of oil disposal into a source of revenue.

Can you think of a complementary product you might develop or a service you might provide for the growing number of electric car owners? If it provides them real economic value in addition to enhancing their environmental creds, you'll probably have a winner.

Quick Opportunity Screening

While Chapter 5 addresses the science and art of validating your opportunity, making an initial assessment of an opportunity is critical during the search phase. How can you tell whether your opportunity contains a nice sustainable business or one that might even explode into the next Facebook? Or perhaps it's a money pit that will consume your time and resources without producing results.

The essence of a business is capturing profits. In order to do that, you need some competitive advantage in the marketplace. Recall that according to Michael Porter, there are just two basic business strategies: differentiation and price (see Chapter 3).

Consider your opportunity. Customers with a pain point or in need of joy are surely using some sort of solution currently. What is it? Is it adequate? Can you imagine a significantly better solution? If not, can you imagine that there would be a way to make a solution that is significantly cheaper? If the answer is that you can't do it better or cheaper, people probably won't switch from their existing solutions; this is simply not a business opportunity. Move on. That's all there is to the quick screening process!

A negative answer can be difficult for the entrepreneur to see, and once seen, difficult to accept. You, of course, want to believe that you are creating something valuable, and your mom, spouse, and friends will surely agree! Fooling yourself is such a big problem that much of the discussion of validation in Chapter 5 is designed just to protect you from it. The greater the level of realism you bring to this quick screening process, the more time you'll save yourself and other people who may have to deal with the really bad ideas you should have rejected in the first place.

Experience and the Power of Naivety

By definition, new ideas require the ability to defy assumptions and question common beliefs. People within a system adapt to accept its limitations and operate within a cultural context that makes challenging it unlikely. For this reason, a naïve or even foolish outsider is often in the best position to change things.

The American sport of baseball is a big business with a 150-year history. Much of its appeal is based on the time-honored traditions ingrained in the sport. A conservative respect for these traditions permeates everything in that business. Anyone who questioned these traditions was considered to be hopelessly naïve. Billy Beane, a former player turned talent scout for the Oakland Athletics (A's), was naïve enough to question the entire practice of baseball recruiting. Beane, whose career inspired the book and movie *Moneyball*, chose players based on their optimal statistical results rather than qualitatively choosing individuals based on anecdotal observations of their demonstrated skills. Instead of following tradition and going out to watch players practice for an afternoon, Beane analyzed their career performance, usually in the minor leagues. Beane realized that observation was biased in favor of spectacular events that captured the attention of the scouts and overlooked the consistent "small ball" play of many great players who actually got on base more than others. Beane skipped over big-name home run hitters and instead collected lower-paid players who could simply get on base. This was a disruptive approach that led the previously down-and-out A's to a winning season and shifted the paradigm of the sport.

Naivety paid off for Beane and the A's, and that is why Steve Jobs famously advised young people to "stay foolish." However, unproven ideas in markets where a lot of smart folks thinks they have it all figured can be risky. There are times when a crazy idea really is just a crazy idea.

The A's famously built a winning team on the cheap.

Source: Eric Broder Van Dyke/Shutterstock.com

The Cue Cat turned out to be a solution for a problem that did not really exist.

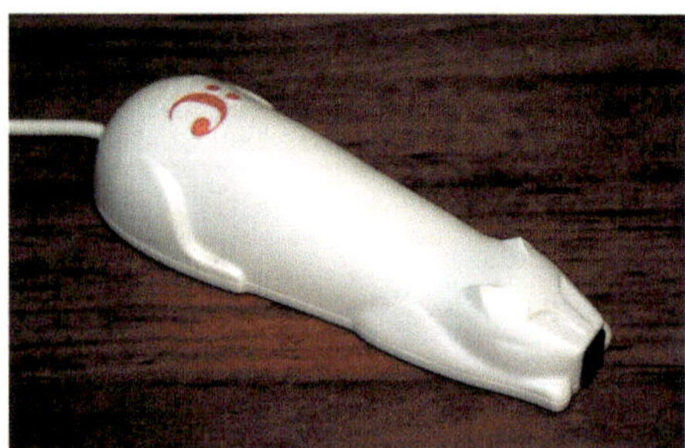

Source: https://commons.wikimedia.org/wiki/File:Cuecat1.jpg

In 2000, a startup called Digital Convergence Corporation released the Cue Cat, a small plastic barcode scanner that was shaped like a cat. The firm's founder, J. Jovan Philyaw, realized that companies like Coca-Cola were spending a lot of money building fancy websites but had trouble getting users to spend time there. He concluded that problem was that typing a product name into a search bar wasn't easy enough for customers. Philyaw's idea was that if customers wanted to know something about a product, say a bottle of Coke, they would plug in their Cue Cat, scan the product's barcode into their computer, and then special software they had installed would take them to a website related to the item. It turned out that almost nobody wanted a barcode scanner shaped like a cat and that it was a lot easier to type in "coke.com" than mess with the weird plastic cat and its attendant software. This may seem obvious now, but Philyaw raised $185 million from investors including $10 million from the Coca-Cola Corporation. What Philyaw didn't see was that while people loved to drink soda, they didn't care to spend time reading about it on the internet. Nothing was going to make them spend their time at coke.com if there were sports, games, and cat videos elsewhere. Even a weird plastic cat wasn't going to lure them into doing that. Performing extensive research, or **due diligence**, before investing your time or other people's money into a seemingly crazy idea is a pretty sane approach.

due diligence

The research and analysis done by a reasonable person to assess a business idea or opportunity.

Geographic Opportunity

Sometimes the best way to start an innovative business is to begin by copying an existing product and improve it as you expand. Walmart's original source of competitive advantage had nothing to do with its current "Everyday Low Prices" model but rather was based on geographic potential. At that time, Kmart was the leading low-cost provider in the competitive U.S. retail market, but their stores were centered in big city hubs. Kmart was happy getting 5 percent of the retail business in St. Louis or Atlanta. Walmart founder Sam Walton realized that stores located in suburbs and smaller cities such as Omaha, Nebraska, or Redding, California, could avoid competition from Kmart. His chain was big enough to easily beat the local main street retailers and snag up to 45 percent of those smaller markets, capturing the same level of revenues and profits that Kmart was getting in the big cities. Walmart used this low competition market to optimize its logistical model so well that it easily overtook Kmart on cost as it expanded into the larger markets.

Additionally, think of what sort of biases and opportunities come with markets and geographies. In the Sahara Desert, there is a greater demand for water; in NYC is there is a greater demand for transportation. Patients in Xiangyang, China, may be less willing to visit a Western medical clinic, while an acupuncture clinic may not find many clients in Elkport, Iowa. What comes with the locale or culture? What makes one population more likely to purchase a product or service than another? Similarly, think about how these factors can affect your business as you start out or expand.

Is Buying a Franchise or Licensing for Me?

If you can't innovate, you can copy, but it's best to do this legally. Licensing and franchising offer opportunities to do just that. **Licensing** the rights to use a trademark logo is a way to add instant value to a generic product like a backpack or pullover. Generally, licenses are relatively inexpensive and have fewer obligations. The buyer or licensee simply has to respect the terms of the agreement and use the trademark appropriately. For example, former Microsoft entrepreneur Paul Allen has the National Football League (NFL) franchise for the Seattle Seahawks. While Allen actually owns the huge business that runs the stadium and hires players, smaller entrepreneurs can acquire licenses from the NFL to develop and sell merchandise branded with the Seahawks' team logo as long as they follow specific rules on its use and pay fees. Allen's business might even buy some of those Seahawks shirts, hats, or magnets to sell in their team store or online.

licensing

Buying the rights to use a trademark (a logo or product) with restrictions on quality. See also *franchising*.

franchising

Buying the rights to use a business model, trademark, marketing, and other assets for operating a standardized business.

franchisee

An individual or company paying for the right to use a business model, trademark, marketing, and other assets for operating a standardized business.

franchisor

A company offering the right to use a business model, trademark, marketing, and other assets for operating a standardized business.

turnkey

A complete and ready to run operation.

Franchising is paying for the rights to use a business model as well as the trademarks and associated marketing collateral of a brand. You're probably familiar with popular retail franchises like Wendy's, Subway, and 7-11. These stores all look like they are the same company, but many of them are owned by local businesspeople who live in your community. Such a businessperson is a **franchisee**, and the brand they are working under is owned by the **franchisor**.

A franchise usually requires an upfront fee and royalties on all future profits. For many popular retail and food franchises, the initials fees are typically between $50,000 and $200,000, and the royalties are a few percent of all sales. The franchise rules can be very restrictive to a business and include things like the layout of the store, the products to be sold, employee uniforms, and customer service procedures. Everything from the menu to the employee training process is predetermined by Subway corporate and carefully documented. In fact, the franchisee is prohibited from deviating from the model on even minor things like the bright yellow and green color of the fixtures in their restaurant.

Good franchisors offer their franchisees a lot of support. The franchisor will likely provide management training and run national promotional campaigns. An owner of a Subway franchise gets a business that is nearly a **turnkey** operation. All the franchisee needs to put in is money and effort.

Most importantly, franchisors usually offer exclusive rights to a geographic area for the use of their highly recognized brand. Want to see this in action? Use Google Maps and look at the McDonald's restaurant franchises in any U.S. city, such as Cheyenne, Wyoming. You'll find they are fairly evenly distributed based on the population density of the area. McDonald's will not grant you a franchise to operate within walking distance of an existing store.

McDonald's franchises in Cheyenne Wyoming are carefully distributed in a relatively small town.

Source: Screenshot, Map Data © 2019 Google

There are several other types of franchises besides the familiar retail brand restaurants and stores. These include the product creators as a franchisor offering the right to produce the products they design and brand. Coca-Cola bottlers are a good example of this. The popular coke products delivered to your store are likely produced in a factory owned and operated under a license from Coca-Cola to use their formula, packaging, and branding. Clothing brands such as Levi's also license the right to manufacturer their popular products. Levi's now focuses almost entirely on design and marketing of clothing, not manufacturing. They closed their last company-owned U.S. factory in 2003. Their jeans and other gear are made by global manufactures and shipped directly to retailers, including the Levi's owned stores. Levi's and Coca-Cola issue strict guidelines designed to ensure that their customers always get what they are expecting from these valuable brands. The brands also conduct quality inspections to ensure compliance with these guidelines.

McDonald's is the most successful franchise operation in history.

Source: ATIKAN PORNCHAIPRASIT/Shutterstock.com

Another franchising situation is where the franchisor is a wholesaler of products, and the value they bring is in aggregating and managing the supply chain for you. Many Main Street-type businesses don't have the capacity to deal with hundreds of different companies, so they join franchise groups that handle that. These firms may also provide branding and marketing support but tend to be much less prescriptive about the business setup and operations. Ace Hardware is one such company that helps small hardware companies across the United States stock their shelves as well as offering a known brand name to operate under.

The question of licensing versus franchising comes down to an entrepreneur's appetite for risk and desire for independence. On the one hand, franchisees benefit from a tried-and-true formula but must adhere to strict rules. An entrepreneur who wants to work with certain brands but maintain independence might forgo the security that comes with a proven business model and become a licensee if that is an option. Many others simply won't want to deal with any limitations outside of their control and will strike out on their own.

In the New Entrepreneurial Dynamic, finding the right opportunity is always up to you, the individual entrepreneur. Spend the time to know yourself well and use that to frame your opportunity search. Starting out right will go a long way toward crafting an entrepreneurial destiny that is most rewarding for you.

NED Factors That Influence Opportunity Search

Globalization: Entrepreneurs can easily search global markets for new products and services to bring to their locale. Small businesses can also easily exploit arbitrage opportunities across geographic markets.

Technological, Political, and Cultural Trends: Entrepreneurs, particularly younger ones, are often more in touch with new technologies and fashions than the busy managers at large firms.

Open Innovation: Startups are able to make the open innovation choice easily whereas the legal departments in established firms are very likely to oppose and delay the use of IP the firm does not control.

Disruption: Entrepreneurs are inherently disruptive. Keeping that disruptive spirit imbedded in your startup culture is critical to maintaining a competitive advantage over larger, established firms with more resources.

Key Takeaways

- If you see high-profile startups entering a de novo market, there are probably lots of opportunities for smaller startups in the new industry.
- Think outside the box about the supplies and services a new industry requires.
- Watch out for fads that won't last long enough to support your startup dreams.
- Don't fear entering new markets you lack experience in.
- Always perform the due diligence before taking a risk on a radical new idea.
- Consider the value of buying into a franchise to reduce search costs and risk.

4.6 Case Study: Fred Ross Takes the Entrepreneurial Plunge with Deckside Pool Service

Traci and Fred Ross (center) with the Deckside Pool team

Source: Fred Ross

Fred Ross had made a career as a highly respected business development exec in the booming enterprise IT world. He had worked as a general manager, director, and vice president of sales for a series of major computer services and networking firms providing IT support to corporate America. Fred had developed a reputation for being a "turnaround" executive. Companies would assign him to the most underperforming branch or regional office, where he would put a new team, new process, and a new culture in place—often resulting in record-breaking sales and profit. Implementing the leading-edge systems and traveling the world for meetings with top executives offered an exciting life. Ross recalls, "I was working with the industry 'movers and shakers' and doing things like flying up to Silicon Valley to pitch outsourced data centers to Meg Whitman, CEO at eBay." However, Ross says the pace was literally killing him, "The pressure, pace, 24/7 working hours, travel, and politics were destroying my health and my family."

Fred was at the pinnacle of his industry, but something important was missing in all that. Fred admits, "Everything in that world was filled with dramatic corporate politics, and I was really tired of the relentless, unreasonable goals and soulless world of tech." The down-to-earth Iowan admits, "I felt like I was putting on a fake smile and steel plate armor before going to work each day to do battle with people in my own company!" The obvious solution was to become his own boss and set his own agenda as an entrepreneur.

Fred's first inclination was to go right back into the industry he knew best, corporate IT, and he launched eNetCentric, a startup to provide services for the "dot.com" firms of the early internet age. In hindsight, not only was the timing poor, as the internet boom was just about to bust, but it wasn't really the radical change he was looking for in his life. Supporting a big firm's "mission-critical" infrastructure as an entrepreneur meant the stress was about the same, but the paychecks were less reliable. Pausing, he adds in a gentle Midwestern accent, "I really just wanted to work with good people and add some real value to their lives." Fred concluded that to experience a real change, he would have to define his own abilities more broadly. He had an entrepreneurial epiphany that he summed up like this:

People get stuck in this trap of "I'm a network engineer," or "I am in aerospace or insurance, and that's all I know." That's not true. I began to think about what skills do I REALLY have like problem solving, recruiting and hiring, operational efficiency, critical thinking, managing, leading, organizing and, of course, hard-working just to name a few. I have skills that go far beyond my specific education. I can succeed in a lot of industries, and there is no need for me to focus on one that is highly competitive and filled with drama.

Ross began to methodically evaluate businesses of all sorts. The only criteria were that he would be his own boss and apply his operational and critical thinking skills with determination. He considered a variety of retail franchises and opportunities, those being a popular route for corporate execs looking to escape the daily grind. Fred didn't see those as an escape, noting, "I don't want to work seven days and open at seven and close at ten!" He also thought about real estate, another popular gig for business development professionals, but he really didn't want to focus on sales or fight over commissions.

Fred had a vision of turning an old-school business into a more sophisticated model and creating a bit of industry disruption. "I wanted something that didn't have an insane amount of competition, and I was looking for a business that was still fragmented, but that wasn't so attractive and large that it would be gobbled up by big corporations," he explains. He says, "Look at the marijuana business. It's new and hot, but it is already so big that you're going to be competing with major companies."

At a family get together, Fred's brother-in-law, Chance, mentioned that he talked with a friend who was happily running a successful swimming pool maintenance business. Fred recalls:

Chance starts telling me about it, and I'm like, "Really, that kind of business still exists in the United States?" Good gross margins, minimal competition, highly fragmented, low tech. I had never actually owned or even cleaned a swimming pool but had been on many swim teams in my youth. I had no real exposure to the swimming pool industry, but I was still excited by the simplicity of the business.

Fred started doing research about the industry and quickly realized how many pools there are in the U.S. (more than seven million) and that the biggest concentration was in Southern California (more than one million). He exclaims, "I was living right in the center of that market." It was a big enough niche but not so big or exciting that it attracted outside strategic players. Pool service firms also had other lines of revenue you might not think about. When a customer's system needs a new pump or filter or heater, they go to the guy who maintains their pool. That stuff is like free extra money. Fred decided to dive in!

If you're in a new industry, starting from scratch and building to a critical mass of customers is really hard and takes a long time. Fred explains the advantage of "buying versus building" when entering an established market:

In many industries, I could easily go to a broker and buy a small business with existing customers, operations, brand name, etc. After more careful financial analysis, I decided to "buy versus build" to reach a critical sustainable level of volume. The initial investment was in a small route of 50 pools for 12 times the monthly gross revenues. That cost me around $40k to achieve a quick and a very solid start.

Fred's wife, Traci, was skeptical at first. She was asking him, "Why would you leave your $300K VP job and get into a Ford Ranger and go clean swimming pools for $20 an hour?" That was a good question, and Fred had to assure her that he wasn't giving up an entire career to become a low paid blue-collar tradesman. As he told his wife, "I was starting a business that would let me spend more time with my family." On top of that, buying the existing business required a series of equity loans on their home in Coto de Caza, California. Traci was quick to point that risk out as well!

Still, it worked. Fred beams, "As soon as we got in the pool business everything seemed to flow, and each day I thought 'Wow, this is where I was meant to be.'" That positive attitude, lessened travel, and no late-night corporate emergencies and politics won Traci over too. Fred brags, "There was a lot of satisfaction in a job well done. I knew the family whose pool I was cleaning was going to enjoy their weekend, and I was proud to help." And while the work was sometimes grueling, it usually ended at 5:00 p.m. or earlier, and the money rolled in. He beamed, "This was fun, I lost weight, I got back in shape, and I was making good money. It was a personal win/win!"

You might wonder how a one-person business operation can handle dealing with life. How do you go on vacation, or what if you get sick? Fred was able to schedule a couple weeks off with his home clients in the winter when most people didn't use their pool much, and his research had revealed that the independent operators handled that with a trade association called The Independent Poolman's Association or IPSA. IPSA provided Fred with insurance, a certification program, and educational programs that included "lunch and learns" from manufacturers of pool equipment and supplies. Most importantly, if you went on vacation, you could get someone to cover for you.

Fred notes that, "If a guy breaks his leg or gets really ill, the members will all get together and cover for you, and they'd do it for free." He recalls being pretty satisfied at this point:

I had decompressed from the stress of the corporate world. We had grown the business to about 130–140 pools and upped the fees to about $80 a month, which brought in about $135,000. Plus, we had the good repair business going. At first, I outsourced things like installing new heaters, but I quickly figured that out, and that made me even more money. With basically no overhead beyond a truck, I got to keep almost all of that.

While all this was rewarding, it was indeed just the sort of blue-collar work he'd promised Traci he would not get stuck in, and it did not satisfy his competitive nature nor stop his mind from thinking of bigger things. "One day, I was in the truck driving to the next pool and wondering "What is a guy with an MBA and a new BMW in the garage doing cleaning pools?" It was time to get back to that vision of a more sophisticated business.

Around this time, Fred and Traci were at a Bible study and began talking to Chris, who ran a large commercial pool company called Deckside. He had done well but was tired of his business and just wanted to move on. Commercial pools are owned and operated by cities, hotels, apartment buildings, high-schools, colleges, amusement parks, and even water parks. Fred knew that these big installations were intimidating to the typical suburban backyard pool cleaner. He said, "My colleagues would go in and see these 2 million BTU heaters with rows and rows of sand filters and 480-volt circuits, and they would throw up their hands." To Fred, on the other hand, that situation was "just like the way a small-time computer repair person looked at those big server farms I had been setting up." For Fred, the challenge was simply a matter of training and scaling. Taking a crew to do several hours of work at one location could be a lot more efficient than getting back in the truck and heading to a new home for each and every billable hour.

Fred agreed to buy Deckside but then thought about where he was going to get the $300,000 to do it. "I'm like Chris, I love the business, but I just don't have $300,000 laying around." Chris didn't expect a single big payment and taught Fred that most businesses get sold for a little bit of cash, a lot of sweat equity payments over time, and a check at the end. Fred dove in and pulled it off. There were times when he and Traci had to borrow money just to make the monthly payment, but the business grew and making the final buyout was not a problem.

Deckside already had three employees who knew what they were doing, and they brought Fred up to speed while he juggled maintaining his residential pool business.

I quickly realized, "I gotta get rid of the residential pools and focus on the commercial. I quickly realized they were two different markets with unique customer demands. If we tried to service both, we would fail."

He sold some of the residential pools in groups to friends in the business for the standard rate of 10–12x monthly billings. For one really sweet group, a number of pools lined up in a tight neighborhood, and he got 14x. For the rest, he used a broker, just like the one he had bought his first business from.

In 2003, Deckside was generating $300K a year, but it had more overhead. In fact, Fred wasn't billing his own time. He was now 100 percent overhead, so the net income was less. Fred was in the office doing customer service, scheduling, purchasing, hiring, and marketing but always focused on growing. Fred tried servicing large apartment ownership groups and even some huge million-gallon pools at amusement parks and the U.S. National Water Polo training facility in Los Alamitos, California. He found those customers and their tendency to be "vendor beaters" was not profitable. He quickly discovered that his firm's sweet spot was the 25-yard junior Olympic type pool found at apartment buildings or homeowner associations (HOAs) and explains:

The large HOAs became our bread and butter customer. They wouldn't nickel and dime us. Their requirements and demands were as predictable as the seasons. They were also the best of the best customers, nice to do business with, willing and able to pay, and you can keep the contracts forever if you don't screw up. In short—a niche within a niche.

Focusing on growth paid off for Fred, and Deckside grew to annual revenues over $3 million a year. The business was generating EBITDA of between 8 percent and 15 percent each year. He paid himself a good salary and had great perks like a company car and generous expense accounts. Eventually, he used the money to make other investments and pursue his passion for sailing and bought a boat he named "No Drama" as a reflection of his new lifestyle.

After a while, maintaining the growth began to get harder because of a strong economy and doing business in a very highly regulated state. "I'd run an ad, and almost nobody would show up. Worse, those who did didn't want to work." Fred started looking into robotics and IT solutions in the hopes of reducing labor by maybe 30 percent. At the same time, to compound the problem, the California Department of Environmental Regulations adopted new CDC (Center for Disease Control) recommendations that every public/commercial pool had to be chemically tested each day. Fred explains, "The CDC had discovered that many bacteria had become more resistant to chlorine." This shock to the industry could double or triple the cost of pool ownership! Customers didn't want to pay for those extra stops.

The regulatory shift and labor climate had killed the fun and was a signal to Fred that it was time for him to move on. He put Deckside on the market and found a New York investment banker who had worked with VCs and startups and who wanted to get out of that rat race. This potential buyer had already bought up over 1,000 residential pool contracts in San Diego and Orange County. Fred notes:

We did serious due diligence on his background with his former employers. His wife is an MD, and he's super smart: MBA from a big-name school and operations experience in multiple VC-backed highly successful startups. Most importantly, he was not afraid to work hard and get his hands dirty; he's got some experience in residential.

Fred and Traci Ross on the *No Drama II.*

Source: Greg Autry

Fred valued the business at an EBITDA 5–7x (see Chapter 13), which came out to a little over $2 million. The deal closed in January of 2018, and it included a requirement that Fred stay onboard for 12 months to run things. Fred recalls that for the first month, he was "as busy as hell training the new owner on all our systems." But by the second month, he says, "I was running out of stuff to do by noon." By the third month, he'd check in each morning at 7:00 a.m. and ask, "Do you need anything?" and they'd say "No," and Fred would just go home. Still, it turned out that the new owner needed Fred more than he imagined. Fred recalls:

I told him, "Go through one summer" before you change anything, but as soon as I'm gone, he's changing everything. He wants to change the name of the company, which had been in the market since 1981. He changes the culture. Then lo and behold, in early July, I get a call and he's telling me, "We lost our ass last month," and I had to tell him, "You didn't listen to me about processes!" It was all just 100 little mistakes like letting his techs go to the wholesalers without an official purchase order (no control) and losing focus on the dashboard of metrics we had developed. He had overly focused on sales and marketing to the detriment of operations—ambitious but not practical. Fred got his buyer back on track. The payments are coming in, and he is confident the deal will end well. He and Traci are happily spending their time visiting friends and family back in Iowa and sailing on a new boat named the *No Drama II.*

Endnotes

1. Schumpeter, J. (1945) "Creative destruction." *Capitalism, Socialism and Democracy*, 82–5.
2. See also creative destruction. Clayton Christensen: http://www.claytonchristensen.com/key-concepts/.
3. Christensen, C. (2013) The innovator's dilemma: When new technologies cause great firms to fail. *Harvard Business Review Press*.
4. http://www.everipedia.com/97c46756-89ea-4683-b187-a89cde649e89/
5. https://techvibes.com/2015/01/07/facts-stewart-butterfield-slack-2015-01-07
6. Thanks to Danny Charlton for suggesting the great example of Slack.
7. It has been attributed to Seneca the Younger.
8. https://web.archive.org/web/20071023034940/http://www.nike.com/nikebiz/nikebiz.jhtml
9. http://whartoniteseekscodemonkey-blog.tumblr.com
10. Chesbrough, H., Vanhaverbeke, W., & West, J. (Eds.). (2006). *Open innovation: Researching a new paradigm*. Oxford University Press on Demand.
11. De Toqueville, A. (1835). *Democracy in America*. New York: A Mentor Book from New American Library.
12. https://www.fastcompany.com/3035816/hit-the-ground-running/what-paypals-cofounder-can-teach-U.S.-about-embracing-weirdness
13. This is because American corn syrup production is subsidized by the federal government and sugar imports face a U.S. high tariff.
14. Goran, M. I., Ulijaszek, S. J., & Ventura, E. E. (2013). High fructose corn syrup and diabetes prevalence: A global perspective. *Global public health, 8(1)*, 55–64. https://www.ncbi.nlm.nih.gov/pubmed/23181629
15. The Tesla P100D accelerates from 0 to 60mph in just 2.5 seconds.
16. https://www.sba.gov/sites/default/files/files/Q Environmental Article.doc(1).pdf

CHAPTER 5

Feasibility Analysis and Opportunity Evaluation

Advice is what we ask for when we already know the answer but wish we didn't.
—*Erica Jong*

There are tools to test the likelihood that your entrepreneurial vision will succeed.

Source: © Shutterstock, Inc.

Just because you can do something doesn't mean you should do it. There are an infinite number of business ideas that will not produce the results that the founder had envisioned. Before stepping out into the marketplace, you can do several things to ensure that your startup vision has a fair chance of success. That is the purpose of this chapter.

5.1 Feasibility Analysis

Learning Objectives

1. Understand that most ideas have probably occurred to others and have either been rejected or have failed.
2. Understand that investors are looking for a team that can execute on your idea better than others.
3. Recognize that your initial approach will likely require a course adjustment or pivot.
4. Understand the importance of market research.
5. Understand that every business contains a firm value chain.
6. Understand that every business operates in an industry value chain.
7. Understand technical feasibility analysis.
8. Understand resource feasibility analysis.
9. Recognize that not all ideas scale equally.

Vetting

Investors will ask an entrepreneur two fundamental questions before digging into the details of the proposed venture:

1. Why hasn't this already been done?
2. Why is your team the best team to do this?

vetting

A thorough and diligent review of a potential hire or investment.

Regardless of whether your business requires outside investment, you should also ask yourself these **vetting** questions before you put your own time and money into the venture. If you can't answer them in a way that would make an outside investor put her money down, should you invest your own time and resources into the venture?

The first question, "*Why hasn't this already been done?*" doesn't presume that you are planning something incredibly radical such as developing an electric passenger airplane. Your "new idea" might be something as mundane as opening a pancake restaurant near your campus where one does not currently exist. The question of why there isn't already a good breakfast option for students may lead you to consider which customer and supply-driven factors would prevent someone from having already done it. In this process, you might discover an important fact like *few students wake up early enough to enjoy a traditional sit-down breakfast.*

The second question, "*Why is your team the best team to do this?*" also applies to any business. Imagine that you're a medical student, planning to be a surgeon, with a deep and abiding love for classic American blues music. Your fascination with this genre and the stress of your career lead you to imagine yourself opening a retro vinyl record store as a relaxing side business and a way to help pay your school bills. It would seem that virtually anyone could launch and run this business. It's not brain surgery, right?

Thinking through this scheme, or any business idea, means considering the resources your business idea needs. Sourcing your product will require poking through bins of records in dusty antique stores, lurking at garage sales every Saturday, and cruising Craigslist. Marketing will require slowly building a community of blues aficionados. Operations will require categorizing and adequately maintaining a large, physical inventory of records and having a very knowledgeable person there when people come in to browse. You will quickly realize that the significant resource this business consumes is *time*. And that means *your* time because you can't just hire student workers to do this work; it requires expertise and passion.

Carefully consider any business idea.

Source: © Shutterstock, Inc.

Running a vintage record store is a lifetime commitment, not a part-time hobby. Unless you want to drop out of school and dedicate your life to this while trying to pay off the student debt you've already collected, it isn't going to work. If you've got the skills to actually do brain surgery, that's probably the career you should focus on. When your career gets going, you'll be able to buy all the vinyl you want and invest in a record business run by an entrepreneur with a similar passion but not as distracted by other life opportunities.

When you share a new business idea, you'll find that most of the people you present your concept to fall into two categories. Your mom and those who love you make up the first group. With them, you cannot lose! Mom might even hang your business plan on the fridge with a magnet! This information has little value because it is completely lacking in objectivity and will very likely lead you into wasting time and money.

The second group you will encounter is made up of skeptics who wish to protect you from the ignominy of failure and the spiteful who are jealous of your creativity and entrepreneurial aspiration. With them you can't win! All your ideas are naïve, overly ambitious, or outright preposterous. While you must never let the spiteful dispirit you, real challenges to your plans are very useful. Every objection you receive that you can overcome with a logical argument will make your business case better, and the process itself will armor you for the more powerful criticism you will face in the real market. The German philosopher Friedrich Nietzsche famously said, "What does not kill me makes me stronger," and countering criticism is a faster and cheaper way to learn than entering the arena of the marketplace with an unchallenged idea.

To do this right, you should conduct a methodical and scientific **feasibility analysis** of your plan. It is not sufficient to emotionally reject a doubter's arguments. You must *prove* that you have identified real customer pain points or ways to delight those customers. You must prove you and your team have the skills to effectively and profitably address these needs. You must show you are capable of gathering the resources required to launch this business and see it through to sustainable profitability. Most importantly, to make a truly scientific argument in support of your plan you must have reliable data. You need to understand your industry and your market and know exactly how your business fits in and creates value for customers. These data may include market statistics, customer interviews, consumer surveys, and detailed reviews of your supply chain and costs model.

feasibility analysis

A review process undertaken in order to ensure that your business idea fits you as well as it fits the market.

This text has repeatedly cautioned that entrepreneurs must be honest with themselves to succeed. That trait is more important at this stage of the business development process than any other. Any real analysis of a business opportunity will uncover flaws. You must be prepared to admit they exist and take the hard action of changing your plans to avoid them. Depending on the nature and severity of the flaws uncovered in your analysis, you will need to make minor changes to your model or do a major **pivot** toward a very different idea. This chapter is about that process of feasibility analysis.

pivot

A shift in strategy to pursue a different business model when a previous model has proven untenable.

Your Market and Industry

Understanding where your product or service idea fits into the broader economy is critical. If you're in an established market, you need to research it thoroughly. How big is the market, and how much of it might you actually capture? Make sure you know who the incumbent players are and why they've been successful in capturing market share and profits. What do they do well? What are their weaknesses?

If you're launching a café, for example, your industry is the broad, global restaurant industry that does billions of dollars in revenue annually. The restaurant industry itself is part of a bigger and more complex food services sector. Big global chains like KFC, McDonald's, and Outback Steakhouse may be some of your competitors. If your long-term goal is to launch a similar corporate chain business or a mega-franchise operation, then your potential market may be customers in the world who eat out or might do so. That is a lot to chew on!

On the other hand, if you're retiring from your corporate job to set up a café in the style of a main street small business, you might define your market as people who eat at restaurants in your town. These customers include the locals and the visitors, if there are any. Your competition is probably the chain operations and some other small businesses. Remember from the discussion of Porter's Five Forces in Chapter 3 that you also must compete indirectly with substitute providers—other means by which people might satisfy their hunger—including grocery stores, pizza delivery, and fast-food outlets with drive-thru windows.

Market Size

Your first important task is determining is the size of your market. If you're competing in a national or global industry, you can usually find lots of valuable data online. Government agencies such as the U.S. Census Bureau offer some useful info there. You'll find volumes of data in downloadable Excel spreadsheets with breakdowns of every industry by sales and employees as well as by state and country. There are also private companies like Hoover's, Statista, and IBISWorld that consolidate data and provide detailed reports on industries for a fee.

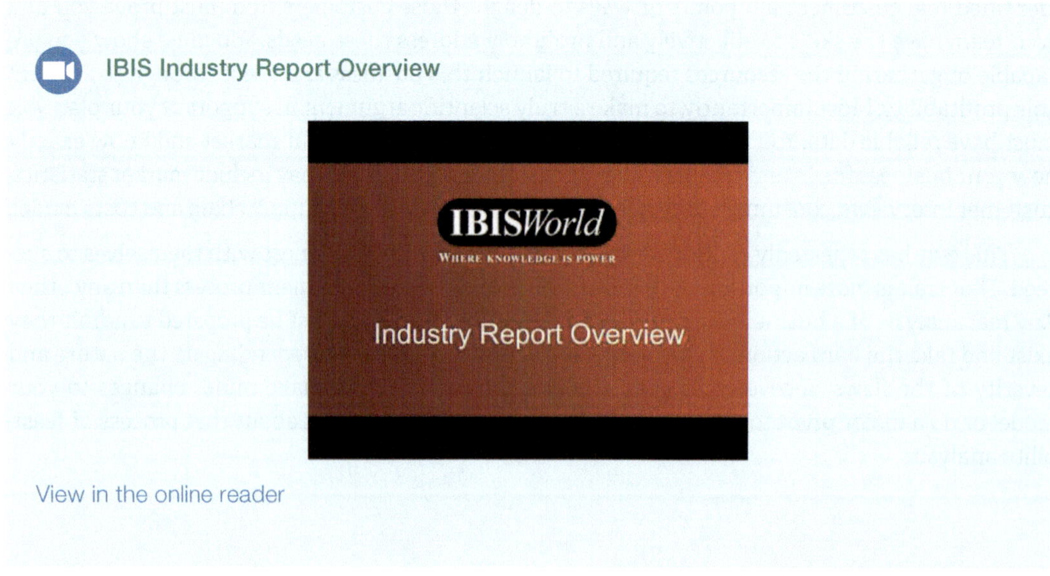

You should be aware of the life cycle of industries and figure out where you are entering on the curve. Looking at several reports across both old and new markets you will note that new industries have a shallow emergence phase when a handful of companies are working to make their new ideas into businesses. If they succeed, the industry typically enjoys relatively rapid growth. In these de novo industries, many new companies enter the market. While most will crash and burn, this is where new fortunes are most often made. Think of the personal-computer industry in the 1980s or the smartphone industry in the 2000s.

FIGURE 5.1 Industry Life Cycle

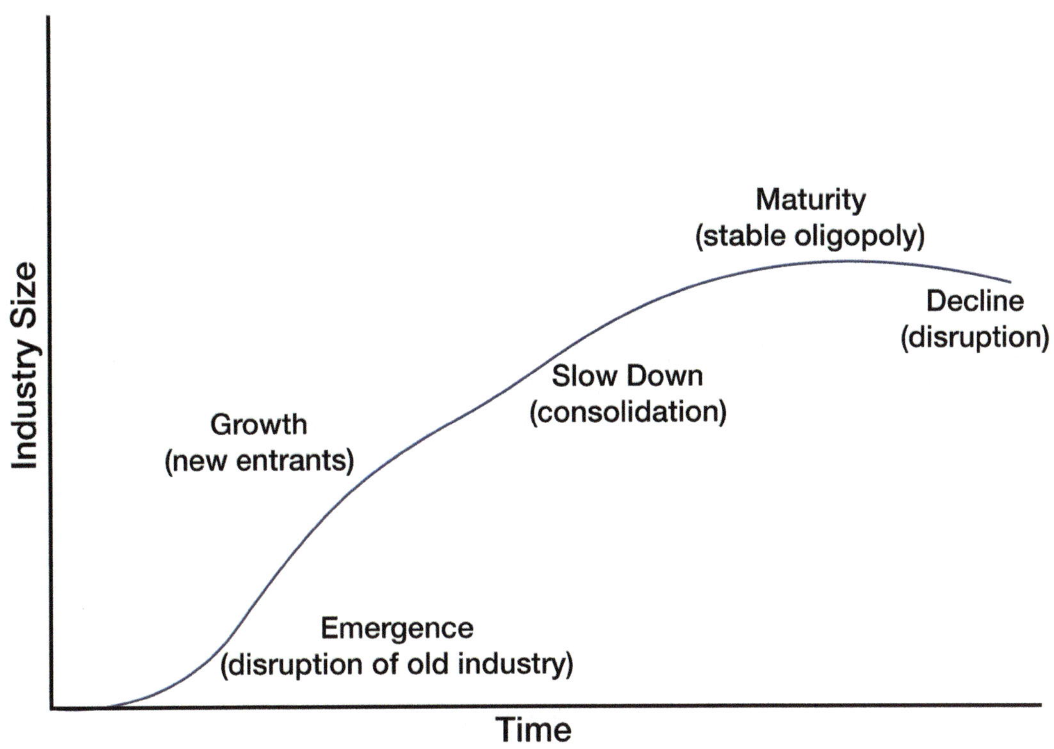

Source: Greg Autry

Eventually, the market for the new product becomes saturated and growth stalls. During this slow-down period, competitive pressures build. Seeking economies of scale, firms merge and are bought out by bigger competitors. Some fail as profit margins shrink. As we noted in Chapter 3, many industries end up in a state of stable oligopoly, where a handful of firms dominate the market. This period may last decades or even a century. Most industries, such as restaurants, are in the "mature" state, the longest phase of the cycle. The American automobile industry has been in this mature state for more than seventy years.

The Value Chain

Another important step toward understanding if your product is worth launching is to determine if it actually *adds value* to the target market. This added value is not merely theoretical. If your new phone app can make raisin toast somewhere in the cloud, that's really swell, but it is valueless unless somebody is willing to pay for it. Since people can't consume virtual toast, this isn't likely to delight anyone; it adds no real economic value.

value chain

The entire set of activities and processes performed by a company to deliver value to its customer, including, but not limited to, manufacturing, distribution, and marketing.

A traditional firm adds real value by taking in materials (for example: flour, sugar, water, etc.) and producing a product (cake) via a process (recipe) that utilizes labor (mixing, baking, frosting), marketing (coupons), and distribution (cupcake vending machine). It may also provide services (clean up) required with the product. The different elements in this process make up the firm's **value chain**.

Look at the illustration of the firm value chain for a manufacturing company in Figure 5.2. It shows these fundamental steps along the bottom as well as the required *support activities* needed for them to flow smoothly. In our cupcake store, inbound logistics is the process of receiving the flour and sugar from your supplier's truck and putting it in your storage cupboards. The support activity *procurement* is the work of ordering the flour. *Outbound logistics* may be the process of shipping the cupcakes off to the customer or just handing them over the bakery counter. Where do you think the mixing, baking, and frosting fall in Figure 5.2?

For software or app companies, which essentially convert mental labor into a product, the firm value chain would combine *inbound logistics* and *operations* into *development*, but the basic concept would remain consistent.

You might be surprised to find that in reality, the value chain extends far beyond your cupcake store. Your suppliers add value when they buy sugar and flour by the truck or railcar load and put them in convenient bags for your store. In turn, their suppliers mill wheat and sugar cane into the flour and sugar. If you sell your cupcakes wholesale to a restaurant, they add value by putting them on the menu and serving them. What happens to the price of the material in each of these steps in the chain?

FIGURE 5.2 Firm Value Chain

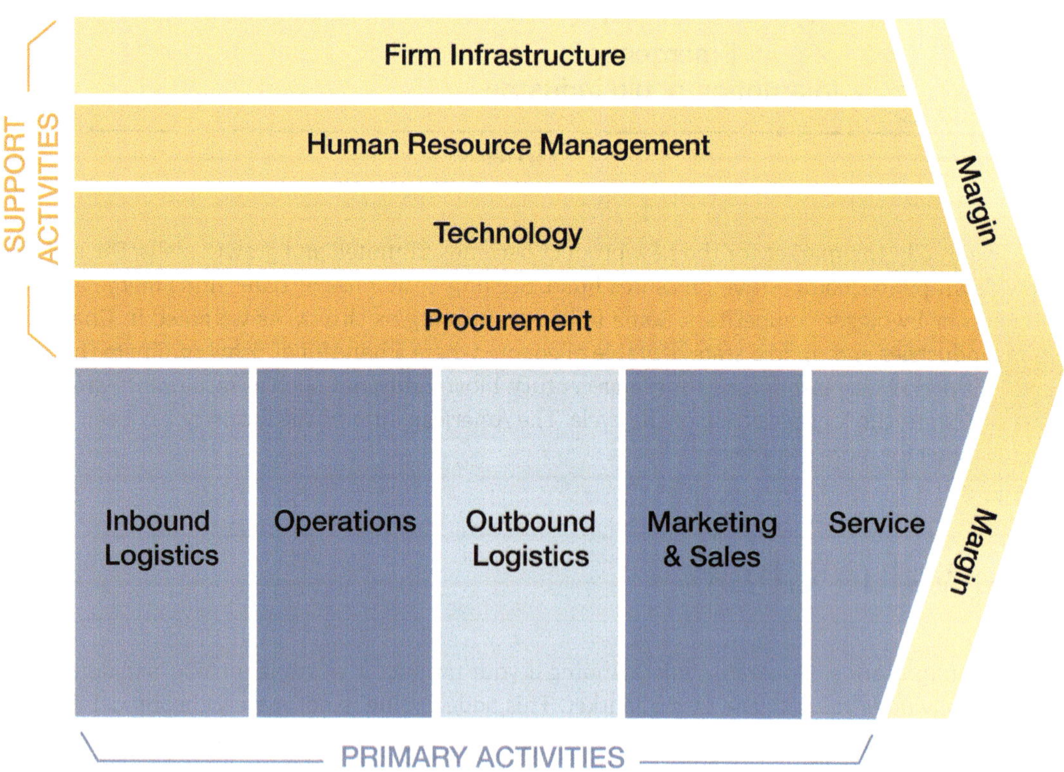

Source: Based on https://commons.wikimedia.org/wiki/File:Porter_Value_Chain.png

industry value chain

The entire set of activities and processes performed by many firms to support the production of products or provision of services.

Look at the illustration of the **industry value chain** for a laptop computer. You can see there are a lot of raw materials that will go into the product to be refined by various firms along the way. The bottom row traces the path followed by crude oil, which is made into plastic, then into a keyboard, which is integrated into the laptop. The finished computer is sold to a wholesaler who ships it to a computer store, where a customer purchases it.

FIGURE 5.3 Industry Value Chain for Laptop Computer

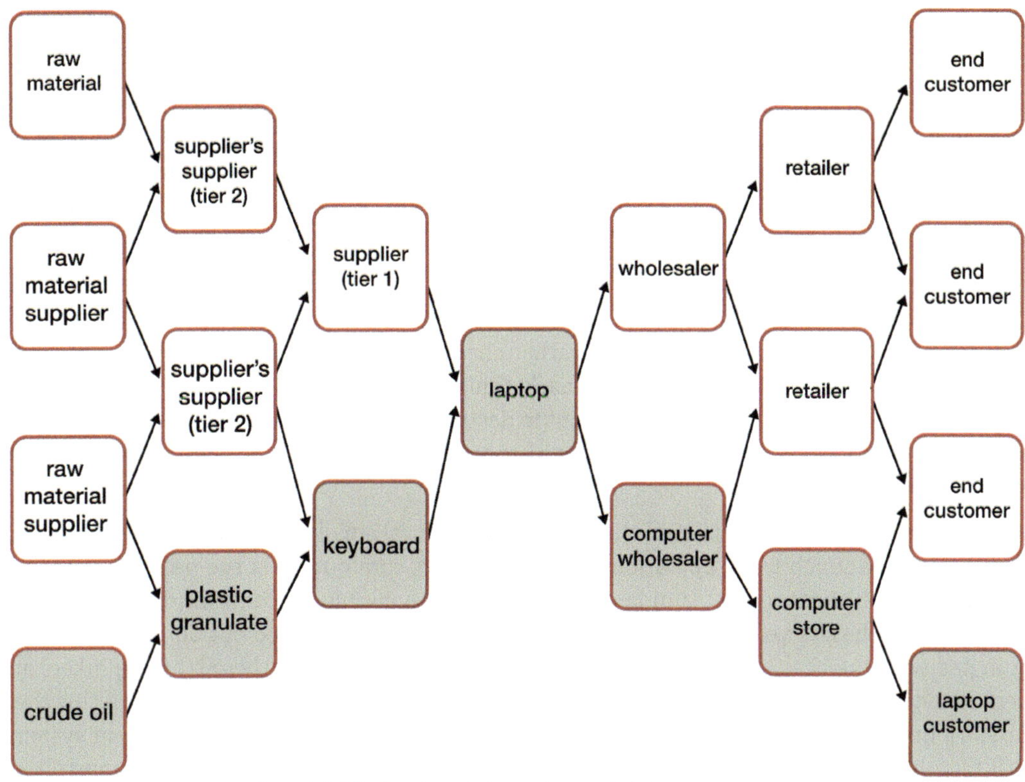

Source: https://commons.wikimedia.org/wiki/File:Supply_and_demand_network_(en).png

Value Mismatch

Sometimes the value added doesn't match what the market desires. Let's consider the case of the Ouya, a video game console that drastically reduced barriers to game development and reduced the size of consumer consoles. Based on this theoretically sound idea, the company was able to raise more than $8 million on Kickstarter. The problem is that Ouya prioritized size and cost over performance and quality. It turns out that gamers would rather spend a little more money for a better experience. They're also unwilling to take a step backward in gaming power. Doing everything on the cheap left Ouya without a market because it just did not provide any value to customers. Had Ouya understood its customers better, they could have avoided this problem either by developing a stronger product or by not selling the inferior one in the first place.

The Ouya game console.

Source: https://commons.wikimedia.org/wiki/File:OUYA-Console-set-h.jpg

Once you understand what it is that your customers value, you need to consider what they are giving up by switching to your product and how that might affect the value chain. You might build the best, cheapest smartphone ever, but chances are you won't break the death grip Apple has on the smartphone market. Apple has brilliant marketing and high brand awareness and provides a complete ecosystem that includes computers, an online content store with music, movies, and books, a payment system, relationships with all the major mobile network providers, and hundreds of first-rate retail stores with support services. Simply having better technical specifications isn't going to beat all that. So even if your product fits nicely into the value chain, consider that there may be barriers set up around the value chain that can block you.

Technical Feasibility

Recall that we opened this chapter with the question, "Why hasn't this already been done?" A major component of that question revolves around the issue of technical feasibility. The world is full of ingenious people constantly facing the same problems you do. If you were in the consumer electronics market, for example, you would want to seriously ponder the question of, "Why hasn't Samsung or Google or HP done this?" If leading technical firms full of brilliant engineers haven't pursued this path, perhaps there is simply not a feasible engineering solution. Look at your specific category and consider the reasons why your idea is not already a reality.

It is possible, as we have discussed in earlier chapters, that the incumbent firms are simply unable to grasp the next big thing, and the market might be open for disruption. It's possible that Google is the next Xerox, and your idea is about to destroy them. However, these firms are now very aware of the theory behind disruption and the history of their predecessors. They are working hard not to miss the next big thing.

Technical issues can bedevil even the simplest traditional small business. Imagine that you've decided to start a lunch truck operation servicing a resort community in the nearby mountains. There aren't a lot of convenient dining solutions for the many high-income outdoor enthusiasts that flock from the city year-round to hike, fish, and snowboard. The food options are limited and not in line with the healthy lifestyles of the upscale clients. You're sure these starving hikers and skiers would be willing to pay good money for a healthy and filling meal. If you research this clientele, you'll find they like to pay nearly everything with credit cards or app-based payment systems. You'll then likely settle on a solution from Square or PayPal running on a tablet or smartphone. Great! You're good to go, right?

So you get all that credit card tech set up with your bank and invest $150,000 in an amazing lunch truck, stock it full of kale salads and free-range chicken breasts, and arrive outside the most popular ski resort parking lot on a busy holiday weekend! People start awkwardly running over in their clunky boots as soon as you park. By the time you get the awning up, a line has formed! You're ready to rake in the bucks, and you smugly ask yourself, "Why hasn't somebody done this already?" The answer comes to you as you ring up your first order and process her credit card: "No cell service!" That's why there are no lunch trucks in the mountains.

Resource Feasibility

Our second question was, "Why is your team the best team to do this?" The feasibility of your new business is constrained by your own capabilities and resources, or your ability to obtain the necessary resources. You can't launch a software startup if you can't program or can't find competitive programmers. You can't open a successful restaurant if you can't cook or hire a chef. You can't start the sort of rapid growth necessary to do a big tech disruption if you don't have access to the massive capital necessary to enter those markets.

So, before you waste your time or other people's time with your grandiose vision, take some time to consider *if you can actually implement it*. If not, your next question should be, "Can I learn to do this in a reasonable amount of time and with reasonable effort?"

Most folks simply aren't ready to learn a whole new industry or embrace a new skillset. However, entrepreneurs are remarkably flexible. While Steve Jobs or Elon Musk epitomize that concept in a big way, many smaller business owners have made successful transitions from corporate accountant or marketing rep to restaurateur or deep-sea fishing guide. It's a lot easier to do this if your new business has been a long-standing personal hobby or passion. If you never cook at home, you're probably not going to flourish in the kitchen of that new pancake restaurant. On the other hand, if you spend every day off work out on at sea hunting for albacore, you've probably developed a lot of the basic understanding necessary to manage a charter fishing boat.

If you've concluded you're not the one to do this, then you'll need to ask: "Can I find the right experts to join me?" Recruiting isn't as simple as placing an ad for a short-order cook or an experienced boat captain. Cooking and captaining are critical core competencies in your business, and as we've cautioned, they should probably not simply be outsourced. For the best chance of success, your business must excel at its core functions. You can outsource the menu design and the boat maintenance, but the food and the fishing have to be great. That means that your recruits should be part of the founding team. They need to care about your business in a way that transcends a simple contract or employment agreement. You should be looking for partners to assume these critical functions and share your business with you.

Most business ideas require teams to execute.

Source: © Shutterstock, Inc.

Commercialization and Scale Feasibility

Walmart purchases products by the hundreds of thousands or millions. Doing so captures massive economies of scale, allowing Walmart to pressure its suppliers into cost reductions. Satisfying the demands of this sort of massive volume approach is practically the only way to keep the megastore chain's business. Additionally, to maintain the lowest possible consumer prices, products will likely be globally sourced to locations with low labor rates, low taxes, and pliant environmental rules. Running a business such as Walmart requires expertise in global sourcing. You need trustworthy employees with local knowledge to help you select reliable factories and then keep an eagle eye on the pace of production and quality of output.

While not every business needs to supply Walmart, every business has to be able to reach a level of scale where they are profitable. Beyond meeting your minimum requirements for scale, more is not always best. Just because you could find a factory in Bangladesh ready to make a million T-shirts with your grinning frog illustration does not suggest there are a million customers who would appreciate your design enough to pay for it. If your pancake restaurant serves only two meals a day, do you think you'll be able to afford to pay the rent, utilities, and salaries? Even if each of those couple of meals were incredibly profitable and your rent was low, it is unlikely you could cover your costs. We will discuss how to determine your firm's costs and profit requirements in future chapters on accounting and cashflow.

Regardless of how good your product is, you need to do some research to determine if your market is big enough and if you can capture a large enough share to support your operation. You also need to figure out how much of it you must capture to remain viable. Can you stay a small fish in your industry's pond? If your target industry is small-town restaurants, the answer is yes. A quick look around any town will show you multiple examples of successful single location establishments.

However, if you've decided to build your car and enter the automobile manufacturing industry, the answer to the question to "Can I stay a small fish?" becomes a resounding "no." In order to deal with the complex regulatory environment and to capture any economies, you must scale that business to thousands of cars or charge a very high price per car. You succeed as a mass-market car maker like Nissan by selling half a million cars each year at reasonable prices. You may also succeed as a specialized, high-end car company like supercar maker McLaren, which sells 1,500 ultra-high-end cars for up to $1.5 million each. Either way, an automobile manufacturer must take in at least hundreds of millions of dollars per year to survive. Within the current layout of that industry, an automobile firm simply cannot be a small business.

Many great artisanal manufacturers produce small runs of high-quality goods with love and care. These products are priced much higher than goods at Walmart, and the higher profits on each item sold can go a long way toward making up for low volume. In fact, many small vendors have collapsed trying to make the transition to high volume at low prices. They have found that they lost money taking huge, low-cost orders from corporations like Walmart and that fronting the funds required to build those orders pushed them into bankruptcy. Even if you think you can avoid bankruptcy to pull off that sort of Walmart scale, you may also find that the stress of this situation disrupts your personal life to an unacceptable extent. Often the artisanal path is both more profitable and personally rewarding.

The New Entrepreneurial Dynamic does not pursue growth at all costs. It encourages you to find a profitable balance between the nature of your product or service and the real-world needs of your customers, all in the context of creating a business that satisfies your own needs.

Key Takeaways

- Find out why previous entrepreneurs rejected your idea or failed at it.
- Be sure you truly believe that your team can win with your idea and why they are the right team.
- Be willing to challenge your own idea and change it to fit the reality you find in the marketplace.
- Research your market carefully before entering. The data is out there.
- Be clear on what value your firm will add within the industry supply chain and find a profitable niche.
- Make sure your idea can scale to where you want to go.

5.2 Opportunity Valuation

Learning Objectives

1. Understand the limitations and appropriate use of surveys and focus groups.
2. Understand the application of Blank's customer development model.
3. Understand the processes of customer discovery and customer validation.
4. Understand the difference between your customer and the user.
5. Recognize the value of a minimum viable product (MVP).
6. Understand your responsibility in making a safe and environmentally considerate product.

Talking to Customers

The very best source of information about the sales viability of your product or service in the marketplace will always come from those who plan to buy it—potential customers. Traditional firms often solicit the opinions of consumers via **surveys** or **focus groups** to determine if there are willing buyers for a particular product.

survey

A formal set of questions presented to a statistically relevant sample of respondents, such as target customers.

focus group

A small gathering of potential customers designed to provoke conversational insights into proposed products, features, and designs.

Listen to potential customers.

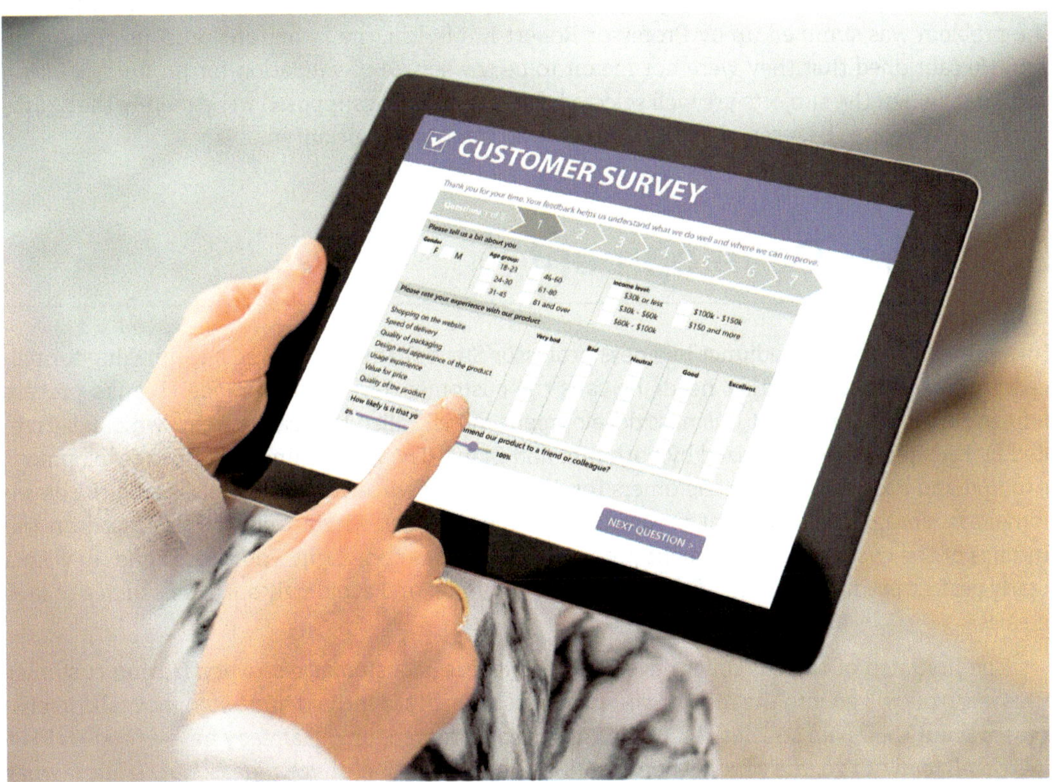

Source: © Shutterstock, Inc.

While surveys can be very useful tools when you want to price out or define the feature set of a fairly mature concept, they can be extremely misleading when you are trying to flesh out an innovative new idea. Although surveys may have open-ended questions, they are essentially one-way, asynchronous communications. Meaning you can't look at a survey response and quickly ask the respondent to clarify or expand on their point or say, "Ah, I see what you mean, but what if we did it this way?" What you need at the launch of a new business is a deeper, more nuanced conversation with potential customers.

What about focus groups then? Focus groups are a time-honored marketing technique of bringing a small number of potential customers into contact with a potential product. This could be anything from a car to a new movie—and in fact, I've personally participated in focus groups for both of those product categories. The idea is that the marketing team will use a few questions to provoke a dynamic discussion among the customers about the benefits and shortcomings of a potential product. During this discussion, the customers will quickly reveal their real feelings. The problem is that the record of a product, like a new TV series, vetted by focus groups is rather dismal. Professor Gerald Zaltman of Harvard Business School sums it up this way: "The correlation between stated intent and actual behavior is usually low and negative."[1] That's a nice way of saying that people lie, even in focus groups. Can you think of why that is?

Further research has shown that people in focus groups are keenly interested in how smart and informed they appear to the rest of the group and they want to be liked by the marketing person leading the group, who is viewed as authoritative. To stand out, they tend to be either too kind or too critical of the products they are evaluating. This is a natural process, and since many people are paid to participate in focus groups, they want to be invited back. Praising the product presented would be a natural strategy to gain favor, and criticizing it might make you appear to be bold and smart. The problem here is the focus group participant is thinking about the dynamics of the process, not the product. Worse, once one or two members of the group show a preference, the group as a whole often falls in line with the "group think," making it hard to get honest responses.

While they were very popular in the second half of the last century, focus groups have fallen out of favor with many innovators. Steve Jobs famously rejected focus groups and liked to quote Henry Ford who said, "If I had asked people what they wanted, they would have said faster horses." The problem was summed up by Professor Robert K. Merton, the father of the focus group concept. He cautioned that they were not meant to be the source of validation for products. Merton said, "Even when the subjects are well selected, focus groups are supposed to be merely the source of ideas that need to be researched." If focus groups aren't the solution, what is?

Customer Development

Entrepreneur, writer, and adjunct business professor Steve Blank has offered a compelling formalized process of finding market needs he calls the customer development model. Blank's process defines part of an important business development model called the lean startup, which was created by Eric Reis and popularized by both him and Blank. The idea behind customer development is to find and even nurture the customers for your product while you develop it. You do the development in an agile development process, where the product is iteratively refined based on the findings of the customer development process. When this is done right, you should end up with a nearly perfect product-customer fit when you go to market and avoid ugly surprises, such as a lack of sales.

The first step of the customer development process is customer discovery. During customer discovery, you will go into the market you have most broadly identified and listen (not talk) to customers about their pain and desires. While any eager entrepreneur will already have a product idea, or several, ready to go, the process here is not to seek validation of your ideas, but to learn what customers really need so you can develop a product for which they will pay. The questions you ask during customer discovery are only there to prompt the interviewees into sharing their needs. Never presume that you already understand those problems or that you know how to solve them. Once you have identified that a likely group of customers has a problem that you can likely solve with the resource you have, go to your iterative development process and start solving the *customer's problem.*

Customer Validation

customer validation

The process of verifying product-market fit by testing the basic assumptions of a business model. See also *alpha test; beta test; customer discovery; minimum viable product.*

After you've designed a product and a business model to deliver it, you should verify that you have correctly interpreted and fulfilled your customer's needs before you invest more time and other people's money into mass producing this idea. The process of **customer validation** involves showing, *absolutely never selling or pitching,* your concept to actual potential customers and seeing if they might pay for it, and if so, how much? This can be accomplished with further interviews, surveys, and the sale of a very simple product (see Section 2).

During this process of customer engagement, you should be aware of the risk of exposing your concepts to a lot of people who could offer your ideas to competitors. However, experience suggests the much greater risk lies in making a product that customers won't buy or use. Assuming everyone wants to steal your idea and has the time, money, and the resources to make a go of it is usually a conceit of the entrepreneur rather than a real threat. Once your product is on the market and is successful, you can surely expect imitators and even counterfeiters to appear. However, thieves are lazy; they want you to do the hard work of customer validation and product development first.

An Apple Watch in use.

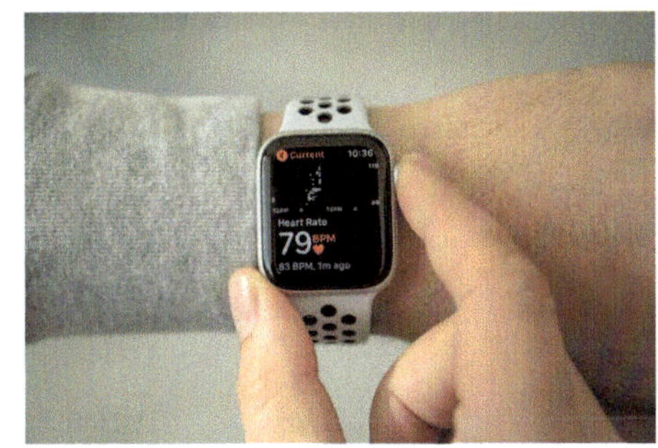

Source: DenPhotos/Shutterstock.com

The Apple Watch underwent years of secret product development before it was introduced in 2015. Renowned Apple designer Jony Ive was sure that everyone would want this product and famously stated with the release of the Apple Watch, "Swiss watchmakers were #$%^&@!" (We can't print what Jony actually said.) However, initial public adoption of the Apple Watch and competing smartwatches from Samsung was muted at best. A number of techy people bought these products at first to try them out, but few people persisted in wearing them. It turned out that having a small computer on your wrist didn't really solve many real-world problems or add enough value for most people to wear a clunky gizmo that had to be charged every day. Worse, you had to carry around a smartphone just to use the watch, so what was the point? Potential users' problems were already being sufficiently addressed by mechanical watches and the always present smartphone. Breaching their secrecy wall and doing some significant customer discovery would very likely have enabled Apple to discover all this before the firm invested so much time and credibility in the watch. To Apple's credit, they listened to customer feedback, and by late 2018 their Series 3 and 4 watches, which were able to function untethered from a phone, gained significant traction in the market and returned profits to the firm.

Blank's Lean Startup Model is heavily focused on the customer demand side of the business model. That's not a bad thing because, as Chapter 2 stated, in the New Entrepreneurial Dynamic, "Customers are required; everything else in a business is optional." However, this customer focus makes the Lean Startup Model best for rapid growth startups entering unproven markets with new ideas, like a new tech product or app. I strongly recommend Blank's book (with Steve Dorf), *The Startup Owner's Manual*[2] for entrepreneurs pursuing rapid growth/Silicon Valley startups.

The model is much less appropriate for businesses entering proven, mature markets without a revolutionary product. If your customers are already proven and your competitive advantage is going to come from cost rather than differentiation, you'll want to pursue a more supply-side focused approach. That does not mean you should ever ignore your potential customers; you may still discover something unexpected by talking to them.

Customer and the User

During this process of customer development and in your future marketing and sales efforts, you must always be aware that the person paying for the product or service you sell, your customer, may or may not be the person using or consuming it, your user. Consider McDonald's. Most of the time, the customer at McDonald's pays for his or her meal and then eats it. In this case, they are also the user. What if Dad takes the kids out for chicken nuggets? Who is the customer for a Happy Meal? In this case, the user, the kids, is distinct from the paying customer, Dad. McDonald's must develop a product that the kids desire but for which the parent will pay. This involves making sure the product is tasty to young palates raised on sugar and fat, while convincing at least one adult that the meal is sufficiently nutritious. In this case, the parent is a **third-party payer**.

third-party payer

The organization or individual paying for a product or service to be consumed by another party. A scholarship or health insurer are common third-party payers.

Many big markets like education and health care depend on third-party payers. In K–12 education, this is often the government, which funds the schools most students attend. However, it could be a church or parent paying for tuition at a private school. As a higher education student, there is a good chance much of your tuition is being covered by some combination of loans, scholarships, grants, or parents. If you are in the education business, you need to make sure that your institution is accredited with organizations that will permit these loans, scholarships, and government support—as well as to sufficiently impress the parents. In many countries, health care is funded substantially or entirely by the government. In the U.S., a complex mix of insurance, government, and patient copays funds the system. Making sure your drug or medical device will be covered by both public and private insurance systems is super critical before you go to market.

Beta Testing and the Minimum Viable Product

alpha test

Process by which a firm tests its own unfinished product in-house to determine market readiness. See also *beta test*; *minimum viable product (MVP)*.

beta test

Process by which a firm tests its own unfinished product by providing it to actual consumers to use in real-life situations to determine market readiness. See also *alpha test*; *minimum viable product (MVP)*.

early adopter

A consumer who will use a new technology or product as soon as it becomes available.

minimum viable product (MVP)

A version of product with the fewest features to deliver maximum customer validation. See also *alpha test*; *beta test*; *customer discovery*; *customer validation*.

Ideally, before you invest a lot of time and energy in a full-blown product and business model, you will have conclusively determined that there is a market for your basic concept by generating customer feedback. One approach to this is an **alpha test**, whereby your own firm's staff work with and test a functional but unfinished version of your final product in real-life situations. A **beta test** provides a select group of real-world users with an unfinished product to find out how they like it and identify any bugs that need fixing. Following this path is standard operating procedure in the software world. Keep in mind that in most cases, you can't charge customers for a product that has been released for testing purposes.

A related approach is to develop the simplest finished product you can that captures your value proposition and sell that to **early adopters**. Some people may be entirely satisfied with a minimalist implementation of your basic idea, or simply so attracted to new things that they will be excited to get their hands on the first iteration and wait for a more robust solution later. Business consultant Frank Robinson christened this a **minimum viable product (MVP)**, and the idea has been promoted by authors Eric Reis and Steve Blank as part of their Lean Startup Model. An MVP gives you early-stage feedback before you get too far along in the design of the complete product. The important fact that you sell (not give away) your MVP means that it also validates your claim that you are adding value for customers. It also doesn't hurt at all that you get paid.

In the early 2010s, it became clear to a number of technologists that a software-driven, self-driving car was possible. Tesla Motors, Google, and Apple all launched efforts to exploit this new opportunity, and each took a different route to development. Apple kept their car project, like the iPhone and Apple Watch, a secret and developed it primarily in a hidden laboratory and test track. Google openly displayed their product under development and launched an extensive alpha test program with Google engineers supervising the vehicles in operation in real-world environments.

Elon Musk chose the MVP route at Tesla. Rather than making a fully self-driving vehicle that could take you door to door, the company developed a product that used cameras, radar and ultrasonic sensors to maintain the vehicle's speed, keep its following distance safe, hold it within traffic lanes, and avoid obstacles. This system presumed the driver would remain alert to road conditions and in control at all times. It could detect if the driver was holding the wheel, and failure to do so would trigger an alert or automatically slow the car. The software also provided auto parking features, limited remote control from your smartphone, and collision avoidance technologies that would move or brake the car in the event the driver failed to react to an imminent threat. Tesla released this "autopilot" solution as an option for $2,500 with the vehicle purchase or as a software download for $3,000. The firm generated millions in revenue, a lot of press for being the "first to market with self-driving," and collected millions of miles of real-world road data. Can you think why Tesla's MVP data might be more valuable than that collected under the Google alpha test or by test drivers on Apple's test track?

Tesla automobiles continuously capture real world data.

Source: TierneyMJ/Shutterstock.com

From the data acquired from real driver behavior in a self-driving car, Tesla learned that customers don't always follow directions! Just about anyone who has released a product to the world can tell you horror stories of how customers misinterpreted or abused their product in ways the manufacturer never imagined. In some notable cases, autopilot customers crashed their vehicles by using it inappropriately or in unforeseen circumstances. Tesla was able to make significant software improvements and develop new hardware based on these incidents and other data.[3] Google also had some accidents, but because they used their own employees, you can well imagine that the testers may have been careful not to significantly challenge their own system. Test drivers on Apple's test track are surely going to simulate all the difficult scenarios that they can anticipate, but until they hand over the product to real customers, they aren't likely to find out what can go wrong.

The MVP approach is a central part of the New Entrepreneurial Dynamic. Whenever possible, find ways to test your products in the real world before committing your time, resources, and other people's money to a full-blown implementation of your small business idea or startup vision. If you're planning to launch that small café near campus, why not test your fare on students by getting a gig catering events at the university? You could also consider a cart or food truck. If you're planning a cake shop, you might offer your cakes to local restaurants before opening the doors of your bakery. Whenever possible, set up a small e-commerce site and sell some products directly to consumers before you attempt to do wholesale distribution through retail outlets. This will allow you to test the market, establish the best price point, and gain valuable customer feedback. The additional profit margin you capture when selling direct at retail prices rather than discounting for wholesale pricing is also very helpful in the early stages of your operation. This makes even more sense if ramping up production is difficult and you have not captured the **economies of scale** or have a limited quantity of product to deliver.

economy of scale

The inverse relationship resulting from increased production driving down the price per unit due to the overall cost being spread out among a high number of goods sold. See also *fixed costs*.

Safety and Environmental Concerns

If you make something or provide a service, you must make sure your product is safe for consumers. You should be particularly careful with anything that is likely to be handled by children or is present at any facility where children may be. Children make choices that adults simply can't predict and can find danger in the most benign environments. Failure to put safety first could result in lawsuits that may quickly put your small business out of business.

Beyond simply thinking through what is safe or doing your own testing, there are many commercial labs that conduct product safety certification. Underwriters Laboratories certifies electrical appliances as "UL Approved" for instance. Keep in mind that paying for certifications can be expensive.

You'll also want to consider whether your product is safe for workers to make. Can it be disposed of in an environmentally friendly way? Is the manufacturing process compliant with environmental laws? You may be surprised to find that processes like painting and sanding can be heavily regulated because exposure to dust or vapors can be hazardous and emitting them into the atmosphere can contribute to dangerous smog. If you outsource, inspecting the factories where your products are made can be burdensome, particularly overseas. One strategy is to ride on someone else's inspections. Many high-profile multinationals like Disney must maintain a high level of manufacturing oversight because they are subject to a lot of media scrutiny. Factories in places like China will tout being "Disney certified," and you can choose to use those manufacturers with some assurance that they meet basic levels of safety and environmental responsibility.

Keeping your own workers safe requires you understand the jobs they are doing or hire experts who do. Ensure that your workers are properly trained and equipped with appropriate safety gear for the tasks at hand. Simple things like eye protection are inexpensive preventors of costly injuries. The law and/or your insurance provider will also likely require that you document the proper procedures and policies for performing any potentially dangerous tasks that include requiring the use of safety gear. Have your employees sign off that they have read and are familiar with these documents. That is to make sure they actually pay attention and to protect you in the event they chose not to do the right thing when you aren't looking.

Keeping workers safe requires proper equipment.

Source: © Shutterstock, Inc.

It is particularly important to ensure safety in facilities that are open to customers. For instance, if you own a retail shop or restaurant, you must be sure there are no inherent hazards, such as oddly placed or sized steps, low beams, or exposed sharp edges on furnishings. You and your staff must also be constantly on the lookout for temporary risks such as broken glass, slippery liquids, or power cords on walking surfaces.

Sadly, you must also know that in the United States, there are **predatory plaintiffs**, people who actively look for opportunities to intentionally "injure" themselves and sue inattentive small businesses. They have relationships with corrupt doctors and lawyers who are experts at extorting payment from business owners and their insurance companies. If anybody appears to have injured themselves in your business, be sure to provide prompt medical assistance and document everything that occurred, including taking photos of the area or anything the injured person claims was hazardous. You may need this evidence in court. At the same time, be careful to avoid confrontation and don't offend real customers by assuming a hostile attitude.

predatory plaintiffs

Litigants who actively seek opportunities to sue businesses for claimed injuries.

The New Entrepreneurial Dynamic favors entrepreneurs who think ahead and operate ethically—even when nobody is looking. Your business should protect its workers, customers, and the environment because it is the right thing to do, because you don't want to incur liability, and because your reputation is invaluable.

Key Takeaways

- In the end, delivering a product customers will pay for is what counts.
- Don't rely on surveys because they are easy and avoid contact.
- Listen to your potential customers; don't sell to them.
- The person who pays for your product or makes the purchasing decision may or may not be the user of the product.
- Run an alpha and beta test on your product before selling it.
- Make an MVP, if you can, before trying to build the perfect complete solution.
- Keep your workers safe and document your firm's safety procedures.
- Being considerate of your customers' safety and the environment is the right thing to do and it is probably the best thing to do as well.

5.3 Financial Feasibility

Learning Objectives

1. Understand that the capital requirements of each startup are different.
2. Recognize the possibility of bootstrapping your startup rather than seeking outside investors.
3. Understand that identifying profitability is fundamental to validating any business model.
4. Understand the demographics of your clients.
5. Understand the basics of variable and fixed costs.
6. Learn to apply the economics of one unit model.

Capital Investment

As the adage goes, "It takes money to make money," and there are very few businesses you can launch without **capital investment**. The easiest route to getting started is to save up money or be lucky enough to borrow it from mom and dad or some close friend. That said, the New Entrepreneurial Dynamic rewards those who creatively **bootstrap** their small business. Bootstrapping is the process of creatively financing the startup costs of a firm when you don't have the time to save or access to easy cash. Can you think of alternative ways entrepreneurs fund the costs required to start a business?

capital investment

Funds invested to support a startup with the expectation that they will be recovered through future earnings. See also *bootstrap*.

bootstrap

Creatively financing the startup costs of a firm using existing resources. See also *capital investment*.

Some of the most common bootstrapping techniques include using personal credit cards, negotiating deferred payment on rent, equipment, and inventory, and collecting advance payments from customers. To put those things in context, let's imagine that you are going to set up a small artisanal manufacturing business making ceramics. You'll need a workshop location, a potter's wheel, a kiln, and other specialized ceramics equipment like bats, cones, brushes, and sculpting tools. You'll also need initial supplies such as clay, coloring agents, and glazes. How do you get all this with minimal investment?

Capital is required to grow a business.

Source: © Shutterstock, Inc.

If you are willing to locate in a distressed area or run-down property, you may be able to convince the landlord to accommodate you with reduced rent in exchange for improving the facility. A ceramics factory certainly doesn't need to look fancy, so a property in need of some love may work very well.

The best way to get any sort of equipment or supplies for your startup—from office furniture to specialized ovens—is to look for similar businesses that are going out of business. They may be selling their gear and supplies in a liquidation sale, or they may have already gone bankrupt, and the gear may be offered at auction. Such equipment usually sells for pennies on the dollar. Machines that cost $10,000 new can often be purchased for $1,000 at auction. However, "buyer beware" always applies when purchasing used equipment. In the cases of auctions, you are often unable to test the equipment before bidding. It helps to have a practiced eye and to assume in advance that what you buy may require maintenance. In some cases, you may be able to connect with a business owner who is going out of business and negotiate to take their equipment from them on a payment schedule. Rather than default on their existing financing arrangement, bankrupt business owners may be willing to exchange their equipment for an agreement to take over payments. If you do this, be careful to ensure that the owner is, in fact, using your payments to pay their debt—otherwise, the lienholder could potentially seize the gear that you've been paying for.

You may also be able to pick up supplies from a failed business, but you'll probably have to buy some too. Some bootstrapping options here include negotiating with suppliers for delayed payments and using your personal credit cards to get stocked.

Finally, getting money up front is always the best solution to early startup **cash flow** challenges. How about running a crowdfunding campaign on Kickstarter or Indiegogo to get customers to prepay for some of your ceramic creations? You might use the wheels and kilns at school to make some great looking prototypes and film yourself in action tossing clay!

cash flow

The incoming and outgoing of money in a business.

Chapter 7 will address all this in more detail, but what is important now is for you to rigorously investigate feasible ways for you to get the funds you need to launch your business. Initial capital requirements of this sort can be guesstimated from basic research and consultations with experts, manufacturers, and suppliers. Experience also suggests that you should include a significant buffer for unexpected expenses. If you conclude your idea requires a great deal of additional startup capital, you may need to find investors. Do you know any investors? Do you have a network that can help you find investors?

Pricing, Margins, Affordability, and Demographics

profit margin

The amount by which revenue from sales exceeds costs in a business. See also *gross profit*, *net profit*.

When you look into the feasibility of a product, one of the most important things to look for is a realistic **profit margin**. If you cannot sell your product for more than it costs you to produce or procure, then you are not adding value. If you are not adding value, then you don't have a business. You may design the ultimate toothbrush, but if each one costs you $200 to make, it will have to retail for $400 or more. At that price, it's unlikely you'll find enough buyers to support your business. To reduce price, you may have to cut features or quality. This balance between features, quality, and cost must serve your target customer. Some people are willing to pay exorbitant prices for haute couture clothing and wouldn't buy fast fashion if it were nearly free. That doesn't mean that Zara hasn't made billions by providing such clothing as cheaply as possible. Your demographics will dictate what prices you can support and, in turn, what your costs must be in order to support workable margins.

It is essential to research the portions of the industry value chain that are downstream from your business. That means you must understand who you will sell to, who they sell to, and know how many steps there are between you and the final consumer. If you're a manufacturer of artisanal pottery, you might sell directly to consumers at fairs, and the price you charge is both the customer's price and your revenue. On the other hand, you might sell to an international distributor who sells to a local distributor, who sells to retailers, who sells to customers. In this case, to discover the value chain, you might visit a retail store that sells pottery and ask the manager, "I'm thinking of selling my pottery in stores like yours. Who do you buy your pottery from?" They will likely be happy to put you in touch with their distributor, who, if they like you and your product, will explain the industry value chain to you.

Each organization between product production and the customer adds value, and each will charge for that value. So, your revenue may be a lot less than the price the customer pays. For instance, if a customer pays $100 for a pot, you are likely to have gotten something like $20 for that same pot from the international distributor. The international distributor might sell the pot to the local distributor for $35, who sells it to the retailer for $50. Since most retail stores want margins of 50 percent or more, meaning they double the price of items they sell, your pot now carries a price tag of $100.

Variable Costs, Controlling Unit Costs, COGS, and EOU

variable costs

Business expenses that change with each unit of production, for example, the cost of supplies, labor, and energy.

fixed cost

The expenses that must be paid by a company regardless of business activity, for example, rent and insurance. See also *economy of scale*; *variable costs*.

Variable costs are the costs that change with each unit of production. If you run a hot dog cart, then hot dogs and buns are variable costs because the number of hot dogs and buns sold will change day to day. The cart itself is a **fixed cost**—it stays the same regardless of how many hot dogs you sell. Dealing with your variable costs may require some optimization calculations to figure out the ideal batch sizes. It's tricky to figure out how many hot dogs you are going to sell. Interestingly, hot dogs typically come in packs of ten and buns in packs of eight. So, forty and eighty are natural inventory targets.

The **economics of one unit** (EOU) model is a technique to analyze your financial feasibility. The first step is to determine what your unit of sale is. For our hot dog cart, it's one hot dog. Now we want to know what it costs us to make a hot dog or what our **cost of goods sold** (COGS) per unit is. To calculate our COGS per unit, we need the cost of the hot dog and the bun along with the condiments and the napkin. Let's cost that out:

Hot Dog Cost of Goods Sold per Unit		
Hot Dog	$	0.70
Bun	$	0.20
Condiments	$	0.05
Napkin	$	0.05
COGS	**$**	**1.00**

So, if we've determined that we can sell our hot dogs to the public for $2, are we making money? On a per-unit level, YES! We are making a **gross profit** of $1 per hot dog ($2 sale price – $1 COGS = $1). The next question is: Do we sell enough hot dogs, profiting $1 each, to cover the cost of our cart and other fixed costs? Let's take a look at what we think a hot dog cart would cost per month to cover the cart lease, a city sidewalk vendor permit, and insurance.

Monthly Costs for Hot Dog Cart Business		
Cart Lease	$	200
City Vendor Permit	$	50
Insurance	$	50
Fixed Costs	**$**	**300**

So, how many hot dogs must you sell each month to break even? If you said 300 hot dogs per month, you're correct. At $1 gross profit per dog, you need to sell 300 to cover the fixed costs of $300. Sounds easy, right? But realize that leaves NOTHING for you. At 300 hot dogs per month, you are only covering costs, not earning any **net profit**—money left over after costs that you could take home. What if you sold 1,000 hot dogs per month? That's a lot, and you'd take home $700—nothing to write home about for sure. You might as well just get a job at McDonald's unless you can sell thousands of hot dogs each month. The hot dog cart is a pretty tough business.

That choice to take the job at McDonald's is a real option, and if you don't do it, you've given up the opportunity to earn some money. That economic concept is called **opportunity cost**—the value of what you give up when you choose to do something else.

If you're a manufacturer, one way to control for the variable costs and reduce the need for storing large quantities of parts is to try to incorporate as many of the same parts into multiple products. Using the same rivet in all of your shoe collections or the same processors in all of your devices will allow you to reduce the inventory needed, which in turn will reduce storage costs and money stuck in product.

economics of one unit

A systemic method of analyzing the cost and sales price of a product at the unit level. Essentially answering the question: "Can we sell this product or service for more than it costs us to make or provide?"

cost of goods sold

The total cost to produce a good or service to be sold. See also *fixed costs, gross profit, net profit, profit margin, variable costs.*

gross profit

A company's revenue after deducting the cost to produce and deliver goods or services. See also *net profit; profit margin.*

A hot dog vendor at work.

Source: https://commons.wikimedia.org/wiki/File:Hot_Dog_Cart_(37004358434).jpg

net profit

A company's total earnings, after all business expenses are deducted, over a specified period, often a year. See also *gross profit; profit margin.*

opportunity cost

The potential benefit given up when one choice is made over another.

Key Takeaways

- Don't start a business that isn't going to make you money or takes so much money it will never recover the investment.
- Know who your customers are.
- Understand what your fixed costs are and if your profits can overcome them.
- Honestly consider what other thing you might be doing instead of investing time and money into this project.

5.4 Difficult Distribution Channels

Learning Objectives

1. Understand access barriers at the distribution level.
2. Recognize that the Porter model applies to opportunity analysis.
3. Recognize the challenge of overcoming consumer brand loyalty.

Access Barriers

As we saw in Chapter 3, which covered competitive advantage, barriers to entry often involve production challenges and access to customers in retail markets. There are times when you know that you can make a great product at the right price, but simply getting your creation into the hands of consumers is difficult. Securing space on shelves at supermarkets is so competitive that new brands often actually pay the market to put their products out there. Can you think of any other points in the value chain where customer access is limited?

Often, this customer access barrier is created at the distribution level. Imagine that you love beer and you enjoy making your own microbrew. Your friends tell you that your IPA is so good that you should sell it. Production, in limited quantities, is no problem, and you know you can make a profit. This sounds like a pretty easy business to get into on a small scale, right?

It turns out that beer is an extremely difficult industry to "tap" into due to a complicated **distribution system**. In the U.S., an unusual set of regulations around the sale of alcohol emerged after **prohibition** (a period when alcohol production and consumption was illegal in the United States), regulating the sale of alcohol. Firms are only allowed to manufacture, distribute, or sell beer, but in most cases, they may not engage in *more than one* of these activities. This means if a small craft brewery opens up, it has to get a distribution contract or else it will not get any sales. However, distributors will only handle beers that customers have demanded. That's fine, but how can a customer know they want something if the distributor is not carrying it? So, beer becomes an unbreakable loop unless the brewer's salespeople are truly amazing at convincing distributors to take risks they don't need to. So, for the beer industry, the distribution challenge is bigger than the product development or manufacturing challenge.

One of the best ways to overcome these barriers is to develop and use your network. If you're going to be in the beer business or any other, you should cultivate relationships with actors in that industry. There are many reasons to do this, but for beer, the major reason is to get the opportunity to pitch your product to the industry gatekeepers, the distributors.

distribution system

How a product or a service is transferred from its source to the consumer, for example, internet download, direct mail, or trucking from a wholesale warehouse to a retail store. See also *value chain*.

prohibition

The period between 1920 and 1933 when the production, distribution, sale, and consumption of alcohol was prevented by law in the United States.

Market Attractiveness

Chapter 3 detailed the use of Porter's Five Forces model to determine if your small business or startup can enter an existing market and operate profitably. Before entering a market, it is critical to understand these forces of industry: rivalry, supplier powers, buyer powers, threats of new entrants, and threats of substitute products. Conducting this industry analysis could save you the pain of entering an awful market or help you develop a strategy for effectively dealing with the barriers to entry.

Now you may wonder how you are supposed to analyze a de novo market, one that does not yet exist or is just emerging. In these cases, the data are sparse. You may need to rely on your gut, but another good option is to consider investigating similar industries. If you are contemplating leaping into the space tourism business, understanding how the commercial airline industry evolved could provide valuable insights. If you are thinking about entering the wearable computing app space, understanding how the early smartphone and app markets functioned will tell you a lot of things—for instance, that first-mover advantage in the app space is critical in order to get the attention of influential early adopters. With very low barriers to entry, everyone makes an app as soon as they believe the market is real. After a certain point, gaining customers' attention becomes nearly impossible. So, if you actually believe that people will use smartwatches or clothes, move early!

Overcoming Loyalty in Existing Markets

Some markets have very stable brands that command tremendous loyalty from their consumers. Breaking into such markets can be notoriously difficult. Sometimes loyalty is based on the success of a particular product, but often it is the consumer's deeper respect for the firm that makes the product successful. Brands like Sony, Nike, BMW, Harley Davidson, and Louis Vuitton have built a following that transcends their individual products. We call such brands "iconic."

Consumer loyalty is most often based simply on conservatism and the fact that existing products work. Trying something new isn't worth the risk in time and negative outcomes. People are notoriously brand loyal in personal hygiene products like shampoo, hair dye, and razors. They buy the same things because reliability matters a lot in their daily routine. If a new hair dye might potentially turn the user's hair an unintended shade, the high cost of that result will dampen consumers' appetite for novelty.

signal

The passive transmission of information among consumers or within a market.

Finally, in some markets, loyalty is based on the way a brand serves as a **signal** or a source of social identification for its consumers. Users of Apple laptops believe that the firm's sleek aluminum machines convey the message that they, as users, are hip, modern, and ahead of the technology curve. Some drivers buy Mercedes Benz vehicles because they wish to convey the message that they have "made it" as much as they enjoy the actual craftsmanship of the German-built luxury car.

Personal grooming products enjoy strong customer loyalty.

Source: © Shutterstock, Inc.

In the small business world, loyalties can be very personal. People eat at Joe's Diner because they know and love Joe. He's been behind the counter since they were kids, and he is an institution in their community. Such personal affection is immensely hard to overcome. Just trying out your new place across the street might make them feel guilty. Going to your café could be a personal affront to somebody they see as family.

When brands command loyalty for any of these reasons, it can be very hard for a new firm to break into the market. You must be realistic about this before you decide to proceed, and if you do proceed, you must have a plan to deal with it. For instance, the loyalty in the men's razor market kept it stably dominated for years by a handful of firms—Gillette, Schick, and Bic. But that doesn't mean you can never break into these markets. You simply can't do it half-heartedly. You have to go the extra mile to get people's attention and find ways to break the distribution barriers. The founders of the Dollar Shave Club gained traction with a famously amusing video debut and a strategy of outflanking the U.S. retail distribution barrier by selling direct to consumers on the internet. Another razor company, Harry's, similarly used the direct-to-consumer route but focused on establishing differentiation via a higher-end experience.

Key Takeaways

- Understand the laws and structure of the market you are entering.
- Use the Porter Five Forces model to see if you can find profits in your target market.
- Understand how your potential customers relate to their existing brands.
- Recognize your target customer's loyalty to their current brand choice.

5.5 Does the Idea Really Fit the Entrepreneur?

Learning Objectives

1. Learn to analyze whether an opportunity suits the entrepreneur.
2. Recognize the reality of the entrepreneur's age as it relates to business opportunities.
3. Consider again if your idea is ready for the market.
4. Recognize that abandoning your idea may lead to a better one.

Business-Entrepreneur Fit

A critical function of your feasibility analysis is to ensure that your business idea fits *you* as well as it fits the market. This takes us back to our second question: "Why is your team the best team to do this?" If you've come up with a brilliant idea, but you are not the right person to do it, then you should probably not proceed. If you are the right one, then go for it. This goes beyond the question of whether you can hire the right team members. The New Entrepreneurial Dynamic is all about recruiting and outsourcing the best resources to get the job done, but it requires a fundamental business-entrepreneur fit. If, as the leader, you are not passionate about your business, it won't succeed, no matter how well qualified your team is. To put it another way, you really shouldn't try to sell pet products if you don't like animals.

There is also the question of whether you're qualified, as yet, to lead an organization into a field. While Mark Cuban did run a bar before he was old enough to legally drink, you probably shouldn't try to enter a field you aren't qualified for or allowed to be in.

Many fields, such as finance, place a great emphasis on credentials. If you want to start a bank, then it would help to have a degree in finance and some banking experience. While there are always exceptions—for example, Elon Musk's youthful determination to disrupt the banking industry with his X.com, and later PayPal, startups—it is recommended that you attack markets in which you are likely to succeed. This is particularly true when your effort will require outside investment. You need to look like you're going to succeed before most investors will support your efforts.

That doesn't mean being young is always a disadvantage. If you're 19 and want to take on the app gaming world, investors may see your youth and inexperience as an advantage in that market. In fact, having a mature and successful career can sometimes actually inhibit your attractiveness to investors. A 50-year-old launching that app game company would probably never be able to secure backing because she would be perceived as less innovative and out of touch with the core youth gaming market. More importantly, older, successful entrepreneurs are often viewed as less dedicated. They probably have some money and some income, and they aren't hungry. Investors may assume older entrepreneurs have less physical energy and stamina, so they will be less likely to stay up all night working on the project. They may also have a lot of other obligations to manage, including families and personal investments.

Business Model Transformation: When Your First Idea Isn't Quite the Thing

In the end, this process of feasibility analysis may result in a wise decision to abandon your idea. That's okay. Don't panic! Maybe you just file that one away for later, when you have the right resources, and move on. The process of analysis might also help you discover a different path. A lot of great startups begin their journey down a certain path, but when confronted with the reality of customers or production, discover that they must pivot to a different, often related, idea to capture a market.

PayPal's Peter Thiel was actually discussing replacing the U.S. dollar with electronic currency years before Bitcoin and the blockchain revolution. Reality forced him to pivot and join forces with Elon Musk to pursue a more realistic and smaller niche in the financial industry—electronic payment transfers for online auctions. That niche turned out to be worth more than $3 billion when PayPal was sold to eBay. Do such pivots occur in small businesses?

A small business can do the same thing that Musk and Thiel did. While you might be disappointed to discover that your dream of opening a new café in town is doomed because of immense customer loyalty to Joe's Diner, a lunch truck could still be a winner. It might turn out that because the lunch truck business is inherently cheap and mobile, it is also more scalable and geographically expandable. Soon you're serving several nearby towns with a fleet of trucks and ready to start selling franchises. That opportunity would never have arisen if you'd opened a traditional diner across from Joe!

Doing a solid feasibility analysis is costly and time-consuming, but it is a small investment that will allow you to avoid ideas that really aren't going to work before you invest your time and other people's money. With that information, self-honesty, and your creative nature, the tools of the New Entrepreneurial Dynamic will allow you to build a business model that will make you wealthy and happy.

Factors That Shape Feasibility

Listen to customers. You can always tell a customer—they are the ones with the money—but you can't tell them much. Don't tell them what they want; listen and hear about what they need.

Start with a small commitment, then iterate. Minimize your risk and maximize the information you gather by starting with an MVP and learn from that experience before you "go all in" with your idea.

Let your financial failures happen in the model. Use EOU and build a model that will help you determine if you have gross profits. If you do, can you scale to the point to overcome fixed costs? If not, don't proceed.

Analyze in real-time. The business environment is far too dynamic for monthly reports. You need to build a dashboard, maintain it, and listen to it.

Key Takeaways

- Be sure the opportunity fits your life and plans before proceeding.
- Never be afraid to walk away from an idea or reboot your startup.

5.6 Case Study: 121C, Inc.—The Skateboard MVP

Ryan Olliges, an aerospace engineering student at the University of Southern California, worked as the composites lead in the university's student-run Rocket Lab. Realizing that his lab threw out a significant amount of aerospace-grade carbon fiber trim scrap, he began to ponder potential reuses for the material as well as the bigger issue of carbon fiber disposal in the aerospace industry.

Ryan might have decided to build a complex, high-value product like a carbon fiber racing bicycle. Such a product would have captured a lot of revenue. However, a bicycle is a relatively complex piece of equipment with dozens of moving parts and hundreds of components. Ryan settled on the skateboard because he loved skating and the nearly flat deck of a skateboard was easy to process. Further, the additional materials required to build a complete skateboard—trucks, wheels, and bearings—were simple to obtain and integrate.

Ryan built a carbon fiber skateboard and began to take it around campus to collect feedback on the design from student riders. Skaters liked the idea of a new stronger and lighter material at a reasonable price. They also liked the idea of a board that looked entirely different than traditional wood decks. Ryan used this feedback to refine his design, moving away from a traditional surfboard style to a sleeker shape inspired by aircraft.

He also began to talk to business school professors about his plan to build a carbon fiber skateboard business. He brought the board to a professor at his school's Center for Entrepreneurial Studies because he had heard that the professor was well connected in the space industry. The professor indeed knew several companies that had literally tons of this material to dispose of. He was excited by the opportunity to solve an important environmental problem as well as by the chance to manufacture a variety of carbon fiber products in the U.S. at a significant cost advantage. While many other products would offer bigger markets, higher prices, and larger profit margins, the professor felt Ryan's skateboard would be the perfect MVP. The skateboard would be a great way to demonstrate the more significant concept of sustainably handling the material.

In fact, the entrepreneurship professor and a fellow instructor from the accounting school joined Ryan's father, Paul Olliges, in funding the new firm. Ryan named the company "121C" to commemorate an important personal achievement in building a tool to reach that temperature, a critical requirement to cure the thermoset resin in the carbon fiber composite. With his entrepreneurship professor's introductions and assistance, Ryan was able to secure supply contracts with two local spacecraft manufacturers generating carbon fiber scrap. A third major company also occasionally provided material. After an initial attempt to outsource production failed, the firm brought the deck pressing operation in-house.

The final skateboard design was designated as the "Aileron" and became the firm's first product. It launched the next summer with the support of a successful $44,000 Kickstarter campaign. The following year, 121C managed to generate more than $250,000 in skateboard sales with the Aileron.

Carbon fiber Rover skateboards.

Source: Greg Autry

A second skateboard, the "Rover," was launched the following summer, and this time the firm raised $102,000 from Kickstarter backers. Paul designed and built a new, heavier duty press for the Rover that allowed them to press multiple boards at a time. More importantly, sales eventually exceeded costs, and the firm reached a cash flow positive position. Most critically, the MVP demonstrated to potential investors and suppliers that this startup firm could deliver on its basic model of upcycling industrial waste into a profitable consumer product—something much bigger and better-funded competitors had not achieved.

Based in large part on the success with the MVP, the 121C team was able to raise more than $1 million in private funding to expand the operation and attract the attention of larger angel investors. Today the firm makes frames for drones, cylinders for snare drums, and sheets for high-end office furniture. In fact, Ryan has renamed the firm Elevated Materials and is selling off the skateboard business in order focus on these higher volume products.

Endnotes

1. Zaltman, G. (2003). *How customers think: Essential insights into the mind of the market*. Harvard Business Press.
2. Blank, S., & Dorf, B. (2012). *The startup owner's manual: The step-by-step guide for building a great company*. BookBaby.
3. Tesla maintains that their data demonstrates that vehicles operating under autopilot are safer per mile than cars driven by human beings.

CHAPTER 6

Team Building and Leadership

6.1 How to Entrepreneur

Learning Objectives

1. Recognize that some people may be predisposed to leadership or entrepreneurship.
2. Understand that anyone can learn to be a better leader or entrepreneur.
3. Recognize the skills that will enable entrepreneurial leadership.
4. Understand the styles of leadership.
5. Recognize the prevalence of networks in the startup world.
6. Learn to build a cohesive environment.

Nelson Mandela, the former dissident and eventual president of South Africa was a charismatic natural leader.

Source: https://commons.wikimedia.org/wiki/File:Nelson_Mandela-2008_(edit).jpg

Recent research suggests that leadership and management skills have a genetic component,[1] and this should not be surprising. History is full of individuals from the fourth Macedonian conqueror, Alexander the Great, to the anti-apartheid leader and South African president, Nelson

Mandela, who seem to have been born to lead. Today there is a great mystique surrounding famous natural entrepreneurs such as Richard Branson and Jack Ma.

Jack Ma

Source: Frederic Legrand - COMEO/Shutterstock.com

It's very important to realize that these naturally charismatic geniuses are in short supply and that while they can be great for rapid-growth startups, they might actually be dangerous in an organic-growth small business, where their ambitions might far exceed the organization's scope and resources. Most of the leadership skills you will require as an entrepreneur can be learned and refined.

Learning Leadership Skills

A short walk through any traditional bookstore or a brief search of the internet will reveal abundant literature on leadership. You'll also quickly discover that there is an entire industry of seminars and motivational speakers dedicated to transforming you into a successful leader. Much of this material is of questionable value, but if reading a good book or listening to an inspirational speaker makes you feel more confident and empathetic, it might not hurt.

Skill Building

Reading through the leadership literature, the following list of traits and skills are a distillation of the qualities that are truly beneficial to the entrepreneurial leader.

Honesty: This one comes first because, without honesty, all the work you do will lack credibility. Your employees, investors, vendors, and customers *must* believe that you are telling them the truth and can be trusted to do the right thing by them.

Confidence: A leader must project sincere confidence. Employees can smell fear. If you don't genuinely believe in the future of your enterprise and can't convey that faith to your team, nobody will follow you.

Communication: Communication errors plague all organizations. In a small business with little hierarchy, the communication between the leader and his team is critical. Leaders must be able to convey their vision and strategy to the team. When you discuss procedures with your direct reports, you need to be clear and concise. Just as important, an effective leader is a good listener. You must understand what your team is telling you about the business and their needs, and the team must believe that you are listening.

Delegation: Handing off responsibilities to the right people at the right time and with the right expectations is key to effective leadership. Team members want to contribute, and leaders who cannot delegate effectively have no followers. Setting realistic expectations for delegated tasks is also important. Leaders who simply "dump" on their employees or expect too much will not get far.

Inspiration: Leaders also need to inspire their teams. If you have confidence and communicate well, you can pass your vision on to a team that will carry it forward without constant oversight. If you have the right team members and they truly want to get to the same place in business as you do, your business nearly runs itself.

Drive: A leader needs to wake up each morning ready to take on the challenges of the day. If you're not driven, your team isn't driven, and the organization isn't going anywhere.

Mentoring: A great leader is also a teacher. When you mentor your employees, you make them more valuable, and in turn, they respect a boss who transfers value to them. When team members fail you, it's rarely an intentional act. A leader finds out why members failed and gets them the training or support they need to do better the next time.

Leadership Styles

Successful leaders have many different approaches or **leadership styles**. Psychologist Kurt Lewin defines three different leadership styles.

The traditional view of a leader is a king-like individual who makes decisions without consulting the team. He issues orders and expects them to be obeyed. This is **autocratic leadership**, and most individuals find this sort of leader to be demoralizing. If a leader is highly charismatic, he may succeed in compelling a team to follow his vision through the power of his personality. Autocratic leadership is effective when decisions must be made quickly, as in a crisis. Consequently, military leaders are often autocratic.

A leader who makes decisions based on input from the team is a **democratic leader**. This style works best when there is time to solicit and evaluate multiple opinions. Employees generally prefer working in democratic organizations.

Some leaders are relaxed and let employees find their own path to success. Such a leader does little more than provide the resources employees need to execute their tasks. Lewin calls this **laissez-faire leadership**. It works best in simple businesses with clear goals. Employees who are independent thinkers will have high job satisfaction under such a regime. However, democratic and laissez-faire leaders can be ineffective in a crisis or in highly competitive situations that demand swift and clear decisions.

leadership style

The manner in which the leader establishes cohesion and motivates the team to pursue organizational goals.

autocratic leadership

A leader who unilaterally makes decisions without consulting the team.

democratic leader

A leader who consults with his team before making decisions.

laissez-faire leadership

A leadership style in which the manager empowers employees to make most decisions on their own.

participative leader

A leader who establishes credibility by proving he can do his employees' work and works alongside his team.

transactional leader

A leader who is focused on minimizing the cost of transactions with clearly defined, impersonal, contractual relationships.

transformational leader

A modern leader identified by their ability to raise the performance of an organization through inspired mutual change in the organization.

Many additional leadership styles and frameworks have been proposed since Lewin. One important style is the **participative leader**, who works hand-in-hand with the team to achieve the goal. Employees usually appreciate a leader who understands their work intimately and is willing to do it. The risk here is that the leader has other responsibilities to attend to and being "just one of the guys" may cause the staff to lose respect for his authority.

The **transactional leader** approaches the management relationship like a contract. Rewards and punishments are the result of employees succeeding or failing to adhere to agreed-upon goals and measures. This impersonal style of leadership tends to reward ambitious, self-motivated employees but does not bond the team together.

James McGregor Burns introduced the concept of the **transformational leader**, and Bernard M. Bass refined it. The transformational leader strives to improve her own performance in concert with her organization. She sets clear goals and has high expectations of her staff. Her personal integrity and inspirational nature bring everyone along. A transformational leader establishes a two-way, trust-based relationship with employees. She seeks feedback from her team and has the integrity to correct her own shortcomings when they are identified. The New Entrepreneurial Dynamic favors the transformational leader because a leader who is self-aware, trusting, and capable of improvement can best adapt to and exploit changing environments.

The Elite Network

In Silicon Valley, a close-knit group of entrepreneurs nicknamed the "PayPal Mafia" has established an informal and elite network in which selected startups can grow and prosper. Those who are chosen obtain inside access to capital and priceless industry connections. Rather than making crime pay, this "mafia," whose members are the founders of PayPal, have made technological innovation and market insight pay. After selling PayPal to eBay for $1.5 billion in 2002, Elon Musk, Peter Thiel, and Max Levchin have individually gone on to found billion-dollar companies. Their firms include SpaceX, Tesla Motors, LinkedIn, Yelp, and YouTube.

Peter Thiel

Source: https://commons.wikimedia.org/wiki/File:Peter_Thiel_by_Dan_Taylor.jpg

PayPal was not the result of a single visionary CEO and founder single-handedly leading a brilliant tech startup to inevitable success. The now-ubiquitous internet payment system was the result of a merger of two small struggling firms, Musk's X.com and Thiel and Levchin's Confinity, Inc. Making a success of the combined organizations necessitated real **teamwork** with multiple members playing off one another's strengths and weaknesses. The process involved a lot of disappointment and compromise. Musk did not get the chance to completely disrupt the global banking system, which was his original aspiration. Thiel and Levchin were not able to pursue the development of security products for handheld devices. However, Musk's banking insights combined with Thiel and Levchin's security skills produced a trustworthy online money transfer system that the evolving internet economy required, and it made them all very rich.

teamwork

The combined action of a group of people, notably an organization like a business.

While you are not likely to become a billionaire, the lessons of the PayPal founders speak directly to small business success. Great teams work together to find great business models. Small business used to thrive under a single, determined leader supported by a set of homogenous employees dedicated to doing their job well. A myopic focus on excellence in execution—doing the same thing over and over, very well—was the proven formula for success in the old, static business world. Today, that same formula is a recipe for failure. Under the New Entrepreneurial Dynamic, great execution remains important, but it no longer offers the small business owner a strategic advantage. Can you think of why that is?

Building the Right Team

Professor Noam Wasserman, an expert on team founding, cautions that "nothing can bedevil a startup more than its 'people problems.'" Making the right choices as you add members to your team, particularly early on, is critical to success in any business. Wassermann advises that for a team to be highly functional, "Three Rs" must be in sync: relationships, roles, and rewards.

While entrepreneurs are most comfortable building their team out of close friends or family members, it is unlikely that the people you know best are the best ones for the job. Further, even if your friends are extremely talented and hardworking, relationship-based firms often lack **diversity**. Management researchers have long known that heterogeneous teams composed of people with a broad range of life and work experience outperform those composed of very similar individuals. One simple reason is that your friends' experiences are very likely similar, and their **social networks** overlap with yours, offering a limited number of redundant connections. Professor Wasserman's research suggests that teams built of past coworkers perform best. In such a situation, the founder has a real-world understanding of the team members' capabilities and work habits without being so close that their experiences and networks are too similar.

Roles are the defined areas of responsibility that a person takes on in the organization and are typically reflected in their title. Startups and small businesses require a smaller team to take on a wide array of challenges. These organizations function best when team members are versatile **generalists** who "wear several hats." If the organization grows in scale, it can benefit from the efficiency of **specialists** who excel at particular tasks.

Rewards are the value that team members extract from their involvement in the business. These include immediate monetary rewards like salary and bonuses as well as promises of future financial returns from ownership shares or options. (Splitting ownership is a particularly tricky dilemma to be discussed later.) Rewards may also include fewer tangible benefits such as lifestyle and flexible hours. There is the "cool factor" of being involved in an attractive new industry or of just being part of a startup at a time when entrepreneurship is hot.

Cohesion and Team Building

Successful leaders often establish group **cohesion** indirectly by generating a constructive environment in which their team feels more homogenous than it is. When people share personal interests and goals, they develop a "sameness" that can help them excel in other areas. For instance, the PayPal Mafia discovered that they all loved science fiction (*Star Wars*, not *Star Trek*), played video games, and shared a passion for establishing a digital currency. Elon Musk made a point of supporting these interests in the team and engendering this "sameness." This sense of shared identity helped unite a team of strong egos and keep them on track toward their common goal of creating a practical internet payment system. Can you use a similar technique to bring your team together?

Here are some suggestions of places to look for and build commonality among your team members based on their own inclinations.

1. **Are they interested in watching sports?** Take the team out for an evening at a local ballpark. Find a minor-league team to get the group interested in to avoid their lifetime loyalties to popular big-name teams (every firm has one diehard Cubs fan). Another option is to create a fantasy league or a (low-value) betting pool on the season.
2. **Do they like to play sports?** Establish a softball team or a bowling league team. Engage the nonplayers as fans and find ways for them to participate, such as designing the shirts and bringing the food.

diversity

The characteristic of heterogeneous organizations; having a variety of team members based on skill, experience, and demographics.

social networks

The human connections that an individual brings to an organization, composed of friends, family members, and business associates that they regularly interact with. It may also be judged by how well it is connected to other important networks.

roles

The specific functions that an individual performs in an organization.

generalist

An individual who is capable of performing a wide variety of tasks. The opposite of specialist.

specialist

An individual who is an expert in one narrow area or endeavor and not skilled in a variety of tasks. The opposite of generalist.

rewards

Incentives offered to employees to increase their performance.

cohesion

Holding together. A group is cohesive if it maintains its identity as a team through trials and tribulations.

3. **Do they appreciate good food?** How about bringing in lunch or dinner one day a week from a different local eatery and reviewing it together. Make it more than a meal; make it an event. After sampling everything, pull out your phones and post your reviews on Yelp.
4. **Do they play games?** Set up a competitive video game league.
5. **Movies?** Schedule a movie night once a month.

These are just ideas. Almost any small team can find some area of mutual interest, and as a leader, your job is to engage the "strays" with the activities. This isn't always as easy as it seems. People are busy and have other serious commitments in life beyond work. Make sure you understand everyone's reality. Someone who has to care for their sick mom at home may participate less. However, partners or employees who obviously *do not want* to engage with the team outside of simply doing their daily job for pay are not ideal for a small business. They see nothing special in your business, and they are not going to put in the extra time or effort when a real crisis arrives. Get them out of your organization.

Some things will almost surely break down team cohesion. Religion and politics are famous for fracturing families, friendships, and teams. You may have strong opinions on these topics yourself, and unless you are specifically recruiting people based on their religion or politics—which is often illegal discrimination—you are likely to have team members with conflicting personal beliefs. To create unity, it is crucial that you respect everyone's points of view and make it clear that you expect the same from all your team members. While your religion and your political views are valuable tools in guiding your choices and they will be positively reflected in the ethics of your organization, you should scrupulously avoid introducing the particulars of any belief system or political party into the work environment.

Team building rarely goes smoothly. When you get frustrated by the process, recall the adage that says, "Rome wasn't built in a day." The perfect team isn't going to materialize in your first week, and you are not going to tie it together with some pop team-building exercise like building a bridge out of marshmallows and toothpicks. Leadership, like most other tasks in a small business, requires consistent hard work.

Key Takeaways

- You and your startup will be stronger if you call on others to build it.
- Being a leader requires being part of a team.
- Find shared values and passions on which to build your team.
- Always be networking and stay open to becoming part of a band rather than a soloist.
- Avoid introducing contentious issues into your team environment.

6.2 The Organizational Chart

Learning Objectives

1. Understand the organizational chart.
2. Understand traditional positions and titles.
3. Understand that traditional titles may not fit entrepreneurial endeavors.
4. Recognize that startups need multifunctional team members.
5. Recognize that investors want fully committed team members.

Structure

Businesses are organizations and, by definition, must have some structure. In large organizations, this means formal titles and job descriptions that carefully define individual roles and responsibilities. In small firms, founders who are friends are sometimes reluctant to establish any formal roles. However, lacking hierarchy or defined responsibilities, the foundation of your company will be too unsteady to support even minimal growth. The best **organizational chart** or "org chart" leverages the strengths of your team. It is a contract that states who is responsible for what and the title they get to put on their resume, in as formal or informal a structure as the team needs and desires.

organizational chart

The nature of power relationships and personal interactions within an organization such as a business.

FIGURE 6.1 NASA Headquarters
A large organization has very formal titles and reporting structures.

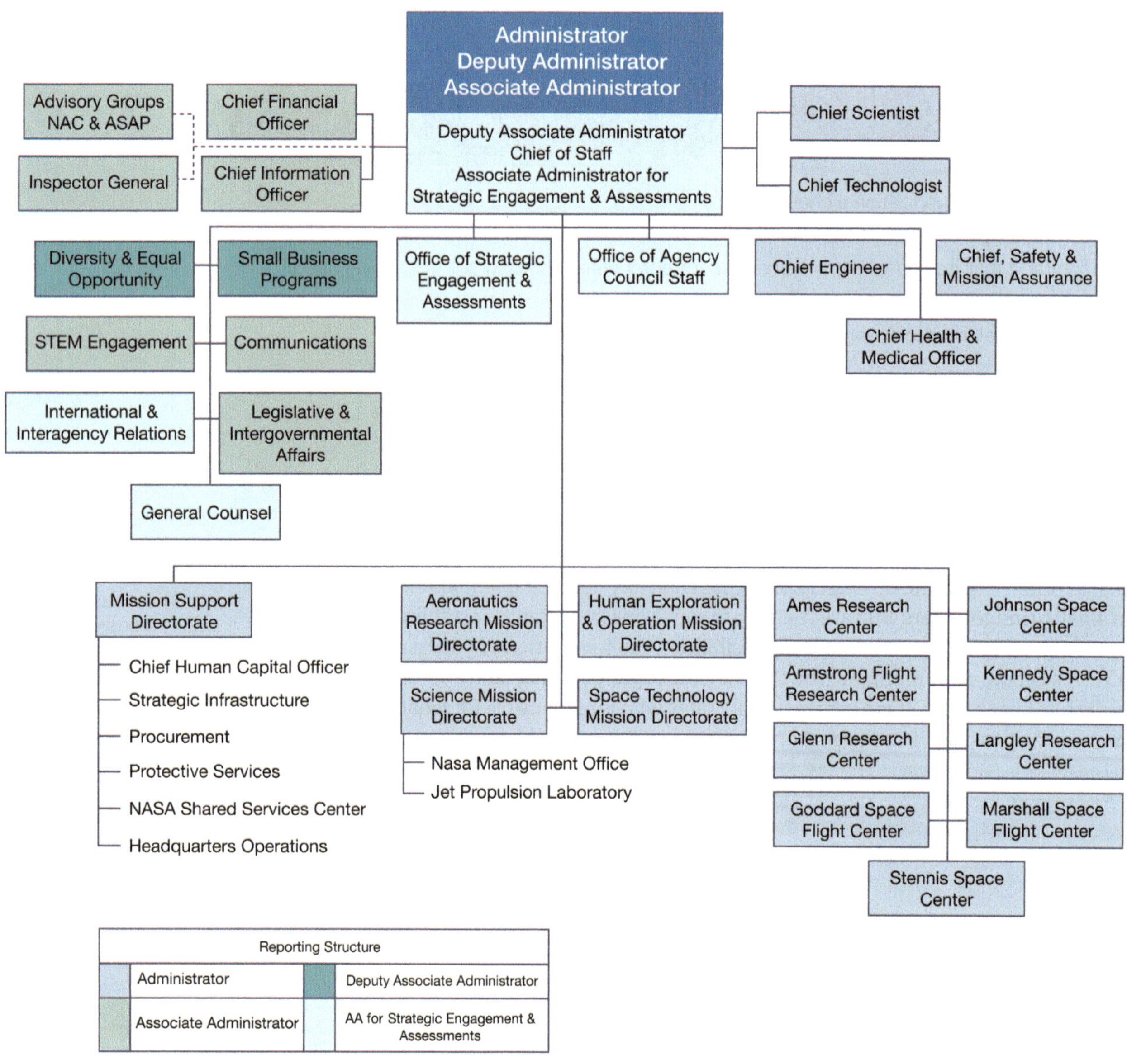

Source: NASA

External contingencies, including governmental agencies and banks, will require you to fill specific titles, including president and secretary, if your business is a corporation. Your customers or vendors will expect to find traditional titles like sales director or purchasing director for them to interface with as well. While small businesses aren't encouraged to adopt all these titles, the "C-Suite" positions that head up a traditional company are listed in Figure 6.2.

FIGURE 6.2 Sample Small Business Org Chart
A smaller organization has a simple reporting structure and is more flexible.

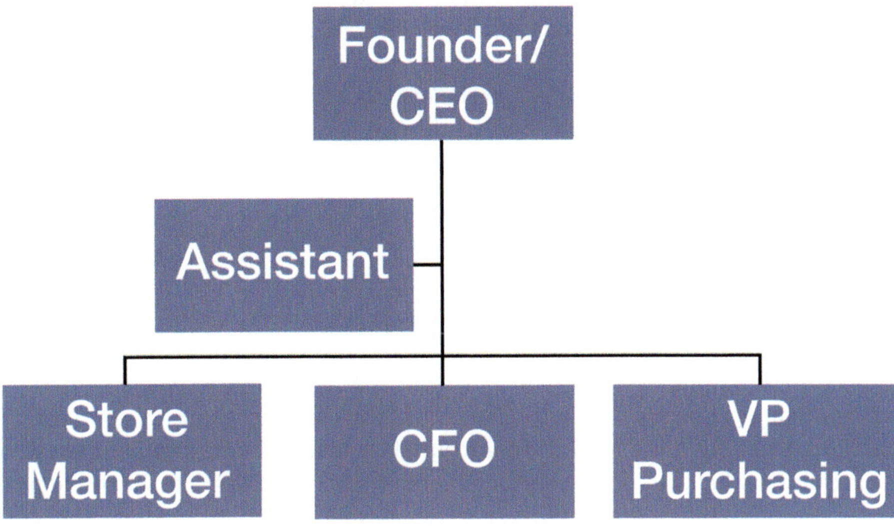

Source: Greg Autry

Traditional Positions and Titles

1. **Founder or CEO.** The founder or CEO is ultimately responsible for the startup. Whether or not the venture takes off is due to the efforts of this individual who is calling the shots and setting the course for the company. This is your Elon Musk or Steve Jobs: straight innovator and leader.
2. **Chief Technology Officer.** What is a startup without a product? This position creates and maintains products for the startup, whether it be the service/merchandise itself, the company domain, or some other innovative gizmo. Decisions requiring expertise and technical knowledge pass by this person's desk. Think Bill Gates or Mark Carges: techy.
3. **Chief Financial Officer.** This is the "money person" who takes care of the books, manages margins, and balances the infamous debits and credits. When it comes to the bottom line, this is the main person. Indra Nooyi was once Pepsi's CFO before her meticulous nature led to her promotion to CEO.
4. **Chief Marketing Officer.** One of the biggest concerns with new companies is user acquisition, which is the domain of the CMO. Managing the face of the company, advertising, and user development all on a lean budget is the duty of the CMO. Beth Comstock and Nikesh Arora are two of the most recognizable names of folks responsible for bringing a well-defined product campaign to market.

Many naïve entrepreneurs attempt to emulate the large firm approach to corporate structure, believing they are following in the footsteps of the great business legends. They will define all sorts of roles more suited to a larger business and make their organization more complex than is necessary or helpful. A traditional title can also be limiting; it says as much about *what you don't do* as what you do. If your business card says "CFO," customers simply will not expect you to be able to sell your product or to support them with technical issues.

In reality, your business needs someone who makes a product, someone who sells a product, and often an individual to make this process flow. The New Entrepreneurial Dynamic takes the business jargon out of team positions. Feel free to be creative and even have a bit of fun with your small business titles. For example, "leader," "designer," "hacker," and "hustler" are great titles. The leader's role is obvious. The designer handles product or service development and customer-facing issues. The hacker is a problem solver who makes the backend of things work, and the hustler searches for new customers and markets.

Designing the Dynamic Team

The problem with adopting corporate formality is that you can't move quickly—you can't be nimble. Formal titles don't play in the New Entrepreneurial Dynamic. More important than what team members are called is what they do. In very small firms, traditional titles actually sound pretty silly to sophisticated people: picture Marge White, a young entrepreneurial baker operating a food trolley. Marge has boldly titled herself chief executive officer. Imagine her going around saying, "I'm the CEO of Marge's Muffin Cart." If you chuckled at how ridiculously pretentious that is, you're not alone. "The Muffin Maven" would be way cooler and generate smiles rather than smirks.

In the early days, most firms require just three roles:

1. Designing your product or service
2. Building the product or delivering the service
3. Getting customers or users to buy

Depending on the scale of your initial rollout, there may be more than one person in each role. In most cases, a firm probably has multiple people building the product or delivering the service, and they may have more than one salesperson as well.

Virtualizing Positions

Beyond the roles listed just listed, everything else can be farmed out. The New Entrepreneurial Dynamic firm simply doesn't require a CFO, a chief counsel, or a VP of human resources; you can outsource accounting, legal, and HR. For a small business, outside professionals are the only thing that makes sense. For a startup with growth expectations, filing those roles with the perfect individual can wait until you have sufficient work to keep these specialists busy. You might even farm out the sales and manufacturing. In many modern small businesses, the only core roles are product design and marketing.

Switch-Hitting

Stepping away from the security of a steady job and out on the limb of small business can be terrifying. So, many entrepreneurs continue to work a day job and launch their business as a side passion. This approach provides the business founder with income stability and benefits like health insurance while they develop their product and recruit customers.

Switch-hitting may seem like the ideal choice for getting a new business off the ground, but having two jobs and going between them can be incredibly hard to do well. This scenario also consumes a lot of time, and it offers a real challenge to anyone with a family or who wants to maintain a social life.

As noted in Chapter 3, failure to commit fully to your business by "burning your boats" may cause it to remain underdeveloped and other people sense that. Recruiting great employees to work on your dream can be difficult if you aren't willing to totally commit to it yourself. Investors are also highly skeptical of part-time entrepreneurs.

Utility Players

A startup or small business often does not have the luxury of building a full-fledged team of expert specialists. Ideal team members can pitch, catch, and field the variety of tasks that arise daily in a small business. When you recruit, look deeply into the experiences of your candidates and see who has demonstrated the versatility and willingness to handle a number of roles. Individuals who are obsessed with their qualifications and see themselves as privileged professionals probably won't be willing to get their hands dirty or take on dull or mundane tasks. These people are better off in a corporate job, and you should avoid them no matter how smart or credentialed they seem to be.

In the New Entrepreneurial Dynamic, nothing beats adaptability and the willingness to work. Stock up on utility players and set the expectation within your organization that all positions are subject to change. Do not let anyone feel entitled to their position. They earn it each day and the moment having them in a particular slot is not optimal for the future of the organization, things must change. That isn't to suggest that loyalty isn't important, but rather to be clear with everyone that you aren't going to sacrifice everyone else simply to keep one team member's ego unbruised.

Key Takeaways

- Stay dynamic. Consider your team as flexible as any other part of the business.
- Consider that a title is a contract for performance of a job.
- Don't give important titles to individuals who won't grow to fill those important jobs.
- Never use a title to make yourself appear important.

6.3 Slicing the Pie and Valuing Startup Inputs

Learning Objectives

1. Understand that an equity split should be a formalized and fair process of negotiation.
2. Understand the potentially disastrous consequences of an informal or ambiguous agreement on equity.
3. Understand that a quantitative model can be developed to value the individual inputs to a company.
4. Understand equity is in exchange for uncompensated value delivered by individuals to the firm.
5. Recognize that some individuals bring skills or networks that make their time more valuable than others.

The Equity Split

equity split

The division of shares of ownership of a company.

equity

Firm ownership usually represented by stock shares.

Establishing the correct division of ownership, or the **equity split**, is a complex calculation that many would-be business partners simply won't address directly. But when ownership is not discussed, misperceptions begin to build among the founding team as to what their fair share should be. Often, you'll find that if you add up the expectations a group of founders have about their individual percentage ownership, you get something like 150 percent total. If this problem is not dealt with honestly and openly, arguments and even lawsuits are sure to follow. The more successful the firm becomes, the more dissatisfied the participants may be. The tragic story of the Facebook **equity** split and the ensuing lawsuits detailed in the film *The Social Network* should stand as an object lesson to every entrepreneur.

Deciding the equity split should be a transparent process.

Source: © Shutterstock, Inc.

The simplest way to determine the value of each individual's input is to identify the launch and growth activities and who contributes to them. These activities then should be evaluated on their weight of impact to success. For instance, in a highly technical product, the inventor, who develops the fundamental value behind the product, is likely to be more important to the firm's eventual success than the co-founder, who manages marketing. It's probably pretty easy to find a competent marketing person and relatively hard to find a brilliant engineer. On the other hand, if you're working on a branded fashion line, the marketing genius behind the product positioning might actually be more important than the clothing designer. In these cases, everyone probably intuitively understands the relative value of these contributions, but if they are not openly addressed, the situation will eventually become awkward.

It can be very attractive and far too easy to simply divide equity evenly in the spirit of friendship in the "Three Musketeers" model of equity formation. However, when the inputs in value and time are imbalanced, the equity distribution inequality will begin to gnaw on those who got the short end out of the deal. In turn, they are likely to contribute less effort to the firm, and this costs everyone money in the long run.

Another reason to consider doing the due diligence on the equity split is that it serves as a signal to outsiders about the seriousness of your firm. Research by Noam Wasserman and Thomas Hellman[2] suggests that firms that chose simple equal equity splits are less attractive to investors. This may be because taking a shortcut around the ownership conversation is an indication that the team members are unable to have an honest conversation about important issues or are simply unrealistic about how equity is divided.

Establishing a mutually acceptable equity division from the start is clearly critical for entrepreneurs. So how exactly do you do that? Is it just a matter of sitting down and arguing with each other?

Entrepreneurs must take the most documented and systematic approach possible in preparing for equity divisions. Using data helps avoid emotional discussions, which are nonproductive. One method of providing rigor to equity division is a simple, four-step process that has been successfully applied to startups.

Take the example of Superior Casers. This startup plans to make unique custom covers for phones and tablets. Superior was founded by four students from a small business management class: Young, Sally, Dylan, and Loc. The four founders are trying to determine how to divide up the stock in their company. The amount of actual cash that each member puts in is easy to determine, but the intangible assets are less clear.

Step One: Identify the Most Important Value Creating Activities

Most founders can identify a handful of critical activities that create value in their business. Each member of Superior Cases submits a list of high-level activities they think are critical to the startup, and then together they reduce the list to four simple factors:

1. **Product Design:** Who came up with the initial ideas and will design the merchandise?
2. **Unpaid Labor:** Who will do the actual work before it is possible to pay anyone for their time?
3. **Personal Networks:** Who has access to suppliers, investors, and retailers the firm will need to succeed?
4. **Marketing and Sales:** Who is going to establish a brand that will attract customers and resellers?

Four major activities are a reasonable count for a very simple business. You might find you need six or eight for your startup. Avoid going much over eight because the process becomes unwieldy, and some of your activities will surely overlap each other, leading to confusion.

Step Two: Value Those Activities

The next step is deciding how *relatively* important each of these activities is. Clearly, the cases must be designed before anything else can happen, and they need to be great, or nobody is going to buy them. So the team agrees that product design is the most critical function and sets that at 40 percent of the company's value. The team also concurs that the people working for free while the startup is growing are critical and set it at 25 percent. Marketing is also determined to be 25 percent. Finally, some team members bring valuable relationships to the firm and can connect the company with suppliers, customers, and investors. Those personal networks are valued at 10 percent.

So, we now have the following functions and values:

- Product Design: 40 percent
- Unpaid Labor: 25 percent
- Marketing: 25 percent
- Personal Networks: 10 percent

Total: 100 percent (It's important to verify these add to 100 percent.)

Step Three: Rate Each Person's Contribution to Each Activity

Step three is deciding how much each individual contributes to each of the activities that have been defined. The Superior Case team started by asking each member to rank their value in each activity on a scale of 0-5, where a 0 indicates they provide no value and a 5 that they are completely indispensable in this area.

At Superior, Young knows he has designed a unique electronics case and has given himself a 5, and everyone agreed. He also believes he will be doing most of the unpaid labor of production and logistics, so he gave himself a 4. He has a strong set of networks, including investors and a family connection with a Korean firm that operates a factory in Shenzhen, China, where the cases will be made. Young, therefore, gives himself a 5 under personal networks. Young does not intend to get involved in branding or sales, so he gives himself 0 there. In this case, the partners all agree with his ratings.

Sally helps with product design and suggests she be given a 3, but the team politely disagrees that her contribution is that strong, and they settle on 2. She proposes 2 for the labor and 4 for networks as she is well connected in the retail sales channel for mobile accessories. She will be handling the major branding, marketing, and sales work and gives herself a 5 in that activity. Everyone agrees on these points.

Dylan and Loc similarly propose their contributions, and the team makes consensus adjustments. Finally, we are ready to calculate everyone's relative contributions.

Step Four: Calculate Each Person's Relative Contribution

In Figure 6.3, you will see a row for each of the Superior Case team members.

FIGURE 6.3 Potential Equity Split
Example of potential equity split for Superior Case.

	Contribution	Product		Unpaid		Personal		Customer		Weighted	
Team Member	Criteria	Design	weight	Labor	weight	Networks	weight	Relations	weight	Total	Equity %
	Criteria Weighting	40%		25%		10%		25%		100%	
Young	(0–5 contribution)	5	2	4	1	5	0.5	0	0	3.500	42%
Sally	(0–5 contribution)	2	0.8	2	0.5	4	0.4	5	1.25	2.950	35%
Dylan	(0–5 contribution)	0	0	3	0.75	3	0.3	0	0	1.050	13%
Loc	(0–5 contribution)	0	0	3	0.75	1	0.1	0	0	0.850	10%
									Total	8.350	100%

There is a column for each value-adding activity: product design, unpaid labor, personal networks, and customer relations. Each of those columns is followed by a "weight" column, which simply multiplies the number in the activity column (Young's 5 in product design) by the weight for that category (40 percent) and displays the result (5 × 0.4 equals 2 in this case). All of the weighted columns are totaled for each team member, and the results are 3.5 for Young, 2.95 for Sally, 1.050 for Dylan, and 0.850 for Loc. The total of all the columns is 8.350. Dividing each of the team members' weighted total by this value provides an equity percentage out of 100.

The final results suggest Young gets 42 percent of Superior, Sally 35 percent, Dylan 13 percent, and Loc 10 percent. The members reviewed this breakdown, and all agreed. With this done, actual stock can be issued in proportion to the ownership percentages. The Superior Case team took this to their attorney, who issued certificates for 100,000 shares of stock. Young received 42,000 shares, Sally 35,000, Dylan 13,000, and Loc 10,000.

Dynamic Equity Adjustment

The essence of the New Entrepreneurial Dynamic is change and adaptation. That applies to equity splits as well. Actual contributions from individuals, as well as their personal perceptions of their contributions, and the contributions others make, change over time. It's critical for the team to have continuing discussions about compensation and equity to make sure they remain in alignment. When equity, pay, and contributions get out of alignment, bad feelings arise. Companies should establish regular meetings, every year or so, to review and adjust the ownership to reflect reality. During the first few years, they might want to do that even more often.

At Superior, Sally's mom became very ill, and Sally had to cut back her contributions to the firm during some critical months in year two. Loc stepped up and took over a lot of Sally's work during this period. As the startup didn't have the cash flow to pay him for this time, the team agreed to award him some additional shares for his effort. Loc was pleased by the recognition, and the quality of his work increased.

Whenever new shares are issued, everyone's percentages drop in proportion, but the team did not reduce Sally's shares because of her absence. That would have been a reasonable topic of conversation had it bothered the other members. Upon her return to full-time work, Sally made an extra effort to make up for her absence because she was aware of the graciousness of her fellow team members in this decision.

Whose Intellectual Property Is It?

Intellectual property (IP), the valuable ideas that a company uses to gain competitive advantage, can be even trickier to slice up than equity. Do these patents, trade secrets, copyrights, and trademarks belong to the company and are thus included in the equity, or does the individual who created the idea hold the rights? What factors might influence how you decide?

intellectual property (IP)

The valuable ideas a company uses to gain competitive advantage that may be protected as patents, copyrights, and trade secrets.

If you were the sole genius behind a patentable idea and developed it entirely on your own, you may choose to hold the IP in your name individually and license it to the company. If the idea was developed with resources paid for by the firm, then the company and its stockholders have an interest in it. If you're seeking investment in your firm, remember that investors will view the patent as a particularly important part of the firm's value. If you add your patent or patentable idea to the firm, be sure you are adequately compensated.

In the circumstance where others inside or outside of the firm contribute to the development of a basic idea into a patentable device or process, the situation can be more complex. Consider the debacle at Snapchat, where three friends discussed their idea for an awesome app and toyed with it, but only two ended up launching the now ubiquitous app and doing all the hard work. Reggie Brown, the third "founder," ended up suing Evan Spiegel and Bobby Murphy for his third stake in the multi-billion-dollar startup. If anyone conceivably contributed to your IP, you need to have an agreement with them that specifies what, if anything, they are going to receive. If you've got a valuable idea, it is important that you consult a lawyer.

Such problems are endemic to successful companies, large and small. A failure to deal with things correctly upfront can result in painful conversations later. Many an entrepreneur has found themselves in court fighting with a former partner, employee, friend, or family member over their claims of contributions to the firm's initial ideas.

Key Takeaways

- Take the time to make the equity split fair.
- Establish a model that accurately quantifies the value of founder's contributions.
- Understand that equity split can be a dynamic process.
- Be clear from the start about who developed the intellectual property behind your product.
- If someone outside the founding team contributes to your business be sure their relationship and contribution is clearly defined.
- It is better to engage a lawyer to set things up correctly than to hire several to argue over it later.

6.4 Evolving Roles as Your Business Matures

Learning Objectives

1. Understand that as firms grow their leadership needs to change.
2. Learn to build a company culture that will last.
3. Recognize organizational inertia.
4. Understand the importance of recruiting in building firm culture.
5. Appreciate the value of diversity to firm performance and growth.
6. Learn to set clear expectations of employees and be prepared for problems.
7. Learn to handle terminations with grace.

The Challenges of Growth

lean venture

A startup that minimizes investment in capital and human resources and maximizes flexibility in the allocation of these, aka "lean startup."

It would be a little shocking if Mark Zuckerberg was still writing code for Facebook websites or apps. With more resources come more flexibility, and it is important to keep an eye on the future so that when flexibility allows movement, a company can adapt and properly fill its new capacity. For example, in a nice traditional **lean venture**, the founder will probably be functioning as the CEO/CFO/CTO as well as doing sales, marketing, and perhaps a handful of other jobs. A good team has members who can address any number of challenges on any given day and are open and willing to work under a job title, unconstrained by antiquated expectations and practices.

Mark Zuckerberg

Source: Frederic Legrand - COMEO/Shutterstock.com

The most important lesson to learn, though, is that your company is a business with employees who ought to help the business grow. If a cofounder or employee was instrumental in the ideation or product development phase but no longer serves a purpose in the growth of the sales phase, compensate them for their work and let them go. This may seem harsh, but what is the purpose of keeping a developer who can do nothing but prototype if there is nothing left to prototype? As the company grows, its needs will evolve, and you and the company should make sure every person on board is serving a purpose. Discarded early employees and founders may find themselves wealthy from increases in their stock holdings, without putting in any additional work.

Life Cycle of a Growth Business

A startup does not simply become Facebook overnight, and Facebook does not simply stay Facebook perpetually. The average company lasts eighteen years in today's market conditions, which means that if it is average, Facebook will only be in business until 2022. However, if Mark Zuckerberg is the innovator that he appears to be, Facebook will continuously evolve and avoid this expiration date.

Jack Ma, the founder of Alibaba, has famously stated that he has designed his firm to last for 100 years. It's been around for a couple of decades already, and to persist, it has had to transform its model several times. Can your small business do the same?

The New Entrepreneurial Dynamic acknowledges that businesses must change over time to survive.

Culture Change and Inertia

Every company has an **organizational culture**, and the culture of a business is an incredibly important factor in its success. Most importantly, in light of the New Entrepreneurial Dynamic, your company culture should be purposefully established upfront because it is difficult to change.

organizational culture

The beliefs and behaviors that define interactions within an organization and who the organization appears to and engages with outside entities.

Dozens of models of organizational culture that divide organizations into four, five, or more types. A useful framework from professors Kim S. Cameron and Robert E. Quinn at the University of Michigan's Ross Business School places businesses in a two-axis matrix with four quadrants.[3]

FIGURE 6.4 Competing Values Framework

Flexibility and Discretion

Internal Focus and Integration

CLAN

ADHOCRACY

HIERARCHY

MARKET

External Focus and Differentiation

Stability and Control

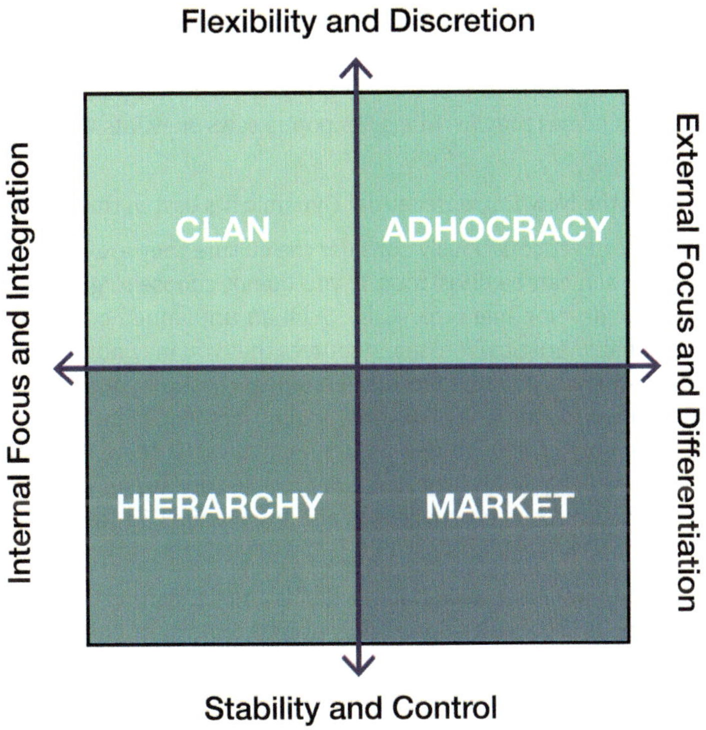

Source: Cameron, Kim S., and Robert E. Quinn. Diagnosing and changing organizational culture: Based on the competing values framework. John Wiley & Sons, 2011.

In this Competing Values Framework (Figure 6.4), firms are evaluated based on their organizational flexibility and whether their culture is internally or externally focused. The more flexible an organization, the higher on the vertical axis it is placed. Conservative organizations that seek stability are lower on this axis.

Organizations that develop and maintain their unique cultures internally and focus on their own attributes are mapped on the left side of the horizontal axis. Those firms that actively incorporate external influences into their culture and are highly engaged in interacting with their market and competitors are placed to the right. Together the two axes divide organizations into four quadrants: Hierarchy, Market, Adhocracy, and Clan.

Hierarchy Culture

A culture with strongly defined roles and top-down management structure. Decisions are made in an autocratic manner.

Market Culture

A closely controlled organizational culture that is focused on capturing market share.

Clan Culture

A collaborative culture based on shared values and experiences. Leaders adopt a mentoring style. Feedback is seriously considered, and individuals are very loyal to the group.

Adhocracy Culture

An extremely flexible company culture and leadership style. Such organizations are externally focused, often on a temporary goal.

The **Hierarchy Culture** is internally focused and control oriented. It is a very traditional business culture, best suited to large firms that focus on consistent delivery and avoid spontaneous innovation. Any changes in this organization come from the top. Leaders are authoritarian and are not looking for input from employees or customers. Workers on the front lines, interacting with customers, have no autonomy. This culture is great for the military, but in today's kinetic business world, it is very difficult for firms to survive with this traditional and nonflexible model. This culture is completely incompatible with the New Entrepreneurial Dynamic.

The **Market Culture** is focused externally on its customers and maintains stability and control. These firms are results-driven, very demanding, and even harsh toward their staff. Taking a dominant market position or exiting that market is a typical strategy. Large corporations looking for efficiencies in their transactions adopt this culture. Its lack of dynamism makes it less compatible with the needs of most small businesses that must compete on adaptability, not scale efficiencies.

In a **Clan Culture**, the team collaborates to excel. Their cohesion comes from shared values and goals. The opinions of employees, customers, and vendors are all considered. Employees are empowered and loyalty is earned. Leaders assume a mentoring role to develop the skills of their teams. The clan culture is the natural form adopted by small, family-run businesses.

The **Adhocracy Culture** is externally focused on its goal and very flexible. This organization is dynamic, special purpose, and even temporary in its very nature. In the Hollywood entertainment industry, film companies are formed just for the purpose of making a single movie. Adhocracy works great for small businesses that do things like popup sales or events where each one is unique and specialized.

Where do you think the New Entrepreneurial Dynamic fits best in this framework?

Many entrepreneurs never consciously consider the culture they are building and just sort of "get to work." This approach can be disastrous. If you do not choose to guide the culture of your company, your team will develop one organically. Such an unplanned cultural development will come with quirks and characteristics from many sources that you may not find desirable. From the outset, sit down and truly think about what sort of culture is best for you, your company, and your business model. In addition to thinking about the current moment, think about where your company is going and what sort of culture will be required to get it there. Will you take a Zappos approach where everyone is equal and the company focuses on fun and personality, or will you take a SpaceX approach and focus on challenges and innovation? There is no right answer, but there is often a wrong one.

It is very important to understand that it is difficult and dangerous to try to switch organizational cultures. Throughout this book, you are encouraged to *pivot* or change the aspects of your business that aren't working well. However, while moving to a Plan B can be attractive, research suggests that keeping a bad culture intact is less risky than switching to a good one. So, whatever culture you adopt in the beginning is likely to endure for the rest of your corporate career. Choose wisely.

Recruiting

Recruiting top-tier talent for a small business that isn't going to take over the world or for a startup that is little more than an idea is difficult. Not having money, a gorgeous corporate campus, or the cache of a name like "Google" can make it seem nearly impossible. However, as with most things, small businesses actually have some special powers. Employees are not just looking for money or prestigious employers. They also care about things like their families, location, lifestyles, and personal passions.

If you can't compete on pay and spending, you can compete on things like flexibility, integrity, and compassion. You may not be headquartered in the hustle and bustle of New York or Shanghai, but the pace and livability of a small town or the suburbs might be exactly what a lot of great employees are looking for. Finally, you'd be surprised how many good workers have simply been "burned out" or "worked over" by multinational corporations. They've had enough of the rat race and feeling as though all their hard work is lost in a giant, soulless machine. They'd love to work in a small business where they can see their effort actually making a difference and adding value to the lives of real customers.

This isn't to say you want to hire corporate cast-offs or rejects. You still want the A players, but you want the ones who can think differently. Make sure you do your due diligence in the hiring process. Check the references; spend the time to get to know them. Make sure they know their stuff and they truly appreciate what your firm offers. Additionally, "A-hires" bring in "A-hires"—each recruit counts twice because the better the employees you bring in, the better employees you will attract. Never settle, always reach, and make sure every individual brings the greatest value possible to your venture.

Homogeneity versus Diversity in Management

Many leaders talk about the importance of drawing from a multidisciplinary range of management fields to increase diversity. While diversity and breadth of knowledge can be useful, especially when it comes to specialization and adaptation, the most important quality for a startup's management team is to have one common passion and similar personality. Embarking on a startup venture will be the wildest ride of your life, with ups and downs, and you need to know that through it all, you can count on the person next to you to hold a similar goal and stick with it through thick and thin.

Networking in the Online and the Real Worlds

Networking may be the single most important skill for any small businessperson. In an effort to help you remember others and get to know others, maintain a positive online image; be open to connecting via social networking in both your business profile and personally. Although the social media marketplace is dynamic, LinkedIn and Facebook are great general sources for finding employees.

In most cases, there is a lot of online networking you can do for free. Your only cost is the value of your time. However, if you don't have a lot of time, paying to play can get your job listing out in front of a lot of eyes quickly. Websites such as Monster.com and Indeed specialize in this. You can find contract workers in places like Upwork. These services let you target engineers, salespeople, marketing experts, or whatever specialists you might need.

The group's founders of Capital Cities met via Craigslist.

Source: https://commons.wikimedia.org/wiki/File:Capital_Cities_rockin'_the_'hoo!.jpg

Ryan Merchant and Sebu Simonian, founders of the pop band Capital Cities, met on Craigslist when Sebu posted an ad offering production services. If Merchant had not had the courage to connect with a stranger, they would never have made their 2013 Billboard Hot 100 hit song, "Safe and Sound." That success produced a lot of income and a great deal of fun! The moral of that story is that in order to have the perfect network, you merely need to be outgoing and receptive to any opportunity or relationship that presents itself.

With all our focus on our virtual networks, it remains important not to overlook the real world. The best connections still happen there. Attend the regular conferences for your industry. Even if your firm is too small to set up a booth at the trade show, you will meet people in the halls and at the lunch tables. Don't limit the search to traditional events either. If you're on vacation or attending a bar mitzvah, wedding, or even a funeral, make a point of meeting people and finding out what they do. They could very well turn out to be your future team members, or they may help you find the perfect recruits. Additionally, never be afraid to reach out to friends, family, or acquaintances for introductions. When it comes to networking, just remember that "one never knows."

Stealing Talent from Competitors

Often, the most obvious pool of talent can be found at your competition. If you run Sandra's Taco Stand and need workers who can cook, serve food, and run a cash register, then Bill's Burger Joint across the street would seem like the perfect recruiting ground. If there are problems with the culture at Bill's—maybe everyone hates the night manager—then bringing them over to your team should be easy! However, if the competition is doing well by their employees, you'll find it a lot harder to recruit them. In those cases, you might have to pay more, and that risks creating a bidding war that could needlessly drive up labor costs for both your firms.

Being too aggressive about this sort of thing can also damage your reputation in your local business community or within your industry. You never know when you might want Bill's help. He might make an introduction for you to a trusted vendor. The two of you might need to work together to fight a new city parking law that makes it hard for customers to get to your businesses or combat a signage ordinance that makes it hard for people to find you.

These same general ideas apply whether your business is fast food or technology. If you are in the technology field, an important concern might be what intellectual property they might bring from your competitor. While having access to the inner secrets of your archrivals might seem great, it is a very real possibility that your new employee could be constrained from working on certain things by his previous employment contract or a noncompete agreement he may have signed. Even if he inadvertently duplicates some process or design from his previous employer, you may find that you're facing a lawsuit over IP theft. Be very careful with this. Discuss it with any potential new hires and be sure they understand that your organization operates ethically and openly.

Another important consideration is the process of integrating outsiders into your firm and incorporating them into your unique company culture. Your new hires are used to operating in a somewhat different business environment and leadership style. The success of their assimilation will depend on how different your management style and other cultural aspects are from your competitors. Think about that and realize that if the company they came from is significantly different, the transition will take longer, and you will need to be more involved. Make a point of getting all your employees engaged in the process of greeting and integrating new team members. Ask them to include new hires in both work projects and work-related social activities. Consider bringing new hires to your home or out to dinner with your family so they know you really care about them personally.

Management Competencies

Zappos, the online shoe store, is famous for having all newly hired executives learn by working in their phone centers first because it is integral to their business. Pulse, a California startup, starts all prospective employees in short trials as low-level office workers. They use these trials to test the candidates' team interaction and cultural fit, which is far more valuable information than anything you can find on a resume.

Finding efficient managers with passion is not easy. Since you will be operating on a tight budget, finding a manager who has a knack for squeezing every last penny out of an office budget or optimizing manufacturing supply chains allows for you to get the biggest bang for your buck. Last, being a manager for Marge's Muffin Cart or even XYZ tech startup will be less alluring than the same position at Apple or Goldman Sachs, so make sure your manager is in it for thelong haul and is zealous about what you are doing. It will allow for a better office environment and a greater chance of retention.

Building an Ethnically Diverse or Global Team

Researchers have demonstrated the value of a team with diverse backgrounds. The major benefits of diversity are not in the team members' physical characteristics such as their outward ethnic identity, but rather in the variety of their life experiences, skill sets, and connections. It is likely that a team built around these points of diversity will also be ethnically mixed. Business owners in ethnically diverse areas also realize that building a company that "looks like the community" sends a positive signal to potential customers. In some cases, your government may compel or encourage you to hire minority candidates—or at least you should not appear to be discriminating against any group. In any case, while getting the best candidate for the job must remain the top priority for your small business, how can you best locate and recruit great candidates who will contribute to a diverse team?

Diverse teams perform better.

Source: © Shutterstock, Inc.

Your ability and your need to recruit diverse candidates will depend significantly on where you are. In some cities, like Hong Kong, London, or Los Angeles, the diversity and integration of ethnicities and cultures run so deep that it would be hard to form a homogenous team. In these cities, businesses with staff of a single ethnicity appear clannish and can be intimidating to outsiders. On the other hand, if you're in a small town in America's rural Midwest or Japan, where ethnic identity is more homogenous, you might find it much more difficult. Regardless, your best bet is to be open and hospitable to everyone. Your marketing is the most obvious outward manifestation of your company culture. By including different faces and languages in your materials, you can signal to candidates that everyone is welcome here. You can also be direct in your job advertising by including a proactive phrase such as "We are building a diverse and talented team!" It is important that you go beyond the required governmental verbiage such as "We are an equal opportunity employer" or "Discrimination in employment is prohibited by law," or you are not actually providing any discernable signal.

Be aware of the anti-discrimination laws of your nation, state, or province. Your larger customers may even be interested in your diversity program. These rules can be difficult to comply with despite your best intentions. For instance, you may be legally prohibited from asking a candidate about their ethnicity during the application or interview process in order to prevent active discrimination—yet you may be required to track and report such data to prove that you're not discriminating. You may think you recognize diversity in its physical appearance but remember you are also looking for diverse experience. Do not conflate these two qualities. The best approach is to simply ask candidates to share broadly about their life experience and how they believe such experiences would benefit your firm. An American small business owner may be very surprised to find that the "white" woman he is interviewing grew up in Kenya and Singapore and speaks four languages. He might also find out that the "Asian-looking" candidate was adopted by a white family as a baby and that he grew up in rural Minnesota speaking only English!

Gender diversity would seem to be an easier goal to achieve. While the world has made significant progress toward integrating women into all professions, much work remains in terms of equal pay and promotion. This success also varies significantly among nations. Women entrepreneurs are an important part of this progress, and small businesses can contribute significantly by giving young women their first opportunities in management. Attracting female workers involves treating them as equals. If your competitors aren't doing that you have an advantage.

Today's gender environment is more complex than your grandparents could have ever imagined. The LGBTQ+ community drives a number of gender identification issues in the developed world. This may complicate your hiring practices as well as policies surrounding benefits, the definition of maternity leave, and employee and customer bathroom access.

The global experience of your team can be very important. If a startup requires outsourced and inexpensive manufacturing, adding a team member with active ties to China or Vietnam could be really helpful. If it is about outsource services, an employee with connections to India could help. If the firm wants to expand into Latin American, African, or European markets, then clearly hiring an employee from those regions would be a great asset. Hiring immigrants or first-generation immigrants is an excellent way to achieve this. And research data[4] suggest that immigrants are predisposed to small business. For instance, in South Korea, the business landscape is dominated by enormous conglomerate firms known as chaebols. Many young Koreans in Seoul aspire to lifelong corporate positions with firms like Samsung or LG. However, about a third of Korean immigrants to the United States are involved in small businesses that range from import-export firms to dry cleaners.[5]

It is important to remember that foreign countries are not really the stereotypical uniform national entities sometimes imagined. They have their own diverse social, cultural, religious, and business communities with many differences. The government of China recognizes fifty-five "official" minority groups within their borders, but in actuality, there are many more. India combines a dizzying array of cultures and languages. Simply getting someone from country X who is properly educated to do the job is not enough. Many nations have complex class or clan systems or customs that can bedevil the naïve foreign businessperson's attempts to quickly enter a market.

FIGURE 6.5 Linguistic Diversity
Language families of the Indian subcontinent.

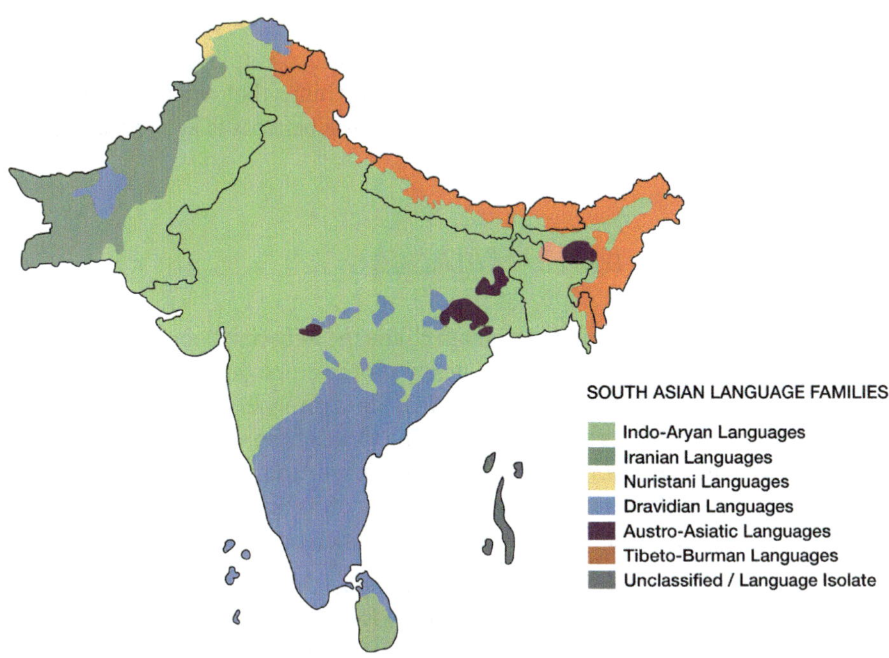

Source: Wikimedia https://commons.wikimedia.org/wiki/File:South_Asian_Language_Families.jpg

Tying your firm to the wrong person early on may inadvertently brand your firm as tied to a particular group or subculture. This can send the wrong message to some customers and permanently damage your brand with important constituencies in that nation. Do your homework and conduct many, many interviews to determine that you are getting a person who will let you cross cultural boundaries and can get you into the network you actually need to be in. While incorporating these members into the team, try to account for geographic and cultural differences. Will they work from a different location, and how would this affect organizational flow, legal workings, and communication? Additionally, if there are cultural or language barriers, how do you plan to overcome them for a seamless company culture?

Establishing an Attractive Package

While top talent flocks to famous names like Google or trendy startups like Uber and Airbnb, unknown companies don't attract the great candidates automatically. In fact, less desirable **b-team** players often target small businesses they think are less demanding. A small business has to maintain the highest standards and sell itself to candidates. If you put your best foot forward, you can attract winners to your interviews, but you're going to need to craft an attractive employment package to get them on your team.

b-team
Second rate employees who are not top competitors in their respective fields.

Designing a package that is a talent magnet requires research. Important considerations for an attractive package include salary, benefits, and stock, as well as fun perks that can help build company loyalty and morale. First, you have to know the ranges for salaries, benefit packages, stock options, etc. of your industry.

You need not offer the highest pay in your industry. Small businesses have the advantage of flexibility. You can craft attractive packages tailored to the needs of individuals. Maybe your dream worker needs to be at home every Thursday to meet with a specialist who helps his father with a health problem. You can credibly promise to make that happen, whereas a big corporation's promise to accommodate that might ring hollow!

The very nature of your business can also be a lure. Startups can be "cool," leveraging that mystique in recruiting. Your company culture may be hip, or perhaps what you do is socially popular at the moment. Some firms offer discounts and free merchandise to employees if the demographic of their workers matches their consumers as well. Identifying things that will fire the passion in your ideal employees and creating packages that emphasize these benefits is key to the New Entrepreneurial Dynamic.

Screening Resumes and References

In the movie *Confessions of a Shopaholic*, the main character, Rebecca Bloomwood, obtains a job at a financial magazine by "fudging" her resume. Luckily for the employer, she somehow managed to be a perfect fit, but unluckily for startup founders, real life is rarely like the movies. You must complete your due diligence on resumes and references. The value of the words on the resume does not always equal what they imply. If you run an app development company and the prospective new hire for the position of CTO claims he worked in a variety of hackathons, quiz him about the projects. Give him some real tasks to code and observe his competence firsthand.

Before checking employee references, identify the things that are going to be really important for you to know. Is this person adaptable enough for the New Entrepreneurial Dynamic? How does this person perform in a team? How reliable is he? How driven? If possible, ask for anecdotes that reveal the prospective new hire's characteristics. Remember that the previous employer may not be telling you the absolute truth. Former employers may be covering for this person because of friendships, financial obligations, or simply to avoid being sued for damaging the candidate's reputation—a factor that pushes many former managers into near silence. Validate minor but specific claims the employee made during the interview. Finding inconsistencies may actually be easier in the seemingly less important areas because any major cover-ups are likely to be well protected.

You might also perform formal background checks. For a fee, some organizations will verify the potential employees' references, check their criminal and driving records, give you their credit score, and let you know if they've ever been involved in a lawsuit. Taken together, this information may suggest a pattern that can be helpful in your hiring decisions. While any good candidate might have a bad mark in one of these areas for a variety of reasons, a systemic pattern of irresponsibility is a bad sign. One speeding ticket or lawsuit shouldn't eliminate a candidate, but if you find a person who is consistently in trouble with the law, doesn't pay her bills, or is routinely in civil court, keep looking.

Last, look at candidates' hobbies or after-work activities that they are willing to share. These may portray a different side of them. What do these things suggest about their character and their fit within your organization? Spend a moment and visualize what it would be like to have this person in your small business?

Once they've passed all the screening, do your best get to know the candidate, his character, and get a sense of how he will perform in your company. Take him out to dinner, introduce him to everyone on the team. Have him work on a trial basis for a day or two if that is legal in your area and agreeable to everyone.

Avoiding Troublesome Hires and CYA

To paraphrase Smokey Bear, "Only you can prevent business fires!" Bad puns aside, problematic hires turn into problematic employees who turn into problematic ex-employees. If an applicant sets off a funny feeling in your gut, trust your instinct, and try to figure out why you are suspicious.

Additionally, when something seems too good to be true, that's often exactly the case. Imagine you're interviewing the former vice president of sales of some Fortune 500 firm. You're excited to have somebody of this caliber at your small company. You note that they left the large employer over a "difference of opinion," but they claim they "feel passionately about your project." Still, you pick up a sketchy vibe about the whole thing. Don't ignore that feeling.

If you end up in the unfortunate situation of having a problem employee on your hands, first try to mitigate the issue. If someone simply isn't doing the job, it may boil down to either training or setting clear expectations. Those problems can always be fixed. The very worst new employee problems always manifest as people issues; the new candidate simply won't fit into your culture and is damaging to morale. Other employees avoid him, and maybe some have even left your organization. Do your best to document these incidents and counsel the offender. If he is open to discussing the problem and seems genuinely willing to accommodate change, there is real hope. If the individual is immediately defensive or belligerent and you get the sense that he's probably been through this at other jobs, you've likely got a big problem on your hands. Proceed with caution.

Once you conclude the situation is irreparable, take the only possible route and CYA—call your attorney. Often these troublemakers are **litigious**, and you don't want to end up with a lawsuit. Consult your lawyer to ensure that the actions you take next are properly documented and handled. Your best option is often to convince the employee to leave the company voluntarily with a mutually positive outcome. This is very likely how they ended up in your organization in the first place—nobody wants to give a bad reference to someone who may be vengeful. When they do leave, ensure you have a nondisclosure agreement in place.

litigious

An individual or organization that is prone to engaging in lawsuits, filings, and other legal actions.

Conducting Interviews

When interviewing prospective employees, consider every aspect of what they will bring to your company. Your small business is truly an aggregation of its employees, and a scalable startup will always bear the imprint of those first hires. Your interview style must reflect the culture you are seeking to establish. Category Five Boat Shoes, a startup based in Boston, takes a much more relaxed and friendly approach with its interviews because the company has a democratic leadership style. Furthermore, the company asks about the prospects' ambitions and passions because the company itself wants and targets passionate millennials. Just as you must gauge the customer's willingness to pay to correct their pain points, you also must assess the **willingness to work** of prospective employees, as a pool and as individuals.

willingness to work

The amount of effort an individual is willing to give for their organization.

When looking for particular skill sets, rather than simply asking how qualified they might be, test those skills. Picky firms like Elon Musk's SpaceX puts employees through a gauntlet of technical tests remotely, and then, if they pass, they work them even harder in person. If you need a coder, have them write code; if you need a manager, give them a trial run in managing the office.

An active interview and testing process will give you a sense of how these individuals would perform in your company and what it would be like working with them. Intentionally plan for some little things to go wrong with the interview process. For instance, ensure that there not enough chairs in the conference room when you start the interview. Then observe if the candidate is stressed by this minor inconvenience, inclined to leap in and help solve the problem, or just stands back and waits for other people to fix things. Do minor disruptions annoy him? Which of these responses do you think you'd like to see in a small business employee?

Many job interviews are now conducted online.

Source: © Shutterstock, Inc.

Problems and Terminations

Small businesses have uniquely personal issues in resolving employment disputes and conducting terminations. What if a long-time employee runs into trouble? Or worse, a founder no longer provides adequate value for the venture? How can you deal with firing someone from a two-person team? What if the firm's revenue will not support both your salary and that of your partner and best friend?

There are no easy answers to these hard questions, but you can try to moderate them in advance. The best way to avoid these situations is to clearly define relationships with partners and employees before entering into a work environment. Couples have the highest mortality rate in startup ventures because stress at work comes right home with them. There is nowhere to escape the problems of the day. Husbands and wives need to clearly understand the demarcation points between work and home and make their family a priority.

Setting Expectations

gamification

The process of making a task more interesting by framing it as a friendly competition.

Try to ensure that employee expectations are clear and that they fit the company culture. Make sure that you have policies on performance and that you document them regularly—not just when a problem develops. This proactive process starts on day one with your choice of titles, assigned obligations, and job descriptions. Always attempt to update and maintain clear goals and expectations for deliverables. This can be particularly difficult for small businesses that are striving for dynamism. The process may seem counter to the principles of adaptability, but efforts such as performance programs that set reasonable competitive goals for employees from the beginning act as a sort of **gamification** that engenders some "friendly competition" between individuals or teams.

In terms of nondeliverables, there should be an upfront consideration of where the boundaries are in the work relationship. Do you and your employees grab dinner together after work? What is the level of professionalism expected? Are you Facebook and Snapchat friends, or do you keep your social lives separate? Additionally, when it comes to giving and receiving feedback, what is the formalized process (e.g., weekly sit-downs, a comment box)? These decisions will largely set the culture for the work environment, so it is best to think about what you hope that culture will be and make these expectations clear even during the hiring process.

Employee Education

The Boston Beer Company serves as a great example of the power of employee education. The firm brews Samuel Adams beer and is well known for educating its employees about the industry. The salespeople are very knowledgeable about what makes a good beer and why Sam Adams is a great one. The same training drives product innovation by creating a knowledgeable R&D team that can appraise new and quirky tasting beers.

Startups usually don't have a lot of assets; they have employees. The best way to increase outputs and value is by ensuring your employees are working efficiently. Knowledge is power, so ensure your sales, tech, marketing, and all other employees have the knowledge they need to perform at the level required of them. Multidisciplinary instruction is great for small business teams as well. Supporting continuing education, both external and internal, is also a good way to keep employees connected with their small firm.

Evaluations

Effective employee evaluations depend on clearly set deliverables and expectations. Establish clear metrics that you can measure and hold employees accountable to them. For instance, you can set a revenue quota for sales staff, a production goal for manufacturing workers, or a customer satisfaction rating for retail workers.

When your employees fail to achieve their goals, don't get punitive—ask them why they think it happened, provide them your analysis, and offer them tools to improve. Keep evaluations positive and encourage hard work. Coaches and managers who punish engender temporary obedience and long-term resentment. It is also important that you set goals for yourself and other managers. It shows you understand that neither you nor anyone else in the company is perfect or above scrutiny. This makes it a whole lot easier for employees to confront their own shortcomings.

Keep the evaluation process transparent and simple. Large firms often build up complex systems over time that become confusing and irritating to the employees subjected to them. In many cases, the human resource department is so busy with the process of evaluations and defending that process that little value is created for the firm or the employees.

Dispute Resolution

Some disputes are irreconcilable, no matter how hard you try. There was a software startup (which will be left unnamed) with a new hire called "Stephanie." Stephanie performed well in the main office in Philadelphia, and she was transferred to the company's new San Francisco office at her own request. Unfortunately, she felt underappreciated amid the Bay Area software stars, and she started spreading negativity. Stephanie was called out on this attitude, and the CEO met with her to discuss the problem. He quickly concluded that her behavior was unacceptable and gave her two weeks to shape up or ship out. The next day Stephanie maliciously deleted all the company's source code, the crown jewels of the organization. The small firm folded in a few weeks. While screening out malicious employees is a good idea, just about anyone can make a really poor choice under pressure. The lesson here is not to jump to disciplinary action.

Avoid initiating meetings that will result in arguments.

Source: © Shutterstock, Inc.

Do not be afraid to cut negative players, but make sure that all options have been explored first before reaching for the easy axe. Honest discussion aimed at finding a mutual agreement and resolution is a much better tactic. Avoid initiating any meeting that is likely to simply devolve into an unproductive argument.

Layoffs Versus Sharing the Pain

When finances get tough in a small business, hard decisions have to be made quickly, and they are often personal. Imagine that you run a small coffee shop with your brother. Revenues are down, and you cannot afford to pay for two salaries and upkeep. Should you lay off your brother or sacrifice yourself? Or do you try to "share the pain" and cut both your wages in half? This dilemma is a very real one that could happen in any struggling startup attempting to grab market share. The answer lies in a rational evaluation of the state of the company. If the company cannot run without your brother and you can both survive on lower wages, obviously that would be the way to go. However, if you cannot survive on lower wages and can make ends meet running the company yourself, you will need to make the hard call of laying off family. At the end of the day, this evaluation may seem harsh, but your company comes first, and you come second; look at what is in the best interest of your company and then yourself.

Termination

Firing an employee is perhaps the most disagreeable task an entrepreneur faces. For the small business owner, your employees are often your friends, and there is no distant HR department to do the dirty work anonymously. Ultimately, the only way to make the process easier is to point back to the clear expectations set at the beginning of the employment. Explaining the mismatch in performance and expectations can present both important educational feedback and lend some rationale to an emotional experience. If the termination is due to a change in the company life cycle or a mismatch and not a performance problem, try to help with a transition out of the company, such as finding a new employer or offering letters of recommendation.

The other important consideration with firings is the effect on company morale and culture, as the employee is likely to be a friend of your other employees. Explain to the other workers, just as you explained to the employee being discharged, why the situation occurred, and reassure them that it was not an easy decision but one that had to be made. Do not assure them of their positions and appear weak, but also do not appear heartless. Remember, taking the time to provide continuous feedback all along prevents ugly surprises.

Departures

When employees step down or retire, your first consideration should be finding a replacement. The new candidate may come from inside or outside the company. If you decide to recruit outside, always be careful not to snub an aspirational employee hoping to climb the ladder in your organization. Another important consideration is what happens to employee's ownership if they hold equity? They own the share fairly but are no longer contributing, so the question arises, do they deserve to claim dividends? Working out realistic contracts and documented expectations at the start of employment will make departures that much easier. In most cases, partners and employees should have stock buyback agreements that require them to sell their stock back to the firm or to another stockholder when they depart. Otherwise, you may end up with a greater and greater percentage of your firm being held by people who are not engaged in its daily success.

Networking for Life

The New Entrepreneurial Dynamic view of team building is not constructed from a series of disconnected efforts, forming one startup, hiring one key player, or making one great business connection at a conference. NED is about blending all of your entrepreneurial moments into the arc of a life well-lived.

The interactions you have today may not yield any immediate results, but they could very well determine future events. The talented individual you can't afford to hire today may be a great fit down the road when your firm is better funded. He may end up working for an important potential customer, supplier, or investor. If someone leaves your firm today, she may want to come back later and with more experience and better skills. She might even turn out to be your boss at a company that buys out your firm. Most industries are led by a fairly small community of players; people move from organization to organization but stay within the community. These reconnections literally happen all the time. The lesson here is to find value in every team-building interaction. When you have to say "no" or "goodbye," always do it in a positive way that keeps the communication channels open and maintains mutual respect.

Key Takeaways

- As organizations mature, the players become more specialized.
- Organizational culture is an important component of a firm's success.
- Treat recruiting strategically. Get the best.
- Diversity is valuable, but cohesion is essential.
- Always be networking.
- Time spent integrating a new hire is time well spent.
- Keep the evaluation process transparent and simple.
- Consider alternatives to layoffs.
- Understand the complexities of firing employees.
- Consider stock buyback agreements so that employees who depart do not take significant equity outside the firm.

6.5 Case Study: Brian Fitzgerald and Future Point

Brian Fitzgerald set his pen down, leaned back in his chair, and considered. Signing the documents in front of him would end his entrepreneurial career, and the thought of giving up what he had built at Future Point made him melancholy. On the other hand, the offer from Blizzard Entertainment held a promising future and was generous to his team. It made a great deal of sense for the operations of both groups. What path should he take?

Fitzgerald, a pioneering entrepreneur in the video game industry, had been through a long series of game startups. While there were successes and moments of excitement, none of these ventures ever reached their potential. Should he consider this opportunity to sell his latest firm, to what was arguably the world's most respected game company, as a vindication or another premature entrepreneurial ending?

As a high school student in the late 1970s, Fitzgerald had partnered with his best friend, Greg Autry, to launch his first venture, H.A.L. Labs.[6] The teenagers' initial plan to build a personal computer proved far too ambitious for their few hundred dollars in seed capital. Out of funds and shy of a working prototype, they began to focus on the idea of developing software for successful early computers, like the Apple II. Autry and Fitzgerald were both avid players of arcade video games like Lunar Lander, Space Invaders, and Asteroids. A number of amateur programmers had tried to bring these titles to home computers, usually with mediocre results. Fitzgerald felt he could do a lot better. During his freshman year at the University of California, Irvine, he developed a brilliantly accurate knock-off Pac-Man, a game that was then taking the world by storm. Autry worked on marketing and sales of the game. They named it TAXMAN, and the two soon found they had a big hit on their hands. H.A.L. Labs quickly became a highly regarded, though undercapitalized, video game publisher in the early 1980s.

By 1984, the firm was pushed out of the retail game market by an influx of well-financed competitors. Fitzgerald and Autry turned to securing contracts to do development for other companies, but both were also eventually forced to take corporate jobs in order to support their struggling firm. The development of a programming environment for the new Apple II computer was a technical triumph, but a commercial failure because that platform was overshadowed by Apple's original Macintosh computer and the growing popularity of IBM's PC. Eventually, Autry moved on and launched a computer services startup. While H.A.L. Labs hadn't lasted, Fitzgerald learned that a partnership of complementary individuals was a useful way to run a startup.

Fitzgerald stuck with the effort and was determined to make another stab at game development. He searched for new partners and, with two creative friends, Robinson Huff and Ron Myers, established Big Science Software. The trio began development of an innovative approach to chess for the Macintosh, inspired by Myers, who was a master-level chess player. Although their game's potential market was limited—chess isn't Pac-Man after all—the demo was good enough to secure a solid publishing offer from Changeling Software. Fitzgerald felt the new firm was off to a solid start. However, he quickly found out that his very practical approach to business, honed by years of hard knocks at H.A.L. Labs, wasn't shared by his new partners.

Huff and Myers, more artistic and less experienced in business, were inclined to be skeptical of the intentions of businesspeople. They bristled at the defensive legalistic clauses in the Changeling contract. Fitzgerald recognized this language as the boilerplate protections all publishers inserted into their agreements, but he could not sway his partners to accept them. Against his better judgment, Fitzgerald worked them through the details and produced a counterproposal to the Changeling contract.

Although taken aback by the smaller firm's presumption in dictating terms, Changeling played along and responded with a more accommodating contract. Huff and Myers were still dissatisfied with the language and wanted to counter again with even more rewrites. Fitzgerald urged them to accept the terms based on Big Science's desperate need for cash, the positive personal relationship with Changeling's leadership, and the firm's good reputation. Fitzgerald had seen a lot of contracts and had come to understand that it was always the personal relationships between the parties that actually determined how businesses treated each other. He saw the contract language as a detail that would only emerge in the direst of circumstances. However, Huff and Myers still viewed every contingency in the contract as a very possible or even probable outcome. Unable to convince his Big Science partners, Fitzgerald sent Changeling another revision to the contract. Frustrated, Changeling chose to simply drop negotiations with what they saw as an immature company.

Fitzgerald expressed frustration with this period, "That was tough because, by this point, I'd started focusing most of my energy on the game and had been slowly accumulating lots of debt." He was living on credit cards and going broke while his partners chased away a solid cash deal for the project they all wanted. The partnership structure that had worked so well in the first business was a disaster in the second. Worse, the partners were unhappy with his taking on unrelated contract work to make ends meet, and everyone felt the situation was inequitable. Something was going to have to give, and the Big Science trio split with some acrimony.

During this period, Fitzgerald had been attending program meetups hosted by Quicksilver Software, a successful Irvine-based game developer. He saw the meetups as a great opportunity to network, a task that wasn't his favorite thing but something he recognized as important. At one of the events, he discovered that Quicksilver had been offered and declined the opportunity to do some ports (conversions) to the Macintosh for a new firm, Blizzard Entertainment. Seeing the opportunity, but not wanting to engage it with the disintegrating Big Science team, he introduced his company as Future Tense Software, establishing a new sole proprietorship to exploit this opportunity.

Disappointed by partnerships, Fitzgerald was determined to build a team, but also to maintain direct control over the firm's directions and finances. He signed up the Blizzard contract and renamed his startup Future Point because to secure the URL for FutureTense.com would be too difficult. Fitzgerald quickly recruited Dave Lawrence out of one of the firms he had been doing contract work for. Together they ported Blizzard's new *Warcraft* game from Microsoft DOS to Macintosh. A contract to port *Warcraft II* to both Macintosh and Windows quickly followed, and Fitzgerald brought on an old high school friend, Tony Tribelli, to help. The success of those two titles resulted in contracts for a Mac port of *Diablo* and some critical design work on a space game called *Starcraft*. Fitzgerald brought in younger interns who were excited by the chance to work on Blizzard's now-famous games.

With the volume of work increasing and payroll costs escalating, Future Point's finances got tight. Fitzgerald discovered that as Blizzard's products became more complex, their schedules slipped considerably. Blizzard's team kept making changes to *Diablo* and *Starcraft* that required Future Point to rewrite code they'd already finished. The fixed price bids he had provided for the work on *Diablo* and *Starcraft* were simply too low to be profitable. Despite working on some incredibly successful products and having a very promising future, Future Point lacked outside capital and credit and was unable to reliably pay Fitzgerald or his team.

When Blizzard requested bids for *Diablo II* and *Warcraft III*, Fitzgerald made sure his bids were higher and provided for the contingency of Blizzard delaying the process. Blizzard began to see that if the Future Point team was entirely focused on Blizzard projects and their pricing was getting higher, they might as well be an internal Macintosh development team. Responding to the new bids, Blizzard suggested that picking up the entire Future Point team would be an option and outlined an acquisition package that was very attractive to both Fitzgerald and his hardworking employees. Brian Fitzgerald now faced the most important decision of his career.

Endnotes

1. De Neve, J-E., Mikhaylov, S., Dawes, C. T., Christakis, N. A., & Fowler, J. H. (2013). Born to lead? A twin design and genetic association study of leadership role occupancy. *Leadership Quarterly, 24(1)*, 45–60. https://www.ncbi.nlm.nih.gov/pmc/articles/PMC3583370/
2. Hellman, T. F., & Wasserman, N. (2011). *The fist deal: The division of founder equity in new ventures* (Working Paper 16922). National Bureau of Economic Research. vhttps://www.nber.org/papers/w16922.
3. Cameron, K. S., & Quinn, R. E. (2005). *Diagnosing and changing organizational culture: Based on the competing values framework*. John Wiley & Sons.
4. https://www.inc.com/jessica-stillman/immigrants-play-an-outsize-role-in-small-business.html
5. Park, K. (1997). *The Korean American dream: Immigrants and small business in New York City*. Cornell University Press.
6. Note: H.A.L. Labs should not to be confused with the Japanese firm HAL Laboratory, though both were inspired by the computer in the Arthur C. Clarke's book and Stanley Kubrick film, *2001: A Space Odyssey*.

CHAPTER 7
Funding

> Statement: It's not about the money.
> Reply: It's always about the money.
> —*Traditional*

Dragons' Den is a hit BBC television program that plays on the public's growing interest in entrepreneurship. This fascination with startups is a global phenomena, and the *Den* has spawned a Canadian spinoff of the same name. The popular American show *Shark Tank* is a copy of that Canadian series. All of these shows feature real-world entrepreneurs pitching their startups in hopes of securing funding from successful businesspeople. The "dragons" and "sharks" in these series are **angel investors**.

angel investors

Wealthy individuals, most often successful businesspeople, who typically make investments in the range of $50,000 to $1 million in exchange for an interest in a new firm. See also *seed capital*, *startup funds*.

Dragon's Den—Biggest Deal

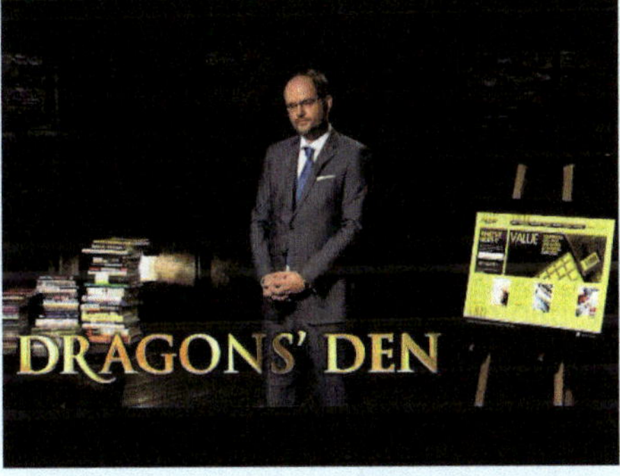

View in the online reader

7.1 Source of Capital

Learning Objectives

1. Understand how to estimate necessary startup funding.
2. Be able to identify various sources of seed capital.
3. Be familiar with different investment rounds.
4. Be familiar with angels, venture capitalists, private equity, and family offices.

5. Know what an accredited investor is.
6. Understand what different types of investors look for and why.
7. Understand the appropriate use of crowdfunding.

Early Capital

Popular TV shows, business articles, and the curriculum in our business schools have created a false belief among would-be entrepreneurs that getting outside investment is fundamental to launching a business. For most firms, this is not the case at all.

Look at Figure 7.1 from the Kauffman Foundation, illustrating how *Inc.* magazine's 5,000 fastest-growing firms are funded. You will note that very few of these notable small businesses actually access venture capital (6.5 percent) or angel investors (7.7 percent), while the vast majority used personal savings (67 percent). It is important to understand that these data represent investment in the fastest-growing small companies in America, a set of firms that have the very best access to capital in the world. The average small business is much less likely to have formal outside investors. According to Kauffman, less than 3 percent of U.S. firms use angel investors, and less than 1 percent secure venture capital investment. For global small businesses, such formal investors are even less relevant; they simply don't exist in most of the developed world.

FIGURE 7.1 Fast-Growing Firms' Sources of Funding
Each year, *Inc.* magazine lists the 5,000 fastest growing companies in America. In 2014, the Kauffman Foundation surveyed firms listed by *Inc.* since 1996 to learn about their sources of funding.

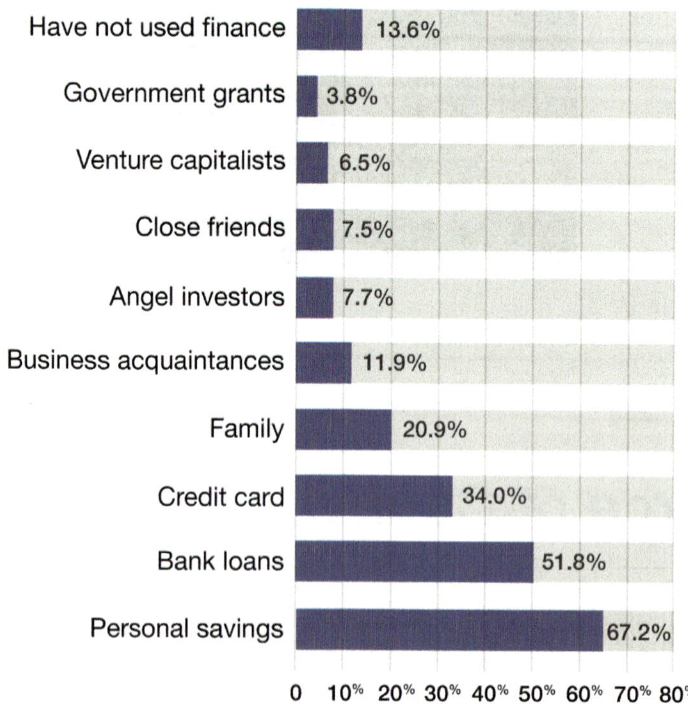

Source: Data from Ewing Marion Kauffman Foundation; http://www.kauffman.org/what-we-do/resources/entrepreneurship-policy-digest/how-entrepreneurs-access-capital-and-get-funded

While very few entrepreneurs are ever going to get cast on a national TV show, young entrepreneurs are often eager to secure money from "dragons," "sharks," or other angel investors. Why do you think that is? Why don't they just sell their product or service to make a profit? Can't they just borrow from the bank when they need to?

Money invested in a business is referred to as **capital**. The initial money used to get the business off the ground is known as the **seed capital**. Every small business requires some seed money, some more than others. Your goal as a startup founder should be to minimize and yet never underestimate your small business' initial cash requirements. As an entrepreneur, nothing is more frustrating than opening the doors to your new shop or factory, turning on your e-commerce store, or launching your new app and finding you have to shut down your business because you can't afford to service the customers who are pouring in. Sadly, this happens all too often. In the end, businesses fail because of a lack of cash, just as humans may suffer from any number of ills. Even if you have customer goodwill and ongoing sales, you will have to close your door without the cash to pay the bills. Having cash on hand is so important and not having it is such a common disadvantage that many businesspeople will tell you that "Cash is king!" Can you think of any famous and large startups that faced a demand induced cash flow crisis? How can you avoid this trap?

capital

Money or other assets used to finance a startup or investment. See also *seed capital*.

seed capital

Funding required to launch a business. See also *startup funding*; *three Fs*.

The best option would seem to be to gather a lot more money than you think you will need. That's easier said than done. Most startups are growing on a shoestring budget, and like a low-calorie diet, that may be healthy. Oddly, however, being cash-rich has not always proven to be a good option for startups. In fact, having too much money has also killed a lot of new firms! Can you imagine how having excess wealth might imperil a group of entrepreneurs?

In his legendary commencement address to the graduating class at Stanford University, Steve Jobs famously advised students to "Stay hungry. Stay foolish."[1] Jobs' message to young entrepreneurs was that if you were eager to work hard and willing to challenge conventional assumptions, you could do great things! As soon as you've got enough money and enough resources to "relax and think," your endeavors may actually be doomed. Once they've obtained a "nest egg," many entrepreneurs become more conservative in their thinking and much less likely to invest either their time or money into radical ideas. It's important to note that Jobs himself seemed immune to this "spoilage." Despite having made billions more than once and having the resources of the world's greatest company at his command, he maintained a relatively modest lifestyle and continued to be obsessed with the products he produced. Jobs could "stay hungry" in a banquet hall. In fact, he seemed to enjoy self-denial. That's a powerful skill for entrepreneurs.

Elite bicycle racers in the Tour de France push themselves up mountain passes.

Source: Radu Razvan/Shutterstock.com

While the New Entrepreneurial Dynamic encourages entrepreneurs to avoid overindulging themselves or their team, it is not about becoming a monk. Success in any endeavor usually requires that you learn to *enjoy the process of overcoming adversity*. Watching an elite cyclist struggle up one more mountain pass to complete a race, you may think he or she looks absolutely miserable, but you'd probably be wrong. Pushing themselves to the limit is something these extreme athletes enjoy, or they would not do it.

For better or worse, overfunding and too many resources are problems with which very few entrepreneurs ever grapple. The rest of this chapter will be focused on the task of gathering enough cash and resources to get your business going and to maintain it during its growth phase.

Determining Startup Funding Requirements

financial feasibility

The potential of a business venture to be profitable.

startup funding

The monies required to purchase fixed costs like facilities and equipment necessary to launch a business.

In Chapter 5, we contemplated the **financial feasibility** of your business model. We will now drill down on a key element of financial feasibility: your ability to obtain **startup funding**. Startup funds are the monies required to pay for fixed costs, such as facilities and equipment needed to get started. These funds also cover variable costs, such as salaries and inventory of operations, until your firm makes enough money to break even. These concepts will be detailed in Chapter 13.

Imagine you've noticed that a town is completely lacking in bicycle shops. You do your customer discovery and conclude that there are sufficient riders in the area who would prefer to shop locally. You've located the perfect spot for a shop. What you need to do now is pay the first and last month's rent and security deposit, set up the utilities, purchase some insurance, buy some racks, display cases, and tools, stock a lot of bikes, hire some staff, and open the doors. How much will all that cost? Let's do a quick estimate in a spreadsheet.

TABLE 7.1 Startup Expenses for a Bicycle Shop

First Month Rent	$	4,500
Last Month Rent		4,500
Security Deposit		3,000
Tools		25,000
Furnishings		75,000
Utilities		1,200
Insurance		800
Initial Bike Inventory		250,000
Three Sales People per Month		15,000
Service Person per Month	$	4,000
Total	$	383,000

This is a pretty simplified model; you may find you have dozens of other smaller needs—things such as signage and a locksmith and window painting for your grand opening. You should build in a contingency of 20 percent or so. Adding a safety margin of $70,000 to the total of $383,000 indicates that this bicycle store needs to raise about $450,000 to open. How many prospective bike shop owners have access to $450,000?

A lot of small business entrepreneurs begin to panic when they think of startup funding requirements like $450,000. Don't panic! Let's look at this systematically. What funding sources can you tap? The obvious ones are things like personal savings and family money. Most entrepreneurs then begin to think about outside investors. However, that is only a small part of the funding story. You can secure seed capital in more creative ways.

Which of these startup requirements is the most expensive? The $250,000 inventory of bicycles accounts for more than half of the capital required! Did you know that the bicycle manufacturers and outside lenders will likely provide you with the money you need to stock all those bicycles? Advancing products and allowing you to pay for them later is called **net terms**. Borrowing to fund the items for sale in a store is called **inventory flooring**. Each of these concepts will be covered in more detail in Chapter 13 and Chapter 14, but suffice it to say it may be possible to open your bicycle dream shop for as little as $200,000 ($450,000 – $250,000)! Now, where might you get $200,000, that is besides getting on *Dragons' Den* or *Shark Tank*?

net terms

Advancing product for payment later.

inventory flooring

Borrowing to fund items for sale in a store. See also *net terms*.

Personal Credit and Savings

The first money most entrepreneurs tap is their savings. In the developed world, savings is usually a bank account balance or money invested in stocks and bonds that can be easily sold. In the developing world, many smaller businesses are initially launched with "mattress cash," physical currency saved up for just such an opportunity or a rainy day. While personal savings is easy to access, can you think of why you might not want to use it?

By putting all or most of your available savings into your business, you are risking personal disaster if the business fails and you don't have other steady income. If a major problem comes up just after you invest your rainy-day fund, you could be in a pinch. Imagine your car breaking down, your spouse losing his or her job, or an illness in the family that requires money. In such a situation, you may find yourself unable to meet your personal financial obligations or trying to "unwind" the investment from your businesses by backing out of a lease or selling equipment you just bought at a discount. For this reason, you may consider a mix of financing sources, even if you have enough personal cash on hand to proceed.

Personal savings is usually the first source of funding for a startup.

Source: © Shutterstock, Inc.

Workers in the U.S. often have the majority of their savings in tax-deferred accounts such as individual retirement accounts (IRAs) or 401(k) retirement savings plans with their employer. While entrepreneurs do often tap these savings to fund their startups, withdrawing funds from these accounts before your eligible retirement age is generally not recommended. Everyone should be saving for retirement, and withdrawals from these accounts are subject to significant taxes and penalties. Be sure to consult with your financial advisor or a tax accountant before touching these funds. It is often possible to borrow against your retirement savings rather than withdrawing the funds. Borrowing may avoid early withdrawal penalties and allow your investments to remain tax-free when you pay them back. However, a loan will incur interest, and you are still risking the funds themselves if the business fails and you are unable to pay back the loan. Be very cautious and consider a mix of funding sources so you do not undermine your family's future.

Another common but even more perilous source of funding for entrepreneurs is short-term personal credit, usually in the form of credit cards. Using a Visa or Mastercard to buy equipment, supplies, and inventory for your new business can make a lot of sense—if it is done wisely. You're likely to have up to one month (depending on where you are in your billing cycle) to pay the bills. You may also generate some sort of valuable "reward points" with your bank that you may redeem for business or personal use. Anytime you can use your card and then pay it off when the bill comes due, you probably should. However, running up a balance on your card or taking cash advances with the intention to repay with future earnings you don't have in hand is very risky. The interest rates on credit cards are notoriously high. If you fail to make the payments, you may undermine your credit rating—an asset that is invaluable to both your personal and business future. Worse, you could find personal assets, such as your home or automobile, attached to repay credit card debt, most of which is likely to be accumulated interest and penalties. Again, credit cards should be part of a mix of funding sources for your start up, rather than a major financing strategy.

The advantage of all these sources is that they are entirely personally controlled and readily available. They also do not dilute your equity position in your firm—meaning you do not need to give up either ownership or control of your new business to others. However, as previously cautioned, they each put your personal financial situation at risk. Funding a business with your own capital and credit and then growing it organically is known as bootstrapping.

The Three Fs

three Fs

Family, friends, and fools—a source of easily accessible startup funding. See also *seed capital*.

After the options of personal savings and credit, the next place most entrepreneurs turn to is a group sarcastically referred to as the **three Fs**: family, friends, and fools. Tapping money from people that you have easy access to and borrowing from those who know your character best makes a lot of sense, which is why so many entrepreneurs take this route.

As Figure 7.1 shows, 21 percent of fast-growing firms used family money. For Main Street entrepreneurs, this figure is much higher. When Tiantian Qui (Chapter 1 Section 5) had a vision for a new kind of Chinese restaurant, she went to her father, a successful businessman, for backing. Mr. Qui loaned her $350,000 to build out and launch the Hip Hot Café in Monterrey Park, California. It was a risky investment in an unproven young entrepreneur. Smart positioning, brilliant execution, and hard work built her beautiful little restaurant into a local success story. Within two years, she had saved up more than $400,000 from profits. Tiantian was ready to pay her father back, but he encouraged her to use the savings to build a second restaurant. Hip Hot Café is a classic story of a family business investment that went well. Can you think of what might go wrong with an entrepreneur taking family money under different circumstances?

In reality, all money comes with obligations attached. If you fund your business with money from the bank, with credit cards, or with a home loan, and the business fails, you are likely to be caught up in an uncomfortable and penalizing legal process involving collection agents and lawyers. These debt professionals may harass you on the phone and through the mail. Still, that's nothing compared to the quietly accusing stares you'll get from loved ones if you lose their savings. You can't escape family, and even if they don't say a word, your sense of guilt may transform joyful family events into obligations that you dread to attend. Financial stress of this nature can result in divorce or other permanent family divisions. Think carefully before taking family funds.

Imagine that you are a young woman who has a difficult relationship with your father-in-law. You feel that he has never really approved of you or saw you as worthy of his son. You feel that one way to prove yourself to this difficult man is by succeeding in your own business. Your mother-in-law, who is sympathetic and will deny her son nothing, offers you a hand up with a personal loan. You know that if the business hits a rough patch, you'll find out just how judgmental your father-in-law can be. That's an added level of pressure that might either provide you with extra motivation to succeed or an unneeded level of stress.

Business and financial connections can disrupt family relationships.

Source: © Shutterstock, Inc.

The situation with borrowing startup funds from friends is similar, though usually not as fraught with potential downfalls as it is with family. Friends have chosen you, not inherited you. They must bear some responsibility for their decision to invest, and if you fail, they tend to be less judgmental. Still, many a good friendship has been permanently damaged or even ended over a misunderstanding involving an investment.

To avoid the difficult situations described here, never borrow money that the lender cannot afford to lose; be abundantly clear about the risks involved and communicate regularly about the status of the firm. If things go badly, do not hide the situation from your investors. If something very bad occurs, you are much better off if you've kept them honestly worried about outcomes. If you've always painted a rosy picture and then one day have to say, "By the way, I've lost all your money," you'll not only look like a failure, but much worse, you'll look like a liar. If it becomes obvious that you've been lying all along, what's to keep your investor, rich aunt, or generous friend from imagining that you've actually stolen their money and are lying about the business having consumed it? As the saying goes, "Honesty is the best policy."

Angels

One of the advantages of going with formal angel investors over the three Fs is that these experienced entrepreneurs and investors will speak more honestly with you, and if things go badly, they will view the situation within the context of a business relationship. In fact, professional startup investors expect many if not most of their investments to fail. It goes with the territory, and it isn't personal. Additionally, they will share the lessons of success and, more importantly, what they've learned from investments gone wrong. Where do you think you might find angel investors?

Angel investors typically invest $50,000 to $1 million and operate both independently and within networks. They are equity investors, buying stock in a firm. Angels are usually looking for a significant amount of **equity**, though usually not a **controlling interest**, in the new firm. A controlling interest normally requires owning more than half of a firm.

equity

Ownership of a portion or all of a firm at a specific value.

controlling interest

Holding a majority of the stock in a company.

accredited investors

An investor who has met Security Exchange Commission income or net worth requirements to demonstrate that they are qualified to invest in stock offerings that the agency does not regulate.

Under U.S. law, for these angels to invest in unregistered (not controlled by regulators) stock offerings, the angels must be **accredited investors**. An accredited investor must demonstrate that they have annual income of at least $200,000 per year individually or a net worth in excess of $1 million. The purpose of this is to keep predatory entrepreneurs or scoundrels posing as entrepreneurs from luring those who can least afford it into a situation where they might lose all their money. This means you cannot simply go out to average people and ask them for money to fund your company.

These groups are surprisingly easy to find and contact—after all, they *want* to talk to startup founders. You can find these groups by talking to others in your local or investor startup community or to other successful former entrepreneurs that you may know. If you're a student in an entrepreneurship program, you may have a leg up. The business school of your local university is a great place to connect with these investors, who themselves are often looking for opportunities to invest in student startups. They may be alumni of the school and looking to give back. If you are in a smaller school that isn't directly connected to such networks, consider participating in a prize competition at a school that is. Some of these competitions are open to outside teams, while others may require that you join an existing startup or recruit a partner from the sponsoring school's student body.

Another way to find angels is by groups or networks they form to share and to vet investment opportunities. Angel networks strive to make themselves available to entrepreneurs. They can easily be located online with a Google search for "angel investor network." Many are regional, such as the Pasadena Angels, a group from Southern California. Other angel groups are industry-specific, such as the Space Angels Network, which invests in commercial space firms. They also facilitate the syndicates of investors who pool their money in single-purpose funds to make larger investments in startups.

There are also online angel search services, such as AngelList at angel.com, which exist specifically to connect investors with entrepreneurs. They help sort investors by region, industry, and size. Crunchbase.com tracks investments in tens of thousands of startups by thousands of investors from small to huge. You can search its database to find a good fit for your startup based on firms they have previously invested in. If it is that easy to find an angel, the next questions are: What should you be looking for in an angel, and how do you convince them to back you?

You want to find angel investors who are going to be compatible with your approach to business. An angel investor is most often a successful entrepreneur who has retired or an established businessperson with a lot of experience and income. They firmly believe they know what they are doing, and in addition to giving you money, they expect to give you advice and have you take it. Some entrepreneurs feel they know more about their business than anyone and don't want that sort of interference from investors. In that case, you should probably consider the home loan route and avoid angels. But if you are open to it, finding an investor you admire and are willing to take advice from can be incredibly important.

You also want angels who bring more to the venture than simply their checkbooks. It is essential to find angels who have experience in your industry, so their mentoring is of practical value. Great angels also bring networks of business connections. They should be able to introduce you to potential customers and suppliers. They will have reliable and trustworthy relationships with bankers, accountants, lawyers, and other professionals upon whom you can call. Without the intervention of an angel, connecting with these kinds of resources may require an exchange of equity in your company. Finally, many angel groups feed into some more prominent money investors known as venture capitalists. If you are going to need millions of dollars in the future, it's best to find angels who can take you to the venture capitalists (VCs) when you are ready.

Venture Capitalists

While virtually no small businesses and very few startups will ever have the need or opportunity to engage with VCs, a disproportionate amount of entrepreneurial literature is focused on helping founders find ways to attract or please VCs. The most popular business books, entrepreneurship TV shows, and articles in business magazines might lead you to believe that getting money from VCs is the actual goal of a startup, rather than generating returns and other tangible benefits for its founders. Many business school courses in entrepreneurship feature a similarly misguided approach.

The New Entrepreneurial Dynamic is less focused on capital acquisition and much more focused on delivering value to the founders. It encourages you to minimize the use of outside money and only recruit investors who share your vision and bring significant nonfinancial contributions to your startup. In most cases, VCs should be the last thing you worry about in a new business. However, there is one class of startup where these high-powered investors are essentially required.

Rapid growth or scalable startups (per Steve Blank), particularly in the tech sector, fit the VC model. It's no coincidence that pioneering firms like Apple and Microsoft evolved alongside the top VC firms. It's why so many of these tech firms and VCs are side by side in the San Francisco Bay area and nearby Silicon Valley. If you have a new software-enabled solution or a disruptive technology where the manufacturing is outsourced, VCs will be interested.

That doesn't mean VCs are suitable for all growing firms. They are generally less attracted to services that involve lots of real employees or to hardware projects where manufacturing must be done in-house. They are surprisingly uninterested in firms with relatively low-risk plans. If you have a surefire way to generate double-digit growth in a new machine tool business, you probably shouldn't bother the VCs! On the other hand, if you have a new app with a nine-in-ten chance of total failure but a one-in-ten chance of delivering a 100X return, the VCs may love you.

Venture capitalists differ from angels in several ways. First, VCs invest more money. Most VCs are looking to invest $3 million and usually much more in a startup. Anything less than that will not generate enough return to be worth their time. Secondly, they usually come in after the angels. While most small businesses won't need to get beyond the angels, those that fit the VC model will go through a formal series of VC investment stages once they have demonstrated they have a somewhat viable product. Figure 7.2 shows this process.

FIGURE 7.2 Rapid Growth Funding Cycle

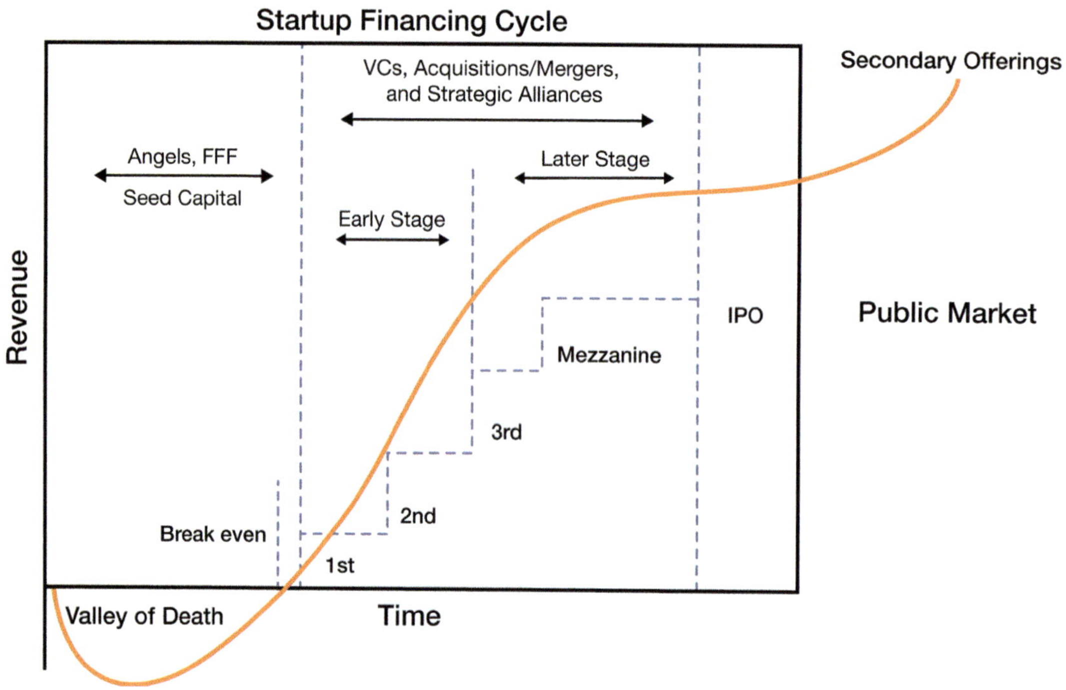

Source: https://commons.wikimedia.org/wiki/File:Startup_financing_cycle.svg

The section on the right side with its first, second, third (or more) funding stages reflects the investments of venture capital funds. Before each **funding round**, the VCs will reevaluate the firm's investment potential and are likely to push for changes to the product, team, or business model before providing the funds necessary for the firm's growth. The rounds are often labeled as A, B, C, or first, second mezzanine.

Officially the first money in the formal investing process is the **pre-seed money** put in by the founders themselves. Pre-seed funding is usually tens of thousands of dollars. The **seed round** is the first official outside investment, usually made by angel investors, and is typically some hundreds of thousands or maybe a few million dollars. Venture capitalists then come in with the **Series A** round and typically invest $5 million to $20 million. The investments and the pool of investors grow with additional Series B, C, etc. These investors generally all know each other and often invest together in groups. Some VCs and other funds will only invest as ride along investors with large VCs that they know have done the due diligence on the startup.

VCs specialize in some specific area of this sequence with the more risk tolerant ones entering early on in the seed rounds and Series A investments, where the startups have little track record. These early investors stand to make the most from a successful exit. More risk adverse investors follow on in later rounds.

In most cases the **valuation**, or price of the stock, increases with each round. If you've watched Shark Tank you've seen valuations in action. If Mr. Wonderful (Kevin O'Leary) agrees to pay $100,000 for 10 percent of a beehive manufacturing firm, what is that firm worth? The answer is $1 million. Can you see how that valuation is calculated?

funding round

A period of time during which a business accepts outside investment, typically divided into Seed, Series A, B, C, etc.

pre-seed money

The money put into a rapid-growth startup by the founders and their close associates, before any formal outside investment.

seed round

The first round of formal investing, usually from angel investors.

Series A

Usually the first round of investment usually engaging venture capitalists. Followed by Series B, C, etc.

valuation

The total value of a company based on the amount paid for shares in its latest investment round.

If $100,000 = 10 percent, the valuation must be ten times that amount because 10 percent is one-tenth of 100 percent. The formula would be: $100,000 × 100%/10% = $1 million. If 10 percent = $100,000, then 20 percent would be $200,000, and 90 percent would be $900,000, and therefore 100 percent must be a cool million. We call this the **post-money valuation**, because it includes the 10 percent put in by the investor, in this case Mr. Wonderful. The **pre-money valuation** is the value of what the investors brought to the deal, not counting the investment funds. In this case that would be $900,000 because $1 million – the $100,000 investment leaves $900,000.

post-money valuation

The value of a company after the recent investment is put in.

pre-money valuation

The value of a company not including the recent investment put in.

Can you figure out what the post-money valuation would be if O'Leary got 20 percent for his $100,000? If you said $500,000, you are correct. $100,000 × 100%/20% = $500,000. The pre-money valuation would be $500,000 – $100,000 = $400,000.

Sometimes a firm falls on bad times or the macroeconomy (see Chapter 15) is in a slump, and investors do not have a lot of money to invest in startups. If a company must raise money under these circumstances, they may have to offer a lot of stock and take a lower valuation than they got in the last round. This is called a **down round**, and you might imagine it is very unpopular with previous investors who paid more for their stock earlier on.

down round

An investment round where the firm receives a lower valuation than in previous rounds.

It is very important for business founders to understand that if venture capitalists have invested millions of dollars during each of several funding rounds, the firm will become dependent on them to continue its growth. While you're likely to get other VCs to invest, these folks are sitting on your board, and they are good personal friends with all the other VC firms in their sector. If they decide, and they often do, that the founders are not the right people to continue management of the firm as it enters a new stage, they will replace you and your partners. Many a young CEO has been fired from his own company to make way for more experienced management. Steve Jobs' firing from Apple Computer in 1985 is a classic example of this cautionary tale of what can happen once you've given up control of your firm.

At the end of the cycle, the firm may enter the publicly traded markets in an initial public offering (IPO) of stock. A successful IPO makes the VCs and most everyone still on the team very wealthy. It's the entrepreneurial equivalent of winning Olympic gold! The IPO, however, is actually a very rare event. In a really good year, there may be a dozen or so IPOs in the market, and during economic downturns, there may not be any at all for years. In most cases, VCs choose to sell the firms they have funded to larger competitors rather than pursue an IPO. A sale is a much easier, cheaper, and more reliable way of cashing out on the investment. Everyone still profits, but control is handed over to the buying firm.

Founders must understand this critical fact: VCs look at your firm as an opportunity to see a return on investment, not as your dream. The bottom line is this: *If your vision is to build and manage your own business empire, venture capitalists are much more likely to squash that dream than make it come true.*

Finally, and most importantly, venture capitalists are working with **other people's money** or "OPM." Venture fund managers administer a **venture capital fund**, which includes some of their own firm's money but is mostly composed of investments from wealthy individuals, pension funds, insurance companies, foundations, and other organizations with large amounts of money to invest. This obligation to return money to other people ties the hands of VCs from acting on their own inclinations. Your VC may actually love you and want you to learn and grow as an entrepreneur, but he isn't going to risk millions in other people's money to give you that chance. He is going to do what is required to maximize returns for the fund's investors.

other people's money

Investment funds belonging to shareholders, customers, or clients rather than the person investing it.

venture capital fund

An investment fund made up of money from wealthy individuals, pension funds, insurance companies, and other organizations managed by venture capitalists (VCs). See also *other people's money*.

Interview with Tim Ellis

Tim Ellis

Source: Tim Ellis

I first met Tim Ellis and his future cofounder, Jordan Noone, when they were student leaders in the Rocket Propulsion Lab (RPL) at the University of Southern California, where I taught entrepreneurship for seven years. I had the pleasure of observing and occasionally offering advice as these young entrepreneurs built a vision of 3D printing rockets into one of America's most exciting new companies, Relativity Space. That firm is now valued at over $4 billion. I sat with Tim at the Space Symposium, in Colorado Springs, Colorado to discuss his entrepreneurial journey.

Prof. Autry: When you were younger, did you picture yourself as an entrepreneur and business owner?

Ellis: My dad ran a business doing kidney dialysis architecture. It was always a small business and very niche. I saw him face failure on many occasions but always persevere. I was fortunate to see that sort of grit early on.

I went into college thinking that I would become a screen writer. I got a half-tuition scholarship to the University of Southern California as a Presidential Scholar and on my application, I said, "my dream job is either to be a fiction writer or CEO." I wasn't that entrepreneurial from the standpoint of knowing that I was going to launch a startup, but always cared about creativity and big impact. I've learned during my time with Relativity that engineering is just creativity with physics and I've been able to use that inner passion to drive change in the business world.

Prof. Autry: What is it that led you into aerospace engineering and into propulsion?

Ellis: I got into USC undeclared and switched to aerospace engineering because it started with an "A" and was at the top of the majors list. I tried to change my freshman year when taking a class called MATLAB, because it scared me the same way writing did, which was being alone in a room and having to be creative. I thought, "Crap, now I'm going to be alone writing code." Luckily, I found the USC Rocket Propulsion Lab, which was working to be the first student group in the world to launch a rocket to space. After seeing my first rocket engine test I was hooked. It was the most visceral, loud, bright, crazy experience I ever had. Ironically, I ended up writing the MATLAB code to design those rockets.

Prof. Autry: Several entrepreneurs came out of the RPL. What do you think it was about that experience that drove people into entrepreneurship as opposed to just going and working for large companies?

Ellis: College shapes the DNA of who you grow up to be. Colleges have cultures just like companies. USC is one of the highest producers of entrepreneurs in the United States. It has this population of very bright people with a little bit of a chip on their shoulders. USC has attitude, but in a good way; you have to be gritty and disruptive. The USC Rocket Propulsion Lab culture very much embraced that. Our unofficial motto was "Space or Nothing" and this was emblematic of this idea of being all in. Grit and relentlessness maps to the number one quality you need to be successful in a venture-backed startup.

Prof. Autry: When you left USC and the USC Rocket Propulsion Lab you were you still thinking you might do something entrepreneurial, or did you picture a corporate career?

Ellis: I started my career as an intern at Masten Space Systems, a really small company, but moved to Blue Origin, Jeff Bezos' space company. I started as an intern when the company was about 150 people and stayed through about 500 people. I launched the metal 3D printing division at Blue Origin. Nobody told me to do that, and in fact, I faced a lot of headwinds. My boss felt it was a waste of time, but I believed 3D was the future. Soon, I was using metal 3D printing in all of my projects, and it was working, surprising everyone, including Jeff.

Prof. Autry: So that means you started thinking you wanted to go do it on your own?

Ellis: I met my wife, Richelle, when we were both giving TEDx talks at USC. She's an artist and when I was at Blue Origin, we were actually writing a business plan to start a science art gallery called "Relativity Gallery." So, we wrote the whole business plan. I was launching the 3D printing division at Blue and this art gallery idea that made me realize that I was probably hooked on entrepreneurship.

The business idea came out of thinking why aren't more firms besides SpaceX trying to get to Mars to make humanity multiplanetary? I was also wondering, why are we still building rockets one at a time, with hundreds of thousands to millions of parts, in giant factories filled with fixed tooling and little automation. I felt that the next sixty years couldn't possibly look that way and if it did, it would be very depressing. There had to be some company in humanity's future that would build an industrial base on Mars. That was the genesis of 3D printing entire rockets.

Prof. Autry: And so you have an idea, but where does one go to get money to 3D print rockets on Mars?

Ellis: The first Relativity email I sent was to the only investor I could think of, Mark Cuban. I guessed twenty different versions of "MCuban" and "mark.cuban" whatever at yahoo and gmail. My subject line was "Space is sexy and we are 3D printing an entire rocket." We were raising a seed round of $500k and asking Cuban for $100k. One of the email addresses worked and I guess we got his attention because he replied within five minutes offering to do the whole round. The same week we got into Y Combinator and started incorporating.

Prof. Autry: I remember, your cofounder, Jordan Noone, came to me about that time and asked me "Should we go with Y Combinator or Cuban," and I said "That's not a question, take both."

Ellis: I remember that. That's how naïve we were. I thought there was no way we could do both, but of course obviously we could. We raised our series A right out of Y Combinator. That was ninety pitches in thirty days or something like that. Everyone said "no," except Social Capital, who agreed to lead the round. Series B was 140 pitches over three or four months and Playground Global decided to take the lead. We started to hire an executive team from SpaceX and other private space companies and signed our first customer contacts. Our big printing technology was working. With that credibility, later funding rounds moved fast. We've learned what investors look for and with the close of our series E we've raised over $1.3 Billion.

Prof. Autry: What golden nugget of advice do you have for aspiring entrepreneurs?

Ellis: I've always focused on, "Where can I learn the most and where can I learn the fastest?" Never stop pulling on that thread of learning and then not being afraid to hire people better than you. In fact, that is your job, you need to hire people better than you, because that's how you learn even faster.

Autry: What's next for Tim Ellis? If you look to a post-Relativity standpoint, if there is one, have you thought of going back to arts or writing or anything with the wisdom and resources you have acquired?

Ellis: I want to build an industrial base on Mars and help to build a multi-planetary future for the world. Helping put a million people on Mars. I want to see more people launching ambitious companies with a vision that adds up to something pretty amazing, should they succeed.

My wife and I are still very passionate about the arts. I work a lot with her on her projects. She refuses to let me give her help or make connections. She wants to stand on her own two feet, which I respect a lot.

Other Sources of Equity Capital

equity investment

An investment in a company made in exchange for stock or a percentage of ownership in the firm.

liquidating

Selling off the assets of a distressed company and dividing the proceeds of the sale up amongst creditors and shareholders.

There are many other organized **equity investment** structures. Some of the more popular ones include the following.

Private Equity Funds are generally limited partnerships organized to invest funds from individuals and institutional investors to be invested into businesses. Venture capital is a type of private equity that focuses on startups. There are funds that focus on buying and restarting or **liquidating** distressed businesses, buying out diversified firms and selling off their parts, and a lot that focus on real estate development.

Family Office Funds manage the money of high net-worth (wealthy) individuals and their heirs. They tend to be cautious in their investments and are often good sources of funding for firms that aren't as fast growing as venture capitalists prefer but are already generating cash and offer less risk to the fund.

Hedge Funds are private funds designed to take advantage of certain market conditions. They may for instance short the market or a class of stocks to protect the investor from an economic downturn. Hedge fund managers usually take a significant portion (20 percent) of the gains as a performance fee.

Classes of Stock

Not all company stock is equal. Many firms issue different classes of stocks with different agreements associated with them. Most commonly they are labeled as Class A, Class B, etc. Common stock refers to stock that provides for equity ownership of a firm and voting rights, including electing the board of directors. Preferred stock may have more powerful voting privileges and a priority position to be paid back if the firm fails and is liquidated.

Some classes of stock may have no voting rights. If you sell small amounts of stock to a number of individual investors you may wish to make these nonvoting shares. This means when important decisions are made, you don't have to spend the time to collect ballots from these individuals who, having a small portion of the equity, won't make a difference in the outcome of the vote in any case.

Crowdfunding

Another increasingly popular way to fund small startups is through crowdfunding. Sites like Kickstarter and Indiegogo allow entrepreneurs to connect with a community of like-minded consumers who are eager to support the next cool company. A startup will construct a video in support of a fundraising "campaign" that usually lasts 30 to 45 days. Customers who are willing to pay upfront to acquire one of the first products from the firm will make a pledge and receive a product later as a "premium." Under this model, the monies received as "pledges" are really donations to the firm, and the product to be delivered as premiums are thank you gifts in exchange for that pledge. The important point is that it is not a loan, nor is there any legal obligation for the firm to either deliver the product or return the money, though Kickstarter won't invite you back again if you fail to deliver. It's a relatively risk-free way to get the money you need upfront in order to deliver a product later. Would crowdfunding work for any business?

A problem with crowdfunding is that it works best for particular classes of products that appeal to generally younger folks who do a lot of online purchasing and share campaigns via social media. Products like skateboards and games have often been well received. Campaigns that appeal to technology aficionados also do better than nontech products. Products with environmental or social benefits like electric vehicles are popular in crowdfunding. Online crowdfunding also requires that you have the skills to produce a compelling video to sell that product. Experience has shown that the most successful crowdfunding campaigns are consumer products that cost a few hundred dollars or less. Finally, to maximize returns from fundraisers on Kickstarter and Indiegogo, you must wage global campaigns. One champion of crowdfunding has been Pebble, a smartwatch firm that has run three campaigns, each of which raised in excess of $10 million in the early days of Kickstarter. Pebble watches cost between $69 and $300 and are targeted at tech-savvy folks.

A Kickstarter campaign.

Source: Greg Autry

Do you think you could get the Kickstarter community to capitalize your new car wash in Boise, Idaho? What could you offer as a premium besides car washes? Why would tech people care about this? How could that possibly appeal to someone in Barcelona or Hong Kong? It probably wouldn't. You might be able to sell dozens of car wash tickets in advance, but you won't make enough to buy a $200,000 machine and lease a place to set it up.

If you do launch a crowdfunding campaign, you must do it well! Research by Ethan Mollick of the Wharton School at the University of Pennsylvania suggests that campaigns that signal quality have a much higher degree of success. For instance, the production value of the marketing video is very important. Mollick found that even a single spelling error in the campaign can reduce the likelihood of a campaign succeeding by 13 percent![2]

Crowdfunding Equity

Another option for startups is to gather funds from their audience in crowdfunded equity offerings. According to a report from British Business Bank, "Crowdfunding is having a significant impact on seed-stage activity in the UK equity investment market" since its introduction in 2011. The business research firm Beauhurst reports that it is now the most active investor category in Britain (see Figure 7.3), with the website CrowdCube leading the category.

FIGURE 7.3 UK Crowdfunding Deals and Investments by Six Months

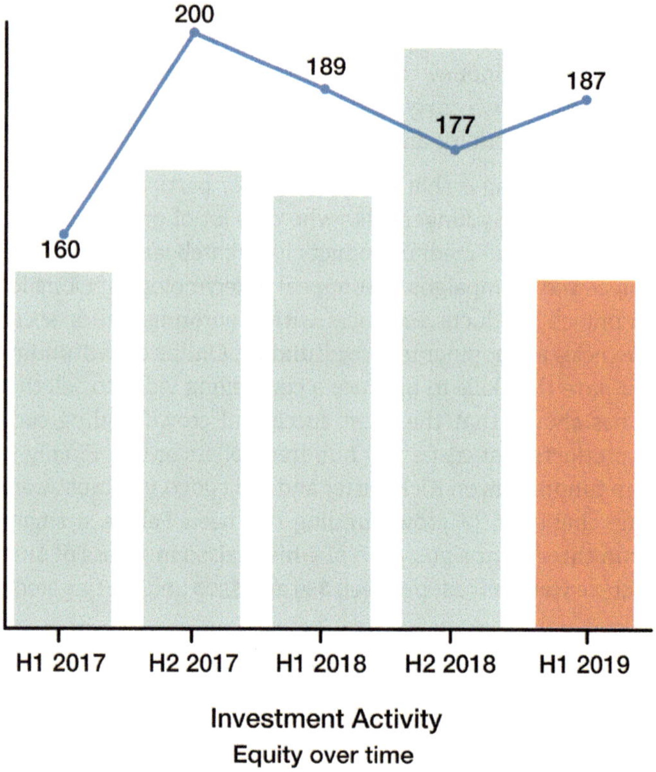

Source: Data from Bearhurst, https://www.beauhurst.com/blog/uk-crowd-funding-landscape-2019/

In 2015, the Securities and Exchange Commission (SEC) introduced rules for similar online crowdsourced equity funding in the U.S. The rules limit who can participate and how much they can invest. The regulations are somewhat complex to execute but, in essence, provide small business owners with access to a "mini IPO." Start Engine is an equity crowdfunding platform founded in response to this rule change for which its founders had previously advocated. The site offers an opportunity for relatively small investors with perhaps a few hundred dollars to invest in startups. In 2016, Elio Motors, a prospective manufacturer of three-wheeled cars, raised $17 million on the Start Engine.[3] In 2018, Start Engine used its own platform to raise $10 million for itself from thousands of small investors. The investor category of "fools" has been expanded far beyond just the people you know!

Be aware that even the "simplified" SEC paperwork for these offerings can be complex for a small entrepreneur and possibly generate thousands of dollars in legal fees. Start Engine and its competitors do provide entrepreneurs with some support for those wishing to sell stock. They also have networks of lawyers familiar with their processes.

Other Prepayment Financing Schemes

Kickstarter isn't the only way to get your customers to pay you upfront. Sometimes if you have a truly innovative product and you can demonstrate your ability to deliver, you may be able to get your customers to **advance** payment to complete development. This sort of arrangement is especially common in professional services; for example, lawyers usually insist on collecting a **retainer** before providing services. It is also standard practice in custom software development. Talented programmers may demand 30 percent or even 50 percent payment upfront before they begin work.

advance

Payment for a product prior to delivery.

retainer

An upfront fee charged by a consultant, lawyer, or other professional before they will provide professional services.

exclusive license

An agreement to withhold the same rights, within a scope or field, from other licensees.

Prepayment options are less common with physical products, but if you design a product that offers your customer a significant competitive advantage, you may very well get paid upfront to finance your operation. This usually occurs in a situation where you can license some technology or brand to a company that will be able to increase its market share simply because of access to your product. In that case, they won't want their competitors to have the same advantage. In exchange for offering the customer an **exclusive license**, you should be able to demand significant payment upfront. In this situation, you've agreed to sell your product only to this customer for a predetermined period of time. The license should usually cover only a single market as defined by a product category or geography. Can you see how that might help you get even more money upfront?

Imagine you've invented a new type of shoe sole that is incredibly comfortable and water-resistant. You see that your solution can be used by shoe manufacturers as well as scuba and snowboard boot producers. A company in each of those markets should be satisfied to have access to your product in their category. In fact, they may *have to license your product* even if they don't use it! Why is that?

The leader in a particular product category may not want to see disruption in their successful dominance of a market. In fact, the last thing they want to do is innovate and disrupt their production by including a new, potentially troublesome component. However, if you license your solution to their upstart competitor, their hold on the market could be lost. A conservative brand that dominates the ski boot market may potentially pay you some amount of money simply not to sell your product to any other firm in the ski boot category for a couple of years while they consider adding it to their product line in the future. It's like money for nothing!

In 2013 and 2014, Apple advanced nearly $1 billion to GT Advanced Technologies to manufacture unscratchable sapphire-class screens for their watches and phones.[4] Sadly for Apple, GT failed to deliver the screens. Because of horror stories of this nature, most firms will do some serious due diligence investigation of your actual manufacturing capabilities before proceeding. Be prepared to convince them that if they give you their money, you will deliver for them.

Key Takeaways

- Always be thinking about how much money your startup is going to require.
- Try to avoid using other people's money for as long as possible.
- Be cautious with your own savings and assets.
- Recognize that money from friends and family can complicate your life.
- Look for angel investors that add value beyond cash.
- Only think about venture capital if you need large amounts of cash.
- Consider crowdfunding if it fits your product.
- Always be looking for ways to get paid before delivering products.

7.2 Debt Financing—Loans

Learning Objectives

1. Appreciate the risks and benefits of debt financing.
2. Understand how to choose a bank and the importance of building a personal relationship with a banker.
3. Appreciate that getting net terms from a vendor is like getting a loan.
4. Recognize the importance of personal credit.
5. Understand that investors who have turned you down may come back to fund the startup.

Remember our car wash financing dilemma in Boise, Idaho? Kickstarter wasn't going to work for that startup, but there are still some good options. The small car wash business is very well understood and fairly predictable. There are thousands and thousands of them across North America and Europe. Existing data shows what the costs and revenues are likely to be for one placed in a particular geography. Knowing the number of cars in the area, the income of the individuals, and the distance from the nearest competitor is very likely to predict your profitability with reasonable accuracy. Can you think of why this level of predictability would be an advantage?

risk analysis

A review of the potential risks associated with a business venture.

debt financing

Money borrowed to be paid back with interest, for example, a loan or a lease.

backend

Part of a financial deal resulting in the payment of a fee to the facilitator of the deal.

Having that sort of high degree of confidence that a firm will be profitable is incredibly valuable. In the finance world, this ability to analyze the likely future outcomes of a business is called **risk analysis**. A company whose analysis indicates very low risk, like a car wash, can secure **debt financing**. Debt financing is when you borrow money to pay back with interest, as in a loan or a lease. It is usually much preferable to equity financing because, as with crowdfunding, you are not giving up ownership or control of your business. Who do you think might loan you money to set up a car wash?

First, the manufacturer of the car wash equipment will have one or more financing partners who understand their product and your business. They will be the easiest source of funds to get set up. However, you must be aware that when somebody who is selling you something (a house, car, equipment, or franchise) introduces you to a lender, there is a good chance they are not only helping you buy their product, but they are also making money on the **backend**, meaning they are getting paid some percentage of the fees or interest you are paying for your loan. That will increase the cost of your loan above what you might get if you secured your own financing.

You can also approach friends and family for loans on a simple business like this, as it is a business that even a non-businessperson should be able to understand. You'll sleep soundly at night knowing no one's made a risky investment, provided you've done your homework!

Small Business Bank Loans and Government Programs

personal guarantee

An individual's promise to repay charges to a business credit card.

Although banks are generally averse to lending to newly established businesses, if you are pursuing a very simple model like the car wash and have solid credit and some business experience, they may be willing to loan to you. It is important to understand that even if your business is an independent operation and incorporated, the bank will ask you (and your spouse) to sign a **personal guarantee**. This means you are individually responsible for paying the loan back and that if the business defaults on the loan, the bank can seize your personal income (paycheck) or assets (house, auto, etc.)

to collect on their loan. Bankers want entrepreneurs to be "all in" on their firms. They believe that the founder will work harder to make the business a success and pay back the loan if they are personally invested.

If you search "car wash business financing" online, you will find banks and specialty lenders advertising such loans as well as blogs and messages from other entrepreneurs sharing their experience in securing financing.

In the U.S., the Small Business Administration (SBA) is likely to approve a loan for this sort of business as well. In this case, the SBA guarantees the loan, making the lending decision easier for the bank. If you are starting a relatively simple business in an established category, you should investigate your ability to get an SBA-backed loan from a local bank. The SBA process itself is a bit bureaucratic, so be prepared to spend a good deal of time chasing paper and on your computer detailing your personal and business finances. Start the process by looking at the loan checklist online at sba.gov or by visiting a local bank approved for SBA loans.

In Europe, individual countries, as well as the EU and European Central Bank (ECB), provide financial assistance to small and medium-sized enterprises (SMEs). SMEs make up the bulk of the European economy, but according to the *Economist*, banks have recently been reducing their lending in that sector. The EU, several member states, and the UK have all moved to prop up that critical source of cash with subsidies and guarantees. You can investigate a number of European and national programs by visiting the EU's "Access to Finance" portal page.[5]

Home Loan

The very best source of funds for your new business may be your home. While many entrepreneurs are wary of attaching any obligation to their family's residence, a home loan or line of credit can be the best financial choice for several reasons. First, if you have sufficient equity in your home, meaning you owe much less than the home is worth, you can usually easily get a loan in a few weeks. Loans backed by real estate usually offer some of the lowest rates available. A home loan is nearly always many times cheaper than credit card debt (perhaps 4 percent versus 18 percent). Even better, in the U.S. and some other countries, much of the interest on a home loan may be **tax deductible**. Money borrowed at 4 percent on your home may only cost you 2.5 percent after taxes. This is very attractive.

tax deductible

Item or expense that can be deducted from taxable income.

It is essential to understand that any loan on your home does, of course, **encumber** that asset, meaning it becomes tied up by the lender, and selling or transferring it is more difficult. Further, if you fail to make the loan payments or pay your bills, your home could be foreclosed or **repossessed**, meaning it could be seized and your family evicted so the house can be sold by the lender to cover your debt. However, the same thing is even more likely to happen if you run up credit card debt because of the higher interest rates incurred. If you decided to borrow against your home to fund your dream business, be sure that you and your family have considered the risks.

encumber

To make a claim against property owned by a separate entity.

repossessed

When property used as collateral for a loan or bought on secured credit is seized for repayment or because of nonpayment.

creditworthy

Deserving of credit based on proven financial reliability.

collateralized

To pledge an asset to a bank or other lender to secure a loan. In the event of default, the lender can seize and liquidate the asset. Typical assets include real property, equipment, and contract revenues.

As previously noted, you should establish a personal relationship with your banker before you apply for a loan. You also need to get your business into **creditworthy** shape. Unlike investors, banks are not betting on your future growth; they are lending to profitable firms that are already able to make payments and can prove it. On top of that, they want the loans **collateralized**, which means some tangible asset (starting with the cash in your bank accounts) can be used to cover your debt if you fail to pay. There is a truism among small business owners that "banks only loan to businesses that don't need loans."

Requirements vary by bank, industry, location, and the economy, but in general, your business should have at least a year of demonstrated profitability, good reasons to expect revenues and profits to continue to grow, a solid credit history, and assets to secure the loan. Be prepared to prove all this with solid accounting and clear answers to financial questions.

Be aware that most business loans are based on a variable rate, usually as some number of interest points above prime, as in "prime plus two." The prime rate is the rate that commercial banks charge their very best, low-risk customers, typically big businesses. If one of these major companies is getting loans at 2 percent, then your prime plus two loan is at 4 percent. If inflation increases, the government and banks will raise all their rates. When the prime jumps to 4 percent, you will be paying 6 percent.

Selecting a Bank

Finding the right bank for your car wash or any other startup is a critical first step for your small business. There are a lot more things to consider in the selection process than simply the convenience of multiple branch locations or thousands of ATMs.

Developing banking relationships early is critical for startups.

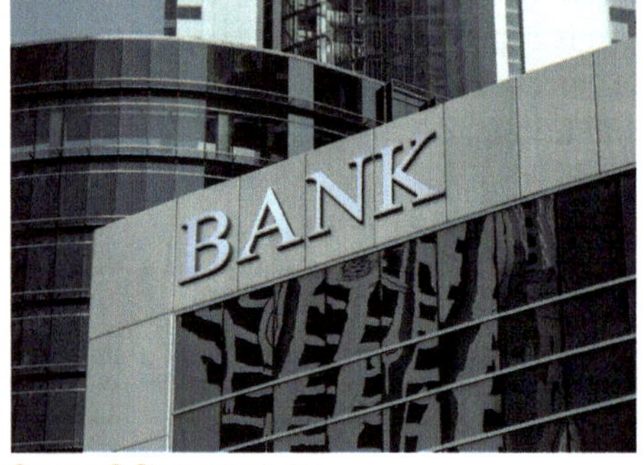

Source: © Shutterstock, Inc.

Remember that your banking priorities as an individual differ from your needs as a business. Consumer banking transactions are relatively simple and routine. Even the more significant decisions such as granting a home loan or financing a personal car purchase are handled entirely by mechanical processes based on your credit rating, your job, and the appraisal; very little, if any, human judgment is involved.

Business banking, on the other hand, remains very relationship driven. Establishing a good personal rapport with bank officers who have the authority to make lending decisions is much more important. Lending to a business requires a lot more understanding on the part of the bank. Your banker will need to know and trust the members of your team. She will also want to know who your customers are and why they need your business. In a local market, she may even know and speak directly to those customers. She should also understand your strategic plans and how that will influence your future lending needs.

Having a thorough understanding of the context in which your business operates enables your banker to make better, faster decisions about lending requests that could mean the difference between life or death for your small business. Finding a bank that understands your market, your area, and your industry is essential. For this reason, regional banks are usually the best choice for a small business owner. The *Wall Street Journal* sums this up nicely in their online guide, "How to Shop for a Bank."

Smaller, regionally focused banks may be better because they know local market conditions. They often provide more one-on-one access to a loan officer and put more emphasis on a borrower's character rather than just applying a credit-score model. And they can be more flexible during tough times, such as covering overdrawn accounts without imposing stiff penalties.[6]

The *Wall Street Journal* qualifies this by noting that if you are interested in getting an SBA-backed loan, a larger institution might be worth considering because they are often more in tune with federal programs. On average, interest rates at larger banks also tend to be lower.

Here is a list of criteria to consider when evaluating a business bank:

- **Attitude:** Do the employees and managers seem happy to see you, and do they want your business? Do you feel they will be on your side when you request a loan or an exception to the normal banking rules?
- **Access:** Can you establish a direct relationship with lending decision-makers?
- **Locations:** Can you get to the bank when you need to? If you travel, do you need access to branch offices or ATMs?
- **Hours**: Is the bank open late or on Saturday—if you need that?
- **Online banking solutions and apps:** Can you deposit checks from your phone? Does their system interface to QuickBooks Online (or whatever accounting program you use)?
- **SBA relations:** Is the bank qualified and eager to make SBA loans?
- **Minimum balance requirements:** How much money do you need to keep in your account to avoid paying onerous fees?
- **Familiarity:** Does this bank understand your business or industry?
- **SBA workout:** Does this bank have a history of good faith efforts to negotiate a workout on seriously delinquent loans?

Interview with a Regional Banker

Interview with Ken Clark, senior vice president of Citizens Business Bank, a successful regional bank in California.

Prof. Autry: Ken, can you describe the basics of a small business banking relationship and why it is important?

Ken Clark: One of the unsung heroes of the American way of life is the banking system that has made our economy strong over the last couple of centuries. Just like a solid banking system is important to a country's financial health, I believe that a solid banking relationship is critical to a business's financial health. If a business has access to capital, it can grow, it can expand, and it can invest in new ventures and new equipment to increase efficiency.

When a business starts in the garage, the banking relationship may be nothing more than a checking account. As the firm grows over time, they will need loans for equipment, receivables, and other things to support growth or to help growth accelerate. As the firm grows, they may need a building, which can also be a great investment for the owners of that business—part of their retirement plan. When a company can do this and still have cash, they can deal with things like 401(k) plans for their employees. Banks make that possible.

Finally, banks can assist with exits and succession plans or moving the business to the next generation. All along that curve, access to banking and those tools really helps the business. If the small business owners didn't have that relationship, they would be restricted at every stage of that curve.

Prof. Autry: What do you think a small businessperson should look for in a bank?

Ken Clark: The common wisdom is that a business needs a good CPA, a good banker, and a good attorney, though hopefully not too often on the attorney! It is really true. A CPA, a lawyer, and a banker deal with a lot of businesses in a lot of industries. If they've been doing it for any length of time, they can guide a businessperson, alerting them to hurdles and opportunities they are likely to encounter. They will say, "Have you thought of this?" or "Look out for that."

Find a banker who has some experience, not one right out of school. Get somebody who has seen a little bit, especially in your industry, when possible. However, to my mind, especially for a small business, the number one thing they should look for is simply good communications. If you can sit down with a banker and communicate your expectations and aspirations—what your business needs are today, what they may be five years down the road—then you've formed a team with the banker. This trust and communication is critical. If their bank doesn't have the tool you need at a particular time, a good banker will be able to direct you to the appropriate partner, perhaps even to another bank to help you with that need or opportunity.

Prof. Autry: What do you think are the advantages and disadvantages of considering a local, regional, or national bank?

Ken Clark: National banks have two specialties. One is dealing with the masses of consumers. They are dealing with millions and millions of accounts and individuals, and they want to do that with the utmost efficiency. The advantage is that the national banks would rather put technology upfront to deal with those masses rather than have those millions of clients using up the time of employees. So, if what you need are automated systems, mobile apps, web services, and things like that, a national bank will have those products right away. The other thing that national banks like to do is deal with very large companies, in many cases, multinational corporations. Of course, that doesn't help the small businessperson at all.

The flip side of this is the community bank. If you go to a community bank, it may have a single branch in your town or maybe up to 20 throughout a small area. They can't afford to develop leading-edge technology because they don't have the masses to support that sort of investment. What they do have is people; people that you can sit down and really talk with.

Regional banks are in the middle. They will get those automated products more quickly than community banks. You can still easily talk to people, but you may need to drive a little farther because they don't have branches on every corner. They will often have specialty areas. In Southern California, for instance, some banks specialize in the entertainment industry. In California's Central Valley, many are expert in the agricultural industry.

If you're a small business and all you think you need is automated and off-the-shelf products, and you don't see that a lot of customization may be needed for you now or in the future, then a large bank may work well for you. If you see that you could use more guidance or that you're going to need a line of credit or some sort of loan that is not necessarily straight off the shelf, a community or regional bank is a better fit.

Prof. Autry: What would you say to an entrepreneur about maintaining their banking relationship?

Ken Clark: As I mentioned, communication and visibility [are] really important. Reinforcing and building that communication is also important. Sitting at your banker's desk for five minutes every month or buying them coffee makes a big difference. They'll remember you if you do that and kind of watch your back to the extent that they can. They may even call you out of the blue with an opportunity! So, I think communication is the most important thing.

It is really important for a small businessperson to remember that your banker is on your side. If you need a loan, it is in the banker's personal interest to give you a loan. There are some things that can't be done, but if it is possible, they are on your team. Getting you that loan helps with their bonus and their goals. In Japan, bankers and business owners have such a tight relationship your banker may call you at the end of the year and say, "Draw on your line of credit for a week, so I can make my bonus." That's an extreme example of the team approach.

If you spread your relationship over five banks, you're not going to have a strong relationship. There may be reasons you need two banks, but try to establish a strong primary banking relationship and give them good business. Keep your face in front of them. That's the number one thing.

Prof. Autry: What other words of advice do you have for entrepreneurs?

Ken Clark: Be aware that there are business cycles. Your business may have a loss year occasionally; banks understand that. A banker's rule of thumb is that two out of three years are profitable for a business. You should be showing enough profit to support the loans and other things you're asking the bank to help with. At times a business will avoid showing profits or show a loss for tax purposes. You can shove all your expenses into the current year, you can make adjustments, and your CPA can help you with those kinds of tax strategies. That's understandable, but realize that showing losses won't help your banker give you what you need, like that equipment loan you may be planning on. You must find a happy medium. If you're showing a profit, you're going to have to pay taxes on that, but if you show a loss every year, it's going to be very hard for your banker to support your growth. By showing a profit, you are contributing to your capital base and demonstrating that you are working with your banker to expand your business. That's teamwork.

Establishing Your Business Credit

As with personal credit, establishing business credit is important to the long-term financial success of your firm. It is also a slow process, requiring diligence and integrity on your part. As with your personal credit, your firm's repayment history and financials will be rated by outside agencies. In the U.S. and many other countries, big and small businesses are tracked by Dun & Bradstreet (D&B). This firm, based in Millburn, New Jersey, maintains records on more than 300 million businesses worldwide. When you launch your firm or begin to seek credit, you will want to get a D&B number. You can obtain this from the D&B website at dnb.com. D&B will ask for regular updates from you about your financial status and collect information from vendors with which you have **net terms**. Your bank, vendors, and other potential creditors will check your D&B rating before extending credit.

net terms

An arrangement in which a firm receives goods or services and pays for them later, on an agreed schedule.

Net Terms

Establishing business credit often begins with securing net terms from your vendors. When you first go to purchase something, your vendors will surely demand cash on delivery (COD) terms or a credit card payment before delivering goods or services. After a few successful transactions, you can usually ask for net terms and get an invoice payable in 15 days. Be sure to pay those promptly. After establishing a track record, you'll have referenceable vendors who can tell other potential vendors, bankers, or lenders that your firm has honored its obligations.

Your personal credit rating is also incredibly important to the establishment of successful business credit. Your bank and other lenders are likely to insist on checking your personal credit rating before granting a business loan. So, even if you don't have a business idea currently, always work on establishing and building your personal credit rating. Protect your personal credit rating from fraud and identity theft—the last thing you need when you are trying to close an important round of business financing is to explain that your bad credit score is due to someone running around damaging your personal credit.

Maintain Your Relationships and Join the Network

Your small business banking relationship does not end when you open the account. If all goes well, it's the beginning of a lifelong relationship. As with any relationship, your small business banking partnership won't sustain itself; you must nurture it. Don't use the ATM. Instead, take the time to go into the branch, make your deposits in person, and be seen. Stop and say "hey" to the vice president (often, everyone at a small bank seems to be a vice president), branch manager, or whomever you work with on a regular basis. They usually sit at desks out in the open for that very purpose. Get to know the assistant manager or senior tellers by name—they will eventually move up the chain. Ask them to lunch, and you'll find they will probably both agree and pick up the check! Take up golf; bankers love to play golf with clients.

This relationship-building isn't just about socializing; it's a process that creates the opportunity for you to build trust. It's a chance for your banker to understand your business and your personal circumstances better as well. Bring your family to an event where your banker will be. When a loan officer is thinking about your kids, saying "no" to your credit line request is a lot harder. That's one reason you need to establish this personal relationship *before* you apply for a loan.

The worlds of angel investors and venture capitalists are similar. These individuals all know each other, and they discuss opportunities. If you don't get funding the first go 'round, don't worry. Investors rarely say, "Get the heck out of my sight." They may not give you money today, but they may want to see how you do. Update them on your progress and, if possible, maintain a social relationship. You and your firm may grow on them, or they may introduce you to the investor who is right for you.

If you work on this, you'll eventually find that you've become an integral part of the local "good old boys" network. Although it's not just for boys anymore, there really is a small group of professionals who run things in most communities or markets. These business owners, bankers, accountants, lawyers, and politicians support each other in the development of their city or industry. While most of them do not intentionally discriminate against "outsiders," the fact remains is that if you're not "in" a group, you are "out" and at a serious and unfair disadvantage. As a business owner, it's much better to be on the inside, and a local banker is a key connection to entering the network. Eventually, you may join the local chamber of commerce, assume a leadership position in an industry organization, or be elected to public office. Always remember where you came from and give those who lack connections the chance to network and prove themselves. Who knows where this may lead? You might even find yourself on *Dragons' Den* someday as one of the dragons!

NED Factors That Are Important in Financing a Business

Firm and Founder: When it comes to raising money, the entrepreneur(s) and their startup are nearly inseparable. Your credit becomes the company credit. Your networking skills determine access to capital. Your credibility closes the deal.

Multiple Paths: New entrepreneurial financing is dynamic. You should tap multiple sources and always keep your options open so you can pull in money when you need it most.

Network, Network, Network: The importance of relationships to securing equity investment and loans cannot be overstated. Network!

Less Is More: You may be struggling each day, but you are learning, learning to innovate because you must, learning to be efficient because you can't afford not to.

Key Takeaways

- Establish business credit early.
- Setup up a D&B number as soon as you establish your business.
- Use debt financing if you can get it.
- Make the effort to develop a banking relationship.
- Always consider running a Kickstarter before going into debt or selling equity.
- Spend the effort to build your firm's credit by getting net terms from suppliers.
- Expand your network by keeping your banking relationship going.
- Work your way into the "in-group" in your community or industry.

7.3 Case Study: Embedded Ventures

Jordan Noone was at a crossroads. The cofounder of Relativity Space had built an amazing commercial space startup and raised more than half a billion dollars in venture capital. His firm was opening a big new corporate headquarters in Long Beach, California, and was refurbishing a 200,000 square foot manufacturing facility at NASA's Stennis Spaceflight Center in Mississippi. They were only about a year away from actually launching the first 3D-printed orbital rocket from one of the firm's two space launch facilities. Still, Noone had the nagging feeling that he should be doing something different. Should he see this journey through to its eventual goal of putting a rocket on Mars or take the plunge on a new venture?

Jordan Noone

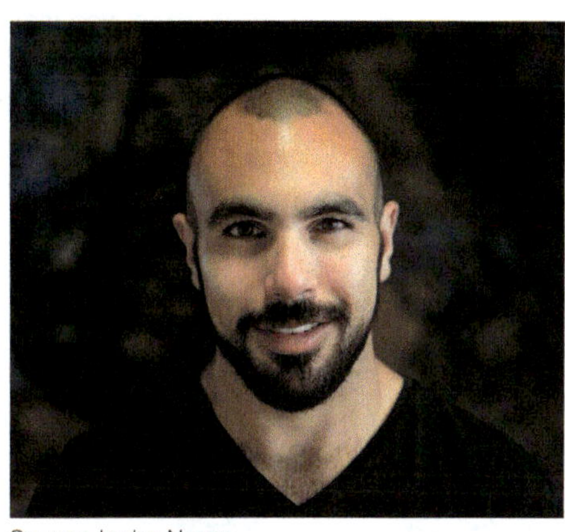

Source: Jordan Noone

Noone grew up in South Pasadena, in Southern California's ethnic melting pot. "Noone is a name most folks can't place, but it's Irish, and I'm a mix of European, Armenian, and Filipino ancestry." As a high school student, he had applied for a scholarship through the Navy ROTC program. "My dad had been Air Force ROTC, so this seemed natural, and I discovered that aerospace engineering was the major most likely to attract military scholarships." The Viterbi School of Engineering at the University of Southern California (USC) was a global leader in that field and would keep him close to his SoCal roots. Things did not go exactly as Noone and his family had planned. "I got into USC, which was amazing, but before I started, I developed emergency appendicitis, and the surgery prevented me from qualifying for the ROTC." Noone's parents had to foot the bill for the expensive private university, an investment which, in hindsight, turned out to be a very good call.

Noone was hungering for a creative outlet that would "let me do something with my hands and take some risks." He adds, "I loved doing things like rebuilding cars, and now all the work was going to be very theoretical and entirely on paper or a computer." Luckily for the future rocket entrepreneur, students from USC's Rocket Propulsion Laboratory (RPL) came to class during the first week to recruit incoming students. He recalls being instantly attracted to the student rocket geeks. "The RPL team appealed to me because they seemed like a band of rebellious misfits. That was very different from the other campus clubs that focused on very achievable personal goals, like pitching some design on paper to a captive audience of pretend investors inside a classroom. The RPL guys wanted to build stuff that would go to space and take it out to the desert and launch it on their own, with basically no supervision. It was a bit crazy, and I loved that."

Just as importantly, Noone also met his future business partner, Tim Ellis, and began to work with him in the rocket lab. Noone took over leadership of the group during his junior year. Although he graduated in 2014, the team he helped build would launch the first student-built rocket to reach space in the spring of 2019.

Noone had received an internship at Elon Musk's SpaceX and eventually went to work full time on the firm's Dragon spacecraft. Ellis moved to Kent, Washington, to work for Jeff Bezos' space startup, Blue Origin. Both of the former RPL buddies suffered through traffic-filled commutes. They began to synchronize that time so they could talk on the phone about many things, including opportunities in the space business. Noone and Ellis had both encountered metallic additive manufacturing (3D printing) at their respective firms but were convinced that a lot more could be done with the technology than they were seeing. The two decided to make the leap and establish a company that would print an entire orbital rocket, eliminating most production labor costs and allowing for unprecedented flexibility in design. Noone sent an unsolicited investment pitch to celebrity investor Mark Cuban and surprisingly received a check for $500,000 to seed fund the crazy idea. Relativity Space was born!

Noone and Ellis were also able to enter the prestigious Y Combinator accelerator. They soon raised $14 million in Series A funding from Silicon Valley VCs Playground Global and Social Capital. This round valued the firm at $35 million. The two used the funds to develop and build the world's largest 3D metal printers and were producing full-sized rocket fuel tanks as well as engines, combustion chambers, and nozzles. Performing well, they were able to close a $35 million Series B round at an $80 million valuation from the same group.

In 2019, things got serious as the team went for a $100 million-plus Series C round from several new investors. Noone notes, "There is a disconnect at this point where you have to communicate professionally to that class of investor." They closed it with $140 million. In late 2020, Relativity Space brought in another $500 million investment, and the firm now had a valuation of $2.3 billion. The two entrepreneurs had everything needed to go to space. The firm had operations going in four states and more than two hundred employees. That was exciting, but managing all that was not the part of the startup process that Noone loved. He says, "I really enjoy the riskier 'zero to one' part of the process where you take a totally new idea and see if it can be turned into a business." Jordan had also learned that he liked finance and communicating with professional investors. The same itch for a little more risk and disruption that had attracted him to the RPL team was working on him again. Although he didn't have any specific idea in mind, he began to feel that he'd rather be exploring and funding a new venture rather than managing and scaling one that was well on its way to success.

Jenna Bryant

Source: Jenna Bryant

Meanwhile, Jenna Bryant had moved to Southern California from Alabama to finish a degree in design and pursue her passion as a hip-hop dancer. At the same time, she picked up a side gig recruiting engineers for hard-to-fill technical roles at early-stage startups. Through this, she realized her passion for working with early-stage tech companies and the engineering community around them. Her first mentor, MySpace co-founder Colin Digiaro, encouraged her to take this newly found passion and turn it into a recruiting firm of her own. She did this and quickly attracted an overwhelming number of clients across the entire tech ecosystem. This also got the attention of Riot Ventures when they relocated their early-stage VC fund to Los Angeles. After multiple attempts to recruit her to join their firm, she finally agreed to join as a partner after realizing the need for someone like her to improve the venture capital industry.

Bryant began hosting "secret" events in order to expand her network of "hard tech" CTOs and technical founders, and Jordan Noone was one of the top targets on her list, given Relativity's growth. After Jordan attended one of her defense-focused events, they began a regular discussion about things they wanted to see improved in the venture capital community. During the 2020 Coronavirus pandemic, Bryant and Noone were constantly on the phone, and Bryant shared her desire to form her own investment firm—with a different twist.

Bryant became increasingly more passionate about providing a different option for early-stage startups, driven by questions she was asking herself. "Early-stage investing is about predicting where science and technology will meet in the future, and the technical competency and leadership qualities of the founders. So why do most early-stage VC's have pure finance backgrounds versus hands-on technical and startup experience? Early-stage hard tech startups need resources beyond what capital and connections can provide. They need expensive physical resources like lab space, rocket launch pads, and manufacturing facilities. So why is there so much distance between early-stage startups and large corporations who can grant access to these resources and possibly even be their first customer? If data prove that diverse teams perform better, why is the VC industry so far behind when it comes to diversity?"

She also noted that engineering-focused entrepreneurs lacked a financial vocabulary and an initial network. "This is the land of warm introductions; nobody gets anywhere near the money unless they have the right friends." That wasn't the best system for optimizing success, and it wasn't fair. Bryant notes, "The lack of diversity in the tech sector holds up a mirror to the VC vetting system."

She also saw that big firms needed access to the innovative cultures of the small ones but couldn't always do the due diligence on the technology. With this in mind, she decided to focus on the defense sector where the Department of Defense and large organizations didn't mesh well with traditional VCs. The key in that market was trust, and as a successful recruiter, she understood how to establish that.

When Jordan Noone finally decided to take the plunge in the fall of 2020 and leave Relativity Space on a quest to find his new venture, Bryant was practically the first person to know that. She immediately saw the potential of Noone as a partner. Here was a guy who understood the technology from hardware to software, could talk finance, and had been through the reality of building and funding a successful startup. Who would be better at the due diligence than Noone? Bryant comments with a wry smile, "I just knew I had to get Jordan on board; lucky for him, he was game." Embedded Ventures was about to launch.

Endnotes

1. Steve Jobs' 2005 Stanford Commencement Address https://youtu.be/UF8uR6Z6KLc.
2. Mollick, E. (2014). The dynamics of crowdfunding: An exploratory study. *Journal of Business Venturing 29.1*, 1–16.
3. To date, Elio has not produced a vehicle for sale.
4. http://www.wsj.com/articles/inside-apples-broken-sapphire-factory-1416436043
5. http://europa.eu/youreurope/business/funding-grants/access-to-finance/index_en.htm
6. *Wall Street Journal*, "How to Shop for a Bank," http://guides.wsj.com/small-business/funding/how-to-shop-for-a-bank/.

CHAPTER 8

Launching

> The critical ingredient is getting off your butt and doing something. It's as simple as that. A lot of people have ideas, but there are few who decide to do something about them now. Not tomorrow. Not next week. But today. The true entrepreneur is a doer, not a dreamer.
>
> —*Nolan Bushnell, founder of Atari*

8.1 Reducing Launch Risk

Learning Objectives

1. Appreciate that entrepreneurs don't seek risk but seek to manage it.
2. Understand the benefits of various organizational forms.
3. Recognize that a partnership is simply a legal agreement.
4. Understand that corporations exist primarily to shield individuals from legal liability.
5. Understand the tax advantages of S corps and LLCs.
6. Understand what a stock option is.
7. Understand which forms of business will support acquisitions and IPOs.
8. Recognize the purpose of the benefit corporation and the importance of stakeholder theory.
9. Understand that a firm with a clear purpose and operational goal is likely to be more successful.

Entrepreneurs do not have to risk their lives as Philippe Petit did tightrope walking the Twin Towers.

Source: Alan Welner/AP

In 1974, a French tightrope walker and his assistant snuck onto the roofs of the World Trade Center's Twin Towers in New York City and tied a cable between the buildings. Phillipe Petit then famously walked across the gap, over 1,000 feet above the city. Petit wasn't paid for the work; in fact it cost him thousands of dollars and his daring stunt got him arrested. Why on Earth would anyone do that? The answer appears to be that some people thrive on risk-taking and the attention they get from their risky behavior. Popular culture often assumes that entrepreneurs are also thrill seekers.

Smart Entrepreneurs Don't Seek Risk, They Manage It

The New Entrepreneurial Dynamic rejects the assumption that successful entrepreneurs seek risk. Rather than viewing entrepreneurs has high-stakes gamblers, NED views entrepreneurs as informed speculators, willing to accept some level of risk when necessary but always endeavoring to minimize it.

existential risk

A risk that could result in the failure (death) of the enterprise.

Minimizing risk means analyzing it and managing it. Many of the **existential risks** that rip many startups apart are actually "baked in" to the company from its founding. This chapter is about avoiding those and setting off on the right foot.

The Organizational Form

Do you use transportation services like Uber and Lyft? Are the rideshare drivers these apps deliver independent entrepreneurs contracting with you for temporary work, or are they essentially employees in the service of the app company you've chosen? Think about it from both sides for a while, and you should find that the answer isn't entirely obvious. Is it important?

The question of whom an Uber driver is working for has economic, legal, and tax implications for Uber, the driver, the customer, and for the government at various levels. It's become a central theme of the debate over what is often called the **gig economy**, a key feature of the New Entrepreneurial Dynamic. The gig economy is really a collection of markets such as transportation, graphic arts, or app coding, in which customers can now connect directly with independent contractors on an as-needed basis, and in situations where these contractors are not officially employed by any firm. In many ways, the contractor is liberated from the burdens of employment in the traditional economy by being able to choose things such as their working hours, vacations, and tools of the trade (car, computer). However, they may also lose the guarantees of set hours of employment and benefits such as sick leave, health care, or unemployment insurance. The theoretical employer, Uber, or another firm, benefits from reducing the complexities of employment associated with such things. They don't have to estimate market demand and pay drivers to sit around if they are wrong. They are off the hook for a lot of government-mandated benefits, paperwork, and taxes.

the gig economy

A collection of markets in which technology has reduced the cost of connecting customers with independent contractors, reducing the requirement for traditional firms and employment.

It may surprise people, but management scholars have actively debated the question of "why do companies exist?" These arguments fall under the general heading of the **theory of the firm**, and for many years much of the debate has centered around the difference between contracting and employment. Free market economists have long asked, "Why don't individuals simply contract with each other for products and services they need at the time?" One of the primary answers involves **transaction costs**. Ronald Coase concluded that if the time required for customers and contractors to search for each other and negotiate terms for each job was too expensive, a firm would then arise that would organize this process and reduce the cost of transacting. For example, going to a supermarket is simpler and cheaper than contracting directly with farmers, ranchers, and bakers even though the cost of the goods is actually lower at the source.

theory of the firm

A collection of economic and organizational behavior theories that seek to explain why companies exist and are structured in the ways they are.

transaction costs

The nondirect cost associated with making a trade for goods or services in an economic market. This is not the price of the good or service itself, but rather the additional expense required for each of the parties to find each other and settle on agreed terms.

In the past, an organized taxi fleet, operated by a firm with advertising and centralized dispatchers using radios to deliver cabs, was better than wandering the streets hoping to find a ride. Uber simply removed that transaction cost by leveraging the ubiquity of the smartphone. Their entire business was based on that recognition, and the economic justification for the existence of the traditional taxi firm vanished overnight. Recall that in a previous chapter, it was noted how a change in technology establishes opportunities for new businesses to emerge.

In the end, the environment determines if a business adds enough value for the customer to support it, and it will also determine how it is organized. This environment is a mix of the market forces previously discussed and government regulations designed to constrain those forces. In many places, governments reacted negatively to Uber and Lyft. London banned them entirely to protect their traditional black cab service. Other governments reacted by taxing the transactions or requiring the service to provide certain benefits the government did not want to assume the cost for.

When you establish your new firm, you will need to be aware of this environment and do your best to fit both the market demands and legal requirements. One of your first major choices will be the **legal form** or business structure of your organization. This refers to whether your firm will be set up as a **sole proprietorship**, a **partnership**, **corporation**, or some variance of these. This choice is important and must be made before conducting any business and requires that you think carefully about the future of your business. It will depend primarily on whom you plan to include in your business and what you plan to do.

What Will You Call It?

If you go into business by yourself without setting up a specific legal structure, you are by default a sole proprietorship. This choice is the very simplest and most common form of business. Recall that in Chapter 1, it was noted that most businesses in the U.S. had only one employee, the founder. Most of those "one-person shops" are sole proprietorships. If you conduct your business operations under your own name, the only requirement in most places is that you report the business income and expenses on your taxes. If you chose a different name for your business such as "Fancy Farms Goat Milk," then you must file a **fictitious name statement** or **DBA** (Doing Business As), which usually involves registering at the local county or city office and placing a public notice online or in a local publication indicating that you are the responsible party behind the operation. The purpose of this is that if your business fails to pay its bills or does some harm, those you owe or those who have been victimized can pursue legal action against you as an individual. That's a concept called **liability**, and it is a very important point we will come back to.

legal form

Also referred to as business structure or legal entity, this is a choice among the several defined forms described by the government for purposes of taxation, regulation, and jurisprudence. The traditional choices are sole proprietorship, partnership, and various forms of corporations.

sole proprietorship

A business run by a single individual for their own benefit. In such a business, the proprietor is individually liable for the activities and the taxes of the firm.

partnership

An agreement between two or more individuals or entities to enter into business operations together.

corporation

A legal structure that creates an entity with many of the same legal functions as a person for purposes of distributing proceeds and protecting the individuals involved from direct liability for the firm's actions.

fictitious name statement

See *DBA*.

DBA

Doing business as, fictitious name statement, a legal notification that a business is operating under a different name than its legal name or of the individual founders.

liability

Financial responsibility for a firm's action.

If your business is called "Sally's Personal Cartoons," and you hand draw caricatures of people from photos they send you over the internet, a sole proprietorship is a reasonable business model. To be clear, Sally's Personal Cartoons could hire employees or pay contractors to help do the drawing, but as long as Sally is the only one putting in **capital** or funds to start the business, and she is the only one claiming an **ownership stake**, then she has ultimate responsibility and takes all the profits from the business. What happens if Sally wants to work with some friends who contribute some money or whose unpaid work constitutes an **in-kind** value that deserves some stake in future business outcomes or ownership? If Sally and her friends decide to start a business and define the terms of ownership and record their obligations and benefits in a verbal or written agreement, they have formed a general partnership. Like a sole proprietorship, the owners of a general partnership are generally liable for the work they do and all the debts and liabilities of the business. Again, while it is easy to set up, a general partnership would not be a good choice for a business that could incur any serious liability.

capital

Funds used to develop infrastructure and acquire resources.

ownership stake

An equity holding (stock) in a company.

in-kind

Products or services traded directly rather than for cash.

A Partnership Is an Agreement

While in most places, you can legally start a partnership with a handshake or some notes scribbled on a napkin, producing a carefully considered and written **partnership agreement** is a very important step in avoiding problems. The most important part of a partnership agreement outlines the contribution each partner will make and the rules for the distribution of profits not reinvested in the business. Additional critical information should also be included:

Launching a partnership is fun, but you need more than just a group high-five!

Source: © Shutterstock, Inc.

- **Legal name:** What is the partnership to be called on legal forms?
- **Purpose:** A brief description of the planned business activities.
- **Names, identifying information, and contact information:** A list of the individuals involved in the agreement and where can they be found. This should include legal names, dates of birth, legal addresses, email addresses, and phone numbers.
- **Capital contributions:** The cash and other noncompensated contributions made by each partner. This includes unpaid labor and resources like computers, cars, or other items placed into the partnership.
- **Expectations:** A list of specific commitments partners will make, usually in regard to contributing time or future assets to the partnership.
- **Ownership interest:** The percentage of ownership agreed upon for each partner. This obviously must total 100 percent. (See Chapter 6 for suggestions on allocating ownership.)
- **Distributions:** A description of how and when profits will be distributed. Losses may also be allocated for tax purposes.
- **Management:** The rules of how the partnership will be managed. This may include noting whether voting by partners is by ownership interest or some other formula. Special rules may be established for things like requiring a **supermajority** to remove a partner.
- **Addition, departure, and removal of partners:** Rules for how the partnership may add a partner, account for the death or disability of a partner, for the voluntary departure of a partner, or involuntary ejection of a partner.
- **Dissolution:** Definition of how and when the partnership can be dissolved. This should include a description of how the assets and liabilities of the partnership will be divided. It will document who gets what's left over in cash, equipment, or contracts, and who is responsible for paying any debts.

partnership agreement

A contract between two or more individuals planning to manage and operate a business.

supermajority

A number larger than 50 percent, such as two-thirds, required by some voting rules.

Templates for partnership agreements are available online, and they can be created using common legal tools from popular services like LegalZoom and Nolo. In general, if you are uncertain of how to proceed or if there are unusual special agreements you want to establish between partners, getting professional legal guidance up front may be the best investment you make. In the United States, you might expect to spend $1,000 to $3,000 to have a lawyer draft your partnership agreement and help you file the legal documents required to establish your firm.

operating agreement

The rules for running a business, including distribution of profits and dissolution. See also *partnership agreement*; *corporate bylaws*.

corporate bylaws

A legal document establishing the rules by which a corporation functions, including voting requirements, stock issuance, distribution of profits and losses, appointment of officers, and dissolution.

Sometimes the partnership agreement is also referred to as an **operating agreement**. It should be clear that any business, large or small, will require rules similar to these in order to avoid conflict between individuals over the control and distribution of profits. The basic components from the partnership agreement are included in documents for more advanced forms of organization such as corporations, where they are referred to as the **corporate bylaws**.

What Do You Plan to Do?

In our society, every person is financially responsible for any economic damage or personal injury that they cause or contribute to. Such damages commonly arise during automobile accidents. In most states in the U.S. and in most countries, a driver who is found to be at fault is responsible for the repairs to the other driver's vehicle and any medical bills the other party generates. You may also be subjected to additional penalties for causing "pain and suffering," and these can sometimes be very significant. For this reason, drivers are usually required to carry an insurance policy that is sufficient to cover even a major accident. You probably know this, but have you considered what might happen if you owned a pizza restaurant and the driver of an uninsured campus food delivery service struck a pedestrian while delivering a pepperoni and pineapple pie from your shop to a nearby fraternity house?

liable

The state of being legally responsible in law, often for damages caused to some victim.

If you operate a business and your customer, employee, contractor, or anyone else is injured directly or even indirectly by the operation of your business or by the product you produce, you may be **liable**. For this reason, businesses also carry insurance, but that may not be enough. Imagine that Sally decides that rather than draw cartoons, she will produce organic, nonpasteurized goat milk products. Pasteurization is a process whereby a food product is heated to a temperature sufficient to kill most bacteria present in the food and has been a common food safety process since the nineteenth century. Sally, however, believes that this artificial heating process reduces the inherent nutritional value and ruins the natural flavor of dairy products. Many customers agree, and Sally is suddenly selling thousands of pints of goat milk around the country. That's great, but what do you think might happen if a large batch of her product were to be accidentally contaminated with dangerous E. coli bacteria and hundreds of people became ill and several died?

lien

A right to take possession of a person or firm's property until a debt is satisfied.

It's likely that Sally's insurance policy could not cover the damages associated with the rash of major lawsuits that will surely follow such a tragic occurrence. When an insurance policy falls short, the operator of the business is responsible for the remainder of the damages. Without any further protection, she would literally lose everything she owned and likely have a **lien** against her future earnings, possibly for the rest of her life. Given that sort of jeopardy, why would anyone, no matter how passionate or meticulous, ever risk entering the food industry?

The Corporation

It's hard to imagine how you could cause any serious injury with a business like Sally's Personal Cartoons. But, for the goat milk business, there is a preferable legal form, the corporation. A corporation is a legal entity, essentially an "artificial person" for legal purposes. You are creating an entity that will conduct your business and assume responsibility for it. You may be the owner and operator of the business, but the corporate entity is responsible for its economic actions and, in most cases, assumes all the legal liabilities generated by the business. In practical terms, this means that if someone is poisoned by some nasty bacteria that inadvertently got into a batch of Sally's Goat Milk, only the company is legally responsible, and Sally herself is not, provided the corporation has been properly formed and maintained. The assets of Sally's Goat Milk would be forfeited to pay a judgment from a lawsuit by the victims but not Sally's home, car, retirement, etc. You may indeed lose your business in such a disaster, but you will not lose your home, car, and future.

This protection offered by a corporation is often referred to as the **corporate veil**, and it is why most serious businesses are corporations of some sort. Any business operations that could conceivably result in serious economic or physical injury should be set up as a corporation from day one—before any business is conducted. It can be tempting to do a little business before you spend the time or pay for incorporation—but don't! If you sell just a few pints of goat milk before you get around to the legal formation, you could still be at risk of losing everything you own. In fact, it's reasonable to expect that product quality problems are more likely to occur early on in the business before you've built up a great deal of experience.

corporate veil

The protection from individual liability provided to business owners by the corporate legal structure.

Another important feature of a corporation is that it continues to exist as a legal entity even after its owners die. For this reason, it is preferred by those who wish to see their businesses continue without them and allow for a less complex transfer of the firm's assets to their heirs, who simply inherit the firm's stock and assume control if that stock represents a majority interest.

Who Will Pay the Taxes?

Other motivations beyond liability will influence your choice of a legal business structure. Since a corporation is a legal entity, it has tax obligations just like a person. In the United States, a traditional corporation, commonly known as a "C Corp," is required to pay income taxes at the federal level and in almost every state. This makes sense to most people who presume that businesses enjoying the protection of the corporate legal status, using government infrastructure (highways, air traffic system, courts), and other benefits (military protection, technology development) should be required to contribute to governmental operations. In fact, as of this writing, only South Dakota and Wyoming have placed no tax on corporate income or revenues. However, many small business owners find this extremely unfair. Can you think why?

Understand how your choice of business structure will impact your taxes.

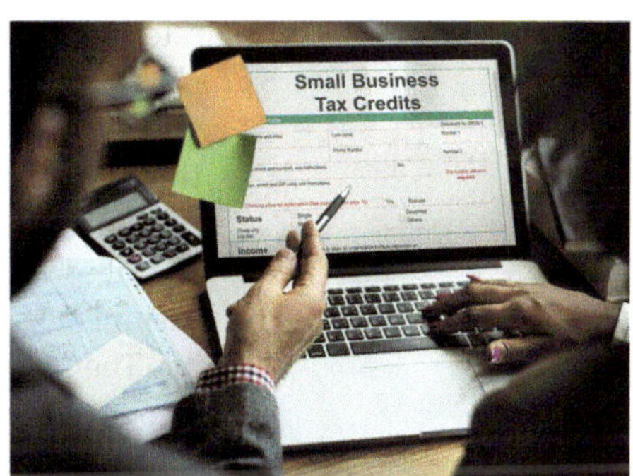

Source: © Shutterstock, Inc.

Let's return to Sally's Goat Milk a decade after its founding. The goat milk market is in a boom as a new study suggests that it may reduce the symptoms of ligma (a tragic illness the victims of which are primarily online game players). The business is now grossing $1.2 million a year, and after all costs, Sally's firm is recognizing tidy profits of $240,000! Sally has clearly made it to the ranks of the well-to-do. There is no reason Sally's Goat Milk shouldn't be paying its fair share to the U.S. government and the State of California where Sally is headquartered, correct?

Sally's Goat Milk, a C Corp, dutifully shells out 21 percent[1] of its profits or $50,400 to the **Internal Revenue Service (IRS)** and 8.84 percent or $21,216 to the California Franchise Tax Board.[2] Sally's firm now has $168,384 left over, and as the only shareholder, Sally issues a **dividend**, or payment of corporate profits, to herself in that amount. Guess what? Sally, the individual, now has income! The IRS would like 32 percent ($53,882) of that, and California would like 9.3 percent ($15,660), leaving Sally with just $98,841 of her $240,000 windfall. Her final tax rate was effectively a whopping 59 percent. She will also have to pay many other taxes and fees, including 15.3 percent for the corporate and personal Social Security and Medicare contributions, reducing her actual income significantly more. While this is a worst-case scenario and Sally could have used many strategic deductions and other techniques to lower these taxes, she still faces the fundamental issue of paying taxes twice on the same income, which is often referred to as "double taxation" and is the bane of small business owners around the world.

Internal Revenue Service (IRS)

The U.S. federal agency tasked with collecting income taxes from businesses and individuals.

dividend

A distribution of a portion of a firm's profit paid to its shareholders.

closely held firms

A company with relatively few owners, as compared to a large publicly traded company that may have millions of shareholders.

shareholders

Individuals or entities who own a portion of a firm.

Luckily, or actually, through the political action of business leaders, there are solutions to this problem, at least at the federal level in the United States. Recognizing that Sally's business would be treated very differently if it were a sole proprietorship, the IRS introduced the Subchapter S election or "S Corp" option for **closely held firms**. A corporation with fewer than 100 **shareholders**, all of whom are legal U.S. citizens or residents, may elect this tax filing option with the IRS and essentially avoid paying federal taxes. Rather, the profits or losses generated by an S Corp are passed through to the shareholders of the company for tax purposes. This means Sally must pay the taxes on all of Sally's Goat Milk profits on her personal income taxes at her personal rate. She will not pay a double tax. Most states follow the IRS S Corp rule, although some, including California, tax at least a portion of the S Corp income. Can you think of any downsides for a business owner using the S Corp structure?

The personal income tax rate can often be higher than the corporate rate, particularly if your business is small and you have other significant income (maybe from keeping your day job). Secondly, what if you prefer to keep the profits in the firm to reinvest in growth? You still must pay the firm's taxes on them on your personal income tax filing! If your fast-growing startup made $500,000 and you wanted to plow it all back into new capabilities, equipment, and additional employees, you could very well owe $200,000 or more in personal federal and state taxes.

These tax implications can be particularly troublesome when you have several owners in the S Corp with different personal tax situations. Imagine a quickly growing medical software startup, established as an S Corp and having three shareholders. Becky and Johan, the founders, each hold 45 percent of the firm's stock for a total of 90 percent and have a controlling interest in any corporate decisions. They have generously rewarded their top employee, Helena, with a 10 percent share in the startup! Becky and Johan are already independently wealthy from selling their previous software enterprise to a large company. They don't need any additional income and really want to keep this new company growing to ensure an even bigger exit and have decided to reinvest the entire $1 million into expanding the offices and recruiting top new developers and sales staff. While Helena is thrilled with the possibilities, she also discovers that she has received a form called a Schedule K-1 that informs her she has an additional $100,000 in taxable income (10 percent of the $1 million profits). The state and federal taxes on that income are over $40,000, more than her entire take-home income for the year! In this case, Helena's S Corp has done so well that she may have to declare personal bankruptcy. She could even face criminal prosecution for failure to pay her income taxes. In the worst of circumstances, the firm could fail, and she'd never even see the $100,000 in profits she paid taxes on, though she might share in the tax loss generated at the time of the firm's final tax filing. How could such a disaster have been avoided?

option

An option is an agreement allowing an individual to purchase shares in a firm at a later date for a set amount. They are often granted to the employees of startups, allowing them to participate in the firm if and when it is successfully sold or goes public. This motivates the employees while avoiding the complexities of having many shareholders during the growth state.

There are several ways to avoid this scenario, but the most important component is communications. One might assume that Becky and Johan didn't intend to ruin Helena's financial life with their generous gift. Had they understood the situation, they could have agreed to distribute enough of the $1 million so that the amount Helena received balanced the additional income tax she owed. Of course, every dollar given to Helena under this plan requires they take $9 out of the firm for themselves, even if they don't want that. Other strategies might include issuing an employee bonus to Helena or, rather than giving her stock at all, offering her an **option** to purchase stock later at some greatly discounted price. These tax issues will be expounded upon later in the text. The point is that the selection of a legal structure must be carefully considered; do not choose one just because it seems the simplest.

Still, most really big companies, and all publicly traded ones, are C Corps. One might ask if the S Corp structure is a mechanism whereby small businesses gain an unfair advantage over larger C Corp firms. In reality, very large corporations have become experts at avoiding federal and state taxes. For instance, General Electric corporation, considered by many to be the ninja of tax avoidance, had profits of more than $40 billion from 2008 to 2015 and paid no federal income tax. In fact, GE was able to structure its finances in a way to claim $1.3 billion back from the government, an effective tax rate of -3.4 percent![3]

Similarly, while Apple notes that it pays 40 percent on its "U.S. profits," the firm has effectively avoided most American and California taxes for years by moving two-thirds of its global income to

Irish corporations that are located in obscure tax havens like the tiny island of Jersey, in a tax avoidance scheme that has raised the ire of both the U.S. and European Union.[4] The bottom line is that corporate taxes amount to less than 10 percent of federal revenues, whereas personal taxes account for half of the revenues, and a great deal of that is paid by sole proprietorships, partnerships, and S Corps. Entrepreneurs ought not to feel guilty when taking advantage of legal structures to avoid paying double taxes.

While the complexities of these tax strategies can be daunting, worrying about how to distribute profits is a good problem to have for any startup. Most startups lose money for the first few years. An important upside of a pass-through tax entity is the converse fact that losses from the business flow onto the personal tax returns of the shareholders in proportion to their holding. This makes them very attractive to investors who are almost always high-income individuals looking for ways to reduce their individual tax burdens. While losses are not sustainable, most investors are happy to receive a Schedule K-1 with a negative number on it during tax season, directly reducing their **marginal income**, the portion of their earnings that is taxed at the highest rates. If Sally's Goat Milk burns through almost all its investments as an S Corp, Sally and her investors will get a good portion of that money back on their taxes. In this way, government policy partially subsidizes investments in risky startups. For this reason, almost all startups choose a legal form that allows pass-through taxation.

marginal income

The last portions of income added to the total income of a person or firm. The marginal income is usually taxed at the highest tax rate.

Lastly, it is worth noting that an S Corp can switch to a C Corp simply by electing that corporate form with the IRS. The C Corp is the required form for a publicly traded firm, so if your organization is so ambitious as to plan for an **initial public offering (IPO)** of stock on a major stock exchange, the C Corp may still be the right choice. There are challenges to choosing the S Corp form, however. Can you think of what they might be?

initial public offering (IPO)

The first time a firm's stock is made available to everyone via its listing on a public stock exchange like the New York Stock Exchange.

Other Hybrid Forms

Among the downsides to the S Corp are the fact that the tax obligations and benefits are doled out proportional to the investment. This often means that a startup founder with little or no income is getting most of the early tax losses for the organization. These losses would be better allocated to the firm's higher-income investors. Additionally, some investors cannot invest in an S Corp at all because of their own legal forms or nationality. The S Corp limits shareholders to 100 U.S. citizens or permanent residents. For instance, partnerships may not be owners of stocks in an S Corp. Many angel investor groups form partnerships or similar legal forms to co-invest.

For these reasons, another legal form called the **limited liability company (LLC)** was developed. The LLC is essentially a partnership that also provides similar protection (though not as thorough as a corporation) of personal assets from business liability and the ability to elect S Corp pass-through tax structure. The LLC allows for avoidance of double taxation while being more flexible on ownership and distribution of taxes. The LLC can include partnerships, corporations, and foreign persons as owners.

limited liability company (LLC)

Legal form of business organization that protects the founders from personal liability and affords "pass-through" tax treatment at the individual tax rate, avoiding double taxation in the distribution of profits. There are several variants of the LLC form including the professional limited liability company (PLLC) and the limited liability partnership (LLP).

S corporations may avoid "self-employment tax" by reporting the owner(s) as employee(s) with standard deductions for FICA taxes (Social Security and Medicare). Corporate earnings after a "reasonable salary" can be treated as unearned income that is not subject to further FICA taxes.

One of the least discussed and most important advantages of the LLC is that it can divide ownership into classes for tax purposes. If Sally's Goat Milk is an S Corp and burns cash during its growth phase and generates tax losses that pass through to its owners, Sally is the biggest recipient of those losses because the taxable profits or losses are distributed on the K-1 in proportion to ownership. As founder, Sally is still holding the majority of the company's stock. Her investors, who own a minority share in the firm, get lesser losses. Can you think of any problem with that?

As an entrepreneur working full time on a startup that is not yet making a profit, Sally doesn't have much income. She doesn't need a tax loss right now. Her investors, however, are high-income individuals and would love that loss. In fact, it's one of the most attractive short-term reasons to invest. The LLC solves that by allowing profits and losses to be allocated as the management sees fit. That means tax losses can go to investors who can apply them now. In the future, tax profits might go to low-income shareholders like Sally, who are in lower tax brackets and are working for the future returns of the company. This allows money to stay in the firm for growth while not punishing the high-income investors. Doing this "tax dance" optimally and legally will require consulting with all the investors before tax season under the supervision of an experienced accountant.

Finally, the legal requirements of an LLC are simpler than with an S Corp. Corporations are required to engage in procedures that include maintaining a board, electing officers, conducting meetings, and recording minutes. In practice, these requirements are relatively simple, but they must be done. The partnership-like LLC, on the other hand, requires only an operating agreement and very little follow-through. In general, most new startups choose the LLC form, and in most cases, it is probably the preferable choice for the widest variety of firms and circumstances.

It is more difficult to move an LLC to a C Corp should you decide to issue an IPO at a future date. LLCs are also required to use accrual accounting, whereas an S Corp can file taxes on a cash or accrual basis. As will be discussed in future chapters, flexibility in this reporting option can enable strategies to reduce tax obligations.

Still Other Forms

In the United States, corporate law is a state-level function, and vary from state to state. There are also some exotic variations on the LLC, such as the professional limited liability corporation (PLLC), which exists in some states specifically for certain professions like lawyers, accountants, and engineers. California has a special limited liability partnership (LLP) structure for only accountants and lawyers; other professions (as defined by state law) must operate under a form called the professional corporation (PC). Neither the LLP nor the PC provides full legal protection for professionals as the state wishes to keep doctors, accountants, and others responsible for malpractice. This is a situation where one should engage experienced legal advice.

Earning Profits for the Benefit of Others

The **benefit corporation (B Corp)** is a recent legal structure recognized in some U.S. states for the increasing number of **social entrepreneurship** businesses. This organizational structure has a primary goal of serving a social need rather than being entirely focused on generating profits for stockholders. The trend began in 2011, and as of this writing, the B Corp is recognized in thirty-three states and the District of Columbia. The assumption that a firm has obligations to a variety of **stakeholders**, including its community, nation, and the environment, has historical roots in the management concept of **stakeholder theory** advanced by R. E. Freeman[5] and the older political doctrine of corporate responsibility. However, in recent decades a growing perception among business leaders and educators has been that a firm is legally bound to maximize shareholder value, and anything that distracts from generating profits and returning them to investors could be seen as mismanagement. Can you see any potential problem with holding the managers of all firms responsible for generating maximum economic returns?

The B Corp is an effort to provide protection to corporate officers and managers who want to prioritize other stakeholders or even outside beneficiaries of their firm's efforts over return on investment. To be clear, a B Corp is not a charity; it is a real profit-generating business with investors. Establishing a firm as a B Corp signals to investors that they should expect their investments to be used to do some social good as well as hopefully return profits. For example, a B Corp might simply give away a portion of its profits to needy individuals or to charities that align with its founding values. It may also conduct a relatively normal business such as running grocery stores but is intentionally locating those stores in underserved or economically depressed areas that offer lower profits and greater risk of failure. A B Corp might choose to employ disadvantaged workers, such as convicted felons, seniors, or those with disabilities, who might not otherwise be able to find steady work.

To further complicate things, there are a variety of new variations on the B Corp model in some states, including the benefit LLC (B LLC) and the low-profit limited liability company (L3C). The scope of this text and the dynamically changing environment for these legal forms don't allow for detailing all the options here. If you are interested in a social entrepreneurship startup, you should do some serious online research and reach out to your accounting and legal professionals before choosing a status.

benefit corporation (B Corp)

A corporate form created specifically for firms with a social mission.

social entrepreneurship

A business with a mission to do some social or other good in addition to its efforts to generate profits.

stakeholders

Individuals or entities holding an interest in the actions and success of an enterprise. These may include employees, shareholders, customers, community members, etc.

stakeholder theory

The concept that management has an obligation to consider the interest of additional parties beyond just the shareholders.

Legal		Personal Asset	Income Tax	Income Tax		
Form	Perpetual Duration	Liability Protection	Rate	Allocation	Ownership	Formalities
Sole Proprietorship	No	None	Personal Rate	100%	1 person	None
Partnership	No	None	Personal Rate	By % ownership	Several People	Partnership Agreement
C Corp	Yes	Very Strong	Corporate Rate	To Corporation	Many People, Partnerships or Corporations	Bylaws, Board, Meetings, Filings
S Corp	Yes	Very Strong	Personal Rate	By % Ownership	100 U.S. Citizens or Residents	Bylaws, Board, Meetings, Filings
LLC	Maybe	Strong	Choose	As Desired	Many People, Partnerships, or Corporations	Operating Agreement
B Corp	Yes	Strong	Choose C or S Corp	Corp or % Ownership	C or S Corp	Bylaws, Board, Meetings, Filings

Start Wisely with the First Step, Regardless of Where You Do Business

Specific examples from the U.S. are described here. Legal forms in the UK, Europe, and other developed countries are similar, but subtly different, particularly in regard to taxes. Also, remember these rules are constantly changing at the national as well as the state or provincial levels. Be sure you understand your current local laws before choosing a legal form. For more details on the American rules, extensive online resources from the government agencies and various business advisory sites can help explain them further. The U.S. Small Business Administration (sba.gov) and the IRS have web pages and downloadable documents of these legal forms. Popular business websites like Investopedia and Forbes do as well. Finally, online providers of legal services like LegalZoom and Nolo also offer valuable information at no cost, though they do wish to sell you additional services.

In the United Kingdom, Companies House, a government resource, provides extensive information on forming startups online.[6] The Federation of Small Businesses, or FSB, is a nonprofit membership organization for small businesses that also offers a wealth of information.[7] In the European Union, the Your Europe site offers information on startup rules and taxes with links to individual EU nations.[8]

In the end, you should probably consult with an experienced accountant and lawyer who understands your local laws and tax rules before you choose a legal form for your startup. An investment in a few hundred dollars, pounds, or euros of professional services may help you avoid thousands in liabilities or taxes later.

Not All Startups Are 100 Percent Fresh

Imagine that Sally has organized Sally's Goat Milk as an LLC and then discovers that camel milk is a growing market with a dedicated base of health-conscious consumers. She decides to try distributing products from the humped ungulates along with her famous goat milk, cheese, and butter. Does she need to form a new company to do that? No, she does not need to form a new company. In fact, Sally could use her LLC to sell anything from music to medical software if she so chose. However, while it might just be a weird enough moniker for an alternative rock band, the healthcare industry isn't likely to trust an **electronic medical record (EMR)** from a company called Sally's Goat Milk.

electronic medical record (EMR)

An enterprise software system designed to record and track medical patient healthcare information.

Sally may just be the next Steve Jobs or Elon Musk, a parallel entrepreneur able to simultaneously tackle some very diverse markets. But there are many reasons that Jobs never merged Pixar with Apple and that Musk kept Tesla and SpaceX generally separate. A primary reason is that the investors for each venture can be very different, and their expectations of an exit strategy may vary. Can you see how this applies to Sally's situation?

Imagine Sally's interest in health outcomes leads her to envision a whole new concept for a holistic EMR. She starts working on it with resources from Sally's Goat Milk, but it quickly becomes clear it can't stay within the goat milk brand or operation. To do this, Sally is required to file an additional fictitious name statement or DBA, letting the world know that her LLC is behind HoloHealth. Unless they go looking for public records, no hospital will know that HoloHealth started as a goat milk distributor. Can you see any problems that might develop as Sally grows both the milk and tool sides of her business?

Sally's Goat Milk business may require only a few hundred thousand dollars, and its friends and family investors are likely to be satisfied taking profits out over time. HoloHealth, on the other hand, will require millions of dollars in product development, marketing, and sales to penetrate the demanding and highly specialized medical software market. The investors in HoloHealth will expect a big exit in the form of an IPO or sale of the startup to a larger firm for billions of dollars. The corporate form for HoloHealth will probably be a C Corp with a formal board of directors who have absolutely no expertise or interest in the goat milk business. Sally needs to set up HoloHealth as a separate business, even if she brings some of her original team or resources into the new company.

Spinoffs, Distractions, and Focus

If a company starts a business and then decides to make it a separate operation because management believes it will create more shareholder value operating separately, this firm is called a **spinoff**. Can you think of any famous spinoff firms? United Airlines was a spinoff created by entrepreneur William Boeing to ensure a large customer for his airplane building business. He achieved this via the acquisition of a number of small air carriers around 1930. United had obvious synergies with Boeing, and that makes a lot more sense than Sally heading off into healthcare software. Sally's HoloHealth must grow larger than its parent company and has no **synergy**. It will suck resources and Sally's time from the goat milk business, putting both startups at risk. Entrepreneurs are naturally curious and creative. They are constantly coming up with great new ideas. Distracting themselves by following unrelated brilliant ideas that do not provide value to their core business is one of the most common ways that entrepreneurs sabotage their own startups. A laser focus on your core business and rejecting distracting opportunities is a critical tactic in minimizing the risk during the launch of a new startup.

spinoff

A startup that is launched from an existing company.

synergy

The additional benefit that arises when complementary parties or ideas come together in an effort.

Sometimes, however, a spinoff is a great opportunity for an entrepreneur. Let's say you're working on a team at a large firm but feeling your entrepreneurial oats. You and your coworkers have been kicking around one of these great ideas, but management says it is too unrelated and too distracting for the firm to pursue. Rather than being frustrated, this may be just the opportunity for you to launch a new venture with some wind at your back! Go to your supervisors and say, "This is a huge opportunity, somebody needs to do it, and we can generate value for our shareholders if we do it in a spinoff." Randy Komisar, who wrote the preface to this book, seized just such an opportunity when he was at Apple. In 1987 Randy cofounded an Apple spinoff company, Claris, with the mission to develop a line of quality software for Apple's computer line that would not directly compete with Apple's third-party developers. Apple funded the startup and provided ready access to customers, any startup's dream. Claris' software packages, particularly it's FileMaker database, were big hits, and Randy netted several million dollars when the firm was sold. The buyer, ironically, was Apple!

Key Takeaways

- Approach risk rationally.
- Make a wise choice on your organizational form upfront.
- Plan for the tax considerations of your choice of organizational form.
- Consider forming a B Corp if you would like your business to be grounded in doing social or environmental good.
- It may be worth spinning off operations that distract from your firm's core mission.

8.2 Getting Going

Learning Objectives

1. Understand what you can accomplish in launching a startup while remaining employed.
2. Recognize the value of developing written agreements.
3. Be familiar with the common causes of company failure.
4. Understand the value of establishing efficient communications norms in a startup.
5. Understand why insurance is important and the various types of insurance a startup may require.
6. Understand the basic options for startup facilities.

Leaving Your Comfy Day Job

One of the ways to mitigate the early risk of your startup going bankrupt is to work another job to pay your own bills so you can invest some time, without pay, into the startup. The challenge here is that you are not giving 100 percent to either your employer or your new venture. If your business is anything more ambitious than selling some stuff online in your spare time, there has to be a point when you will cut the cord. On the other hand, you may hate your corporate job so much that you are far too eager to run away and join the entrepreneurs without adequately planning for the harsh reality of self-employment. How do you know when it's time to risk it all on your new venture?

Choose the moment to leave your corporate job carefully.

Source: © Shutterstock, Inc.

Remember the quote, "Customers are required; everything else in a business is optional," from Chapter 2? It should be your guide here. Once you can be fairly confident that somebody will pay for your product or service, you can take the risk of investing time and money. The process of customer discovery can be conducted relatively easily as a part-time pursuit because it's an asynchronous activity with a schedule driven by you. Many other forms of marketing can be effectively accomplished online, anytime. Basic R&D and initial product design and development of a minimum viable product have been famously accomplished by folks with other jobs. Steve Wozniak was working at Hewlett-Packard when he designed and built the first Apple computer. You can line up your suppliers and get your bank accounts ready.

Recruiting the critical members of your startup team is something you need to do before you launch. Recall what you learned from Noam Wasserman in Chapter 6 about the most effective teams? Professor Wasserman told us that teams formed from former coworkers are often the most effective. That's why many startups, even if they are not officially spinoffs, emerge from workgroups in larger companies. This gives you time to establish relations with your banker, lawyer, accountant, and other professionals.

Most importantly, you can often do some initial **pre-sales**, getting solid purchase orders before delivering the product or service, with select customers, as long as your regular work is the sort that will allow you to respond promptly to customer opportunities. It's a whole lot more comfortable to step away from your job nest and fly into entrepreneurship when you have some real commitments for cash under your wing!

pre-sales

Selling products or services in advance for prepayment. A popular way to improve small business cash flow.

However, once you start delivering products, everything flips, and suddenly you must be available to respond to your customers' needs and on their schedule. Except for businesses that are entirely online, it's doubtful you can accomplish this satisfactorily and hold down another job. An idea that frequently occurs to highly paid entrepreneurs, like skilled engineers holding down good jobs, is to recruit a partner or hire an employee to work full-time handling sales and customer support while they continue to work their day job. This sounds like a dream solution, but in reality, it is nearly always a recipe for disaster. Such an arrangement usually produces dismal financial results because the person most qualified to pitch to the best customers is obviously not fully committed to the product or service being sold. Additionally, the arrangement is practically engineered to breed resentment between the partners or employer and employee. The New Entrepreneurial Dynamic requires full commitment.

Preventing a Lawsuit

It is far better to do the legal work before there is a disagreement.

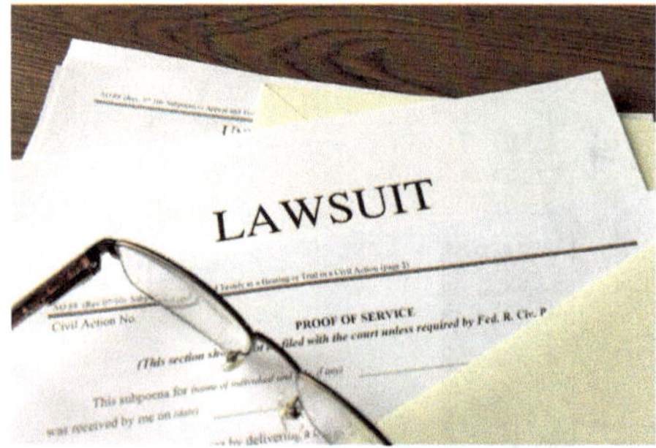

Source: © Shutterstock, Inc.

Every business has multiple important stakeholders; owner(s), customers, vendors, employees, family members, and spouses are some of the most important ones. Often when businesses fail or do exceptionally well, some of these stakeholders will conclude they have not been treated properly. Partners want bigger shares for their contributions. Customers want to renegotiate pricing. Vendors desire better terms. Family members may feel they contributed. Finally, spouses and significant others have broken up as many businesses as they have bands. While some of these conflicts are unavoidable, the vast majority can be prevented with a little foresight, good communications, an open-door policy, and solid written agreements. Let's look at these points one-by-one.

Avoiding Disaster

As the saying goes, "Always expect the worst, and you'll never be disappointed." Try not to depress your entrepreneurial spirit before you launch your firm, but be wise and spend some time imagining everything that could go wrong. If you Google "reasons that business fail," you'll find a long list of articles and studies offering the top 5, 10, or 20 causes for failure. The most common of these are summarized next.

Lack of cash: The business equivalent of "cardiac arrest," running out of money is the proximate cause of death for nearly every startup, often just when they feel they were about to turn the corner to profitability. It's extremely rare to find an entrepreneur who correctly anticipated all the problems and opportunities on the road ahead, most of which need to be addressed by spending money. Consequently, most business plans, pitch decks, and cocktail napkins underestimate the investment required. If you can, raise a lot more than you think you need. As mentioned in Chapter 16, "Cash is king." That said, do not "live large" as a startup. Many dot com firms demonstrated that the sense of wealth created by big investments, when spent lavishly on facilities and goodies, undermined productivity. Plan to keep money in the bank but operate like it isn't there.

Lack of customers: Many entrepreneurs fall in love with their product, and discovering that not everyone feels the need or even wants it comes as a brutal shock. Failure to take seriously the customer discovery and product/market fit concepts discussed in Chapter 4 and Chapter 5 has run more businesses out of funds than any other cause. Typically, what happens is that customer discovery gets done on the fly after the first product is bombing in the real market. The "postmortem" suggests that the basic business concept has merit but wasn't presented in a way that was palatable to consumers. A pivot or major iteration is required, and a new development cycle burns the startup's cash. New marketing and sales efforts are initiated, and liabilities grow. Just as customer orders begin to trickle in, the firm finds itself too low on funds to continue. Do your customer homework up front. Get some pre-sales in hand before you launch.

Wrong team: The original group of friends that were hanging around when the founder or co-founders conceived the business is highly unlikely to be the very best team for taking the product to market. All too often, entrepreneurs grab the resources most easily available to them, including packing the startup with a cadre of buddies who happen to have time on their hands (a warning sign). Later, the harsh realities of product and customer development demonstrate that experienced experts are required. Removing, demoting, or reassigning the wrong people on the startup team later is painful and expensive. It's a distraction and cost that has driven many a promising firm into bankruptcy. Do your research about what skills you will need and get the best from the start. Be brutally honest with yourself up front, and disappointment will be avoided. Be clear about who is "just helping out" and to whom you have made a commitment for full participation in your startup.

Team dysfunction: Sometimes, even a group of highly qualified individuals will produce spectacularly disastrous results. A band composed entirely of all-stars, with their accompanying egos, is unwieldy. Finding the right people and managing them are two different skills. In addition to selecting the best, you want to carefully consider how you will deploy them and keep them satisfied with their jobs, pay, and equity stakes. Understand all the personalities involved in your endeavor and how they are likely to behave under serious stress. Plan ways to keep your team aligned and cohesive from the start, as team-building exercises applied after conflicts emerge are usually doomed to fail. These techniques are best applied proactively, so budget time and money for them from the start.

Lack of dynamism: The only surely predictable thing about launching a business is that the unpredictable will occur. The New Entrepreneurial Dynamic assumes that most startups will need to pivot or iterate their product or service in some substantial way in order to match their market and survive. Flexibility in attitude and organizational structure are the key elements for survival in these cases. Additionally, many sudden business failures come from unanticipated disasters that can range from the emergence of a well-funded and superior competitor to acts of God like floods or earthquakes. Rigid businesses rapidly collapse under such circumstances; dynamic ones quickly adapt, relocate, or reorient and survive.

Good Communications

Ensuring that a team holds together and is rowing in the same direction always depends on rapid, continuous, and effective communication. What this means is that everyone in the management team knows what they need to know. It also means they aren't burdened with useless information or trapped in time-consuming meetings about things they do not need to know. Establishing protocols and systems where people can communicate actionable data to one another is key to the success of your organization.

In an example of proactively managing negative communications, Elon Musk famously sent an email to Tesla employees encouraging them to avoid frequent and large meetings and to walk out of any meeting or drop any call where they felt they were not adding value.[9] This is very sound advice. To avoid these meetings, calls, and unmanageable email boxes, consider using modern digital tools that allow open access to communications but manage them through organized and searchable threads. The Slack app is a great tool for startup teams to coordinate and communicate. Whatever you choose for communications standards, choose wisely and with intent. If you do not define communications standards and establish a communications culture, haphazard systems and inefficient norms will develop organically as your firm grows. If you address this later, you will encounter cultural resistance to change, and the **switching costs** of moving to better systems will be very high.

switching costs

The nondirect costs generated when a customer changes from one product to another, most often the time spent adapting to a new system.

Open Door Policy

Elon Musk's email to Tesla employees also stated, "Communication should travel via the shortest path necessary to get the job done, not through the 'chain of command.'" Musk carries this across firms. In his office at SpaceX, he sits at a desk in an open cubicle that anyone can walk right up to. Of course, the bearer of news had better have a really good reason to bother the CEO.

In addition to enabling better decision-making, another good reason for having such an "open door" policy is that resentment and conflict invariably build within organizations where executive management is separated from those doing the work. As fun as it might be to build an exclusive executive suite, that sort of closed, status-driven environment is toxic to innovation and to the dynamism a young firm needs to survive. Everyone in your organization needs to be available and responsive. Build that expectation into the culture from day one, and establish it with physical facilities that are open and inviting.[10]

Solid Written Agreements

side agreements

Agreements made about the future operations, transfer of ownership or distribution of profits, etc., in a business that are in addition to the regular partnership agreement or corporate documents.

Many of the things that go wrong in an organization can best be prevented or mitigated by the effective implementation of written agreements. As previously noted, an agreement is required to have a partnership or operating agreement, and a corporation has bylaws. Too often, entrepreneurs eager to roll up their sleeves and get down to work eschew the drudgery of drafting these documents and copy boilerplates from their lawyers or some online resource in an attempt to fill the minimum requirements for running their business. These generic documents don't actually deal with the issues that are most likely to arise. A number of written **side agreements** should be considered with any new business. Among these are the following.

Buyout agreement: Startups benefit from those actively working in the firm having "buy-in" or "skin in the game" in the form of ownership. Absentee ownership dilutes the influence of those running the firm in determining direction and is often distracting. If you set up your initial equity split today with the assumption that everyone currently engaged will remain engaged and no significant new players will enter the firm, you're wrong. Someone will decide they have to take a great job offer elsewhere, relocate with their spouse, or they might even get ill or die. A buyout agreement ensures that when a cofounder, partner, or other major stockholder leaves the firm, they leave their stock behind as well. Such an agreement should include a mechanism for determining the circumstances triggering a sale, a formula for the valuation of the stock, and a schedule for payments.

For example, imagine Sally's brother has joined her in running Sally's Goat Milk. She has decided to give Jim a generous 30 percent of the stock in her firm. She worries, however, that he might just decide to return to his old job if the goat milk business doesn't produce quick returns. Sally drafts an agreement with Jim that requires the stock to be returned to the firm if he leaves. In return, he receives a promissory note requiring the company to pay the accounting book value plus 10 percent of net profits after taxes for the current year and promises to do so on a monthly basis over three years without interest. The agreement allows the company's board to consider exemptions to this policy on a case-by-case basis. This clause could avoid forcing a disagreeable decision in the case of a protracted illness or even the sale of the company.

Noncompete agreements: One of the common disasters that befalls small firms is having a key player desert the firm and join a new or existing competitor. When they do this, it is almost impossible for them not to take ideas, connections, and goodwill from your firm with them. In the worst cases, they may blatantly abscond with intellectual property, poach key employees, and steal your best customers. A noncompete agreement is designed to prevent critical individuals from working in your firm's market, usually defined by industry and geography, for some period of time. In many jurisdictions, California, for example, such agreements are notoriously difficult to enforce. However, they will at least make it clear to individuals considering leaving that you don't find that agreeable and will fight. It may also be agreeable to back this stick with a carrot in the form of a concrete financial incentive such as a bonus payable some years from now.

Spousal agreements: A spousal or significant-other agreement, or an agreement with any individual or entity that is heir to one of your key stockholders, is designed to keep stock in the firm and ensure that you do not find yourself in business with a disinterested or even hostile major stockholder.

Recall that Sally's brother Jim has joined Sally's Goat Milk. Keeping ownership in the family appeals to Sally, but she really isn't on the best terms with Jim's wife. Recognizing that if her brother ever divorced or died, her sister-in-law would acquire a significant amount of company stock, Sally requires Jim and his wife to sign an agreement stating that the stock cannot be owned by anyone not working at Sally's Goat Milk. The spousal agreement mirrors the payment terms of the buyout agreement. While Jim's wife likely resents having to sign such an agreement in the first place, she is just as likely not to want to work with Sally if her husband passes. With this solution, her interests are protected, and a difficult process is avoided during a stressful time.

None of this means that you can't choose to be nicer than your agreements require, and the New Entrepreneurial Dynamic encourages generosity. It's simply always better to let renegotiation of terms, including the handing out of additional shares or funds, to be seen as tokens of your personal munificence rather than the grudging accession to lawsuits or threats.

Insurance

Insurance is one of the most obvious ways to hedge against potential problems in your company's future. You should consider a large number of insurance options and they may be legally required for you to launch and run your business. Several of the more important ones are addressed next.

"Key Person" Life Insurance Policies

The most distressing way for a critical member of your team to leave your firm is through death or disability. At such a time, both your business and your life are likely to be significantly distracted. Revenues are likely to be impacted by the loss, and it is not a time to be short on cash or have to dig up cash to pay off someone's heirs for a stock buyback. It is also a time when you may need to spend money recruiting a replacement. In many cases, the solution to this problem is key person insurance, an insurance policy taken out by the firm and payable on the death or disability of a specific individual. The payout can then be used to repurchase the stock held by the lost member and cover other losses the company is likely to suffer through the loss. The good news is that many startups are founded by active young individuals for whom even a million-dollar or higher life insurance policy is relatively affordable. The older your team member is, the statistically more likely their death is, and, insurance being an actuarial business, the higher the rates. Getting key person insurance is relatively easy, and as will be discussed, you should establish a relationship with an insurance broker or agent in any case.

Product Liability Insurance

If you make a product for the general public, you need to have product liability insurance to cover yourself in case of a lawsuit. Anyone can sue you for just about any claim, and defending that can be expensive. Insurance typically covers the legal fees and often manages the confusing legal process for you. The amount of your **insurance premium**, the amount you pay each year, will vary by the risk your product poses and the volume of product you sell. Most policies can be paid every six months or even broken into monthly payments to protect your firm's cash flow.

insurance premium

Money paid regularly to provide insurance coverage.

Lest you imagine your product or service is so safe that you need not worry, note that a woman successfully sued McDonald's for nearly $3 million when she was burned by spilling the fast-food restaurant's very hot coffee in her car.[11]

Errors and Omissions Insurance (E&O)

Commonly referred to as professional liability insurance, this policy covers you against claims made by your customers due to your failure to perform. Essentially, if you mess up doing your job, your customers can not only demand their money back but can also insist that you repay them for any time or business they may have lost due to your failure. For example, if your company supplies a small but critical component for a car manufacturer and a problem with your product requires an entire auto factory to shut down while they find a new source, that manufacturer could sue you for many, many times the value of your sale. You'll want to have E&O insurance coverage anytime that a mistake at your firm could conceivably cause losses to another party.

Worker's Compensation Insurance

Worker's compensation covers the medical costs to employees who are injured on the job as well as lost wages and, in some cases, compensates individuals for the permanent and lasting effects of their injuries. There is no more critical insurance in your firm. Employee injuries are among the highest cost lawsuits to settle, and almost all U.S. states require you have this insurance covering all your W2 employees. Enforcement of these laws is typically extremely serious. States do not mess around with the safety of workers. The cost of worker's comp is usually some percentage of the employee's salary based on the riskiness of their line of work. It's relatively low for computer programmers but for dangerous jobs, like roofing, it can be very expensive. If you're in a profession where employees are exposed to physical dangers, you'll want to make sure you calculate this cost into your business model.

Property Insurance

If you buy or rent a facility, you'll need to insure it and your business property (computers, furniture, machinery, etc.) against fire, burglary, flooding, and other risks. This insurance may also protect you against injuries to nonemployees (customers or visitors) in your facility.

Property insurance is critical to protect against fires and other disasters.

Source: Joseph Sohm/Shutterstock.com

Health Insurance

Health insurance for employees is a very complex situation in the United States. In many cases, the law may require you to provide healthcare insurance for your employees, but even if it does not, it is often an attractive benefit for workers, and a healthy employee is a more productive one. Healthcare insurance options and packages are particularly complicated and change so often that they exceed the scope of this text. There are third-party advisers who will consult for a fee or a commission. It is important to note that the cost of health insurance in the U.S. has been increasing at double-digit rates for many years, so when you build your business model, it is probably wise to assume this cost will continue to escalate. If your nation provides health insurance under a national health plan, you may not be involved in this issue, but in some countries, employers are required to contribute to the payments made by their employees or the state.

Auto Insurance

Automobile insurance will be required for any vehicles your firm owns. You should also discuss coverage with your insurance broker or agent for employees who use their own vehicles for work purposes as their personal insurance is likely not to cover this activity. You may also require that your employees purchase auto insurance that allows them to drive for work and then compensate them.

You may be offered many other insurance options during launch or later. Data breach insurance has become a product as more and more sensitive company and personal information is stored on business computer networks. Your insurance broker or agent and your accountant are good sources of information on these products.

Facilities

Where to locate your business is a choice based on the nature of your business and the market you have selected. For brick-and-mortar retail, the selection criteria are very specific and super important. Manufacturing and fulfillment firms have important logistical constraints in selection, such as proximity to transportation hubs. If your business is outbound service or online, you may have a lot more options. You may even run it out of your home or from your laptop and phone as you travel the world. If you do require a physical location, selecting and negotiating for a facility can be approached a number of ways.

Renting

When renting a location, you are usually compelled to sign a lease that requires you to pay the landlord for some number of years. For small startups, these leases will invariably include a personal guarantee whereby the founders are obligated to pay the rent even if the business fails. Although $5,000 a month may not seem like a lot at first, you could find yourself working a second job, long after your startup failed, to pay for a building you're not using any longer but has two years left on the lease.

For this reason, you should seriously consider ramping up your operation from a minimally viable facility. What is the smallest, least expensive site where you can prove your concept, and most importantly, what is the shortest lease obligation you can find?

For many businesses, getting into a business incubator that has shared office space, copiers, and the like, is ideal. These incubators are often subsidized by government agencies or universities and can be ideal places to share information with other startup founders. Some incubators may be provided by investors who are seeking a portion of your business and may also invest further in successful incubator tenants.

Shared or Coworking Spaces

Shared workspaces are increasingly popular.

Source: © Shutterstock, Inc.

A low-commitment option that is very much in keeping with the New Entrepreneurial Dynamic is a commercial **shared workspace** or **coworking space** provided by firms like WeWork, where you can rent a desk by the month. Companies like Regus also supply executive suites where you can have a dedicated office (or more). These locations usually provide amenities like reception, office equipment, and coffee rooms. Over the long term, these solutions may not be cheaper, but they do avoid long-term commitments.

shared workspace
An office suite sublet to a number of small businesses and startups for daily operations without the commitment to a dedicated facility.

coworking space
An office suite sublet to a number of small businesses and startups for daily operations without the commitment to a dedicated facility.

leasehold improvements
Changes made to a property, usually by the landlord, to satisfy the needs of a current or new business tenant.

tenant improvements
Changes made to a property, by the tenant, to satisfy the needs of the tenant's operations.

Improvements

If you do decide your business requires a dedicated facility, one of the matters you'll have to discuss is getting that building, storefront, or suite configured correctly for your operation. Modifications to an existing facility can either be negotiated into your lease contract as **leasehold improvements** or added later by you as **tenant improvements**. If the real estate market is soft (not going strongly), the landlord may be eager to accommodate your particular need for walls, lighting, carpet, or whatever as long as you commit to a lease of sufficient term. On the other hand, if business is good for landlords, you are likely to find you'll be paying for any changes. For this reason, launching your business during a recession or lull in the real estate market can save a great deal of money over time.

It is always best to explain your plans up front and get them approved. Under almost any lease, modification to the facility beyond moving a piece of furniture or hanging a picture will require the approval of your landlord. You do not want to commit to renting a place for your business and find you will not be allowed to make changes necessary for conducting that business.

Buying

In general, the New Entrepreneurial Dynamic would not suggest locking your business into a permanent facility by purchasing a building and land. Such a significant commitment ties up capital and ties down your geographic and facility options. Under some circumstances, it may make sense for the business or, more likely, the business owner, to purchase a property for investment or tax purposes. In the latter case, the owner can rent the property to his or her own business and charge for things like leasehold improvements, taking a business deduction on improving the owned property. As with renting, timing your commitment to a slow real estate market is likely to save you a lot of money; buying in during a boom can cost your firm dearly.

Planning Never Ends

While there are many more things you will learn in actually launching your startup, this chapter has given you a lot to think about. The New Entrepreneurial Dynamic recognizes that all of these things, from legal form to insurance to facilities, may change as your business evolves. To compete in today's ever-changing world, you must be continually looking forward, identifying potential risks, and planning to mitigate them. Enjoy the launch!

3,2,1 Launch!

New Legal Forms: Around the world policy makers are competing to encourage entrepreneurship in their nations. New advantageous organizational forms are constantly emerging at the national and state level that may provide legal or tax advantages. Be sure you're using the best structure.

New Tech Supports Virtualization: New technologies and services are making it possible to run multi-million-dollar businesses without offices, dedicated IT resources, warehousing, or even employees. Unless your startup absolutely requires physical space for manufacturing or is a storefront operation, you should consider avoiding commitment to any fixed costs and even designing your firm to remain virtual beyond the launch stage.

Globalization: It is getting harder to hold a competitive advantage in any domain without leveraging global resources. Unless your business is committed to remaining a small, local startup, you must consider the global opportunities and competitors from the start. Select a legal structure that will easily allow for foreign shareholders and operations.

Key Takeaways

- Spend the time to write down verbal agreements.
- Make important agreements into actual signed contracts.
- Get insurance *before* you need it.
- If possible, delay the purchase or leases of office space for as long as possible; go virtual or use shared spaces.

8.3 Case Study: An Entrepreneurial Marketing Misfit Finds His Niche

Brett Linkletter (second from right in front) and his Misfit team.

Source: Misfit Media

Brett Linkletter was always a bit of a troublemaker. The aspiring entrepreneur knew his idea of producing and selling a calendar called "Trojan 12" featuring students from the University of Southern California in swimsuits, would become a flashpoint of controversy. What he hadn't counted on was getting into a legal dispute with the university administration over the use of their trademarks or landing a new career in marketing.

Renaming his product "SoCal 12" solved Brett's problem with USC, albeit at a cost. He had already, against his professor's advice, printed thousands of units, and registered a domain name. The product was actually a big success, netting more than ten thousand dollars in sales, but it was not something on which Linkletter felt he could build a career. An opportunity arose when an ad agency owner came in as a guest speaker in one of his business classes. The speaker asked the class, "Does anyone here actually run a business?" Brett volunteered his calendar project, and the visiting businessperson said, "Hey! I've heard about that." The connection resulted in him hiring Linkletter to work with social media influencers, proving P. T. Barnum's adage that "there is no such thing as bad publicity." Although the job didn't really amount to much, it led him to an opportunity to do marketing for an up-and-coming tequila brand with a famous celebrity founder.

Working long hours for someone else, even on cool projects, just wasn't Brett's nature. He ended up acquiring his own clients, getting fired, and founding an agency called Misfit Media. At first, Brett assumed he'd do what everyone else in the marketing biz seemed to be doing, building an eclectic base of clients across a wide variety of domains. He collected a watch company, fashion startups, a skateboard maker, and even launched his own brand of men's grooming products. It was about this time that Jace Kovacevich approached Brett with the proposal that he join Misfit as a partner, on the condition that he could round up some clients. Jace rounded up the clients, and to this day, they remain great business partners. Brett notes, "Having a partner makes everything easier. You just can't do everything yourself, and being able to delegate tasks to someone who cares about the firm as much as you do is an incredible relief."

Being busy and having clients felt kind of like success to Brett, but even with Jace, he was working all the time and barely taking home $1,500 a month. While Brett was honing his skills as a photographer and learning a lot about social media, he was in business to make money, and this clearly wasn't the way to do it. However, one particular client was beginning to shift the financial fortunes of the firm. A family member introduced Linkletter to the owners of Original Tommy's Burger, an LA landmark. The restaurateurs at Tommy's had little insight into internet-based ads or what Facebook or Instagram could do for their business. The social media work that Brett's team brought to this old-school eatery had an immediate and surprisingly measurable impact on their sales. Brett notes, "These guys think we are total geniuses. Whereas, when we pitched to tech-savvy e-commerce business owners, we'd be just another player in the game." It got him thinking about the power of owning a niche market and how that could add an enormous amount of value as opposed to being another player continually struggling to prove themselves in a crowded space.

Linkletter and his partner ran across some marketing training videos from a guy named Billy Gene. "At first glance, the stuff seemed kind of cheesy," Brett remembers, "but he really opened our eyes to the power of the local business space as a target market." Linkletter found that basically, nobody was trying to sell to all these little restaurant chains. They had solid business models, they had customers, and they spent money on marketing. Most importantly, they had been placing ads in local papers, on bus stop benches, and places where they really had zero feedback on the effectiveness of the ad spent. It was different from the e-commerce world, where everyone was counting up their conversions. Misfit was able to develop an automated system that provided promotional offers to restaurant customers who opted into a program they developed, using Facebook's Messenger platform. Their FB Messenger system used "messenger bots" that tracked every single transaction, making them verifiable in-store purchases. This provided the clients with an advertising program backed with proven return on investment (ROI), something they had never seen. The little agency began to ink deals with more and more of the small restaurants and expanded to localities outside of Southern California. Brett recalls that at that point, "We were adding clients and people all the time! We now knew there was a big opportunity in the restaurant space, but we were still keeping and picking up clients in other niches."

Jace and Bret

Source: Jace and Brett

All looked good until suddenly Tommy's dropped them. Misfit had been neglecting their anchor client while they used those revenues to pursue other opportunities. "They weren't getting the attention they were used to, and the expectations weren't clear. That was a huge wake-up call." Misfit began to drop their remaining clients outside of the restaurant space and refine their skills in their new restaurant niche. After his success with Gene's program, Linkletter was looking for more external advice. He found Sam Ovens, another business guru, who owned a site called Consulting.com. Ovens' program was designed to help firms exploit opportunities with niche clients. He showed the Misfit team that getting repeatable systems in place for their clients was critical for maximizing return on their efforts on behalf of those clients. Brett shares, "We learned how to market ourselves better and how to produce new clients on demand." He goes on, "Today we only do restaurants. One industry, one service. We do one thing really well. You can't even reach us unless you go through the application process. For every $100 I spend on ads, I get a call booked with me with a qualified restaurant lead. We then close a third of those leads within 45 minutes.... So every $300 we spend on ads, we gain a new client. Our average client pays us a monthly retainer of $1,500, and the majority of our clients will end up working with us for over six months, so our ROI on our ads is fantastic."

Misfit's sweet spot is a restaurant with two to eight locations. They may all be in one city or across the country, but small is good. Brett noted that larger chains were problematic because "When they get a dozen or more locations, the decision-making processes grind to halt. These bigger companies just have too many people wanting to critique or manage a process they don't really understand. That's frustrating because it's a process that we have totally locked down and where we deliver proven ROI."

This laser focus on a well-defined but ample market provides Misfit with higher profits and Brett with peace of mind. Brett notes, "A lot of advertising agencies live in a state of fear instead of a state of abundance. They are too worried about keeping bad clients rather than knowing there are always more out there. They can't turn down business without stressing. I get stressed if we don't grow by 10 percent or more a month, but only within our competency. I don't care how many things you've marketed; it's impossible to be an expert at every industry. You don't have a brain surgeon doing your teeth. If you go outside your swim lane, you're not building expertise, you're not developing skills, you're not building the case studies you need for your next sale."

This focus also makes scaling easier. In marketing, the biggest investment in growth is bringing on new employees and getting them to be productive. For most marketing agencies, it's super expensive and time-intensive to train new employees. Most newbies at other agencies will screw up their first few clients, so nobody wants to trust them with good leads, and that's expensive if your firm is paying them a salary. Brett notes, "I know the restaurant business so well now that I can turn any untrained marketing person into a restaurant marketing rock star in only a couple of weeks.... I've dedicated 100 percent of myself to owning and dominating this niche."

Things are good at Misfit. Pepsi and U.S. Foods, two big suppliers in the small restaurant world, are now actively encouraging their clients to hire Misfit because it helps their own sell-through. Linkletter proudly shares, "We will be celebrating $100k in revenue this month alone. I can forecast that next month, we will hit $130k in revenue." That's good money for a business with very low overhead and where each revenue dollar is pretty much also incremental profit. He's not slowing down, but Brett has a great new apartment in Venice Beach, is traveling the world and getting more surfing in, all while his business grows.

Brett Linkletter

Source: Brett Linkletter

Looking forward, Linkletter understands that no business model is safe in today's dynamic business environment. He's got to keep moving, capturing the most valuable part of what he calls "the opportunity curve." That's the point where a new idea, like using Facebook Messenger bots to deliver customers to restaurants, is technically possible, but everyone isn't doing it yet. Brett notes, "For now, consumers are still responsive to messenger notifications. They aren't ignoring our offers like they do on regular social media posts or emails, and our competitors aren't all over this yet. We know that won't last." He adds, "I'm always looking for the next new thing."

Endnotes

1. After the Trump administration's tax cut of 2017.
2. https://www.investopedia.com/articles/personal-finance/102115/taxes-california-small-business-basics.asp
3. Institute on Taxation and Economic Policy. March 9, 2017. "The 35 Percent Corporate Tax Myth," https://itep.org/the-35-percent-corporate-tax-myth/.
4. *The Irish Times*. (2017, November 6). Apple's cash mountain, how it avoids tax, and the Irish link.
5. Freeman, R. E., & Reed, D. L. (1983). Stockholders and stakeholders: A new perspective on corporate governance. *California Management Review, 25(3)*, 88–106.
6. Companies House is at https://www.gov.uk/government/organisations/companies-house.
7. FSB is at https://www.fsb.org.uk.
8. Your Europe info is at https://europa.eu/youreurope/business/running-business/ start-ups/starting-business/index_en.htm.
9. Musk, E. (2018). Progress, precision and profit (email to Tesla employees).
10. It is not unreasonable to provide shared, closed spaces where individuals or teams can go to work or think without distractions for short periods of intense work.
11. Burtka, A. T. (n.d.). *Liebeck v. McDonald's*: The hot coffee case. American Museum of Tort Law. https://www.tortmuseum.org/liebeck-v-mcdonalds/.

CHAPTER 9
Brand Building

> Perception is reality.
> —*Lee Atwater*

Cattle brands.

Source: © Shutterstock, Inc.

The original **brand** is a metal tool with a symbol on it that is heated over coals and pressed into the side of a steer, horse, or other commercial livestock. The resulting indelible scar creates a permanent symbol of ownership of that particular animal. While this practice is generally associated with nineteenth-century American cowboys, it remains a common practice around the world. The brand concept has been as permanent as its origin.

brand

A unique image used to identify a product or company.

9.1 Product Branding

Learning Objectives

1. Understand what a brand is.
2. Grasp the power of brand recognition.
3. Understand brand definition and the process involved.
4. Understand the goodwill value of a brand for its owners.
5. Understand what commodity products are.
6. Recognize the opportunity to disrupt stale brands.
7. Appreciate the importance of corporate ethics and how unethical behavior can induce brand disasters.
8. Recognize the importance of brand fit to the market, the entrepreneur, and the growth plan.
9. Learn the value of trademarks.

Perception Management

product branding

The marketing practice of creating an image or identity associated with a specific product.

logo

A graphic, text, or symbol designed to represent a brand.

marketing campaign

A specific, defined series of activities used in marketing a new or changed product or service.

Walking through a modern shopping mall or surfing through Amazon.com is an immersive experience in **product branding**. Our subconscious instantly recognizes hundreds of **logos**—graphic or text symbols designed to represent a brand. We see and process the symbols for Apple, Nike, and Louis Vuitton more quickly than common words, and each of these logos generates an emotional response. That all happens because the large firms whose products dominate the mall and internet landscape have invested millions of dollars into **marketing campaigns** designed to instill positive associations with these symbols in the minds of consumers. Why is so much time and money being spent on ingraining these images in your mind and managing your response to them as opposed to demonstrating the functionality of the products they represent?

We live in a world where information flows are growing exponentially. We are constantly collecting data from our school, work, family, and friends. In addition to in-person interactions and voice calls, asynchronous communications such as email and social media allow this information to accumulate to the point where it must be processed in bulk, consuming more and more of our time. When we add to this a barrage of advertisements on signage, television, computers, and mobile devices, it is simply overwhelming. Most of the information we receive is trivial, and as individuals, we must spend more and more of our mental energy processing, sorting, and eliminating information that we can't afford to consider.

marketers

Those people whose skill lies in developing brands and generating attention for companies.

mass marketing

Effort to reach an entire customer segment through a single strategy utilizing mass media and/or mass distribution.

Today's **marketers**—those people whose skill lies in developing brands and generating attention for companies—understand that, try as they might, they will get very little of your attention. In fact, they will probably only get a few seconds or even a fraction of a second of your conscious awareness as you stroll through that mall. Building the image of a brand at every opportunity and tying it to that instantly processed logo is the key to modern **mass marketing**. What if you don't make a consumer good that would be sold in the mall? What if your customers are all other businesses? Do nonconsumer companies need to worry about branding?

Think about the Boeing corporation. Are you likely to ever buy a Boeing product? Probably not, but you probably do know they are a global leader in the production of large jet aircraft. You'd also likely recognize the Boeing logo. Why do you recognize the logo? Boeing doesn't sell jets directly to consumers (outside of a few billionaires with private 737s), but it does sell to airlines and governments around the world. Those large organizations build fleets of planes that cost hundreds of millions and even billions of dollars.

Boeing (and Rolls Royce) Logo on a 787 Dreamliner.

Source: Ryan Fletcher/Shutterstock.com

Thousands of individuals will be involved in making the recommendation to go with Boeing or with their archrival, Airbus. Having global brand awareness guarantees that when a buying decision is at hand, all the parties involved will instantly recognize the Boeing brand and hopefully have a positive association with that brand. Did the loss of two Boeing 737 MAX aircraft in 2019 impact your overall perception of this brand? You can imagine that Boeing's marketers were working hard to ensure that the perception of their brand stayed positive in the minds of people across the globe. That's quite a task!

As a small business owner or startup founder, your brand is a precious and delicate thing. You must plant, nurture, and protect it at all costs. It is an investment in time, dedication to quality, and an exercise in **perception management**. Good brand building will return value and support your firm in the future at no additional cost. The well-constructed brand is a resource as valuable as gold. The New Entrepreneurial Dynamic requires that brands stay true to their core principles while dynamically adapting to the realities of a global market that is constantly evolving around them.

perception management

Actions taken to guide consumer understanding of a brand.

Defining Your Brand

Every established brand has a **brand definition**—something that it stands for in the mind of consumers. Figure 9.1 shows the rankings of the top-rated brands in the world, according to Interbrand, a brand consulting and marketing firm.

brand definition

What a product or company stands for in the mind of consumers.

FIGURE 9.1 Top 15 Global Brands
Top 15 global brands ranked by Interbrand.

Rank	Logo	Brand	Country of Origin	Sector	Brand Value ($m)	Change in Brand Value
1		Apple	United States	Technology	408,251	+26%
2	amazon	Amazon	United States	Retail	249,249	+24%
3	Microsoft	Microsoft	United States	Technology	210,191	+27%
4	Google	Google	United States	Technology	196,811	+19%
5	SAMSUNG	Samsung	South Korea	Technology	74,635	+20%
6	Coca-Cola	Coca-Cola	United States	Beverages	57,488	+1%
7		Toyota	Japan	Automotive	54,107	+5%
8		Mercedes-Benz	Germany	Automotive	50,866	+3%
9		Mcdonald's	United States	Restaurants	45,865	+7%
10	Disney	Disney	United States	Media	44,183	+8%
11		Nike	United States	Sporting Goods	42,538	+24%
12		BMW	Germany	Automotive	41,631	+5%
13	LOUIS VUITTON	Louis Vuitton	France	Automotive	36,766	+16%
14	TESLA	Tesla	United States	Automotive	36,270	+184%
15	facebook	Facebook	United States	Media	36,248	+3%

Source: Based on rankings from https://interbrand.com/best-global-brands/

Apple's brand is defined as hipness and leading technology; Harley Davidson is rebellious yet patriotic; BMW is luxury and excellence in engineering. Do you see something each of those brand definitions has in common?

Notice that each of these great brands combines two distinct ideas to create a unique identity. Aspiring to something as simple as "being the best in our industry" is great, but not distinctive. You need another "hook" for your brand.

Apple has combined technological savvy with a hip, freethinking, and artistic feel, but their arch-rival Microsoft has done the opposite. The firm from Redmond has combined technology with the reliable, button-down culture of multinational corporations. So, although their products do many of the same things in nearly identical ways, their user bases are distinctly loyal. A college professor today looks out at a sea of Apple logos on the laptops that face him, while many bankers and engineers simply can't imagine using any computer that doesn't run Windows. Does any of this apply to a small business?

Yes, your small business has a brand! Regrettably, many small business owners don't think of that, but they should. Your brand definition will determine who your customers are. Your customers will determine the profitability and longevity of your brand. Consequently, controlling the development of your brand definition is a critical strategic function of your business. As you learned with company culture in an earlier chapter, if you do not consciously define your brand, others will define it for you. Allowing that process to proceed randomly is inherently dangerous.

Without a Brand, You Throw Away Value

Look again at Figure 9.1. Do you see the dollar amounts listed next to each brand? These are the values that Interbrand has calculated for each brand, meaning that if the firm decided to sell its brand and nothing else, it would collect that amount. Interbrand's valuation suggests that Apple could burn its facilities to the ground, fire every top employee, dump all its product inventory in the sea, and still sell the firm for $170 billion simply because the Apple brand creates so much value. It may seem hard to believe, but a cursory look at products without a brand easily demonstrates the power of branding.

In today's marketing-driven world, it is hard to imagine that there are products without a brand! There are. Think of those famously unbranded store products in the plain white and blue packages that say nothing more than "flour" or "milk" or "sugar." Think of generic drugs. What is the main feature that drives consumers to select those choices over their branded peer products? It's price, of course. When your business competes only on price, you are selling a **commodity**, a good for which it is assumed that all competing products are essentially of equal quality and performance. Is that a problem?

commodity

A generic product for which the primary distinguishing feature is price, i.e., salt, flour, oil.

Commodities are a tough place for a small business to make money. They nearly always trade on very slim margins since they attract customers who are only differentiating on price. What cost control that can be achieved is usually based on economies of scale that favor large incumbent firms. Usually, the barriers to entry are very low as well, leaving the threat of new entrants high. Commodities markets are also subject to speculative price variations outside the control of the entrepreneur. These factors make commodities very unattractive markets.

On the other hand, experience shows that consumers will pay more for a branded product, even if it offers no real-world advantages! Table salt is a basic chemical, sodium chloride (NaCl). Most manufacturers add a little iodine as a nutritional supplement. Skipping some exotic cooking salts containing other minerals, there is no patent, additional feature, or other intellectual property to make one container of the white table salt crystals better than another. So, you'd think that all brands of salt would sell for the same price, right?

Stores offer non-branded products at lower prices.

Source: Sheila Fitzgerald/Shutterstock.com

In North America, the largest seller of salt is a company called Morton, whose logo of a young girl walking in the rain with an umbrella is well known. The company's slogan, "When it rains, it pours," is also familiar to many Americans. On Amazon.com, a 26-ounce container of Morton salt sells for $11.99, while a 26-ounce of Diamond Crystal brand salt sells for $5.99. Since Morton's input costs are the same, or even lower, based on their massive scale, the margins it and its resellers capture are far higher than those of the commodity sellers. That is a real measure of the pure value-add of branding: twice the price for the same thing.

The Morton logo dominates its market.

Source: Julie Clopper/Shutterstock.com

Great brands like Apple, Morton, and Coca-Cola are so culturally embedded in the retail landscape that it is hard for consumers to imagine a world without them. Apple's brand helps its users identify themselves. Apple owners feel that their use of the firm's sleek products signals their hipness, affluence, and intelligence. For the amount of profits that it generates, Apple does very little advertising compared to other large companies. Morton doesn't need to advertise to maintain its dominance in salt and keep those higher margins. Parents simply pass on their buying choice to their kids by observation. Consider that Coca-Cola can charge higher margins for clothing and other gear emblazoned with its logo. Another way to look at that is to recognize that people will pay money for the opportunity to advertise Coke. Now that is brand power!

Interbrand uses firm financial statements and their analysis of the brand's role in sales to analyze how much of a firm's higher profits come from its brand value. They suggest that not only does a solid brand generate more money for the firm's shareholders, but it also reduces risk. A stable brand supports a stable firm.

Product Fit

Would anyone buy a Lamborghini if they were not over-the-top about everything? Every brand appeals to some customer identity. Understanding what attracts existing customers and what will bring in new customers is essential to a brand. The branding of the consumer audio equipment company Beats differs significantly from that of its competitor, Sennheiser. Beats focuses on youth appeal and looks since its customers care less about the intricacies of music and more about appearances and the perception of luxury. Their customer wants to pay extra for the sake of everyone else knowing they spent the money. Sennheiser, on the other hand, is a pure quality performer, and thus its image is simpler and geared toward those who are willing to pay for superior technology. Browsing the websites of these two companies will clearly reveal this marketing distinction.

TOMS shoes knew it wanted to give back to the world by providing footwear to those in need. Rather than choosing a wishy-washy approach, TOMS set a simple one-for-one model. This clear branding for its product, centered on charity, allowed the impact of every purchase to be visible to consumers. Visibility is important in all industries, but especially so in non-profits.

Managing the Brand

If you're a fan of college basketball, you know that each team has a unique style of play. Kansas State usually prefers to play it slow, while the University of Kentucky plays quicker and more active. These playstyles define each team as a whole, independent of the composition of players, and are intentionally designed by the management and coaching staff. If a playstyle is not working well, it can be adapted to better suit the competition and the situation, but changing it completely isn't likely to work out well for a team trained to deliver in a particular style.

Every team has its own style of play which defines its brand with fans.

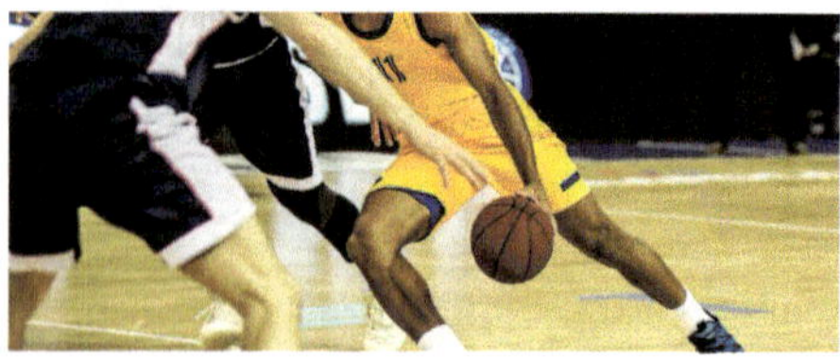

Source: © Shutterstock, Inc.

Great brands are similar. Just by its logo or slogan, a consumer can instantly identify the branded product. Done right, the logo and the product seem inseparable and feel inevitable. Think of Apple's iconic aluminum and glass products. The customer has expectations that a new product from that brand will maintain the style they've come to love and identify with.

For this reason, the product-brand connection must be carefully managed. It is often relatively easy to make a radical technical or physical change in a product or to present a service very differently. However, when that veers away from customers' expectations of the brand—imagine the Kentucky coach asking his players to "slow it down"—what do you think might happen?

A brand's message must stay consistent. This allows consumers to feel comfortable using the brand to signal messages about their identity. They do not want to find themselves surprisingly tied to an image they don't admire. For instance, the Nike Swoosh suggests "active, bold, and assertive." Yet, Nike is aware of current global demographic trends, and the firm understands that the most desirable higher-income consumers in the developed world are aging and gaining weight. So, the sportswear firm does offer a line of plus-sized clothing and products targeted at seniors. While we've all seen not-so-athletic people wearing Nike gear in the real world, there are no pictures of a 300 pound, 60-year-old man smoking while eating a pizza on Nike's website. The carefully crafted home page and the firm's expertly managed social media are dominated by fit young people. Why?

Would aspiring young athletes feel compelled to buy Nike after seeing advertisements featuring overweight guys in Nike stretch pants and old ladies using walkers emblazoned with the Swoosh? Of course not! Even Nike's older and out-of-shape customers do not want to see themselves that way. Great branding isn't about the current reality of the buyer; it's about their aspirations. Understanding this, Nike uses the clever slogan "Where All Athletes Belong," implying everyone is welcome and can feel athletic.

The Nike Story

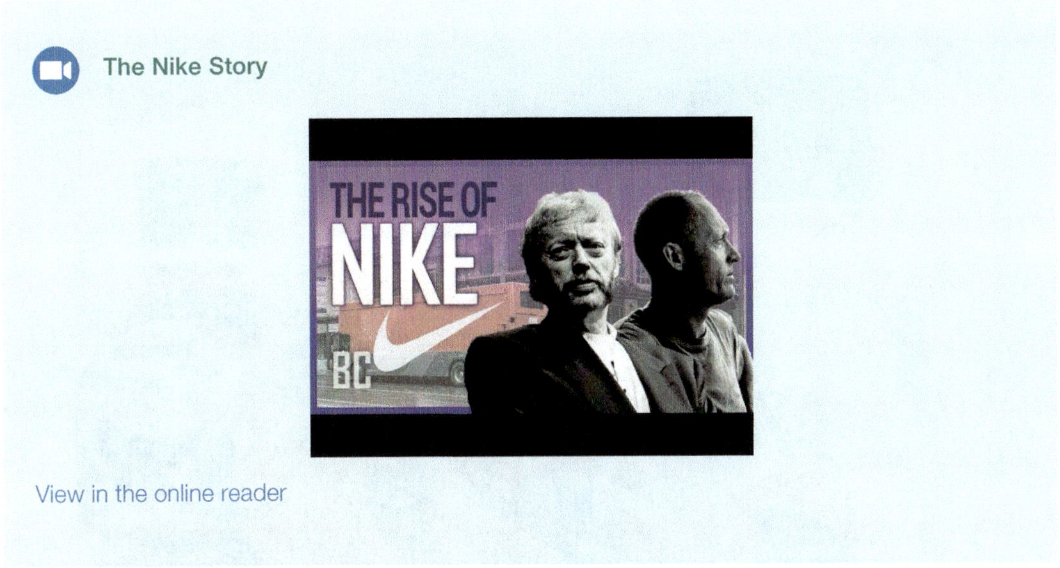

View in the online reader

Customers expect branded products to behave in a certain way, and change is usually punished by those comfortable with the existing paradigm. Remember that noncustomers have already rejected the brand, and that choice will blind them to the attractive nature of the new product—even if the firm designed it specifically for them.

A great real-world example of attempting to deal with customer brand expectations comes from legendary country singer Garth Brooks. With a long series of hits, his trademark black Stetson Tyler cowboy hat, and friendly good looks, Brooks had established an iconic country brand.[1] However, in 1999 the country star decided to make an unexpected detour into popular rock with the release of an album under the pseudonym "Chris Gaines." Brooks figured he could have fun exploring another genre and expand his appeal to those rock fans who disdained country music. He even planned to make a documentary film about his alter ego. Brooks hosted *Saturday Night Live* one evening and introduced Chris Gaines as the musical guest. The connection was obvious to everyone.

When Brooks' fans saw their clean-cut country star strut out in leather pants with shaggy hair and sporting a goatee, they were appalled. They figured he'd gone nuts, and they rejected what was actually a pretty good collection of songs. Rock listeners were not fooled by the pseudonym and generally refused to give the release a try either. The results were as expected: poor album sales with little airplay on either country or pop stations. Brooks' esteem and career suffered a minor setback. Luckily for him, his talent allowed him to slide right back into the country saddle again.

Fans wanted the country music superstar to stick to the country image they had of him.

Source: Sterling Munksgard/Shutterstock.com

The lesson from the Brooks/Gaines story is that it is very hard to be all things to all people. It is best to clearly identify a *market*, develop your brand, and stick with it. This is especially true for small businesses, where resources are limited. If you're absolutely compelled to pursue another market or develop an alternate product, you're better off establishing another brand that captures the nature of that product in a way that won't *pollute* your existing brand.

For an alternate brand to work, you must keep it completely separate in the public's mind as though it comes from an entirely different source, something a celebrity like Brooks couldn't pull off. For instance, PepsiCo, the soda maker, owns Tropicana. Most consumers don't realize this, and

Pepsi doesn't emphasize the connection because the association with unhealthy, corn syrup-sweetened soda would *pollute* these brands and dilute their healthy appeal.

Although the popular global brand is owned by PepsiCo, its health-focused branding is entirely different.

Source: MAHATHIR MOHD YASIN/Shutterstock.com

How do these lessons apply to small business branding? How many "Donuts and Pizza" stores do you see? Don't laugh; there is a very viable business model behind the idea. Both donuts and pizza are popular takeout foods, and the small businesses that serve them operate out of similarly sized and equipped strip mall locations. Most significantly, donuts are generally sold only in the morning, while pizza is lunch and dinner fare. A savvy small business owner would maximize the utilization of a location by serving donuts in the morning and switching to pizza at about 11 a.m. It makes economic sense, but it's a branding disaster. Consumers will be suspicious of a brand that claims excellence in both of those categories. The whole idea of donuts and pizza offers an improbable mix of tastes and smells, and it probably makes most people slightly ill just thinking about it. So, sadly, most small donut stores do 90 percent of their business from 6 a.m. to 10 a.m. and have very low utilization after that.

Great Brands and Brand Value

How do you measure the value of a brand? Consider the amazing brand that is Disney. Tickets to Disneyland in Anaheim, California, are substantially higher than passes to their Southern California competitors such as Knott's Berry Farm, Legoland, and Universal Studios. Yet a lot more people visit Mickey Mouse's home than these other more affordable fun spots. In fact, everyone in the SoCal tourism industry understands that Disneyland is "the destination," and other sites simply compete for tourists choosing a second stop on their California trip.

On the other hand, if a Chevron gas station raises the price on its regular gas by five cents a gallon, drivers on their way to Disneyland will promptly dash across the street to a lower price at Shell.

You can measure the relative value of the Disney brand versus Chevron by looking at the **gross profit margin** in their financial statements. While oil and gas companies make good profits during good times, it's a business based on enormous volume at relatively low profit margins. Valuable brands like Disney create mental switching costs around the branded product and reduce the price sensitivity of customers. Gas is a commodity, and purveyors of it have had a very hard time adding significant brand value. If your small business commands exceptional prices and reports higher margins than your peers, you've probably established some brand value.

gross profit margin

A financial metric calculated by dividing gross profit by revenues.

Imagine a nifty hipster coffee shop near a college campus. This is the hot place to hang out and sip organic, fair-trade, wholesome brew under old-timey lights in red leather chairs. Now imagine this coffee shop moves two miles away, but everyone still chooses to hang out there. Not only that, but they are also charging more than other local shops. This is brand value in action. When the coffee shop owner goes to sell her business, she will command a better price if she can effectively demonstrate this brand value to potential buyers.

New Brands Versus Old Brands

All of this makes it clear that it is difficult to displace a powerful existing brand. Can you imagine being a new entrant with a digital tablet trying to go up against Apple in the consumer market? Even global mega-corporations, including Samsung, Microsoft, and Hewlett-Packard have found that to be a daunting challenge. Occasionally, however, a plucky little disruptor manages to establish a foothold with a new brand in a market long dominated by one or a few powerful incumbents. Can you think of any?

The Dollar Shave Club's disruption of the branded razor business is a great example. King Camp Gillette founded the American Safety Razor company in 1901 and began marketing the first mass-produced, disposable blade razors based on his innovative patent for stamping rather than forging steel blades. He is credited with inventing the famous "razor and blades" business model. The firm sold the razor at cost, locking customers into the brand and necessitating their purchase of expensive replacement blades. This model has been applied successfully across many industries. For more than 100 years, the Gillette brand dominated the higher end of the American disposable blade razor industry. Brands like Schick and Bic competed mostly on price, but most men were willing to pay a bit more every week to not nick their necks. They stuck with Gillette's brand reputation for quality, and the firm could support its relatively high-cost U.S. manufacturing. Today, Gillette is owned by the multinational consumer goods firm Proctor and Gamble.

Mark Levine and Michael Dubin saw an opportunity to make huge margins in the disposable razor business. They reduced costs by importing blades from Asia and selling directly online, enabling them to offer lower prices to the consumer and take a chunk of the retailer's margin as well. Dollar Shave arranged to source product from a Korean blade maker and lined up funding from an incubator to outsource production of the handle and packaging and build their brand. This brand building is where the real magic occurred. Remember, most consumers had been happy with Gillette for more than 100 years. Dollar Shave needed to disrupt that and did so with a brilliantly humorous online video titled "Our Blades Are F***ing Great," which now has well over 20 million views on YouTube. The 2012 video caught people's attention, and Dollar Shave delivered a good product at a good price and demonstrated high customer retention rates. Dollar Shave was now viewed as a credible threat to Gillette and garnered the attention of Proctor and Gamble's international competitor, Unilever. In July 2016, the brand was sold to Unilever for $1 billion. That is the power of brand disruption. Can you do something like that in a local market?

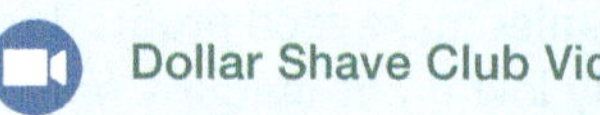

Dollar Shave Club Video

This offbeat YouTube video went viral, establishing a new trend in men's grooming products.

View in the online reader

Yiu has been dreaming of opening an art gallery in a small coastal town. It's a vibrant area with a strong creative streak. It also has a tight-knit group of wealthy businesspeople who view themselves as art patrons. However, the local scene has been dominated for many years by one gallery. Charleston, the owner of the incumbent gallery, has established his shop as the hub for all the popular artists as well as the buyers. He also dominates the social scene. Yiu feels there is room for more than one gallery, but she knows that her competitor will see her entry as a threat and will not be eager to share either his artists or his wealthy clients with her. What can she do?

Yiu will need to disrupt the existing paradigm, and the key to doing that will be to find compelling new local artists or to bring in hot outside talent whose works are substantially different from what Charleston is offering. She must then convince the art buyers that her artists are leading a new wave they need to be aware of. How can she get them in?

Yiu decides to host a charity event and auction off several new pieces to support an important local cause, cleaning up the town's notoriously polluted water supply. This cause engages the support of many community activists who are able to pressure local political leaders into backing the event. These politicians, seeing a way to score points with the citizenry over a popular issue and to solve a municipal problem without tapping into their own budgets, eagerly compel attendance among the town's business leaders. At the dramatic opening, Yiu finds she has a captive audience for her new artists. Once the owners have added a few pieces of the new work to their collections, she is sure they will want to expand their investment. It is an auspicious beginning for her new gallery.

Brand Disasters

Most consumer product companies have opportunities to save money by reducing the quality of their products. They can use inferior materials or reduce the amount of more expensive ingredients. For instance, a candy firm might shrink a popular candy bar or cut back on expensive nuts, hoping buyers won't notice. This is a risky strategy, because if the change becomes a topic of public discussion, the brand could be damaged, and some consumers might switch long-term brand loyalties. Some brand disasters are much worse than that.

Women's clothing boutique chain Lily Pulitzer was proud to be featured in a news article that was going to be based on interviews with executives at their headquarters. Unfortunately, the visiting reporter's eye landed on a doodle taped to an employee's cubicle with a caption reading, "Just another day of fat, white, and hideous. You should probably just kill yourself." This little drawing posted in a private space sent the very public news article in a decidedly negative direction. While the employee was probably motivating themselves to stay in shape, it underscored the fashion industry's dangerously obsessive preoccupation with thinness. Lily Pulitzer ended up in the middle of a negative discussion around fat-shaming rather than getting a load of positive publicity. What is the message here?

The message is that *every form* of communication is a message to the public about the values of your brand. The culture of your company must genuinely reflect the values you wish to present to the consumer. Everyone must be **on message** all the time, and that's easier to do when the message is genuine and natural. The media and the public will latch onto anything that looks disingenuous and tear it apart.

on message

Adhering to the approved message of an organization.

Can you imagine anything being worse than the brand disaster Lily Pulitzer faced? There have been cases where brand disaster created **existential threats** to major businesses. Sometimes these events were well handled, and the brand was reinforced. In some other cases, things went very badly indeed.

existential threat

A problem so serious that it threatens the very existence of the organization.

Malaysian Airlines lost two airplanes in 2014. One plane completely vanished in March, likely the result of terrorism. That July another was mistakenly shot down by a missile while crossing over a war zone in the Ukraine. Hundreds of passengers perished in each event. Perplexingly, the national airline's marketing department then choose to proceed with an ad campaign entitled "Bucket List," asking people to tweet about places they would like to see before they died. Associating flying with dying is a bad idea for any airline at any time, but in the case of Malaysian in 2014, it was a destructive misuse of marketing resources at a time when all public messaging should have been very carefully controlled.

An example of a firm doing a much better job of managing a brand threat occurred in 1982, when a psychopath inserted potassium cyanide poison into bottles of Tylenol brand pain reliever. His acts killed seven people in the Chicago area, beginning with a twelve-year-old girl from Elk Grove, Illinois. James William Lewis did this in an attempt to extort $1 million from Tylenol's manufacturer, Johnson & Johnson. Rather than make a payoff and keep things quiet, the firm immediately warned the public and hospitals, and swiftly recalled 31 million containers valued at over $100 million. Johnson & Johnson incurred a huge financial loss, but it emerged with a golden reputation among consumers and the respect of the global business community. The firm then developed tamper-resistant packaging for its medications, which consumer product companies imitated. When you peel off the plastic seal on the top of a juice bottle today, it's because of this case and one firm's ethical response.

Johnson & Johnson earned the public's trust by responding in an ethical manner to a brand nightmare.

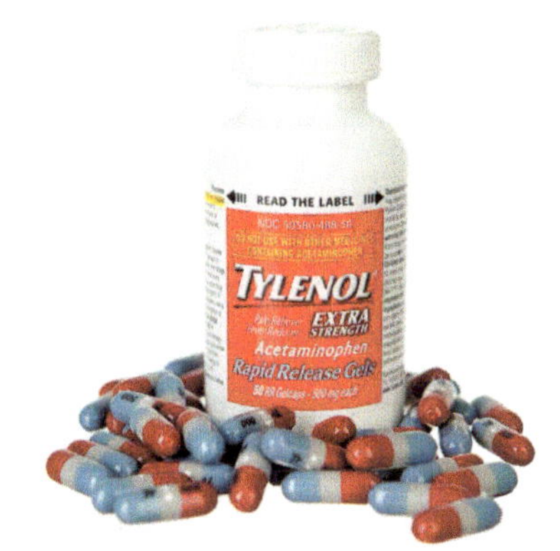

Source: Sean Locke Photography/Shutterstock.com

One company that failed to learn from Johnson & Johnson was the Sanlu Group, a manufacturer of baby formula in Shijiazhuang, China. In 2008, some of the firm's milk suppliers discovered that adding melamine, a chemical typically used to make plastic resins, would cause their milk to test higher for protein content. This **adulteration** of the product increased the milk's wholesale market value. Unaware of the deception, Sanlu paid more for what they thought was better milk. However, consuming melamine causes serious kidney damage, and some Sanlu customers began to get sick. When Sanlu discovered what was going on, they should have admitted that they'd been duped by their suppliers and alerted the public to the danger. Instead, they attempted to cover up the issue to protect their brand's reputation. They even asked local authorities to keep the problem quiet "to avoid whipping up the issue and creating a negative influence in society."[2] Some authorities were paid bribes. At least six children died, more than 50,000 were hospitalized, and as many as 300,000 suffered health problems. In the end, some of the milk suppliers were actually executed by the Chinese government. It doesn't get much worse for a brand than that.

adulteration

Changing the formula of a product in a negative way.

It's unlikely you will have to deal with such life-and-death problems threatening your brand, but honesty is always the best policy, and broadcasting the bad news is usually best done sooner rather than later. Preventing a brand crisis from occurring is another case where a small business actually holds the advantage because a brand image is easier to control for no other reason than *there are fewer people to keep on message*. In a small business, the owner can personally vet all the official marketing material and interview every candidate for employment.

If a brand crisis does happen, a small business is again better equipped to manage the damage control process and to not make it worse. Again, the business owner can keep his or her finger directly on the situation. If you have any employees who may not react well under fire, now is the time to send them on a quick vacation.

Brand and Market Transitions

Cambria is a top producer of high-quality quartz countertops. You might be surprised to learn that Stan Davis started his family's business in 1936 by buying into a creamery, or a manufacturer of butter. Over the years, that firm expanded its dairy processing operations into cheese and developed a variety of brands through several acquisitions and mergers. This is hardly the background for establishing a presence in the fickle interior design market. In fact, the firm's website says, "Nothing about Cambria's beginning was very strategic." Cambria President and CEO Marty Davis remarked, "It just kind of happened."

In 2000, the Davis family saw an opportunity to diversify and acquired a quartz processing operation. Their dedication to quality resulted in a great product. However, the firm was not recognized in the world of interior design or construction. They wisely decided to partner with DuPont and began utilizing the larger, more established firm for distribution of their original quartz tile products. This gave the family a chance to get their production process down while developing their own "Cambria" brand. In just over a decade, they had built a successful operation and a highly admired brand that commands respect in the interior design world.

Targeting: Market and Community Specific Brands

> You can fool all the people some of the time and some of the people all the time, but you cannot fool all the people all the time.
>
> —*Unknown (often attributed to Abraham Lincoln)*

Many people would assert that marketing is not much more than a sophisticated tool used to trick customers into buying a product or service they otherwise would not need. Good marketing should be a process of bringing the perceived value of a *great brand* in line with the value of its *great products*. However, the quote above makes an excellent point: brands must target customers, but they need not and should not court *all* customers. Brands can be laser focused on specific targets by interest, identity, or geography.

A hardworking entrepreneur who had built a successful line of snowboarding clothing and accessories was frustrated by the lack of respect that his parents showed for his accomplishments. When he attended an industry tradeshow or showed up on the slopes, he was a rock star, but none of that prestige translated when he visited home. He was considering expanding his advertising into television or print media that his parents would appreciate. He thought that perhaps it might also bring him some unexpected customers.

GOEXPO Winter 2019 Fair

Source: Aleksandra Suzi/Shutterstock.com

Don't fret if your mom has no idea that your brand is huge as long as the consumers who are most likely to buy your products respect it. We live in an age where information technology allows advertising and messaging to be targeted with almost pinpoint accuracy. The best marketing is so focused and direct that your noncustomer mom will never, ever see it. In fact, if she does come across it, that may be a signal that you're wasting your time and money.

Do not waste your precious brand-building efforts or your advertising budget on people who will never help pay for that effort or produce profits. Marketing simply for prestige, recognition, and ego are signs of a brand about to fail.

Your marketing goal is to drive sales and build awareness within a target audience. Your audience may be defined by geography. For example, imagine you own a hotel laundry service company that targets inns along the Tijuana-Rosarito-Ensenada corridor of Baja California. Alternatively, your audience may be the whole world but limited by specific consumer interests, as with the previous snowboard products example. An audience might also be limited by demographics, as is the case with an auto brand aimed at first-time car buyers in the developing world. Finally, your audience could be some specific mix of all these factors, geography, interests, and demographics, such as for a clothing store in Tokyo that sells only to high-end men's business suit buyers.

Focusing narrowly offers several marketing advantages. The first is that good targeting ensures that the **conversion rate**, or the percentage of potential buyers exposed to your message compared with those who complete an action like learning about your product or making a purchase, is relatively high. In Chapter 10, the mechanics of how to make this happen for your brand will be discussed!

conversion rate

Percentage of potential buyers exposed to your message who complete an action, i.e., learning about the product or making a purchase.

Entrepreneur Fit

Have you noticed how the faces of some brands just fit their products or services? Think about Sir Richard Branson, and then think about flying. Picture Martha Stewart and her conservative home décor. Look at Alibaba's Jack Ma, and imagine huge online sales.

These entrepreneurs fit their companies and their products like a glove. They seem to love what they do, and their customers can sense it. The fact that these famous entrepreneurs are a vital part of their brand works well for them and for their companies. You can do the same with your small business.

self-image
A personal identity.

The trials of small business ownership are hard enough without enduring a bad match between your brand and your own **self-image**. If you cannot agree with your company's model, brand, or product, then it will be a rough ride. For example, if you don't smoke, do you want to open a tobacco store? If you are a recovering alcoholic, is it smart to launch a nightclub? Most likely, the answer is no. So, first and foremost, do something that's both profitable and at least agreeable to you. If you can be passionate about your work, all the better.

Now, just because you fit the product doesn't mean that any business in that category will fit you. If you love scuba diving but cannot stand humidity or mosquitoes, do you want to buy a dive shop in Florida? The New Entrepreneurial Dynamic requires that the brand be an integrated part of the entire entrepreneurial fit. If some aspect of your small business makes it difficult for you to love your work, it will be that much harder for you to build a brand that other people will love. So, if you love to swim with fish, open that dive shop in Hawaii where the weather is better and the mosquitoes are fewer. Your undistracted love for the work will show and make the brand all the better. Just make sure that your brand is something that you wake up smiling about each morning.

Growth Plan Fit

A brand must fit the current and future scale of an organization. If you're a local café, part of the ambiance and credibility is in the authenticity of being a small business. Many people prefer the idea of patronizing a locally owned establishment and expect a higher quality and more unique product from it. They don't want to patronize a large, impersonal, global entity. If you get too professional and "slick" in your approach, you risk looking like just another chain restaurant, and you may reduce the value of your brand to this group of "authenticity seekers."

On the other hand, if you plan to grow your operation into a global franchise, you want to make sure you've got a brand and image that can support that growth. Some customers prefer to patronize a large organization that has strictly defined quality standards. They aren't looking for new experiences, and they want a consistently uniform product. The McDonald's brand is what works for them. This group is comforted by shiny plastic and an assembly line feel that our authenticity seekers eschew.

focus group
A tool for gathering insights from potential customers that brings a group of individuals together to discuss a proposed new product or service and its marketing.

Multinational Conglomerates Dress Up as Small Biz

Be aware that the consumer's perception of the difference between big and small businesses is intentionally blurred by corporate marketers. They are looking to establish brands that capture the authenticity of small business while still leveraging their economies of scale in production and their retail distribution monopolies.

Let's go check out the specialty sauce aisle in a big, chain supermarket. You will see dozens of products in all different categories striving to look authentic to their cuisine. There's Italian marinara, Thai peanut sauce, and Mexican mole with chocolate in it. There will also be a large section of Southern (U.S.) barbecue sauces as well. Our eyes land on "Little Bob's Famous BBQ Sauce." The bottle features a picture of a wise, smiling old man, "Little Bob." The label design is a bit "cheesy" with a big map of Texas on it. It looks like something Little Bob and his family made in their kitchen in Houston and shipped out of their garage. You're thinking, "That's some authentic sauce!"

Many of these brands aspire to appear "authentic."

Source: Niloo/Shutterstock.com

Before you think you're helping an entrepreneur when you buy this stuff, let's consider how many bottles must have been shipped to fill up the shelves of even one major supermarket chain. It's highly unlikely this tasty stuff was bottled at home. Some investigation would show that the BBQ sauce was actually developed in a giant food lab in Minnesota using statistical data on consumer preferences. It was made by technicians and is bottled by several large "co-packing" factories across the nation.

"Authentic" branded products may actually be developed by scientists in sterile labs.

Source: © Shutterstock, Inc.

The Little Bob label was produced by a group of hipster graphic artists in Venice, California. In fact, it turns out "Little Bob" himself was portrayed by a model. Sadly, there never was a person of that name. The photo on the label was selected by interviewing consumers in **focus groups** about which image they felt was most authentic.

Association

brand association

A planned relationship between a brand and something else, i.e., a color, concept, person, emotion, or idea that comes to the consumer's mind when a brand is considered.

Brand association is a powerful psychological tool that marketers have been using for years. At the abstract level, brands tie themselves to things like specific bright colors (Coke, Pepsi), smiles (Amazon), the sun (BP), or other generally positive concepts, expressions, and things.

Iconic public symbols with positive associations are often co-opted by brands.

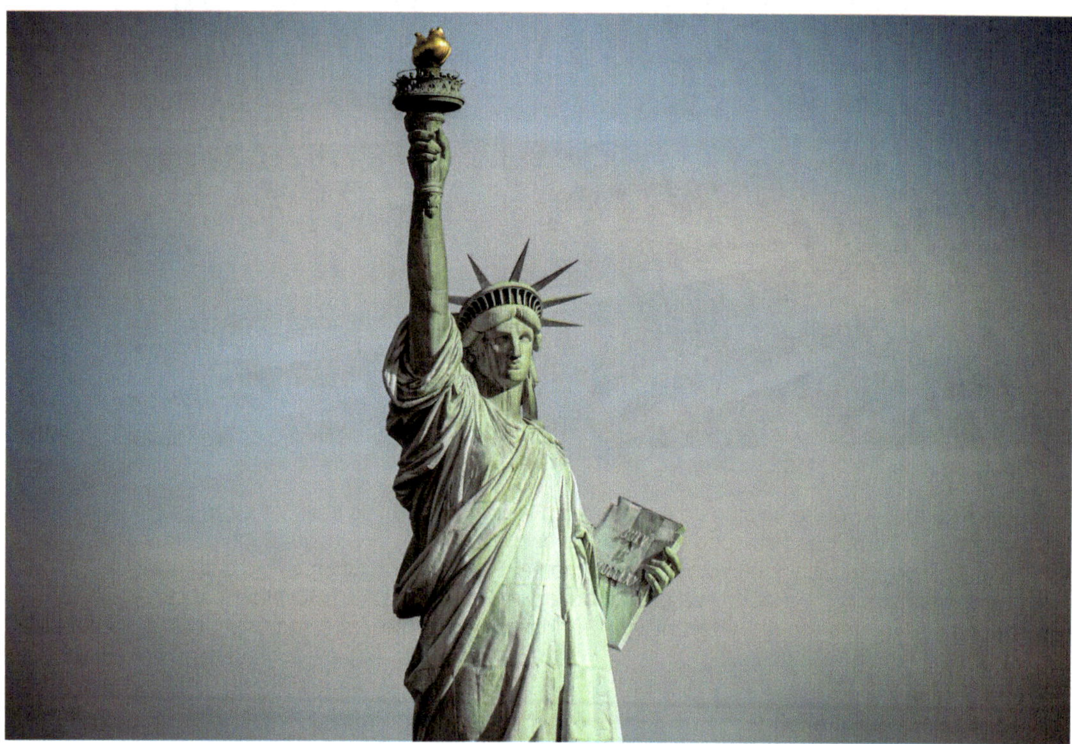

Source: © Shutterstock, Inc.

At the most concrete level, repeated messaging is used to tie the brand to something or even someone very specific. For instance, many companies, such as Liberty Tax Service, have leveraged the public's positive association with the iconic Statue of Liberty. Other brands have tied themselves to famous people, for example, the very successful George Foreman Grill (no, George did not invent that). Some have established artificial personalities who are archetypes of the individual they want to be associated with (see "Multinational Conglomerates Dress Up as Small Biz").

tagline

A catchphrase or slogan used to identify a product or company.

If your small business pulls mostly from the local community, including that community's name in your brand or in a **tagline**, it usually makes the locals happy. If you have a strong reputation in the community, your own name might be a great association as well. Imagine Joe Basher, a retired NHL hockey player, returning home to Maple, the rural town in Canada's Manitoba province where he grew up. Joe still needs income and is looking for a way to leverage his sports-related fame and continue to work in the sport that he loves. Joe buys an ice rink that serves local recreational skaters and hosts a hockey league. The ice rink is called, not surprisingly, the "Maple Ice Rink."

Joe has a number of choices. He could rename the rink "Basher's Sports Complex," an association that would probably attract more hockey players. The recreational skaters, on the other hand, are very fond of the Maple association. Joe might try a combination like "Joe Basher's Maple Ice Rink" or keep the existing name and add a tagline that plays on his fame, as in "Maple Ice Rink: Home of the Basher Hockey League." What is the best way to go?

Remember our discussion of scaling? It applies to associations. If Joe is looking for a relaxing lifestyle business in Maple, he should keep the town's name. On the other hand, if he aspires to build a national chain like Tim Horton did in donuts, he should lead with the Basher brand that would appeal to fans across North America. The first rink could be "Basher's Sports Complex: Maple," and maybe the next one will be "Basher's Sports Complex: Ottawa"!

Association can also be dangerous for your brand. Remember that although you can control your own product quality, you cannot control the independent things or people that you associate your brand with. Nike learned that painfully when their expensive endorsement of Tiger Woods became a nightmare following public revelations of the famous golfer's infamous personal misconduct. Could negative association possibly be that big a problem for a small business?

Imagine that it is 2003, and you are launching a line of authentic Japanese food products from your adopted city of San Francisco, California. Your first product is a seafood seasoning mix. To lend it some authenticity, you name the mix "Fukushima Flavor" in honor of the prefecture on Honshu Island where you lived as a child. The spice sells well, and you add "Fukushima" to all your new product names to keep the brand going! That's all very good until 2011 when a devastating earthquake and tsunami destroys the Daiichi nuclear power plant at Fukushima. Suddenly, the name "Fukushima" is indelibly associated with disaster and frightening radiation leakage.

Trademarks, Brandmarks, Copyright

In 2009, director James Cameron released his blockbuster film *Avatar*. The following year the Nickelodeon TV network released a film adaptation of its cartoon series, *Avatar: The Last Airbender*, which had been running since 2006. However, because Nickelodeon did not properly **trademark** the name "Avatar," they were legally barred from using their own title for their own film project despite being "first to market." Even worse, when they developed a sequel TV series, *Avatar: Legend of Korra*, they were forced to remove "Avatar" from that media as well. Such disasters are easily avoided.

trademark

A symbol, word, or phrase that denotes a specific product and may be legally registered for protection.

In the United States, anyone can simply claim a trademark for their product name or a service mark for their service by placing the ™ or ℠ symbols after the name. No paperwork or registration is required. However, if you wish to go a step further to secure enhanced rights and evidentiary benefits at trial, you can obtain a registered mark ® by filing with the U.S. Patent and Trade Office. If, as in the case of "Avatar," your work is worth millions of dollars, you are strongly advised to file with the assistance of an experienced patent attorney. If you're opening Paul's Fishing Supply on Main Street, you probably don't have to worry much at all. For most businesses, using the ™ is good practice.

You can also use copyrights for slogans, product descriptions, and sales verbiage. Again, you do not actually need to register; simply place the © afterward or note your claim as in "Copyright 2021 Greg Autry." However, if you wish to clearly establish your legal rights and precedent, you may file a copyright notice with the U.S. Copyright Office.

Registered Trademark, Copyright, Trademark, and Service Mark symbols.

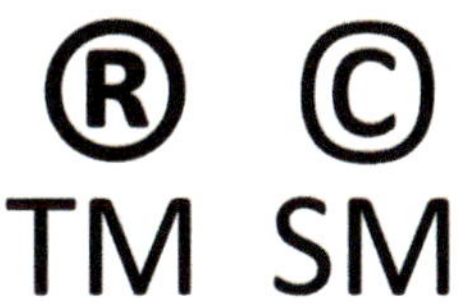

Source: Greg Autry

In Europe, some countries respect a trademark that is not registered, but for full protection in all EU states, it is recommended that you register your trademark online with the European Union Intellectual Property Office (EUIPO). In China, you should register with the China Patent and Trademark Office (CTMO), which is part of the State Administration for Industry & Commerce.

While these intellectual property protections are critical in many arenas, in most small businesses, you can probably safely wait a bit before filing, particularly if the legal fees are a challenge. As with everything in the New Entrepreneurial Dynamic, business names are subject to change. Your original gut instincts on a great name may not be what you eventually run with. For example, Walmart started life as "Walton's Five and Dime." Rather than feeding your lawyer your profits, wait until you know it's the perfect time to file.

Key Takeaways

- Always be building your brand.
- Consider brand impact on every decision you make.
- Know what your brand definition is and why.
- Make sure your brand can grow with your firm.
- Protect your valuable trademarks and register if needed.

9.2 Your Brand in the New Entrepreneurial Dynamic

Learning Objectives

1. Understand that all brands exist in a changing environment.
2. Recognize that brands are tied to feelings as much as rational value judgments.
3. Understand the critical importance of brand coherence.
4. Recognize that brands create value for entrepreneurs and shareholders.

As the art and the science of branding have improved, the marketplace has gotten ever more competitive. The media landscape has also changed. The frenetic pace of social media provides companies with the ability to associate their products with events, people, and fads in real-time, but it also demands 7/24/365 brand management. This can be a real challenge for working entrepreneurs to manage. Big firms have automated systems backed by teams of professionals to manage Twitter. The entrepreneur has her phone, and in today's world of brand management, she can never, ever put it away. Embrace a bit of Zen-like philosophy from the 1984 film *Buckaroo Banzai*, and keep in mind that "no matter where you go, there you are."

Brands must also be dynamic and capable of evolving over time. Adapting a brand to changing conditions and preferences can be a difficult business. In the 1990s, dining trends shifted from classic sit-down chains like Denny's, which generally served awful coffee but were oddly called "coffee shops," to hip coffee-focused venues like Starbucks.

Generational divides present particular problems. Some brands simply age and die with their consumers. The fact that their parents embraced a specific brand causes many young consumers to actively reject them because nothing mom or dad does is ever likely to be cool. This inability to transcend generations is well-known in the music industry—very few discotheques operate today—but it is also present in the auto, fashion, and food services industries.

trend

Current consumer habits or behaviors with potential long-term significance. See also *fad*.

fad

Short-lived consumer popularity. See also *trend*.

It is essential to follow **trends** while avoiding **fads**. Trends are popular new preferences in culture or technology that add value to people's lives and that last for years. Organic foods have been part of a popular trend in the U.S. since the 2000s. Firms that credibly embraced that trend for better quality foods gained long-term positive brand association.

The GPS-enabled augmented-reality smartphone game Pokémon Go was extremely popular in 2016.

Source: Wachiwit/Shutterstock.com

Fads, on the other hand, are short-lived phenomena that don't add enough value to require that they stay around. Fads end quickly, often in a few months. More importantly, when fads fade, they are usually disdained by the very people who adopted them. This is a mental mechanism people use to justify rejecting something they previously embraced. In the spring of 2016, *everyone* with a smartphone seemed to be playing the popular game app Pokémon Go, but by that fall, the fad was over, and it was literally a joke. Companies that spent the summer developing a marketing campaign around Pokémon Go locations didn't just waste their investment, they were mocked by consumers. That's exactly what a brand doesn't want.

Building Your Brand

Brands aren't simply created and then magically leap into the public consciousness. They take time to gain recognition and to take on meaning. A great product, a great name, and a great logo are still not a brand. You must repeatedly position all these items so that they are viewed in the right context by the consumer. The first time a potential buyer sees a new item in the store, an ad, or in the media, they aren't necessarily clear on what it is, what it does, or how they are supposed to *feel* about it. Establishing the brand is about their feelings. Embedding positive feelings about a brand into the buyer's mind demands constantly managed reinforcement.

The first part of this requires simple repetition, getting the brand out there, in front of the consumer, repeatedly until they react to it subconsciously. Like a catchy song, after enough repetitions, your brand will be in their brain for life. The fact that brands can be imprinted onto our subconscious minds has been scientifically demonstrated. Neuroscientists have used functional magnetic resonance imaging (fMRI) machines to look at the brains of consumers while they viewed seemingly random pictures flashed on a screen. When logos for well-known brands appeared, the fMRI data showed that a well-defined emotional network in the viewers' brains was activated.[3] Another study showed that the imprinting of brands begins very early and found that some brain regions associated with motivation were activated in children when they observed food company logos.[4]

Managing Your Brand

brand management

Work done to ensure that a brand is presented consistently and positively and/or mitigate any damage done to a brand.

brand coherence

The consistent application of brand identity.

Brand managers work to ensure that imprinting occurs as quickly as possible and to minimize any negative imprinting that might occur if the brand is viewed in a disturbing context. The best brands work hard to make sure their products, name, and logo are always presented consistently and in an approved context. This is called **brand management**, and its purpose is to ensure **brand coherence**. Large firms establish official style guides and approval processes that retailers must use when presenting their products in the store or in advertising. Do the same principles apply in managing brand coherence for small brands?

Consider Joe Basher's ice rink. Joe has a brand from his pro-hockey days he needs to protect. Joe isn't an experienced businessperson, but he does have that one tool—his own famous name—that he can use to lift the prospects of a struggling ice rink. However, if the ice rink isn't executed well and the consumer experience is negative, he could irreparably damage his brand and reduce its value in other endeavors like product endorsements or personal appearances. Joe needs to make sure the perceptions of the rink are positive and that these perceptions are managed carefully by someone who cares. He might consider hiring an outside consultant to help him manage this process, particularly in the realms of social media.

Cashing In on Your Brand

As previously shown, the value of a company is not always in the intellectual property or resources of a firm. Much of it may be in the brand power imprinted onto the minds of consumers. That power can be very attractive for other companies looking to leverage those imprinted consumers, and consequently, the use of mergers and acquisitions to buy a brand is a major industry. Additionally, mechanisms like franchises, syndication, and licensing a brand allow you to keep control of your brand's equity while still getting paid for its use. At some point, however, you may want to cash in the full value of what you've created.

overvaluation

The act or instance of assigning a value higher than the normal purchase price to an asset being purchased.

The craft beer business exploded in the 2000s and 2010s. At first, the incursion of disruptive firms into their market was seen as a threat by large incumbents like Budweiser's parent firm, Anheuser-Busch (later AB InBev). However, while the customers wanted the hip new brands, the established big companies controlled the distribution system. This suggested that a combination of the two businesses would be more valuable than the firms could be separately. AB InBev went on a buying spree, acquiring firms like Goose Island and Elysian. In doing so, they captured the "hipness" of these companies and maintained their market dominance. For the smaller brands, the deal was all about how "hipness" drove their brand value. The equipment, recipes, and techniques of these companies were of little value to the big brewer. What AB InBev wanted was to cash in on the "craft brew" creds, which their own brands like Bud Light can never claim. AB InBev paid an **overvaluation** for these firms to capture those creds.

Valuing a brand for sale can be tricky due to this intangible aspect. Ultimately, measurements of customer retention, alternatives, and other standard business metrics can be useful, but the emphasis must be on capturing the brand. For example, comparing expenditures to develop the brand and expenditures of competitors to achieve the same or lesser brand can help demonstrate value in the intangible. In the end, a brand, like anything else, is worth what some buyer is willing to pay for it. Think of who stands to benefit most from incorporating your brand or maybe even eliminating it from the market, and you will find your customer. How does this work with small businesses?

Consider two local cafés: Jane's Coffee Shop and the Hipster Café. Jane's Coffee Shop has been on Main Street for as long as anyone can remember. As Jane approaches retirement, she is considering selling the business. Her facility is not fancy. In fact, the façade is a little run down, and its dark interior is long overdue for a style update. The clientele doesn't care or even notice because they have been coming to Jane's their entire lives. Many of them are retired and on fixed incomes. They don't have a lot of money, but they are loyal. Each of them has their favorite booth, and they can sit there for hours enjoying the free coffee refills. They are used to the stained fabric and the worn tabletops. The wait staff has been at Jane's as long as the customers, and everyone knows one another. Jane has never thought about her "brand." She has never used social media nor seen her reviews on Yelp. Without a plan, the little café's brand developed and evolved over many years. It might best be described as "comfort food for seniors."

Across town, José recently opened the Hipster Café. José just graduated from business school and is very brand conscious. Hipster is bright and open with outdoor seating. Everything from the logo to the music has been carefully designed to attract educated young people with higher **disposable incomes**. They pay extra for organic foods and fancy coffees from around the world. They connect with Hipster on Twitter and Instagram to find out about cool "off-the-menu" items, and the reviews on Yelp are all positive and very carefully managed by José and his young tech-savvy staff. Despite being in business for only a year, José is actually considering selling Hipster in order to pursue a new idea he has for a restaurant-focused social media management service.

A modern café.

Source: © Shutterstock, Inc.

Which of these two cafés is going to sell for more? If you asked Jane, she would have no doubt that her long-established business is far more valuable than José's little upstart café. She would be dead wrong. The main asset a buyer would be interested in is the future revenues as determined by the value of the client base. Despite their loyalty, Jane's older and lower-spending diners do not present an attractive long-term investment. There isn't a lot of money there, the clients will literally die off, and they are not connected to the brand beyond their seat in the booth. On the other hand, the potential of growing the Hipster brand from the high-value and highly connected clientele that José has built up is promising. José's understanding of his brand has made all the difference.

disposable income

Spendable money left over after taxes have been paid.

Brand Building in a Dynamic World

Cultural Change: Public expectations and cultural norms are changing at an increasing rate as globalization and technology break down and shift existing social structures. Recently, definitions of personal identity have become a topical issue in the United States. Identity concepts, such as "manly," that have driven some brands (think jeans, razors) for decades may now resonate negatively with younger consumers. Always consider the social and political context in which your brand will be interpreted and how you will adapt to changes in that context. Doing this well is a competitive advantage; doing it poorly may be a serious problem.

Technology: Getting your brand in front of consumers is increasingly about digital exposure. Look ahead and stay connected to what young people are doing in order to keep your brand development efforts at the leading edge. Working on getting your brand used by a character in a mobile game app may be better than buying a billboard.

Globalization: Today, all brands are international. With increasing levels of wealth in formerly developing countries, international travel is exploding. If you don't ship a product overseas, there is a good chance that international customers are coming to you more and more frequently. Keep your brand global aware and language independent when possible. Consider the names, taglines, and images you select with consideration to their possible meaning in other cultures and languages.

Earth has no borderlines, and globalization is blurring them in the markets as well.

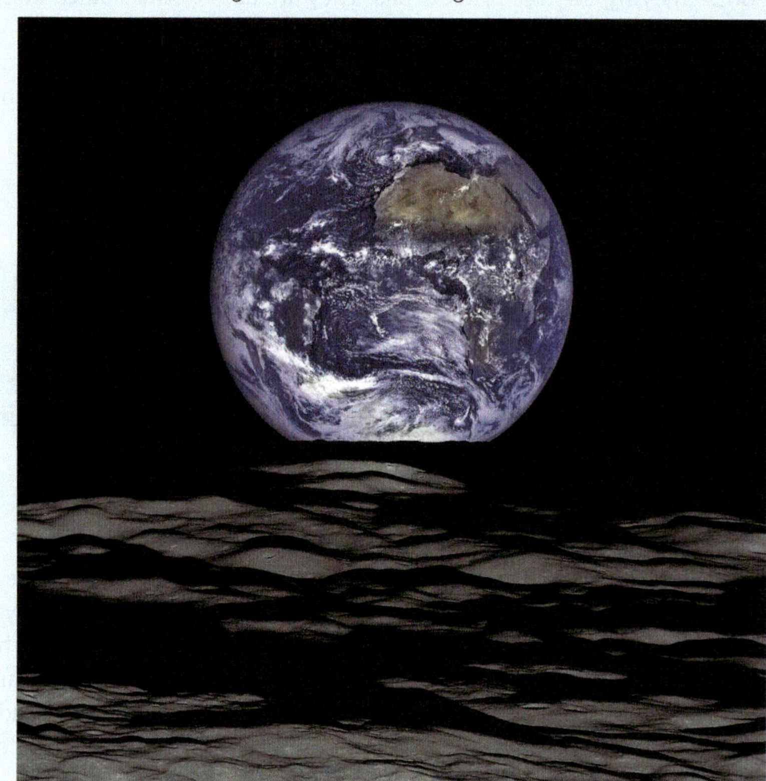

Source: NASA

Key Takeaways

- Avoid attaching your valuable brand to passing fads.
- Always be building your brand.
- Keep your brand coherent and on track at all times.
- Be ready to leverage your brand or even sell it when it is most valuable.
- Customers determine the value of your brand; stay current.

9.3 Case Study: Wahoo's Tacos

The Lee brothers, Wahoo's founders (from left: Wing, Mingo, and Ed).

Source: The Lee Brothers

Ed Lee was born to be a restaurateur. Well, the founder of the Wahoo's Tacos chain was actually *born in a restaurant*. Ed and his brothers, Wing and Mingo, are Southern California surfers of Chinese ethnicity who were born in Brazil. Together, they make famously creative Mexican food fused with unexpected tastes like Korean kimchi. Before settling on the Wahoo's concept, Ed and his brothers experimented with clothing, latex hospital gloves, Asian restaurant supply, and once nearly purchased a bison ranch in Montana. The Lee family is a classic "only in America" tale of entrepreneurship. Wahoo's opened in 1988 and now has 60 locations and annual revenues of over $65 million. The case is presented here in an interview format.

Prof. Autry: Tell me about Wahoo's brand. How did you build that?

Lee: We opened the first Wahoo's in '88, in Costa Mesa, California. The menu was a copy of an authentic place we loved in Ensenada. Then we just went with what we loved. We started infusing other stuff into tacos and burritos. Things like Japanese teriyaki and Korean BBQ. Who does that? We also decorated the store with stickers for surf culture companies and covered the walls with skateboards and cool local stuff. It was totally embracing the Southern California cultural mashup that made the Wahoo's brand so unique.

Prof. Autry: What's the biggest challenge your brand has faced?

Lee: Well, that's an easy one, the "Band-Aid incident!"

Prof. Autry: What was that about?

Lee: Back in 1995, I got a call from our headquarters' office saying, "You need to get down here right away." When I arrived at the HQ, our parking lot was packed with news vans and crawling with reporters. The first reporter I ran into took me aside to warn me what was going on, and she said, "You want the good news or the bad news first?"

I replied, "Give me the good news."

And she said, "The world is safe. There is absolutely nothing terrible going on today anywhere on Earth."

So I asked her, "Then what's the bad news?"

She replied, "You're the news." She went on to explain that a woman was claiming that a Band-Aid had been found in her burrito.

Prof. Autry: How did you handle that?

Lee: Well, firstly, the old adage, "There's no such thing as bad publicity" is true. Our sales the next week were through the roof. We had, like our best week ever.

Prof. Autry: That's pretty surprising!

Lee: We were honest, and that is important. It is also important that it showed. We looked like we cared because we did. We looked like real people dealing with a problem honestly. I told the *LA Times* that the employee felt horrible and that we all felt bad. Customers responded by supporting the Wahoo's brand and coming into the restaurants.

Prof. Autry: So it all worked out that easily?

Lee: Oh no! There was a lawsuit. The lady with the Band-Aid, she was a nurse, and she and her daughter quit their jobs figuring they were going to have a big legal payday on us. Our insurance company told us we were going to lose, and the judgment would exceed our coverage. We were actually preparing to liquidate the entire business. A lot of people were going to lose their jobs.

Prof. Autry: What happened then?

Lee: I wanted that Band-Aid. I told my attorney that if I was going to have to trade my entire business over this Band-Aid, I wanted it as part of the settlement. You know what? She couldn't produce it. There was no evidence! That was pretty much the end of the case. I actually feel a bit sorry for the woman and her daughter.

Prof. Autry: What did you learn from this brand crisis, and what did you change?

Lee: I'd have to say you always need to be level-headed. You need to be really sincere. When things go wrong, you fix them, and you make sure everyone understands. We made specific changes to the food preparation process, including using steel mesh gloves and food processors, but the key thing is just constantly reinforcing our commitment to safety and quality and making sure everyone is on board with that.

Endnotes

1. So iconic, in fact, that his hat has been installed as an exhibit at the Smithsonian National Museum of American History.
2. https://web.archive.org/web/20130215164311/http://www.reuters.com/article/2008/10/01/us-china-milk-idUSTRE48T0L920081001.
3. Casarotto, S., et al. (2012). Covert brand recognition engages emotion-specific brain networks. *Archives Italiennes de Biologie, 150(4)*, 259–273.
4. Bruce, A. S., et al. (2014). Branding and a child's brain: An fMRI study of neural responses to logos. *Social Cognitive and Affective Neuroscience 9(1)* 118–122.

CHAPTER 10

Marketing

> The product is the contents, the store is the packaging, and the communication is the magic. People buy magic and stories.
>
> —*Pietro Becarri, CEO of Fendi*

Disneyland is the physical manifestation of the Disney brand of family fun.

Source: wonderlustpicstravel/Shutterstock.com

Capture the first thought that comes to mind when you think of the following brands: Disney, Toyota, or Apple. It's likely you thought of family fun, reliability, and a sleek electronic device, respectively. How were those brand images implanted in your brain? To a great extent, repeated exposure to carefully crafted commercial messages have permanently connected these attributes to those brands in your subconscious mind. Although each of these global companies delivers a top-quality product and dominates their respective market segments, they don't trust serendipity to lead consumers to their desired brand perception. These firms literally have thousands of people spending many millions of dollars each year to ensure that you perceive their brand in precisely the way they would like you to. Professionals are working in the background managing everything from Super Bowl commercials to Instagram posts. They are called professional **marketers**.

marketers

Individuals who craft and execute marketing plans.

10.1 Beyond Brands

Learning Objectives

1. Understand the difference between marketing and advertising.
2. Recognize that effective marketing drives a variety of functions in support of sales.
3. Understand the concept of satisficing.
4. Recognize that markets have limits and advertising can have diminishing returns.
5. Understand the technology adoption life cycle.
6. Understand the chasm concept, beachhead strategy, and bowling pin effect.

Marketing Versus Advertising Versus Selling

marketing

The activities of a company associated with creating demand for the firm's products or services within their target market.

advertising

The activity of informing potential customers about a product or service via paid public announcements over various media such as print, television, digital, and social media.

While **marketing** and **advertising** are closely related, they must not be conflated. Each does what it sounds like—marketing creates markets, and advertising creates advertisements. Marketing can be broadly defined as the activities of a company associated with creating demand for the firm's products or services within their target market. Advertisements are one useful tool for positioning products within the market, informing potential customers of the existence of the product, and generating demand. Advertisements are generally paid messaging in public outlets, including print, television, radio, web, mobile, and social media. Other useful tools include publicity (spinning the news) and social media. Recall the discussion in Chapter 3 of objectives, strategy, and tactics. How might you apply that thinking in this context?

FIGURE 10.1 Marketing in Context

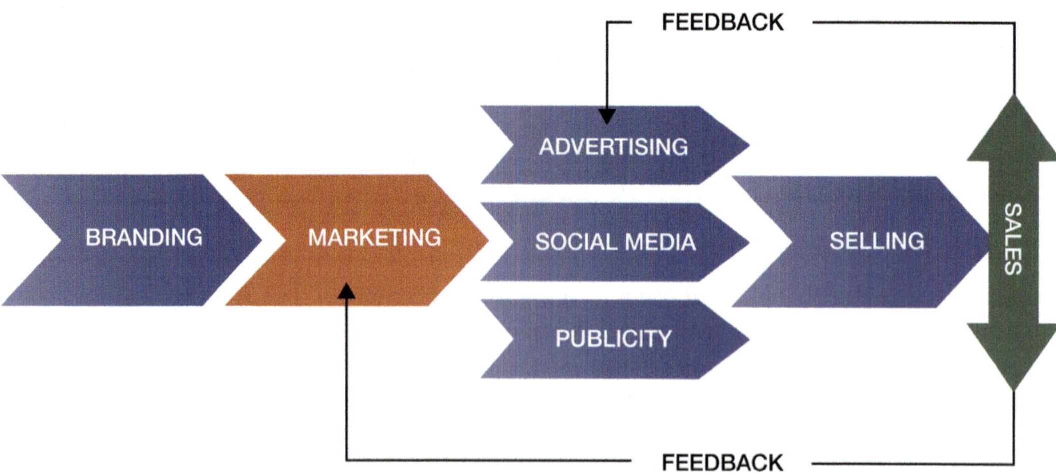

Source: Greg Autry

sales process

The process that comes after consumers are made aware of a product via marketing, and that is designed to result in a closing a deal.

Take a look at Figure 10.1 and imagine you are in just about any business. From Chapter 9, you know that building a great brand should be our overriding goal. Marketing is our strategic plan. Advertising, social media, publicity, and other tactics implement the marketing goals. Advertising and other tactics, in turn, support the **sales process** discussed in Chapter 11. Think of marketing as the overall way that you will plan to shape the market in a way that is beneficial for your firm's revenues. The results, measured in sales units or revenues, provide the feedback you will use to iteratively adjust marketing strategy, advertising, and other tactics until sales are optimized. Why are sales dollars the final measure of our efforts?

Sales is the metric that is used because, in the end, brand value that cannot be converted to sales cannot be sustained. To be sustainable, marketing and advertising activities must generate more profits than they consume. Sales will be discussed further, but good marketing and successful advertisements are always aligned with a successful close. This begins with understanding why customers purchase products and how they come to decisions about specific brands.

Satisficing and Differentiating

You might assume that consumers purchase the best product or service they can afford to buy. The fact is, consumers often choose less capable products or service providers. In fact, they often pay more for the lesser good! Can you think of why this would be?

The reasons people might pay more for less or choose a lesser grade product are complex. However, a great deal of consumer decision-making can be explained by the limited resources of information and time. A buyer can't select the best product if they don't know it exists, and they usually can't spend the time to research every possible product to find the perfect one for their budget. Sound familiar?

Have you gone looking for a restaurant in a strange city and found that Yelp, Google, and other services offered a bewildering array of options and thousands of customer reviews to consider? You know that somewhere in there is the review or set of criteria that will offer you the greatest dining experience. You can only view one review at a time on your smartphone, and you can't remember each review. You could start making notes and go back and forth to compare. However, your stomach is saying, "Must have food now!" and most of the restaurants stop serving at 10 p.m., so you better make a decision. In the end, you do just enough research to assure that you won't have a horrid experience or get completely ripped off. You select the best restaurant that your search capabilities and time permit.

The brilliant business scholar and Nobel prize-winning economist, Herbert A. Simon, defined this concept formally in 1947 as **satisficing** and argued convincingly that people do not seek the optimal solution but rather the first choice that will satisfy their needs. Marketers have long been aware of the idea, and it is why they spend money on advertising. If they can get you information about their product sooner, you may purchase it without doing exhaustive research. You will accept their ad as research to save yourself the investment of time required to do the genuine work.

satisficing

The theory that consumers search long enough to find a solution that meets their needs rather than finding the ultimately best solution.

Herbert Simon

Detail of Herbert Simon from *Family Portrait 2,* 1965

Source: Wikimedia Creative Commons Attribution-Share Alike 4.0 International

> Decision makers can satisfice either by finding optimum solutions for a simplified world, or by finding satisfactory solutions for a more realistic world. Neither approach, in general, dominates the other, and both have continued to co-exist in the world of management science.
>
> *—Herbert A. Simon, in his speech accepting the Nobel Prize in Economics*

Herbert A. Simon was a founder of modern management theory and much, much more. Born in Milwaukee, Wisconsin, on June 15, 1916, Simon developed an early interest in science and particularly the study of human behavior and decision-making. He studied social sciences and mathematics at the University of Chicago, receiving a BA and a PhD in political science. His PhD dissertation was on the theoretical basis for organizational decision-making. Among his major contributions to organizational theory were the concepts of bounded rationality and satisficing. Bounded rationality presumes that human beings (or any system) are limited in their decision-making capability by the bounds of their mental abilities and the time needed to collect information and make the decision. Consequently, people and organizations do not actually attempt to make optimal decisions, but rather make the best decision they can in the time allotted, often choosing the first solution that meets all their required criteria rather than expending more valuable time in further searching.

This sort of thinking lent itself very well to the new science of computing, and Simon was an early contributor to the field of artificial intelligence (AI). His work with Allen Newell developing the IPL computer language and their idea of separating problem-solving code in memory from the data it was applied to revolutionized software design and resulted in his winning the prestigious Turing Award in 1975. The Turing is the highest honor in the field of computer science. Simon's interest in psychology resulted in the development of Elementary Perceiver and Memorizer theory, which, when coded in IPL, became one of the first machine learning programs, thus laying the groundwork for the modern AI that drives many startup opportunities today.

Simon went on to think about the way that the human mind compensates for its limited processing ability by organizing information into "chunks" and using the structural regularity of the environment as a shortcut in making decisions. He even published work on how language and culture (Chinese versus English, for instance) altered the actual organization of information in the human brain.[1] His work in this area formed a bedrock for the science of behavioral economics and organizational theory. Expected utility and other theories that presumed human beings operated like mathematical machines using perfect information and unlimited computing power had to be adjusted to account for the reality of human capabilities.

In 1947, Simon published the seminal work *Administrative Behavior,* a book that analyzed organizational decision-making in the context of business operations.[2] It is still required reading for scholars of business strategy and economics. Simon's insight that perfect decisions are impossible because of incomplete information and bounded rationality revolutionized the science of microeconomics and resulted in Simon's being awarded the Nobel Memorial Prize in Economics in 1978. In 1986, President Reagan awarded him with the National Medal of Science, America's highest award for scientific achievement. He also received the 1995 IJCAI Award for Research Excellence in artificial intelligence, the American Psychological Association's Award for Distinguished Scientific Contributions to Psychology in 1969, as well as APA's lifetime contribution award in 1993.

Simon's personal life was as varied as his professional career. As a teen, he spent his summers working a farm on a marsh in rural Wisconsin. His daughter, Katherine, recalls that he bragged that during his undergrad career he only took one course, which was boxing. The rest of his curriculum at the University of Chicago was self-directed, and he graduated by simply challenging all the final exams.[3] Simon was also a skilled pianist and chess player who had a fascination with the classification of beetles. One of his graduate students remarked, "Every time Simon received a major award, which was often, he would learn the local language to accept it in." He was an avid mountaineer and spent the week of his sixty-fifth birthday wandering through the Alps on his own. Simon passed in 2001.

Advertising Campaigns

Marketing is effective when the cost of the marketing activity is less than the value created by the activity over time. If, for instance, an **advertising campaign** creates demand from enough new customers that the cumulative profits from sales to those customers is more than you spent on the development and **placement** of those ads, you've probably got a winner. As long as the gains are from customers who would otherwise not be aware of or choose your firm's product, you are taking away sales and profits from competing firms in your market. Congratulations, your marketing has become a source of competitive advantage! What should you do now?

advertising campaign

A series of advertisements designed to create brand awareness.

placement

The function of putting an ad into a particular location in media, as in securing an ad space in a magazine.

Measure It to Manage It

One of the most obvious answers is: If something works, do more of it. Should you scale a successful ad campaign by running it more often? The question depends on several factors where you may not have any data. The most important factor is the question of whether you have reached **market saturation** or not. That is, has your advertisement been seen by all the customers in the target market the most appropriate number of times required to move customers toward a purchase? Exceeding market saturation is obviously inefficient, but it can also be damaging. Can you think of why?

market saturation

The point at which additional advertising does not produce profitable returns.

infinitely scalable

A system that is not subject to diminishing returns, where you can continue to invest money and always get consistent returns.

diminishing returns

The concept that as a market becomes saturated, each additional dollar placed into developing it will result in lower returns.

Is there an advertisement that you have seen so many times that it actually irritates you when it pops up in your social media or on television? Does this cause negative associations in your mind with that company? Would you actually be less likely to consume its product or service? Too much of a good thing can produce negative results. So, you can conclude that returns to advertising are not **infinitely scalable**. Advertising is subject to the laws of **diminishing returns**. How do you know where that point of diminishing returns is? What about running the same ads in different outlets or in different markets? Will that generate more profits than expense?

These are good questions, and people have been looking for answers for a very long time. In the nineteeth century, department store owner John Wanamaker famously said, "Half the money I spend on advertising is wasted. The trouble is, I do not know which half." Echoing this a century later, twentieth-century management guru Peter Drucker was fond of saying, "You can't manage what you can't measure." Luckily for you, as a twenty-first-century entrepreneur, information technology and big data tools are answering Wanamaker's questions and fulfilling Drucker's mandate. We'll take a deeper look into the tools for measuring and managing marketing effectiveness later in the chapter.

The Technology Adoption Life Cycle

Every market has a beginning. The smartphone market started with the Palm Treo in 2002. The automobile market began in 1885 with the Benz Patent-Motorwagen. Somewhere long ago, some Neolithic farmers started the grain business, selling a finished agricultural good to others, relieving them of the need to farm themselves.

The first car, an 1885 Benz Patent Motorwagen.

Source: https://commons.wikimedia.org/wiki/File:1885Benz.jpg

Whenever a new type of product enters the marketplace, there is a predictable process of market acceptance referred to as the **technology adoption life cycle**. This life cycle really applies to all products that are new, not just what we think of as tech. In fact, this model was first identified in the agricultural sector in 1956 by sociology researchers George Beal and Joe Bohlen.[4] It was formalized by Everett Rogers in his 1962 book *Diffusion of Innovations*,[5] which represented the process as a normal distribution bell curve divided into categories of innovators, early adopters, early majority, late majority, and laggards.

technology adoption life cycle

The sequential market categories (innovators, early adopters, early majority, late majority, laggards) that a new product or service must penetrate over time.

FIGURE 10.2 Technology Adoption Life Cycle

Rogers' bell curve and categorization of technology consumers.

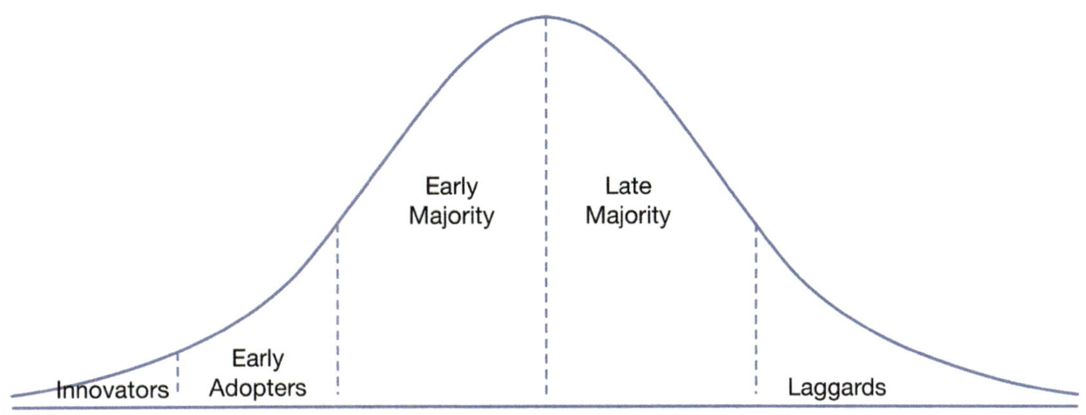

Source: Greg Autry

Beal, Bohlen, Rogers, and many subsequent management scholars have noted that selling a product in a whole new category is a special challenge. When you're marketing something totally new, you have to sell the customer on the very idea, not just the advantages of your product. Benz wasn't competing with other automobile firms; he was competing with horses and walking! Selling the first cars involved convincing people to learn something new, risk danger, and deal with a lot of inconveniences, such as finding and storing their own fuel (there were no gas stations).

It turns out that a small category of folks, the **innovators**, like new things for their own sake and will revel in these inconveniences. You probably know some of these nerds, the ones who brag to their friends about how complex and hard to use their new gizmos are. If it breaks, they are happy to fix it. Selling to innovators requires little more than letting them know your thing exists and giving them an attractive feature set, and the more complex, the better for them. The next category, the **early adopters**, are similar in that they are inclined to new products and like to show them off; however, they generally demand that the stuff actually work and add measurable value to their lives. They are still an easy sell and willing to pay good money to be among the first users of something valuable. Innovators and early adopters tend to be younger, educated, independent thinkers with enough income to take some risk in product purchases.

innovators

The category of buyers in a market who are willing to use new products that are not fully mature and may require a great deal of effort to use.

early adopters

The category of buyers who are willing to try new products as long as they deliver on their promise and come with support.

The Chasm Concept

So far, so good. It seems you can simply change your pitch as you move from one market category to the next. However, markets often include a problematic phenomenon known as the **chasm**. The chasm is a term coined by Geoffrey Moore to describe the difficulty in reaching the third category, the early majority. Moore argues in his seminal work, *Crossing the Chasm*,[6] that fundamental differences in the consumers of this third category from the previous two render the market transition to early adopters a leap rather than smooth migration. This an incredibly important problem.

chasm

The chasm is a term coined by Geoffrey Moore to describe the difficulty in bridging the gap between those who like adopting new technologies and those who just want stuff that works.

A glance at the technology Adoption life cycle suggests that given the normal (bell curve) distribution, no firm can survive without capturing a substantial portion of the very large early majority category. Firms left in the innovator and early adopter market are doomed to obscurity. They will not have the revenue required to keep their product competitive. Eventually, they lose even their own pioneering customers. So, what is so different about the early majority, and how do you sell to them?

FIGURE 10.3 Moore's Chasm

The chasm is a barrier lying between the early adopters and the majority of customers.

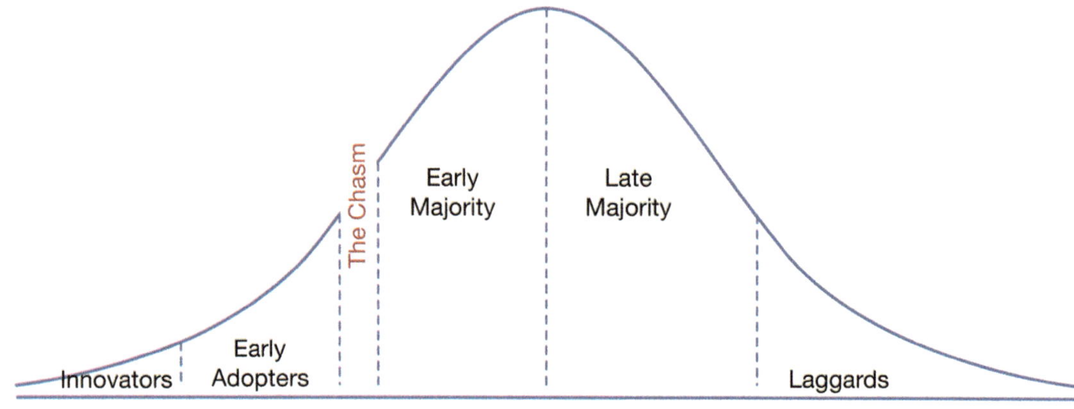

Source: Greg Autry

referential

Customers who insist on receiving positive reviews before they will purchase new products.

The primary difference with the early majority is that they are less independent and more risk-averse than the early adopters. They are willing to try things they haven't used before, but only if they have solid evidence from reliable sources that a new product or service works as advertised. They are highly **referential**, meaning they want to hear good things from their friends—peers in the early majority—who are using the new thing. That presents an obvious conundrum: How do you get traction in this category if you must have customer references from within the category to get traction?

Establishing a Beachhead

beachhead strategy

A strategy involving putting all your resources into a single market at the same time in order to secure a strong foothold that cannot be displaced.

Moore suggests the **beachhead strategy** is the most viable approach to penetrating the early majority category. Like many business strategies, he chooses a historical military analogy to illustrate his approach. Moore argues that the strategy of Supreme Allied Commander General Dwight D. Eisenhower, developed for the massive 1944 invasion of Nazi-occupied Europe from across the English Channel, is a good model for firms attempting to leap from the small early adopter category across the chasm to the large early majority category. Sitting on the island of Britain, General Eisenhower had a huge target, nearly the entire coastline of Europe, to consider. Should he divide his forces and assault several locations, forcing the Germans to spread their defense? Should he pick a handful of locations? Should he deploy his forces all at once or over time?

D-Day Beachhead, Normandy, France, June 6, 1944

Source: U.S. National Archives, https://artsandculture.google.com/exhibit/wRQ7nqwa

Eisenhower's simple plan, called Operation Overlord, focused all available allied resources into the smallest possible area in the shortest possible time, in order to absolutely guarantee the penetration of the enemy defenses. During the D-Day invasion, Eisenhower used more than 5,000 ships to deposit over 100,000 soldiers onto a strip of beaches on France's Normandy coast in a single day. Ten thousand planes and 23,000 paratroopers were used as well. The forces were so close together that the process seemed to be chaotic, and the casualties were enormous, but the German defenders in this small area were utterly overwhelmed. The allied forces secured a permanent beachhead, from which they liberated Europe in relatively short order. How do you think that would translate to marketing strategy?

The early adopter category in any market contains a number of smaller market niches or segments, each with possible distribution channels. Let's think about the self-driving car market. These new devices could be marketed to the average car buyer, and you could sell to them through existing car dealers (like nearly all cars today), direct on the internet (like Tesla), or even through multi-level marketing (like Tupperware). You could also sell to big corporations with fleets of cars and channels using car dealer fleet sales departments or a direct sales force. There are also taxi services, limousine rental firms, town car operators, rental car companies, and food and package delivery . . . you can see there are lots of customers in the early majority to sell a self-driving car. Should you try to dominate all of these segments and try to conquer the whole market or just test them all to see where your product does best?

The reality is, that like General Eisenhower, your marketing resources are limited, and spreading them out into all of these segments and distribution channels will result in a diluted message that will be easily overwhelmed by any competitors who choose to concentrate their forces into one of the segments. Consequently, you must concentrate and pour all your efforts into establishing a beachhead of referenceable customers in one segment. The size of the segment is not as important as being 100 percent sure you can win it. Everything depends on the invasion. It will take a lot of advertising and sales work to get a few customers and then to leverage them into volume sales, but once an early majority market starts to move, they move in a herd, and subsequent sales will be relatively effortless.

Bowling Pin Effect

bowling pin effect

The ability of a firm to leap across market segments from a secure beachhead in the early majority category of one segment.

Once you are entrenched in an early majority market segment, say the corporate fleet market for self-driving cars, getting into another adjacent segment is fairly easy. Rental car and taxi fleet operators use the same principles that corporate buyers do when choosing vehicles to purchase. If they see that your firm has hundreds of vehicles serving Fortune 500 firms, they will be very willing to try your product. You can effectively use a cross-segment reference to get directly to the early majority in any adjacent market. As these adjacent market segments begin to fall, Moore calls that the **bowling pin effect**. Once you obtain that power of using your conquered segments to knock down others, you are on your way to conquering the entire early majority market.

The late majority portion of your market will simply follow the early majority. These are simply a more risk-averse and price-conscious version of the early majority. Finally, there are the laggards, and their business isn't really that important because they aren't big spenders or large in number. Think of your grandparents who initially thought a smartphone would be hard to use and stuck with an old flip phone until they pretty much couldn't find one anymore.

The lesson is that your biggest marketing moment happens after your product is stabilized and you are ready to scale your sales efforts beyond the enthusiasts and into the larger market. At that point, you must identify a niche and a distribution channel you can dominate and then throw everything you have in marketing and advertising at it. How do you identify the right segment?

Key Takeaways

- Use marketing to build your brand and drive sales through several channels.
- Remember customers aren't looking for the optimal solution. They are looking for the easiest solution that stops their pain or provides sufficient pleasure.
- Focus your marketing on an initial market segment you can penetrate deeply.
- Once you've conquered a market segment, spread into adjacent segments where your initial success will carry weight.

10.2 Marketing Strategies

Learning Objectives

1. Understand how brand power can reduce advertising costs.
2. Understand the power of an aspirational brand.
3. Learn to use the news media for brand building.
4. Understand the role of trade shows.
5. Appreciate the role of social media in brand building.
6. Understand the power of granularity available in social media advertising.
7. Understand the importance of search engine optimization.
8. Understand how search ads work.
9. Understand how influencers are motivated to push products.
10. Understand that unethical marketing will not pay in the long run.

Riding Your Brand Power

Sometimes marketing results in permanent value being added to your brand. As noted in Chapter 9, companies such as Coca-Cola, Nike, and Apple possess immense brand power. Their positive associations are so firmly embedded in our minds that their products can outsell their competitors simply by sitting on the shelf with their logo facing outward. Does that mean these firms do not need to continue their marketing efforts and advertising campaigns? Wouldn't sales just continue, and their profits increase, if they stopped spending money on those things?

The answer to these questions is not a simple "yes" or "no." In the short run, cutting the ad budget to zero will certainly drive down fixed costs and increase a firm's net profits if the brand association is powerful enough to sell the product. It's very possible that there would be little change in Coca-Cola revenues if they shut down their Coke advertising for a quarter. On the other hand, Pepsi would not. In fact, the second-place soft drink firm would likely up the ante in the 130-year war between the two brands by boosting advertising. It is reasonable to assume that at some point, massive Pepsi advertising could eventually eclipse the Coke brand in consumers' minds. Coca-Cola must continue to advertise enough to signal to Pepsi that they will protect their dominant brand position. Are there companies that can get away with it?

A writer for *Road and Track* who was reviewing the Tesla Model X shortly after its debut reported, "When I was taking photos of this Model X P100D in a hip part of Brooklyn, every time I raised the doors, people stopped." He also noted that "attendees of a nearby music festival stopped and took selfies" with the car. He finally concluded that the primary purpose of unique Falcon Wing doors was to attract attention; they are, in essence, advertising.[7] Which brings up the question, have you ever seen a Tesla advertisement?

Huy Fong Sriracha Sauce

Source: Steve Cukrov/Shutterstock.com

As of mid-2019, Elon Musk's electric car company had not run an ad during its record-setting sixteen years of sales growth. The marketing plan at Tesla is to let excitement around the unique features of their cars build the brand. Tesla is not the only auto firm with such a policy. Rolls Royce, a one-hundred-year-old super-luxury brand, uses a similar **aspirational brand** strategy. Few drivers can afford to buy either of these cars, but many want to. Even just sitting in a parking lot, these cars are advertisements for the brand. Many of those who could buy these cars were fond of the attention the public admiration of their vehicles brought.

A number of other famous companies have skipped paid advertising. These include warehouse retailer Costco, doughnut store chain Krispy Kreme, and the flaming hot Asian condiment Huy Fong Sriracha sauce. Huy Fong Foods founder David Tran says sales growth for his firm has been constrained primarily by his access to newly ripe chili peppers. As he told Quartz, "I don't advertise, because I can't advertise."[8] Advertising would only drive sales that he couldn't fill. The company's seemingly unsophisticated approach to marketing has actually developed into a powerful and valuable cult brand. The bottles' simple logo with its line-drawn rooster and a cluttered multilingual descriptive text graces T-shirts, phone cases, lunch boxes, and a variety of other consumer goods.

aspirational brand

A product that many consumers wish to own but cannot. The exclusivity of this makes the product more attractive to those who can afford it.

Radio and TV

While new media is all the rage, traditional outlets of print, radio, and television are far from dead. When most people hear the word "advertising," they still think of old school broadcast television spots. The biggest virtual gathering of Americans is still probably the Super Bowl, a television mega-event as famous for its commercials as for the football games, which are often lopsided nonevents. Many people actually watch the show for the advertisements, driving viral videos, memes, and discussions across social media. This rare focus on the ads makes the Super Bowl the world's most expensive and competitive outlet for the marketing efforts of large corporations.

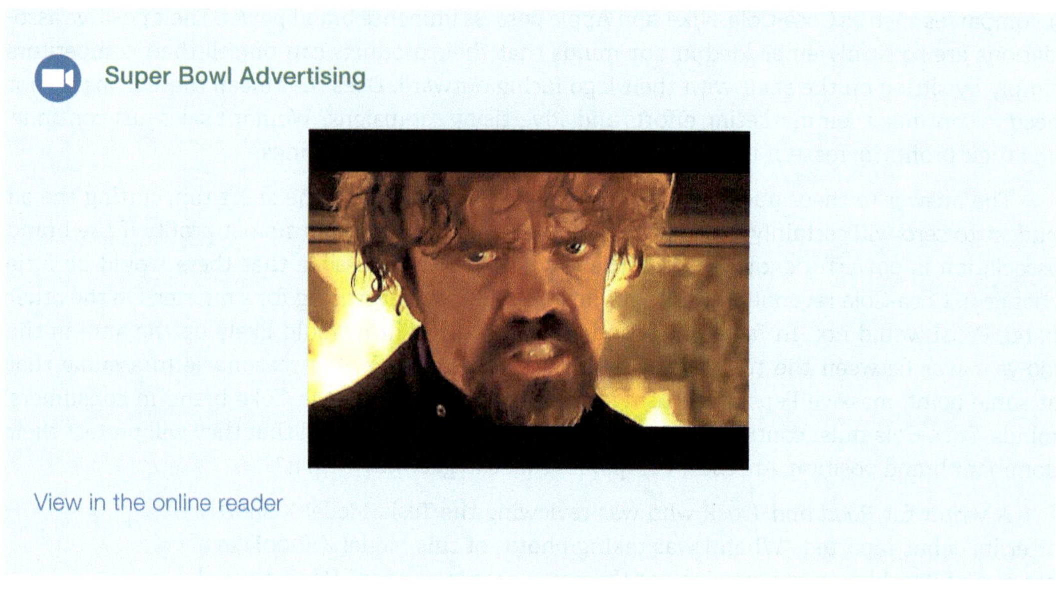

Traditional media advertising campaigns are difficult for startups because they are expensive, harder to target, and the results are notoriously difficult to track. Can you think of why that is?

conversions
Sales driven by advertisements.

The physical infrastructure investments required for broadcast and cable television or traditional and satellite radio are immense. The cost of facilities, antenna towers, miles of cables, and space launches have to be recovered by the networks and regional operators almost entirely from advertising revenues. Consequently, most small startups simply can't participate in anything outside of local cable TV or radio. While those outlets may be suitable for a local restaurant chain, they are entirely useless for a startup fashion brand or smartphone app with a global target market. Unlike social media ads and other internet-based advertising systems, the reach of ads in traditional media is determined by physical limitations of the broadcast, geography, broadcast licensing, and other factors completely outside of your control. You may reach a lot of people, but you can't be sure exactly who they will be, and you probably won't know exactly how many stayed and watched your ad. While you can try "how did you find us" surveys, the reality is that you simply cannot tie traditional advertising expenditures directly to actual **conversions** (sales) the way you can with a good internet campaign. If you have several advertising campaigns running simultaneously it's even harder, if not impossible, to figure which sales were driven by a particular radio or TV spot.

The best way for most startups to leverage traditional media is to make your firm part of the story rather than a paid advertiser. News reporters are always looking for something to fill the dead air on slow days, and many a clever or just lucky entrepreneur has found their fifteen seconds of fame on television for free by tying themselves to some popular trend, coaxing a free celebrity endorsement, or arranging some outrageous stunt that the TV cameras could not stay away from.

The popular television show *Shark Tank* offers entrepreneurs the perfect chance to pitch their product to a nationwide television audience in the guise of seeking investment for their startup. It's a little-known fact that many times the entrepreneurs back out of the deal they had made on TV with Sharks like Mark Cuban or Kevin "Mr. Wonderful" O'Leary because all they really wanted was 10 minutes of free network TV exposure. The founders of a skateboard wheel manufacturer appropriately named Shark Wheels shook hands on a $250,000 three-Shark deal but found that the exposure was worth enough that they really didn't need to sacrifice any of their equity or bring in that investment.

Managing the News

If you can't afford or maybe just don't want to pay for advertising but want exposure in the traditional media, one of the best strategies is to get your brand mentioned in the news. Pay careful attention the next time you pick up an article or see a TV news story about the latest Disney film, the newest Toyota hybrid car, or a major new product announcement from Apple. You'll see the hand of the firms' expert marketers in the crafting of that news story.

Marketers often call the press "lazy" because they are often willing to print or broadcast material they've been handed by companies with very little or no additional research. To be fair, news editors and producers often find they have gaps that need to be filled with something, anything, on very short notice. Reporters are generally very busy and have to work very quickly to meet their deadlines. If you have an interesting story that you can "spoon feed" to the press, they may pass on your marketing as news. That's a double win. Firstly, because you don't have to pay for it. Secondly, because news consumers pay attention to product information contained within news stories, even though they may skip right over a paid advertisement or zone out during a commercial.

The traditional way to achieve this sort of free advertising is to issue a **press release**. A press release (sometimes PR) is a text document containing an announcement from your firm that you believe will be newsworthy enough to get the attention of a news reporter or editor. These press releases can then be sent directly to news outlets you feel are appropriate for your business, based on their geographic coverage or specialty. For firms with national or international markets, it may be worth paying a news service like PR Newswire or BusinessWire to distribute your press release in a stream of information they provide to thousands of media sources around the world.

press release

A written document used to introduce a new firm, product, or service to the world, and often designed to be used as the basis for a news story.

Typical business press releases are about the release of a new product or the achievement of some notable research, production, or sales goal. For instance, you might be eager to share with the world that your Orlando-based roller-skating rink is opening a second location in nearby Tampa! A good press release campaign will be supported with online resources in the form of a **media kit**. A media kit is an online repository of additional materials that will make a news story more engaging and are likely to include company artwork and photographs featuring the products, the founders, the development team, or whatever might be most interesting to the readers of the targeted outlets. For radio, **sound bites** of team members or customers talking about the product can be very helpful. Television producers will expect you to have **B-roll**, video segments they can air in the background while their personalities discuss your firm and product. You might have exterior and interior photos and video clips of your skating rink, or if it isn't complete, an artist rendering of what it will look like. Whenever possible, put people front and center in these images and videos; they are more likely to engage. Video of smiling kids roller skating is a lot more engaging than a shot of the exterior of a building.

media kit

An organized collection of text, images, and video designed to allow news reporters to produce stories about your firm or its products.

sound bites

A short, catchy, and quotable phrase that news reporters love to include in their stories.

B-roll

Background video footage often provided by product developers and event organizers to media outlets about their product releases.

To be honest, the world is unlikely to be as excited about your news you are. However, it is certainly worth emailing your PR to the *Tampa Bay Times* newspaper and the local TV stations. If you pick a slow news day—never issue a press release when there is a major breaking story dominating the media—some editor desperate to fill space or airtime may cover your opening or print part of your PR as is. Still, a new skating rink is going to have to compete with a local senior citizen turning 100 and would easily be displaced by kittens up for adoption at the local shelter. Can you think of additional ways to improve the odds of your skating rink opening story getting covered?

In the U.S. and many countries, the media exists to sell advertising. The content is simply there to attract eyeballs. Boring business stories don't drive advertising sales; exciting ones do. Your job as a marketing entrepreneur is to be interesting yourself or make your business interesting. What would make the grand opening of a skating rink more interesting? One simple way to get attention and attendees is to offer an economic incentive. If you open for free the first day, offer prizes or free food, there is a better chance you'll get the paper to mention that because their readers will feel the information was of value to them. You could also offer to run an ad in the paper if they cover your event. While such deals are considered distasteful by most journalists, the harsh economic realities of the declining local news business mean they happen all the time. Don't be afraid to ask.

What if you brought in a celebrity to take the first run around the rink? Maybe an Olympic speed skater, television star, 80s pop star, or an astronaut? The news cameras are a lot more likely to show up for that, and the story is likely to draw more attendees as well. Maybe you can find a friendly celebrity through your network of friends. If not, you can probably hire a moderately notable person for an hour or so for a few thousand dollars, if you think that is worth it. You can find celebrities for hire via their own websites or through agencies that specialize in such things. Do a Google search, and you'll be surprised who might love to drop in to be your skating rink attention-getter.

You could also consider arranging some sort of record-breaking stunt. Find an athletic local who'd like to break the world record for roller skate jumping (Jeff Dupont, 20 ft. 3.36 in., 2/12/2012),[9] or invent some new record. Let the media know about the attempt and that you'll be documenting it for inclusion in the famous *Guinness Book of World Records*. Better yet, make them a part of the record setting by doing the world's largest skating lesson (545 people, Belagavi, India, 11/10/2018).[10] A big community event like that is a great news story because everyone involved (and their moms) will buy a paper and tune in to watch the local news.

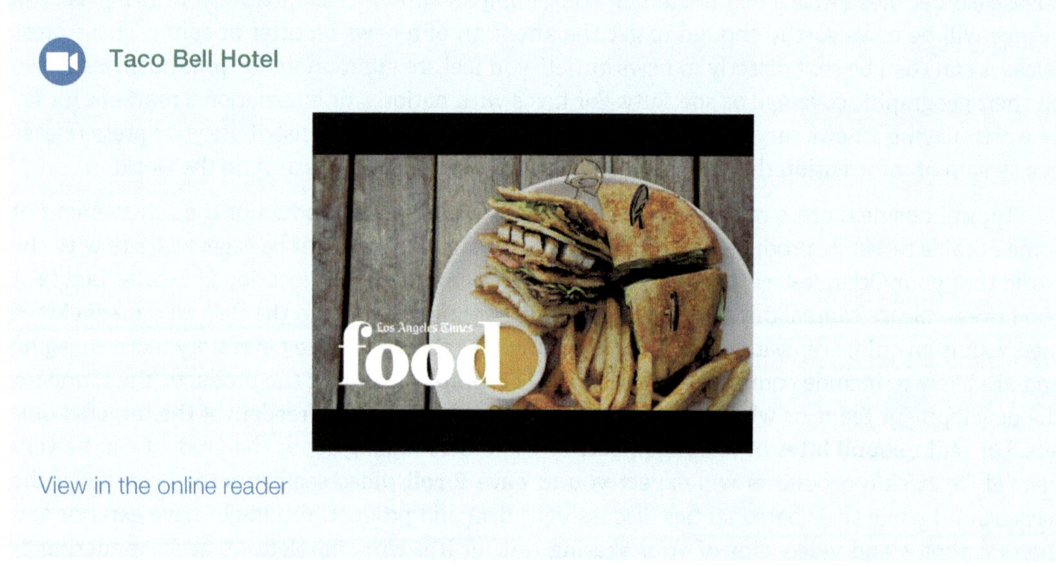

Before you dismiss these sorts of marketing stunts as just silly, consider that even the large firms that can afford traditional advertising indulge in them. In June 2019, Taco Bell, a division of the giant global fast-food chain Yum! Brands, announced the launch of a pop-up hotel chain called "The Bell: A Taco Bell Hotel and Resort" in Palm Springs, California. The hotel would run for just a few days in August of that year, simply for the sake of capturing media attention, and it worked. The story made the front page of CNN.com and was covered by the *LA Times* and many other media outlets.

In fact, the *Guinness Book of World Records* was established in 1955 as a promotional marketing tool by the manager of the Irish beer brewing firm, Guinness. The book is now the most successful copyrighted title of all time and Guinness World Records reports its brand is recognized by 98 percent of the people in the English-speaking world.[11]

Trade Shows

Every market, from plumbing to surfing to satellites, has events where the broader community of vendors, customers, and media gather to share what's new in their industry. These events include conferences, seminars, and trade shows.

Ideal Home Show, London, UK

Source: pcruciatti/Shutterstock.com

At trade shows, sellers present their wares from booths on the floor of large halls. Buyers walk the aisles of these shows looking for specific products and hopeful of the chance they will stumble across a surprising treasure. As an attendee, you may improve the supplier base, but as an exhibitor, it's your job to be that pleasant surprise for your customers. In order for your customers to find you, your booth will have to find a way to stand out from the crowd. Large firms and well-funded startups will have oversized exhibits featuring impressive and expensive signage and displays. How might a smaller startup attract the attention of buyers?

The traditional approach to luring customers into your tradeshow booth is by offering them free items, often referred to as **tchotchkes** or **swag**. These giveaways are typically inexpensive things like t-shirts, pens, or keychains. They come printed with your company or product logo and perhaps a slogan. The main problem with this approach is that everyone else has a giveaway because it's almost expected. Avoid wasting your money on pieces of trash that will just be picked up by individuals not really interested in your product and thrown away when they get back to their hotel room. You might consider offering something like candy to everyone as a general attractant to start a conversation with potential buyers. Then, once you've vetted the prospect's interest and ability to buy, and want them to remember you, you can offer them a higher-quality piece of swag. You can hold these more expensive items back, in a hidden space in your booth so everyone won't be lining up for them.

tchotchkes

Inexpensive gifts featuring your company logo that are used as free gifts to lure visitors to your exhibit at shows and conventions.

swag

Gifts featuring your company logo that are used as free gifts to lure visitors to your exhibit at shows and conventions.

marketing collateral

Material providing details about your firm, service, or product that can be distributed by sales staff at public events.

More important than free gifts are media materials, usually in the form of printed handouts that explain your product or services in detail. These brochures, flyers, or perhaps videos on thumb drives are known *as* **marketing collateral**. *A successful piece of collateral has to survive the hotel room sorting*—where the customer decides what is actually worth reading and what will be trashed as dead weight. A graphically compelling piece is critical for catching the buyer's eye, but as soon as they look at it, they need to feel that your collateral contains valuable information; otherwise, there will be no reason to keep it. Finally, the purpose of collateral is to motivate the buyer to reconnect with your firm after the trade show is over, hopefully by placing an order. At a minimum, it must have appropriate contact information and a website URL. It's also worth considering adding a special discount or bonus offer with a short expiration time frame (maybe one week after the show) that will compel the customer to complete a transaction while it is fresh in their mind.

When you interact with potential customers, make sure you take the opportunity to listen to them as much as you talk at them about the product. What are they looking for? What do they think about your product or brand? Ask, "What was your favorite thing at this show?" and find out how they view your competition. This information can be marketing research gold.

Finally, get the prospect's business card, scan the QR code on their conference badge (most conferences have a system for this), or have them fill out a form with their contact information for your sales team to follow up on. Another idea is to offer them some additional gifts to pull out their mobile device, right then and there, and follow your company on your preferred social media platform.

elevator pitch

The very tight, one minute or less, explanation of your product or service that will encourage the listener to want to learn more.

Guerilla Tactics for Trade Shows and Conventions

Okay, if you're saying to yourself, "Going to a trade show or convention? That sounds very expensive," you'd be right. You could easily spend $20,000 to $50,000 to put in a decent appearance at any significant trade show. That means you need to do your due diligence and be sure the investment is likely to have a return. If you're not already deeply embedded into your target industry, one alternative is to experience the show as an attendee for the first time and poke around. Attending a trade show is likely to cost you just a few hundred dollars.

As a show attendee, you can learn a lot by observing your competitors in action. One approach is to simply go introduce yourself. Try to connect with someone at your own level, the founder, or higher-level executive if they are there. You may be surprised at the collegial reception that you receive from your competitors. When Ryan Olliges of 121C entered the skateboard business, he attended the popular Agenda conference where he found that other skate brand owners were excited about his carbon fiber deck and surprisingly helpful with information about production and marketing techniques. Some even arranged for him to come visit their facilities and learn more. While this sort of reception isn't universal, it isn't uncommon. Competitors in most industries have a basic respect for each other. They love what they do and want to see a healthy industry with quality players in it because that is good for attracting more customers to their market. In some cases, they see themselves in a young entrepreneur and feel obligated to pass on sage advice. If you get that response, make the most of it; it could save you from repeating the painful mistakes of the industry veterans.

Another technique for visiting your competitors is to shift your perspective and assume the role of a potential customer. What do you like or dislike about their product? Do you like the presentation of their booth? Its location in the show? How did the staff handle the interaction? Were they trying to build a brand, or were they just trying to close a sale with you? How did they respond to your questions? Ask them what they think of your firm's product. Have they heard of you? What do they think are their advantages over your offering? They will eagerly tell you, the potential "customer" exactly what they think. Do be offended if they are highly critical. That's their job, and there is probably a grain of truth to whatever criticisms they offer. View it as an opportunity for you to up your game. Understanding how your competitors view the strategic landscape in your market can be incredibly valuable. Collect their swag and marketing collateral for further evaluation.

It might be worth having a senior member of your team take the direct approach and try to connect with your peers in the other organization while a less recognizable employee explores the customer experience with your competitor's sales staff.

Being a trade show attendee can be a good strategy for building your brand and drumming up sales. If you're a supplier to the industry, your potential customers will have booths, and you can go to them on the show floor rather than pay more and hope they come to see you. You can also meet potential customers randomly wandering the floor of the show, particularly around the booths of your direct competitors. Listen to those conversations, and if you feel comfortable, approach the customer later, and tell them about your brand. Trade shows typically prohibit the distribution of sales materials by attendees who are not paying for exhibit space, but that doesn't mean it doesn't happen. Sharing a card or a flyer is likely not going to be an issue. What you cannot do is walk the aisles handing out your collateral *en masse*.

If you're in the sort of industry where there are a very few, but very strategic, customers you need to acquire, then attend a conference or a trade show with a speaker track. Do your research and see who is addressing the conference or sitting on a panel that you want to meet. Typically, at the end of these sessions, the audience will line up to meet the speakers from the panel as they leave the stage. That works, but it's a highly competitive moment, and you have to have your **elevator pitch** ready and finely tuned. Another strategy is to look your target up in advance, learn as much as you can about them, and be able to recognize them. Then look for them in the show, around the coffee cart, in one of the conference meals, or at the bar during an evening reception. This is a much better place to establish a genuine connection and hopefully have more than a few seconds to build your brand, get feedback, and pass on your collateral. Be careful and polite not to interrupt anyone else's conversation. If your future customer thinks you're rude, that won't be a good start. Stand slightly back, but in their line of vision while they finish whatever conversation they are in. Do not appear to be eavesdropping on their conversation but let them understand you'd like to speak next. Also, remember that there is a fine line between doing your research about the customer and their professional interest and being too familiar. Don't come off like a stalker. A compliment to some achievement they've had as in, "Congratulations on winning the industry leadership award last year!" is great, mentioning you saw their kids on Facebook, not so much.

Be sure to research any admission discounts that you may qualify for. Typically, the earlier you register, the better, and discounts are usually available for students. Often there are different levels of attendance, which may include educational sessions and meals. Be strategic about what you need to get your marketing done.

Social Media

In reality, all marketing is social, by definition. Marketing is about reaching out and connecting with people to share ideas. Marketing depends on media to accomplish this. However, in recent years, specific tools have been grouped into the category of social media and have become the hottest territory in marketing. These tools are generally internet-based websites and mobile apps that allow people to connect globally based on their shared interests.

While the origin of social media in the late 1990s and early 2000s is a bit murky, the first platform that garnered significant attention of the general public was MySpace, a personal website-building platform launched in 2003. MySpace became very popular, but it never successfully **monetized**; it just wasn't clear how to make money off providing pages for millions of mostly very young MySpace users to express themselves. That platform was soon eclipsed by Facebook, founded the following year by a team that included Harvard student Mark Zuckerberg.

monetized
Converted to a money.

Zuckerberg is a social media tycoon and multi-billionaire because he and his team developed ways to extract money from the rich user data Facebook collected, specifically by providing a paid advertising platform that could be remarkably well targeted. The very personal information Facebook has about its users is exactly the sort of thing advertisers want to know: Where does this person live? What interests them? What brands do they follow? What kind of work do they do? The answers to those questions can help a marketer craft a very tight audience for their advertisements at a level of **granularity** impossible with regular ads. How do you think this granularity looks in practice?

granularity
The level of detail in a model or plan.

FIGURE 10.4 Audience Definition In Facebook
This screenshot illustrates audience definition in Facebook.

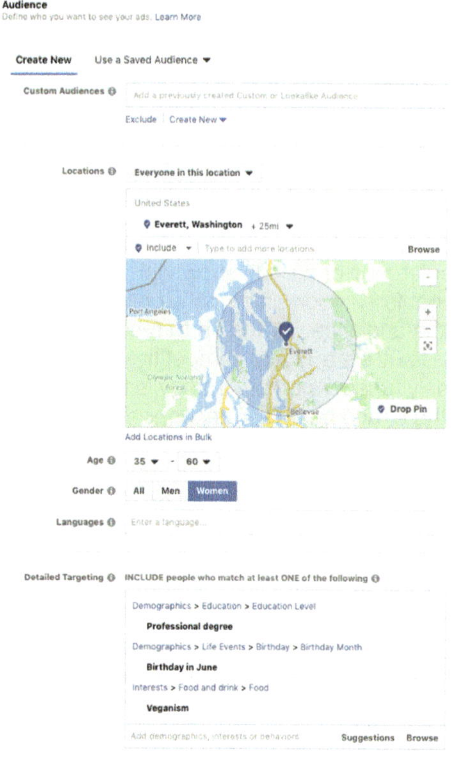

Source: Facebook screenshot captured by author.

Imagine you own a store in Everett, Washington, that makes high-priced organic, vegan birthday cakes with a feminine appeal. You can create a Facebook custom audience that targets professional women of a certain age who are interested in veganism and who live within twenty-five miles of your location. You can do that, and you can even hit them only in the month before their birthdays! The women who see that ad are highly likely to be interested in your product and able to buy a cake from you. Such a targeted social media ad is going to be a lot more effective than placing an ad on KCAL radio and hitting the entire greater Seattle community, even on Gil Chesterton's restaurant show.

Today, there are a number of globally recognized major social media platforms, including Facebook, Twitter, Instagram, LinkedIn, and WeChat. Although they all allow us to connect and share ideas—as well as argue over them—they each have a unique value proposition. LinkedIn, for instance, is clearly focused on making professional connections and facilitating job searches. If your product or service adds value to the employment process or its appeal is tightly linked to a company or industry, LinkedIn is probably a great place for you to market.

It's important to realize that social media is a constantly shifting landscape. Different platforms appeal to different groups and come in and out of favor as things progress. As of this writing, Instagram, a popular photo-sharing platform, is the hot commodity for reaching the most valuable consumer demographic, and that is why Facebook purchased the firm in 2012. In addition to the big names, there are also thousands of niche platforms and social media communities appealing to smaller markets based on very specialized interests, geographic location, or more.

Social media marketing is highly competitive, and the quality of the content is all-important. Social media platforms are determined to keep eyeballs on their screens and will not punish their members with ads that are not engaging. Users can close and even block your ads with a single click. Consequently, although your ad may be paid for, nobody has to watch it if they don't want to; the content of the ad needs to be something the user actually wants to see and chooses to focus on. Instagram ads need to be eye-catching and brilliant; Facebook videos need to be inspiring or amusing; LinkedIn pieces need to actually be informative.

Increasingly, many consumer-focused brands are actually moving to content marketing, where the content is not directly related to the brand, and the brand message rides on that content. These ads may contain stunning photos of some natural scene or video of an artistic performance. The brand plays the role of curator for this customized content and builds credibility with the customer by engaging them with something they love. More importantly, the brand hopes the viewer will share the content with friends, likely to be in the targeted demographic, greatly leveraging their investment in advertising.

Internet Ads

Many blogs and local, national, and international news sites fund themselves by selling advertising. These may include pop-up ads, inline ads, or banners that run along the top or bottom of their sites. Often some of the ads are designed to look like regular news stories on that site, though they may have a small "sponsored" note next to them. It is important to remember that advertising on these sites aligns you with the audiences that frequent them. If you're on a cooking blog, that's your audience. On CNN or Fox, you're going to find somewhat serious news readers; on the *New York Times* or *Wall Street Journal* sites, you'll be targeting a more educated audience. Move further upscale to journals like *The Economist*, *The Atlantic*, or *Foreign Policy* to reach more folks with graduate degrees. Each of these news outlets can offer you demographic details about their audience.

You should also be aware that news is inseparable from policy choices, and each of these outlets also has a general reputation for leaning one way or another on the political spectrum. While policy considerations may not be relevant to your message, the way you frame your product or service and the images you use may resonate differently with the viewers. Think carefully about who will be seeing your ads and how they will react.

Search

Wouldn't it be nice if you knew what your potential customers were looking for and get to them before they even saw your competition? Increasingly, consumers in search of fulfillment will use Google (or in China, Baidu) to locate the products or services they are wanting. Looking for coral-reef-friendly sunscreen? Type that in, and you'll get a screen like the one in Figure 10.5. Note that the first three results have a small green box labeled "ad" next to the URL. Almost any time you search on Google, the first couple of listings are paid advertisements disguised as search results. You'll also see ads with images over on the right side of the screen under the title "sponsored." It's likely the products shown are appropriate results for your search because the advertisers have selected and bid on search terms like "reef-friendly," so most searchers do not feel inconvenienced. However, the result is that products from firms that pay-to-play get to more customers, and the less market savvy or under-financed firms struggle for attention.

Google calls this advertising service simply "Google Ads" (it was formerly known as AdWords), which includes not just search results but also ads on YouTube and other Google-owned internet properties. The cost of these ads is based on a bidding process where more popular search terms are priced higher. You set a monthly budget for expenditures, and Google consumes your money in a dynamic process you can monitor and adjust based on your satisfaction with the resulting metrics. What metrics do you think would matter? What you really want is conversions, people who, upon seeing the ad, click over to your site or app and make a purchase. The second-best result is just getting that click so you know that people have been informed about your product and may return; this is typically what Google charges you for. Google will provide reports that help you manage that. Prices per click through to your site generally fall out between a few cents and a few dollars, depending on the value of the transactions that may result. Ads for expensive items like cars are likely to be bid up by the auto firms because they can afford to pay for a lot of failed clicks for each sale of $30,000 or more. Ads for cell phone cases are popular, but the reality of a $30 product limits how much any firm is willing to pay for priority placement.

FIGURE 10.5
Google search results.

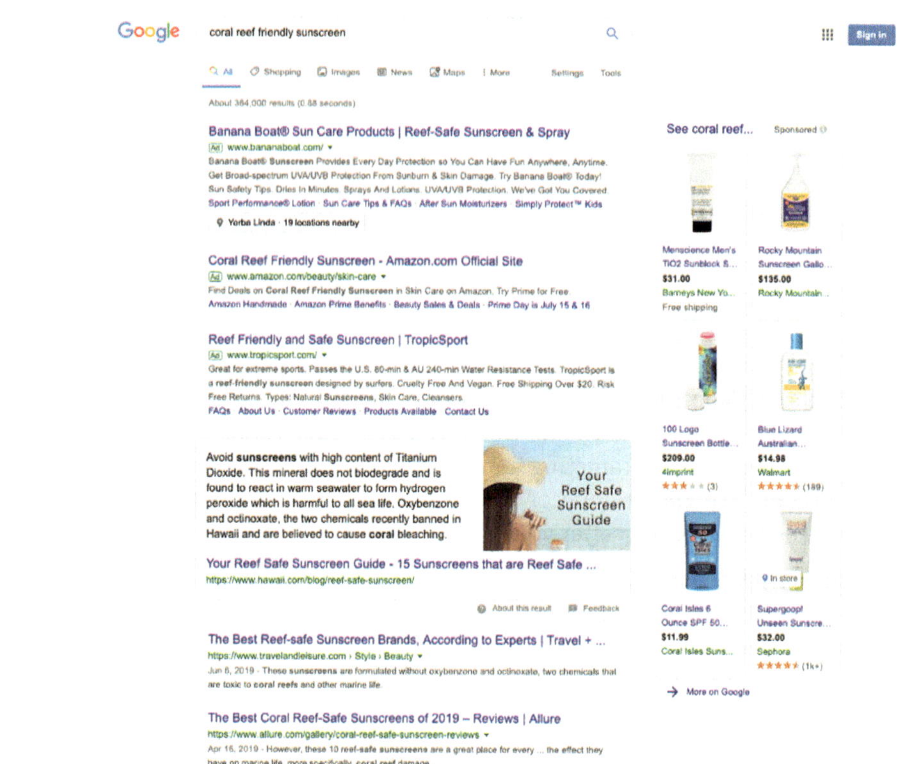

Source: Screen capture by author.

The "trick" with Google Ads is finding a search term that your customers are using but that your competitors are not already bidding on. For instance, maybe "reef safe sunscreen" is a popular term in your market, but just perhaps users are also looking for "green sunscreen" by which they mean "environmental" and not that they wish to look like Kermit the Frog on the beach. The best way to find this out is through a customer discovery process. Ask dozens of potential customers what search terms they would use to find you. Don't suggest any to them (as in a multiple-choice survey). Let them come up with their own as your real consumers would. It's not easy, but stumbling upon the right search term nobody is already paying for is like finding a nugget of gold.

Optimizing Your Search Results

organic search results

Internet search results that are not paid advertising.

The listings below the paid ads and below Google's selected information piece on the topic (from Hawaii.com in this case) are the **organic search results**. Those are the listings that would have been on top if Google's normal algorithm of optimizing search results was allowed to function purely in the interest of the searcher. The ability of Google's algorithm to swiftly produce relevant results from natural language queries is what made the company's engine the go-to choice for the free world (Google has been stymied by governmental censorship requirements in several nations).

There is an entire industry based around optimizing websites in ways that will ensure higher placement in Google searches. This process is called search engine optimization or SEO. In general, you want to make sure of the following:

1. Your website is open to indexing by the **crawlers** that Google (and other engines) use to find websites.
2. The crawler picks the keywords that you wish to be linked to in the search algorithm.
3. Other sites link to your site. The quantity and quality of these **backlinks** are an important metric in the algorithm.

crawler

A software bot that scans websites for keywords to feed search results.

backlink

A link from one website to another. Many links to your site will improve SEO results.

Using experienced commercial website developers will ensure that the first two points are addressed. The third point involves getting placement, with links, in as many news stories, blogs, and other online locations as possible. This can be done by convincing authors and reporters to link to you or by posting a lot of comments on stories. This is why you will sometimes see completely unrelated weblinks that seem to be randomly dumped into the comment section of blogs. Google has developed AI to sense and reject those search spam links.

SEO is a constantly evolving tactical battlefield. Thousands of marketplace competitors are working daily to exploit weaknesses in the Google algorithm, and Google's team is constantly responding with changes to keep the playing field level and free of spammy results. Any specific techniques I offered here would likely have been rendered ineffective by the time you read this. You will find good information on current SEO tactics and techniques on blogs, Reddit posts, and videos, but your best bet, unless you want to take on the nearly full-time job of becoming an expert and staying current on SEO, might be to hire one of the many consultants who specialize in this field. They or you may hire teams to go out and get quality backlinks in place for you as well.

Blogs

As was just noted, links to your site placed in influential blogs can significantly increase your SEO standing, and of course, any sort of positive product exposure may directly drive sales and certainly helps build brand awareness. Bloggers cover a variety of media: there are written (primarily text) blogs, podcasts (audio), and video blogs. They also come with different levels of exposure and credibility. There are amateur bloggers who run their own sites or use popular self-publishing tools to get their messages out, and there are top-tier contributors with regular columns on brand name sites such as *Forbes* or *Consumer Reports*. Getting onto those sites is the gold standard for product exposure and top-quality backlinks.

There are several methods to getting your product mentioned positively in a good blog. The straightforward approach is to identify an appropriate blog your target customers are likely to follow and reach out to the blogger themselves. It's usually possible to find their contact information within the blog or, if not, track them down using a Google search or LinkedIn. When you find them, explain why you feel that covering your product would be valuable to the blogger's readers. Remember, the goal of the blogger is to get more views of his work, and your job is to convince her that your story is relevant and interesting enough to do that. People are busy, and they are inclined to reject most of these sorts of appeals. Don't expect a generic "Dear Blogger, please write about my new business" email to work. Make it short, but personal, and make them feel good about helping you. Explain to them why you personally follow them and what you love about their work:

Dear Samantha, I love your cat blog! It's fun and witty, and I've found so many great cat ideas and products in it. Thank you for doing what you do. I'm sure your readers would get a kick out of our new baked goods for cats. May I please send you some samples?

Remember, their goal is to get more views. If you are going to run an online ad campaign for your product, you could promise to link back to their posting and promote it directly by running social media ads featuring it as in "Read the great review of our Cat Cakes in Samantha's Cat Corner!" Knowing you are going to be working on her side and even spending money to send her readers, Samantha is far more likely to accommodate you. Tell her, "We are budgeting $5,000 over the next six weeks to promote Cat Cakes, and we will link back to your blog post in those ads." Who wouldn't want $5,000 in free advertising for their blog?

pay-to-play

Paying a blogger, reviewer, or journalist to include your firm, product, or service in their stories.

Another tactic that is commonly used is **pay-to-play** writing. This is a gray area in the industry. Bloggers are usually unpaid, and even writers for major press outlets are at best terribly underpaid. This means they are always looking for external means to support their work. Accepting some money, perhaps $500–$1,500, to write a column about a product is not at all unusual. While it is probably against the rules at their publication for a writer to accept outside payments, it doesn't mean they are necessarily misleading the public. Most writers will still only cover material they feel is relevant to their readership. If they bore or mislead their viewers, their days as a blogger are limited. You can offer such payment directly to a writer or hire marketing consultants who work with a stable of bloggers and successful writers who routinely blog or post for money.

influencer

An individual whose credibility in a market, often via blogging, video blogging, or celebrity status, compels consumers to make purchasing decisions and choose brands.

unboxing

The process of opening and reviewing a new product on video.

Video blogs on YouTube and elsewhere work pretty much the same, but the competition is even more intense when it comes to pay-to-play. Many of the most popular **influencers** have been able to demand thousands of dollars as well as free products and other considerations.

Unboxing channels are quite popular for a surprisingly large number of viewers. Vicariously watching another person open up and check out a cool product is a free way of getting the thrill of shopping for something, often an aspirational good you can't afford.

Unboxing Video

Unbox Therapy is a YouTube Channel with 17.3 million subscribers.

View in the online reader

Ryan ToysReview, a YouTube channel run by a toy-loving kid and his parents, has more than 28 million subscribers, and most of his posts receive millions of reviews. Getting your new toy on Ryan's channel could make your product all on its own. Many unboxers do these reviews at no charge. Ryan is living every kid's dream by getting a ton of free toys, and his family collects a share of YouTube ad revenues from his page—banner ads and the video ads they place in front of his videos. Other reviewers are able to charge many thousands of dollars for their services.

 Ryan's World aka Ryan ToysReview

Ryan's family has more than 28 million subscribers; this video has 2 billion views!

View in the online reader

Targeted Marketing

Efficient marketing requires both **precision** and **accuracy**, so let's take a look at what that means using the popular target metaphor. Imagine that you are throwing darts at a traditional round "bull's eye" target. You throw a lot of darts and track each one's location on the target. Figure 10.6 provides four distinctly different outcomes.

precision

A process which, when repeated, consistently produces the same results.

accuracy

A process that, on average, yields result as close to correct as possible.

The lower right outcome, low accuracy with low precision, is terrible; you've missed the bull's eye entirely, and your darts are spread across the top of the target seemingly at random. You clearly aren't consistent and lack precision, and even if you track some average of the X and Y axis values, you will find your "center" is high above and to the left of the bull's eye. That's inaccurate. If this were a social media promotion or ad campaign, you probably didn't get exposure to any of your desired consumers.

The lower left outcome, high accuracy with low precision, is an improvement. While you still can't get them in the same place, your darts are nicely centered around the bull's eye. The average of all your throws would probably be close to the center. That's accurate, and if it were a campaign, you'd be sure to get a few good views.

FIGURE 10.6 Accuracy Versus Precision
Accuracy is getting close to the target. Precision is reliably hitting the same place.

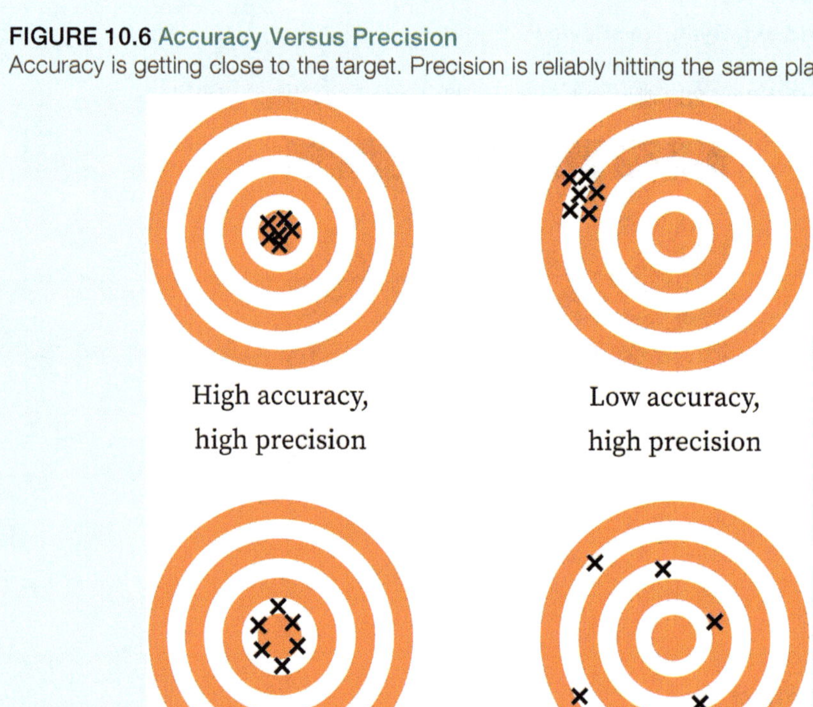

Source: © Shutterstock, Inc.

The upper right outcome, low accuracy with high precision, may be the worst possible scenario. It shows a very precise "grouping" of darts centered completely outside the bull's eyes. There is no chance you hit your target audience with this campaign. Instead, you've very successfully targeted someone else's customers! This is the equivalent of marketing your Baja hotel service business to bicycle riders in Singapore!

The upper left outcome, high accuracy with high precision, is obviously your objective. In this case, the darts are all just where they belong. Achieving accuracy while maintaining precision represents the most efficient utilization of your efforts in darts or marketing. This is a social media campaign where each and every tweet hits the phone of an actual potential buyer. It's a direct mail advertisement for your new café that lands on all the right doorsteps of your town.

Traditional Print Ads

Sometimes just running a plain old advertisement in a magazine or a newspaper still makes sense. As with digital media, the choice of traditional media outlets depends on the readership fitting your product well. Advertising a fashion product in *Popular Mechanics* or technical gizmo in *Vogue* are expensively poor choices.

For ads in newspapers and local journals, the benefit is often a very select geography. Putting a discount coupon into the *Titusville Herald*, a local newspaper, is a great way to drive traffic to your coffee and popsicle store on Merritt Island, Florida. On the other hand, if your business runs wildlife tours around Florida, you want tourists, and they don't often read the local paper. You need to place your coupon in a specialty tourist-focused paper. That might be something like the *Space Coast Visitor's Guide*, a publication specifically geared to the millions of visitors who tour NASA's

Kennedy Space Center each year. Can you think of why a discount coupon in both these cases is recommended?

The space center attracts millions of visitors to Florida's "Space Coast."

Source: NASA, credit Dan Casper https://www.nasa.gov/press-release/kennedy-space-center-visitor-complex-opens-new-exhibit-saturday

Unlike social media, print media does not automatically provide you with data on views and conversions. Using a coupon or **promo code** that customers present when they appear at your store or website will allow you to count the conversions from the ads. These discounts, even if they are built into your pricing model, also make customers feel they are getting something special. In many industries, such as the tour business, they are practically required to get customers in the door.

promo code

A code used to provide consumers with a discount at the point of checkout in an online store.

If you decide to market a national or international product into local outlets across a wide geography, be sure your product and message are appropriate to the customer and culture you are reaching. An advertisement using shocking graphic images might work well in the anything-goes culture of Northern California or New York but confuses or even offends potential customers in more conservative Southern states.

Never run your domestic **ad copy** internationally until you have consulted with local experts. It's extremely easy for a well-meaning message to literally get lost in translation, resulting in no response or even a negative brand image. There is a famous marketing tale about the Swedish appliance maker, Electrolux. In coming to the English-speaking world, the company ran ads for its vacuum cleaners featuring the phrase "Nothing sucks like an Electrolux." In the English-speaking world, "sucks" is a word frequently associated with poor quality. While experts agree that this double-entendre was an intentional attempt to get attention, the lesson on language is still clear.

ad copy

The main text used in an advertisement that describes the message being conveyed.

Electrolux's Double-Entendre

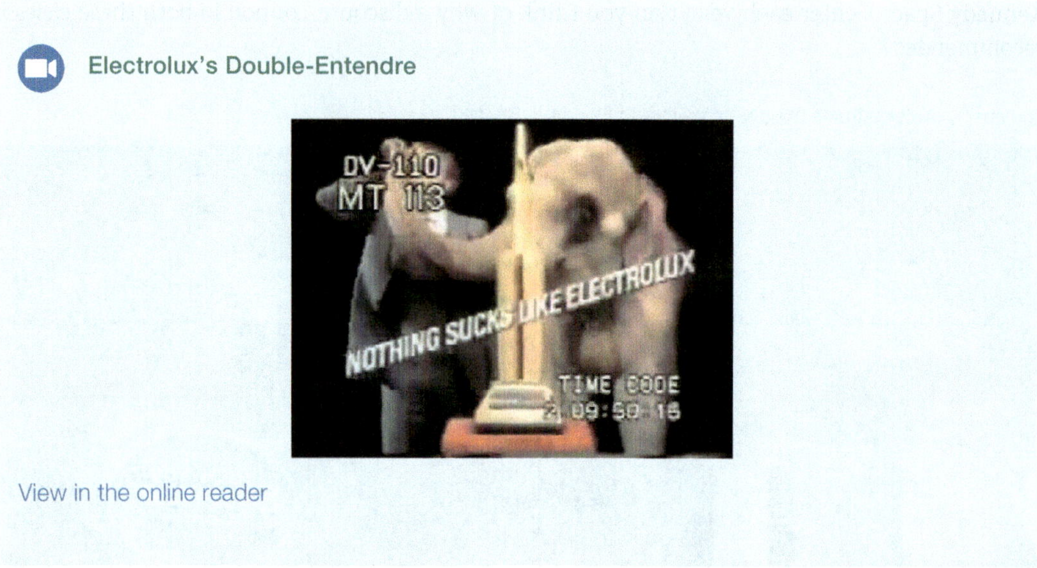

View in the online reader

Marketing Integrity

Soft drinks were originally promoted as health products.

Scientists tell us that all space is an ocean of ether in which our solar system swims, and that all life, animal and vegetable, is derived from the sun's energy, transmitted to our planet by this ether. Plant life organizes this energy for us in natures laboratory. As animals we then partake of natures bountiful store and the sun's energy. Certain fruits, nuts and sugar cane represent this energy and vitality best. We have found this great natural law, and we combine these substances with distilled water. The name we give our combination is Dr. Pepper.

Dr. Pepper is liquid sunlight. As the sun rules and governs the day, so should you govern your appetite. Eat and drink to build up the cells that are broken down by fatigue, mental or physical. Drink a beverage that promotes cell building, not one that simply deadens the sensory nerves. Drink Dr. Pepper. Solar energy-liquid sunshine. Vim, vigor, vitality—that is what Dr. Pepper means. Try it. On sale at all fountains and in bottles. It's made in Texas. It's profits are spent in Texas to promote Texas industries.

DR. PEPPER CO. Waco, Texas

Source: By Dr. Pepper Co. - Abbeville progress. (Abbeville, Vermilion Parish, La.), 21 June 1913. Chronicling America: Historic American Newspapers. Lib. of Congress. <http://chroniclingamerica.loc.gov/lccn/sn88064057/1913-06-21/ed-1/seq-7/>, Public Domain, https://commons.wikimedia.org/w/index.php?curid=32026659

In many cases, marketing and advertising have been used as a tool to mislead buyers by obscuring a product's deficiencies or even outright lying about its benefits. There is a long history of **snake oil** products in the health sector, featuring remedies based on natural solutions, mysterious international sources, and dubious "alternative science." These products prey on desperate buyers who are particularly willing to believe in miraculous solutions to their chronic conditions.

snake oil

A product, often in the healthcare area, with marketing that claims benefits that are not scientifically supported.

At the turn of the last century, Coca-Cola, Pepsi Cola, and many other sodas were marketed as medicinal products designed to invigorate your metabolism. Dr. Pepper was developed by a pharmacist and sold under the slogan "Good for Life" with the prescription that you should drink it three times a day to avoid midday letdowns. The sugar and caffeine in the mix does provide a temporary boost, and the brew's flavor has kept it successful for more than a hundred years.

Today hundreds of drinks still claim to boost energy and improve fitness and mental acuity. While a few come with a bit of real science behind them, it's likely most are created and marketed by entrepreneurs lacking any real medical credibility. Sugar and stimulants will continue to power products like Monster and Rock Star energy drinks in the market.

Regardless of the sector you're in, it's important to be truthful with your customers. In today's world, there will always be someone eager to pounce on anything that smells disingenuous. Don't become their target. The value of your brand is often your most important asset, and the bedrock of brand reputation is honesty.

FIGURE 10.7 Dilbert Cartoon

The Pointy-Haired Boss equates marketing with fraud.

Source: DILBERT © 2007 Scott Adams, Inc. Used By permission of ANDREWS MCMEEL SYNDICATION. All rights reserved.

Our Ever-Changing Media

Communications Technology: Over the last several decades, continual innovation in electronic hardware and associated software systems has resulted in platform and information proliferation.

Information Overload: The technology trend has also accelerated the rate at which consumers receive information and multiplied the means by which they gather it. Many are weary and wary of advertising and other marketing tools. A dynamic marketing effort must be genuine to gather real traction.

Platform Culture: Every few years, younger consumers embrace a new favored online outlet and leave the last one to their parents. Over the first two decades of this century, we've seen the desirable youth market move from email to the web to Facebook to Twitter and then Instagram, while flirting with SnapChat, WeChat, and others. A dynamic marketing effort must be platform independent and ready to quickly test and evaluate the viability of the next new trend.

Regulations: The online regulatory environment has become increasingly complex as governments attempt to ensure privacy and protect consumer from misinformation. Failure to comply could result in massive fines. A dynamic marketing effort must include regular research into the regulatory environment.

Key Takeaways

- Use your brand to drive sales, not advertising, where possible.
- Remember that it is conversions that count in the end.
- Use the news media for free advertising.
- Be creative in maximizing your potential at trade shows.
- Leverage social media both organically and as an ad platform.
- Invest in SEO and effective search ads.
- Learn to manage influencers when they are effective and affordable.
- Always be ethical.

10.3 Case Study: Building One Hot Brand

Sriracha on store shelves.

Source: calimedia/Shutterstock.com

Wherever you may be in the world, there is a good chance you're familiar with the famous brand David Tran created. Tran is the immigrant founder behind the global phenomena of Huy Fong Food's Sriracha Sauce, with its distinctive bottle and green cap. The sauce has developed such a cult following that the Huy Fong's rooster logo is seen around the world, emblazoned on everything from ball caps to shoes. Tran's entrepreneurial journey started as one of the thousands of Vietnamese "boat people" refugees who fled the communist takeover of their home country following the withdrawal of American forces in the 1970s. Determined to settle in the United States, Tran made his way to Hong Kong on a small vessel named *Huy Fong*. He eventually settled in Boston but quickly decided to head west and arrived in California in 1980.

Settling into the growing Vietnamese community in Southern California, Tran quickly realized that the sauces offered to accompany traditional Vietnamese Pho soup in America were a pale comparison to those he had enjoyed in Asia. He attributed this discrepancy to the use of underripe green peppers or previously dried chilis, rather than fresh peppers in the preparation of American-style sauces. Tran found himself hunting for ripe peppers and stirring up batches of sauce in a bucket at home. When asked if there are any secrets as to how Huy Fong's Sriracha sauce is made, David simply said, "No, anyone can make it at home. You just need to get the fresh chili, chop it, add a few ingredients, and that is it. There is no secret or anything; the only difference is the freshness of the chili pepper."

Tran wasn't looking to get rich or establish an iconic brand. He pursued entrepreneurship purely for the sake of offering a better product at a fair price. By enjoying the benefits of running a privately held firm, Tran has been able to focus on that goal rather than on profit-seeking. Early on, he intuitively recognized his personal sense of mission as the source of Huy Fong's brand power in its battle against larger food product competitors like Kraft-Heinz and Hunt-Wesson Corporation. When traditional American hot sauce heavyweight Tabasco entered the sriracha sauce market, Tran was able to dismiss the attempt as a poor imitation of his famous product and powerful brand.

From the very beginning, Huy Fong was blessed with a spontaneous word-of-mouth campaign driven by its product quality and supported by its cult-like devotees. Tran never invested in traditional advertising or marketing beyond maintaining a modest website. He has often stated that he saw no purpose in spending profits on advertising because he has always been able to sell all the sauce his firm could produce from the available chili crop. That does not mean that this successful entrepreneur has not also been an intuitive marketer.

Tran made Huy Fong's celebrated Sriracha bottle image and rooster logo available as a no-cost license to just about any product manufacturer that applied for it. The appearance of the Huy Fong rooster or sauce bottle on skateboards, dog toys, and pajamas constantly reinforces the positive brand associations for Sriracha's dedicated fan base while signaling the exceptional nature of this sauce to those who may not have sampled it. This broad exposure lifted a relatively obscure brand image into the pantheon of iconic corporate logos, alongside the likes of Nike, Coca-Cola, and Apple. Tran shared that his business school-educated son has advocated for Huy Fong capturing the economic value of the logo, but the elder entrepreneur remains very happy with the way things are.

It is the humble jalapeño chili pepper that drives Huy Fong's massive operations. During the peak of the California growing season (August–October), its 650,000 sq. ft. factory in Irwindale, California, receives thirty to forty truckloads of chilis per day. These ripe, red jalapeño peppers must be quickly washed, ground, and processed to create the chili paste. This paste is then stored in 55-gallon barrels that are stacked from floor-to-ceiling in the massive warehouse to await its transformation into the signature Sriracha sauce. While the chili season only lasts for three months, enough chili paste is stored in the factory, roughly 200,000 barrels worth, to accommodate Huy Fong's year-round production. Almost every aspect of the Huy Fong manufacturing process is done in-house, right down to the molding of the plastic Sriracha bottles and the big, blue chili paste storage barrels. The chilis are the firm's only major external dependency. It takes up to three additional months for green chilis to turn red. Leaving them in the field to ripen incurs an opportunity cost for the farmer who could be using his land for another crop. Huy Fong, in order to be able to make the best product possible, needs farmers willing to produce the higher-cost red chilis. That dependency turned out to be the Achille's heel in the famous sauce maker's strategy.

For twenty-eight years, David Tran maintained a very friendly, somewhat informal business relationship with Underwood Ranches in Ventura, California, the exclusive grower of red chilis for Huy Fong. During some parts of their business relationship, Huy Fong guaranteed a payment of $20 million to $30 million up front for the entire chili crop regardless of outcomes. Furthermore, the Sriracha maker provided $87 million in capital in order to buy a harvesting machine capable of picking the 100 million pounds of chilis that Huy Fong's Sriracha operation demanded. For nearly three decades this agreement absolved David's growers of almost all risk and provided Huy Fong with the red chilis for its sauce.

Ultimately there was a falling out between Underwood and Huy Fong, resulting in the parties parting ways and Underwood starting its own competing chili sauce. After Underwood made it clear that it would not grow peppers for Huy Fong, other pepper farmers, well aware of the strength of Huy Fong's brands, eagerly inked deals that kept their chilis in the ground until ripe. Retailers remained loyal to the famous brand their customers loved. Huy Fong Foods greatly reduced its supply risk and supplier power. Tran believes he is now getting better-quality peppers at a better price. Sales and profits are up, and Huy Fong's Sriracha brand is stronger than ever.

At age 74, David Tran still comes to work each day, although he no longer manages the day-to-day operations of the business. Huy Fong's founder delegates most of the operational work to his sister-in-law while he simply enjoys his business for its own sake. Tran says, "I come to work every day because we have the tours, and I like to say hello to everyone on the tour, and that makes me happy."[12] All he ever wanted to do was "make a product for the rich man, with a price for the poor man," and that is an achievement the saucy entrepreneur truly relishes.

Endnotes

1. Zhang, G., & Simon, H. A. (1985). STM capacity for Chinese words and idioms: Chunking and acoustical loop hypotheses. *Memory & Cognition, 13*(3), 193–201.
2. Simon, H. A. (2013). *Administrative Behavior*. Simon and Schuster.
3. Frank, K. S. (n.d.) *Herbert A. Simon: A family memory* http://www.cs.cmu.edu/simon/kfrank.html.
4. Beal, G. M., & Bohlen, J. M. (1956). *The diffusion process* (No. 761-2016-51585, p. 111). https://ageconsearch.umn.edu/record/17351/files/ar560111.pdf.
5. Rogers, E. M. (2010). *Diffusion of innovations*. Simon and Schuster.
6. Moore, G. A., & McKenna, R. (1999). *Crossing the chasm*. Harper Business Essentials.
7. Perkins, C. (2018). "Tesla's silly falcon wing doors have one great function." *Road and Track*. https://www.roadandtrack.com/new-cars/a21722920/tesla-model-x-falcon-wing-doors/
8. Ferdman, R. (2013). The highly unusual company behind Sriracha, the world's coolest hot sauce. *Quartz*. https://qz.com/132738/ the-highly-unusual-company-behind-siracha-the-worlds-coolest-hotsauce/.
9. *Guinness World Records*. (2012). https://www.guinnessworldrecords.com/world-records/97711-longest-forward-jump-on-roller-skates
10. Guinness World Records. (2018). https://www.guinnessworldrecords.com/world-records/501223-largest-roller-skating-lesson
11. Guinness World Records. (2015). https://web.archive.org/web/20150821044202/http://corporate.guinnessworldrecords.com/index.aspx
12. Tours were unfortunately discontinued during the COVID-19 pandemic.

CHAPTER 11
Selling

> You miss 100 percent of the shots you don't take.
>
> —*Wayne Gretzky*[1]

Home purchases depend heavily on the work of sales professionals.

Source: © Shutterstock, Inc.

While you won't have any problems stopping into a corner shop and picking up a candy bar, what if you wanted to buy the building that store was located in? Where would you start? You'd most likely go find a commercial real estate sales agent, and the seller of the building would do the same. Why?

11.1 The Context of Selling

Learning Objectives

1. Understand why people choose to buy things.
2. Understand that the sales process is a social function.
3. Recognize when active personal sales functions add value and when they do not.
4. Understand the role of the salesperson in the modern age.
5. Understand how potential customers move through the sales process or cycle as represented by the sales funnel model.
6. Recognize that marketing and advertising feed the sales process.
7. Understand the value of tightly integrating marketing and sales efforts.

The Process of Selling

charlatan

A fraudulent salesperson.

huckster

A fraudulent salesperson.

customer relationship management (CRM)

The formalized process of interacting with customers.

Professional selling is a critical skill that must be mastered or managed by nearly every successful entrepreneur. Sales is often seen as a domain of **charlatans** and **hucksters**. Outside of the mechanics of **customer relationship management (CRM)**, the sales process is often ignored in university courses. The science of sales attracts significantly less academic research than do the popular areas of marketing and strategy. Modern entrepreneurship textbooks are heavily oriented toward marketing and customer discovery, but few of them directly address the process of selling. This chapter introduces the basics of the sales process and profession.

People Buy Stuff from People

If you're in the market for a new set of noise-canceling headphones, it's likely you might be influenced by advertisements, read online reviews, talk to your friends, and then click "buy" on Amazon or some other e-commerce site and wait for your new headgear to arrive. You'll never interact directly with another human being during the entire process. Today, we view that human-to-software interfacing as entirely natural. If your grandfather had wanted headphones in the 1970s, would his purchasing process have been the same? Would he make the same choice as you today?

A sales meeting in progress.

Source: © Shutterstock, Inc.

Imagine you're a technophile environmentalist and you've been thinking about the benefits of equipping your home with rooftop solar panels. After you do a few Google searches on the topic, the modern engine of marketing kicks in. Algorithms detect your search patterns, and your social media stream is suddenly filled with advertisements for such systems. They suggest you should "act now" before generous governmental subsidies expire. What is your next step? You're eager to make a solar purchase, but these systems require installation and offer a variety of performance specifications, monitoring systems, and payment options. Some of the choices will depend on factors like the direction your home faces, the angle of your roof, and even the shadows of nearby trees. You can't just click on the "buy" button and wait for the box to arrive and set this system up.

People often seek expert advice before making a purchase in a domain where they lack expertise. Some products are complicated enough, expensive enough, or regulated in such a way that no matter how sophisticated a consumer you are, you will have no choice but to complete your order with a person. If you chose to walk into a big box store, such as Best Buy, to talk about headphones or you submit your contact information to the solar panel installer, a **sales process** is initiated.

During the sales process, a **salesperson** will assist you with your selection, and she will likely employ a variety of time-proven techniques designed to guide you as rapidly as possible to a commitment that aligns with her firms' interests and hopefully with yours. However, she may not be labeled as a "salesperson." Your headphone salesperson is likely to be a "customer service associate," and the solar panel salesperson may have a title like "system designer." In the B2B (business-to-business) world, the process of sales is typically called **business development**, and more informally "biz dev." Salespeople are often called "account executives" or "business development executives" Why is that?

sales process

The steps a customer proceeds through during the process of buying a product or service including (but not limited to) awareness, qualification, and closing.

salesperson

The individual responsible for servicing the customer during the sales process. Sometimes referred to as an "account executive."

business development

The more sophisticated name for sales, particularly in the corporate world.

Sales and Business Development

What comes to mind when you hear the word "salesman?" Have all your experiences with salespeople been positive? Most people have experienced uncomfortable pressure from aggressive salespeople or even experienced **buyer's remorse** after being sold a product that was inappropriate, too expensive, or inadequate. Why do we have sales?

buyer's remorse

The psychological state of regretting the expense or choice of a major purchase.

transactional

A relationship based on an exchange of value.

All sales take place in a social context. Long before the dawn of history, early humans likely engaged in **transactional** economic relationships. They negotiated exchanges of material or labor for the things they required: water, food, fire, furs, shelter, and tools. Since these items were mostly necessities, the only discussion would have been fairly simple negotiations of price relative to other barter items. As the human economy progressed, our ancestors began to acquire more luxuries, things that were not required for survival but were desirable. Imagine that a primitive hunter comes to a primitive encampment with a cache of beautiful but very small animal pelts suitable for adornment. A few minutes later, a gatherer who has discovered a batch of delectable berries arrives. Why would the exchange of these items be more complex?

sales art

The techniques and skills utilized to sell a product.

salesmanship

The techniques and skills utilized to sell a product.

When someone wishes to sell you an item that you do not absolutely need or when you have choices on what to purchase, a sales process begins. The vendor must convince you, the customer, that your limited currency should be traded for his offerings. The salesperson's arguments may be rational ones, arguing for the utility of the product to you or its technical superiority as compared to other products. The arguments may also be psychologically based, manipulating your sense of identity, perceived social standing, and self-worth to compel you to purchase. Over the centuries, product vendors have developed a variety of useful psychological techniques designed to separate customers from their money. These techniques constitute the tactical toolbox of the **sales art** and form a set of skills often referred to as **salesmanship**.

Marketing and Ads Fill the Sales Funnel

leads

Potential customers generated and identified by marketing efforts.

sales pipeline

A concept representing the flow of customers coming into and progressing through the sales process.

For a person or business to buy your product, you will obviously need to establish contact with them. It is also much easier to make a sale if the customer is familiar with and respects your brand. It's also great if they know about the specific product offering and the value it might add to their work or personal life. The branding, marketing, and advertising tools outlined in Chapter 9 and Chapter 10 set the stage for sales. Popular brands, effective marketing campaigns, and good advertisements funnel potential customers, also known as sales prospects or **leads**, into a **sales pipeline**.

FIGURE 11.1 The Sales Funnel

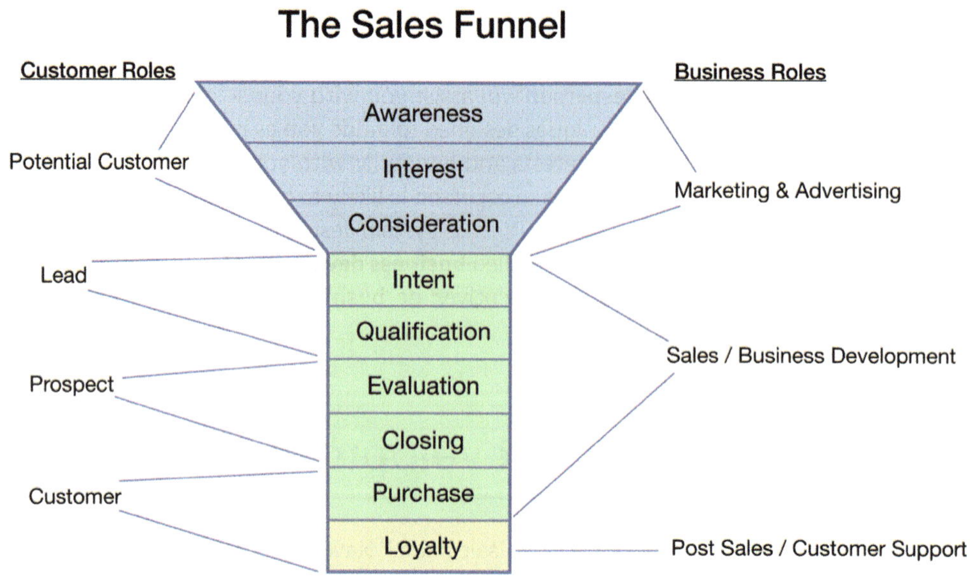

Source: Greg Autry

You can visualize this pipeline as a representation of potential customers passing through a series of stages from identification to handing over their money. Since more customers start the process than are finally closed (you can't win them all), the pipeline narrows as it goes along, which supports a model often visualized as the sales funnel.

Awareness, interest, and consideration are usually functions performed by the marketing and advertising teams. Awareness is the process of bringing your product to the attention of potential customers via advertising, internet searches, product placement, and other tools covered in Chapter 9 and Chapter 10. Interest is the effort to get the customer actively engaged by coming to your website, calling, visiting your trade show booth, etc. Consideration is the phase where you are in contact with the customer, and they begin to think seriously about purchasing a product, solution, or service in your category, but not necessarily yours. Picture a potential customer who has become aware of electric cars from news stories, began to research these vehicles and visited several websites. During the consideration stage, they used online tools and requested more information from Volkswagen, Rivian, and Tesla. They are now a sales lead, a potential customer you have identified, and they have entered the sales process.

Integrated Marketing

Before leaving the world of branding, marketing, and advertising, let us revisit the graphic from Chapter 3 on strategy. Recall that our organization's strategy drives tactics that are executed to produce results. Results are quantified in metrics that are used by management to develop strategies, adapt tactics, and improve execution. Where do those metrics come from?

FIGURE 11.2 Strategy, Tactics, Execution

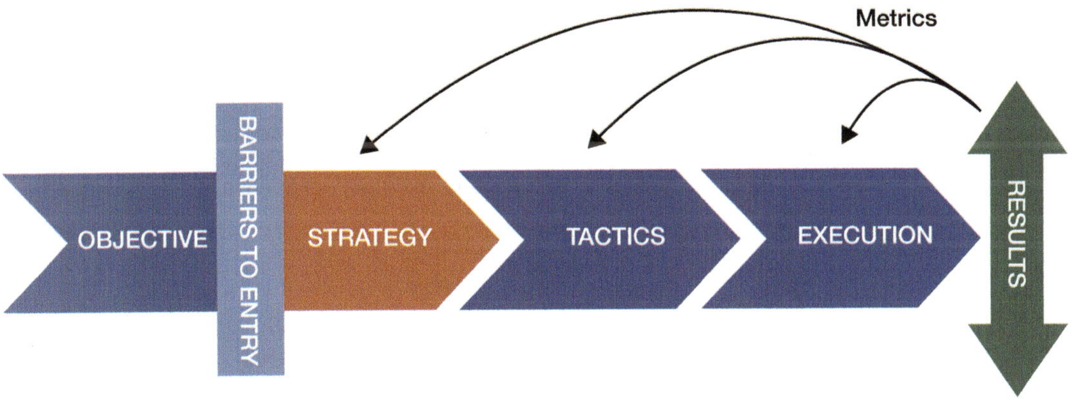

Source: Greg Autry

The sales process is the most important tool in evaluating those business functions. The quantity and quality of sales determine the success of the organization in moving forward to its objectives. The sales process, successful or not, is a rich source of information about evolving customer needs, brand perceptions, marketing strategy effectiveness, and advertising appeal. Salespeople are the first to recognize a marketing problem and are in the best position to identify the causes. Establish a reporting system that generates actionable data from the sales process. Integrate your sales team into your marketing decision-making via this procedure and by including their feedback in strategic meetings on everything from product design to advertising. **Integrated marketing** is a holistic system where feedback obtained during any customer interaction is channeled to the marketing and advertising professionals, allowing them to optimize their efforts to produce a greater quantity and quality of leads to fill the sales pipeline.

integrated marketing

A holistic system where feedback obtained during any customer interaction is channeled to the marketing and advertising professionals allowing them to optimize their efforts to produce a greater quantity and quality of leads to fill the sales pipeline.

An observant salesperson must learn your customers' perceptions of your offerings, brand, marketing, and advertising. She will also pick up valuable information about what your competitors are doing well and what mistakes they have made. These can serve as powerful analogs and antilogs for your marketing efforts. Sales should support an ongoing process of customer discovery and market validation, as discussed in Chapter 4 and Chapter 5.

Key Takeaways

- While sales are increasingly made online, personal sales is "still a thing" in many product and service categories and will remain so.
- The process of buying a product is a multistep cycle with different roles assumed by the customer and the seller.
- Your marketing and advertising systems drive potential customers into the sales funnel.
- In the B2B world, sales is often referred to as business development.

11.2 The Sales Process

Learning Objectives

1. Understand how the roles of the potential customer change as they move through the funnel.
2. Appreciate the important cost of customer acquisition.
3. Understand the varying length of the sales cycle.
4. Recognize the importance of qualifying leads.
5. Understand the qualifying process.
6. Appreciate the need to research your customer.
7. Master basic sales techniques.
8. Learn to cope with rejection and how to build and maintain confidence during the sales process.

> My popularity, my happiness and sense of worth depend to no small extent upon my skill in dealing with people.
>
> —*Dale Carnegie*[2]

Working the Funnel

Recall the sales funnel from Section 1? The sales process begins with **intent** and carries through to **purchase**. The purpose of sales in this integrated process is to transform customer interest into revenues by **closing** the sale.

intent

The stage in the sales funnel where the customer has decided to buy a product in your category.

purchase

The actual transaction where a good or service is financially committed to. This may be signing a contract, providing a purchase order, etc.

closing

The process of securing a final agreement on a sale.

Sales Begin with Intent

At the intent stage in the funnel, the lead has demonstrated an intent to purchase a product in your category. If your sales process is human-driven, it is at this point that a salesperson should engage the customer. In many automated sales systems, this process mimics a human response. In either case, this phase calls for a cautious and careful first contact. In sales, as in fishing, it is extremely easy to spook your prey on their first approach. As noted previously, many customers have had negative experiences or heard horrific stories of aggressive tactics used by some salespeople. At the intent stage, your only goal should be to build trust. Introduce yourself with as few words as possible, let them know you are there to assist them with questions about your firm's product or service and even the product or service category more broadly. Then shut up and listen! Wait patiently for the customer to respond and take the bait.

Qualifying

Once the customer intends to buy a product, they are ready to begin evaluating your offering, and at this point, you could begin to spend a lot of time giving them the information they need to fall in love with it. However, evaluation is a two-way street, and before you invest your time in the lead, you want to be sure your time will be well spent. That process is called **qualifying**, and it should be done before you move on to supporting the customer's evaluation process.

qualifying

The process of determining if a potential customer is suitable, able, and willing to purchase a product or service.

To maximize their time, car salespeople need to qualify buyers.

Source: © Shutterstock, Inc.

During the qualifying process you determine if this potential customer is suitable for your product and your firm. You'll want to identify several lead attributes during the qualifying process, including how well the offering fits the customer, the lead's ability to pay, whether you are working with the decision-maker, and how likely the sale is to close in any case. Let's review these qualifications individually:

Product/customer fit: Is your product really a good fit for the lead? If, during the sales process, they are likely to discover that what you have to offer won't really solve their problem or that another solution is better for them, they aren't a qualified lead.

Ability to pay: If the customer doesn't have the cash on hand, credit available, or won't qualify for financing required to purchase your product, they aren't a qualified lead.

Decision-maker: Often, you may be talking to an individual with interest from an organization that might be able to buy your product, but the lead himself isn't actually authorized to do so. Identifying and contacting the decision-maker is critical to a successful sale. If a lead can't get you a purchase order or make a payment, they aren't a qualified lead.

Likelihood to close: Some folks just have trouble coming to decisions. If a lead isn't likely to reach a decision within a time frame that justifies your investment in the process, they aren't a qualified lead.

To summarize, a qualified lead actually needs or wants your product, has money to buy it, and is ready and authorized to make a purchasing decision. A lead that meets all these criteria advances to the status of a sales prospect. They are worthy of investing significant sales effort into the process as you move to close the sale. If they fail to have all these criteria, they not worth pursuing.

Some marketing systems provide salespeople with prequalified leads. Basic qualification might be handled by a lower-paid, front-end customer service staff. Once they have done their job, they hand over the prospect to the sales experts. Often these first-level staff are interns or apprentice sales staff who will observe and learn the ropes before moving up into a full sales position.

Qualification may also be done by online systems backed with an algorithm or increasingly an AI system that searches many databases, including the lead's social media. Can you think of why it would be valuable to analyze a consumer's Facebook page or Instagram feed?

Seeing the products that a lead already owns can tell you a lot about their preferences, ability to pay, and the likelihood of purchasing similar items. If you're selling new Porsches, you probably don't want to spend time with leads who have ten-year-old Toyotas or Chevys in all their social media pictures. They might like to test drive your 911, but they probably aren't going to be buying one.

Usually, one can find several predictive *determinants of income* in an individual's social media profile. These include the city or area of town in which they live, their educational level, and their profession. While it is not a guarantee that a lawyer with a PhD from Harvard living in Beverly Hills has more purchasing power to buy your Porsches, it's a fair guess. It's important to note that many social profiles are exaggerated or even entirely fabricated. Watch out for the fakers. You should also be aware that many real millionaires are pretty low-key. As Thomas J. Stanley and William D. Danko noted in *The Millionaire Next Door*, spending money isn't the same as having it, and many entrepreneurs are in trades that don't attract a great deal of attention. The owner of a plumbing business or electrical contracting firm is entirely qualified to buy a luxury sports coupe.

Often it is the responsibility of the salesperson to handle the qualifying. They may be given a list of names, email addresses, and phone numbers collected at a trade show or from online advertising. They can start doing some of the research using social media or asking the applicants qualifying questions in the context of socializing, such as "I live in the valley; where do you folks live?" or "How about Alabama in the game last night? Where did you go to college?" or "What do you do when you're not shopping for cars?"

In general, salespeople prefer to receive qualified leads or at least high-quality leads that come from a pool of very likely prospects. Working through a list of the leads that signed up in exchange for receiving a free gift, rather than because they were genuinely interested or able to buy something, can be immensely frustrating for the sales staff.

One of the most important traits of the successful salesperson is the ability to ignore distracting, unqualified leads, and focus all their time on productive opportunities. Directing unqualified leads to a product they can afford or one that actually fits their needs will save you both time and actually give you a reputation as an **honest broker**.

honest broker

A person who is willing to tell a potential customer the truth about the best product for them, even at the expense of losing their own sale opportunity.

Evaluating

Evaluation is among the most critical stages in the sales funnel. It is during this stage that the prospect will move from simply wishing to purchase a product to determining which brand and specific solution will best meet their needs. This is a make-it or break-it moment.

evaluation

The customer's process of determining the value of a product. Evaluation should be carefully guided by the sales team.

Your prospect has already determined they need or desire the sort of product you offer, and in reaching that conclusion, they have probably already come to certain conclusions about the relative merits of your product, service, and organization. If they are working with your organization and entered your sales funnel, it is likely that these preconceptions are generally positive, and your job during evaluation is primarily to reinforce positive perceptions. However, don't assume there aren't some lurking reservations. They may have seen a competitor's advertisement or a product review that suggests your offering is lacking in some way. If those things are out there, you need to be familiar with them and have credible responses that don't appear defensive.

A good way to assist your prospect at the start of the evaluation process is to ask an open-ended question like, "What do you know about our services?" or "What brought you to look at our products?" If the response is super positive, don't be afraid to cheerfully move to a close with, "Great, is there anything else you need to know, or are you ready to make a purchase?" You can save a lot of time with this no-pressure tactic.

If the initial response or the response to an early closing attempt includes concerns, address the technical aspects directly and honestly. If you can, back up your claim with added credibility from some other source like a product review or another member of your team. You might say, "I'm sure you'll be able to use our Model Z for that application but let me bring over one of our most experienced technicians to address your specific concern." Taking the extra time and adding an additional voice of concern for their needs is usually seen as a positive by the client. Let them know it is not just a product they are buying but that your organization will be there to serve them. The value of this transaction and the likely value of repeat business from this customer should guide you in the amount of effort you might invest at this point. Once the prospect has had all their real concerns addressed or you've reached the maximum time you can reasonably expend on education, it is time to close.

Closing

Just because the prospect has decided your product is the best fit does not mean the money is in the bank. The purchasing stage is, therefore, proceeded by the all-important closing process. It is hard to understand rationally, but there is often a moment when the prospect is willing to buy the product, the salesperson is eager to sell it, and yet the transaction never occurs. Can you think of reasons why?

Potential customers often bolt from the sales funnel at this last moment because they are nervous about making a purchasing decision and want to get away from the sales process to think it through. This is particularly common with high-cost items. Other times the prospect is entirely ready, but the salesperson, fearing rejection, continues to sell rather than asking the prospect for the payment or signature required to close the deal. It is the job of a professional salesperson to understand when it is time to close and to have the courage to do it. Dealing with rejection will be discussed later in this chapter.

Before you move to close, you need to know the prospect is ready to commit, correct? Maybe and maybe not. There are two points of view here. One made famous by Alec Baldwin's shocking sales speech in the film *Glengarry Glenn Ross* is "Always Be Closing." Baldwin's character terrorizes the staff of a "boiler room" sales operation where salespeople are driven to push prospects into dubious land deals over the telephone with the most unsavory techniques. The objective is to close the deal no matter what, and there is no finesse. The New Entrepreneurial Dynamic doesn't incorporate this old-school approach.

Always Be Closing

View in the online reader

The other model is the fishing analogy proffered earlier in the chapter. In that scenario, the prospect is your fish, aware that the sales process contains both bait and likely some hook they don't want to swallow. Their job is to avoid the salesperson's scheming, get the best deal, and get out before they get tricked into paying too much or get saddled with the extended warranty or some other expensive and unnecessary add-on designed primarily to increase sales commissions. Your job is to put the fish at ease and get them to take the bait.

The best sales approach is to be the ethical operator and "show the hook" from the start by being as open as possible with the prospect. Make sure the prospect knows *they* will determine when to buy. You will stand back, offer information, and assist them when they have questions, but you will never pressure them. This is the essence of being a customer service representative rather than a "salesperson."

There are situations when waiting for the prospect to decide simply won't support your business model. If you have perishable goods, inventory financed by flooring that must be sold, or your margins simply aren't high enough on each sale to spend hours standing by; you may choose to lose some sales by pushing the customer to a decision. This is when the skill of closing is required.

If the prospect is ready to be closed, they have either made a decision, or there is no additional information or value you can add to the sales process. It is time for you to ask for the order. In most cases, this determination is more of an art than science. An experienced salesperson will have observed enough customers within her domain to intuitively sense the moment to close, often without understanding why. Still, there are some obvious signs you should look for. The most notable clue that a prospect is ready to be closed is when they stop asking questions, but don't leave. Or the nature of the questions may change from asking about the qualities of a product (features, sizes, colors) to the price. If the price is the only thing left on the table, it is time to settle the deal and close on that.

In markets where prices are negotiable—and this may vary by products and cultures—a classic closing technique is to ask the prospect, "If I can get you the price you want, are you ready to buy?" A "yes" from the prospect to that question has pretty well sealed the deal for you, presuming your offering adds enough value to the prospect's life to cover the margin your business model requires. What do you think the best follow-up would be at that point? Should the salesperson propose a price?

No! Never put a price forward in a price negotiation! This may seem counter-intuitive, but your job as a price negotiator is to get the prospect to put up a price, because that price might actually be higher than you would have offered. So, the best response to "Yes, I'd be ready to buy at the right price," is: "What price is that?" If the price isn't right, take it seriously but come back with something that encourages them to move closer to where you need to be. You might offer to add in some additional option or incentive to change the perception of value, or you might say, "That's an honest opening offer, but I've got to be honest with you too, we can't make money at that price. What do you seriously think you could do?" Now, in order to stay in the negotiation, they've got to up their price, and you've not offered any information on where your bottom line is.

Once the prospect comes back with a price you can live with, don't instantly leap at it and say, "Okay, great!" Doing that will let the prospect know they've made a mistake by crossing above your bottom-line price and regret their price offer. You don't want them pulling back or even feeling bad about their purchase, so pause and look dubious. Do some calculations. Go talk to your boss about it, and come back looking like you got yelled at for going too low. Then grudgingly *concede to their terms*. Let your new customer leave feeling like a winner!

Beyond the price negotiation scenario outlined above, there are a plethora of proven closing techniques employed by salespeople. Let's look at a few.

minor close

Some agreement from the customer short of a full commitment to purchasing. A minor close, such as agreeing on a color choice, can bring the customer closer to the final decision.

Minor close: The **minor close** technique involves getting the prospect used to making decisions by presenting them with a series of harmless choices that all presume they are going to eventually make the purchase. You might ask, "Which color do you prefer," or "When you order, would you like to pick up the product or have us ship it to your location?" When the time comes to actually close, all the minor questions are resolved, and the prospect has a sense of commitment, having invested in all these other choices.

Getting to "yes": Dale Carnegie, often considered the founding father of scientific selling, taught that saying "yes" would "set the psychological process of the listeners moving in an affirmative direction."[3] Carnegie similarly noted that getting someone to back off of a "no" statement was difficult because just saying "no" put the person "on guard" and into a state of "physical withdrawal or readiness for withdrawal." The easiest way to leverage Carnegie's yes technique is to query your prospect with questions that will surely result in agreement. You might ask, "Don't you agree that your college football team has been doing great this season?" or "Hasn't the weather been lovely?" With enough of these affirmations made in a row, it becomes routine for the prospect to agree with you, and rejecting your "Can I go ahead and complete the order now?" requires an actual change in their mental and physical state. It's easier to just keep saying "yes."

The assumptive close: Simply assuming that the customer is going to buy is also a powerful technique. Talk about the prospect enjoying whatever you are selling in the future, "When you are out on your new boat . . ." or "During the cruise, you and your husband will. . . ." You can also talk about the purchasing decision as though it has already been made, "Now that you've decided to join our family of happy customers, we can. . . ." Contradicting your assumption may be difficult for many prospects. It's rude to correct someone, and they may even feel they would be calling you a liar. Weak-willed or extremely polite prospects will often go along with the sale to avoid the stress of confrontation.

Intimidation: This isn't a recommended technique, but it is commonly employed in sales. The purpose is to incite confrontation with the prospect that can only be resolved by their making a purchase. A classic example is to state something like, "I don't think you can actually afford to buy this fine an automobile." The statement challenges the prospect's economic and social standing, and it implies he is a fraud. It works even better when done in front of the prospect's family or peers. He can only redeem his standing by purchasing the car. He also can't argue over the price, or he will seem cheap. By paying the asking price, he proves, to his foolish self, that you're wrong and he has plenty of money to throw around!

Walking away: Not being a slave to the sunk cost of time and effort spent in negotiation is a very powerful technique for both a buyer and seller. Simply say, "Thank you for coming. This isn't going to be worth my time," and if you're at the prospect's site, start to leave. The other party is likely to be concerned about the time they have invested and will likely beg you to stay. At that point, you will have the upper hand in the negotiation because now the other party can hardly back out without losing face. Donald Trump famously advocates this technique in his book, *The Art of the Deal*.[4]

If you Google "closing the sale," you'll find countless books, videos, articles, seminars, and training sessions ready to help you master this skill. The quality of these resources varies, but if you are going to be involved in the sales process, and most entrepreneurs are, it's worth your time to explore this fascinating intersection of economics and psychology.

The Purchase

Once the prospect has agreed to buy your product, the remaining step is the actual process of purchasing. In many retail transactions, that may involve no more than the salesclerk scanning a barcode and touching their smartphone on the credit card terminal or the customer clicking on the "Buy Now" button in an app. In other cases, such as selling a car or a large B2B contract, there can be contracts, regulatory paperwork, and financing arrangements to complete. Don't risk losing your customer by making this process unnecessarily cumbersome.

In some businesses, the purchasing phase is used to sneak in additional fees and even product sales. Automobile finance officers are notorious for this practice, and that is one of the reasons many customers dread engaging in the auto sales process. Online sales are making this increasingly difficult in most product categories. This practice is inconsistent with the openness of the New Entrepreneurial Dynamic. Don't do it!

Contract signing is the commitment step in complex sales processes.

Source: © Shutterstock, Inc.

The paperwork involved with completing the purchase should be simple and pleasant. The delivery of your product should be prompt and uncomplicated. Customers often have the ability to halt the purchasing process, even after signing an agreement. They can simply refuse to make a payment. In some jurisdictions, they may be able to renege on a sales agreement within a three-day period. The salesperson must stay engaged in the process at least up until the money is in the bank, but that is not the end of the process. Many people build up a great deal of excitement before a purchase and then feel let down in the post-sales process and do not become return customers. Worse, they may return products or cancel subscription services. You've made a significant investment in acquiring a customer. Keeping a proven customer is cheaper than generating a new one, and satisfied clients bring in new leads and grow your business in a **virtuous cycle**. Loyalty is a post-sales function that will be discussed later in this chapter.

virtuous cycle

A process that repeats in a way that creates value with each previous iteration feeding the next one.

Additional Important Sales Topics

Qualifying is critical because of all the steps involved in moving a potential customer from awareness to purchase, and the hands-on, one-on-one sales process is by far the most expensive. A major factor in this cost is the length of the **sales process**, sometimes referred to as the **sales cycle**.

sales process

The steps a customer proceeds through during the process of buying a product or service including (but not limited to) awareness, qualification, and closing.

sales cycle

The steps a customer proceeds through during the process of buying a product or service including (but not limited to) awareness, qualification, and closing. Same as sales process.

The Sales Process Varies

The sales process varies widely by industry and by product. Selling a pair of headphones in a retail store is likely to involve a few minutes of time. Closing the sale on an enterprise-wide clinical software system to a multi-hospital medical group or a weapons system to the Pentagon will literally take years, dozens of meetings, and many hundreds if not thousands of hours from an entire team of salespeople. Such sales efforts cost hundreds of thousands of dollars. Tying your team up on a major sale also comes with an opportunity cost—they could be working on another target. In these circumstances, it is critically important that your odds of succeeding be good, and proper qualification of your lead is the key to not wasting money or time on the wrong opportunity.

The sales cycle is an important part of the larger **cash conversion cycle** (CCC), which measures the time it takes to convert your firm's investment in inventory or resources (new money or reinvestment of profits) into cash flows from sales. The longer this cycle and the more time invested in the sales process, the higher your firm's profits must be to ensure that the returns to your investors over time are high enough to justify their support.

cash conversion cycle

A measurement of the time it takes to convert your firm's investments in inventory and resources into cash.

Cold Calling/Warm Calling

In some cases, salespeople are tasked with generating their own leads from the target market. Other times a list of leads may be provided that have been identified via a marketing process, but the **target customers** themselves are not aware that they've entered the sales funnel.

target customer

A potential customer identified via a marketing process that has just entered the sales funnel.

Contacting someone who doesn't know they are a sales prospect is called **cold calling**, and it is perhaps the most demanding and intimidating experience in the sales world. The odds of rejection are very high. There is also a fair chance you will get an openly hostile reaction from a lead who values their time and does not want to be distracted with a sales pitch.

cold calling

When a salesperson calls upon an unsuspecting lead in the absence of any relationship. The likelihood of rejection in a cold call is very high.

When a cold call comes in as an email or a text message, the receiver may view it as **spam** and ignore it. If the salesperson has made an unscheduled phone call or shows up at the lead's door, it's harder to not engage them in conversation, though the reaction they get may be unpleasant. To avoid a lead simply hanging up the phone or tossing them out, salespeople are often trained to mislead their prey with a story about taking a survey, offering a free prize, or some other ruse designed to engage the customer's interest and build a conversation that will be harder for the target to terminate politely.

spam

Unwelcome and distracting messages, often in email.

You've probably been the recipient of these unwanted sales pitches yourself. Many businesses organize their telephone and facilities so they can avoid cold callers. All calls go to a receptionist or to voice mail first for screening. The door has a passcode or a reception desk, and if you don't pass screening, you're not going to get to your target. The U.S. Trade Commission even established a national "Do Not Call" registry to help consumers avoid the plague of technology-enabled cold callers, and more than 200 million Americans are registered.

Most people work to avoid uninvited sales pitches.

Source: © Shutterstock, Inc.

All of that is an overwhelming vote of "no" on cold calling, which is increasingly viewed as a waste of time by sales professionals. Statistics are frequently offered to suggest that the success rate of cold calls in moving a target into the sales funnel is 2 percent or less. That means only one out of fifty attempts to schedule a meeting, demo, or consultation works. Worse, it means you've likely irritated forty-nine potential customers, an effect your brand does not need.

The most popular technique salespeople use to avoid the painful rejection of cold calling is the **warm call**. A warm call is when you reach out to a target customer in the context of some already established connection that bestows credibility upon your attempt to establish a rapport. This might be because the customer signed up for "more information" on your firm's website or at a trade show. It might also be because you are able to leverage a mutual association of some kind.

warm call

An initial sales call where a relationship has been established, often through a mutual connection. Preferable to a cold call.

Using a personal referral from a third party that the customer respects is a very powerful way to prevent a target from giving you the brush off. Imagine that you're a very busy executive at a large firm and a salesperson you don't know calls you on the phone. You're in the middle of working on an important report and do not want to be distracted. Consider how you would respond to each of these two telephone openings:

"Hello, I'd like to talk to you about an incredible solution for your company's transportation problems. . . ."

"Good morning, I was just talking to your colleague Shana over at Company X, and she mentioned that your firm has the same logistical problem we solved for her. She suggested I talk to you about how we did that. . . ."

In the first scenario, you're thinking, "Who is this guy, and how do I get rid of him?" You'll probably just want to get off the phone and back to your report and respond with a short, "Sorry, no, I'm busy," and hang up. With the second call, you're now thinking about Shana, whom you enjoy working with, and that establishes credibility to the solution, creates a more pleasant mood, and places the conversation into a social context you value. If you blow this guy off, he's likely to go back to your colleague and say, "Shana, your friend was really rude." Nobody wants to be known as a jerk, so at the least, you're not going to hang up on him. You're probably going to agree to talk now or schedule a time to talk later. Can you think of an even stronger way to leverage a mutual contact like this?

The step beyond the warm call is to get someone else to make a referral. Imagine if Shana called you on behalf of the salesperson and said, "John, I really think you should talk to Jose over at Acme Logistics about their logistical solution; it saved us a ton of money and time."

Getting that to happen is not impossible. If you're the salesperson and you know that your firm has delivered real value for Shana, and she respects you enough, don't be afraid to ask her to help out. This sort of trust in a relationship doesn't happen with one sale; it is earned over time and requires constant maintenance. This level of sales is applicable to the highest end products and services where sales may go on for years and be worth millions of dollars, pounds, or euros. Incumbent firms have these relationships which protect their existing customers and provide them with very warm access to other customers. These relationships constitute a significant barrier to entry in markets such as medical devices and manufacturing equipment. If your startup is in the business of selling expensive, long-term products or services, you have to plan for relationship building. Can you think of any way to jumpstart your sales and overcome the barriers to entry in such a category?

The best solution is often to hire a salesperson with years of experience, industry credibility, and established relationships with the customers you want to capture from the incumbents. Firms in these markets are aware that poaching is a threat, and they know they must keep their best salespeople for years. They compensate them very well, and they protect them with the same dedication they give to their firm's intellectual property and brands. How can your startup compete with the incumbent's superior finances and other resources?

The best tool that a startup has in recruiting is to appeal to the entrepreneurial nature of the recruit. Salespeople are inherently entrepreneurial risk-takers. They are usually compensated for their sales and often see themselves as running their own little business within their firm. Consider bringing on a successful salesperson from one of the incumbents, making him or her the vice president or director of sales and offering them authority and equity they don't have at the big firm that currently employs them.

proxy sales agent

Someone not employed by your firm working to help you drive sales. These are most often customers motivated by an incentive program to bring in referral customers.

If you're pitching consumer goods where a sale occurs once every several years, the opportunity to maintain continual relationships can be more difficult, but getting referrals is possible with the right motivation. Often the solution to a warm call is offering an incentive to buyers that makes them pitch to their peers. With the right motivation, your best customers are transformed into **proxy sales agents**. Have you seen such programs in action?

As discussed in Chapter 3, Tesla faced significant barriers to entry, breaking into an automobile sales market dominated by traditional car dealerships. While their primary strategic play was to go direct to consumers via the internet, one of the firm's best tactics was to offer rewards to clients who provide referrals. They did this via the Tesla mobile app and on social media, where each Tesla user had a referral code that would earn them "loot" in the form of cash, upgrades, or charging credits. The program was immensely successful, and Tesla was able to significantly scale back the cost of the rewards as the firm's products gained market credibility and the barriers to entry had been cleared.

two-for-one sale

A promotion where the customer gets twice as much product if they commit to buying at a particular time.

Referral marketing tactics aren't just for big guys like Elon Musk. Your small startup could easily develop a similar incentive program to convince happy customers to share their positive experience. The trick is in the execution of the program and ensuring that your customers receive their incentives. The risk is that in doing it wrong, you could turn a happy customer into a disgruntled proxy. The simplest version of this technique is a **two-for-one sale**, frequently used in retail. If your customer brings a friend in to your restaurant, one of you gets a free meal. Of course, the food had better be good enough for your customer and her friend to come back for . . . and to pay for.

multi-level marketing

A system that rewards the recruitment of additional salespeople by existing salespeople to rapidly increase sales.

What if your customers each sold three friends and those three each sold three friends and so on? Taking the referral concept a step further leads to a **multi-level marketing** program, discussed later in this chapter.

Corporate Sales

Most of what we've learned so far works for sales to consumers and sales to companies, but somet hings about selling to an organization are unique. Let's take a look at those.

Preparing for the Call

In the corporate world, understanding your customer involves understanding the structure of the organization you are selling into. Which person in a large company is the **decision-maker** who can actually say "yes" or "no" to your product? Who is the **gatekeeper** who can keep a salesperson from reaching the decision-maker? Are there any potential **saboteurs**, individuals who may actively oppose your product or service because it conflicts with their own agendas? Traditionally, the first meeting with a new potential corporate climate is mostly dedicated to figuring all that out. At the same time that a salesperson is learning all this, she also has to establish her credibility with the client. Early impressions count.

Understanding the customer's position in their market as well as what your competition is offering them is a prerequisite for establishing credibility. Researching that before you make the first call is critical, and as research becomes increasingly important, the easier it is to do. An article in the *Journal of Personal Selling & Sales Management* notes, "Customers also expect the salespeople calling on them to become familiar with information available in the public domain and on the internet prior to calling."[5] The article goes on to warn, "Salespeople who attempt to use the first call to obtain background information—because they had not accessed available information prior to the first call—will make a poor first impression and likely fail to penetrate the account."

Little things count too. What is the company culture of your target? Is their communication style formal or informal? How do they dress? Are they a traditional suit and tie shop, or are they proud of their casual style? Contacting them in the wrong way or showing up in wrong attire could label you as someone who doesn't understand how they think. How might you figure that out?

You can Google search for information about the firm or, better yet, use your social media, like LinkedIn, to find a friend who has worked there. If he says, "always email," then email. If he says, "keep calling them on the phone," great. He may even know useful things like "Mondays are always slow, and that would be the best time to get their attention" or "Fridays are crazy, and they will never be able to get the decision-makers in then."

Pictures of the firm at work or your friend should give you some insights into the dress code. This doesn't mean that if you find out that the firm's CEO wears cargo shorts and a Hawaiian shirt as a uniform—as is the case with Palmer Luckey, the founder of Oculus Rift and Anduril—that you should do the same. Showing up like a clone of their unique CEO would be ridiculous, but so would showing up in a suit and tie. The best bet is to choose something you're comfortable in, and that won't look like you "don't get it" or are trying too hard to fit in. A salesperson always does best when he feels comfortable.

decision-maker

A person who can make the final selection of a product or service.

gatekeeper

A person whose approval is required for access to the final decision-maker for a sale.

saboteur

A person, often within the customer's organization, who subverts the sales process. A saboteur's job may be threatened by your solution or they may have a relationship with your competitor.

The author (center), and Ryan Olliges (left) pitch Palmer Luckey, CEO of Anduril (right), in casual clothes.

Source: Greg Autry

Meetings

pitch meeting

A meeting with a customer (investor, etc.) where a solution is proposed.

In the world of corporate sales, you'll most likely be dealing with a group of people who all have input into the decision to buy or reject your product. This means that after the initial fact-finding expeditions and establishment of your basic credibility, you are likely to end up in a **pitch meeting** with the prospective customer's leadership or decision-making team. The objective of these meetings is to establish that your particular product or service solution fits the customer's needs and adds sufficient value to justify the expense. While your goal is to sell your solution, you're very unlikely to reach an actual close in one of these meetings. Corporate teams almost universally defer their decision-making sessions to a later meeting without the vendor present. Pressing for a close in a demo or pitch meeting is pointless and potentially damaging to your relationship with the prospect.

ask

The deliverable, or a request that a salesperson makes of a lead. Signing a contract, for instance.

However, you always want to have some **ask** or specific request at the end of any customer meeting. The purpose of the ask is to keep the customer engaged. You must find a way to obligate the prospect to continue communicating. You may simply ask them to find out more about their specific needs, budget limitations, or such and get back to you. Often the ask is a request for a follow-on meeting, often to demonstrate your solution for them.

At a pitch meeting, you may bring along some support from your own team, but usually, you'll be outnumbered, and the meeting is at the customer's location for their convenience and comfort. These factors make it hard to maintain control of a sales meeting and guide the sales process to the conclusion you are looking for. Can you imagine how such a meeting might go badly?

In any corporate group, there are likely to be disagreements among the potential decision-makers or **influencers**, those individuals who don't have direct purchasing authority, but whose opinion is valued or who may have leverage in other areas they can use to influence decisions. It is essential to identify all these individuals and try to understand where they are likely to stand in regard to your product. Will bringing on your product possibly cause them extra work or expense (retraining, replacing existing systems) or even eliminate their jobs by automating some processes? Is it possible that someone is a close friend or even relative of one of your competitors? While employees should be acting in the best interest of their firms, anyone personally motivated to stop your sales effort should be viewed as a potential saboteur, and they may find ways to derail your sales presentation.

influencer

An independent individual whose opinions, often expressed in blogs, videos, or social media posts, are influential in decisions made by buyers. Influencers can also be professionals within a field whose advice is respected by buyers.

Some things just need to be seen to be appreciated. If your product falls into that category, chances are you are going to have to give a **demo**. It might be a fairly straightforward presentation of an existing, standard product already on the market. Such products are easy to demo because they are fully operational and tested in the real world. You or your staff should be very familiar with them. The challenge comes when you have to demonstrate an idea or prototype. The usual approach is to mockup a prototype or an elaborate presentation and make it look like there is a lot more substance to your solution than there may really be. Such a demo is often referred to in the sales trade as a **dog and pony show**, and it can be highly risky. Demonstrating an app that the software team coded the night before or a device your engineers fabricated without much testing can lead to serious embarrassment during a demo. Even if the product does what it is supposed to, you may have had very little time to learn it. Often these prototypes require a staged demonstration where you go step-by-step through a proven safe operation, avoiding untested features or combinations. If the customer says, "Let me see that," or "Show me what happens when you select the other option . . . ," software might crash or devices might break. It is always best to be honest about the state of your product, but if you must do a dog and pony show, keep control of the demo and the audience at all times.

demo

The process of showing a product or service to a potential customer.

dog and pony show

Doing a major demonstration of a product in front of a customer audience.

Motivation and Rejection

Getting up in the morning and going out to invest your time and energy into an uncertain process filled with potential rejection is daunting. Rejection is intrinsic to the sales process. If sales were assured, we wouldn't need professional salespeople, and businesses would simply hire cashiers and order takers. If you choose to pursue sales, it is very important that you be able to separate your work from your personal life. You must not allow rejection of a product or service you represent to impact your own self-worth, or the sales process will consume you from within.

Learning to manage rejection is a critical business and life skill.

Source: © Shutterstock, Inc.

Sales trainer Brian Tracy states, "The fear of rejection and failure is the single greatest obstacle to success in adult life."[6] He recommends rationalizing your fears by writing them down, analyzing them, and accepting the worst outcomes in advance. If you can do that, you're likely to be pleasantly surprised by what actually happens in the sales process.

This is not to say you should be resigned to failure, simply that you have already dealt with the emotions of that possibility. To accept the possibility of failure and remain confident, you must not take the customer's rejection personally. You aren't being rejected. A product or service offering is being rejected, and the causes are likely beyond your control. Very often, sales don't close because of issues the prospects have that you are totally unaware of. The prospect might have received bad news at work, her stock account took a big hit, or maybe her husband or business partner doesn't like the idea.

Accepting rejection is not easy, and learning to do it can be painful, but the best salespeople are masters at this process. It's a real problem with investors as well. If you are an aspiring entrepreneur who is particularly sensitive to the judgment of others and you don't feel that you can overcome that trait, you're at a disadvantage. Recruiting thick-skinned sales professionals should be one of your early priorities.

It is also worth noting that as an entrepreneur, the sales process is not the only place where you will encounter rejections. You'll experience that any time you seek to work with people who have a choice. You'll find plenty of rejection during fundraising from finicky investors and during the recruiting process from potential startup employees. It's probably best to grow some thick skin yourself and learn to accept rejection as an inherent part of your work.

Key Takeaways

- Qualifying customers is critical.
- Research your customers to understand their motivations.
- Learn to adapt processes from client to client.
- Always be aware of the nonverbal messaging you send to customers.
- It is crucial that salespeople develop emotional and mental resilience.
- Learn to handle rejection.

11.3 Customer Loyalty and Maintenance

Learning Objectives

1. Recognize the value of customer loyalty.
2. Understand the value of good customer maintenance.
3. Understand customer relationship management and CRM systems.
4. Lay the groundwork for the next sale.

Keeping Your New Customer Is Job 1

Congratulations, you've got a customer. Now what? Your first job may be to soften any buyer's remorse your customer may experience. Buyer's remorse is the letdown many customers feel after the adrenaline rush of the new purchase has faded.

If you're selling cheap hats to tourists on the beach, it is likely you will never see most of your customers again. The sales process ends at the purchase, with their money in your pocket. The quality of the hat and the customers' long-term experience with it is not your concern. Is this true with all products? In some businesses, managing the post-sales phase and even supporting the customer through the entire product life cycle is the responsibility of the salesperson.

Nearly all of this vendor's sales are one-time.

Source: Salty View/Shutterstock.com

customer loyalty

Keeping customers that have already been acquired happy and prepossessed to choose your product.

customer acquisition cost

The expense of identifying and closing a single customer. The total cost of marketing + advertising + sales/number of customers sold.

customer relationship

Interactions between the firm, usually the sales staff, and the customer.

referenceable

A customer who is able and willing to recommend a product or service to friends.

Nobody has a bigger interest in customer satisfaction than the salesperson or business development team in businesses where long-term **customer loyalty** is what delivers the profits. With some products, the **customer acquisition cost** is so high that multiple sales over a sustained time period are required to recoup them. Imagine that your firm is spending $100 on marketing in order to drive enough leads into your funnel to close one deal. Your accounting department reports that your net profit per sale is $50. In that case, you need to sell at least two items to each customer just to break even. In these cases, ensuring customer loyalty is not simply desirable but necessary.

For breakfast cereals, customer loyalty is pretty much a matter of production quality and marketing, but when you think of expensive and complex products with fewer customers, such as automobiles or industrial equipment, keeping the customer happy often requires additional personal contact. In B2B sales, a business' constant attention to the customer is typical, and dedicated sales staff are typically assigned to specific business customers or even individual buyers. These **customer relationships** may last for years. Customer relationship management techniques and tools will be discussed in Section 4.

Building and Leveraging References

Too many entrepreneurs work hard to close sales, collect the money from their new customers, deliver the goods, and then move on looking for the next customer. Satisfied customers are among the most valuable assets in any business. From a sales perspective, they are absolutely the most important asset. The best customer is not just satisfied but **referenceable**. Referenceable customers are clients who will take the time to share their positive experience with others either in response to queries or proactively.

You're surely familiar with reviews on Amazon, Yelp, Google, and the like where users of products and patrons of restaurants rate their experiences and share the details of their experiences. These sorts of reviews are increasingly important for B2C (business-to-consumer) firms, and salespeople know it. You can count on unhappy customers or even your competitors to provide negative reviews; taking the time to encourage your happy customers to post is critical. Whenever possible, reach back out to recent customers an appropriate amount of time after they have received their product. If they are in good spirits, encourage them to post, recommend you to their friends, and perhaps provide a quote or two that your marketing team might be willing to share. For significant transactions, like home and auto sales, ask your customers if they would be willing to accept inquiries from other potential customers about the quality of your product and process.

Yes, Yelp can help you find the best tacos in Tokyo.

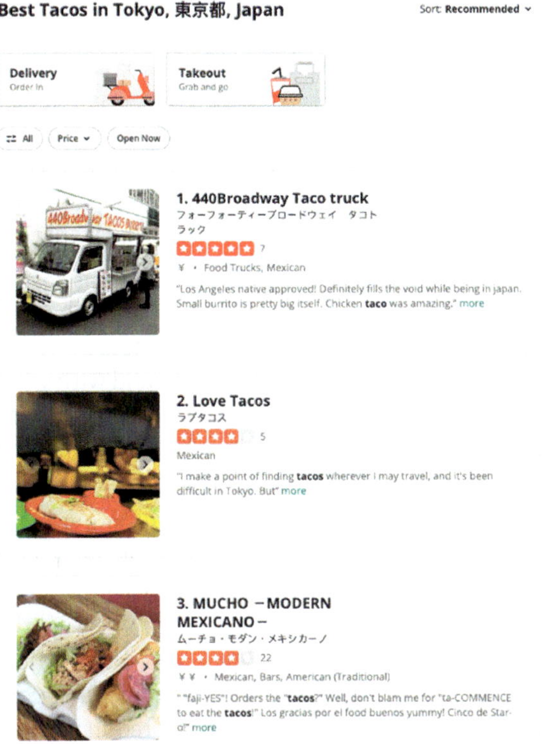

Source: Screenshot by author, 1/15/20 https://www.yelp.com/search?find_desc=Tacos&find_loc=Tokyo, Japan

For B2B business, there are also online rating services, but very often the word-of-mouth reviews shared among industry peers are what count. The conversations over lunch, at industry conferences, or on golf courses often determine who gets the next sale. Having an existing customer tell a potential one, "That was the best solution we ever invested in," could easily be worth a hundred advertisements. As a salesperson, you should be encouraging those interactions and keeping your customer happy, and occasionally reminding them that a well-working product they don't have to think about can be of great value. Asking them to take reference calls or offer marketing quotes is even more valuable in the business realm because your other customers are likely to actually know these individuals. Checking in with former clients is also a great way to pick up any possible problems *before* they become the topic of conversation with your future clients or complaints to your firm.

Handling Complaints and Negative Reviews

Handling complaints about your product or service is the least agreeable part of customer relationship management, but surprisingly, it can be an excellent opportunity to improve a relationship. Well-handled complaints are actually the gold standard in customer service.

The first step is qualifying the complaint. You need to determine if the customer wants the problem to be solved before you invest a great deal of time into the issue. A customer who is unrecoverable is likely just to go away quietly and seek business elsewhere.

Some customer relationships can't be saved. Know when to cut your losses.

Source: © Shutterstock, Inc.

If your customer makes a rational complaint about your product's performance or something your firm has done, even if they are angry, they are investing their time in the hope that you will address their concerns and resolve their problem. This is your chance to turn anger into happiness. The first step in such a situation is to acknowledge the client's concerns and make them understand you are looking into the issue and will get back to them promptly. Responding to genuine complaints with genuine solutions is simply a prerequisite for doing business. However, in all but the most minor matters, solving the customer's problem will not be a sufficient response. Why is that?

In most cases, a problem with a product has cost the customer time, at the least, and may have cost them revenue or embarrassment as well. Imagine that you sell some sort of medical diagnostic system and it fails. Your customer, a local hospital, has patients who require testing, and with your system down, they have had to transport these patients, by ambulance, to a facility across town for the tests. That's not good on several obvious levels. Fixing your machine won't be enough to smooth over the pain and expense of such a situation.

If you want a happy, referable customer, you've got to take it a step further and let them know you and your firm are truly sorry for having inconvenienced them and that you will go above and beyond to make things right. In the case of the hospital, you should first consider providing them with a loaner machine while theirs is being serviced to reduce the cost of transportation and the stress on their patients and medical staff. If the volume of patients justifies it, you might next address the issue of downtime by offering the hospital customer a discount on a second machine. This win/win solution might provide the hospital with the redundancy they clearly need and get you an additional sale, albeit at a lower margin.

Sometimes, however, a customer can't be made happy, and they will throw some sort of "stink bomb" communication on their way out. If you receive a profanity-laden email or phone call, it may be best not to respond in any detail that might provoke further anger. Just let them know you're sorry to hear they aren't satisfied and are ready to address any specific issues. If this is a public communication on a review site or on a social media posting, you will need to address it calmly and rationally in that context.

Make your firm look professional and let others reach their own conclusions about "Mr. Stinkbomb." If your firm has professional social media managers, this work should be delegated to their care. Never get into a tit-for-tat, back-and-forth argument with a customer, either in public or online. It is pointless, time-consuming, emotionally draining, and if others see the mudslinging, it will simply harm the reputation of your firm.

Customer Relationship Management

Customer relationship management, or CRM, is the formalized process of interacting with customers. It includes the sales process, servicing, and forecasting of future needs. A good CRM will ensure that you are in appropriately—not annoyingly—regular contact with your customers to check on their success with your product and respond proactively to their future needs for reorders, updates, etc. Doing this right is a service for the customer and a continuing source of revenues for the client.

Firms with excellent CRM have customers who are more satisfied and loyal, and they capture more value out of each customer. Any startup dependent on sales should build CRM into its DNA from the start. Keeping a record of your customers and managing this data is critical.

While CRM is truly a process, in today's world, that process is usually defined by software solutions, and enterprise-level CRM software is the most successful category of software as a service (SaaS). The leaders in this $40 billion industry are firms such as Salesforce, SAP, and Oracle. The enterprise-level version of these solutions will be unaffordable and require too much overhead for most startups, but most of them offer a scalable cloud-based solution. Some CRM systems are targeted directly at smaller firms designed to integrate with the popular QuickBooks accounting system. These solutions allow salespeople to convert their closings directly into invoices and offer reminders for invoicing subscriptions or contacting customers for reorders.

Salesforce built a multibillion-dollar enterprise out of CRM.

Source: Tada Images/Shutterstock.com

If your startup can't afford any investment in a formal CRM program, you can set up a simple spreadsheet in Google Docs or Office 360 to track customer data and share it with your team. If your sheet database is organized well, it should be possible to import it into a real CRM system later. You'll want to include at least the minimal fields in your simple database:

- Firm name
- Firm description (what do they do)
- Firm location and official address, phone
- Product needs
- Product preferences
- Notes on organization
- Contact name(s)
- Contact email, address, phone
- Notes on contact

Information is power, so collect it and use it to your advantage. Don't be afraid to record reasonably personal things like college, birthdays, favorite sports teams, hobbies, or touchy points (i.e., "don't talk about . . ."). The more you know about a customer, the easier it is to understand their needs and perspective and how they reach decisions about purchases. Giving someone a shout out—like a text message—on their birthday or when their team wins an important game can go a long way to making a sales relationship seem more like a friendship.

As the artificial intelligence (AI) field progresses, more and more of the CRM process will be automated. Reminders about contract renewals, update options, and the rest are already there.

Even those birthday greetings and game day texts could be figured out by your AI and executed automatically. Staying on top of the CRM AI trend will be a source of competitive advantage for startups looking to disrupt mature markets and displace incumbent players.

Key Takeaways

- Customer loyalty may be the single best asset your business can have.
- If your business is scalable, you *must* establish a system to track and optimize customer relationships.
- Remember that references, ratings, and reviews must be managed.
- Strive to turn negative interactions into positive ones.

11.4 Organizing Sales

Learning Objectives

1. Understand how sales outcomes depend on the sales organization.
2. Understand that the motivations and performance of salespeople are closely tied to their compensation.
3. Explore basic compensation systems.
4. Understand the options for outsourcing sales.
5. Understand the power and risks of multi-level sales systems.

> When somebody says it's not about the money, it's about the money.
>
> —*H. L. Mencken*[7]

Sales Compensation

Sales compensation can be very unique.

Source: © Shutterstock, Inc.

Everyone understands that employees need to be paid. They perform jobs that add value to the firm, and they have opportunity costs in that they could be doing something else to benefit themselves. In most areas of the modern firm, from production to marketing, employees are paid for the time they put in, either by hourly wages or annual salaries. They may also get a year-end bonus or other perks, but in general, their expectations of pay are clearly set in advance. Sales is a very different domain when it comes to compensation. Can you think of why?

For a salesperson, motivation is always the primary factor in success. As we've discussed, getting up each day and facing rejection is not easy. Offering a **performance-based pay plan** is the traditional solution to this problem of motivation. Such programs include commissions, bonuses, or other financial rewards tied to sales as a substantial portion of the salesperson's compensation. The lure of increased income and the fear of not making enough have long been the "carrot and stick" of sales.

performance-based pay plan

A compensation system, often for sales staff, based on outcomes such as revenues or profits generated. Generally, a commission-based or bonus-based sales plan.

Salaries and Commissions

Paying employees based on performance is an attractive proposition to most business owners. Ideally, such a plan motivates the sales staff and insulates against fixed costs if sales do not emerge. Paying a percentage **commission** on sales is the most common way to achieve this.

commission

A form of pay where salespeople are compensated with a percentage of the revenues they generate in closed sales.

Imagine a bicycle rental business on the beach. You charge $20 per hour of rental. You could pay the attendants who manage your business $15/hour, or you might pay them a percentage of the revenue for each bike they rent. If your commission rate is 25 percent of revenue, then they would earn $5 per hourly rental and need to rent 3 bikes per hour to make the same $15. This might motivate them to move the bikes out quicker and maybe even to call out to passersby in hopes of selling more rentals. If it rains and things are slow, you won't be stuck paying $15/hour for nothing. Are there problems with this model?

One of the obvious problems is that your attendant might not want to be at risk of having no income just because the weather turns bad. Many products are much harder to sell than bicycle rentals, and salespeople must invest significant time in learning the products and in working leads through the sales funnel. In some industries, the length of the sales cycle can be measured in months. Imagine if you are selling nuclear power plants to developing nations. There is surely a lot to learn about such a product's specification, construction, and advantages, as well as the politics and regulations surrounding it. Spending a year doing that learning might not be unreasonable. When you finally head out to sell, the time between your first contact at the Ministry of Energy and the actual contract signing will be years. It could be another decade before the plant becomes operational and is fully paid for. Salespeople in these sorts of situations must be paid some reasonable **base salary** to support them while they come up to speed. It also makes sense to pay these sophisticated salespeople on **milestones** in the sales process, such as securing meetings with identified decision-makers, signing letters of intent, initiating an order, etc.

base salary

A guaranteed amount of money paid to a salesperson before their commissions are added. Base pay is designed to provide a level of income certainty.

milestones

Identifiable objectives in the sales process that can be used to measure progress toward closing.

What if you allowed your bicycle attendant to negotiate deals on bike rentals in order to increase business? Perhaps he will offer a discount for group rentals or multi-hour rentals? Sounds good? Can you see a problem here?

Let's imagine that the bike rentals cost you $10/hour. At $20/hour your gross profit is a solid 50 percent, or $10. If you pay the attendant $5, you're still doing well with your own $5 profit. Suppose he lowers the price of the rental to $15/hour and doubles the number of rental hours, is that good? Not really, because now you are paying all the profits ($5) to the attendant! If he drops the price to $12/hour and triples rentals, you'll be getting $7 after his commission, leaving you with a $3 loss on each hour of rental. Increasing the volume, in this case, is increasing your losses! How would you solve this problem?

The best way to prevent sales commissions from eating your profits is to align the salesperson's interests with your own by establishing a commission plan tied to profits. If you pay the bike station attendant 50 percent of gross profits if he keeps the price at $20, he still takes home $5. He may offer discounts when it increases total profits, but he will never let the profits drop to anywhere near zero.

spiff

A sales incentive aimed at moving a specific product. A spiff is often paid as a cash bonus on top of the regular commission to the salespeople for each of that item sold.

Often an organization wishes to move some specific product, perhaps because a mistake was made, it was unpopular, or too much of it has accumulated in inventory. In this case, the firm is likely to offer some additional bonus specifically attached to sales of these items. Such an incentive is called a **spiff**. If you're in a store and a salesperson is annoyingly persistent in leading you to a particular item that you aren't really interested in, there is a good chance the store manager has put a spiff on that product.

Goals and Recognition

Sales motivation is often as much about recognition as it is a financial reward. People need money, but salespeople require psychological support as well. Trophies, plaques, congratulatory emails, and articles in company publications can go a long way to patching the ego of your sales staff who routinely face rejection. One of the traditional perks of the sales job in the corporate world has been attending an annual sales conference at some nice destination, often places like Las Vegas or Hawaii. These conferences usually feature a gala dinner where the firms often present the above-mentioned trophies and plaques and sometimes additional generous bonuses. Those who don't win at this year's conference may be motivated to work harder for recognition the following year. Smaller companies can do these things on a less grand scale. Consider taking your sales team on a weekend cruise or a stay at a local beach resort, guest ranch, or a similar destination.

Many organizations host annual awards events to recognize top salespeople.

Source: Pavel L Photo and Video/Shutterstock.com

A Word of Caution about Sales Incentives

While performance-based pay plan programs can be very effective, they can also be difficult to manage and sometimes go awry in a few ways. When things are good, salespeople can, at times, earn unreasonable amounts. There are times when sales success is due to forces outside the salesperson's actual control.

Imagine that you're in a market dominated by two firms, a duopoly, and your competitor makes a terrible blunder that prevents them from delivering product. Sales will flow to your firm because the customer has no other choice. Such a situation occurred in 2019 when Boeing's new 737MAX airliner was grounded for serious safety concerns related to its design and software. With the competition unable to deliver a popular product, you can imagine that the salespeople at Airbus had little trouble closing sales in the narrow-body jet market the 737 had previously dominated. In other circumstances, perhaps your design team came up with an incredible new product that sweeps the market, or your marketing department hit one out of the park with their new campaign. In cases like these, the commissions you pay are on dollars that would have come to your firm anyway.

Overly generous or flamboyant sale incentives can also generate resentment among the other, noncommissioned professionals who are supporting the sales effort. In organizations where the star salespeoples' egos are treated like the lead singers in a rock band, the rest of the "band" can become jealous. You need your drummers and bass players too, so recognize the marketing, production, and services heroes as well.

Outsourcing Sales

Some businesses, such as car dealerships and real estate brokerages, are sales focused. In these firms, the sales organization is the core of the organization and the source of the firm's competitive advantage. In these cases, sales are tightly integrated into everything the company does.

In other businesses, sales may be a very important function but not the core competency of the organization. In a firm where the CEO must focus his or her energies and the company's capital on technology development, production, or delivery of services to maintain an edge, running a sales organization, while necessary, can be a distraction. The New Entrepreneurial Dynamic encourages startups to outsource noncore business functions to outside professionals, and there are several proven ways to do this with sales.

Manufacturer Reps

A traditional way to outsource sales of a product you make is to hire an individual or a company that provides sales services for multiple product companies. They are usually paid with some percentage of sales. These **manufacturers' representatives** or **sales agents** typically focus on particular industries and markets. For instance, there are manufacturers' representatives in the bicycle industry who go out and pitch bike-related products to retail stores, chains, and distributors. They sell bikes, frames, tires, saddles, and accessories of all sorts to several manufacturers.

manufacturers' representative

A firm that represents the business interests of a manufacturer.

sales agents

Outsourced professional salespeople who will represent your product.

The percentage a rep gets get is likely to be more than you'd pay internal commissioned salespeople, because the reps need to fund their own overhead as well. However, you usually won't have to support them with any base pay while they come up to speed on your product. Because they bring industry expertise on a wide variety of products, they often have strong, established relationships with the buyers in your target market. This means that a manufacturers' rep not only saves you the time and expense of recruiting a professional sales team but gets your products to market faster. Their customers are nearly all repeat customers, and you don't have to wait for them to be pushed through the sales funnel! For the customer, meeting with one of these reps is far more efficient as well. For instance, it is more efficient to meet with the buyer for a chain of bicycle shops, rather than meeting with a dozen or more individual salespeople, each with one product. Can you think of any downsides or challenges in this system?

While the buyer loves getting information about a large selection of products from a single source, there may be problems if the products themselves are in direct competition with each other. If the sales rep sells your bike tires as well as a competing line of tires, they can be conflicted.

An additional incentive or spiff from your competitor might cause your virtual salesperson to sell those tires over yours. To avoid this, many manufacturers' representatives try to avoid picking up conflicting lines. This becomes even more problematic as firms expand their product lines. Perhaps your representative only sells your tires, but now you've decided to start making wheels. Any good bicycle rep probably has a long-standing relationship with a wheel maker. What to do? If your tire business is significantly larger than the competitors' wheel sales, you might win the battle over the representation, but if it is the other way around, you'll have a problem. As your firm's product catalog gets more diverse, it becomes more and more reasonable for you to bring your sales in-house.

You can find manufacturers' reps by searching online, at industry conferences where they are very active, or through organizations like the Manufactures and Agents Association or MANA.[8]

Affiliates, Independent Agents, and Multi-Level Marketing

independent sales agent

An individual who hires themselves out as a contractor to sell products or services.

Another option for outsourcing sales is to authorize a large number of **independent sales agents** to represent your product or service to the public. This model was made famous in the United States during the mid-twentieth century by door-to-door salespeople. They literally walked neighborhoods knocking on people's doors to hawk household products like brushes and cosmetics. While that model is much less common, some companies still rely primarily on individuals to sell their products within their networks, often at product-focused home parties. Can you think of any of these?

Some organizations use self-organizing hierarchies to sell their products.

Source: © Shutterstock, Inc.

On the internet today, **affiliate marketing** is a popular way of driving traffic to a sales website. Blogs, news sites, and others may be paid some flat fee or percentage of sales to deliver customer clicks to your e-commerce platform. The lure of generating commissions from scalable autonomous systems on the internet has resulted in the phenomena of **click-bait**, sites that use tantalizing content to lure unsuspecting web surfers to commissionable advertisements.

Amway, founded by two school buddies in Michigan in the 1950s, sells home care health and beauty products through agents. One of the key drivers of Amway's success has been its practice of rewarding its agents for recruiting additional agents. This practice is intended to encourage the sales team to expand their ranks rather than to jealously guard their distributorship. It's been remarkably successful, and Amway is now reported to have $8 billion in annual revenues globally. The practice of incentivizing sales agents to bring on more sales agents and rewarding them for the success of those "beneath them" in the chain is known as multi-level marketing. It has been a very successful strategy for many startups needing to build a large and aggressive sales organizations quickly. Can you think of the potential downsides to this system?

affiliate marketing

Online marketing through third party websites incentivized to drive traffic to you.

click-bait

Sites that use tantalizing and sometimes lurid content to lure unsuspecting web surfers to commissionable advertisements.

In some cases, the financial motivation to bring on new agents can result in the high-pressure recruitment of individuals not well suited to sales. The new recruits can be burdened with product inventory at their own expense, and this pressures them to do the same to their friends and colleagues. There has been significant public criticism of this practice, and in some cases, such systems have been shut down as illegal **pyramid schemes**. A pyramid scheme is a sales system where gaining additional agents is theonly source of sales and business is unsustainable in the absence of exponential growth.

pyramid scheme

A sales system, often illegal, where the sales go into additional agents and where the business is unsustainable in the absence of exponential growth.

Integrators and Value-Added Resellers

Many products require additional services or integration with other products to provide value for the final customers. If you're a small company in Israel making customized CubeSats for university researchers, your little satellites are not exactly a "ready to use" product. They need to be launched into space, and that is something neither you nor your customers can do. Paying $65 million for a SpaceX Falcon 9 rocket to launch your $500,000 payload isn't a viable choice for the customer. Luckily such a large rocket can launch many dozens of such CubeSats. Somebody needs to buy the rocket launch, sell enough payload slots, and make sure everything goes into the payload fairing and works correctly. Payload integrators exist to fill this specific need. In December 2018, one such integrator, Spaceflight Industries, successfully integrated, launched, and deployed sixty-four different small satellites from a single Falcon 9 flight. In general, such firms are called **systems integrators**, and they can be critical partners in the sales process for any firm whose products are part of a complex **technical ecosystem**.

system integrator

A firm that combines several products and services into a working solution for the customer. The system's integrator often participates in or leads the sales process for complex solutions.

technical ecosystem

The technological environment in which a particular product must operate.

The launch of Falcon 9 rocket contained sixty-four small satellite payloads integrated by Spaceflight Industries.

Source: Greg Autry

The customer may buy the product from you and contract with the systems integrator separately. In that case, you are likely to need to work with the salespeople at the integrator. In other cases, the customer is seeking a **turnkey solution** and will want to purchase the entire solution from an integrator. Imagine that you sell an enterprise software solution for analyzing laboratory results. Your customers are large healthcare firms. Your software can't run without hardware like servers and networking gear. It also requires the development of custom interfaces to existing medical databases and clinical systems. Providing these sorts of services could be a significant distraction and cost to a startup that needs to focus on its core product.

turnkey solution

A system that is ready to use without a buildout or customization.

value-added reseller

A firm that combines products and services and resells them as a turnkey, ready for purchase solution, creating value for both the customer and the product developer.

Letting a firm sell your solution bundled with their hardware and integration services would make things easier for you and your customer, and many small software and hardware firms partner with integrators to find, sell, and service their customers. The firms that provide this service are known as **value-added resellers** or VARs. The name implies that they can charge more for your product than your firm because the turnkey solution creates new value for the customer. They also add value for product developers, like you, by finding customers and keeping them happy. Making things easier for everyone funds the VAR's operations.

Everything Is Sales

You may not intend a career as a salesperson. You may even disdain the profession as unseemly. Just remember that in the real-world people make the decisions that will determine the course of your life. Think about these important life events:

Getting into Your Aspirational School: Before you got into the college, university, or academy of your dreams, you likely had to write a cover letter and a theme of some sort and then perhaps sit for an interview. If you go on to grad school, you'll be doing even more selling yourself.

Getting the Perfect Job: More cover letters and more interviews and perhaps lunches or dinners with the boss and the team. All of that time is selling the product that is you!

Romancing and Proposing to Your Spouse: Your special relationship may have been written in the stars, but somebody has to close the deal and that takes the positioning, courage, and determination called "sales."

Renting Your First Apartment: You've got the degree, the job and a family in the making. Great, but now is the time to convince Mr. and Ms. Landlord that you're the right family to rent their townhouse to. Sales, again.

Each of these tasks involves convincing another person to take a chance on you. They require sales skills. Appreciate them. Learn them. Collecting the sales merit badge can take you places in life far beyond collecting commissions.

Key Takeaways

- Outsourcing the sales function enables your team to focus on firm core competencies.
- Outside sales representatives require less time and capital to get sales going.
- As your business grows, it may make sense to develop an internal sales team.
- If your product is complex and requires integration services and support, working with systems integrators or value-added resellers is a good option.

11.5 Case Study: Unboxing the Sales Process with unboXt

Hakeem Atwater and Kendra Ward

Source: Kendra Ward

Kendra Ward was a dual major at Spelman College in math and industrial engineering, and Hakeem Atwater was a business undergrad at Morehouse when the two Atlanta-area students met through friends. Kendra had an idea for an app that would synchronize the remote viewing experience of Netflix for virtualized viewing parties, and she pitched Hakeem right away. He didn't buy it, which was a shame since the same idea later generated millions for another entrepreneur. Still, the two stayed in conversation, became the best of friends, and would eventually become successful business partners.

Atwater was born in Columbus, Ohio, into a family that moved a lot. He recalls, "We went from Ohio to New Jersey to North Carolina and Northern California, and I was always changing schools." While this geographic instability might have been a source of weakness for another young person, Atwater thrived. "I became comfortable sitting alone at the lunch table by sitting back in the lunchroom or wherever and observing the way other students would interact. I learned how to observe the why behind people's actions. This still informs my perspective as a businessperson today."

Atwater went on to hone his skills with internships at Goldman Sachs and PriceWaterhouseCoopers in New York before settling into a job with Fifth Third Bank in Cincinnati, Ohio. He noted that most corporations struggled with the one-to-one management skills required for employee retention, despite having a lot of data in sophisticated human resource systems. The future entrepreneur remarked, "There is a *lot* of unnecessary churn out there." Atwater began to imagine a software platform for improving recruiting and leadership effectiveness that would build team cohesion and increase employee motivation. Atwater recalls, "I saw how we could take highly fractured corporate performance data, identify current areas of concerns with employees, and deliver actionable insights directly to their managers before things got out of hand." Saving employees rather than turning them over would save firms money and increase organizational morale.

Discovering that Ward was attending an event in Las Vegas with her colleagues from Goldman Sachs in Salt Lake City, he drove out from Los Angeles to pitch her on this idea, which he originally called "My Cabinet." Ward understood the idea and began to visualize the solution. What they needed now was a customer willing to share their vision and let them test their insights in the real world. That seemed to be a daunting challenge. Ward asked, "What established company is going to let a couple of unproven young entrepreneurs try out something new on their primary asset, their people?" Surprisingly, it didn't take long to find an apparent matchup.

Atwater had the opportunity to connect with a regional director from a major national insurance company. "She asked me about my side projects, and I pitched her on the My Cabinet idea." The director realized the independent agent network they used to sell and service their business suffered from the exact problems Atwater's solution would solve. Atwater recalls saying to the director, "We can do that!" and suddenly unboXt was a real service with a powerful evangelist inside a big company. However, the regional director's real-world understanding of the problem and how the unboXt solution would address it wasn't shared by corporate leadership at headquarters. Negative customer feedback had alerted the headquarters crowd to the turnover issue within the agencies, but they were disconnected from the full array of drivers behind the problem. Being who they were, the corporate leadership assumed they knew their business better than any outsider and wanted to design the solution themselves. Headquarters had already defined a list of metrics they wanted to change, and they wanted to do that with immediate, targeted fixes, not make structural changes to address the more embedded cultural problems Atwater saw.

One component of the system was a screening function for recruitment, and the headquarters folks attached all their hopes to that solution. They wanted the young entrepreneurs to produce a specific tool just for them, rather than the toolbox of solutions that the entrepreneurs had envisioned. Trying to argue to the headquarters' executives that their original vision was exactly what was needed for the agencies was a lost cause. Ward notes, "Our total lack of a track record made it impossible for us to get them to change their perspective about their business. We had little proof." It was frustrating for the entrepreneurs to get so far, so fast, and then find themselves misdirected at the finish line.

"To this front, Kendra and I saw that we had to make a decision—build a tool to service the client today or move on." What complicated the situation was that mentors they had were either also first-time founders or venture capitalists advised them to "take the money and get the win today," under any circumstances.

Atwater and Ward boldly decided to part ways with their first customer and walk away from a very significant revenue opportunity. Ironically, their connections with the original firm's regional director brought them to the attention of another major player in the insurance market: Allstate. The solution Atwater had originally envisioned worked well for Allstate, and unboXt has had a long and successful relationship with that company and its agents. Other customers followed.

Today, United Parcel Service (UPS) has become unboXt's biggest client, though that sale process had its own challenges. A pilot project with UPS in 2019 went very well. The unboXt team was ready to pitch a proposal for a full rollout into America's largest logistics company! However, pitch day turned out to be the very day in March 2020 when the COVID-19 pandemic pummeled the firm's stock price. Still, UPS leadership saw that the market was wrong and that the pandemic would result in increased shipping. They would need strong leadership to continue to attract, retain, and train the best talent and therefore saw the value in the partnership. Atwater notes:

It's been important for us to remember organizations (large and small) are operated by humans. Humans and organizations, alike, run on trust. Trust is two-sided, competence and character. Character will get you in the room, whereas competence eventually earns you a seat at the table. We adopted this ideal and focused on delivering value, which in turn has awarded us a loyal customer.

Find unboXt on the web at https://getunboxt.com.

Endnotes

1. Commonly attributed to Canadian hockey player Wayne Gretzky, aka "The Great One."
2. Carnegie, D. (2009). *How to win friends & influence people*. Simon & Schuster.
3. Carnegie, D. (2009). *How to win friends & influence people*. Simon & Schuster.
4. Trump, D. J., & Schwartz, T. (2009). *Trump: The art of the deal*. Ballantine Books.
5. Jones, E., et al. (2005). The changing environment of selling and sales management. *Journal of Personal Selling & Sales Management, 25*(2), 105–111.
6. https://www.briantracy.com/blog/personal-success/fear-of-rejection/
7. Commonly ascribed to Winston Churchill.
8. https://www.manaonline.org/manufacturers/online-directory/

CHAPTER 12
Operations

> I am a great believer in Luck. The harder I work, the more of it I seem to have.
>
> —*Coleman Cox*[1]

Running your business well is as important as building it right.

Source: © Shutterstock, Inc.

Delivering on the promise of a great product or service is a much bigger challenge than planning or raising funds for your planned business. As noted in Chapter 3, simply executing well can be a competitive advantage in itself. Doing that isn't simply a matter of committing to excellence. It requires learning, recruiting great people, and gathering the right resources. That is what this chapter is about.

12.1 Execution and Resources

Learning Objectives

1. Understand the importance of excellence in execution.
2. Understand the relationship between tactics and execution.
3. Understand that operations should be data driven.
4. Understand why real-time dashboarding and accounting are necessary for proper execution.
5. Learn about accounting system options for supporting execution.
6. Understand the importance of appropriately locating and configuring facilities in execution.
7. Understand the importance of logistics.
8. Consider the benefits, costs, and challenges of global sourcing.

Execution Is Everything

logistics

Transportation of products to customers or from suppliers to businesses.

operations

The management processes that coordinate people and resources to ensure that a business runs efficiently.

Some firms, like Southwest Airlines, built their entire business on just doing their job well. For a modern and lean startup, product production, quality management, and **logistics** can be a daunting challenge. Luckily, a great deal of research into business **operations** has been done, and well documented best practices are readily available to today's dynamic entrepreneurs. These concepts are backed up with a plethora of software solutions, apps, and virtualized services. Operations is one area of your business where risk is very manageable, *if* you pay attention.

Measuring What You Manage

metrics

Critical and actionable pieces of information you need to see to keep your business on track that can be used to test the hypothesis behind your major assumptions.

Operations are about executing tactics in support of the overall strategy. Recall again the illustration on strategy, tactics, and execution from earlier chapters. You'll note that **metrics** derived from results (primarily sales) should be the drivers for adjustments you will make to your plan, tactics, and execution. Because of this, the adage, "You can't manage what you can't measure," is one of the most common phrases in business. So how do you measure?

FIGURE 12.1 Strategy, Tactics, Execution

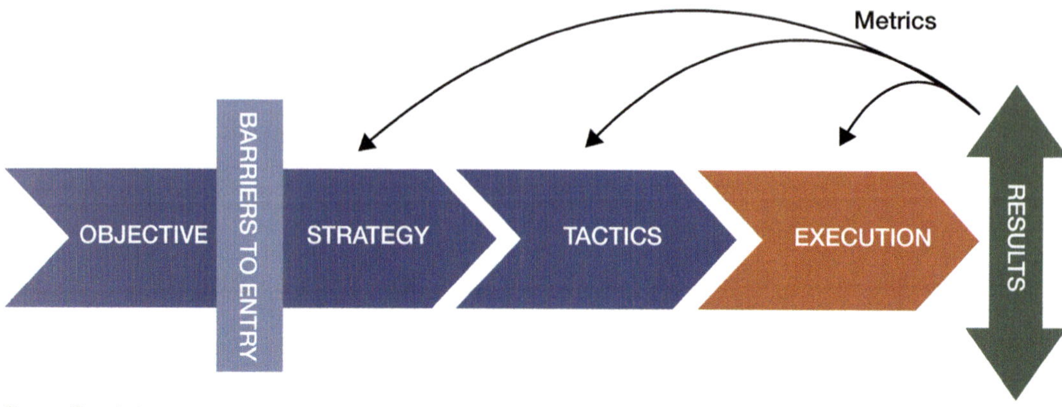

Source: Greg Autry

Dashboarding

In today's competitive business climate, entrepreneurs need to know what is going on and they need to know it almost before it happens. Modern accounting and banking systems allow small business owners to keep their books up-to-the-minute, and that's great because **performance analysis** needs to be done in real time.

performance analysis

Reviewing statistic data to inform and enhance business decisions.

Gauges and displays inform the driver about the state of their vehicle.

Source: © Shutterstock, Inc.

The **dashboard** of an automobile features gauges or electronic displays that keep you constantly informed of important data like your fuel level, speed, RPMs, mileage, and the operating temperature of your engine. An internal combustion engine must be warm in order to operate efficiently, but too much heat will permanently damage it and cost you thousands of dollars in repairs and weeks of downtime. What if your engine temperature data were presented to you as a specific numerical value, say "95° C." Is that good? What should you do if you see that? You (and most drivers) probably have no idea.[2]

dashboard

See *business dashboard*.

To be useful, data must be *interpretable* and *actionable* by the person receiving it and presented in a matter that focuses your attention on the critical items. This means you know which values require your attention, and you also know what to do when you see them. Otherwise, it is simply distracting noise. Consequently, most engine gauges and displays center the appropriate operating range on the gauge and offer colored graphics highlighting the too cold (blue) and too hot (red) **thresholds**. This information is easily interpretable. The driver can quickly glance at the gauge and know things are okay with the engine. Having to stop and think about specific numbers would divert the driver's attention from the more important business of paying attention to navigation and potential road hazards. The data are also actionable; if the temperature crosses the safety threshold, the driver can pull to the side of the road, stop driving, and seek assistance. For good measure, most cars also feature a "check engine" light and even an audio alert to ensure that the driver acts on critical information.

thresholds

The specific data points that validate or reject assumptions.

business dashboard

A tool, often an internal website or actively updated spreadsheet, that presents key performance data.

Managing a business in real time is very similar to driving a car. You're driving your business forward, watching out for obstacles, and scouting for better routes ahead. Similarly, you've got to keep the mechanics of your firm in order and deliver the goods. You've got new customers to acquire, existing ones to service, and vendors to negotiate with. You cannot spend the entire day sitting in front of your accounting system looking at ledgers full of minutia. You need interpretable and actionable data close at hand. The New Entrepreneurial Dynamic encourages the use of a **business dashboard** to gather and present information that is critical to managing a business.

Building a Dashboard

A business dashboard is a tool that allows you to maintain a focus on the things that are most important for your firm while still running your business. It might be a manual system based on paper reports or an Excel spreadsheet. Better yet, if you have the expertise available, use a live database with a web or mobile app on the front end.

sales volume

The number of units sold in a given period.

inventory levels

The amount of stock of products or materials used to make products, kept on hand.

A live database serves two major purposes. Firstly, a dashboard can be used to monitor routine information that will allow you to make minor adjustments in order to keep your business on track. Imagine you own a popular shoe store in a small college town. You will always want to know how your shoe store's **sales volume** of various styles and sizes compare to your **inventory levels**. This measurement is critical so that you can reorder the right shoes in a timely manner. Keeping the right products in stock at the right levels ensures customers are satisfied, sales are not missed, and that unsellable items do not accumulate. Ordering popular items in advance and in larger quantities gets you better pricing and prevents money from being spent on expedited shipping to fill gaps in the shelves.

hypothesis testing

The process of turning assumptions about your business model into specific tests that can be validated or rejected by hard data.

Secondly, a dashboard can be used to test major assumptions about your business. Venture capitalist Randy Komisar and Stanford professor John Mullins are advocates of dashboarding for this purpose. In their book, *Getting to Plan B*, they explain that entrepreneurs enter a market with certain "leaps of faith," ideas that can only be tested in the marketplace. Dashboards allow the entrepreneur to see if these leaps of faith are valid through a process of **hypothesis testing**—turning these assumptions into specific tests that can be validated or rejected by hard data.

Let's go back to your shoe store. Imagine that you've decided that young women are the best customer segment to target with ads because (you believe) that they buy a lot of shoes as women's fashions change more frequently than men's. You might be spending on social media advertising aimed at women ages 16–25 in your town, but how do you know this is working? You've made an assumption about young female buyers, and it should be validated before you invest too much. Rather than blindly pouring money into the campaign, you construct a testable hypothesis and add metrics to your dashboard that will test it. Can you think of how you might do that?

Perhaps you might establish a customer loyalty program with a "rewards card." Ever wonder why your grocery store does that? When customers register for the program, you collect their demographic data (age, gender, etc.). When those reward cards are scanned at the register, you log the purchases by each customer into a system that can slice and dice that data and feed it to your dashboard. In particular, you can analyze it against specific thresholds that will validate or reject your assumption about young shoe buyers. Your hypothesis might be stated as "our average female customer aged 16–24 will make at least 50 percent more purchases than the average (of all) our customers." Your data will tell you if this is true. If it is, continuing or even increasing that focused advertising makes sense. If the data say it is not, save your advertising dollars and move on to a new hypothesis.

The New Entrepreneurial Dynamic builds a dashboard out of five components: metrics, data collection, calculation, analysis, and presentation.

Metrics: Your metrics are the critical, *actionable* pieces of information you need to see to keep your business on track and facts you need to test the hypothesis behind your major assumptions. Defining these metrics is your first step. Once you've identified what you need to know, consider how often you need to know it. To be relevant to your decision-making process, does this data need to be real-time, hourly, daily, or monthly? Finally, you need to set the thresholds for each data point. What is the safe range, and what values should trigger an alert and force you into action?

Data Collection: You may have heard the phrase, "If you can't measure it, you can't manage it." The **data collection** component of your dashboard is about quantifying the phenomena you want to analyze and present a digestible view of the results. This view may contain data straight from your accounting system, such as *revenues per month*. It might also be something that will require you to put specialized systems into place to capture data such as the *average age of our customers*.

data collection

The process of collecting, analyzing, and measuring specific business variables.

Calculation: Sometimes, your dashboard requirement may be for a simple number that requires little or no manipulation, such as *unit sales per day*. In this case, you just count up the sales each day, and no math is required. If you've got a more sophisticated metric such as *sales of $200 or more shipped to EU nations*, you may have to develop an algorithm to look through your sales data, filter the sales by size, and match that up to the information in your shipping logs. This process could be done by hand each day, or the numbers could be typed into a spreadsheet prepopulated with the formulas. However, the best way to do this is with a live database that pulls the numbers from your sales system and your shipping system and does the calculations as well. At this point, you can see how important it is that your various information systems coordinate with each other. It is also critical that you choose systems that give you good access to the data inside them. However, it is unlikely that the system's "canned reports" will provide everything you'll want in your dashboard.

Analysis: So, you've got data, what does it all mean in context? This is where you apply your thresholds. Some of them may be as simple as our temperature gauge example. If sales fall below 2,000 units per day, then ALERT! On the other hand, is there a real difference between 2,001 units and 1,999 units? Maybe that's a single day anomaly? Perhaps you want to issue an alert only if sales drop below 2,000 and *stay* there for three or more days. Another option is to look at the trend. It's one thing if sales dip down to 1,900 units and then trend upward with 1,930 the next day and 1,988 the next; it is entirely another if they fall below 2,000 and continue *declining*. By utilizing a spreadsheet or database, you can build algorithms that alert you to values, trends, or patterns that demand your attention.

Presentation: Finally, your data and alerts need to be formatted and presented to management (that may be just the entrepreneur), in a way that is convenient, attractive, and sensible. This may be a paper report prepared each day or week by your assistant. It may be a spreadsheet full of numbers if you're a data wonk. Some of the best dashboards I've seen are web-enabled spreadsheets or databases. These allow for attractive graphical representations and easy access to your data from anywhere. Many clever young entrepreneurs have the ability to create custom Android or iOS (Apple) apps and gain the comfort of knowing their firm's vital stats are literally in their pocket.

As with everything in the New Entrepreneurial Dynamic, nothing here is set in stone. Your business is a living, breathing organism in a constantly changing environment, and the metrics you need to keep an eye on one year may be different the next. Adaptations could be as simple as pushing out your threshold settings to reflect a growth in sales, or it could be integrating entire new data sources with new calculations. What you do is up to you, but when you ditched the static business plan, you took on the responsibility to maintain rigor via dashboarding. Allowing your dashboard to slip slowly into irrelevancy is akin to not maintaining the safety inspections on an aircraft.

Additionally, some hypotheses that you have tested may be cleared from your dashboard never to be seen again, while some should be continually retested to ensure they are *still valid* in a changing environment. When you create new assumptions or make major changes to your business model, the things that should be measured also change. Komisar and Mullins note, "There's no simple formula for what a dashboard should look like in one company or another, at a given point in time. There's art in their development, and science in their use."[3]

Managing What You Can't Measure

> It is wrong to suppose that if you can't measure it, you can't manage it—a costly myth.
> —*W. Edwards Deming*[4]

The above quote is ironic as the apriorism about measuring being required to manage is often misattributed to W. Edwards Deming. Dr. Deming was an engineer who became the globally recognized master of scientific management. Deming warned against over management and specifically against burdening operations with additional oversight, audits, and paperwork required to track productivity and quality. He noted that it is entirely possible that the work required to gather data might obliterate the gains achieved from managing the process. Some levels of accuracy cannot be obtained, and management must hire professionals and trust them to do their jobs.

What Deming wanted us to do was to establish proven and repeatable methods to achieve quality. He wanted these methods to be based on sound assumptions. In other words, in the absence of measurable data, or where measuring is impractical, make wise choices and stick with them. You may not have the perfect system, but assuming you understand your business, you'll have a good enough one. Recall what you learned from Herbert Simon about satisficing in an earlier chapter.

Writing on school improvement, Deming argues, "Numerical goals accomplish nothing. Ranking and reward of individual people, schools, districts do not improve the system. Only the method is important."[5] So Deming argues that if you understand the theory behind an operation well, you can optimize the method and improve it, even if measuring it closely is inefficient. This is particularly true in a small process that is repeated at great scale, where taking the time to understand the process very well in advance is justifiable but interrupting the process or adding labor to it to measure its outcome is unaffordable. Consequently, certifications like ISO 9000 are aimed at the *reproducibility of processes*; they do not judge the actual efficacy of the operations.

supply chain

A network of external third parties that act together to produce and deliver goods to customers.

W. Edwards Deming

William Edwards Deming was born with the 20th century (October 14, 1900). To a great extent, his singular vision defined excellence in operations during the seminal period in which the modern global **supply chain** developed. Deming grew up on farms in Iowa and Wyoming. He went on to study engineering, math, and physics, eventually earning a PhD from Yale in 1928. He taught statistics at New York University Business School and later at Columbia as well. He became interested in statistical quality control and dedicated himself to making these techniques simpler and more practical.

Deming was particularly interested in making sure that processes were based on data when data were available and on sound theory when it was not. "It is not enough to do your best; you must know what to do, and then do your best," is one of his most repeated admonitions.

Following World War II, Deming took a job with the United States Army to assist General McArthur in conducting a census of the occupied nation of Japan. He found Japanese industry to be eagerly receptive to new methods and worked with the Union of Japanese Scientists and Engineers (JUSE) to help the shattered Japanese economy rebuild. Deming is widely credited as the major inspiration for the Japanese quality revolution that occurred over the next two decades. Companies, such as Toyota, starting with Deming's statistical process model, were able to produce superior products at lower cost than their American peers. These firms rapidly gained global market share and achieved astounding profitability. The Japanese Prime Minister awarded Deming an Imperial medal in 1960, and U.S. President Ronald Reagan presented him with the National Medal of Technology in 1987.

W. Edwards Deming

Source: By FDA - http://www.fda.gov/oc/initiatives/criticalpath/stanski/stanski.html, Public Domain, https://commons.wikimedia.org/w/index.php?curid=3239071

Deming remains highly regarded in Japan and is recognized by JUSE with the "Deming Prize," the world's most prestigious award in what is now known as Total Quality Management. In 1993, he founded the W. Edwards Deming Institute in Washington, D.C. Many of Deming's archive materials are stored in the Library of Congress.

Facilities (or Not)

Since the turn of the millennium, the rapid development of e-commerce and digital virtualization has rendered the concept of a physical location for many businesses as less important or even irrelevant. Still, some types of businesses still require dedicated and often specialized facilities in which to conduct their regular operations. Manufacturing, for instance, is hard to virtualize, though a variety of small manufacturing devices such as 3D printers are creating new options for small operations. Retail sales of highly perishable and time-sensitive items, like the donuts and bagels that morning commuters like to grab on their way to work, are also often facility-dependent.

Keep It at Home or Go Mobile

The 2020 COVID-19 crisis accelerated the trend toward business virtualization by forcing reluctant organizations to test the ability of employees to work from remote locations. Many businesses were pleasantly surprised by the results and made plans to shed offices and cubes.

Traditionally, sales, service, and consulting jobs have long been conducted from home offices. Most B2B businesses learned long ago that dispatching salespeople directly to customer sites from their homes across the country or the globe made more sense than flying them out from a centralized location or opening dozens or hundreds of regional offices. This home-based sales model is scalable from the startup to the enterprise. Many larger corporations even have regional sales managers working from home, supervising sales teams in their areas that are all home-based as well.

Service and repair work can be performed under a similar model. Repairs of office machines and home appliances have long been handled by mobile service personnel, often dispatched from their homes by phone or electronic messaging. This trend is expanding beyond its roots in copier and dishwasher service. Tesla Motors, a constant innovator in the auto industry, has moved much of its lighter repair work, including nonpaint body work from the garage to the driveways of its customers. Why inconvenience the customer and limit your potential service volume by tying it to a physical service bay when any piece of concrete will do as well?

Many independent consultants or small consulting groups flourish in a virtualized environment. Creative individuals often relish the flexibility to work remotely from home or even more idyllic locales. Other than the obviously tempting distractions, there is no reason that most research, interviewing, and report generating work can't be accomplished from a beach cottage or a ski lodge.

In many ways, the hard lessons from COVID-19 have been good lessons for businesspeople. Under the New Entrepreneurial Dynamic, if your startup or small business can avoid the cost and complications of dedicated facilities, it is generally a great idea to do so for as long as possible. Owning property, being locked into leases, and having commitments to physical structures and locations limits your options in reacting to a changing environment.

People often think of restaurants as the classic location-dependent facility. Proximity to diners, visibility, parking, and other factors have played a key role in the success of cafés, pubs, and fine dining establishments for years. Holding such locations even produced a barrier to entry for the competition. How could a restaurant survive without those sources of competitive advantage?

Restaurants are traditionally very location-dependent businesses.

Source: © Shutterstock, Inc.

Under the New Entrepreneurial Dynamic, it is assumed that the environment may change, turning previous location advantages into liabilities. Consider a lunchtime café in Evansville, Indiana, serving the workers of a large factory and its nearby suppliers. An unexpectedly bad year results in the factory being suddenly shuttered and the workforce dispersed to other jobs across the region. A café that owns its property or operates under a five-year lease can't just up and move to a better location when the biggest employer in the neighborhood suddenly shuts down, right? However, a lunch truck can do just that. It is protected against location risks. A lunch truck business is also easier to **scale** than a traditional restaurant; it is easier to add trucks to a fleet than purchase and build out a chain of physical locations.

scale

The process of growing a small enterprise into a large one. A scalable concept is one that is inherently able to grow.

Once again, a crisis highlighted the power of the New Entrepreneurial Dynamic. Food delivery and pickup services boomed, and in fact, many traditional restaurants found their very survival dependent on services like Postmates and Grubhub.

Suitability, Location, and Price

If you cannot or do not wish to virtualize your operation, and you must have a traditional physical location, often referred to as **brick-and-mortar**, you should consider several factors including suitability, cost, and location. Almost all startups lease their offices, storefronts, or small manufacturing facilities. Tying up capital in real estate is a poor choice for a business focused on growth or on returning cash flows to investors. Some mature firms, both large and small, may own their facilities, but for the purposes of this discussion it is presumed that you are leasing property.

brick-and-mortar

Used to describe a building in which a business offers face-to-face services.

A **lease** is simply an agreement between a property owner and the **tenant**, a business owner who desires to rent the property for a specified period. The lease will provide the property exclusively to the tenant for an agreed-upon amount of time, for an agreed-upon amount of rent. The term or length of the lease is typically from one to five years. The rents are usually paid monthly, in advance. The lease will likely include additional down payments. First and last month's rent payments are often required in advance, and there will probably be a **security deposit** that is paid back when the tenant exits and the property is deemed to be in good order.

lease

An agreement between a property owner and the tenant, a business owner who desires to rent the property for a specified period.

tenant

A person who occupies the land and premises of another for a period of time.

security deposit

Money paid to a landlord as a good faith demonstration of intent to take care of the property and collateral against damage to the premises.

leasehold improvements

The amount a landlord will spend to improve the premises so as to encourage and secure occupancy by the tenant.

tenant improvement allowance

Money the landlord may provide to the tenant or deduct from the rent to permit the tenant to make improvements to the property.

tenant improvements

Changes a renter makes to the landlord's property that must be approved in the lease or another agreement.

The suitability of a facility is the measure of its fit to your operations. Is it large enough? Is it appropriately divided into space like offices, manufacturing floor, and warehouses? Does it have sufficient electrical capacity for your manufacturing equipment? Does it offer sufficient parking for both employees and customers? If the facility is lacking in some regard, can changes be made? Will the city allow you to modify the building to accommodate your needs? Such **leasehold improvements** might be part of your demands before signing a lease and required to be undertaken by the owner. Alternatively, the owner may allocate some funds paid to you or discounted from future rents to cover the improvements in what is called a **tenant improvement allowance** (TIA). Finally, the owner may not be willing to pay for improvements but might concede to allow you to make such changes at your own expenses. Changes you make to the owner's property must be approved in the lease or another agreement and are referred to as **tenant improvements**.

Improvements may be paid for by the landlord or the tenant depending on agreements.

Source: © Shutterstock, Inc.

"Location, location, location" has long been the favorite aphorism of the real estate market. This is particularly true for retail establishments. If your customers can't find your store, can't get to it, or won't go there, you don't have a business. Factors that influence the value of a retail sales location include visibility, proximity to customers, transportation access, and neighborhood desirability.

High profile corners or locations in major shopping centers or districts provide the awareness value of advertising along with instant accessibility while that awareness is active. There is no better time for your offering to enter the customer's mind than when they are right outside your location; a sale is just a few steps away. When a shopper sees your brand on the storefront, the odds of them walking in are far higher than if you had spent money on a print or digital ad that required them to journey to your store.

step-up lease

A contract that allows the landlord to increase rent payments over the term of the lease.

Once you've determined a facility is suitable and in a proper location, the remaining issue is simply price! You will likely find that there is no perfect facility. The best building will not be in the best location. The best location will not be affordable. You will need to find the best compromise between all these factors. Remember that your lease payments will be made out of future cash flows. You might be able to convince your landlord that your business will grow and negotiate a **step-up lease**, with rents that start low and then increase when you can afford to pay more.

Most business leases include more complex conditions and esoteric terms, so it is highly recommended that novice entrepreneurs seek the counsel of an experienced friend or colleague during the negotiation process. If you don't have an associate to call on, hire a lawyer to review the lease before signing anything.

Sharing and Saving

Many startups reduce their costs and their commitments by sharing space. Many business **incubators** offer limited office space and other physical amenities startups need to operate while they gather resources and investment. Depending on the organization behind the incubator, these spaces may be provided free of charge or in exchange for equity in the startup. **Colocation** facilities provide similar services to businesses for payment. They also handle all the little issues like utilities, repairs, and cleaning. If your business doesn't really need a full-time conference room and you don't want to clean the breakroom or unclog the toilets, its seriously worth considering these options.

The incubator or colocation environment can be beneficial in other ways. Being in the same space with other entrepreneurs facing similar dilemmas can be encouraging and rewarding. Often colocated businesses recognize synergies. They share experiences, expertise, and networks. It's a great place to find access to suppliers, angel investors, and advisors.

incubator

An organization that helps startup companies by providing essential business services.

colocation

Joining more than one business in a single location.

Manufacturing

Speaking of facilities, no sector of the economy is more facility-dependent than manufacturing, though the nature of their facilities has shifted in response to changes in manufacturing technology. Cottage manufacturers of the middle ages were aggregated into factories during the industrial revolution in order to provide space for new powered machinery and to capture the economies of scale required to fund the purchasing of such expensive capital equipment. From the late eighteenth century onward, the quest for economies of scale has driven a trend toward ever-larger production facilities. Cottage industries became factories, and factories became huge manufacturing centers. Everyone in the supply chain adapted to these environmental shifts, and dynamism was critical to success.

Eventually, entire cities became defined by their industrial focus. In the United States, Detroit was the center for automobile manufacturing in the twentieth century, and it became known as "The Motor City" or "Motown." The major U.S. automakers, including Ford and several firms that later formed General Motors, were all located in the greater Detroit area. The component suppliers for things like brake systems and hydraulic hoses for the auto industry all located in Detroit or other cities along the Great Lakes to be in close proximity to the auto manufacturers.

Enabled by commerce on the Great Lakes, the Motor City became the center of U.S. auto production.

Source: J. A. Dunbar/Shutterstock.com

Recognizing the economic advantages of such regional coordination, the Chinese government has intentionally guided the development of specialized industrial zones to support its export-dependent economy. Under this centralized planning model, cities may specialize in producing commodities from clothing to electronics, and the necessary component manufacturers have located around these hubs. Hundreds of companies working in the Datang area of Zhuji, a city in China's Zhejiang province, produce nearly a third of all the world's socks.[6]

While such a policy provides guidance and support for entrepreneurs, it also limits their options. Datang probably has a lot of young people who don't find the sock business very exciting, and somewhere in Shanghai a young lady might have an obsession with making innovative socks. While a determined entrepreneur can do anything, people's options are constrained by this centralized planning.

factors of production

Inputs needed to create a product or service.

finished product

A product that is ready for sale or distribution.

value-add

An additional amount, above the cost of the materials, that provides funding for the manufacturing process, the distributor, and the retailer.

Manufacturing businesses are firms that get paid to make things. To be more technical, manufacturers add value through a process of modifying and combining **factors of production** in order to produce a **finished product** that they sell to other businesses or individual consumers. Factors of production (or factor inputs) are the raw materials or components that the manufacturer uses to build whatever product it is making. Aircraft manufacturers buy aluminum sheets, jet engines, and electronic assemblies to build airplanes. Clothing factories buy cloth, thread, zippers, and buttons to make shirts and dresses. Window makers buy silicon sand to melt down into glass.

The special skills, facilities, and processes the manufacturer has gathered allow them to charge customers more than the price of the materials they have purchased. Perhaps some lawyer in Spain makes her own dresses because she enjoys the craft. A dedicated, trained workforce of sewers in a factory equipped with commercial cutting and sewing equipment can do the job faster than a home sewer. And although the home seamstress doesn't have to pay herself, she does incur opportunity costs on her own work. She could be doing something other than sewing a dress and getting paid for that work. If buying a dress lets her focus on her legal career, it makes economic sense to pay a significant premium for ready to wear clothes. In fact, few of us are skilled enough or possess the right equipment to make our own clothes quickly and with professional-grade results. It would cost us a lot to develop those skills and buy proper tools and sewing machines. This **value-add**, the additional amount above the cost of the materials, funds the manufacturer, the clothing distributor, and the retailer where the consumer shops.

Supply Chain Management

Professional manufacturers have an additional important source of advantage over their less sophisticated competitors, **supply chain management (SCM)**. Can you think of what SCM might be? Consider the cost and source of sewing materials. Would our Spanish home sewer from the last section pay the same price as the factory does for her sewing materials? Would she have access to the same variety of choices? She is probably limited to what is available in a few retail sewing supply stores. The factory, on the other hand, buys directly from textile mills and component manufacturers around the world. They buy in massive quantities to capture economies of scale, and they have dedicated professional buyers who are experts in negotiating purchases. They may be large enough to specify the actual items to be produced, such as custom-designed prints and buttons in the size, shape, and color to match. While our amateur seamstress may enjoy the quality and joy of her own work, she can't compete with that advantage economically.

supply chain management (SCM)

The science of efficiently managing the factor inputs to production in a business.

Graham Stevens described the objective of supply chain management as an effort "to synchronize the requirements of the customer with the flow of materials from suppliers in order to effect a balance between what are often seen as conflicting goals of high customer service, low inventory management, and low unit cost."[7] Experts in SCM ensure that factories get the best price and the best quality materials exactly when they need them. Keeping your onsite supply of materials low reduces business capital tied up in that inventory and is an important process known as **just-in-time (JIT)** inventory management. JIT can also reduce facility space requirements for supply storage and the time spent in handling that inventory in warehousing.

just-in-time (JIT)

An inventory management strategy that ensures factor inputs to manufacturing are synchronized with production to reduce capital tied up in onsite supplies.

TQM, Continuous Improvement, ISO 9000, Six Sigma

Optimizing the process of manufacturing a product is both an art and a science in manufacturing. Experienced manufacturing experts know how to redesign products for production and set up the workflow to get them made. These experts are known as **production engineers**. Production engineering is the process of taking a design and making it into something that can be manufactured in an efficient and reliable manner. Just because you can build one unit of something doesn't mean it is put together in the manner best suited to producing millions of units reliably. Reducing the **part count** or the number of components in the product, the labor involved in assembling them, and removing uncertainty and likely points of failure from the process are all essential to competitive manufacturing.

production engineers

Experts skilled in redesigning products for mass production and the setup of the workflow required to make them most efficiently.

part count

The number of components required to build a product. Reducing part count often reduces material costs and assembly time in the manufacturing process.

Scientific management techniques ensure production quality and efficiency in a modern factory.

Source: © Shutterstock, Inc.

total quality management (TQM)

A process of detecting and improving errors in manufacturing and improving employee skills to ensure positive outcomes for customers.

continuous improvement process (CIP)

A system of incremental improvements where processes are constantly evaluated and improved to increase speed and quality of production.

Designing processes for building a product efficiently and consistently was an obsession with twentieth-century managers. Experts like W. Edwards Deming introduced scientific thinking to what had been a craft, and entirely new disciplines like **total quality management (TQM)** and **continuous improvement process (CIP)** emerged. TQM works to ensure that the quality of production is consistent, and the goal of CIP is to see that it is incrementally improving based on feedback from quality controls. Formal programs exist to train managers and to certify that production systems are consistent and have very low rates of defects.

ISO 9000 is a set of published standards from the International Standards Organization, and third-party companies use it to certify that manufacturing processes adhere to a set of specific requirements defined in the ISO 9000 standard. It has been a globally popular standard, but it is important to understand that the standard is more about consistency of processes involved in making a product and ensures that the product itself is useful or of high quality.

Six Sigma, a popular quality-improvement program, is a statistically driven process developed at Motorola in the 1980s. Six Sigma seeks to reduce defect rates of a process to the statistically insignificant level of one in 3.4 million, significantly improving customer experiences and reducing manufacturing costs. The Six Sigma "Black Belt" has become an extremely popular certification for production managers around the world.

In addition to quality and cost, safety is a paramount consideration in the design and operation of manufacturing systems. The factory environment is often a place filled with powered machinery, sharp edges, and potentially hazardous materials. Every entrepreneur and manager has an ethical obligation to take reasonable steps to ensure that the people producing their products are safe from harm during their work and that their operation does not present a threat to the surrounding community. From a purely self-interested standpoint, injuries disrupt production and cost factories time and money.

Beyond that, the consequences of injuries include potential liability for medical expenses and compensation for suffering or disabilities resulting from work injuries. In many countries, government regulators provide strict oversight over the health and safety of production environments. In the United States, the Occupational Safety and Health Administration (OSHA) may levy fines or close facilities that they find are not in compliance with worker safety regulations. Some individual states and even municipalities have their own safety regulations and enforcement agencies. Be sure you are familiar with the regulations that apply in your country and region. Again, there are professionals in this area, and entrepreneurs should consider hiring a consultant with experience to help them design their process and provide a formal safety plan for dealing with accidents when they occur.

New Manufacturing Technologies Yield Strategic Advantage

Some manufacturers have recently made bold attempts to capture enormous economies of scale, such as the "Gigafactory" Elon Musk built to drive down the cost of battery packs for his Tesla automotive company. Located outside of Reno, Nevada, the Gigafactory is huge and highly automated. The building is designed to have the largest footprint of any on earth. Suppliers can operate within the massive facility, reducing logistical challenges and costs. For instance, Japan's Panasonic produces the cells for Tesla's battery packs right inside the facility, saving the time and expense of shipping these components across the Pacific. While some factories may be getting huge, there is also a boom in small scale production and even the reemergence of the cottage model. Can you think of why?

Aided by continuous improvements in underlying technologies, automated manufacturing tools have become smaller, more affordable, and easier to use. Sophisticated machines like automated routers, laser, etchers, and embroidery machines are now suitable for operating in the smallest of businesses and even home use. Startups are using this equipment to win deals in specialized niches across the economy.

The boom in additive manufacturing (aka 3D printing) has driven a revolution in the production of prototypes and small volume parts. Many plastic printers are suitable for home operation and have become popular tools for those in the Maker Movement. **Makers** are folks interested in new production techniques and systems for fun, education, and sometimes for profit. In a 2017 paper, Sofia Papavlasopoulou, Michail N. Giannakos, and Letizia Jaccheri described the maker culture as "a philosophy in which individuals or groups of individuals create artifacts that are recreated and assembled using software and/or physical objects."[8] Makers share ideas online and work from home or from a **makerspace**. Makerspaces are shared facilities that provide access to the equipment needed for small scale production. A popular magazine, *Make*, focused on this phenomenon. And an event catering to the makers, Makerfaire, flourished in the late 2000s and early 2010s.

makers

Makers are part of a growing movement built around the fabrication of physical objects; many of them are dedicated to restoring cottage industry manufacturing.

makerspace

A place where individuals come together to work on projects of mutual interest.

Makerspace, Sydney, Australia

Source: haireena/Shutterstock.com

During the COVID-19 pandemic of 2020, thousands of makers across the world produced a huge volume of personal protective equipment (PPE), including 3D printed frames for face shields and masks. Working from quarantine at home, they produced engineering prototypes and sold a variety of items online, including jewelry, game pieces, kitchen utensils, and decorative items.

This philosophy has expanded to some unlikely industries, including aerospace. A variety of manufacturers producing products from drones to satellites have used small scale automation to compete with big-name players. Relativity Space, a startup founded by two millennials, has raised $175 million to 3D print orbital class rockets and has ambitions to print them on Mars someday.

Outsourcing and Offshoring Manufacturing

contract manufacturer

A firm that produces products for other companies to market.

Today, Hon Hai Precision Manufacturing, a Taiwanese firm better known as Foxconn, operates a facility commonly referred to as Foxconn City in Shenzhen, China. This massive factory employs nearly half a million workers, more than two hundred thousand of whom live full time in dormitories within the facility. Hon Hai is a **contract manufacturing** firm that produces products for other companies to market and then sell. You've probably never heard of Hon Hai or Foxconn City, but the odds are you own something made there. The majority of Apple's products, including the iPhone, are made there or at other Foxconn facilities in China. Hon Hai also produces laptops, phones, and other products for most global consumer electronics brands.

Products for Apple and other global electronic brands are made here at Foxconn City, Shenzhen, China.

Source: Greg Autry

More importantly, Hon Hai doesn't just make a product that Apple designed in a process that Apple specified. Rather, Hon Hai manages production engineering for Apple products. Hon Hai's customers work closely with the firm to take their prototype designs for new gizmos and rework them so they will flow off a massive assembly line faster, cheaper, and better.

The production engineering process might involve decisions like replacing the screws that hold the case together with snap-together joints to simplify manual labor or allow for automation. Making that change might require changing the outline of the circuit board near the snap joints. That may require relocating the chips on the board and rerouting the wires that connect to it. A contract manufacturer might suggest changing out some material, such as the plastic on a case, to one that is simpler to source, cheaper to buy, or easier to handle in production. Firms like Hon Hai have amazing experience in this and add significant value to the final product. They may actually contribute 5 percent to 15 percent of the final design of the brand name products you use.

How could your startup ever compete with that sort of scale advantage? The answer is that you don't have to! Why compete with the power of outsourced manufacturing when you can leverage it? As previously noted, Apple is not the only customer at Foxconn City. Apple's huge volume supports the economies of scale, but much of their production comes in waves centered around Apple's new product introduction cycles. That means Hon Hai has extra capacity to accommodate other products. Beyond Hon Hai, there are thousands of other contract manufacturers across East Asia, eager to bid on making your gizmos at the lowest possible price. Today, the vast majority of global consumer goods and a great deal of B2B hardware come out of these contract manufacturing facilities.

Handing over your manufacturing to an outsider and often offshore firm does not come without challenges. Among these challenges is a lack of direct oversight into the process, which can result in surprises involving delivery dates, quality, and the nature of your products. Often a contract manufacturer may get a bigger and more important gig and put off your production to accommodate it, leaving you and your customers waiting. Getting your contract right, including penalties for late deliveries, is important. Sometimes what you get shipped from China isn't exactly what you expected, and if that is a full sea container of product, it may be too late to change it. Getting little things just right, like colors, may involve you flying across the ocean fairly regularly.

A classic problem associated with contract manufacturing is **quality fade**. In this situation, your manufacturing partner starts out doing everything just right but slowly makes adjustments in materials or their processes to save money, and that may result in unexpected problems for you or your customer. For instance, a company making stainless steel shower squeegees was very pleased with the initial samples and ordered thousands of units from their factory partner in China. At some point, an individual in the factory figured they could save a penny or two per unit by substituting cheaper nonstainless screws into the handle. Nobody could see the difference, but months later, hundreds of customers began to return rusting squeegees and posting angry, negative reviews online showing the damage the rust had caused to their showers and tubs. There is no way to fix that sort of loss or damage to your reputation caused by someone else's penny-pinching.

quality fade

The gradual reduction in quality of manufactured output from a contract manufacturer, often caused by unapproved component substitutions and other actions of the manufacturer to reduce their costs.

Another unfortunately common problem is pirating of products. Many firms have discovered that their own contract manufacturing partner will take their proprietary designs and simply start making copies of it for sale through other channels and even directly to competitors in their market. Sometimes individuals in the factory will copy the tooling and process and set up their own line and ship the product into a different international market or just start selling it on Alibaba. These counterfeit products are a source of constant irritation and sometimes a threat to the survival of firms that only design products and outsource manufacturing. If you keep your manufacturing internal to your firm it is harder, though not impossible, for counterfeiters to effectively **reverse engineer** and copy your gear.

reverse engineer

The process of disassembling a product and analyzing its construction in order to duplicate it.

Enforcing your trade secrets and even U.S. or European patents against a company in China is an exercise in frustration. Their courts and local authorities are seldom willing to see a foreign firm win such a contest over a domestic competitor. You can purchase insurance against counterfeiting, and the companies that provide it will go after U.S. distributors and retailers that sell your products, but controlling the online marketplace is very difficult.

You can find contract manufacturers by searching online. In fact, if you simply put up a website featuring a manufactured product, you will soon find your email inbox and LinkedIn message box filled with offers from China and Vietnam. However, it is strongly recommended that you reduce your risk by using only firms that provide solid, verifiable references. Find a friend or colleague who has some years of experience with contract manufacturing and ask for their recommendation. If you don't know anyone, make meeting them a priority. Attend conferences or webinars on manufacturing or join an industry organization. Find someone whose product line is similar enough to yours that their manufacturing advice will be useful but not a direct competitor in your market who might feel conflicted in helping you. For instance, if you are going to make a new electronic keyboard for the music market, a company that makes a line of computer keyboards might be able to help you find a manufacturer. Once you've found the right factory, you can ship them a sample or two along with your CAD files, schematics, etc. and get a bid on pricing and timing. After you agree to terms, you'll usually receive a series of prototypes before actual production begins. However, as noted previously, it is probably worth your time to fly over and inspect things before the factory ramps up production.

Counterfeit markets are common in much of Asia.

Source: hkhtt hj/Shutterstock.com

During recent decades, manufacturing activity declined in the United States, Europe, and Japan as a percentage of economic activity. However, higher-end product manufacturing still flourishes in these nations. Luxury automobiles, airplanes, military equipment, and spacecraft are examples of manufacturing markets where these countries have maintained dominance. Statista reports that in 2019 the top five luxury car brands in the U.S. market were BMW, Mercedes-Benz, Lexus, Audi, and Tesla.[9] All of these cars are manufactured in North America, Europe, or Japan. American Boeing and European Airbus still rule the international commercial airliner market, though China's state-owned enterprises are seeking an entry point into the lower end of that market. Large firms like Boeing and Toyota (Lexus) support a sizable network of suppliers who manufacture assemblies and components for their aircraft and automobiles in domestic and foreign factories. These suppliers often make products for many different firms, including smaller startups.

domestic manufacturing

Production done in the firm's home nation.

Where margins are high, quality is paramount, and close connections between the designer and the factory are desired, **domestic manufacturing** is still often preferred. For instance, you will still find sewing shops manufacturing high-end fashion and designer denim jeans in Los Angeles, California, one of the world's most expensive and highly regulated labor markets.

FIGURE 12.2 Japan's Manufacturing Value Added as a Percentage of GDP (1981–2017)
Manufacturing has been in decline in Japan for a generation.

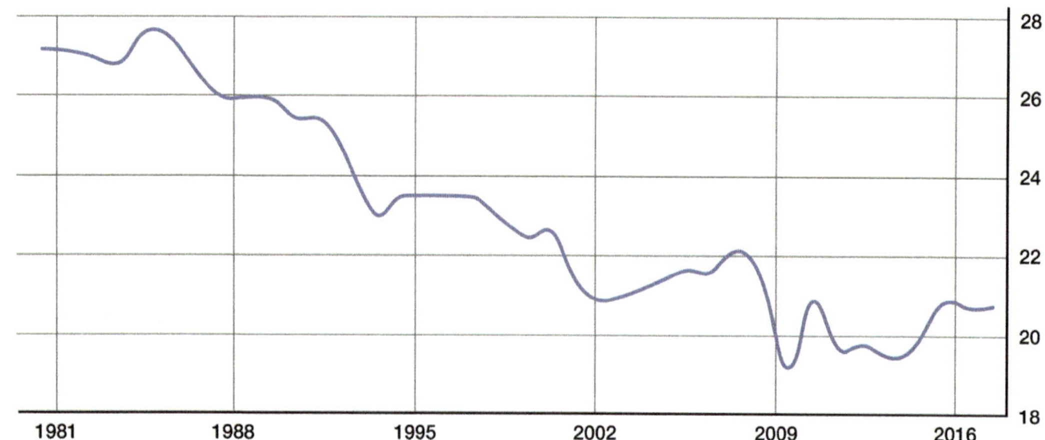

Source: Trading Economics https://tradingeconomics.com/japan/manufacturing-value-added-percent-of-gdp-wb-data.html

If your product, or at least the initial target market, doesn't require massive volumes and your margins are high enough to support it, having a manufacturing partner within driving distance can be a real advantage. This is particularly true for first-generation products where you may be tweaking the design constantly with iterative improvements.

Logical Outsourcing

Making things is one thing; selling them, delivering them, and servicing them is another entirely. The skills involved in consistently producing a quality product at a low price are not the same as those required for business development and distribution. The capital and human resources dedicated to manufacturing do not leverage these other business functions. An expensive 3D printer is of no value in managing inventories or shipping. A chief operations officer who is an expert at manufacturing is unlikely to be competitively skilled in these other domains. Purchases of sales automation tools and shipping robots must necessarily reduce investment in your core manufacturing operations, presenting a difficult choice to a cash-strapped startup. What can be done?

The big firms and their partners are already doing this. If you order an iPhone or laptop from Apple's website, it will be manufactured, packaged, and individually shipped via FedEx from Shenzhen, China. Your new Apple product will arrive at your doorstep without seeing the inside of any Apple facility and without any Apple employee ever touching it! By leveraging business partnerships such as these, Apple can focus entirely on its core competencies of designing great products and maintaining one of the world's most highly respected brands.

Does this leave a startup at an insurmountable disadvantage? Again, the answer is "no." **Logistical outsourcing** of this nature is commonly available to businesses of any size. Thousands of regional firms around the world will warehouse your inventory and ship it to your customers in a process commonly known as **fulfillment services**. In some cases, the fulfillment service may handle online or phone order taking as well.

logistical outsourcing

A service that provides for warehousing and transit of products for product companies.

fulfillment services

An outsourced service that handles the management of physical product inventory, delivery, returns, and other customer-related services.

The largest fulfillment services are run by e-commerce giants like Amazon and Alibaba. Under its "Fulfilled by Amazon," or FBA, service, the e-commerce giant leverages economies of scale to provide smaller firms a world-class platform. FBA provides entrepreneurs with order taking, automated warehouses, and shipping rates negotiated with the advantages of their massive volume. In fact, unless the shopper looks closely at the product advertisement, they often believe that the product is actually an Amazon sale. Of course, there is a cost to the service; Amazon charges a small monthly fee (currently about $40/month) and takes about 15 percent of each sale for being on their platform. They then charge you for shipping and handling, but this will likely be less than what it would cost your startup to manage that process, and shipping fees are often paid by your buyer. You will encounter additional fees when customers return or exchange products.

A fulfilled by Amazon (FBA) product.

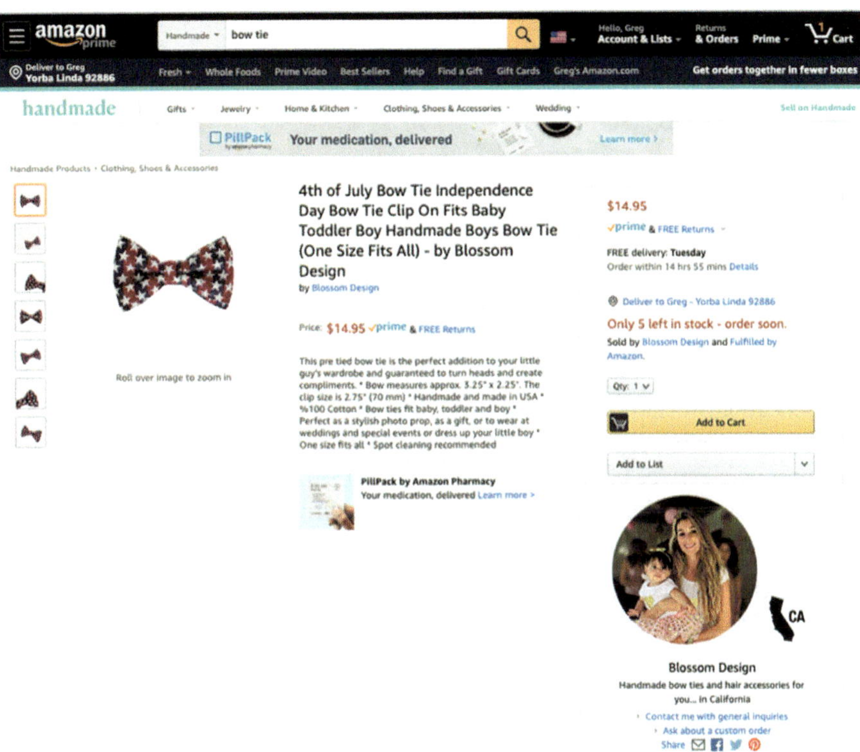

Source: Author's screenshot of Amazon page https://www.amazon.com/July-Independence-Clip-Toddler-Handmade/dp/B07DK6M7WP/ref=sr_1_21

Outsourcing logistics is excellent idea for any startup and for most small businesses. A key component of the New Entrepreneurial Dynamic is maintaining focus on your sources of competitive advantage. Unless storing, packing, and shipping are what differentiates your firm, leave those mundane tasks to the experts.

Service and Retailing

While recent environmental trends have entrepreneurs challenging every business assumption, as already noted, some retail sales and service businesses still effectively exploit the advantages of physical locations. Regardless of whether your business is virtualized or a brick-and-mortar operation, a number of important factors are specific to retailing.

Maintain Consistency

As you learned in previous chapters, building a brand requires consistent messaging. Your retail location, real or virtual, is much the same. The user's shopping experience must be consistent. Have you noticed that while the displays are constantly updated, the basic layout of your local supermarket never changes? The bakery and bread stay on one side of the vast expanse, and the produce stays on the other. You instinctively know where to find the soda and the toilet paper.

abandoned cart

When an e-commerce customer adds items to their shopping cart but abandons the website before completing the purchase.

As you may recall from our discussion of satisficing in an earlier chapter, people value their time and seek to optimize their search time when making purchases. Consequently, they value the consistency of their shopping experience. You cannot depend on your customers to invest the time to track you down at a new location (or URL) or to navigate new store layouts (real or virtual) in order to make purchases. If your website reboot caused your buyers to take more than a few seconds to track down what they want on their phone, they may just take an incoming call, and you end up with an **abandoned cart**.

Customer Satisfaction

Consistency is a fundamental driver of satisfaction. Can you think of others? A highly cited Danish study[10] on customer satisfaction and loyalty across several industries suggested that image was the strongest driver in determining both customer satisfaction and customer loyalty. Essentially, customers wanted to feel good about their choices, so branding and marketing are important. However, product quality factored significantly for food products, and customer service was an important factor for banks, fast-food restaurants, and telephone service providers.

A 2002 publication in the European Journal of Operational Research[11] concluded that good service performance was the second most important driver of customer satisfaction in retail, and more importantly, *poor service performance was the most significant driver of dissatisfaction*. The "retail experience" was the other critical component. This driver included the store layout (attractiveness, consistency) as well as the service component of the sale.

Given these insights, it is clear that customer service, at the point of sale and after, is the most actionable driver of satisfaction in the retail business. To ensure good service, you need to understand the factors customers value, be able to measure them, and act on them. The following four factors are nearly always at the top of any list of customer service deliverables.

Response time: Customers value their own time and want to be serviced promptly. When they have problems, they want quick solutions. Poor response time is usually resolved by increasing the customer service staff. Additionally, optimizing the script and process the staff use and training them to handle customers with alacrity can help.

Communications: The quality of verbal and written exchanges is a critical satisfier in customer relationships. It is particularly important that customers feel they are being listened to, not spoken at, and that the business actually understands their *unique* problem. Problems with communications may be based on the skills of the customer service staff. Hiring for communication abilities is critical in this role. It has been common for firms to offshore call center work to locations where labor is cheaper. This solution risks customer frustration when language and cultural barriers hinder clear and quick communications. Good training for customer service staff is mandatory as well.

Empathy: Once quality communications are established, the customer must feel that the firm and the individual servicing them care about the situation. All too often, customer service staff have seen the same issues over and over, and they therefore tend to treat these concerns as commonplace. For the customer, their problem is new, immediate, and irritating, and they are put off by a casual response. They want a sense of concern for their particular circumstance and a sense of urgency in resolving it. Hiring empathetic individuals to handle customer services is key. Training for empathy is difficult, and you cannot order staff to be empathetic. They may try, but customers respond very negatively to insincerity.

Professionalism: The customer wants to believe that the customer service system at your firm is properly managed, and the staff are trained and empowered to resolve issues for them and are supported by management. An unfortunately common behavior among retail customer service staff is that they overempathize at the individual level and may suggest they are making special accommodations for the customer outside the policies of the firm as in, "The management doesn't want us to do this, but I'm going to replace your item for you without the receipt." This brings the customer into a conspiracy with the staff member positioning the firm as an opponent, exactly what you do not want to occur. The better response is, "It is our store policy that a receipt is required, but our company values your business and will be happy to make an exception."

TABLE 12.1 Customer Service Factors

Factor	Metric	Action
Response Time	Average Response Time, Observation	Increase Staff, Train
Communications	Survey	Hire Right, Train
Empathy	Survey	Hire Right
Professionalism	Survey, Observation	Train

Source: Greg Autry

Measuring average response time online or in a call center is easily accomplished with software. In a brick-and-mortar operation, you can use observers to clock response times. For both telephone and in-person service, observers can also monitor professionalism. However, it is important to note that the mere presence of such observers tends to motivate staff to perform better. This biases the observations, but it also inherently improves the customer experience, which is why professional call centers randomly record or monitor customer calls.

Customer surveys are usually the go-to tool for evaluation of customer service experiences. Customer service surveys are often conducted digitally via a web link from an email or app. Typically they will present a small number of questions in Likert format, where the customer is asked to select from a scale of "Strongly Agree" to "Strongly Disagree" or "Very Positive" to "Very Negative." The five-item Likert scale is most common, and one is shown in Table 12.2.

TABLE 12.2 Typical Customer Survey Using a Five-Item Likert Scale

The staff member who assisted me was:	**Strongly Disagree**	**Disagree**	**Neutral**	**Agree**	**Strongly Agree**
Responsive	☐	☐	☐	☐	☐
Courteous	☐	☐	☐	☐	☐
Professional	☐	☐	☐	☐	☐
Able to resolve my issue	☐	☐	☐	☐	☐
Please tell us more about your experience:					

Source: Greg Autry

Some survey designers prefer a four-item scale that removes the neutral option, forcing all respondents to express an opinion. Others will use a continuous slider to allow respondents to be more nuanced in their ratings.

Surveys come with a bias in that customers with the most extreme experiences or predispositions will take the time to respond. Consequently, survey results tend to be bifurcated into the very negative and very positive camps. It can be difficult to get the average customer to respond. It is usually advisable to have a senior customer service representative or the business owner, if the firm is small, follow up on negative customer surveys. Customers whose comments express genuine complaints in a professional manner expect a response; those that resort to vitriolic anger are probably best left alone.

Key Takeaways

- The best technology and the greatest business model are useless in the absence of competent execution.
- A business dashboard is the most important tool for management insights into execution.
- Selecting an accounting system that fits your operations is critical.
- A cloud-based system is the right choice for most startups.
- Establishing good processes and executing on them consistently can fill in where data are not available.
- Physical locations offer both competitive advantages and liabilities that must be built into your plan.
- Plan for the location your business is going to need, not the one sufficient for today.
- A well-managed supply chain is a very important source of competitive advantage.
- Startups can compete with big firms by carefully leveraging outsourcing.
- Customer service is as important as sales.
- Focus is the key to operational excellence.

12.2 Managing Growth

Learning Objectives

1. Understand that for most startups, growth is an exploitable assumption.
2. Understand that desirable leadership qualities vary with the size and growth rate of the firm.
3. Learn techniques for maximizing cash flow.
4. Understand how strategic, rather than tactical, recruitment supports long-term growth.

> My popularity, my happiness and sense of worth depend to no small extent upon my skill in dealing with people.
>
> —*Dale Carnegie*[12]

Planning to Grow Dynamically

The New Entrepreneurial Dynamic is all about adapting to and exploiting change. Some changes are unanticipated external events like the 2001 terror attacks, the 2008 financial crisis, and the 2020 COVID-19 pandemic. Such **black swan events** are difficult to plan for, but building dynamic capabilities is always the answer in preparing for them. One change you can count on, however, is the growth of your own organization. For most startups, growth is not optional, at least in the beginning. If your firm can't reach breakeven and survive without growing, you might as well build growth into your plans.

black swan events

Rare events that occur without warning, have a major impact, and which in hindsight appear to have been foreseeable.

As has been already noted, growth impacts your choices of facilities and accounting systems. Beyond that, your growth will change your cost structure, usually for the better, by engaging economies of scale in both your cost of goods sold (COGS) and your overhead costs. Growth will also change the internal culture of your firm and the nature of its external relationships. Fast-growing startups and bigger firms attract the attention of the public, and that is usually good. Vendors are eager to support firms they see as on the way up. Customers view firm growth as a reinforcement of their good choices. However, you will also catch the eye of some folks you might rather not encounter, including competitors, regulators, and aggressive lawyers.

A Leader for Each Phase of the Growth Firm

Different sized organizations need different resources at all levels, including leadership. Many young entrepreneurs are shocked to find themselves replaced at the organizations they founded. The most famous case of this phenomena was the firing of Apple founder, Steve Jobs, by the firm's board of directors, a decade after he founded the iconic computer startup.

Venture capitalists are notorious for doing this and with good reason. Randy Komisar writes in his book *The Monk and Riddle*, "Silicon Valley veterans share a tacit understanding that what a startup needs isn't one CEO, but three—each at successive stages of the startups development." Each of these CEOs has very different traits and competencies. Komisar uses dog breeds as a metaphor to describe them. He sees the first CEO as "the retriever," capable of finding the product, the initial team, and money. The second CEO is "the bloodhound," who must find the actual customers. The third CEO is "the husky," who is there to pull the established company for the long haul.

The CEO who runs an established firm is the equivalent of the husky.

Source: © Shutterstock, Inc.

It turns out the young Steve Jobs was a retriever. Jobs found a genius engineer, Steve Wozniak, gathered money, and built a new type of computer. That was great for the nascent Apple Computer. However, as Apple matured, the young entrepreneur failed to identify viable markets for Apple's increasingly sophisticated machines. Additionally, his aggressive and disruptive personality, which had been well suited for quick deal-making in a small startup, alienated many of the career professionals brought in to run the multi-million-dollar corporation his startup had become.

A decade later, he returned to the firm as a more mature and nuanced leader capable of being the bloodhound Apple lacked. Jobs quickly identified opportunities in digital music, smartphones, and tablets and led Apple to global dominance in each of those product categories. Today, Apple CEO Tim Cook is the husky that has pulled Jobs' proven products and business model during the most profitable corporate decade in history.

It's important not to let your ego decide if you are the rare individual who can lead a firm through all these phases. It's perfectly fine to discover that you like being the retriever, always launching new organizations and then stepping aside when the paperwork and bureaucracy get burdensome. Handing the firm over to the bloodhound and the husky and reaping the rewards of their hard work as a stockholder isn't a bad deal. You can stay on as chief technology officer or use your profits to fund a bold new venture of your own.

Inventory Management and Cash Flow

cash flow

Money that passes in and out of a business.

Chapter 14 looks closely at **cash flow**, but for now, it is important to understand that growing firms need all the ready cash they can get to fund growth. Money invested in equipment, inventory, or employees needs to be laser-focused on producing quick returns. Machinery that isn't operational, products sitting around on the shelves, and employees in training aren't generating revenues for you. A key operational job for a manager is to reduce the amount of money tied up in resources and keep those resources as productive as possible. Can you think of some good ways that good managers do that?

The best way to keep cash in hand is not to spend it. Seriously, if you don't need something, holding on to your cash until you do gives your firm the flexibility to spend it *where* you need, *when* the opportunity arises. As the popular business aphorism goes, "Cash is king." That available money is called **working capital**, and maximizing it is core to the New Entrepreneurial Dynamic.

working capital

The money a company uses to fund operations.

It takes money to make money; firms need working capital.

Source: © Shutterstock, Inc.

If you do need something, it's always good if you don't have to pay for it. I'm not suggesting you steal it. I am suggesting you find a way to use the resource now and pay for it later, out of the profits you earned using it. That is why most equipment can be leased, and your inventory can be financed. As long as you expect your increased earnings generated from the purchase to exceed the interest you pay to finance it, it's likely a good choice to hold on to your own cash for other purposes.

Another great way to improve cash flow is to get folks to give you money for nothing. Again, I am not suggesting fraud, but rather getting paid *now* for delivering the goods *later*. A lot of great businesses operate on the upfront payment model, online retailers being a prime example. Though they usually ship products quickly, they usually take your money before they place the order with another firm. Getting their funds in, including the profits before generating any cost of goods sold, is a **negative working capital** model, and it is the dream of any corporate CFO. Amazon has developed negative working capital into an art. Often the items you purchase as "Fulfilled by Amazon" are already sitting on consignment in the Amazon warehouse, but Amazon doesn't pay the supplier for it until *after* they have the customer's funds in hand. Suppliers and customers finance Amazon's growth.

negative working capital

A situation in which the firm receives funds before having to expend them on product production or delivery of a service.

If you do have to run a more traditional working capital model that involves purchasing inventory, selling to customers, and then waiting for your payments, the key is not to wait too long. Carefully managing the accounts receivable and knowing how to incentivize customers to pay early and how to lean on them without losing them are skills every account manager should acquire. Always look at your accounts receivable aging report with an eye to the reliability and the importance of each customer who owes you. If they get behind in payments and you feel they may be in financial trouble or aren't critical to your business, lean on them hard. If they are big, stable customers who are just taking advantage of you, find a way to incentivize them to pay with the offer of a discount or some extra service. When the economy gets tough, many businesses get slow to pay, and many will fail. Be extra vigilant the moment you sense a recession coming on or a downturn brewing in your sector.

The Challenge with Staffing

Along with equipment and supplies, the biggest expense for most firms is labor. Maximizing the value of employees and specifically their ability to generate revenues for the firm is critical to maintaining strong cash flow. A good dashboard measurement of this would-be revenue per employee measured as something like sales per day/employee headcount. A key strategy is to focus your investment in human resources on employees who generate sales and deliver the goods and minimize overhead employees in administrative positions that run your bureaucracy. This isn't to say that you don't need accountants, human resource staff, and regulatory compliance officers, but they cost you money every month and do not directly produce any.

For a nascent startup, the staffing required to accommodate growth can be very daunting. If you're a sole founder, hiring your first employee will double your head count. It's likely you're not paying yourself well (or at all), so the impact to costs will be huge. On the other hand, a large firm may hire several employees a day, and it will be nearly invisible on their income statement. The New Entrepreneurial Dynamic will encourage you to find ways to use contractors and consultants at first, rather than employees. Contractors can be paid on performance; their contracts can be terminated swiftly, and they don't require the plethora of governmental paperwork and taxes that are associated with having employees.

Many entrepreneurs are reactionary. They wait until they *must* hire someone before doing so and then hire the person best suited to address their immediate, tactical concerns. This process often results in suboptimal choices that are not aligned with the firm's long-term strategic needs. You should forecast hiring and consider running a continual hiring process where you are always looking for good candidates. Network with your peers and friends and find individuals working for your competitors or elsewhere who admire your business model. Stay in contact with them until an opportunity arises, and then hire from this pool of pre-vetted candidates. In this manner, you can always be prepared to address a crisis by hiring an individual you know will be well suited to growing your company over time.

Managing Organizational Culture

Have you noticed that every firm, every sports team, every nonprofit, has its own feel? Have you noticed how these organizations attract a certain type of person, or maybe that individuals actually adapt themselves to the organizational culture when they join? All organizations have a culture, and they appear to be fairly permanent artifacts. Many management and psychological studies have verified this perspective. More importantly, the culture in a business impacts the financial performance of the firm. In a 2001 article in the *Journal of Management Development*, Golnaz Sadri and Brian Lees conclude, "A positive culture can provide a significant competitive advantage."[13] That's great if your culture is, as the authors suggest, "consistent with the environment in which the organization operates."

That fit between the firm and its environment is central to the New Entrepreneurial Dynamic. Where does an organizational culture come from? To a great extent, organizational culture is a manifestation of its founder(s). The founding team and early employees in an organization generally come from the network of the founder(s). If he or she likes an aggressive risk-taking posture, the organization usually develops along those lines with a brash culture. On the other hand, if the founder is cautious, methodical, and thoughtful, the organization is likely to be quieter.

Organizational cultures do not have to develop randomly. They can be consciously established. Most importantly, they can be intentionally managed to suit an evolving environment. Sadri and Lees note:

While it is best to establish a positive culture with which employees can identify during an organization's infancy, it is possible to change an existing culture. Such change is best accomplished by modeling desired behavior at all levels of management and by planning events that foster frequent interaction among cross-functional employees.

When management chooses to act in a particular way, employees will emulate that. Such intentional behaviors might include always being highly respectful of customers, being environmentally conscious, or being tolerant of failure in new ventures. For example, if you want your employees to treat your customers like royalty when you are not watching, you must always do so yourself, even when you encounter a customer whose demands or behavior wears on your patience. If you want them to be good environmental stewards, you have to make visible economic sacrifices in that effort yourself. If you want your managers to encourage your employees to be risk-takers and try new things, you cannot punish them when these risks don't pan out. Organized events and training sessions can reinforce organizational values like these.

Remember that for a firm seeking optimal financial performance, the goal should be to develop a culture that best fits your market. This is not necessarily the culture that will emerge as a reflection of the entrepreneur's personality or ideology, factors that often shape how organizations view the world. Be honest with yourself about that and diligent in your intentional development of organizational culture.

However, while profits are necessary, the New Entrepreneurial Dynamic recognizes that maximizing them is not the only reason people start and run businesses. No entrepreneur should feel *compelled* to sacrifice their personal integrity in defining culture, nor must they concede to the societal whims of the moment. The choice between your values and profits may occasionally be a difficult one.

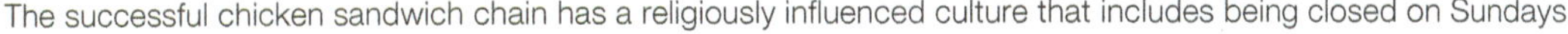

The successful chicken sandwich chain has a religiously influenced culture that includes being closed on Sundays.

Source: DW labs Incorporated/Shutterstock.com

Samuel Truett Cathy, the founder of the wildly successful Chick-fil-A fast-food chain, was deeply committed to his Christian beliefs and kept his restaurants closed on Sundays despite an expectation among American consumers that fast-food service should be as close to 24/7 as possible. While Cathy chose an organizational culture that wasn't perfectly aligned to the market, the profits lost in not pursuing a seventh day of business do not appear to have significantly hindered his firm's growth. In 2019, *Business Insider* reported that Chick-fil-A was the third-largest U.S. fast-food chain by sales with 2018 sales up 16.17 percent.[14] Perhaps the firm's culture, or simply the sincerity of its convictions, appealed to many customers.

Key Takeaways

- Being dynamic is key to growth.
- Taking advantage of change requires working capital.
- Managing cash flow is critical to dynamic advantage.
- Reducing outlays for equipment and materials is key to good cash flow.
- Strive for a negative working capital model in your business model.
- Stay on top of your accounts receivable.
- Focus your salary expenses on revenue-generating employees.
- Consider options to minimize hiring employees.
- Constantly be connecting with potential future employees to build a pool of candidates, so that hiring can address strategic as well as tactical needs.
- An organizational culture that fits the environment in which your firm operates is a source of competitive advantage.
- Organizational culture can be consciously managed.
- The entrepreneur may be compelled to choose to balance their own cultural preferences and those of the market.

12.3 Globalized Operations

Learning Objectives

1. Recognize that the world is interconnected, and global markets are nearly unavoidable.
2. Understand that you can outsource the logistics and bureaucracy of global business to expert organizations.
3. Learn about the advantages and challenges of asynchronous communications.
4. Understand the advantages of remote collaborative work environments.
5. Learn about options and best practices for language translation.

The Global Imperative

In an increasingly interconnected world, it is becoming difficult to keep many products or service businesses local, regional, or even national. When your website, product listings, or social media go up, folks from around the world will find you. They may want to buy your products, or they may be selling you their services. Even if your strategic intent is to constrain your firm's growth geographically and avoid the complexities of remote and transnational business, you will find it hard to turn down. Unless you are running a small, Main Street business, you should probably plan for the complexities of globalization from the start.

Nearly every product is now available in nearly every city on earth.

Source: Sudpoth Sirirattanasakul/Shutterstock.com

We've already discussed in this chapter how outsourcing production, sales, and logistics can help you scale your operations with minimal capital investment. These lessons go doubly for international businesses. The global export/import process presents unique challenges, and this is another reason to outsource your fulfillment. Orders shipped to other countries require special paperwork for the receiving nations' customs and border inspection agencies to process the incoming items. There are often tariffs or other fees that must be paid. If these forms and fees are not handled precisely according to regulations that vary by country, your products can be stuck in limbo or even lost forever in a bureaucratic process. That will make your customer unhappy and leave your invoices unpaid. Payment fraud is also much more common with international orders, its perpetrators knowing that they are often out of your legal reach. Attempting to track lost packages halfway across the world and arguing with foreign shippers and governmental bureaucrats in distant time zones and across language, political, and cultural barriers are not things upon which a focused startup should be spending its time.

Services such as Fulfilled by Amazon are a good choice. Amazon promises to "help you identify which of your products are eligible for FBA Export, fulfills international orders, handles import duty and customs clearance, and ships your product to the international buyer's address." For a small firm, there is a lot of value to capture by avoiding the opportunity cost of getting caught up in the bureaucracy of international trade.

Managing across Space and Time

Managing virtualized activities across the globe is a modern challenge.

Source: © Shutterstock, Inc.

Modern technology has eliminated the price of distance in communications and reduced the price of travel significantly. Virtualization tools like Microsoft Teams, Zoom, BlueJeans, and WebEx are routine parts of business today, providing video conferencing and screen sharing in online meeting spaces. If there was an upside to the tragic events of 2020, it was that almost everyone learned to virtualize during the pandemic.

While virtualization is a great way to run a business across a country and a continent, it isn't as helpful working across the globe. If it is noon in California, the time is 12:30 a.m. in India. The two are on opposite sides of the globe, and if it weren't for the peculiarity of the subcontinent being thirty minutes out of sync with everywhere else, they'd be exactly twelve hours off. There are no "business hours" at one site that correspond to any business hour in the other. That makes meetings between your Santa Monica design team and your programmers in Mumbai rather inconvenient to schedule, and the weird half-hour thing just adds to the confusion. The best you might do is have your California team get up and skip breakfast to be online at 7:00 a.m. while the Indians miss their dinners to meet at 7:30 p.m. their time. Too much of that and nobody will be happy because virtual meals are unsatisfying.

You could, of course, travel to Mumbai for an in-person meeting or invite the programming team to your cool new beachfront offices. That flight, with a likely connection in Europe, would literally take all day—about 24 hours of travel each way! You'd likely need a day of rest after the trip. What to do?

Asynchronous Communications

asynchronous communication

Communication between parties that does not take place in real time.

For a lot of traditional businesspeople, email would seem to be the best solution. Email is an **asynchronous communication** system, meaning that you can send a message and the receiving party does not have to be simultaneously (synchronously) online. Your programmers in Mumbai can open it later and reply when they wake up. Likewise, you'll wake up and find their reply in your inbox. Perfect, right?

From real-world experience, we all know that email communications can be confusing. Trying to explain the intricacies of an intermittent software glitch in words can be hard. Sitting in your office in Toronto, Canada, and describing just how a mechanical part machined in a shop in Malaysia doesn't quite fit into the casing made in Tijuana, Mexico, can be immensely frustrating. The best solution is to add photos and, better yet, video in your asynchronous communications. Still, email can be frustrating because you don't even know if the receiving party has even looked at your message, much less if they are acting on it. Additionally, as emails go back and forth, the conversation diverges from the original subject line of the email, and communication chains can be confusing to reconstruct when you go back to find something.

One software development team, working on a complex game called *Glitch*, ran into just these problems. Looking for a solution, they created their own internal web-based asynchronous communications system to speed development. The game was a flop and shut down after a year, but the communications software lived on as the popular collaboration platform, Slack. Today there are a number of web and app-based collaboration systems such as Asana and Microsoft Teams.

Email also presents challenges for file transfers. Email servers have file size limits, and revision control is very messy when users start sending files to each other.

Language

Even when you can connect in real time or your asynchronous tools are working well, language can be a limiting factor. While your development team in Mumbai is likely to be fluent in English, other than their British idioms, you may find your customers in Thailand are another story. What to do?

Google and other firms provide decent but imperfect automatic translation systems. If you avail yourself of these computerized solutions, be sure to notify the receiving party that you are depending on machine intelligence, and they will understand that there are likely to be awkward phrases, potential errors, and occasionally outlandish or offensive word choices in your communications. Alternatively, you can hire a professional translator as a consultant. Many popular work-for-hire websites like Upwork or Fiverr can help you find a translator.

Global business may demand you hire translation services in person or virtually.

Source: © Shutterstock, Inc.

Many of us have encountered oddly worded product documentation, clearly written by a second language learner. It is usually best to recruit a translator who will translate from your language and compose in their native language. It's easier to "figure out" what someone is saying in another language than to write perfect copy in it. If your product is going to be sold in Thailand, get a Thai national to write the manual from your English (or whatever) original. The same goes with important customer proposals and all legal contracts or any area where no mistakes can be tolerated.

If a great deal of your business is going to be conducted in one specific foreign language, it might behoove you to bring on a fluent team member and try to learn it yourself.

multitasking

Doing more than one thing at a time.

micromanaging

Controlling behavior that includes intense scrutiny and oversight of the performance of employees.

Focus on Success

The NED key to doing a job well is focusing on doing it well. Minimize distractions and maintain a consistent pace. Military trainers often teach recruits that "slow is smooth, and smooth is fast." Speed induces errors, and errors cost time, and in a battle that means lives. This adage is a favorite of one of the world's richest people, Amazon founder Jeff Bezos. Bezos put a tortoise into the coat of arms for his space startup, Blue Origin. The artwork also features the slogan "*Gradatim Ferociter*," Latin for "Step by Step, Ferociously," underscoring his firm's determination to reach its goal with careful, incremental approaches. In an interview with *Inc.*, Bezos said of this philosophy, "I like to do things incrementally."[15]

Source: By https://www.inverse.com/article/14059-the-mystery-behind-blue-origin-s-turtle-friendly-coat-of-arms, Fair use, https://en.wikipedia.org/w/index.php?curid=52012824

Build a work environment free of distracting visual and audio. This doesn't mean work should be boring, particularly in creative endeavors where serendipity adds value. Consider the workflows required to accomplish tasks in your firm. Create comfortable physical and virtual spaces that optimize workflow. Avoid layouts that require employees to move from one location to another or navigate through nonrelevant areas in a software environment to get to the next task.

Reduce or eliminate **multitasking**, doing more than one job at a time. When we multitask, we reduce our commitment to any one job. When we are eager to get back to some other task that needs doing, we often rush the job at hand. These human tendencies reduce operational effectiveness. Empower employees to manage their own time so they can achieve this and restrain management from interrupting employee efforts by **micromanaging** their work. Reward employees on goals completed successfully.

Key Takeaways

- The world is likely going to be your market, whether you chose that or not; be prepared for it.
- Travel is expensive in time, and time zones are expensive to productivity. Do not ignore the costs of a global supply chain.

- Learn to be savvy users of virtualization platforms and asynchronous communication tools.
- Treat translation as seriously as the particular communication demands.

12.4 Case Study: Shifting Operations at Nikki's Kitchen

As a young girl, Nikki Hernandez loved to cook and always envisioned owning a small café. She recalls, "I loved the idea of creating a welcoming space and inviting people into it for good food and company." Still, she postponed that dream in order to raise a family and to support her husband, Tom Ware, in building his custom construction business, Progressive Builders. Years later, with that firm running smoothly and her kids old enough to look after themselves, Nikki's thoughts returned to the food business.

Nikki was particularly fond of baking. She says, "My homemade cookies had always been a popular neighborhood treat and I figured I could sell them." A friend who ran a local pizza parlor offered to sell her cookies there as a dessert option. The cookies were wildly successful, and she began to sell them by the dozen as treats to go. Soon, some customers were coming in just for the cookies, and Nikki began to wonder if her backing might really support her own shop.

In early 2018, the location next door to the pizza parlor became available for rent, and Nikki grabbed it. Tom spent several months of his spare time building out a counter and dining area in the former hardware store space. Nikki decorated the place with cozy country charm and opened the doors in December of that year. She also brought in her daughter Cailyn as a partner. Nikki's Kitchen was born.

Nikki's Kitchen

Source: Nikki Ware

At first the plan was to sell cookies and other baked goods to go and provide some seating for breakfast diners to enjoy a pastry and coffee. Soon however, Nikki's customers were asking for a fuller breakfast menu as well as for sandwiches at lunch. They also wanted her to cater local events. She adapted to the customer demand, though doing short order grill work was a very different business. Operations were suddenly more complex than Nikki had originally planned for. Just keeping up with the dishes was a growing hassle. Nikki recalled, "I experimented with paperware, but it wasn't an environmentally friendly choice, and it also was not what our customers were looking for in a dining experience at a cozy café." She ended up with a full-time dishwasher as well as a short-order cook. The business and staff grew together, and 2019 ended with a much larger operation than Nikki had anticipated. 2020 looked like it would be a great year to optimize the model for profitability.

A customer enjoys breakfast at Nikki's Kitchen.

Source: Nikki Ware

In March 2020 the COVID-19 pandemic hit hard, and the governor of California issued orders that locked down the state's restaurants. Nikki recalls, "We had this big weekend of catering lined up, and I wasn't sure how I was going to fill all the orders. Then suddenly it all vanished, and we had to close the café as well." With no solution to the pandemic in sight, Nikki was forced to lay off most of her staff and refocus on take-out orders. Nikki wasn't sure that Nikki's Kitchen would survive the year.

While the change wasn't Nikki's choice, the financial results of the operational shift were pleasantly surprising. She says, "I found we could just get by with three people, and it was easy and super profitable." The federal government's Paycheck Protection Program (PPP) provided an additional cash infusion, and the landlord offered a rent deferral, so Nikki was able to reinvest her increased profits in adapting her business to the dynamically changing COVID-19 regulatory environment. When California adjusted the lockdown to allow for outdoor dining, Nikki was able to quickly convert an empty lumber storage area next to the shop into an attractive outdoor dining area available to her customers, and the patrons of the pizza parlor and ice-cream shop she shared the center with. The state then reallowed limited indoor dinning with additional mandates such as the use of disposable containers for condiments. Nikki was puzzled by many of these rules. "People are allowed to roam through Costco touching everything and a lot of that product goes to local restaurants as well." She also noted, "In the restaurant business we have *always* been focused on cleanliness. We wipe down everything by nature. Clothing stores can't sanitize their merchandize, which everyone handles, but they stay open while we are the industry that gets singled out under the COVID rules."

COVID-19 didn't just require masks; it turned operations upside down.

Source: Greg Autry

When the winter came, coronavirus infections skyrocketed, and the governor issued another shutdown for restaurants, but let the malls stay open. However, local authorities made it clear that they were simply not going to enforce those seemingly arbitrary rules that would ruin the livelihood of many business owners and leave their employees unemployed for the holidays. Most restaurants ignored the new lockdown order and did their best to survive.

Nikki continues to grow her business, focusing on keeping her customers safe while maintaining an inviting atmosphere. She remains hopeful that the pandemic will subside, and things return to normal by year-end, but she takes nothing for granted. The adaptable entrepreneur is experimenting with delivery service. "Our POS system offered a ninety-day free trial for the interface to the Grubhub app, so we gave it a shot and it is going well." She notes, "This has been really hard, but it's been a good education. I'm actually glad my daughter experienced all this chaos early in her business career. She has learned quickly that operations have to be adaptable if your business is going to survive."

Endnotes

1. Variously attributed but sourced to Cox, 1922. https://quoteinvestigator.com/2012/07/21/luck-hard-work/.
2. In case that was bothering you, 95° C is a fine operating temperature for most gasoline engines.
3. Ibid., Chapter 2.
4. Deming, W. E. (2018). *The new economics for industry, government, education*. MIT press.
5. Ibid.
6. Xinhua, "Across China: Sock capital on the front foot," November 23, 2017 http://www.xinhuanet.com/english/2017-11/23/c_136774699.htm.
7. Stevens, G. C. (1989). Integrating the Supply Chains, *International Journal of Physical Distribution and Materials Management, 8*(8), 3–8.
8. Papavlasopoulou, S., Giannakos, M., & Jaccheri, L. (2016). Empirical studies on the maker movement, a promising approach to learning: A literature review. *Entertainment Computing, 18*. 10.1016/j.entcom. 2016.09.002.
9. https://www.statista.com/statistics/262921/global-production-of-luxury-cars-by-make/
10. Martensen, A., Gronholdt, L., & Kristensen, K. (200)0. The drivers of customer satisfaction and loyalty: Cross-industry findings from Denmark. *Total Quality Management, 11*(4–6), 544–553.
11. Conklin, M., Powaga, K., & Lipovetsky, S. (2004). Customer satisfaction analysis: Identification of key drivers. *European Journal of Operational Research, 154*(3), 819–827.
12. Carnegie, D. (2009). *How to win friends & influence people*. Simon & Schuster.
13. Sadri, Golnaz, & Lees, Brian. "Developing corporate culture as a competitive advantage." *Journal of Management Development* (2001).
14. Taylor, K. & Yuan, Y. (2019). How Chick-fil-A took over America, explained in charts. *Business Insider*. https://www.businessinsider.com/chickfil- a-fast-food-domination-explained-charts-2019-8
15. https://www.inc.com/lisa-calhoun/digging-into-how-jeff-bezos-landed-customer-1.html

CHAPTER 13
Accounting

> It's dull. Dull. Dull. My God it's dull, it's so desperately dull and tedious and stuffy and boring and des-per-ate-ly DULL.
>
> —*Michael Palin, of Monty Python, describing accounting*

Businesspeople are often portrayed as obsessed with accumulating money.

Source: © Shutterstock, Inc.

income statement

A numeric document that illustrates a firm's financial performance in a given period of time. Also known as the profit and loss statement or P&L, it shows how revenues, cost of goods, and fixed costs result in net profits or losses on a monthly, quarterly, or annual basis.

balance sheet

A numeric document that illustrates a firm's balance of assets, liabilities, and shareholder equity at a specific moment in time. It shows what your business owns and what it owes. What remains is the value of the firm owned by its shareholders.

profit margin

A ratio found by dividing net profit (money left after costs have been subtracted from sales) by revenues (firm's sales).

The general public often associates business with the tasks of accounting. In popular media, business owners are often portrayed as modern-day Ebenezer Scrooges, obsessed with money, counting stacks of bills, constantly monitoring their **income statement** and **balance sheet**, worrying over **profit margin**, and maneuvering to avoid paying taxes. For most entrepreneurs, nothing could be further from the truth. They are often too busy growing their business and dealing with crises to think about their accounting. That can be a deadly mistake for any startup.

13.1 Managerial Accounting

Learning Objectives

1. Understand that accounting is a critical entrepreneurial skill.
2. Understand the importance of measuring sales revenues continuously.
3. Understand what a profitable firm is.
4. Recognize the difference between variable and fixed costs.

Basic Accounting Skills

best-in-class

The highest quality product or service of its type in its particular price range. Firms like Apple and Toyota strive to produce best-in-class solutions.

When you think of the most famous entrepreneurs like Facebook's Mark Zuckerberg, Amazon's Jeff Bezos, or Oprah Winfrey, do you think about accounting? Most likely, you don't. You likely think about the cool services they provide, the great products they've created, or the amazing brands they have built. There is a good reason for this. Each of these successful businesspeople has focused most of their energy on delivering the **best-in-class** to their customers, whether that was a social media system, an online store, or a media empire. The mantra of modern entrepreneurship is knowing that if you make truly great things and add value to people's lives, the money will follow. Under this paradigm, entrepreneurs often see accounting as an annoying distraction rather than as a source of competitive advantage.[1] Do not be misled!

cash flow

The monies that move in and out of a business as sales are made, and employees, vendors, and taxes are paid.

cash flow statement

A numeric document that illustrates the entry and exit of cash (or equivalent) from a firm. In a healthy company, it shows how much actual money is being generated by the business operation over a given period of time. In a fast-growing or an unprofitable firm, it shows how fast money is being consumed by the business operations.

Bezos, Zuckerberg, and Winfrey are not oblivious to things like profit margins and **cash flow**. Any of our industry moguls could instantly spot emerging trouble in a **cash flow statement**. Growing their businesses aggressively often required these modern captains of their industries to ride very close to the line of solvency, and doing that successfully required a thorough appreciation of accounting. As maturing entrepreneurs, they have each learned that competence in accounting is a source of competitive advantage that allows them to deploy their financial resources more efficiently than their competitors. Today's small business owners must learn to do the same!

Imagine that you own a local delivery company, and you need to maintain your delivery vans. Understanding how your vehicles actually work can provide you with an advantage over the average fleet operator, *even if somebody else is doing your repair service.* A lot of drivers have discovered that their ignorance of basic auto mechanics rendered them vulnerable to deceitful auto salespeople and unscrupulous repair shops. This weakness could leave an entrepreneur stuck on the side of the road with a load of undelivered goods, watching the competition drive on by. Similarly, many a startup founder has come to regret their lack of accounting skills only after it was too late.

While a basic understanding of accounting is critical for any business owner, you don't actually have to do all this work on a daily basis. Entrepreneurs rarely handle the mechanics of accounting themselves. In a fast-growth startup, accounting is delegated to an outside professional accounting firm or the CFO and his staff. In a small business, they are typically farmed out to an outside bookkeeper and a CPA. Choosing the right accounting resources for the business is an important task for the entrepreneur and will be addressed later in this chapter.

As the opening quote for this chapter suggests, a lot of people feel that accounting is dull and are therefore disinclined to study it. The modern entrepreneurship curriculum is also so heavily focused on the excitement of technology, customers, and marketing that many founders are beginning their careers with an appalling lack of accounting literacy. These young entrepreneurs are often forced to learn the basics of accounting in the **school of hard knocks**, after a financial crisis wrecks their dreams. While counting your money should never be your focus, knowing where it is remains an indispensable skill.

school of hard knocks

The experience of learning a skill in the field, usually after having suffered a setback from the lack of formal education on the topic.

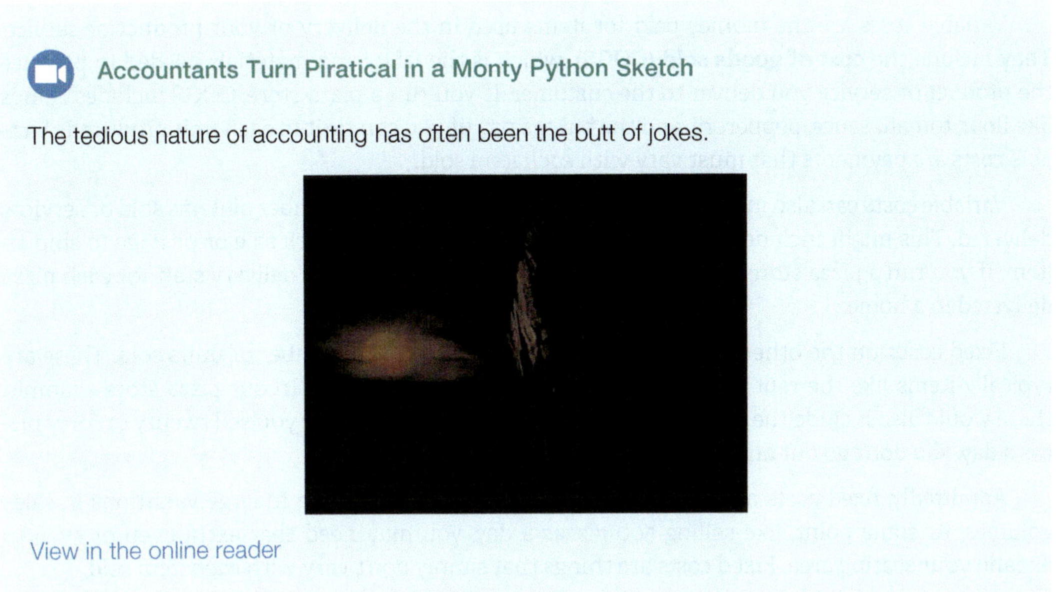

Accountants Turn Piratical in a Monty Python Sketch

The tedious nature of accounting has often been the butt of jokes.

View in the online reader

Revenues

Businesses collect money from customers when they sell a product or deliver a service. These **revenues** are the basic sustenance of business. Without revenues, you are not running a business; you are playing with a hobby, or perhaps you are operating a charity. A primary economic goal for most businesses is to maximize revenues. This is typically achieved by attempting to determine the highest price that the market will allow and then expanding operations as much as possible in order to increase **sales volume**. Expansion can be achieved through capturing more of an existing market via marketing or moving into other markets through geographic extension or by entering new product categories.

revenue

The money collected from sales of your good or service. The total of what all customers have paid you.

sales volume

The number of units of a good or service that are sold during a particular period of time, e.g., donuts sold per day at a bakery.

expenses
Money that must be paid out by your firm to conduct its operations.

profitable
A state where the firm's sales revenues exceed its combined costs in any given period of time.

variable costs
The monies paid for items used in the delivery of your product or service. Variable costs vary with each and every additional unit produced. These include the basic inputs to your product and labor associated with producing it.

fixed costs
The monies paid for items required to support your business operations that are not directly tied to production costs. They remain fixed regardless of normal variations in production volume. These typically include things like rent for facilities, administrative payrolls, and insurance.

cost of goods sold (COGS)
The direct labor and material required to produce the product you sell or the service that you deliver.

However, many business owners have goals that override simply maximizing sales. They may wish to keep their business a "manageable" size, wisely choose to focus on product quality for long-term success and higher profits, or wish to fill some social mission. In the end, the most important thing is that sales revenues exceed the business's **expenses** or costs during any given period of time. Such a firm is **profitable**.

Variable Versus Fixed Costs

Business expenses, or monies that must be paid out by your firm to conduct its work, usually fall into two main categories: **variable costs** and **fixed costs**.

Variable costs are the monies paid for items used in the delivery of your product or service. They include the **cost of goods sold (COGS)**, which is the labor and materials needed to produce the product or service you deliver to the customer. If you run a pizza store, COGS includes things like flour, tomato sauce, pepperoni, and the baker's pay (if you can tie it to each unit produced). Variable costs are payments that must vary with *each* item sold.

Variable costs can also include other things that vary with the number of items sold or services delivered. This might include things like sales commission paid on each sale or postage to ship an item. If you run a pizza store, this might be a set price you pay to your delivery staff for each pizza delivered to a home.

Fixed costs, on the other hand, do not directly vary with the number of units sold. These are typically items like the rent for your facility, insurance, and utilities. In our pizza store example, these would also include the pizza oven and its maintenance. Whether you sell twenty or forty pizzas a day, you don't go out and buy a new oven.

Admittedly, fixed costs are not entirely unchangeable or immune to large variations in sales volumes. At some point, like selling 500 pizzas a day, you may need that extra oven or even to expand your seating area. Fixed costs are things that simply don't vary with *each* item sold.

The balance between fixed and variable costs is critical to the health of any firm. A proper investment in fixed costs, such as buying automation equipment designed to lower the cost of production, can pay back many times its cost by actually reducing the variable costs for each item sold. If you get a pizza-making machine that cuts your labor in half and you sell enough pizzas, you'll eventually pay for that investment in per-pizza savings. After that payoff period, the extra profits go into your pocket rather than to the extra employees you might have hired to make all those pizzas by hand.

The ingredients in your pizza are variable costs.

Source: © Shutterstock, Inc.

However, it is also critical to realize that if you don't sell enough mechanical-made pizzas to pay what you owe the vendor or bank for the pizza machine, you may face a very serious problem. Poor choices in fixed costs commitments such as renting expensive locations, buying fancy vehicles, and ill-conceived marketing campaigns are the number one cause of death for small businesses. When in doubt, an important mantra for any entrepreneur is to "contain fixed expenses." Cash on hand is never a bad thing to have. It is far better to have money in the bank than an underutilized piece of equipment or a big, empty store.

Key Takeaways

- Good entrepreneurs master the accounting skills required to track their money.
- Variable costs increase with each new unit produced.
- COGS is the variable cost of items that go into each item you sell.
- Fixed costs do not change with each item you sell.

13.2 Financial Accounting

Learning Objectives

1. Understand the purpose and timing of the income statement.
2. Learn the differences between cash and accrual accounting.
3. Understand the cost of holding inventory.
4. Learn about ways to manage accounts receivable and inventory.
5. Recognize capital investments, how they depreciate, and how to amortize them.
6. Learn the purpose and components of the balance sheet.
7. Learn the purpose and components of the cash flow statements.
8. Understand the importance of the Accounts Receivable aging report.
9. Be aware of varying international accounting standards.

Income Statements

An income statement, also known as a profit and loss (P&L) statement, tracks the income and costs of a company over a given period of time. They are typically generated monthly, quarterly, and annually. The components of a very simple income statement are:

A very simple income statement has the following components:

Revenue: The money your firm receives from its business activities via the sales of products or delivery of services. In most cases, what your customers pay you.

Cost of goods sold (COGS): The cost of materials and direct labor (usually variable costs) used to produce your product or deliver your service. These are generally equivalent to variable costs.

Gross profit: Revenue – COGS. The money you (hopefully) have left over after selling your goods or delivering your service and paying for all the direct costs used to manufacture or deliver.

Operating costs: The cost of non-direct labor and other services and materials needed to run your business. This is all non-production staff, rent, utilities, insurance, etc. These are generally equivalent to the fixed costs previously discussed.

EBIT

Earnings before interest and tax. This is your net profits with any interest or taxes paid added back in (not considered).

Operating income or earnings before interest and taxes (EBIT): Gross profit – operating costs. The money you (hopefully) have left over after subtracting your operating expenses (fixed costs) from your gross profit.

Taxes: Monies your firm must pay to various levels of government on its income, real estate inventory, and countless other things.

Net profit: The money you (hopefully) have left over after paying taxes from your operating income (EBIT).

Actual income statements may include any number of more specialized items that the firm wishes to track. This may include things like **interest** paid on loans to finance materials or **assets**. The Sample Income Statement illustration shows line items that reflect profits generated in a related joint venture (associates) and investments (non-controlling interests) in other firms.

interest

Money paid as the fee for borrowing funds, usually expressed as percentage per year.

assets

The cash and other items of value owned by a business.

TABLE 13.1 Sample Income Statement

Dexterity Inc. and Subsidiaries Consolidated Statements of Operations (in millions)			
Year Ended December 31	**2009**	**2008**	**2007**
Revenue	$ 36,524.9	$ 29,827.6	$ 21,186.8
Cost of Sales	(18,545.8)	(15,858.8)	(11,745.5)
Gross Profit	17,980.1	13,968.8	9,441.3
Operating Expenses			
Selling, General, and Administrative Expenses	$ (4,142.1)	$ (3,732.3)	$ (3,498.6)
Depreciation	(602.4)	(584.5)	(562.3)
Amortization	(209.9)	(141.9)	(111.8)
Impairment Loss	(17,997.1)	–	–
Total Operating Expense	(22,951.5)	(4,458.7)	(4,172.7)
Operating Profit (or Loss)	$ (4,971.4)	$ 9,510.1	$ 5,268.6
Interest Income	25.3	11.7	12.0
Interest Expense	(718.9)	(742.9)	(799.1)
Profit (or loss) from continuing operations *before* tax, share of profit (or loss) from associates and non-controlling interest	$ (5,665.0)	$ 8,778.9	$ 4,481.5
Income Tax Expense	(1,678.6)	(3,510.5)	(1,789.9)
Profit (or Loss) from Associates, *net of tax*	(20.8)	0.1	(37.3)
Profit (or Loss) from Non-Controlling Interest, *net of tax*	(5.1)	(4.7)	(3.3)
Profit (or Loss) from Continuing Operations	$ (7,369.5)	$ 5,263.8	$ 2,651.0
Profit (or Loss) from Discontinued Operations, *Net of Tax*	(1,090.3)	(802.4)	164.6
Profit or Loss for the Year	$ (8,459.8)	$ 4,461.4	$ 2,815.6

Cash Versus Accrual Accounting

cash accounting

A system of accounting that looks at business assets and liabilities as a snapshot in time. As opposed to accrual accounting, cash accounting does not consider accounts receivable or payable. Cash accounting is appropriate for only the simplest of businesses or for use in some tax strategies.

So far, we have looked at businesses operating in a **cash accounting** framework. Cash accounting is a simple system that only considers what concrete monies a company has *right now*. It counts the money you have in the bank after customers have paid you, and you have paid your bills. When you receive money, you post it under sales, and when you pay out money, you list it on cost of goods sold (COGS) or operating expenses. That is fine if you buy bags of oranges at a market and then walk over to a street corner to sell them for cash. Can you think of why such a system is insufficient for running anything but a very simple business?

Cash accounting is a bit like managing your personal bank account by only looking at your ATM statement balance and just ignoring bills you have due or overlooking undeposited checks you might have in the mail. An individual could get into a lot of financial trouble by thinking, "Hey, I've got money in the bank. I can go shopping!" In fact, doing so will leave them unable to pay the car insurance bill they have sitting on their desk. The same problem could threaten the operation of your small business. This framework does not address money you owe your vendors or monies owed to you by customers who have not paid you yet.

net terms

An agreement between a buyer and seller whereby the buyer pays for the product sometime after they have received it.

transit time

The time a product is in shipment and not available to the buyer for resale.

Outside of very small retail stores, most business transactions do not happen on a cash basis. For bigger stores, most purchases come in a day or more later from credit card transactions, and in the business to business (B2B) world, most firms ship goods to each other on **net terms**, where the product comes with a bill that is due to be paid sometime in the future. Typically, such terms are fifteen or thirty days, but they may be as long as ninety days or more.

On an invoice, you will see the terms listed as "Net 30," for example, meaning you must pay this invoice within thirty days. "Net" refers to the amount due. You may have paid some part upfront or on delivery or have received some sort of discount. The net is the balance that you owe. The number following "Net" is the terms in days in which you have to pay it. The clock starts when the seller ships the product or delivers the service. As the buyer, you are generally responsible for the **transit time**, and if you want your goods sooner, it is your responsibility to pay for a faster shipping method, like FedEx overnight.

Sometimes invoice terms can be more complex. In the United Kingdom, the phrase "net 30, EOM," where EOM means "end of the month," is commonly used to indicate that the bill is due 30 days after the start of the next month.

onerous

Terms that are excessively burdensome or difficult to accommodate.

If you don't understand the terms of an invoice, call the seller and ask what they are expecting rather than risk running afoul of their credit rules. To encourage you to pay in a timely manner, your seller may add a penalty or interest rate to any payments made after the agreed net terms. These may be defined on the invoice or in your contract or agreement with the vendor. Be careful as these terms can often be **onerous**.

A seller may also tempt you with a discount to pay early, which in turn, has positive ramifications for their own cash flows. To do this, they may send you an invoice with terms that read "2% 10, net 30" or "2/10 net 30," for example, which means that you can choose to take a 2 percent discount (pay less) if you pay within ten days or simply chose to pay the normal amount in thirty. Taking such discounts is usually a great idea if you can spare the cash on hand. You'll never find such easy money. After all, what is the annualized interest rate at 2 percent a month? Is that a good rate compared with what you might earn at the bank or elsewhere?

As a buyer, payment terms are an important point of negotiation with your vendor. Can you think of why a buyer would not be willing or able to pay for items the moment they arrive or why the seller would be willing to wait so long for a customer to pay for items they are delivering today?

The Harsh Reality of Collecting Accounts Receivable

In the real world, purchasers often do not pay their bills on time. The cause may either be that they simply don't have the cash on hand or because they pointedly choose to hold on to other people's money and profit from investing it. Depending on your customer and the economic conditions, the average time for collecting a net 30 invoice may easily be forty-five days or more. As a seller, you must be aware of this reality.

In fact, when dealing with smaller businesses, you may often need to offer them a discount when they run late, just to get them to pay a bill they already owe you. In some cases, they may simply never pay, and you may need to sue them, which can be expensive and time-consuming. Finally, your customer can go bankrupt, leaving you stuck with little or nothing. Be very careful how you extend net terms and to which firms you extend them. Techniques for determining this will be discussed in Chapter 14.

Additionally, the power balance (or imbalance) between the buyer and the seller often determines how quickly bills are paid. In general, a larger company has more leverage over a smaller one and can expect its bills to be paid quickly. As a small shop owner, you *will* pay the power company on time because the power company will simply shut you down if you don't. Your window washer isn't so lucky, and you may wait to pay her until you've paid everyone else. Larger firms also have professional collection departments, and if necessary, lawyers on staff who are skilled in making the life of a small businessperson very uncomfortable. If you repeatedly pay your bills to large firms late, your business credit rating can be impacted as they report to agencies like Dunn and Bradstreet, who collect such information. If your business is organized as sole proprietorship or partnership, a business collection group may attach your personal assets or report negatively on your personal credit rating.

Conversely, as a small business owner, you will find that large firms often do not feel compelled to pay your bills in a timely manner—again, largely due to issues of power imbalances.[2] Your business needs their regular, big purchases, and they probably don't need you nearly as much. Other small firms are eager to acquire their business. Most large corporations knowingly make money by **floating** the money they owe to small businesses. By making many thousands of these invoices a few days late, they build up millions of dollars in **float**, money they can keep in their cash flow to finance their operations. That's money they do not have to borrow at interest. As shocking as it is, large businesses *will* do this to your small firm, and they don't care what that means to you, even if it drives you out of business.

Worse, when you, the small business owner, try to solve this dilemma by innocently sending a larger firm one of the those "2% 10, net 30" invoices, they are likely to pay in forty-five days or whenever they darn well feel like it *and still take the 2 percent "early payment" discount*! Should you call to complain about such an abuse, you will likely find yourself working through a maze of bureaucrats who will take up your time, but none of whom are authorized to solve your problem. In fact, you'll often find that big firms have a system whereby nobody even knows who is authorized to take action in favor of the vendor. If you decided to sic your main street lawyer on a big firm, their Ivy League legal eagles may not only beat your guy in court but will leave you with a pile of legal bills far larger than the money that was at stake. In any case, your big customer would surely drop you as a vendor for annoying them, and you'll lose a great deal of business and credibility going forward. This power imbalance is an unfair reality that small business owners must simply learn to live with.

floating

Holding monies that belong to vendors or customers to increase a firm's working capital or to collect the interest on it.

float

Monies belonging to vendors or customers being held for a time to increase a firm's working capital or to collect the interest on it.

The Need for Accrual Accounting

Imagine you own a bicycle shop, and the Christmas holiday season is approaching. From experience, you know that customers are willing to pay more for holiday gifts and that your sales revenues in November and December may account for more than half of your annual income. This is the "make it or break it season" for your shop, so it is really important that you have as many bicycles in stock as possible. The problem is that since the rest of your year is relatively slow and the rainy fall is particularly bad for sales, you don't come into November with a lot of cash on hand. However, you want to double up on the bikes you keep in stock. These items ready for sale but as yet unsold are called **inventory**.

inventory

Product you produce or sell that has not been sold yet, but that you are holding for sale.

The bicycles for sale in a bike store can tie up a lot of the business's cash.

Source: © Shutterstock, Inc.

Now, the bike manufacturer also *wants* you to have a load of their bikes on hand for customers during the peak buying season. They've also been in this business long enough to understand that you and all your peers will have money *after* you sell the Christmas bikes. Therefore, the manufacturer will essentially loan your shop the money to buy all these bikes from them with the expectation that you will pay them in January after you've sold the inventory. If they will not make this accommodation, another bike manufacturer is likely to do so, and customers will find your (and other) stores packed with their competitors' products during the holidays. You can see that it is very important that you and the bike manufacturer accurately forecast the coming holiday season. If you underestimate the number of bikes you can sell, you'll be leaving money on the table and will be weaker in the coming slow season. If you overestimate, you may have many unsold bikes and not enough cash to pay for them, an even more desperate situation.

accounts receivable

Monies owed to you by customers for products they have received but not yet paid for.

accrual accounting

Accounting that takes into consideration transactions where cash has not yet been exchanged, where monies are owed but not yet paid, the accounts receivable and payable.

If you have received product—say bikes for your bicycle shop—and have yet to pay the bill that came with them, your accounts are payable. If customers owe you money—imagine you're the bicycle manufacturer—you've got an important asset in your **accounts receivable**. In order to know how your business is really doing, it is important to account for what you actually owe people and what they owe you. Consequently, these payables and receivables should be visible on the income statement. The accounting system that includes such statements is called the **accrual accounting** system. For all but the simplest business, accrual accounting is required to manage operations effectively. In most cases, and in this book, assume accrual accounting is being used.

Inventory Flooring

Imagine that you're a bicycle manufacturer. You have to build a lot more bikes in preparation for the holidays and to do so, you've got to pay for extra parts and labor. You may not have unlimited cash to loan to thousands of bike shops and then wait months to be repaid. What can you do about that?

Even an unsold inventory of things like bicycles has solid value. Those bikes can always be sold at *some price*, even if it were 50 percent off. Consequently, small businesses, like bicycle shops, can borrow money against part of the value of this inventory. This is a type of **inventory financing** call **floor planning** or **flooring** (because it puts product on the shop "floor"). Many banks and specialty firms provide such flooring and make a profit by charging interest either to the shop or the manufacturer.

Most cars for sale on a dealership lot are financed via floor planning.

Source: © Shutterstock, Inc.

At the consumer level, the buyer also wants to purchase more product, particularly during the holidays, than he can directly afford to pay for. As a bike shop owner, you probably can't afford to loan them your own money to buy their bike. Again, banks and finance companies are happy to step in with an **installment loan** or specialty credit card that allows a consumer to make small payments over time for large purchases. This allows the consumer, at least for a while, to live beyond their means.

This sort of product financing is the grease of the consumer economy, and it keeps sales going. When there is plenty of money to loan at low interest rates, businesses run very smoothly. When loans are hard to get, and rates are high, these firms cut back on expenses like salaries and purchases, and that means jobs for workers in retail and manufacturing. This is a major reason why the interest rates are of such concern to economists and government policymakers. Can you see why making too much money available at too low of an interest rate all the time might be a problem? This will be discussed in more detail in Chapter 15.

inventory financing

A loan secured by inventory held for manufacturing or for sale.

floor planning

See *flooring*.

flooring

A financing arrangement where a bank or specialty lender loans money to pay for merchandise for sale by a retailer. When the merchandise is sold, the loan is repaid. Interest is usually due on the loan each month.

installment loan

An agreement for a buyer to make payments on a product over time, usually with interest, to a third party who pays the seller for the product at the time of sale.

Amortization and Depreciation

capital investment

Significant monies put into to facilities, infrastructure, or machinery necessary for the operation of the business.

Many small businesses require a relatively large **capital investment** in something like a machine to make donuts or a special truck for delivering panes of glass. Some business owners may even choose to buy the building that houses their store or factory. While these business owners believe that their investment will pay back in years to come, the initial outlay for these items may be so large that they distort the financial statements.

Imagine that you own a donut store that sees a consistent $500k a year in revenues and after COGS and normal fixed expenses, always yields a respectable net profit of $50k.[3] Now, imagine what happens if once every fifteen years you need to buy a new donut maker for $200k. Well, in that year, your net profit will sink to a loss of $150k ($50k–$200k) and then suddenly pop back up to $50k the next. A graph of your profits would look like the Net Profits Per Year illustration.

FIGURE 13.1 Net Profits Per Year
Under a cash accounting system, one large expense can distort the firm performance for that year.

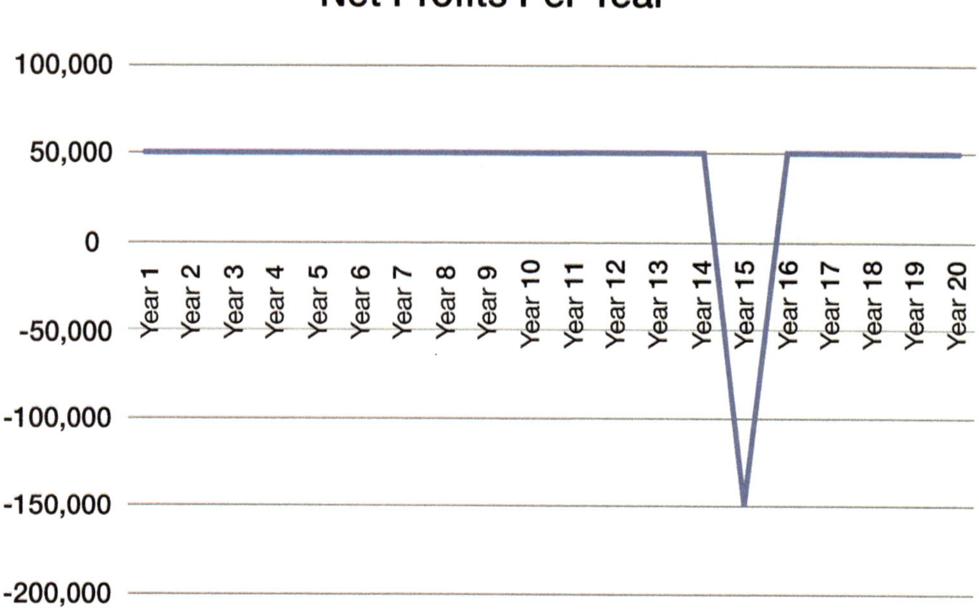

Source: Greg Autry

depreciation

A method for distributing long-term costs of a tangible asset over time, usually the length of its useful service.

tangible asset

A physical item owned by a firm, such as property, vehicles, or machinery.

Does that accurately reflect the actual profitability of your shop over time? No, it's a ridiculous distortion. What would your banker think if you turned in those financials in year 15? At first glance, it looks as if some disaster occurred, even though your business was going steady, just as in every other year. Since your donut machine will provide value to your business over fifteen years as it wears down slowly, its cost should be spread across that time as well. To account for that, the concept of **depreciation** can be used. Depreciation tracks how much of an item's value is used up over time, and applies to a **tangible asset**, which is a physical item that your business owns, such as machinery, real property, or furniture.

Your business may also possess **intangible assets**, which are valuable nonphysical items. Examples of intangible assets include things like patents, a special privilege to use a popular team logo, or exclusive rights to sell a product in some territory. Since intangible assets don't wear out, they are not depreciated. However, they may be valuable for a specific amount of time, like the fifteen-year term of a U.S. design patent, so their cost may be accounted for using the concept of **amortization**.

intangible asset

A nonphysical but valuable thing owned by a firm such as a patent, contract, or established relationships with customers or vendors.

Another option for small businesses to spread the costs of major purchases over time is to rent, lease, or finance big-ticket items like stores, vehicles, and machinery. Doing so not only makes your books look better, but it also spreads out your expenditure of cash over time. After all, how many donut stores have $200k sitting around in the bank to buy a new donut machine? That's probably not a good use of their capital. These options will be discussed in more detail in the Chapter 14.

amortization

The spreading of expenses, usually for an intangible asset, over time.

Balance Sheets

Accounts payable, accounts receivable, and those tangible and intangible assets are items that show up on your firm's *balance sheet*. A balance sheet shows a firm's assets (cash and value of what it owns), liabilities (what it owes), and the equity (what the firm is worth).

accounts payable

Monies you owe to your vendors for products they have shipped to you but that you have not yet paid for.

A very simple balance sheet has the following components:

Assets: Money in the bank and assets that have value, such as equipment, inventory, and money owed to the company by others.

Liabilities: Money the firm owes to other companies, including bills for materials or services and taxes that it has not yet paid.

Net worth: Assets – Liabilities. The (hopefully positive) difference between what the firm has and what it is required to pay. As this money is the rightful property of the firm's owners, it is often referred to as **owner equity**.

owner equity

The value of the firm, which is the value of its capital from investors along with any retained earnings. Same as stockholder equity.

net worth

Assets of a firm minus its liabilities. Usually identical to owner equity and book value.

retained earnings

Net profits kept in the firm and reinvested to fund growth.

book value

The value of a company calculated by subtracting the liabilities from assets. Essentially identical to *owner equity* or *net worth*. Typically, the minimum value for which a firm might be sold.

liquidated

When a firm's assets are all sold for cash and its debts all repaid, leaving the net worth of the firm as cash. Typically, liquidation results in the ceasing of firm operations.

goodwill

An intangible asset that usually arises in acquisitions. Typical goodwill items include valuable customer relations, brand names, or intellectual property.

acquisition

The purchasing of one firm by another.

Actual balance sheets may include any number of more specialized items that the firm wishes to track. The Sample Small Business Balance Sheet illustration includes cash (in the bank), accounts receivable (monies owed by customers), tools and equipment, notes payable (a loan the company owes to a bank, firm, or individual), and accounts payable (money the firm owes its suppliers or vendors). The **net worth** or owner's equity is represented by **retained earnings** (profits saved) and capital stock; it is also known as the **book value** of the firm's stock. This is what the firm would be worth if it were **liquidated**, meaning everything was sold, and the bills were all paid.

TABLE 13.2 Sample Small Business Balance Sheet

Assets (Current)		Liabilities and Owners' Equity	
Cash	$ 6,600	**Liabilities**	
Accounts Receivable	6,200	Notes Payable	$ 5,000
Assets (Non-Current)		Accounts Payable	25,000
Tools and Equipment	25,000	Total Liabilities	30,000
		Owners' Equity	
		Capital Stock	$ 7,000
		Retained Earnings	800
		Total Owners' Equity	7,800
Total	$ 37,800	*Total*	$ 37,800

Balance sheets may also include an interesting catch-all category labeled as **goodwill**. Goodwill includes many items that are difficult to (precisely) value, such as the value of your customer and vendor relationships, or how great your employees are. Goodwill is often the subject of negotiation during the **acquisition** of one firm by another firm. The seller often reaps the rewards of having built his small business from the valuing of this goodwill, since the tangible assets are all things he probably paid the market price for and is unlikely to make a profit on selling to another company. The goodwill is the unique value he has built up over time that cannot be acquired elsewhere. This will be discussed in more detail in Chapter 16.

Cash Flow Statements

If revenue is the sustenance of your business, cash flow is its blood. Cash flow is the movement of money in and out of a business from revenues and expenses. The most important thing about cash flow is that it is uneven. If your business isn't a pure cash-based retail establishment, there will be times when your business has plenty and occasions when money is tight. This is caused by the fact that the timing of your customers' payments will not be perfectly timed with when supplies must be paid for. For nearly every small business, there will be times you will owe more money than you have on hand—even if your customers owe you even more than that. Cash flow statements help you monitor that problem.

Look at Table 13.3. The firm depicted here started the year with $1,000 and took in a net positive of $10,500, ending the year with $11,500. This is a very healthy cash flow, resulting in a significant increase in cash on hand.

TABLE 13.3 Simple Cash Flow Statement

Cash Flows From (Used In) Operating Activities		
Cash receipts from customers	$ 9,500	
Cash paid to suppliers and employees	(2,000)	
Cash generated from operations **(sum)**	7,500	
Interest paid	(2,000)	
Income taxes paid	(3,000)	
Net cash flows from operating activities		$ 2,500
Cash Flows from (Used In) Investing Activities		
Proceeds from the sale of equipment	7,500	
Dividends received	3,000	
Net cash flows from investing activities		10,500
Cash Flows from (Used In) Financing Activities		
Dividends paid	(2,500)	
Net cash flows used in financing activities		(2,500)
Net increase in cash and cash equivalents		10,500
Cash and cash equivalents beginning of year		1,000
Cash and cash equivalents, end of year		$ 11,500

Things are not always so positive. Table 13.4 shows a firm's progress through three years (from right to left) with a variance. It's possible that a firm could have a negative cash flow and see a decrease in cash on hand in a year. How might a firm handle that situation?

TABLE 13.4 Multiyear Cash Flow Statement

XYZ Co. Ltd. Cash Flow Statement (All numbers in millions of Rs.)			
Period ending	*31 Mar 2010*	*31 Mar 2009*	*31 Mar 2008*
Net income	$ 21,538	$ 24,589	$ 17,046
Operating activities, cash flows provided by or used in:			
Depreciation and amortization	2,790	2,592	2,747
Adjustments to net income	4,617	621	2,910
Decrease (increase) in accounts receivable	12,503	17,236	—
Increase (decrease) in liabilities (A/P, taxes payable)	131,622	19,822	37,856
Decrease (increase) in inventories	—	—	—
Increase (decrease) in other operating activities	(173,057)	(33,061)	(62,963)
Net cash flow from operating activities	13	31,799	(2,404)
Investing activities, cash flows provided by or used in:			
Capital expenditures	(4,035)	(3,724)	(3,011)
Investments	(201,777)	(71,710)	(75,649)
Other cash flows from investing activities	1,606	17,009	(571)
Net cash flows from investing activities	(204,206)	(58,425)	(79,231)
Financing activities, cash flows provided by or used in:			
Dividends paid	(9,826)	(9,188)	(8,375)
Sale (repurchase) of stock	(5,327)	(12,090)	133
Increase (decrease) in debt	101,122	26,651	21,204
Other cash flows from financing activities	120,461	27,910	70,349
Net cash flows from financing activities	206,430	33,283	83,311
Effect of exchange rate changes	645	(1,840)	731
Net increase (decrease) in cash and cash equivalents	2,882	4,817	2,407

Aging Reports

Another set of reports you should be looking at regularly are your **aging reports**. Your accounting system will be able generate these. The accounts receivable aging will show you how late in time your accrual-based payments from customers are. A full aging report shows each invoice grouped by customer in the vertical axis and its amount by the number of days out (how long the invoice has been due) in the horizontal. Figure 13.2 shows such a report for a company with just two clients.

aging report
A report that shows the time, in days, for payments due from your customers or owed to you vendors.

FIGURE 13.2 Sample Accounts Receivable Aging Report

Receivables Aging Schedule Details

Organization: USA As Of Date: 01-06-2012 Accounting Schema: Main US/A/Euro

Business Partner	Document No.	Document Date	Current	1–30	31–60	61–90	91–120	Over 120	Credits	Net Due
Customer A										
	1/30	01-01-2012					150.00			150.00
	1/36	01-03-2012			300.00					300.00
	1/34	01-03-2012			450.00					450.00
	1/35	01-03-2012			500.00					500.00
	400044	01-05-2012							(1,000.00)	(1,000.00)
			0.00	0.00	1,250.00	0.00	150.00	0.00	(1,000.00)	400.00
Customer B										
	1/31	01-02-2012				250.00				250.00
	1/32	01-02-2012				300.00				300.00
	1/37	01-04-2012		50.00						50.00
	1/38	01-04-2012		100.00						100.00
			0.00	150.00	0.00	550.00	0.00	0.00	0.00	700.00
Total										
			0.00	150.00	1,250.00	550.00	0.00	0.00	1000.00	1,100.00

A simpler summary report can show just the customer totals (not each invoice) or simply the bottom line of all your billings grouped by days out. You should look at the aging report with the same critical eye an investor or banker might, and anything out more than sixty days is going to look seriously dodgy—meaning that if your customer hasn't paid you yet, are they really ever going to?

FIGURE 13.3 Sample Accounts Payable Aging Report

05/11/2007 05:17:26 PM National Office Supply USA

Printed by: Supervisor **Forecast Aging Report**

Invoice #	Inv Date	Due Date	Past Date	Due	1–15	16–30	31–45	46–60	Over 60	Total
Vendor #: AFF1 (Aero Furniture Factory, Inc.)										
INVOICE5006	01/10/2006	02/09/2006			206.48					
INVOICE5089	01/21/2006	02/20/2006				4,735.95				
	Total for AFF1:		0.00	0.00	0.00	4,735.95	0.00	0.00	0.00	4,942.43
Vendor #: CBA32 (Creative Business Accessories, Inc.)										
P2995	01/21/2006	02/20/2006			206.48	1,520.00				
P2154	01/25/2006	02/34/2006				60.00				
	Total for CBA32:		0.00	0.00	0.00	1,580.00	0.00	0.00	0.00	1,580.00
Vendor #: CTB01 (Citibank VISA Card (Credit Card))										
1000000029	01/18/2006	01/18/2006	1,456.23							
1000000032	01/25/2006	01/25/2006	5,000.00							
	Total for CTB01:		6,456.23	0.00	0.00	0.00	0.00	0.00	0.00	6.456.23
Vendor #: HLS1 (Henderson Lighting Systems)										
INV50015	01/15/2006	02/14/2006			150.00					
	Total for HLS1:		0.00	0.00	0.00	0.00	0.00	0.00	0.00	150.00
Vendor #: LWM1 (Lerner Wilson Manufacturing)										
LW960554001	01/13/2006	01/13/2006	788.06							
LW9658481002	01/13/2006	01/13/2006	15.00							
	Total for LWM1:		803.06	0.00	0.00	0.00	0.00	0.00	0.00	803.06
Vendor #: LWM2 (Leather Works of Montana, Inc.)										
T2005	01/30/2006	01/30/2006	202.18							
	Total for LWM2:		202.18	0.00	0.00	0.00	0.00	0.00	0.00	202.18
	Total For This Report:		7,461.47	0.00	356.48	6,315.95	0.00	0.00	0.00	14,133.90

Look at Figure 13.3. This is basically the same idea as the accounts receivable aging and shows you how you are performing in paying your vendors. An investor or banker will want to know how much of your cash flow comes from delaying payments. The firm in this illustration is responsibly paying all its bills within thirty days.

International Accounting Standards

In Europe and much of the world, accounting principles are dictated by the International Financial Reporting Standards (IFRS), originally created by the European Union (EU) and now overseen by the International Accounting Standards Board (IASB). In the U.S., the similar, but still significantly different, standards of the Generally Accepted Accounting Principles (GAAP), established by the Securities and Exchange Commission (SEC), are dominant.

Every action in business has some tax consequence, and understanding the tax environment in which you and your firm do business is critical in defining your business strategy and tactics. You may find that the choice between investing your time and resources in pursuing one line of business or another comes down to the tax treatment of that business. For instance, the State of

California levies a relatively high sales tax on goods sold at retail but does not tax labor services. Many small California businesses find ways to purchase expensive products from out of state suppliers to avoid the 7.5 percent tax. Additionally, you may find that being responsible for collecting and handling that money for the benefit of the state is an unrewarded burden. For this reason, if you're a computer professional in California with an entrepreneurial bent, it may make more sense to leap into computer services as opposed to selling computer hardware.

The process of declaring taxes due to the government may also require or call for particular accounting approaches. Often the accounting documents that you and your CPA produce for taxes, while they must be "true" in their own right, may look very different from the accounting reports you use to actually manage your business. For example, a small business may find that while accrual accounting is preferable for actually managing their operations, using cash accounting for filing their income taxes is a better choice. Can you think of why this would be?

If a business shows a loss at the end of the year, it will, in most cases, owe no income tax or even be able to pass a loss onto the business owner's personal returns. Timing this properly can be very beneficial for the owners of the business. Consequently, choosing the cash accounting method can be helpful. Consider that if your customers owe you a lot of money at the end of the year and you pay all of your bills before January 1, you can end up with very little cash on hand and likely show a loss on a cash basis, in which case, you likely will not owe any taxes. On an accrual basis, your firm may look very healthy now, with no liabilities (you paid those bills) and a lot of accounts receivable (those customer checks you are waiting for). In fact, you may even want to pay your rent a month or two in advance and just not go to the mailbox after Christmas (where customer checks might be sitting).

Governments may also require small businesses to follow some very arcane accounting rules. A common example of this is tax depreciation schedules that mandate that specific types of equipment be accounted for over a certain number of years, regardless of how long it actually lasts for your particular business. For example, the IRS might require that you depreciate your laptop computers over a five-year period, even if you actually must replace them every other year in order to remain up to date. The actual rules for depreciation are based on tables with different linear and nonlinear schedules. Worse, they are subject to change from year-to-year to suit the desire of politicians to promote the purchases of some types of equipment. Therefore, you should consult an accounting professional before making significant purchases of capital equipment or property.

Tax strategy for small businesses will be discussed in Chapter 14 and Chapter 15.

Finding and Selecting Accounting Professionals

The first level of accounting service providers is **bookkeepers**. Bookkeepers are useful for doing the regular job of making sure your revenues and expenses are properly entered into your accounting system. Bookkeepers also do the legwork of generating accounting reports and preparing the firm's books for tax preparation by an accountant.

bookkeeper

An individual who manages the posting of revenues and expenses to a firm's books, prepares reports, and may assist an accountant or tax preparer in readying a firm's books for tax filings.

accountant

A person who performs accounting functions or provides accounting services to businesses and individuals. In most cases, this title implies no specific qualifications, education, or certification.

trained accountant

An accounting professional with some schooling, usually a four-year degree and work experience.

certified public accountant

A certification of accounting competence in the United States that requires education, experience, and the passing of a rigorous exam.

qualified accountant

A member of any one of six accountancy bodies formed by royal charter in the United Kingdom.

chartered accountant

An accounting professional who has passed a series of examinations and is registered with the Institute of Charted Accountants of England, Scotland, Ireland, or another Commonwealth nation. Equivalent to the U.S. CPA designation.

In many cases, if someone says they are an **accountant**, the title may say very little about their actual training, credibility, capabilities, or certification. Outside of specific areas of practice, such as tax preparation and auditing, anyone can claim to be an "accountant." Typically, a **trained accountant** has a two- or four-year college degree and some practical work experience managing a firm's books but holds no specific educational qualifications or certification. This isn't to say such an individual might not be very good at what they do. Trained accounts can be very helpful in the preparation of internal financial statements, simple tax returns, and reports. After passing a test, a trained accountant can be authorized to practice before the U.S. Internal Revenue Service (IRS) as enrolled agents.

In the U.S., a **certified public accountant** or CPA is a person who has passed an extremely rigorous exam, spent at least two years working for another CPA, and in most cases, also has an advanced college degree in accounting or finance. CPAs add the required credibility to financial statements for outside users such as banks, flooring companies, and other lenders. They also prepare complicated income tax returns and calculate business valuations for a variety of purposes including the sales of businesses. CPAs are also valuable as expert witnesses in court cases.

In the United Kingdom, a **qualified accountant** is a member of any one of six accountancy bodies formed by royal charter. The UK **chartered accountant** title is basically equivalent to that of CPA in the U.S. Chartered accountants must pass a series of examinations and be registered with the Institute of Charted Accountants of England, Scotland, Ireland, or another Commonwealth nation.

You can find accounting professionals through many different avenues. By far, the best way is by personal recommendation from a colleague who runs a business similar to yours. Don't be afraid to ask the owners of other small businesses in your community for a recommendation. Other good referral sources are your commercial banker, your attorney, and your insurance broker. You can also search the website of the accounting professional society in your state. For instance, the California Society of CPAs maintains an extensive list of its members and their areas of specialization.

Accountants often operate together in partnerships large or small. Bookkeepers are typically independent operators. Of the two, it is typically harder to secure a good bookkeeper because the good ones tend to very quickly acquire a maximum load of clients, whereas accounting firms have the ability to add capacity in the form of interns and new hires.

As with any professional you hire, the final responsibility for selecting accounting service providers is the business owners'. This is important. Research their qualifications and check their references carefully. If you can, check their personal credit and criminal records—you probably don't want an accountant who has gone bankrupt or a bookkeeper who has been jailed for fraud, unless that sort of expertise adds value to your particular business.

Key Takeaways

- You must regularly generate and review your financial statements.
- If your money is in your customer's hands and in your inventory, you can't use it.
- Your vendors or lenders may help fund your inventory so you can use your cash.
- Use financial statements to determine if you are profitable.
- Remember being profitable is not always the same as generating usable cash.
- Hire the right professionals to manage your books, accounting, and taxes.

13.3 Accounting Systems

Learning Objectives

1. Recognize the importance of choosing an appropriate accounting system.
2. Understand the importance of finding a solution that will scale with your business.
3. Understand that changing your accounting system is very difficult.
4. Plan ahead for a change if your business is going to scale.
5. Understand the advantages of cloud-based SAS solutions.
6. Recognize the value of keeping your data in a professional data center.

Software

As discussed in Chapter 12, dashboards are a perfect source of feedback for managing execution and making tactical adjustments in the short run. The effectiveness of your longer-term strategies is most visible in the accounting data covered in this chapter and the financial ratios in following chapters. Quarterly and annual review of this data will let you know if your strategies are paying off, literally.

While not all companies chose to utilize dashboards, accounting is an absolute necessity. In fact, in most any jurisdiction around the world, it is a legal requirement for companies to track sales and costs and calculate their profits for tax purposes. Choosing an accounting system and making the right choice up front is critical. For anything bigger than a lunch cart, a paper-based accounting system is out of the question. Even for the smallest of businesses, there are expense and sales tracking apps add real value.

Your business may not always be small, however. As with facilities, your choice in accounting systems should be forward-thinking and support your company today and in the foreseeable future. The switching cost of changing accounting systems can be very high. It takes a lot of time to retrain your staff and move all the data from one system to another. Since the software vendors do not benefit from your leaving their platform, the tools to export that data are rarely simple to navigate and far from universal. You can expect to spend a lot of time doing manual entries any time you change systems from something simple like QuickBooks to a more sophisticated enterprise financial system from Oracle or SAP.

Today, nearly all business accounting and related functions are managed by software systems.

Source: © Shutterstock, Inc.

On the other hand, installing a feature-rich system designed for a much bigger organization can burden a nimble startup with complexities that will slow it down. Training, maintaining, and complying with the requirements of a system like SAP could undermine your primary source of competitive advantage, speed. The cost of such a system may also be completely out of line. In the end, planning for at least one software transition during scaling may be inevitable. It shouldn't surprise you that there are firms and consulting experts who specialize in helping growing firms do just that.

Online Solutions

Another important choice to consider is local versus cloud-hosted solutions. Traditional accounting systems reside on servers within your organization's network. Cloud-hosted systems keep your data in remote data centers accessible over the internet. Having everything online and accessible from a variety of devices is a basic tool of the New Entrepreneurial Dynamic. Most modern accounting systems offer these options. QuickBooks online, offered by Intuit, is currently the most popular solution for small and medium-sized businesses and startups, particularly in the service sectors. Other choices to consider include Xero and Sage 50cloud. For single-person firms, Zoho Books and Intuit's QuickBooks Self-Employed are good choices.

When the software application itself, along with the data, is hosted offsite and provided to you via a web interface or app, it is commonly referred to as Software as a Service or SaaS. Such systems solutions are commonly purchased as a subscription, which includes support services.

While having everything at your fingertips anywhere you travel and being able to share your accounting data with your outside CPA is great, security is a critical consideration as well. Accounting data is a top target of cybercriminals. Your competitors, as well as cybervandals and extortionists, can be a very real threat to your accounting system. According to UK insurer Hiscox, cyber-attacks cost firms an average of $200,000 per incident and have put many out of business.[4]

At first glance, it might appear that an internally hosted system would be more secure. Still, the reality is that few small firms have the expertise or time to maintain servers properly, keep the backups, and provide world-class data security. Updating applications and keeping the security patches in place is just extra work that can be avoided in a SaaS solution. Professional cloud data center providers, like Amazon Web Services, do that for you. Being secure and reliable is their competitive advantage.

If you chose to run your own accounting system, you would still do well to host it on a virtualized server in the cloud, hosted by a professional organization. Unless you keep your accounting server on a completely separate network, inaccessible from the internet, you're likely at risk to external hackers. In any case, those with access to your facilities (including custodial staff and visiting contractors) are also potential security threats. Online accounting providers like Sage and Intuit are also security pros, and you are probably better off if you can leave the accounting IT issues to them and focus on your firm's core competencies.

In making these choices, you should consult your peers, other business owners with similar needs to yourself. They can very likely help you avoid mistakes in the first place, help you when you make them, and point you to qualified accounting system consultants.

Gamify Your Biz! *Accounting Need Not Be Dull*

The traditional way of looking at accounting is to approach it as a task required for operational, legal, or tax purposes. When you are required to do something and to do it in ways that are very precisely defined by others, it can be less than exciting. This is particularly true for the most creative sorts of entrepreneurs, who are by their nature disruptive rule breakers.

The trick to making accounting less of a chore is to realize that *accounting is the score keeping system in the game of business*. When you work in your accounting system you are actually racking up the points you've accumulated from your competitive work in the market. Visualize reviewing your monthly financial statements as if you've reached the end of a game section and are "leveling up." Picture the reward part of the game where your character pauses while coins flash, music plays, and your bonus points are tallied up. With this perspective, making those numbers better each month can become a virtuous obsession, driving you to work harder and to even look forward to reviewing your financial statements.

Key Takeaways

- Carefully consider your accounting system choices from the start.
- Plan for scaling but don't burden your business with undue complexity.
- When in doubt, keep your applications and data in the cloud.
- Consider asking your peers for advice on accounting solutions.

13.4 Case Study: When Things Go Bad, Very Bad: An Accounting Nightmare

It was early Monday morning, and the woman in the sharp suit with the briefcase standing at the back door did not look at all happy. When she thrust her credentials at him, Joe Singleton[5] wasn't happy either. He read the laminated ID that proclaimed the lady was "Ms. Baker, Revenue Agent." Ms. Baker was from the Internal Revenue Service, the IRS. Joe wasn't expecting this. Why had a revenue agent, an accountant for the U.S. federal tax agency, come pounding on the back door of Joe's small office equipment business? Whatever this was about, it was unlikely to be good. IRS agents did not hand-deliver refund checks; he was pretty sure about that.

The formalities were quickly over, and Joe quickly came to the reality that his company was in the middle of an underpayment of taxes investigation that he knew nothing about and that this woman had an appointment with his office manager to collect payment and determine penalties. That office manager, Sophia, was not in yet.

Somehow, Joe was not surprised. Sophia had been acting rather oddly as of late, and being honest with himself, he'd not been paying much attention to the accounting. Joe had been focused on sales opportunities with several big accounts in town, and Sophia had been really running the place for months. He'd always depended on Sophia. She'd been a friend of the family for years before she came on to help at the firm. Sophia's husband, Tony, was well off enough that they really didn't need the money, but she was smart and enjoyed the work and being part of a team. Things had gone really well for several years. But lately, Sophia had been under a lot of stress outside of work. She seemed distant, and maybe she was hiding something.

Joe knew what that "something" was now. The IRS had been communicating with Sophia, or at least trying to, for months. She had, for whatever reason, not shared this information with Joe. It appeared the firm owed tens of thousands of dollars in wage withholdings, money that Sophia had deducted from the employees' checks for their taxes but not forwarded to the IRS as required. Instead, it had been spent. This was not only a financial nightmare, it was a potentially criminal act. An employer has a fiduciary commitment to handle employee tax money properly. Intentional failure to do so is a felony. Joe had a sudden vision of the inside of the nearby prison, which his firm provided services to. It was a very unpleasant visualization.

He set Ms. Baker down in the conference room and went to find his wayward office manager. Sophia had not come in at her usual time that morning. That wasn't too abnormal; nobody punched a clock here, but it was now more than an hour into the day, and Sophia was apparently totally AWOL. Calls to her home and mobile phone went unanswered. "How convenient," Joe thought. With absolutely no data on hand or any idea of what their excuse might be, Joe turned to the IRS agent, apologized profusely, and threw himself upon the mercy of the federal government. He was really, really wishing he'd paid a lot more attention to the books.

It appeared to be Joe's lucky day; perhaps Ms. Baker was less officious than her peers or the IRS's reputation for being hardnosed about such things was overblown. In any case, while the matter was very serious, it didn't look like Joe was going to be working out in the prison yard any time soon. Ms. Baker showed him the payment records, and he quickly understood what was going on. The timing was the problem. It was clear to him now. He could see how his focus on sales to big, slow-paying customers like the city government had sucked cash out of his firm just as he was hiring new technicians to cover the expanded business. Sophia must have run out of money to pay the government and, for whatever reason, had decided not to tell him. He assured Ms. Baker he'd get to the bottom of this promptly and get the monies repaid. She said she'd seen this before and would give him two weeks to report back with a status and plan for repayment. Joe was thankful to see her leave on cordial terms and eager to find out what the hell was going on.

Sophia never returned, apparently suffering from a mental health crisis. Joe was forced to get his wife to take time off her work to come in and help. As the couple dug into the accounting, it turned out to be a bit of a mess, with paperwork scattered, and some of it even intentionally hidden in a bathroom cabinet. Slowly a pattern of deception emerged. When their credit line at the bank had been maxed out, Sophia had begun to try creative things like selling inventory from the shop back to the firm on its one credit card, generating cash today that wouldn't be due for thirty days. When that wasn't enough, she had begun to divert the funds that should have gone to the government to cover the critical bills like rent and electricity. Occasionally, Sophia had been able to catch back up on the payments, but each time the amounts got larger, and the situation only got worse. Eventually, they were hopelessly behind. Joe knew that he was busy and could react emotionally to negative news, but he could still not fathom why Sophia had never told him. It was as though she'd taken one step down the wrong path and found she could never own up to the situation. The bottom line was that they were going to have to find money and seriously reduce expenses for some time to pay all of this off.

At the end of the week, Joe called a general meeting with his dozen employees and told them the bad news that the firm had "made an error in judgment" and owed the government a great deal of money. He was dreadfully sorry, but everyone was going to be impacted by this situation. He would begin by cutting his own salary in half and was asking them all to take a temporary 10 percent cut, which he promised he'd make up. The only other option was to shut the firm down and liquidate its assets, and that wouldn't be good for anyone. As it was, they were going to have to sell some equipment, delay upgrades, and make do with less for a year or more. The employees, while less than happy themselves, agreed to the plan and committed to getting this done.

The following Monday, Joe called Ms. Baker and made an appointment to present his findings and plan. The agent was able to come out the same day and was pleased with the firm's quick response to the situation. She approved the repayment schedule Joe proposed and was even willing to reduce some of the penalties to help Joe pay off the debt more quickly. Joe took the good news to the employees, and they set to the task at hand.

Joe set to work by negotiating a deeper credit line with the bank, convincing his big customers to pay more quickly in exchange for a small discount, reducing expenses across the shop, and moving some of his vendor payments out to longer term. Within eight months, the IRS was paid off, and employee salaries were returned to normal levels. Joe's own salary stayed at half for more than a year, and that was not easy, but it was a lesson learned, and he was thankful he still had a business.

Endnotes

1. Peteraf, M. A. (1993). The cornerstones of competitive advantage: A resource-based view. *Strategic Management Journal, 14(3)*, 179–191.
2. Casciaro, T., & Piskorski, M. J. (2005). Power imbalance, mutual dependence, and constraint absorption: A closer look at resource dependence theory. *Administrative Science Quarterly, 50*(2), 167–199.
3. Note that "k," as in "kilo," has been used to represent a thousand dollars, so $500k is $500,000. This is a common verbal shortcut used in small business financial discussions.
4. https://www.hiscox.com/documents/2019-Hiscox-Cyber-Readiness-Report.pdf
5. Due to the sensitive nature of this case, the names and identifying characteristics of the business and individuals have been changed.

CHAPTER 14
Managing Cash Flow and Finance

Sometimes I think it's a sin
When I feel like I'm winnin' when I'm losin' again.
—*Gordon Lightfoot, "Sundown"*

Running out of money is the event that declares a company dead.

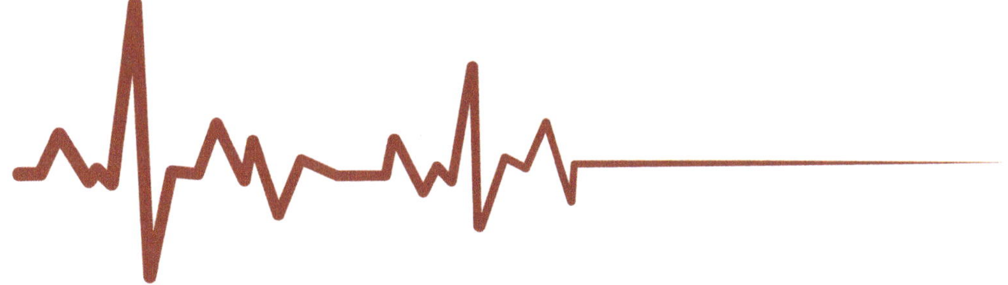

Source: © Shutterstock, Inc.

Cash flow is the blood flow of a firm. Just as death may be officially declared when a person's heart stops beating, businesses are "pronounced dead" when they run out of money. A firm without money on hand is unable to pay the bills that keep the doors open, the website up, and the employees working. We call this condition **bankruptcy**. Just as a person suffering heart failure may be revived with CPR or a defibrillator, some firms do survive bankruptcy and live to do business again. A firm that is not bankrupt, one that is able to pay its bills, is called **solvent**. This chapter is about the financial management tools that can help your firm remain solvent.

bankruptcy

The condition of a firm or individual being unable to meet their debt obligations. Bankruptcy officially occurs when a creditor, such as a landlord, vendors, or employees, sues for payment, or the firm proactively seeks protection from a court. Bankruptcy may be resolved in several ways.

solvent

The state of being able to meet all current obligations; not bankrupt.

14.1 Cash Flow

Learning Objectives

1. Recognize that lack of cash is what kills firms.
2. Understand how to recognize a cash flow crisis.
3. Be aware of options to avert a cash flow crisis.
4. Learn critical financial ratios.
5. Understand what bankruptcy is and how to use it if necessary.
6. Appreciate a variety of tools that can improve cash flow.

Analyzing Data

Basic accounting skills are critical for small business owners. However, simply counting your money is useless. You must analyze your financial data in the context of your business strategy and be prepared to make timely adjustments to your business model.

Is your business moving in the right direction? Are sales up or down? Are customers responding to your marketing? Are vendors delivering products on time and at the costs you anticipated? Are there particular areas that are underperforming? In the past, business managers would look at accounting statements and reports generated each quarter or year to determine how their business was doing. In the twenty-first century, things move far too quickly for that. Repeating a mistake for three or twelve months might kill your small business!

The Overriding Importance of Cash Flow

The most obvious cause of financial distress in business is lack of revenue—the failure to find sufficient customers and sell them the product or service. Another cause is a lack of net income—the inability to demand a market price sufficiently high enough or to hold the cost of goods sold and fixed costs low enough to make a profit on sales.

However, something that routinely shuts down even profitable small firms is a **cash flow crisis**—the tragic mistiming of accounts receivable and accounts payable. This comes to a head when some perfect storm of bills hits just when sales or collections are also slow.

cash flow crisis

A situation in which a business, otherwise profitable, is temporarily unable to meet its obligation because of the timing of cash flows in and out of the firm.

Imagine your spouse and you have long dreamed of living on a lovely island in the Caribbean. You carefully plan and invest in a lifestyle business, renting beach gear at a resort not far from the port. In the fall and winter months, sun-seeking cruise ship passengers from Canada and the Midwest states arrive by the thousands weekly. These are your most **anchor customers**. In fact, groups brought to you from the excursion services of the cruise lines account for more than half of your income.

anchor customer

The customer or customers who provide the bulk of a firm's revenue. Anchor customers are a dependable source of income that makes the variations of smaller clients less significant.

In order to protect itself from lawsuits associated with potential passenger injuries on the beach, the cruise lines require your firm to maintain liability insurance for $1 million and to also list their firms as "additionally insured" on your policy. Such requirements are an increasingly common part of business service agreements. Usually, the smaller firm is burdened with providing insurance to protect the larger partner as they are the bigger target for any potential lawsuit. The annual premium for the renewal of your insurance policy is due each October 1, the date you originally opened your operations and activated the original policy.

Your rental business has done well each year, but revenues are seasonal. Every year the hot summer months are slow, and come fall, it's hard to make ends meet. Your normal payroll, rent, and utilities are also due at the start of each month. However, you've always managed to find the money on October 1, and things look fine by November when the snowbirds begin to flock south for the winter.

This year, two unseasonably late back-to-back hurricanes threatened your island. Disaster was averted, but the big cruise ships all canceled their port stops for two weeks in late September. Your revenues completely evaporated, but your bills did not! Forced to choose between not paying your employees, the landlord, the utilities, or the insurance company, you had to opt for delaying the insurance payment until you got caught up. The insurer is required to notify the "additionally insured" cruise lines that your policy has lapsed. Even though you manage to scrape together the cash and reinstate the policy within weeks, your liability-conscious customers instantly moved to one of your older and seemingly more stable competitors. The remainder of the year's holiday revenues are dismal without the cruise customers, and by January, you are unable to pay the rent or your employees. You're forced to close the doors and head back to your miserable desk job in the big city. Your Caribbean dreams have been crushed by what you'll call "bad luck," but it was actually bad financial management.

Natural disasters can completely upend your business model.

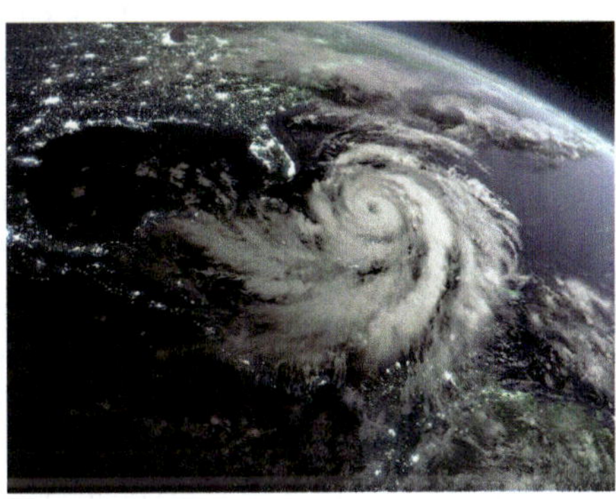

Source: © Shutterstock, Inc.

The previous scenario, or one much like it, is sadly familiar to bankruptcy lawyers and courts the world over. Managing cash flow well is an art and a science that every small business owner must master to avoid this fate! There are several things you, our hypothetical beach rental operator, might have done to save this blissful business.

The first task would be to make sure that no major bills are due during your most vulnerable period, the end of the slow summer season. The insurance premium was due annually on October 1 because that was the date the business originally began operations. You had actually strategically positioned yourself for a holiday season launch so that your new business would start out in the healthiest possible revenue environment. However, clearly understanding the cyclical nature of your economic environment, you should have looked ahead and seen that the annual insurance renewal would come one year later, at the end of the summer dry spell! And experiencing that very tight squeeze several years in a row should have also alerted you to how dangerous this timing was. Prepaying some of the insurance premium in the spring or asking your insurance agent to change the billing cycle would have prevented this problem and saved your dream! Another good option is to have either an **emergency cash reserve** that is sacrosanct outside of a crisis or to have established a **line of credit** with your banker in advance.

emergency cash reserve

Money a firm keeps saved and allocated for a "rainy day" crisis.

line of credit

An arrangement between a bank and a business to preapprove borrowing up to a certain limit. Similar to a *revolving credit agreement*.

Financial Analysis and Ratios

Not surprisingly, certain valuable metrics are common to many, if not all, businesses. Over the years, accountants and investment professionals have developed a helpful array of accounting-based metrics called *financial ratios*. You may find these are powerful additions to building an actionable dashboard of the sort described in previous chapters.

top line

The revenues or gross sales of a firm.

free cash flow

A measure of a firm's financial performance. It is calculated as operating cash flow—capital expenditures.

When you look at your financial statements, how do you know if you're doing well? Is your **top line** (sales revenues) looking good? Let's say you're selling $1 million a year in product. Is that good? Well, for a donut shop, a million dollars a year in sales is excellent. For a car dealership, not so much. Just as in our engine temperature example, context is everything.

Now, if your donut shop sells $1 million in donuts in a year, that is fantastic! However, it's not good if you achieved that feat by selling donuts cheap while loading them up with expensive, high-quality ingredients and advertising heavily. In that case, the cost of making donuts and selling them could exceed your revenues. If you're spending $1.2 million a year to sell $1 million in donuts, your gross profits are actually gross losses! Even if your profit margins are great, what if your **free cash flow** is negative because you are selling a lot of donuts wholesale to a grocery store chain on net terms, and they do not pay quickly? That might be fine if you've got enough money in the bank to survive until your accounts receivables come in. If you don't have the money in the bank to pay the rent, all that wholesale business could be a bad thing.

Let's get more specific. Imagine that on a typical day, your gross profits are $1,500. Is that enough profit? Without context, $1,500 a day doesn't mean anything. If your total fixed costs (rent, salaries, utilities, insurance) are running $600 a day, then that's pretty good because you've got $900 ($1,500 – $600) in net profits each day to take home or reinvest in your business. If fixed costs are $2,000 a day, then it's not gonna fly. You're going to have to put in $500 ($1,500 – $2,000) each day in cash to keep this business running.

financial ratio

The relative magnitude of two or more selected values from an accounting statement that illuminate the overall or specific financial condition of a firm.

What if you considered your gross profits relative to your fixed costs? That could be really useful information! For example, $1,500 in gross profits divided by $600 in fixed costs equals 2.5. That means your daily gross profits are 250 percent of your daily fixed costs. As long as your gross profits/fixed costs result is greater than 1 (or 100 percent), you're making money. On the other hand, $1,500 a day divided by $2,000 in fixed costs equals just 0.75 (75 percent), and that means you've got a problem. This is a very simple **financial ratio**. Such ratios are valuable additions to your dashboard.

A financial ratio is a simple calculation that contrasts the relative magnitude of two important data points. Ratios are among the most important tools in your entrepreneurial toolbox. A quick look at the right ratios can reveal a great deal about a firm's situation. Ratios help to identify danger points as well as opportunities.

Looking at your profits at any one moment in time is pretty straightforward, but what about your growth rate? Is your business moving in the right direction over time? Are sales up? Are profits up year over year? Financial ratios can also be used to analyze the performance of your business over time. With the dozens of data points on your financial statements, there are a lot of possible ratios, but not all combinations are useful.

Let's review a sampling of common financial ratios favored by small business managers, accountants, bankers, and stock analysts. The ratios indicated with stars (*) are the ones most often recommended for small business managers.

Current ratio: A measure of liquidity or your firm's ability to pay its debts. It's calculated as current assets/current liabilities. A firm whose assets (the value of its cash, things it owns, and what others owe it) exceed its liabilities (how much it owes) has a current ratio of greater than 1.0. A firm with a ratio of less than 1.0 may be in trouble, and if it were forced to pay what it owes today, it would go bankrupt. If you find your current ratio is under 1.0, you had better be counting on adequate future growth in profits coming along to pay your obligations that are all due.

Quick ratio: A measure of a firm's ability to meet its immediate obligations. It is calculated as (current assets – inventories)/current liabilities. That means cash on hand, cash in the bank, and the accounts receivable divided by the bills that are due now. A firm with a ratio of less than 1 is currently unable to meet its obligations. While many payments can be delayed past their due date, a firm in this situation may be in serious trouble. For that reason, the quick ratio is sometimes called the "acid test" ratio.

Cash ratio: Similar to quick ratio but does not include the accounts receivable. It's just the cash on hand over the bills that are due now. It is calculated as cash/current liabilities.

Return on assets (ROA): A measure of how well you are using your assets to generate profits. It is calculated as net income/total assets. A firm that has a high ratio is generating a lot of income with relatively few assets. If you see this ratio dropping, it could be an indicator that you may not have purchased the right mix of assets for your operation.

Return on equity (ROE): A measure of how efficiently a firm is using the investment of its shareholders. It is calculated as net income/shareholder equity. Again, we'd like this to be a higher ratio, with more net income relative to equity. If you see this ratio dropping, it could be an indicator that your investments are not delivering.

Return on investment (ROI): A measure of the profitable use of investments. It is calculated as (revenue from investment – cost of investment)/cost of investment. For a firm past its startup stage (favoring growth over profits), a negative ROI value is a serious indicator of trouble.

Return on capital employed (ROCE): A measure of the efficiency with which a firm uses its capital (money invested). ROCE is calculated as earnings before interest and tax (EBIT)/capital employed. Investors are very interested in this ratio because it indicates how well your firm is using its money. If your firm is self-funded, you should be just as concerned because it's your money in operation.

Debt ratio: A measure of a firm's *leverage* or the ratio of its obligations to its assets. It is calculated as total debt/total assets. A firm that is *solvent* will have a value of less than 1. The actual appropriate ratio depends on the industry the firm is in, the interest that it pays for its debt, and how effectively it utilizes that debt. If the value is greater than 1, the company's debts exceed its assets, and if there is no additional funding on its way, that firm is technically bankrupt.

Debt-equity ratio: Another indicator of leverage. It shows the ratio of liabilities to the firm's shareholder equity (the value of all it owns minus what it owes). Debt equity ratio is calculated as total debt/(total assets – total debt). Again, the correct value depends on the industry, and anything above 100 percent (1.00) is a serious indicator of trouble in a mature business.

Capitalization ratio: Yet another debt ratio that focuses on a firm's long-term liabilities, which are the debts that are usually invested in capital equipment like facilities, tooling, and vehicles. It is calculated as long-term debt/long-term debt + (total assets – total debt). Note that the last term (total assets – total debt) is our shareholder equity.

Interest coverage ratio: Designed to determine a firm's ability to service or pay the interest on its debt, it is calculated as EBIT/interest expense. Simply put, if interest payments are a large percentage of your earnings, you may have issues. If this value is less than 2, then you are paying more than half your earnings out as interest. That means you are literally working for someone else (your lender) more than for yourself, and that's probably not the reason you went into business.

Cash flow to debt payment ratio: A ratio that shows how much of a firm's operating cash flow is consumed by debt payments (interest plus principal). It is calculated simply as cash flow from operations/debt payments. It is important to note that units of time specified for both terms must be identical (month, quarter, year).

Fixed-asset turnover: A performance measurement that shows how a firm is able to generate sales from its investment in fixed-assets. It is calculated as sales/fixed assets. The higher this value, the more efficient the utilization of fixed assets is. This ratio is appropriate in firms, like manufacturing firms, where fixed assets are significant.

Inventory turn ratio: A very popular measurement of how often a firm replaces its inventory. This is a very important metric for retailing and distribution firms because items sitting on shelves in stores and warehouses cost money. Turning your inventory more frequently generates higher profits and healthier cash flow. This ratio is calculated as sales/inventory for a given period (month, quarter, year).

Revenue per employee: A simple calculation that shows how much your average employee contributes to firm sales. This figure varies based on industry. A software firm can have an astoundingly high ratio, whereas a "high-touch" service firm like a restaurant will likely have a low one. It is calculated simply as sales/employee count.

EBITDA

Earnings before interest, taxes, depreciation, and amortization. EBITDA is basically your sales, minus your COGS, minus your fixed costs.

EBITDA versus net sales: Looks at the percentage of profits to your sales. It is calculated as EBITDA/revenue. **EBITDA** is earnings before interest, taxes, depreciation, and amortization. EBITDA is basically your sales, minus your cost of goods sold (COGS), minus your fixed costs. It's the same as EBIT (covered in Chapter 13) but with any depreciation or amortization added back in. Don't panic; accounting systems will likely be able to provide you with EBITDA.

Build Your Own Ratios

Picking the right ratios that really matter for your company is important. In fact, you can build your own ratios out of metrics that are unique to your firm. Imagine you operate a company manufacturing customized tableware. You and a small team of artists and craft workers design a unique pattern for a customer, and after they approve it via your website or mobile app, you are able to print the image onto unfired blanks, fire up your kiln, and produce amazing custom stoneware and porcelain. The process of creating and getting the design approved is labor-intensive and the most expensive part of your business; however, you offer it to clients for free in the hopes they will order and reorder a great deal of your product over the years. When plates break or their family grows, you expect them to come back for reorders, which are relatively inexpensive for you to reprint and fire. What sort of metrics would this business want to track? It would seem the ratio of revenues to the number of new designs would be really valuable. It would be calculated as revenue / new designs. The higher that number, the better things are going. You might also want to track reorders per customer per year or sales per customer per year.

Bankruptcy and the Return of the Living Dead

As noted in the introduction to this chapter, a firm that cannot pay its bills is bankrupt. The legal condition of bankruptcy occurs when either the creditor(s) files a petition with the court demanding the firm be liquidated for payment or the debtor firm files a petition with the court seeking protection from the actions of its creditors. In most cases, it is the debtor firm that files the petition.

liquidated

An asset that is sold or a business whose assets have all been sold off.

Once this happens, the court must determine what assets the firm has and what they are worth. In a **Chapter 7 bankruptcy**, the company's assets are then **liquidated** to repay a portion of outstanding debt. When the bankruptcy is closed, the firm no longer is obligated to pay any debts that it incurred prior to filing for bankruptcy protection. In the U.S., there are three major types of bankruptcy defined by the chapters of the Federal Bankruptcy Code.

trustee

A government-appointed administrator who oversees bankruptcy reorganization or liquidation.

Chapter 7 bankruptcy occurs when the court or the debtor conclude that the bankrupt firm cannot be saved. Operations are halted, and a **trustee** is appointed by the court to shut the firm down and liquidate the nonexempt assets.

Chapter 11 bankruptcy occurs when the debtor believes its operations are profitable, and the court concurs that the firm can regain solvency if its operations or its debt are restructured—that is, the payment amounts, interest rates, and schedules are adjusted to make the debt manageable given the firm's cash flow. A firm typically needs to be profitable and have a positive cash flow to gain Chapter 11 protection. The debtor will submit a plan, to be adjusted by the court based on the creditor's concerns, to operate the business and repay the debts in a timely manner. Usually, the firm is left to execute this plan on its own behalf. If there is an indication that the firm's management has been corrupt or incompetent, the court may appoint a temporary trustee in a Chapter 11 case.

Chapter 11 bankruptcy is notoriously complex and costly in legal fees; however, a small business bankruptcy provision reduces the time and cost of the process for firms that owe less than $2,725,625.[1] The most important provision is that the court can prevent[2] the creation of a creditors committee—a method whereby many of the creditors' accounting and legal fees associated with the process fall onto the debtor. Under this procedure, there are shorter time limits, some additional filing requirements, and more oversight from the federal trustee's office.

Chapter 13 bankruptcy is reserved for individuals and sole proprietorships who owe less than a specific amount ($419,275 in **unsecured debt**, and $1,257,850 in **secured debt**, as of April 2019). It is generally simpler and less costly in time and legal fees, but corporations and partnerships may not apply for this protection. A trustee is nearly always appointed in a Chapter 13 bankruptcy.

unsecured debt

A loan that is not guaranteed by any asset pledged by the borrower.

secured debt

A loan that is guaranteed by some asset pledged by the borrower.

It is certainly best to avoid bankruptcy, but if your firm finds itself in that situation, it is critical to handle the process well. Learn about bankruptcy procedures. Excellent resources are available online from sites like Nolo.com. Listen to what others who have gone through the experience have to say. The mistakes they made are hard lessons you need not repeat.

Finding a skilled and honest lawyer is critical. While you can file for bankruptcy on your own, unless your business is very, very simple, legal assistance is required. A firm or individual in bankruptcy is likely to be in a depressed emotional state and often feels that they are at fault (they probably are) and therefore are not entitled to demand much out of this process. They and their remaining assets are easy targets for shysters of all kinds. Skip the bankruptcy pity party; at this moment, the most important thing is either getting your firm back on its feet or cleaning it up efficiently so you can get your creditors and employees paid and move on with your life in the best situation possible. Do not rush off and hire the legal firm that has the most ads on bus benches. If your relationship with your accountant is good, ask him or her for a legal reference. Take a day or two to ask around and get references from your peers if you can. Check with your local chamber of commerce or other business association.

Bank Credit Helps You Avoid Bankruptcy

The best way to handle bankruptcy is to avoid it. The best way to do that is to not get trapped in a cash flow crisis. And the best way to not get trapped in a cash flow crisis is to have a solid relationship with your bank and to establish a **revolving credit agreement**. Such an agreement allows you to tap the bank for money at any time without additional paperwork or explanation. With just a phone call or online transaction, thousands of dollars (or more) can be transferred into your company checking account. The credit agreement will also allow you to pay back the principal and interest over time. The important thing about such an agreement as compared to a traditional loan is that you have done all the paperwork upfront to satisfy the bank of your creditworthiness and arranged to secure the loan with appropriate assets such as facilities, inventory, equipment, or even accounts receivable. When a crisis does arrive, the last thing you need to be doing is spending the time to fill out a loan application and waiting for a bank to approve it—something that is much less likely to happen when you're in a crisis. (See the discussion on banking relationships in Chapter 8 for more information.)

revolving credit agreement

An agreement with a bank that allows you to draw cash when it is required and pay it back over time.

Banks loan money to firms they know can pay but that need cash to fund growth or manage cyclical cash flow challenges.

Source: © Shutterstock, Inc.

Renting and Leasing

Another important way to keep your cash flow smooth is simply to hold on to your cash in the first place. The best way to do that is to not pay for things upfront that you can pay for over time. Renting your facility instead of purchasing it is a major chance to not tie up your funds. For other expensive fixed assets like vehicles, computers, furniture, and manufacturing equipment, leasing is often the intelligent thing to do. Leases come with different terms. Depending on the life span of the asset, you may choose to lease a product for amounts of time from one to five or even ten years. The **disposition** of the property at the end of the lease is also a very important consideration. In a lease, the property technically belongs to the lessor (the firm you're borrowing from), and when the lease is up, they own it. You may or may not have the option to purchase the item, and that **buyout** price may be calculated in different ways. In a **true lease**, you will pay the **fair market value**, whatever the item could be sold for on the open market at the time the lease ends. A **capital lease** is really a loan constructed to look like a lease, and the buyout is an amount specified in the terms of the lease, very often as low as a token $1. The payments on a capital lease will be higher than those on a true lease.

disposition

The action or manner of disposing of a business asset, such as selling it.

buyout

Money required to complete the purchase of a leased or financed item.

true lease

A lease where the item being leased remains the property of the lessor at the end of the lease agreement.

fair market value

The price an asset can actually be sold for.

capital lease

A lease agreement where the lessee actually pays for the leased item in the payments and pays a token amount, usually $1, to transfer the property at the end of the lease.

Leasing can make machinery costing hundreds of thousands of dollars affordable to startups.

Source: Greg Autry

While the sellers of most major products will probably offer you a lease, it is very likely that they are offering you convenience and not the best rate. Occasionally the leasing deals offered to small businesses by auto and equipment dealers are outrageously abusive. You should take whatever they offer to your banker and see if he can do better. Different types of leases may also offer you varying state and federal tax advantages. Checking with your accountant on how to best structure a lease is also a good idea.

Negotiating Net Terms and Flooring

While leasing is appropriate for your fixed costs, is there a way to avoid paying for your COGS? The first thing to do is to negotiate the best payment terms on your material inputs or inventory. As noted in Chapter 13, if you run a bike shop and can get the bike vendor to give you net 60 or net 90 terms, you might actually collect money from your customer *before* you have to pay for the product. That sort of cash flow management is magical for a growing business. You are using someone else's interest- and equity-free money to finance your growth.

In Chapter 13, we mentioned that large companies and government agencies would take advantage of their relative power over your small firm to pay you slowly. This improves their cash flow, and you can do the same with your vendors. Paying a net 30 invoice in forty days probably won't ruin your relationship; on the other hand, it won't earn you friends either, and as a small buyer, you've got little power over these vendors. If you are seriously and/or repeatedly late in payments, your firm's credit rating may suffer. Typically, your smaller vendors and individual contractors are unlikely to be reporting to D&B. Picture the guys who repainted your shop or the lady who does your windows. They are also less likely to be legally aggressive. If you have to delay payment, these are usually the folks who sadly will suffer.

There are some things you simply can't be late on. Among these is payroll. In many jurisdictions, you have a legal obligation to pay your employees on time, and you may face serious fines or even criminal charges if you fail to do so or if you write a bad check. Paying sales taxes that you've collected from customers and payroll taxes you've withheld from employees is very serious (see Chapter 13 Section 4). These monies don't belong to you or your firm, and you have a fiduciary obligation to forward them to the government in a timely manner. Failure to do so could shut you down and lock you in jail. Similar laws apply to employee retirement funds.

If you can't get long enough payment terms, another option is flooring, also described in Chapter 13. In this situation, a third-party finance firm will pay for the inventory you keep on hand for sale. Either you or your vendor will pay the interest on this debt, and the inventory itself secures the debt—meaning the lender can seize it if you don't pay up.

Key Takeaways

- Cash is king.
- Leverage outside money to keep your working capital.
- Lease rather than buy when possible.
- Learn common financial ratios.
- Develop your own ratios.
- Integrate ratios into your dashboard and monitor them.

14.2 Finance

Learning Objectives

1. Understand the variety of business assets that can be collateralized.
2. Recognize the availability and risks of assuming personal debt for business purposes.
3. Understand the risks inherent in debt.
4. Recognize that small business and startup debt can put you personally at risk.

Collateral for Loans

Speaking of inventory, your banker may be willing to collateralize (secure a loan with) that as well. What other things do you think your business might have of value that your banker or a specialty lending group could lend against? Anything that you can show that you own and that might be reasonably liquidated or easily sold on some market is an option. In addition to inventory, this could include any fixed assets that are not already leased, accounts receivable, the value of future contracts, or the value of your patents or copyrights.

When a lender agrees to loan you money based on collateral, you cannot use that same collateral to secure another loan. In the U.S., the lender will file a document under the Uniform Commercial Code with the office of the secretary of state for their state. This UCC-1 filing states that they have first claim to a particular item. Other lenders will search this record before allowing you to make a loan against it and wait a bit to make sure you aren't doing two or more loans simultaneously on the same asset. For this reason, a loan approval process usually takes at least a few days.

invoice discounting

A lender advances money to a business based on invoices that have been issued to customers but are unpaid. The advanced money is discounted by some amount, typically about 10 percent, which the lender keeps when the customer pays.

factoring

A process of borrowing money against accounts receivable, the money owed to the firm by customers. Typically, the right to collect the invoices is transferred to the factor (lender).

Using your accounts receivable, the monies your customers owe you, as collateral for a loan is a special case known as **invoice discounting**. In that case, you show your bank or other lender your sales ledger, and they advance you funds equal to some percentage of that money. As you collect money from the customers, you pay the lender back with interest and fees.

Another popular option, particularly for manufacturing firms, is **factoring**, where you are essentially selling the invoices you've given your customers. The factoring company will pay you now, and they will collect the money from your customer when the bill is due. For that service, they take out a percentage of the monies invoiced. In this situation, your lender is more confident they will get paid, but the customer is aware that you are financing their payments. The lender may also be more aggressive in collecting than you would be. This can be helpful if you're not good at collections but may also alienate your clients if some rude collection person mistreats or frustrates them. Remember, the factoring company knows nothing about your product or service, and if the customer wants to dispute some detail of the invoice, they aren't likely to be helpful about that with your client or happy with you as the borrower.

Using Personal Debt

As was the case in funding a startup (Chapter 7), in many sole proprietorships or closely held firms, there are times when you may choose to use personal loans to finance business activities. For instance, borrowing against your home with a second mortgage or line of credit is comparatively easy, offers attractive interest rates, and is usually deductible against your personal income tax. This may be a very sensible choice, but you should work closely with your accountant to ensure that you are handling the transfer of monies to your firm properly for tax purposes. If there are other shareholders involved, it's important for everyone to understand how your infusion of personal cash impacts the equity of your firm. You're taking a significant risk on behalf of the firm, and there should be compensation. Are you expecting to be issued new stock, or is this a loan you are making to the firm? If it is a loan, are you entitled to interest?

We discussed the use of personal credit cards to launch a startup in Chapter 7, but it is worth revisiting credit cards here as well. *Entrepreneur* magazine reports that "credit cards are among the most popular sources of startup financing,"[3] but we also know that many small business owners use personal credit cards for ongoing business financing. An entrepreneur with a good credit history and some income will find it very easy to acquire multiple credit cards and can use those to purchase goods and services for the firm or even to get cash advances that are transferred into the firm.

Using personal credit cards to fund a business in this way can be extremely dangerous. *Entrepreneur* cautions that "the use of personal credit cards can be a very risky means of financing business operations. MasterCard and Visa weren't designed for this purpose."[4] The first reason for this is that credit card interest rates are notoriously high, and they are also variable. The credit card "agreement" is very one-sided in favor of the issuing bank, and so the minimum monthly payments, annual fees, and other terms can also increase without renegotiation. More importantly, when you acquire money in this manner, you are not forced through the financial and planning "due diligence" that a banker or investor would require. Even your mom would ask more questions than Citibank Visa will. This makes it much easier for you to be self-deluded about your firm's prospects as you "authorize" your own loans via credit card. If you've tried, and you cannot convince anyone else on earth to fund your enterprise, you must ask yourself, "Is this really a good investment or simply my personal desire?"

An entrepreneur must also differentiate between funding growth versus a desperate rescue attempt. If your gizmo factory suddenly receives a solid order for 100,000 gizmos that you know you can produce at a high profit, but for which you don't have the cash on hand to order the parts, then, by all means, reach for your credit card. Don't let that big order get away just because of cash flow. However, be sure you pay yourself back promptly when the customer's check arrives. Oh, and don't forget to pay your credit card off as well.

The same idea applies if your business has suffered a truly one-time and temporary setback. Imagine you run a hardware store in a small town in Oklahoma, and a tornado has just decimated Main Street. Your shop is in ruins, but your insurance company is solid, and you know that you are also in line for federal and state emergency assistance money to rebuild. All that paperwork will take a while. However, you want to open your doors the day after tomorrow to help your neighbors rebuild. Using your credit card to rent a construction trailer and purchase the basic inventory you need to get what had been a working business back in business might be a fantastic idea.

Credit cards can get you back in business while you await an insurance payment.

Source: © Shutterstock, Inc.

On the other hand, imagine that instead of a tornado, the Home Depot opens a new megastore just outside of town. Your small hardware store simply can't compete with their massive inventory, professional marketing, and low price plus high volume strategy. If you engage your personal credit to just keep the doors open at a shop with hopelessly declining sales, you are simply transferring a bankruptcy from a corporation onto yourself. Your personal credit should not be used to extend the painful life of a business model that is no longer working. It can be very hard for entrepreneurs to let go of their dream and very tempting to "ride it all the way down." Don't do it. Close the doors and save what you have to put into your next entrepreneurial dream.

Partner Financing

One of the biggest reasons small businesses find themselves in a cash flow crisis that requires financing is funding the expansion of their business. A bigger facility or new location will increase rent, utilities, and insurance. It will require expensive capital investment in equipment or fixtures, and new employees will need to be hired and trained. Usually, revenues will lag investment as the new location takes time to gather a customer base and/or get running at full speed. Paying someone good money to manage a money-losing new operation is extra costly.

A common solution to both the cash and labor problems is bringing on a new partner to help fund and run the new facility. A partner that can put in some cash and work for less—or even for free—can be a perfect solution. Such an arrangement does require giving up equity, however. Perhaps you'll attract a partner with the promise of letting them share in your existing success, or perhaps you'll only include them in a percentage of the new endeavor. You may simply create a contract to pay your partner a percentage of revenues, or you may actually offer them equity in your firm. To accomplish the latter scenario, you can establish a separate corporation or LLC with a different ownership mix than your existing one; consult your lawyer and accountant on how to best structure this.

Be extremely careful with this plan. Many people will be eager to join the expansion of a successful business! Spend the time to make sure your potential partners are the right fit to manage that relationship. The key to a successful partnership most often lies in personal compatibility, setting realistic expectations, and keeping communications open. Resentment can easily build between business partners who are too different, have different visions of their own value and rewards, or who don't talk regularly. A relationship failure could result in the failure of your new venture or even bring down your existing business.

A Cautionary Word on Debt

If you can get it, debt financing can often be the best way to build your business. It's flexible, and most importantly, it doesn't require that you give up equity or control of your business. Putting the value of all your firm's assets to work in funding a growth firm or one with profits that exceed any interest you pay can make sense. Borrowing is a particularly good choice when rates are low.

A personal guarantee may mean losing your home if your business fails to meet its obligations.

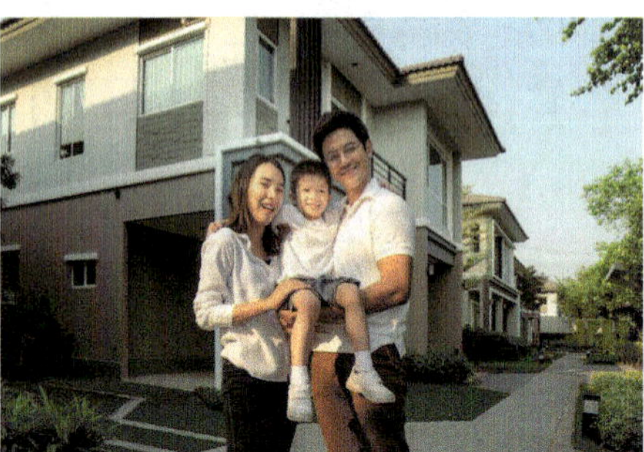

Source: © Shutterstock, Inc.

That said, you are strongly cautioned against running yourself or your small business into debt. While getting your first loans or credit cards can be very hard, once a credible lender trusts you with their money, you'll quickly find that everyone wants to lend you more. Debt can be easy to come by. You may find it to be the easy way out of too many dilemmas, and relying on it can be addictive. We recommend you regularly consult with your CPA or banker about the appropriate level of your total **debt load**.

debt load

The amount of money a firm owes.

There also may come a time when your growth phase is done and you don't expect to need so much cash on hand for operations. You may want to use your business to save and invest. Interest rates also vary over time (we will discuss this in a future chapter), and at times they can be relatively high. Under those circumstances, paying interest to others is not attractive unless the tax advantages are overwhelming. You may instead choose to purchase your facilities as a good long-term investment and even invest in real estate to rent to other firms. Again, consult with your banker and accountant.

It is also essential to note here how closely tied your business and personal debt obligations can be. Even if your firm is organized as a corporation, you may still be personally responsible for loans, leases, and flooring. This is because it is very likely that your creditors will require you to sign a **personal guarantee** to secure a business loan. This means that business bankruptcy will not protect you from repaying this debt and that the bank can attach your personal income and assets—including seizing and selling your home—to fulfill your obligation.

personal guarantee

The requirement that the business owner(s) agree to pay back a loan themselves if the business defaults. This puts the owner's personal assets, such as their home, at risk.

Flexibility and Creativity

> Raise money when you don't need it. When you need it don't go out to raise money, it's too late.
>
> —*Jack Ma*[5]

Today's small business owner should *always* be thinking of *creative* ways to secure money for when it will be needed. Finance and accounting are traditionally areas of very conservative thinking, but today's entrepreneur must be financially creative in order to survive. As this chapter shows, your banker is not sitting patiently waiting for you to run in and request help with a cash flow crisis. You need to prepare in advance for that day and to have multiple alternatives to your bank in mind as well. Financially, the New Entrepreneurial Dynamic is a fusion of preparation and resourcefulness.

Key Takeaways

- Utilize personal debt with care to bridge short-term cash flow issues.
- Avoid taking on long-term personal debt.
- Always think of your assets as potential sources of cash.
- Watch your debt load daily.
- Be aware of your personal obligations for business loans.

14.3 Case Study: Betting It All: An Unorthodox Cash Flow Gamble by Your Author

So, this crazy thing really happened—a lot of great business stories begin that way. In my late twenties, I (text author Greg Autry) owned a computer store and repair shop in Riverside, California. Business was going very well, and we had recently brought on a couple of larger corporate accounts and contracts with school districts and state and local governments. We were well on our way to doubling our $1 million a year business and looked really profitable according to the accrual financial reports. All this new business required rapidly expanding inventory and employee headcount. We were ordering a lot of parts on cash on delivery (COD) terms and recruiting new employees. Expenses were also increasing rapidly, but not as fast as revenues. So, I felt that everything looked great.

However, these new, larger clients paid much more slowly than our traditional individual and small business customers did. A lot of this profit had been accumulating in our Accounts Receivable (AR), which had ballooned to over $100,000. If I'd had a better financial education, such as this textbook on small business management, I would have seen a cash flow crisis coming, and I would have secured factoring on very high-quality AR to even out the cash flow. Lacking this expertise, I inevitably found myself faced with a serious cash shortfall as one of our new, larger payrolls came due.

I knew things were tight but disregarded the bookkeeper's warnings, fully expecting one or two large checks to arrive on time. Come Thursday afternoon, we had about half the money we needed to pay our employees the next day. Our two-week payroll ran about $20,000, but there was just over $10,000 in the bank. This was an immensely frustrating position to be in since *our customers owed us more than a hundred grand*!

I got on the phone at the last minute and tried to collect from every customer. As I recall, I was pretty blunt, "Hey, you guys owe us money, and I can't pay my staff. Have you mailed a check? If not, let me come pick it up today!" Although the bureaucrats who managed the AP at these big organizations seemed sympathetic and were willing to move payments along in a week or so, it would take multiple internal steps and approvals. Bottom line: we weren't going to get paid today or tomorrow.

I called my banker, Ken. He wasn't eager to make an emergency loan without going through all the due diligence either. Despite years of business with the bank and the fact that the clients who owed us money were the tops names in the county, the best Ken would offer was that he'd be "happy to send over a loan application." Approving that would take days or weeks. Meanwhile, the payroll checks had already been printed by Paychex. Half of them were good, but the slowest ones to the bank would find that their checks had bounced.

I considered what would happen if half the employees didn't get paid: not good. The inequality of the situation would be blatant. The employees would be up in arms, and who was I to decide who the winners and losers should be? That was a no-win situation. I also pondered writing new checks, giving all the employees half their wages. I knew these guys. Like most service employees, they lived paycheck to paycheck and needed every penny. Half a paycheck wouldn't cover their rent. It was clear that from my perspective, no check or half a check would both be equally unpopular outcomes that would undermine employee morale and impact productivity. I would surely find a few of my top workers running to my competition, where I knew they had standing offers. I concluded that any half-pay scheme would do as much damage as delaying paychecks entirely for a week—when I was sure we'd have more than enough money to pay them. This was one of those all or nothing situations, and I decided to roll the dice, almost literally.

Las Vegas is about a four-hour drive from Riverside, three and a half if you don't stop for the bathroom. At about 4 p.m., my business partner and I went to the bank, emptied the account, and headed for Nevada. Like many entrepreneurs, we were inclined to gamble, within reason. I even considered myself a skilled card player, primarily at poker. While poker is the gambling that comes closest to doing business, a game where strategy and sales skills count, it takes time to accumulate serious winnings. Being in a rush is the worst possible position for a poker player to be in, and big money poker tables are full of frighteningly good competitors who can smell desperation. What we needed then was a game that could double a bet quickly—or lose it all just as fast—and that game was blackjack.

We planned to go to a casino that still dealt single-deck blackjack—important if you want to count cards to improve your odds—and play small hands, waiting for the right moment to make a series of big bets with the $10k I had. This time it worked. Within an hour, we had well over $20k and a really nice free dinner—whether suspicious or superstitious, casinos often "comp" successful gamblers with meals or show tickets in order to "break their streak" or at least encourage them to "move along." We were more than happy to be "moved along." Early the next morning, we were red-eyed and bedraggled but parked outside our bank with a bag of cash, waiting for the doors to open. The employees never had a clue that there had been a problem. The customers paid up, and everyone was happy except our accountant—who had to figure out how to book $10,000 in cash income.

Needless to say, this was a very risky endeavor. I absolutely do not advise playing blackjack as a business financing strategy, particularly at modern casinos where high-tech surveillance and continuous card-shufflers keep the odds firmly in the house's favor. That said, I later discovered that we were in pretty good company.

According to Roger Frock, FedEx's first general manager, the overnight delivery firm's founder, Fred Smith, successfully used the very same tactic to pay the iconic firm's jet fuel bills during its early days. In his history of the firm, *Changing the Way the World Does Business*, Frock wrote, "By mid-July, our funds were so meager that on Friday we were down to about $5,000 in the checking account, while we needed $24,000 for the jet fuel payment."[6] Frock continues, "However, when I arrived back in Memphis on Monday morning, much to my surprise, the bank balance stood at nearly $32,000." Smith explained to Frock, "I knew we needed money, so I took a plane to Las Vegas and won $27,000." Underscoring the do or die nature of the situation, the wily entrepreneur adds, "What difference did it make?" FedEx would have been dead without the gamble, and today Smith is worth nearly $4 billion.

You can bet that for each of these lucky successes, there are dozens of failures you'll never hear about; entrepreneurs who left their businesses on a table in Vegas, Monte Carlo, or Macau. It is also important to note that in my case, I was gambling more with time than the final outcome. Our employees would all have been paid anyway, albeit a week late.

Endnotes

1. 11 U.S.C. §§ 1181-1195, Subchapter V.
2. If the bankruptcy court has determined the creditors' committee is insufficiently active and representative to provide oversight of the debtor. 11 U.S.C. § 101(51D).
3. https://www.entrepreneur.com/article/81822
4. https://www.entrepreneur.com/article/41520
5. Clark, D. (2018). *Alibaba: The house that Jack Ma built*. HarperCollins Publishers.
6. Frock, R. (2006). *Changing how the world does business: FedEx's incredible journey to success—The inside story*. Berrett-Koehler Publishers.

CHAPTER 15

The Business Environment and Government

> Entrepreneurship is a field rife with policy-relevant implications and yet we have little knowledge of the role of states in the entrepreneurship dynamic.
>
> —*Kaye Schoonhoven & Elaine Romanelli (2001)*[1]

Laws enacted by governments around the world impact startups.

Source: © Shutterstock, Inc.

Small business owners are often surprised to discover how influential the government can be in crafting the cultural environment and technical environments in which businesses must compete. A 2011 report of the Organisation for Economic Co-operation and Development (OECD) concluded that 42.5 percent of the U.S. economy is controlled by local, state, and federal governments. This figure is higher in Europe. Under the **state capitalism** economics of Russia and China, it is often unclear where the company ends and the government begins. Given that government is such a major environmental factor, it is surprising that it is often ignored in most business management texts.

state capitalism

A hybrid of socialism and capitalism where state-owned enterprises compete aggressively in international markets with economic and political support from their governments.

15.1 The Business Environment

Learning Objectives

1. Understand that firms must adapt to the business environment.
2. Recognize the legal, economic, cultural, and technological factors that shape the business environment.
3. Understand the roles government plays in defining the business environment.
4. Understand different types of government.
5. Understand regulations and taxes.
6. Understand compliance strategies.
7. Understand legal options.

Factors of the Business Environment

Some clothing is still custom made by hand for the client.

Source: © Shutterstock, Inc.

fashion

A popular cultural trend in products, typically clothing.

Imagine you own a boutique men's clothing store in Lima, Peru today. Does your business operate in the same way as a tailor's shop in nineteenth century London did? Could you apply the same knowledge set and skills to succeed? Obviously not, but why is that? Why does simply selling clothing to men vary so much with the change in time and place? There are obvious cultural differences, such as language and **fashion** choices. The money and the climate may differ. Though it is hard to imagine how these would significantly impact the process by which clothing is sold. Think about how and where clothing is produced in each case.

In the Victorian English tailor's shop, each and every piece of clothing was measured, hand cut, and sewn in the back of the shop for the client out of raw cloth. Your shop would have been one of several shops on the same High Street that looked and operated very much the same. While a few of these **bespoke** tailors still serve wealthy clients, almost everyone on Earth wears **ready-to-wear** clothing today. Your Peruvian store is filled with racks of ready-to-wear clothing items that were *made halfway around the world* and tailoring is limited to adjusting the hem on pant legs. Your shop probably looks a lot like others in Lima, and for that matter, it isn't likely to look much different from a small clothing store in Mumbai or Vancouver. Why is that? Inexpensive global transportation, lightspeed communications, and major shifts in national trade **policies** have made producing clothing thousands of miles from the consumer's purchase economically practical. These changes, generally referred to as **globalization**, have shifted the **business environment**, the conditions under which your business must operate and compete.

bespoke

A product an individual produced for a specific customer. Not mass-produced.

ready-to-wear

Clothing products that have been mass-produced in advance in a variety of predefined sizes for sale in a retail store to customers who will not have them tailored to fit.

policies

The particular course or action of government manifested in laws and regulations.

globalization

The cumulative process of internationalizing businesses, the disbursement of markets, supply chains, and production across the globe.

business environment

The external factors that define the opportunities and limitations of the market in which your business operates. Regulations, taxes, cultural norms, and customer expectations are some of the more common factors.

Most of our clothing is sold off the rack, ready to wear.

Source: © Shutterstock, Inc.

The business environment shapes the way businesses look and operate. Every business, big or small, grows and operates within an environment that provides opportunities yet also restricts its possible pursuits. Four major factors shape this environment: the legal, economic, cultural, and technological conditions.

These factors combine to define entire industries and how businesses within them succeed or perish. The New Entrepreneurial Dynamic also recognizes that these conditions will change over time. To survive, businesses must match their current environment and be prepared to adapt to the emerging one.

selection process

The evolutionary process by which firms that do not optimally fit their environment fail and leave the better-adapted competitors to continue.

mimetic isomorphism

The process whereby firms in a market copy each other and assume similar characteristics.

archetype

A very typical example of a type of person or thing.

Management scholars have long known that startup firms, just like Darwin's animals, are subject to a **selection process** that weeds out those that are not well adapted to their environment. Through a process known as **mimetic isomorphism**,[2] firms emulate competitors that they perceive as having the best environmental fit. Eventually, all of the businesses in a particular category begin to look very similar.

Let's consider American gas stations. Regardless of its brand or whether the station is an independent small business or one operated by a major oil company, they generally look and operate the same way. Consumers can easily find them, and they do not have to learn anything new in order to utilize their services. Gas stations are nearly always located on the corner of a major street intersection (sometimes all four corners); they are decked out in garish colors, are roughly the same size, accept credit cards at the pump, and have a convenience store selling a variety of unhealthy snacks, drinks, and tobacco products.

Industry and firm **archetypes**, like these gas stations, remain stable until some legal, cultural, economic, or technological change disrupts their environmental fit. In the past, economic conditions such as fuel and labor costs moved gas stations from full-service operations to self-serve, and technological innovations (satellite and internet connections for credit card processing) enabled pay at the pump. The growing complexity of modern auto electronics and the increasing reliability of cars drove stations to replace their service bays with convenience stores. In the near future, electric cars may significantly disrupt this business. Fuel pumps may change or vanish entirely, transforming these businesses from fuel stations into corner stores or something else. Remember that in the New Entrepreneurial Dynamic, *environmental change is opportunity*.

Legal Environment

smuggling

The illegal business of bringing products into a country outside the legal process. Smuggled products may be entirely illegal products or simply ones where the importer has avoided tariffs.

contraband

Products that are illegally imported or exported.

In most countries, a surprising myriad of laws dictate what sort of business you can and cannot establish and how you may run it. Did you know that if you own a corner shop in Singapore, it would be illegal for you to sell chewing gum? The government of that small city-state is extremely protective about cleanliness, and a law was enacted in 1992 to prevent people from disposing of their gum in a public place. It can be difficult to run a business when your product or service is in conflict with the law. This book isn't about selling or **smuggling contraband**. However, even perfectly legitimate businesses are often stymied by ill-considered laws, some of which may even have been promoted by their competitors, eager to erect legal barriers to market entry.

A Ukrainian border guard seizes American cigarettes smuggled across the Polish border to avoid Ukraine's tariff.

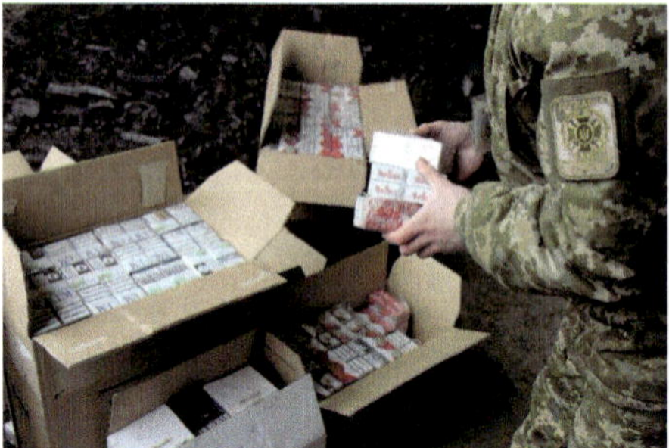

Source: Ivan Semenovych/Shutterstock.com

Economic Environment

Opportunities to found successful new enterprises or run existing small businesses are limited by the economic possibilities of their place and time—location matters. You can guess that it might be difficult to sell luxury goods or mobile apps in North Korea, where most people are very poor and don't have smartphones. The economic environment also varies over time in an inconsistent up and down sequence known as the **business cycle**. Even in **developed nations**, many businesses selling nonessentials suffer during economic recessions and major wars.

business cycle

The up and down pattern in national economic growth, usually measured as a change in real (inflation-adjusted) GDP.

developed nations

A country that is industrialized and has a sophisticated consumer economy, first-rate infrastructure, and a generally high standard of living.

Cultural Environment

Cultural norms are extremely important to businesses. The expectations of consumers for the nature and presentation of products and services vary by nation. It's not uncommon in parts of Spain to find bare legs of ham with hooves attached hanging in a corner market. In China, it might be whole ducks. These inviting gastronomical displays tend to shock visiting Americans who prefer their meat to be hermetically sealed in plastic and refrigerated. Americans expect their corner shops to offer sugar-packed junk food in bright plastic packages. Cultural factors also vary by time, driving what we call fashion. When a particular genre of music or movie is popular, it's easy to sell downloads and pack theaters with those products, but a few years later . . . not so much.

Cultural expectations of food presentation vary by nation and region within a nation.

Source: Greg Autry

Technological Environment

Engineering innovation is perhaps the most visible factor that a modern small business must adapt to. Technology is changing much more rapidly than any of the other factors, and most of the time, technical change is a positive factor for small businesses. Small businesses can evaluate and adopt new technologies quicker than large businesses. These new technologies often simplify or reduce the cost of doing business in ways that level the playing field. A good example can be seen in the retail cash register business. Traditional large retail stores have invested millions of dollars into cash registers and credit card processing systems from companies like NCR or IBM. A single register at a major retailer like Nordstrom's might cost $10,000. These systems were reliable and integrated into sophisticated reporting systems that provided big stores with a competitive advantage in managing operations. Today, any kiosk in the mall can use a $300 tablet equipped with a Bluetooth cash drawer and a card reader to achieve the same or better results.

The Biggest Environmental Influence Is Government

Now that the four major aspects of the business environment have been identified, let's consider what forces define them. How are the parameters of these environments established? Do they change, and if so, why? Turning again to the analogy of natural selection, scientists and theologians disagree on whether the environment that animals contend with is the result of a series of random cosmic accidents or the creation of a supernatural being. In the business environment, there is no doubt that the gods exist; they take the form of governments.

It's obvious that governments define the legal environment for business. A quick glance at the financial news will inform you that all modern governments actively manipulate their national economic environments to various extents, some more than others.

Types of Government

In her book, *Organization and Management in the Embrace of Government*, Professor Jone Pearce, of the Paul Merage School of Business at the University of California Irvine, established a framework for categorizing governments by their approach to business creation. Pearce places the form of a government on a continuum between "impeding" and "facilitating."

In Pearce's model, an authoritarian-communist government like North Korea, opposed to the creation of independent organizations, is *impeding*, while a democratic-capitalist government like the United States, which encourages them, is *facilitating*. These forms are manifestations of characteristics that describe the attitude (hostile/supportive), stability (erratic/predictable), and strength (weak/strong) of the government. For an independent business, the worst government is hostile, erratic, and weak. The best is supportive, predictable, and strong.

This does not suggest that a government behaves as a single, monolithic entity. Governments interface with business through a variety of bodies, offices, and agencies at the national, provincial (state), and local levels. Figure 15.1 below illustrates a model of governmental roles, which builds upon the Pearce framework. You can see that at the lowest level, the government implements specific *policies*. These are the laws, regulations, procedures, and taxes that define the environment in which a business operates. These policies are enacted and enforced by different government agencies acting in specific roles that might include tax layer, regulator, lender, or customer.

FIGURE 15.1 Government Roles

Levels of Analysis of Government Influence

Abstract → Concrete	Definition	Examples
Form ↓	A continuum along which governments may vary in support of independent organizations.	*Impeding—Facilitating (Pearce, 2001)*
Characteristics ↓	Specific dimensions in which governments vary along the above Impending—Facilitating continuum.	*Hostile/Supportive, Erratic/Predictable, Weak/Strong (Pearce, 2001)*
Role Categories ↓	Groups into which roles are naturally organized.	*Resource Provider, Imagemaker, Rival . . .*
Roles ↓	Distinct functions that governments assume and through which they manifest the above characteristics.	*Regulator, Tax Later, Client, Competitor . . .*
Policies	Individual laws and regulations undertaken by government acting in the above roles.	*R&D initiatives, tax subsidies, export restrictions, etc.*

Source: Greg Autry 2014

Regulations and Taxes

> I've always felt that the nine most terrifying words in the English language are, "I'm from the government and I'm here to help."
>
> —*President Ronald Reagan*[3]

Considering the roles that government plays, you should see that the relationship of your business with the government will probably be both positive (loans and purchases) and negative (taxes and regulations). There are times when a business owner finds simply understanding all the ways in which they must interact with government overwhelming. Regulations and taxes can be complex and occasionally even contradictory. Officials from different layers of government don't coordinate with each other on the minutiae of regulations. You may find, for instance, the State of Colorado has legalized the sale of marijuana, but it remains illegal under U.S. federal law, leaving pot entrepreneurs there at risk.

Rules Create Barriers to Entry

Just because something is a great idea and consumers love it doesn't mean you can turn it into a business. Small businesses and even entirely new industries often find barriers to entry in the form of government rules, taxes, or regulations designed by their competitors. Recall from Chapter 3, that the American state laws favor car dealers over Tesla's direct sales model. In China, government censors have banned American social media applications like Twitter and Facebook.

In both America and China, **incumbents** were exploiting their government's ability to keep competitors out of their lucrative markets. In Tesla's case, local car dealerships, backed by the automobile manufacturers who depend on them, lobbied state legislators to block Tesla and rewarded those who supported them with donations to their political campaign.[4] In China, aspiring domestic champions like TikTok and WeChat understood that American firms would be slow to abandon free speech. Invoking China's censorship machine was a convenient way to establish a virtual trade barrier.

incumbent

A business already securely in place in an industry that startups entering the market must compete with.

A Plethora of Taxes Awaits You!

I don't mean to give you the idea that everything governments do is unfair or corrupt or that every law is an insider deal. While you must be aware that these injustices are real, most laws exist simply because lawmakers truly feel they are needed. However, even a well-intended rule can be an obstacle for entrepreneurs, and large incumbents can afford to be much more tolerant of regulatory and tax code complexity than small firms can. Big corporations have entire departments to handle environmental, tax, and employment paperwork defined by hundreds of thousands of pages of federal, state, and local laws. Most businesspeople generally have little time for regulatory compliance. It's hard for them to even figure which laws apply to their firms, much less comply. What to do?

U.S. federal, state, and local regulations fill hundreds of thousands of pages.

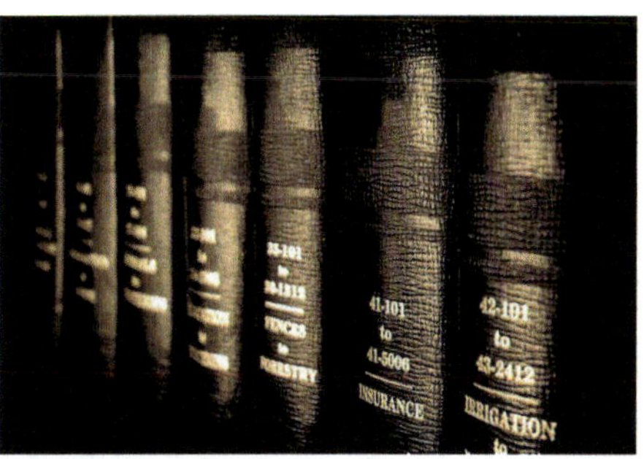

Source: © Shutterstock, Inc.

Small businesses often chose to outsource compliance. For example, services like Paychex and Intuit's QuickBooks Online will handle most of the payroll tax filing complexities for a small U.S. business at a reasonable cost. Similar solutions are available for regulatory posting requirements, 401k plan administration, and more. It is beyond the scope of this text to alert you to every possible law affecting your small business. You should consult with an experienced lawyer and a professional accountant.

As many regulations may be local or particular to your trade, your best bet is to consult your peers. Venues like the local chamber of commerce are perfect for this. Often you will find that even your competitors can be remarkably sympathetic to another small business owner. Following are a few of the legal requirements you will need to be familiar with if you are starting a business in the United States.

Federal and state business income tax: If you're a corporation, you need to acquire a federal tax id number or employer identification number (EIN). You must also file taxes as either a C Corp, which pays the corporate income tax rate, or an S Corp or LLC (LLP), which do not pay taxes directly but rather pass their taxes on to the owner's personal income tax returns (see Chapter 8).

State and municipal sales tax: Most U.S. states have a sales tax, and the rules vary from state to state. Some states tax both material goods and labor the same, and some differently. Individual counties within a state typically have their own taxes added on to the state tax. Some products, notably alcohol and fuel, may incur additional taxes. If you ship goods from one state to another, you are responsible for knowing the rules in the destination state and for collecting and remitting the tax to that state.

State and municipal property tax: Taxing your income and your sales is not enough; the government is going to go after your stuff as well. States will typically tax your real property (buildings and land). Cities and counties may lay a tax on the value of all your assets from computers and inventory down to your chair. Accounting for this is a nightmare for a small business.

Business license: Your city or county will likely require a license to conduct business, as well as the publication of a *Fictitious Name Statement* or *DBA*, documenting who is behind your company.

Professional licenses and certifications: Many states and some counties will require that you be tested, licensed, or certified to engage in specific types of work such as construction and (obviously) medicine.

Construction permits: You can't simply decide to build or improve a facility and call it a store, shop, or factory and open for business. Any significant construction you do, from putting in a wall to moving the toilet, requires local governmental approval. In fact, making one small change can open you up to being required to bring your entire facility "up to code." A California firm that wanted to add a women's restroom discovered that state and local mandates to bring their 1939 building "up to code" were so severe that it would be cheaper to build a new facility, which they decided to build in Texas.

Americans with Disabilities Act: This is a well-intentioned federal law designed to ensure that folks with identified disabilities can navigate and fairly access buildings. However, it has gotten out of control. A small business owner in California, who biked to work, added a personal shower to the existing private bathroom adjoining his personal office. The state inspector required him to remove the entire bathroom because it was upstairs and not accessible to the disabled, even though the business owner had never intended to share access to the shower with anyone. A cadre of trial lawyers actually prey on business owners who have inadvertently failed to comply with some detail of the ADA. They roam around with measuring tapes looking at counter heights and pay bounties to disabled people who are willing to file lawsuits that will generate legal fees for them.[5]

Value-Added Tax (VAT)

A tax placed on products each time they are resold in the supply chain.

In most other countries outside the U.S., you will also need to establish compliance with the **Value-Added Tax (VAT)**, a system of taxes that collects money at each point a product passes from one organization to another. A VAT tax usually allows for rebates on taxes paid for the inputs to your production on products you export. Collecting those rebates is very important; I've spoken to business owners who reported that collecting the national VAT export rebate comprised their entire profit margin.

This is by no means an exhaustive list of regulatory and tax matters that may ensnare a well-meaning entrepreneur. Please consult your accountant, lawyer, and peers to be as familiar as possible with your legal obligations before launching your business!

Thinking Strategically about Taxes

> There is nothing sinister in so arranging one's affairs as to keep taxes as low as possible.
> —*Federal Judge Learned Hand*[6] *(Yep, that's really his name!)*

Not all taxes are created equal or applied equally. It is important to understand that how you position your company, account for your costs, and conduct your sales can change your tax position dramatically. For example, prior to 2018, the 35 percent U.S. corporate tax rate was nearly the world's highest. This motivated big corporations like Apple to avoid taxes by moving most of their profits into foreign shell corporations and Caribbean banks. However, small businesses couldn't play that game and got stuck paying the federal corporate tax plus their state corporate tax, and the owners were taxed personally on their dividends. Going "by the book," an entrepreneur could end up paying 50 percent or more of her profits to the government. In 2018, the U.S. corporate tax rate dropped to 21 percent, still higher than many other countries and high enough to warrant strategic thinking on how to legally minimize your firm's obligations.

If you are tax-savvy or have good advice, you can legally avoid the corporate tax in several ways. The simplest approach is to make an "S Corp election," which relieves your firm of the corporate tax and pushes your business income onto your personal income tax return based on ownership. Each shareholder must account for business profits or losses within their own taxes. LLCs are treated in a similar manner. This is usually preferable in a small, closely held firm.

If your shareholders can't handle the complexity of an S Corp or LLC, you can still avoid the corporate tax via strategic timing. Have your accountant file your business taxes on a cash basis rather than on an accrual basis (see Chapter 13), then simply make sure you have little or no profit left in the company at fiscal year-end. Done correctly, this will mean you don't owe corporate tax. How can a small business owner ensure that his firm has no money left at year-end and get by?

A common method to reduce annual profits is to pay yourself and your employees year-end bonuses. These are subject to personal income tax but are an expense for the business. To avoid going bankrupt on January 1 (because you have no money left), the firm can borrow funds from the bank for a short period of time. This loan can easily be secured by your personal bank account (which should have the bonus sitting in it).

If you feel guilty about legally avoiding the federal tax, just remember Apple is keeping about $200 billion in foreign **shell companies** for the same reason. Most every large corporation is exploiting some similar mechanism. It's your money; you earned it, so please keep as much of it as you *legally* can. If you still feel guilty, you can donate your savings to the charity of your choice.

shell company

A corporation with no real business operations, established purely to manage financial transactions, often in another country and often used to avoid taxes, regulations, or law enforcement.

Big tech firms avoid paying U.S. and California taxes by moving assets to foreign shell companies they control.

Bloomberg the Company & Its Products | Bloomberg Terminal Demo Request | Bloomberg Anywhere Remote Login | Bloomberg Customer Support

Menu Search **Bloomberg** Sign In Subscribe

Photographer: Chris Ratcliffe/Bloomberg

Technology

Facebook Shutting Irish Units at Center of Tax Dispute: Times

By Andrew Davis
December 26, 2020, 1:14 PM EST

LISTEN TO ARTICLE ▶ 1:20
SHARE THIS ARTICLE

Facebook Inc. has moved to wind down several Irish holding companies that had allowed it to shift billions of dollars in profit to the country, where it was lightly taxed, the Times of London reported, citing company documents.

Source: Screenshot by Author, Bloomberg, https://www.bloomberg.com/news/articles/2020-12-26/facebook-shutting-irish-units-at-center-of-tax-dispute-times

This book cannot be a formal tax guide. Be sure to consult your accountant and lawyer about tax strategy before taking action. Any laws discussed here or their interpretation may have changed or be different in your jurisdiction.

When the regulatory or tax environment reaches the point where it is unbearable, one option is to use the same trick the big firms have used against you and lobby your government for a policy change. This is harder for entrepreneurs because they don't have the time, money, or political leverage to work the system. The best solution is to join or form an industry association or coalition and combine the interests of many small businesses that face similar problems into an organized force for political change. Nearly all industries have such organizations.

This text constantly repeats the mantra "change is opportunity," and this applies to regulations as much as anything. When regulations change, somebody will lose, and somebody will benefit. It's the job of the business owner or manager to see change coming and adapt to it more quickly than the competition. Change might be something as simple as your city outlawing plastic bags at your specialty grocery store. Rather than fighting the regulation, embrace the change, go green, and sell your customers environmentally friendly reusable bags. You'll be moving a cost (giving away disposable plastic bags) to a revenue center (selling reusable bags), and you can feel swell about doing the right thing by the planet too.

Subsidies, the Anti-Tax

set asides

Government contracts designated for particular classes of vendors, such as small or minority-owned firms.

There are times when the government is the entrepreneur's friend. The Small Business Administration has a variety of programs designed to give small businesses a leg up. These include educational services, federal guaranteed loans, and **set asides** for government contracts.

Some communities work to attract new businesses, particularly those in technology industries they believe will generate high paying jobs. You can get tax waivers or even outright payments to build your new headquarters in their area. The State of New Mexico will subsidize a significant portion of the payroll of newly hired technology staff. As mentioned earlier, federal and state governments often have particular industries they want to support—currently alternative energy—and they may loan or give you money to launch your startup.

Alternatively, the government may subsidize your customers. At the time of this writing, consumers purchasing an electric car could receive a $7,500 tax credit from the federal government and $2,500 from the State of California. Now an electric car company is NOT a small business, but you might consider that each electric car owner is getting $10,000 back on their taxes. How could you exploit that as a small businessperson? What product or service might you market to these new car owners? Think strategically.

Lawsuits

When relationships with partners, suppliers, customers, or vendors break down, the solution of last resort is to go to court. If this book can offer you one very frank piece of advice that will make your small business career more enjoyable and profitable, it is this:

While U.S. courts are generally corruption free, the process is slow, expensive, and often unpredictable.

Source: © Shutterstock, Inc.

Avoid lawsuits, court actions, and lawyers whenever possible.

I've set this one very strong suggestion out on its own to underscore how seriously you should take it. Experienced entrepreneurs have learned that only lawyers consistently profit from lawsuits, even the lawyers who do all they can to avoid the courtroom itself.

Lawsuits are nothing like a TV legal drama. They are months of expensive paper chasing, followed by a brief and confusing decision-making process with a judgment that often appears to have been randomly generated. Even if you win, you'll be too exhausted to gloat, and it is highly unlikely you will get enough money out of the deal to make it worth it. Much of the money you do get will be vacuumed up by your attorney. If you lose, you may be paying your opponent's attorney as well. This describes the relatively uncorrupted U.S. legal system. In much of the world, justice is reserved for the political elite or sold to the highest bidder by officials who openly accept bribes.

The secret to staying out of court is following these two simple rules:

1. Always produce a clearly understandable contract upfront.
2. Only do business with people with whom you would never *need* that contract.

These two admonitions may seem contradictory, but they aren't. The point of the first rule is that a written document can ensure that what parties *believe* that they are agreeing to is indeed what they *are* agreeing to. Verbal negotiations can be remarkably ambiguous, and that often leads to later heartache. Even the best of friends may end up at odds if they've been working under a false assumption.

The purpose of the second rule is to note that *whom* you do business with is actually more important than *how* you do business. Avoid dealing with criminals, sociopaths, and generally difficult or weird people—even if they seem to have a lot of money. Anyone who brags about filing lawsuits, for instance, should be avoided. That goes for customers, employees, vendors, and, most importantly, business partners.

Finally, if you must argue a contract, try to take it to mediation or private arbitration. Mediation is a guided process where the two parties may come to some settlement or reconciliation. Arbitration is an out-of-court settlement process where an arbitrator—often a retired judge—hears the arguments from both parties in a less formal process and quickly reaches a binding decision. Even though its results may be just as unpredictable as court, it is a lot less expensive in time and money. Many contracts today specify in their terms that any disputes will be settled in arbitration.

As discussed in Chapter 8, it is better to pay a good lawyer to draft proper legal documents that will prevent a lawsuit than to engage one later. Your partnership agreement, corporate bylaws, stock agreements, as well as major contracts with customers and vendors should all have been prepared with sound legal advice. The government will not always see the meaning of self-drafted documents in exactly the way you intended them. It is the primary job of a lawyer to translate your intentions into "governmentalese."

An exception for the U.S. small claims system can be made, as it actually does operate in a manner very similar to the *People's Court* TV show. The small claims process is swift, inexpensive, and generally based on common sense. It can be almost enjoyable if your case is strong and you've got your ducks all in order. The main thing to remember is the judge is busy. Don't waste the judge's time: "Just the facts, ma'am." If you are a small business owner who extends credit or net terms to customers, you *will* have a lot of collection actions. Also, you're busy too, so line up all your small claims suits and file them all at once so you can get a single court date.

Bankruptcy court, which provides insolvent firms' protection from their creditors, is discussed in Chapter 13. A general bankruptcy is a more efficient and agreeable process for all parties than individual court cases where lawyers get most everything. You will still need a lawyer, but the opportunities to suck you dry are much narrower in bankruptcy, where the judge will determine nearly everything.

Key Takeaways

- Four major aspects of the business environment are legal, economic, cultural, and technological.
- Government has a significant impact on small business operations; therefore, it is important to know which laws and regulations apply to your industry.
- Pay attention to taxes you're obligated to pay and understand how to legally avoid those when possible.
- Understand the legal system and your legal obligations; lawsuits are costly and should be avoided when possible.
- Small claims court is a reasonable process for small business owners.

15.2 The Macroeconomic Environment

Learning Objectives

1. Understand the Keynesian economic concepts governments use to manage the macroeconomy.
2. Learn how governments measure and manage the macroeconomy.
3. Understand what government is trying to accomplish in economic intervention and how that may impact your startup.
4. Understand the business cycle and its impact on business.
5. Learn how to forecast the business cycle.
6. Understand secular macroeconomic trends.
7. Recognize how national circumstances and policy may impact your firm.

> If you put two economists in a room, you get two opinions, unless one of them is Lord Keynes, in which case you get three opinions.
>
> —*Winston Churchill*[7]

Keynesian Economics

Since the Great Depression of the 1930s, most governments have presumed that their duty is not merely to establish and enforce economic rules but also to actively manage the business cycle, with the goal of reducing the frequency, severity, and duration of recessions. This belief is founded on the theories of the legendary British economist John Maynard Keynes and is often referred to as *Keynesian economics*.

Lord Keynes believed that in normal circumstances, the forces of supply and demand would, as eighteenth-century economist Adam Smith had proposed, balance prices in an automatic system that benefited businesses and consumers. However, Keynes also postulated that there are times when unexpected events result in **market failure**. Keynes was concerned with the human behavior that made markets imperfect. Unlike classical economists, he did not believe that a large mass of people could *always* be counted upon to make rational pricing decisions. Rather, Keynes believed that groups reacted with emotional herd instincts that he referred to as **animal spirits**. He believed external events could precipitate sharp drops in market prices that would result in consumers *expecting a continued decline*. This *expectation* of lower prices in the future would cause them to delay purchases. Reacting to this drop in sales, firms would cut back on production, and investors would shy from putting money into businesses. Workers would be laid off, and sales would further decline. This **death spiral** would lead to a continuous reduction in national economic activity with no automatic correction. Keynes was convinced that it was the duty of the government to step in at these points and stabilize the markets.

market failure

A situation in which economic circumstances do not result in optimal efficiencies or stable prices.

animal spirits

Economist John Maynard Keynes used this phrase to describe the nonrational behaviors of investors, consumers, and businesspeople that resulted in economic outcomes that didn't match mathematical theory.

death spiral

A situation in which one negative event precipitates further negative events and circumstances continually become worse.

The Great Depression was a global economic downturn that impoverished millions in the 1930s.

Source: https://commons.wikimedia.org/wiki/File:Entre_détresse_et_désespoir_pendant_la_grande_dépression.jpg.

Gross Domestic Product

gross domestic product

The total economic activity of a nation calculated as the sum of all final transactions or as the sum of consumption, business investment, net exports, and government spending.

This national economic activity is measured with **gross domestic product** or GDP. GDP is the sum of all final[8] goods and services in an economy, and Keynes offered the following simple formula[9] to model the behavior of a national economy:

$$GDP = C + I + NX + G$$

The variables or *GDP components* in this equation are the following:

C = consumer consumption—the amount of goods and services purchased by individuals and businesses.

I = business investment—the money invested in facilities, development, equipment, etc.

NX = net exports—the difference between the goods and services a nation sells abroad and those imported from other countries.

G = government spending—the amount of money the government puts into the economy by purchasing goods and services, employing people, and subsidizing individuals and businesses.

GDP components

The subcomponents of national economic activity: consumption, business investment, net exports, and government spending.

The relative importance of these **GDP components** varies by nation. According to the World Bank,[10] in the United States, consumption accounts for nearly 70 percent of total national GDP, whereas in Germany, it is 55 percent, and in China, about 36 percent. Germany's trade surplus provides that country with a positive net export figure of around 6 percent, while China adds about 4 percent. The U.S. *loses* about 3 percent of GDP to its chronic trade deficit.

The business cycle is measured by the change in *real GDP*. "Real" means adjusted for **inflation**. Inflation is the measurement of the national currency's purchasing power, and it shouldn't reflect an actual increase in consumption in the GDP calculation.

Economists generally expect an economy to grow a bit each year. The amount of growth that is possible is a function of population and the opportunity for improvement in the efficiency of the economy. Developed nations have lower growth rate expectations than developing countries. For the United States, a growth rate of 3 or 4 percent is considered healthy. China, which has depended on double-digit growth for many years, is seeing its economy mature, and the Beijing government now officially targets a more cautious 7 percent in annual growth. Both the U.S. and China have recently had trouble meeting those modest expectations.

Why do governments care about the business cycle? A lack of GDP growth is bad for businesses, and that means people are either losing their jobs or finding it difficult to get jobs. This is called a **recession**, and the job problem is measured with the **unemployment rate**, the percentage of people who are able and willing to work that don't have a job.[11] Governments want low unemployment because people without jobs eventually blame their leaders and seek a change in government.

When the economy is robust and GDP is growing rapidly, nearly everyone has a job. Businesses seeking to hire new employees must continually offer higher wages, driving up their costs. The same bidding process occurs over **factors of production**. Businesses pass these higher labor and material costs on to consumers by raising prices. A general increase in prices across many markets is the phenomenon called inflation. Inflation above zero but comfortably below GDP growth is generally considered acceptable. When inflation is much above GDP growth, consumers get fewer goods for their money. Workers usually react to this by demanding higher wages, and business again must raise prices and so on. This vicious circle is known as an **inflationary spiral**. Inflation that gets into the double-digit rates is known as **hyperinflation,** and it can ruin an economy.

In democratic countries, like the UK, a recession or inflationary spiral can result in a change in power. The minority party may come to power, and they will select a new prime minister with new economic policies. In a totalitarian state, economic troubles may, unfortunately, lead to riots, a **coup d'état**, or even civil war. It is wise for governments to make sure their people are busy working and enjoy a lifestyle they consider adequate.

inflation

A broad trend of increasing prices over time with a corresponding drop in purchasing power.

recession

A period of economic slowdown. In the United States, this is officially defined as two consecutive quarters of decline in the GDP.

unemployment rate

A percentage measure of people without jobs who are actively seeking work.

factors of production

The material inputs to the manufacturing process.

inflationary spiral

A situation in which workers demand higher wages in response to rising prices and businesses raise prices to cover those wage increases.

hyperinflation

A situation in which the inflation rate grows into double digits or more.

coup d'état

The swift and forceful seizure of governmental power by the nation's military.

Fiscal and Monetary Policy

fiscal policy

Governmental actions of taxation or spending designed to stimulate or restrain economic growth.

monetary policy

Governmental actions designed to stimulate or restrain economic growth by expanding or contracting the supply of money in the economy.

stimulate

Governmental spending or tax cuts designed to increase economic activity under the Keynesian model.

contractionary

Causing or relating to the contraction (decline) of a country's economy.

open market operations

A percentage measure of aggregate prices over time.

expansionary

Economic policies that increase the supply of money in hopes of boosting economic activity.

A government has two basic toolkits for influencing the macroeconomy, **fiscal policy** and **monetary policy**. Fiscal policy is the ability of the government to either add or remove money from the economy through spending and taxation. By spending more or taxing less, the government attempts to **stimulate** the economy by adding money to encourage businesses to invest and consumers to spend. This is known as *expansionary* policy.

When inflation threatens, the government tries to do the opposite. The government increases taxes and reduces spending, money is removed, and investment and consumption decreases. This is known as **contractionary** policy.

Savvy businesspeople pay attention to government fiscal policy. Increased spending means opportunities for government contracts, and increased taxes are painful. Increase inventory in preparation for new government business or sell it to book profits before a tax hike. In the U.S., knowing what the government is going to do in advance isn't really that hard, as these policies usually take months to wind their way through Congress and acquire the president's signature and are well covered in the press.

Monetary policy involves the ability of the government to control the value of money by managing its quantity and by setting key interest rates. Governments can adjust the amount of money in the economy by simply creating more of it, lending to banks, and adjusting the rules that determine how banks can loan. Governments are often able to control key interest rates directly. In the United States, the Federal Reserve Bank is a semi-autonomous entity that enacts monetary policy. The Fed, as it is commonly known, manages the money supply through **open market operations**, a process where it participates actively in the commercial bond market. The Fed can also set the reserve requirement—the amount of money U.S. banks must keep on hand. Lowering the reserve requirement increases the cash available for loans to businesses, and raising the requirement lowers the available cash. More money in the economy is an **expansionary** policy, spurring economic activity. A reduction in the money supply is a contractionary move targeted at controlling inflation.

The Fed also has the power to set interest rates for the overnight money exchanges banks use to keep their reserves balanced as well as to loan money directly to banks in need at specific interest rates. Lower interest rates generally increase lending and the availability of money in the economy, and higher rates reduce lending.

Savvy businesspeople pay attention to current rates as well as indicators in the financial press about future trends. Rate moves will change the cost of doing business and impact competitors.

Deficits and Debt

budget deficit

The shortfall between tax revenues and government spending for a given year.

national debt

The accumulation of budget deficits that account for the total amount of money owed by a national government.

Like a consumer or a business, governments can spend more money than they take in from taxes and tariffs. This is called deficit spending or a **budget deficit**. When a government engages in deficit spending, it makes up the shortfall by borrowing money, usually by issuing bonds that will be repaid sometime in the future along with regular interest payments.

The accumulation of a nation's annual budget deficits is known as its **national debt**. According to the U.S. Treasury,[12] the United States has accumulated a national debt equal to almost $28 trillion or about 130 percent of U.S. GDP of $21 trillion. This means America owes more than an entire year's worth of economic activity. For Germany, that number is under 100 percent. In Japan, where the government has been struggling for years to stimulate an economy hampered by demographic trends, the national debt has surpassed 200 percent of GDP. Some countries, such as Norway and China, have a surplus of funds that the country invests or loans out to other nations for interest.

However, these numbers don't tell the entire story as provincial (state) and municipal governments may also accumulate significant debt, as is the case in both the U.S. and China. Governments may also have incurred significant obligations to provide payments or services for **entitlements** such as Social Security, Medicare, veterans benefits, or national health services. For a shocking real-time view of America's debt, go to https://www.usdebtclock.org, and look at the "U.S. Debt Clock."

entitlements

Nondiscretionary governmental payments or services guaranteed to some recipients based on their prior contributions or status.

The U.S. debt clock, December 19, 2020.

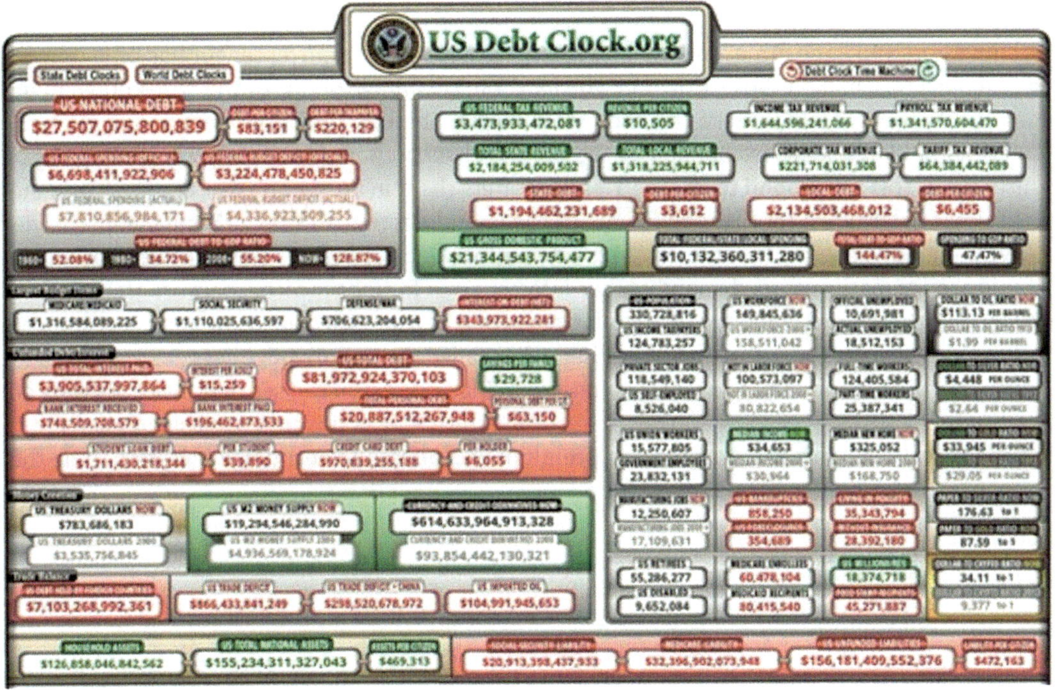

Source: https://www.usdebtclock.org

Why does this concern an entrepreneur? Firstly, the debt must be paid back at some point, possibly with higher taxes. As a nation's debt rises, it is likely that the government will be forced to offer higher interest rates on its bonds. This raises all interest rates within the nation, including business loans and consumer financing. Also, money spent on paying interest cannot be spent on infrastructure and activities that might benefit businesses. If the holders of your government's debt are foreign, then those interest payments are not spent at home and are a **leakage** from the national economy that may slow future economic growth.

leakage

Money that flows out of a country's economy.

The Business Cycle and Your Business

> How did so many experts, including me, fail to see it [financial crisis] approaching?
>
> —*Alan Greenspan, former Chairman of the U.S. Federal Reserve*[13]

Economic forecasting, like weather prediction, is an imperfect science and a bit of an art. Both employ theoretical models and historical observations to forecast the behavior of a complex system. While physical forces such as heat, moisture, and wind drive weather systems, the rational and emotional decisions of human beings move our economies. Both show systems that demonstrate patterns over short and long periods of time. Even though weather predictions are imperfect, we use them to plan our clothing and activities. Macroeconomic forecasts can be similarly valuable for your business.

Economic predictions for the immediate future aren't very accurate, and they aren't useful either because knowing what is going to happen tomorrow doesn't provide sufficient time for businesses to make strategic changes to exploit them. However, the good news is that smaller firms react faster than large ones, a real strategic advantage. Stay abreast of the global economic and financial environment and start each day with a fifteen- to twenty-minute scan of the financial news and markets.

yield curve

A graphic representation of the rates paid for bonds for various lengths of maturity. A normal yield curve ramps up, showing that investors demand higher annual returns for longer commitments.

bond term

The length of time until a bond reaches its maturity. Bonds are issued with specific maturity, at the end of which the capital is returned to the bondholder, and interest payments cease. Examples include a 30-day, 1-year, or 10-year bond.

bond yield

The rate of return an investor realizes on a bond. For a newly issued bond, this is simply the coupon (interest) rate the bond pays. For a bond being resold, the lower the bond's purchase price, the higher the yield on the bond. When bonds are in demand, usually as a safe investment, prices for bonds rise, and yields fall.

opportunity cost

The loss incurred by making suboptimal economic choices. The additional monies you could have earned had you been doing something else that is more profitable, rather than what it was you actually chose to do.

Investors and large firms have many forecasting tools, but the entrepreneur has little time and little money to spend on those. However, you can take advantage of one of the best-known indicators of future economic activity, the bond **yield curve**. The U.S. Treasury offers bonds to finance America's public debt. These bonds pay the investor back in periods ranging from thirty days to thirty years; this is the **bond term**. The Treasury offers them in an auction format whereby a market price is determined for the interest rate of each bond offering; this is the **bond yield**. The yield curve is a graph showing the interest rates offered for bonds of various terms. Under normal economic conditions, investors demand higher interest rates for longer terms because there is a risk involved with tying one's money up for a longer period of time. Without ready cash, investors risk missing out on better use of their money; that risk is called the **opportunity cost**. So, a normal yield curve looks like the one from July of 2003, shown in Figure 15.2. You can see that investors were getting slightly less than 1 percent annual interest for a thirty-day bond and more than 4.5 percent for a twenty-year commitment. A significant premium was offered to encourage investors to tie their money up for so long.

FIGURE 15.2 The Yield Curve

The Yield Curve on July 1, 2003.

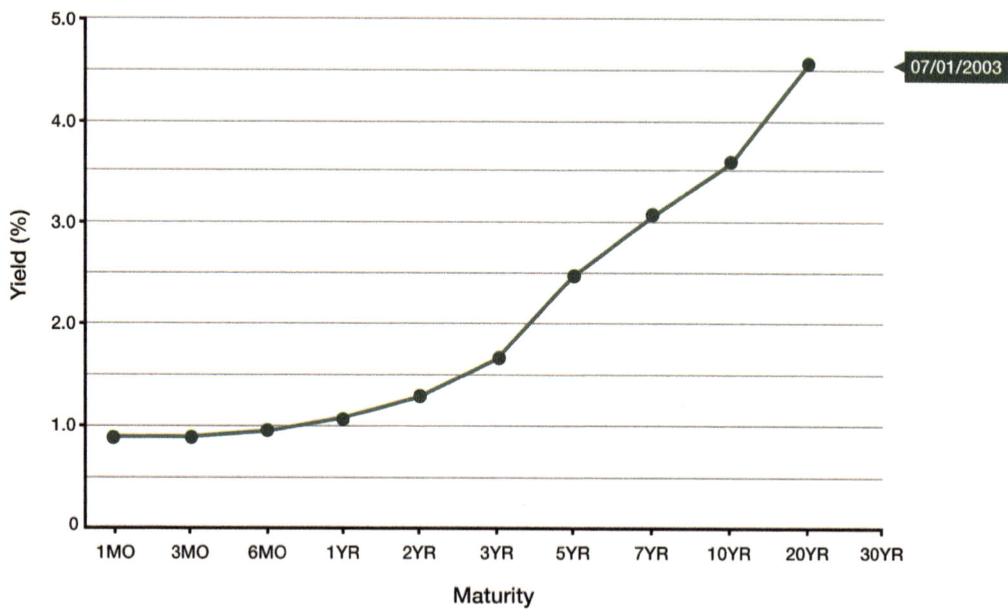

Source: U.S. Treasury: https://www.treasury.gov/resource-center/data-chart-center/interest-rates/Pages/TextView.aspx?data=yield

Let's jump ahead a few years to December of 2006. Figure 15.3 below shows the yield curve along with the 2003 curve. You can see that while the long-term, twenty-year commitment is almost exactly the same at 4.5 percent, the short-term rate has shot up to over 5 percent! (You will also note that the thirty-year bond was introduced that year.) This rare phenomenon is called an **inverted yield curve**. Why would investors be willing to tie their money up for longer for a lower rate, and why would they suddenly want so much for a short investment?

inverted yield curve

A circumstance in which bond buyers are willing to take a lower return for longer term bonds. The inverted yield curve is considered an indication of a coming recession.

FIGURE 15.3 The Yield Curve

The Yield Curve on July 1, 2003 versus December 1, 2006.

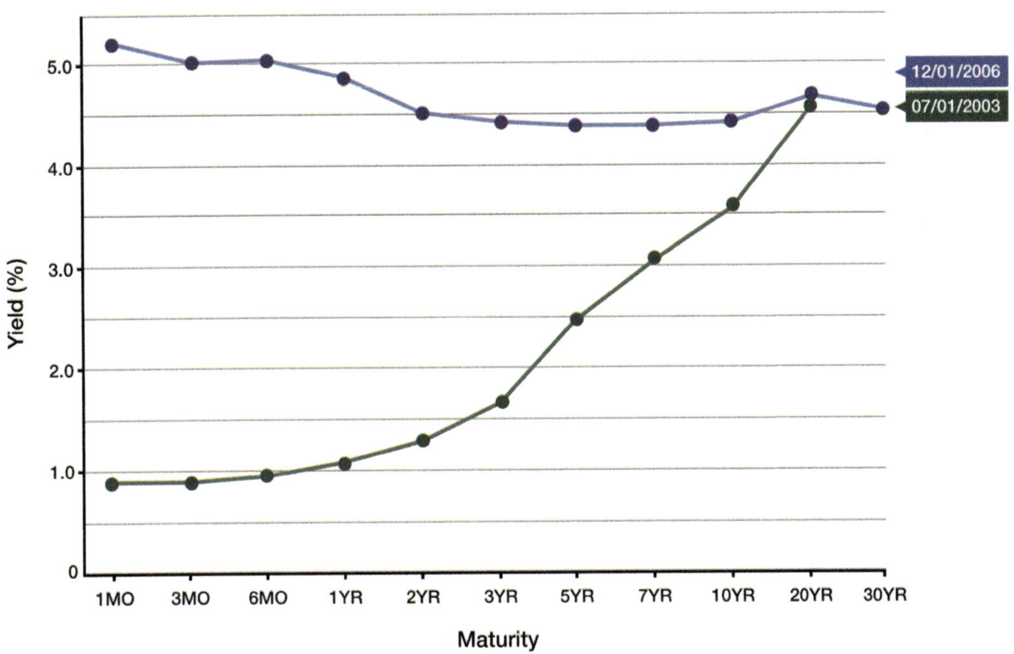

Source: U.S. Treasury: https://www.treasury.gov/resource-center/data-chart-center/interest-rates/Pages/TextView.aspx?data=yield

The explanation is that bonds pay higher yields and can be resold for a premium. Demand for long-term bonds was higher than for short-term bonds in late 2006 because bond investors were *anticipating that yields would drop*. They wanted to lock in the current high yields and own valuable high-interest bonds that could be sold at a profit when yields on new bonds drop. What are the bond traders expecting? What future event do you think would cause a sudden drop in interest rates?

If you guessed "recession," you are correct. Economic activity declines during a recession, and demand for loans drops; lenders tend to lower rates to find customers. More importantly, the government's go-to recession response is to stimulate the economy by lowering rates. Bond traders know this, and bond traders are among the smartest people on earth. Big banks and hedge funds pay millions of dollars to the world's top finance graduates and math whizzes, and they back them up with amazing computing power running mathematical algorithms designed by Nobel Prize winners. An inverted yield curve means that the world's smartest people believe that a recession is coming, and they are betting billions of dollars on it. You should listen to them!

Many economists offer economic forecasts as well. The Economic Cycle Research Institute or ECRI is a leading forecasting group. Their methodology has been a fairly reliable indicator of recession. Applied to the last fifty years, it predicted all recessions with just one "false alarm" (a 2012 slow down that came close to a recession). Though the detailed ECRI reports are available only with a subscription, their weekly index value can be found on their website at www.businesscycle.com, and many news organizations offer excerpts of their predictions.

How reliable are the yield curve and the ECRI weekly index as predictors? Figure 15.4 shows their combined predictive performance over the last three recessions.

FIGURE 15.4 The Predictive Power of the Yield Curve and ECRI Weekly Index

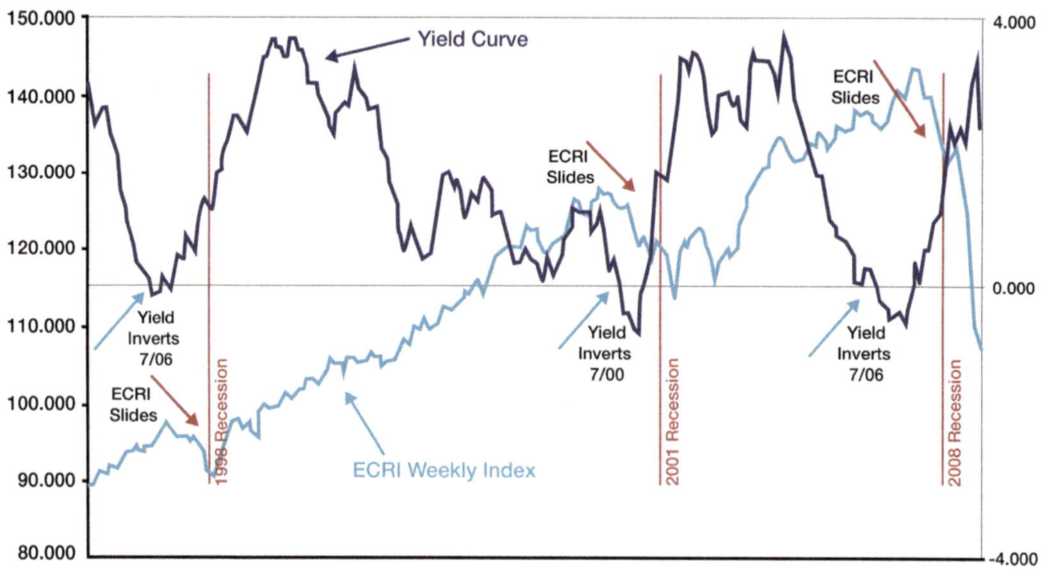

Source: Greg Autry

Global Secular Trends

secular trend

The long-term economic trend that occurs over decades.

The longer, multi-decade economic trend is known as the **secular trend**. It is driven by demographic shifts, major technology shifts, and resource utilization. Such trends can set the overall business climate in a nation for a generation or more. A historical example of a demographic shift influencing the secular trend would be the wave of immigration to Canada that allowed that new nation to develop the resources in its Western regions during the late nineteenth and early twentieth centuries. An example of technology shift influencing the secular trend would be steam power and the Industrial Revolution, which drove long-term growth in manufacturing countries—notably Britain, Germany, and the United States—throughout the nineteenth century. Both of these events created immense opportunities for small businesspeople to prosper. Many entrepreneurial fortunes were made during these periods of long-term economic growth, and many great firms were founded.

While it is impractical for a textbook to discuss the current business cycle and tell you how the business climate is going to be next year, long-term trends are worth noting. Four important markets will be briefly reviewed—Japan, China, the United States, and Europe—to give you an idea of how to think like an economist about the future business environment. These are simple analyses focused on one or two issues, and it is important to realize that many important factors to consider have been omitted.

Japan

A frightening illustration of a bad secular trend can be found in Japan's "lost decade." During the latter portion of the twentieth century, Japan enjoyed a major economic boom, fueled by efficient, quality manufacturing that drove robust automobile and technology exports. However, by the late 1990s, Japan's fortunes had taken a sharp turn for the worse. Growth slowed to almost nothing, and **deflation** threatened. The government attempted to address this with the traditional business cycle tools of fiscal and monetary policy. However, massive deficit spending by the government and sustained interest rates near zero had only short-term impacts. None of the usual treatments could cure this moribund economy, and the "lost decade" extended to more than twenty years. The two major causes of Japan's economic morass have been the island nation's low birth rate and the rise of competition from less expensive Chinese manufacturing.

deflation

The process of dropping prices reflecting the higher purchasing power of currency. Deflation is often an indicator of low aggregate demand and typically occurs during a recession.

A primary driver of domestic consumption is population growth: More people buy more things. Japan has experienced several years of declining population as working Japanese parents have developed a preference for single-child families. At the same time, millions of cheaper Chinese workers moved into enormous new factories funded by investments from foreign banks and corporations. Facilities like the enormous "Foxconn City" plant in Shenzhen, where hundreds of thousands of employees build products for American brands like Apple and HP, undermined Japan's manufacturing advantages. Even Japanese brands like Sony and Honda set up shop across the sea to exploit the opportunities in Shanghai and Guangzhou. Japanese corporate earnings fell, and Japanese salarymen lost their jobs.

Is there any silver lining to this? Small businesses might consider adopting products and pricing strategies such as importing cheaper Chinese goods that might appeal to less affluent Japanese. They might also avoid businesses dependent on domestic Japanese manufacturing as long as they believe China will continue to dominate. Economy-savvy entrepreneur will keep their eye on the secular trend for signs of change. However, things like birth rates don't change quickly and have a significant lag time in their effects.

FIGURE 15.5 Japan's Long Economic Slide

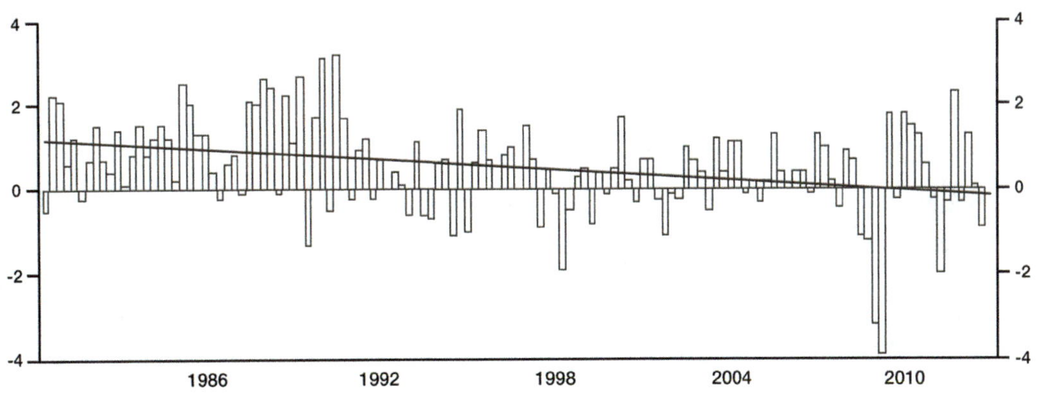

Source: https://commons.wikimedia.org/wiki/File:Japan_GDP_Growth_Rate.png

Japan is not alone in facing a declining and aging population. Most countries in Asia and even many in Latin America and Africa are seeing declines in growth rates or actual drops in their populations as they move from poor agricultural economies, where children are a valuable source of farm labor, to manufacturing and service-dominated economies. In a service economy, children are a costly burden to raise and educate. Taiwan, for instance, now has one of the lowest birth rates in the world.

China

Like Japan, China experienced a period of rapid growth, and from a technology development perspective, it is still a land of opportunities. However, the nation faces a particular self-inflicted demographic challenge. China's government-mandated "One Child" policy collapsed its population *before* it had completed its transition to a service economy, and this threatens its fundamental engine of growth. Moving into the second decade of the twenty-first century, the problem has showed itself in worker shortages, particularly in the faster moving Eastern coastal cities. Wages increased, and some foreign manufacturers relocated to lower-wage nations and highly automated facilities in Europe and North America.

Although One Child has shifted to Three Children, the draconian law established demographic imbalances in China that will last for generations. A high ratio of older retirees to young workers is placing pressure on China's social services system. A cultural preference for male children combined with the One Child law resulted in significant shortage of female births. Female workers dominate China's manufacturing assembly lines. This gender disparity will slow China's manufacturing-driven economy for a generation. Moreover, the lack of young women will further reduce Chinese births and depress economic growth into the next.

China's active population control policies have impacted economic growth.

Source: Greg Autry

Would the risk of a potential Chinese slow down matter to a business owner outside of China? It does if your product requires a component manufactured in Shanghai or if you make a product that Chinese consumers adore. Several resource-rich nations have become dependent on exporting to China rather than developing their own manufacturing industries. Australia (iron and coal), Peru (copper), and Nigeria (oil) will suffer if Chinese demand falters. Imagine that you own a roadside café near an Australian iron mine or a Nigerian oilfield. If the mine or the oilfield shut down, what do you think will happen to your café? Always keep your eye on the global economic environment.

America

Until recently, the United States has maintained relatively robust population growth due to its high rate of immigration. First-generation immigrants are the biggest contributors to its population growth. There are complex political factors that threaten this immigration flow, but without it, the U.S. birthrate would fall below the replacement level, threatening a Japanese-style secular slump and leaving America with a Chinese-style age imbalance that could undermine the Social Security and Medicare programs.

On the upside, America has a variety of mature industries that support a very diverse economy. In addition to autos, agriculture, and basic resource production, the U.S. is the undisputed world leader in the development of new technologies. The personal computer and internet booms fueled American growth for the last thirty years, and both need a refresh. It's hard to know where the next major technological breakthrough will come from, but putting a bet on the United States will still give the best odds. America's research universities are the best in the world and attract the smartest students from around the globe. These schools are tightly integrated with the best angel and venture capital networks. Despite major investments in R&D centers across the globe, it is reasonable to conclude the U.S. will continue its technical dominance for a generation.

America's natural resource base also remains strong. This large nation is blessed with abundant mineral and agricultural wealth. A significant improvement in energy efficiency combined with a recent boom in oil and gas production achieved by hydraulic fracturing (fracking) has eliminated the need for fossil fuel imports. However, recent social and political divisions that have rocked American society might impact long-term economic growth.

America's technology-enabled agricultural production is the most efficient on earth.

Source: © Shutterstock, Inc.

Europe

Europe is in a similar position to the U.S., with many mature industries and a focus on new technologies. It also has a similar declining population of ethnic Europeans now augmented by immigrants primarily from Africa and the Middle East.

The European Union (EU), a political and economic federation of European states, will remain an important factor in Europe's business climate. Many EU countries are also members of the Eurozone and use the common currency known as the "euro." The EU and euro have made doing business across Europe much easier for businesses, large and small. People and goods travel across borders with minimal resistance. Tariffs are eliminated, and within the Eurozone, currency conversions no longer complicate transactions. These are upsides for small businesses that have few resources dedicated to dealing with complex international trade systems. It also makes it much easier for American and Asian firms selling into the single market.

The European Union creates both cross-border market opportunities and regulatory challenges for startups in Europe.

Source: © Shutterstock, Inc.

However, an increasing number of small firms have concluded that EU regulations and taxes are not worth the advantages of the single market. This issue, combined with a sense of national identity, resulted in the United Kingdom voting to extract itself from the EU in a difficult process known as "Brexit." Germany has disproportionately dominated the continent economically, as a major exporter of many goods, including autos, chemicals, and machine tools. Debt problems in Southern European nations like Greece and Italy have repeatedly destabilized the Eurozone.

Key Takeaways

- Fiscal and monetary policy are important for entrepreneurs to understand.
- There are reasonable tools that can help entrepreneurs forecast the future business climate.
- Stay abreast of the financial news.
- It is critical to be aware of global economic events and trends that may impact your business.

15.3 Cultural Environment

Learning Objectives

1. Recognize that cultural variations influence consumers.
2. Recognize that cultural differences offer business opportunities.
3. Recognize that culture is dynamic, not static.
4. Understand how government influences culture.
5. Understand how culture drives markets.

If you've had the opportunity to travel far, you've surely noticed that consumer product and brand preferences vary from country to country and even from region to region. As a visitor to a foreign land, you are likely to encounter and try foods, clothing, and entertainment you didn't even know existed. You may fall in love with many of these exotic items. You may find some of them simply puzzling. You may even be offended by a few. This phenomenon is a manifestation of **culture**, the customs and institutional norms of a particular group of people. The culture in which they grew up will always influence your customers' buying preferences and the behavior of your business associates.

culture

The customs and institutional norms of a particular group of people.

The Culture of Doing Business

The aspects of culture surrounding the sale of goods are known as **consumer culture**. In the U.S., consumer culture has become so important that American citizens are routinely referred to as "consumers" in the media, and supporting policies that serve the interests of these consumers are important to elected officials. Non-democratic nations are less motivated to reward the average citizen with material wealth. Historically, many authoritarian cultures have focused on using much of their economic production to support their ruling class, huge building projects, national arts, and religious institutions.

consumer culture

The manifestation of culture centered around the acquisition and use of goods.

The unique ways in which business is conducted in a particular nation or community is the **business culture**. Business culture includes very obvious rituals such as handshaking, hugging, or bowing upon meeting or departing. Those raised in nations influenced by British standards tend to go with the handshake. Southern Europeans can be fond of hugging their best business associates, and kisses are an Eastern European tradition. Asian cultures have a variety of unspoken bowing rules that may recognize the relative social or business standing of the various participants.

business culture

The unique ways in which business is conducted in a particular nation or community.

In Japan, bowing is an important gesture of respect when greeting or departing.

Source: © Shutterstock, Inc.

More importantly, these surface-level behavior differences hide very important social and business rules you must understand to successfully conduct business abroad. For instance, in the U.S., businesspeople generally accept that the legal system will enforce their contracts and protect them from fraudsters. Therefore, Americans are usually eager to save time and move quickly from a proposal to an agreement. This "get down to business" attitude of Americans can be grating in nations where personal trust must be fully developed before any substantial financial arrangement is agreed to.

expats

Expatriates; those living outside of their native country.

If you will be doing business internationally or with international customers in your own market, you would do well to learn a lot more about global business cultures, and in particular, those of the countries in which you will be working. There are many excellent books to be found and online blogs written by **expats** living and working in many countries.

Globalization

American consumer culture has spread far and wide. Today, globalization and the accompanying growth of multinational brands and retailers have reduced the appearance of locality. On the surface, our cities are starting to look less unique. Nearly every major city (except maybe in North Korea) will have Starbucks, McDonald's, and Walmart or some close copy of those. Still, regional and national culture remain strong under the surface, even within the United States. In Hawaii, the McDonald's menu includes local favorites like the Portuguese sausage breakfast with rice and the taro pie. In Maine, you can get a lobster roll at the Golden Arches. What does this suggest?

McDonald's adapts their menu to accommodate regional cultural preferences.

Source: Greg Autry

When you do business abroad, you need to be culturally aware to be successful and adapt to the reality you will be doing business in. You can also tap underserved markets by catering to travelers and immigrants with different cultural perspectives. Capturing these customers by making them feel at home in a strange land is a great way to avoid going head-to-head with larger competitors who will be slower to react to demographic changes or uninterested in what they see as niche markets. The best way to do that well is to hire and empower employees who understand these customers the best—members of your target community.

Dynamic Culture

Let's consider fast food culture and business. You may be surprised to find that food eateries go back to ancient times. The Roman city of Pompeii, buried in volcanic ash by the eruption of Mount Vesuvius in 79 CE, contained hundreds of street cafés, called thermopolium, where food was served from countertops that look surprisingly like a food court counter found in any modern city. Britain's popular "fish and chips" was a grab and go meal from the nineteenth century that was originally sold across a counter and served in a disposal wrapper of used newspaper.

Ancient Roman café counter, Pompeii, 79 CE.

Source: Wikicommons https://commons.wikimedia.org/wiki/File:Pompeii_thermopolium_interior.jpg

While much remains the same, the New Entrepreneurial Dynamic is always focused on the opportunity created by change. Culture is no exception. As previously discussed, culture is not the same across space, and it is not static in time either. The process of globalization has recently changed behaviors and consumer preferences. Cultures are constantly rubbing up against and changing each other.

The classic American hamburger that defines today's fast food was developed sometime around 1900, coinciding with the beginning of a period of American economic and geopolitical ascendency. By the end of that century, it was probably the most popular meal on the planet. Cuisine exchange has been a two-way process for Americans, and today, a food court in a mall in Houston will offer foods with inspiration from Japan, Mexico, and Mongolia. Foods and other products fall out of favor as this process promotes some options and disfavors others. Influenced by South Asian eating habits, many Americans have opted to become vegetarians or vegans since the 1960s. Similarly, Western perceptions have reduced the popularity of dog meat in East Asian countries where it was once common fare.

The Shoppes at Marina Bay Sands is one of Singapore's largest luxury shopping malls.

Source: Sorbis/Shutterstock.com

Of course, this process is not limited to food. During the twentieth century, European clothing styles overwhelmed the business and casual dress standards of most of the world. In particular, a wide variety of traditional men's clothing styles gave way to pants, shirts, and jackets. Today you can be fairly sure that if you attend a business meeting anywhere from Lima, Peru, to Seoul, Korea, most of your male peers will be comfortable wearing a suit that would be welcome in London a half-century ago.

Government and Culture

Surgeon General's warning on U.S. cigarette packages.

Source: © Shutterstock, Inc.

Governments have significant influence over consumer culture. The tobacco industry serves as a notable example of consumer culture manipulation. For example, the U.K. and U.S. governments have consciously undermined the popularity of tobacco products with health warnings required on packages, public service announcements, and educational programs aimed at dislodging what had been a major cultural touchstone in both nations. Twentieth-century movie scenes featuring glamorous smokers were countered by graphic commercials featuring individuals disfigured by cancer and breathing through tracheostomy tubes. This government-funded manipulation of culture has been accompanied by a near total ban on advertising for tobacco products, blocking the ability of cigarette companies to promote their products or fill the market with images that glorify the use of their dangerous products. The American anti-tobacco campaign has been extremely successful, with U.S. smoking rates dropping from more than 42 percent of adults in 1962 to less than 18 percent in 2013. Most of those still smoking say that they want to quit.[14]

In contrast, China's communist government owns, runs, and promotes a state tobacco monopoly that serves a population still heavily addicted to smoking. Chinese smokers are not unaware of the risks they face, and there have been some public anti-smoking campaigns. However, the government's conflict of interest has slowed progress, and cigarettes remain very popular. Bloomberg reports that Chinese government tobacco firms have "sponsored" elementary schools and one installed signs for young students that read, "Genius comes from hard work. Tobacco helps you become talented."[15] An aspiring tobacco entrepreneur is probably better off opening a smoke shop in Shanghai than in San Francisco.

The broader lesson is that you need to consider the government's perspective of your product and anticipate whether they are likely to bless it or oppose it in the future. If you are considering going into the e-cigarette or "vaping" market, you will find that the U.S. government is beginning to react to this new trend. Do you believe they will let it flourish? Probably not. A few campaigns to oppose this new habit are already appearing, and you should expect a lot more regulation in the future.

On the other hand, if you start a business in an area the government considers a "social good," you may very well find yourself supported by the taxpayers. Governments in Europe and North America have been particularly eager to subsidize firms in the alternative energy sectors like solar and wind power. They do this in the hope that these technologies will reduce both local and global pollution. Entrepreneurs in these industries have wisely promoted the social good their products promise in order to keep the government on their side.

Key Takeaways

- Your customers' consumption habits are attached to the culture they were raised in.
- Culture varies regionally and globally.
- Culture varies over time and is heavily influenced by globalization.
- Governments can influence the public's perception of a product.
- Governments will support products that align with their policy goals.

15.4 Technical Environment

Learning Objectives

1. Understand how technological change creates opportunities.
2. Understand how government policy influences technological developments.

A common perception is that new technologies spring fully formed from the garages of Silicon Valley. In our mind's eye, we see smart engineers working diligently alone or in small groups. They are conceiving, designing, and commercializing amazing new products and services that will revolutionize our world. The reality is that these transformative geniuses are actually embedded in a complex technology ecosystem. More often than not, the "new" products they create are recombined and disruptive applications of existing technologies or the practical application of basic scientific discoveries made elsewhere. "Elsewhere," in this case, is usually a university laboratory. Many of these are funded by grants from the National Science Foundation, Department of Defense, or other government agencies.

A picture of the garage in Los Altos, CA, where Apple was born.

Source: turtix/Shutterstock.com

Picture Steve Wozniak and Steve Jobs in that proverbial garage. The garage itself is very real. In fact, it is still there. If you are in the area, you can drive by and take a look.[16] You'll find it looks just like it did in 1975 when the two Steves were sitting in there, quietly preparing to change the world. You will not notice the invisible hand of government there, but it was very present.

While there is no denying the genius of these two great entrepreneurs, it is important to note that they did not "invent" the computer nor fashion the basic components that went into their creation. Woz's real genius was in the most efficient arrangement of "off the shelf" technology in the form of integrated circuits ("chips") into a home computer. The first digital computers and much of the basic science underlying the circuits they used had been developed in the proceeding decades with funding from the U.S. government and military. The military and space program have also served as important **anchor customers** for many American tech companies.

anchor customer

A single early, large, and dependable customer that provides a stable revenue source that enables a business to pursue other clients.

In his authorized biography by Walter Isaacson, Jobs notes that military research and the Army surplus stores around Silicon Valley provided an environment in which "technology geeks" could flourish. Jobs learned to program on a NASA timesharing computer at the nearby Ames Research Center. That trend of exploiting hybrid government-private technology has been found in every Apple product. In her book, *The Entrepreneurial State*, Sussex University economist Mariana Mazzucato writes, "Nearly every state-of-the-art technology found in the iPod, iPhone, and iPad is an often overlooked and ignored achievement of the research efforts and funding support of the government and military." Examples of U.S. military-developed technology in your iPhone include the "Siri" voice recognition system and the GPS satellite system that supports the maps app and popular geocaching games like Pokémon Go.

The internet itself was created by the U.S. Defense Advanced Research Projects Agency (DARPA). To complement that, the first web browser[17] was developed in 1991 by Tim Berners-Lee, a British scientist working at the CERN nuclear research center. CERN is supported by a coalition of European governments. Berners-Lee's design for the World Wide Web was inspired by a 1980s Apple product called "HyperCard," and he even developed the web on a NeXT machine, the computer developed by Steve Jobs after he left Apple. Commercial firms quickly commercialized CERN's web interface. Today you'll find a browser on every computer, tablet, and phone. You'll even find them in cars.

This constant feedback between government-funded research and commercially focused entrepreneurs has driven the technology business forward for years. How does this relate to your small business?

It may be that your electronics kiosk or game app is simply the passive beneficiary of cool new tech products, but if you are in the tech development business, I suggest that you pay attention to where government research is *headed*. What is DARPA working on today? They are actually pretty open about their research and even host public events and competitions to engage the tech development community in this two-way process.[18] Currently, robotics, artificial intelligence, unmanned aerial vehicles, and nanotech are some of their major areas of focus.

Key Takeaways

- Government-funded research and purchasing create opportunities for startups.
- Entrepreneurs should stay abreast of governmental interests and needs in technology.
- Always be thinking of how a government-developed or subsidized technology might add value in commercial markets.

15.5 Government as a Customer or a Vendor

Learning Objectives

1. Understand the role of government in your market.
2. Recognize the benefits and challenges of the governmental customer.
3. Recognize that access to government business or resources may depend on access and status.
4. Recognize that the government can be a competitor.

For many entrepreneurs, the idea of winning a contract from a municipality or regional government is a very attractive idea. A government contract would provide a steady source of revenue from a dependable customer and add prestige to the firm. After all, if the city or state uses their product or services, shouldn't everyone? Government business is not without its downsides, however. Can you think of what the problems might be?

power relationship

The relative positions of social power between two individuals or organizations (firms).

Having the government as a customer can be much harder than dealing with a commercial client. Governments have a well-deserved reputation for being unresponsive clients and vendors. They know they are the very biggest customer or supplier in your world, and that makes for a very unequal **power relationship**. You need them, and they probably don't need you. Even if your product or service is much better or far cheaper, governments are not subject to the immediate concerns of economic competitiveness that drive your commercial partners; they generally never go out of business.

deference

A humble and respectful submission to another.

Another problem is that government jobs are much more secure than their private-sector counterparts. Government salaries are determined by formula or favoritism (depending on the nation), not on performance or customer satisfaction. Unfortunately, this often shows in the attitude of individual government workers you encounter. Not dealing fairly with your business is hardly going to cost them their job or paycheck. It is usually best to approach governmental employees with charm and some **deference**.

While outright corruption is rare in developed economies like the United States or Britain, in many **developing countries**, it is often assumed you will have to bribe a government official just to get them to do their job.[19] A survey of Indians reported that 62 percent admitted to paying bribes in order to obtain fair treatment from governmental actors in situations from paying taxes to obtaining health care.[20]

developing countries

Nations that have not fully industrialized nor developed a sophisticated consumer economy and have a lower average standard of living than wealthier countries.

The government also has the unique ability to set the legal requirements as well as the terms of your agreement and isn't as likely to enforce the same rules upon itself. Even if everything you deliver is entirely satisfactory, they will simply not pay if the paperwork isn't 100 percent completed perfectly or if some trivial service is not performed precisely to specification.

In some cultures, an envelope full of cash is as expected as a handshake when agreeing to a large deal.

Source: © Shutterstock, Inc.

The Inside Track

Governments in much of the world are plagued with institutional corruption. This includes most of Latin America, Asia, and the Middle East. In these countries, valuable government contracts are often handed out as political favors. Being a friend or a family member of an important local official is often the surest path to success for a small businessperson who aspires to government contracts. The second-best option is to support the likely winner in their election bid or power struggle. The downside of this is that when your faction loses its grip on power, you may lose some or all of your business. You may even be the victim of intentional regulatory abuse by a new regime resentful of your support for their predecessor. My ethical compass requires me to encourage you to avoid doing business with corrupt governments, though I know that is not always possible.

In nations with a better-established **rule of law**, there is usually a desire to ensure that public monies are well spent and the purchasing decisions of governmental agencies are more transparent. A 2011 OECD report noted that "Estonia, Iceland, Italy, Japan, and Korea stand out as making the most types of procurement information available to the public." Purchasing choices are also routinely audited to discourage corruption.

rule of law

The circumstance under which governments follow their constitutional rules and firms can predict the legal outcomes of their behavior.

To ensure that the taxpayers receive the best value, it is common that contracts are awarded to the lowest-cost qualified bidder in a very formal process. In such a process, the agency requiring services or products will issue a **request for proposal** or a **request for bid** or similar document. This is a form filled with questions designed to determine the suitability of your organization to accommodate the agency's needs as well as your pricing. The firm that offers the lowest price *and* answers all the questions to the reviewers' satisfaction is awarded the sale or contract. However, don't believe that this system is perfectly fair. Preferences for friends and family still exist, and there are many creative ways to circumvent the process.

request for proposal

A document asking potential vendors to propose a solution to a problem by defining a project.

request for bid

A document asking potential vendors to provide pricing on a defined project.

Managers who run government agencies prefer dealing with vendors they've had success with and that are run by people they can depend on. They direct purchasing to these familiar organizations because it makes their work easier and the outcomes more predictable. As the new firm on the block, you will face many barriers to entry. However, once you do get "in the system," it can be an important advantage. The key to success is to find an opportunity to prove yourself and make friends within the system. Gaining the trust of **bureaucrats** takes time and patience. Pushing angrily from outside may label you and your firm as a troublemaker.

bureaucrats

The individuals who do the work in a complex governmental system.

The lowest bidder process often results in government vendors working on very thin margins. Those small profits can leave vendors unable to deliver a high-quality product or service. Hence, the sarcastic saying, "It's good enough for government work" is often used to excuse inferior workmanship.

This combination of low margins and the slow payment processing of government contracts is particularly difficult for entrepreneurs. The cash flow challenges of winning a government contract have been known to actually put small companies out of business! The good news is that the government usually does have the money to pay, and when properly pushed, it will eventually cough up the check. That means that getting accounts receivable financing or factoring on your government purchase orders is usually possible. However, the low margins in government work can make the choice to pay interest or fees on such loans unappealing. If you decide to pursue government work, don't simply look at a big sales figure; make sure you're capable of living on the margins and waiting for the payments.

Sometimes being a small business can actually offer opportunities to do business with the government. Many national, regional, and local governments have programs to help small businesses acquire or compete for government contracts. These programs include set asides that provide explicit preference to small businesses as well as those owned by minorities, indigenous peoples, women, or the disabled. Such preferences may include requiring that agencies award a specific percentage of contracts to small or medium-sized enterprises. Agencies may also be allowed to accept bids from such firms that are up to some specific percentage higher than those of their larger competitors, or they may have special, streamlined application processes for small businesses. A 2012 World Bank study noted that the following countries have significant programs to increase governmental contract access for such firms: Australia, Canada, Malaysia, the United Kingdom, the United States, and South Africa.[21]

The United States is particularly aggressive in this area with an explicit requirement that at least 23 percent of all federal contracts be awarded to small businesses. It also has targeted subgoals:

- Women-Owned Small Business—5 percent
- Small Disadvantaged Business—5 percent (ethnic minority-owned)
- Service-Disabled Veteran-Owned Small Business—3 percent
- HUBZone—3 percent (economically disadvantaged areas)

In the United States, the requirement for "ownership" in these subgoal categories is a simple majority or 51 percent. This suggests that in partnerships, it may be advantageous to award majority ownership to female, minority, or disabled partner(s). It is not uncommon for wife-husband businesses that are interested in pursuing government contracts to choose to be "woman-owned" in anticipation of having an advantage in government set asides.

Note that that 51 percent of shares must be held by members of one of these groups, and that you can qualify for two groups but not via a combination of less than 51 percent in each. For instance, if a Hispanic woman founds a business and retains a controlling interest of 60 percent, that firm qualifies in two categories (women-owned and economically disadvantaged). However, a firm gains no advantage if it splits an allocation of 50 percent to a white woman and 50 percent to a Hispanic male. Be sure you understand the rules of these set asides if you intend to pursue them. The U.S. Small Business Administration website provides details.

Governmental Competitors

Did you ever consider that the government may be a competitor for your small business? In many countries, the government is a major owner and operator of businesses. Although national companies are usually pictured as large transportation and resource firms, they can be serious competitors for small businesses.

The United States is generally considered to be relatively free of state-owned enterprises. However, they do exist and do compete with small businesses in many ways. If you're running a bicycle courier service in New York City, you're always competing with the low base rate set by the U.S.

Postal Service. If people can wait one day, they are going to let the government-subsidized service deliver their paperwork. If you own a small café south of the U.S. Capitol building in Washington, D.C., you're competing with the congressional cafeterias located in the basements of congressional office buildings that offer low-priced fare to politicians, government workers, and visitors. Many utilities and local transportation systems are owned by government-controlled corporations.

Europe has generally been privatizing business, particularly, government ownership in things like oil, mining, and aerospace. However, as in America, its hand can still be seen in many places. If you own a local tour operation in Dublin, Ireland, one of your competitors for tourist dollars is the "Ghost Bus Tour," which promises "The most terrifying experience in Dublin!" The Ghost Bus is run by Dublin Bus, part of Córas Iompair Éireann (CIÉ), an Irish statutory (state-owned) corporation.

In China, various levels of government own and operate manufacturing firms, banks, airlines, and more. If you own a corner store in Shanghai, you must count the government among your most serious competitors. The state-owned Shanghai Bailian Group owns several of the nation's largest retail store chains, including the popular Lianhua Supermarkets, which have more than 5,000 locations nationwide.

The secret to competing with government firms is usually to either find a niche they can't fill or find a way to leverage the government's investment to your own advantage. The U.S. Postal Services is unlikely to go into same-day delivery, so small operators flourish in that niche. If you're in Dublin, you might just dig up a good tale about a romantic murder in order to get your small restaurant included as a stop on the Ghost Bus Tour.

Key Takeaways

- The government can be a very large customer for your firm.
- Entrepreneurs may have advantages in qualifying for some governmental business opportunities.
- Even though government contracts offer benefits, working with the government can be challenging due to low margins and slow payment processes.
- The government can be a direct competitor to your business.

15.6 International Trade

Learning Objectives

1. Understand the international trade environment.
2. Recognize the significance of the governmental regulation of trade.
3. Understand free trade zones.

Millions of products are shipped between thousands of ports across the globe.

Source: © Shutterstock, Inc.

importing
The process of bringing a product into a country from abroad.

Apple is a famous American brand, and its products all proudly proclaim, "Designed in California." However, if you own a florist shop in Cupertino, and you go to Apple's website to order an iPad to use as a cash register for your florist shop, you are engaging in international trade. You will be **importing** a product. American-based Apple contracts the manufacturing of that product to Taiwanese-owned companies who actually make it in Shenzhen or Chengdu, China. Apple's online systems forward the order directly to the factory who will ship it across the Pacific Ocean, on a FedEx plane, to your business.

importer
One who brings products into a country from abroad.

During the spring and summer, most of the flowers your shop sells will come from California's central coast, home to some of the highest quality and most productive flower farms in the world. However, during the winter, you will be selling flowers flown in from South America. Your inventory needs also make you an **importer**.

If you own a kiosk in a shopping mall in Ottawa that sells smartphone accessories, you're probably buying them from Alibaba's online marketplace. Products listed on Alibaba.com come from all over the world, and the majority of smartphone cases, cords, and the like will come from China. In today's global economy, it is nearly impossible to run a business without importing equipment and/or inventory from some other country.

exporting
The process of sending a product to another country.

If you're a flower farmer in California, you may ship products to Japan. If you own a small factory outside of Shanghai making smartphone cases, your customer may be that kiosk owner in the Ottawa mall. When a company sells goods to a business or consumer in another country, they are **exporting** their product.

When any of these products cross a border, they are subject to inspections by **customs** agents. Customs is a government office for managing trade. Governments control the flow of products and services across their borders for economic, revenue, political, and national security reasons. The manner in which governments manage international trade relations is extremely important to businesses large and small. Governments generally charge some fee or **tariff** for products or services entering or exiting their country. A tariff accomplishes several tasks, including funding the customs service, generating additional revenue for the government, and increasing the prices of imported goods to discourage their consumption. Why would your government want to increase the price of a product you are buying from abroad? Can you think of why they might want to discourage the consumption of some goods from some countries?

customs

Governmental officials or offices charged with regulating international trade.

tariff

A tax charged on imported products designed to protect the competitive advantage of domestic products and raise government revenues.

Consider cigarettes. In the 1980s, the country of Thailand banned the **import** of American tobacco products in order "to protect the health of Thai citizens." The U.S. government protested against this "trade restriction." Would you agree that preventing the importation of a dangerous drug was a legitimate function of government in this case? Did the Thai government do the right thing?

import

The process of bringing products from a vendor in another country into this country for the purpose of sale.

U.S. tobacco companies are huge conglomerates. A Thai government monopoly, actually called "Thailand Tobacco Monopoly," controls all production and distribution of tobacco in that nation. So what does a trade dispute like this have to do with small businesses?

This decision was frustrating for Thai shop owners as their customers literarily craved those American smokes that brought larger profits. They understood the Thai government actually promoted and subsidized domestic cigarette production. Cynically, the government's real interest was probably in protecting its own business, not the health of its citizens. The U.S., backing its big tobacco firms, pushed for a hearing before the General Agreement on Tariffs and Trade (GATT) panel. The GATT panel concurred with this assertion, and its ruling forced Thailand to accept the American products.

Like most international trade issues, a much deeper issue was actually going on in the Thai-U.S. tobacco argument. Governments and large businesses fight each other over bilateral and multilateral trade agreements. Small businesses, like Thai corner shops, are often stuck in the middle of all this. If your business imports or exports significantly impact trade agreements, it is important you understand this.

A **quota** that limits the quantity of imports establishes trade barriers that keep foreign firms out of the domestic market. This can be an advantage if your small business competes directly with imported products. If your European firm makes rubber boats in Finland and Chinese imports arrive that sell for less than your cost of raw materials, you're in deep water. You'd like a law to limit the number of those imports.

quota

A limit on the quantity of imports of a particular product from a particular country.

Your competitors may also gain an advantage from lower cost or higher quality imports. Imagine that your family has owned a shop in Addis Ababa, Ethiopia, selling locally made clothing for years. You have strong personal relationships with the small factories and in-home seamstresses who make these products. In recent years, the shops around you begin filling with clothes imported from huge factories in Vietnam, Malaysia, and Bangladesh. The imported clothes have a finer finish, are more in touch with global fashion trends, and are cheaper. Your store has a serious problem, and you'd probably like to see a high tariff on imported clothing.

Trade barriers are bad if you are exporting a product into a nation that has high tariffs or imposes quotas. As with the Thai corner shops, it can also be a problem if your business depends on reselling or using imported products. What do you think happens when a government bans the importation of a product or service that many people want?

In many cases, resellers and consumers simply find ways to circumvent trade barriers. For instance, China bans the use of many U.S. smartphone apps and websites like Facebook and Twitter, but sophisticated users in Shanghai or Beijing routinely post on these sites anyway, using technical tricks to circumvent government censors. Individuals and companies may also import illegal physical products by hiding them in containers of other products. While I don't recommend smuggling, it has been a competitive advantage of small businesses throughout history, as it is more difficult for higher profile large businesses to get away with this sort of thing.

globalism
A world view and policies that encourage the rapid economic and cultural integration of all nations without regard to national boundaries.

Most economists believe that reducing trade barriers increases global wealth and prosperity. Very large businesses benefit immensely from global trade. They promote this economic idea of **globalism** and encourage politicians to support free trade arrangements such as the European Union or the North American Free Trade Agreement (NAFTA), which reduced barriers between Mexico, Canada, and the United States. Often, the consequences of these agreements can be disastrous for small businesses in the higher-priced markets. Thousands of small U.S. factories shut down when NAFTA made manufacturing in Mexico attractive.

Interview with Congressman Darrell Issa

Darrell Issa is a congressman from the State of California.

Source: Katherine Welles/Shutterstock.com

Darrell Issa is a successful entrepreneur who made his fortune by developing and marketing innovative car alarm systems in the 1980s. He was a member of the United States Congress from 2001 to 2018 and again in 2020. He has maintained an interest in innovation and entrepreneurship and legislation that affects small business. The following interview was conducted in his office in Washington, D.C.

Prof. Autry: How did you get your start in business? Were you always an entrepreneur?

Congressman Issa: You know, I started out as a young kid with the usual entrepreneurial opportunities, like selling Thin Mints to pay for my YMCA camp summers and other things for Boy Scout camp. That sort of work gets you to understand the art of hustling and whether you can do it or not. More importantly, after the sixth grade, I was growing up in a neighborhood in which a lot of people owned small businesses. I got to see a lot of what it was like to own a small business. I could see these were people who earned very good money. They usually worked long hours, but made far more money than my dad ever did working for General Motors. Also, I came to understand that the risk of owning a small business is a balancing act, and that was probably the only way I could make more money than somebody made working for somebody else. So, by the time I was in college, I had a small business selling 8-track tapes, the car audio format of the 70s. I was a wholesaler, and I had customers all over the Ohio area.

Prof. Autry: Where did you go to school, and did that help with business?

Congressman Issa: I was at Kent State; I didn't start there, but my business developed during the time I was at Kent. I had learned that I could make a lot of money if, in fact, I could buy at a dollar and sell at two dollars and do that in volume. I was able to make more money there than I would have ever been able to in a work-study program. After graduation, though, I had to return to the Army, and that business came to an end.

Prof. Autry: What did you do after your military service?

Congressman Issa: By the time I left the Army, I had no doubt that I wanted to be an entrepreneur. I initially joined a failing company in an effort to turn it around. I did turn it around, and along the way, I experimented with a number of products. These were outside the box products that didn't always succeed. One of them is sitting over there (pointing), a little electronic bug zapper to your right in that brilliant box you cannot miss even in the dark. We also made a half a dozen other products. None of which were great success until I got into radio frequency products, car alarms, security devices, and ultimately car audio. That was extremely successful.

Prof. Autry: How successful? Was it easy?

Congressman Issa: It wasn't easy at all. The business climate was disastrous. I had started my business during a time, in 1980, when we had unemployment in double digits, interest rates in double digits, inflation in double digits. Throughout the 80s, I quietly built my business from zero to $60 million, with about $20 million of EBITA.

Prof. Autry: What made you transition to a political career, and how does your business experience inform that?

Congressman Issa: I was involved in signing the front side of a paycheck and was concerned about making payroll. I was working hard to make that happen, and along came politicians telling me that I was part of the "greed of the 80s." The hubris of that coming from a governor or a president telling small businesses that they weren't contributing positively to the nation bothered me. So, I started donating to candidates who understood how to run a business. I was also little bit involved in a trade association, which got me here in Washington. Those two paths eventually led me to run for office. When you have all these experiences rubbing up next to members of Congress, you figure out that politicians aren't anything special; they're just citizens like you and me. At the same time, I saw a lot of how you have to work to teach people in government how business works because few in government have any idea.

Prof. Autry: Can a politician truly understand entrepreneurship by being told about it?

Congressman Issa: I don't think anyone understands entrepreneurship unless they've taken the risk and at least somewhat paid the price. There are plenty people who are extremely financially successful who have no idea about entrepreneurship. You know, entrepreneurship is risk-taking, and unless you really feel the risk, I don't think you really know what it is to be an entrepreneur.

I had lots of people come to lectures and seminars over the years, particularly MBA students. They all seem to want to collect a salary while they are innovating and get protected from risk by investing other people's money. I have to explain to them that those who put in the lion's share of the money and take the lion's share of the risk expect to get the lion's share of the reward. You can't get anywhere in business without risking it yourself.

Prof. Autry: Is there a balance to that?

Congressman Issa: Well, those that just put in money and expect a return miss the point that they are working off the backs of others, and your employees have to be motivated if you're going to be successful. Conversely, employees often underestimate, particularly in a union environment, what the value of capital and return on investment is. It's a balance of viewpoints that our system handles better than most. I sit here in Washington and see a government that doesn't understand that, particularly when they are using federal dollars.

Prof. Autry: How do you work to improve the situation?

Congressman Issa: Our representative system depends on the people trusting their leaders to make the right decisions, but it also requires that there be a level of transparency so that trust is not blind. We all know that behind closed doors, human beings don't always do the right thing. So, I've made it my biggest priority to work on expanding transparency, improving the Freedom of Information Act, and trying to bring accountability broadly to the federal work force, including contractors and political appointees. That's been a lot of what I focus on as a member of Congress, and I believe it is good for business, big and small.

Adapt to Your Government or Change It!

The New Entrepreneurial Dynamic recognizes that businesses must adapt to the reality of their environment. As this chapter shows, the government is a major component of that environment. There may be circumstances where your firm simply cannot make that adaptation because the government of your nation or region is opposed to your business. If your government doesn't allow you to run your business, you may want to change the government!

In a democratic country, you can work to change the law. If this is a local regulation, perhaps a zoning issue that won't let you rent out rooms in large unoccupied homes, it may be relatively easy to change the rule. If it's a state or provincial issue, it may be more of a challenge, but it can be done. An example of small businesses changing a major law was the California ballot proposition that legalized medical marijuana clinics. National laws, however, are notoriously difficult for small businesses to change.

If it is not possible to change the law, you can relocate your business to an area where it will be easier to run. This may be moving from a high-tax and regulatory environment, such as New York, to a lower-tax and less-regulated state like New Hampshire. It may also involve immigrating from a highly restrictive country, like Vietnam, to a developed nation like Canada. Millions of businesspeople immigrate every year to pursue their entrepreneurial aspirations. Follow your dreams!

Key Takeaways

- International sales offer both significant opportunities and unique pitfalls.
- Entrepreneurs should be familiar with international trade requirements on their business, such as importing, exporting, and tariffs.
- Entrepreneurs facing burdensome governmental challenges can work to change them or relocate.

15.7 Case Study: A Young Entrepreneur Learns about Taxes the Hard Way

The following dialogue is based on the actual experience of the textbook author as a young man encountering the government for the first time in his business career.

"What's a 1099?" asked Greg, a young computer programmer who had gone into business selling video games a couple years back as a high-school senior. Apparently, it was some sort of form that came in the mail. Greg had not recalled seeing anything called a "1099," but as a nineteen year old, he wasn't particularly attentive to his mail, other than the envelopes that looked like they contained checks. Envelopes that looked "boring" had a tendency to pile up and get lost in the general mayhem of his home office space. Apparently, something about this "1099" had earned him an "audit interview" at the IRS office in the local federal building.

The IRS agent on the other side of the table was not looking happy. This auditor wore a suit with a vest and had thick glasses that made a very serious looking face look even more intimidating. He explained dryly, "The 1099 is a form that your customers or contract employers use to report income that they've paid to you so that we can ensure that you have reported it correctly on your tax return. The problem here is that we don't see that income on your tax return."

"Oh. Is that a big problem?" replied the young entrepreneur.

"It certainly can be," replied the auditor sternly. "If you have not claimed this income and you don't have expenses to offset all of it, you could owe taxes as well as penalties and accumulated interest."

"Would that be a lot?"

"The penalties are substantial, and since the return is from last year, you've got some significant interest to worry about as well. If you were found to have intentionally avoided declaring this income, you could be subject to further to . . . well, let's not worry about that yet." The auditor adjusted his glasses and looked across his desk at the long-haired, teenage businessperson slumped casually in the chair. Greg was wearing a rumpled aloha shirt, shorts, and sandals. Not your typical audit candidate. Normally, they sat bolt upright and were conservatively dressed and respectful.

"Worry about what?" asked Greg sheepishly.

"Never mind. The first thing we need to know is, did you, in fact, receive the monies reported by Kent-Samuel Compuworks? Did you do work for them in the year in question? Did they pay you approximately $100,000 during that year?"

"I don't know. I mean, I guess so. I didn't really count it all. I could ask the bank, I think. You know, which checks I deposited and cashed and stuff."

The auditor looked puzzled, "Couldn't we just look at your accounting records? Who manages your books?"

"Books?"

"Who enters information about your transactions into your accounting system? Can we speak with that person? Do you have a bookkeeper or a CPA?" Looking down at Greg's handwritten tax return, the auditor seriously doubted there was any professional accounting involved here.

"I don't know. I mean, I just look at the bank balance and make sure I have enough."

"Oh dear," mumbled the auditor. This was not looking good for the beach bum programmer kid.

"Sorry!" volunteered Greg, who was now beginning to share the auditor's nervousness.

The auditor sensed this nervousness and used a slightly friendlier voice, "Okay, let's assume the reporting is accurate. Do you have any expenses against this income that you did not claim on your return? I don't really see any expenses here at all."

"Expenses? You mean, like money I paid to people?" asked Greg.

"Exactly!" the auditor responded hopefully.

"Oh yeah, I had to pay a lot of people to do the programming and graphics for the games."

"Good. I don't suppose you issued them 1099s?" asked the auditor before answering himself, "No, obviously not." He paused and then continued, "Could you get me copies of the checks you wrote to these programmers?"

"Uh, well, not really."

"Why not? Your bank should have mailed them back to you or can reprint them. Though they may charge you a fee to reprint."

"I didn't use checks."

"Well then, just how did you pay these programmers?" the auditor was beginning to look agitated and sounded unfriendly again.

"I just gave them money. I mean cash," Greg offered meekly.

"What?! Cash? Why on earth did you pay them with cash?" the auditor had leaned forward and was almost out of his chair. "They don't have bank accounts, I think?" Greg volunteered helpfully, "They were pretty young."

"Young? How young were these programmers?"

"I don't exactly know. They're just kids from around the neighborhood. Freshmen, maybe some were in junior high, like twelve to sixteen."

"Oh, my God," the auditor buried his head in his hands.

"What?" asked Greg and then suggested, "I've got some notes here!"

"Notes? Records?"

"Yep!" Greg was more positive. He reached under the chair and produced a shoebox full of 3x5 cards and scraps of notepaper. "Each card shows the game they worked on. There were a LOT of these games. We did them real cheap, like $1,000 each, for this company in L.A. I don't know what they wanted them for because they all sucked, but they didn't seem to care."

"Kent-Samuel were using them as a part of a tax credit scam. That's a separate issue we are looking into. Just let me see your notes." The auditor reached across the table for the box.

The IRS agent removed the lid and rifled through the box. "Hmm," he said, "this one says, 'Flying Battle Monkeys!' Is that the game?"

"Yes, and underneath are the names of who worked on it and how much I paid them."

"That's good. Ok, it says 'Marcus - $200.' Who is Marcus?" the auditor asked.

Greg explained, "Marcus is one of the programmers I trained. Well, they aren't really programmers; I just showed them how to modify the existing code to make a slightly new game with different shapes."

"Fine, fine, but who is Marcus, and how old is he?"

"I'm not sure. I think he's a freshman. Fourteen, maybe?"

The auditor shook his head, "Are you aware that hiring workers under 18 requires permits and that it may not be legal at all to hire those under 16?"

"No. Well, I mean, I guess I hadn't thought of it that way," Greg said. "I guess I had to get a work permit for my job at the library when I was 16, so I guess, well, I don't know. How am I supposed to know about all those rules?" Greg was figuring that ignorance was the best play at this point.

The auditor paused for a very long time. He looked at Greg and the collection of cards and scraps of paper in the shoe box.

Greg fidgeted anxiously in the suddenly uncomfortable chair. He was beginning to see this would turn out to be a much bigger problem than just wasting his time with paperwork. Maybe this was a criminal violation? He began to think, "Can this dude put me in jail for hiring kids? Or is that another agency he'd have to refer this to? How much are these taxes going to be? How will I pay them?" He looked back over at the auditor.

The auditor adjusted his glasses again and looked directly at Greg. After what seemed like forever, he said, "It's common for young entrepreneurs to be unfamiliar with certain aspects of the tax and labor codes. It's important you invest the time in understanding what those rules are before you do business. There are a number of federal and state agencies you have to be familiar with and a lot of rules to follow."

"Yes, sir," Greg replied with a newly found, respectful tone. Suddenly he wished he'd dressed more professionally for this audit interview. "I'll find out about that," he volunteered, trying to sound eager to please.

"Right. Anyway, for right now," the auditor continued as he replaced the lid on the shoebox and pushed it back across the desk, "everything seems to be in order here."

Greg blinked and replayed the last sentence: "Everything seems to be in order." That sounded really good. Lucky break. "Uh, thank you," he replied, picking up the box and rising. The young entrepreneur felt a strong desire to exit the room before the auditor changed his mind. "Thanks," he offered again as he opened the door.

"Oh, and one more thing," the auditor called to stop him.

Greg turned in the doorway and saw the man in the suit was smiling at him. "Yeah?" Greg asked.

"Do NOT let this happen again, young man," the IRS agent said and waved him out.

Endnotes

1. Schoonhoven, C. B., & Romanelli, E. (2001). *The new entrepreneurship dynamic: Origins of entrepreneurship and the evolution of industries*. Stanford University Press.
2. Meyer, J. W., and Rowan, B. (1977). Institutionalized organizations: Formal structure as myth and ceremony. *American Journal of Sociology, 83*(2), 340–363.
3. Ronald Reagan, White House Press Conference, August 12, 1986. https://www.youtube.com/watch?v=xhYJS80MgYA.
4. Crane, Daniel A. "Tesla and the car 'dealers' lobby." Regulation 37 (2014): 10.
5. As of the date of this writing, small businesses with fewer than fifteen employees are not subject to ADA requirements; also, an employer who is subject to ADA requirements does not have to provide a reasonable accommodation if it would cause an "undue hardship." https://www.dol.gov/agencies/odep/publications/fact-sheets/americans-with-disabilities-act.
6. Hand, Billings Learned. *Commissioner v. Newman*. 159 F.2d 848. 2d Cir. 1947.
7. Commonly ascribed to Winston Churchill.
8. It is very important to understand that you only count the last time an item sold. A manufacturer might sell a widget to a distributor who sells it to a retail store who then sells to individuals. In this example, you only count the final sale to the consumer who buys it at the store.
9. https://www.bea.gov/system/files/2020-04/GDP-Education-by-BEA.pdf
10. https://data.worldbank.org/indicator/NE.CON.TOTL.ZS
11. Governments have a tendency to fiddle with the way these numbers are calculated, perhaps to make their constituents feel better about the economy. In the United States, the unemployment rate has been adjusted downward in recent years by simply not counting the "long-term unemployed" and "discouraged workers." Many U.S. economists therefore prefer to track the labor force participation rate, which is less subject to interpretation.
12. https://www.treasurydirect.gov/govt/reports/pd/pd_debttothepenny.htm
13. Greenspan, A. (2013). Never saw it coming: Why the financial crisis took economists by surprise. *Foreign Affairs, 92*(6), 88–96.
14. http://www.cdc.gov/mmwr/preview/mmwrhtml/mm6347a4.htm?s_cid=mm6347a4_w, http://www.cdc.gov/tobacco/data_statistics/tables/trends/cig_smoking/
15. http://www.bloomberg.com/bw/articles/2014-12-11/the-chinese-government-is-getting-rich-selling-cigarettes
16. The Apple garage is located at 2066 Crist Drive in Los Altos, California. This modest home is in a quiet residential area. So, if you visit, please be respectful of the occupants and neighbors. Most recently, Jobs' stepmother was living here. Just ten miles away you'll find the Hewlett-Packard garage, known as the "birthplace of Silicon Valley," at 367 Addison Avenue in Palo Alto. The HP garage is open to visitors as a privately run museum.
17. You can still visit the very first web page at http://info.cern.ch/hypertext/WWW/TheProject.html.
18. Want to help DARPA find a way to fight a swarm of attack drones? They'd like to hear from you: https://www.fbo.gov/utils/view?id=13ac36e8189939fa78f5b3dfc925b126.
19. Paying bribes to foreign government officials violates the U.S. Foreign Corrupt Practices Act (FCPA) and applies to both private and publicly held companies. https://www.justice.gov/criminal-fraud/foreign-corrupt-practices-act
20. https://web.archive.org/web/20130811123343/http://www.iri.org.in/related_readings/India Corruption Study 2005.pdf
21. https://consultations.worldbank.org/Data/hub/files/meetings/Procurement_Policies/BP-DIVERSITY-THROUGHSUPPLIERPREFERENCES.pdf

CHAPTER 16

Exiting and Harvest

> If you don't know where you are going, you'll end up someplace else.
>
> —*Yogi Berra*

Business magazines feature inspiring stories of success.

Source: Spech/Shutterstock.com

Browsing the magazines at an airport convenience store, you'll see titles like *Inc.* and *Entrepreneur*. Think about the covers of those magazines. When was the last time one of them featured the headline "Obscure Small Business Fails: After Years of Fruitless Struggling, Founder Broke" above a picture of a sad-looking shopkeeper? Never, of course. Invariably, the cover story is about amazing entrepreneurs doing amazing entrepreneurial things and making it look amazingly easy! Reading this sort of "entrepreneurship propaganda" lures many aspiring business founders into believing that just about any smart young person with a dream might scoop up some venture capital, launch an initial public offering (IPO), and walk away a billionaire. Sadly, that is not the case. This book is written to prepare you for reality.

16.1 The End of the Road

Learning Objectives

1. Understand different types of liquidity events.
2. Recognize there are many different potential buyers of existing businesses.
3. Be able to assess the advantages and disadvantages associated with various exit and harvest opportunities.
4. Understand how the worth of a business may be determined.
5. Understand what makes a business self-sustaining or not, and the associated strategies.

Should You Stay or Should You Go Now?

confirmation bias

The tendency to interpret new information as supportive of existing beliefs.

The messages that would-be founders receive from the business press, media, and even textbooks are rife with **confirmation bias**; only the most outrageously successful firms get the attention of these outlets. In a good year, only a handful of high-profile companies execute an initial public offering (IPO) of stock and make their founders rich for life. In 2019, a very good year for the market, just 235 U.S. firms went public.[1] In a really bad year, the number is close to zero. However, reading about Mark Zuckerberg and Elon Musk, again and again, establishes their very exceptional experiences as the standard expectations of entrepreneurship. It's essential to correct this misconception by putting it into context. For each Facebook or Tesla, hundreds of companies burn through their investors' hard-earned cash, blow up in battles of litigation, or simply fade quietly into obscurity. There are also tens of thousands of ambitious startups that never even get an investment. Does this suggest that entrepreneurship is a dead end? Is it too risky for any but the most extreme risk-takers to pursue?

An IPO is a rare but exciting way to harvest funds from a very successful startup.

Source: © Shutterstock, Inc.

Remember, while many entrepreneurs desperately pursue the elusive dream of spending Other People's Money, millions of small businesses open their doors each day, serve their customers, pay their employees from profits, and provide a good living for their founders. Many of these small businesses make their founders wealthy for life, but they do it quietly. How do they achieve that? How could you achieve that?

In their book, *The Millionaire Next Door*,[2] Thomas J. Stanley and William D. Danko tell us that the secret to achieving our personal financial dreams lies in the accumulation of prodigious wealth. Working hard, investing wisely, and maintaining a standard of living below your income level enables you to build up a surprisingly large nest egg. A small business is a great platform from which to execute this plan. If you like, you can run your business as a lifestyle business until you retire or die. In fact, the clear majority of small business owners do exactly that. On the other hand, if you have bigger dreams, you may look for a **liquidity event** that will allow you to **harvest** money, exit the business, and pursue those dreams.

liquidity event

Typically, the conversion of the ownership equity held by a company's founders and investors into cash via merger, sale, or IPO.

harvest

Extracting cash from your business by selling part or all of it.

A liquidity event is a mechanism to exchange the value you've built up in your business for cash. While an IPO is one such event, given the number of businesses founded each year globally, the odds suggest that not a single person who reads this textbook will ever take a firm to the IPO stage. Ironically, there are far more books on how to bring a Silicon Valley startup to IPO than there are entrepreneurs who will actually do that. So this chapter will not dedicate a lot of time to that model.

For average small business owners, cashing out means selling their businesses. Who buys small businesses? Some of the answers to that question are obvious, and others may surprise you. One of the most likely buyers for any business is a direct competitor. Can you think of why that is?

Imagine you own Joe's Muffin Shop on Main Street. Your archrival, Jane, owns an identical establishment just down the block. The two of you are in the same market, and you are competing for the same customers. The laws of microeconomics tell us that this competition and an abundant supply of products will result in lower prices. If there was only a single muffin shop in town, that store could charge the locals more. Customers should be willing to pay more, at least up to the cost of having to drive to the next town for their muffin fix. This would drive revenues up significantly.

Being the only muffin shop in town would be a competitive advantage.

Source: Andriy Blokhin/Shutterstock.com

By increasing the sales and production volumes, a combined muffin empire would be able to capture greater **economies of scale**. The new mega-muffin store should be able to negotiate better prices with vendors of flour, sugar, and napkins in exchange for commitments to larger purchasing volumes. The reduced costs of goods sold will drive higher gross margins for the business.

Your two shops are also duplicating resources such as rent, equipment, and staff. It is very likely that a single muffin shop could do the business of both with the resources of just one. You should be able to go to each landlord and renegotiate the lease based on the argument that you're going to exit one of the facilities. Cutting all those fixed costs should increase net profits dramatically.

Higher revenues, higher margins, and higher profits: what's not to like here? You should both see that one of you must go. Does it make a difference who buys out whom? Economically, it shouldn't. Given efficient negotiations, the **net present value** (NPV) of the **future cash flow** the buyer can recognize from the combined operation should be split between the two parties in the sale. The choice should be determined by whoever loves selling muffins the most or, conversely, whoever wants out of that business the most. One of you will be the town's muffin magnate, and the other will retire as a muffin millionaire.

economies of scale

The inverse relationship resulting from increased production driving down price per unit due to the overall cost being spread out among a high number of goods sold.

net present value

The current value of a future set of cashflows, when the buyer considers what they might earn in interest from an alternative investment. What is appropriate to pay today for income in the future over time.

future cash flow

The expected amount of cash and cash-equivalents moving in and out of a business.

acquisition

Taking control of a company by purchasing it outright or acquiring a majority of its stock.

opportunity cost

The potential benefit given up when one choice is made over another.

roll-up merger

Acquisition in which several smaller companies are purchased and combined to create a larger company thus better positioned to take advantage of economies of scale.

Capturing the Value You've Created

While there are several types of liquidity events, anyone who gives you money for your business is looking to make an outsized profit in the long run by leveraging the value you have created in your firm. For you, it's an opportunity to apply that value elsewhere.

There Must Be Fifty Ways to Sell Your Firm

Acquisition is by far the most common exit strategy for small business owners. As in the muffin shop example, acquisition involves one company taking over another in exchange for payment. An acquisition benefits the acquirer because of reduced business development costs and aligned business synergies. The point is that the buyer obtains business components like customers, completed facilities, and intellectual property for less than it would cost them to duplicate these on their own.

It is very important to understand that, in this case, the concept of "cost" involved in duplicating those sorts of business assets includes both money and time. This means a buyer may pay more cash for a facility or customer base to avoid the **opportunity cost** of spending years in the process. This cost is generally higher for larger organizations. Consequently, large businesses often buy up small businesses to quickly enter markets with an established infrastructure and customer base.

A classic acquisition strategy for large firms buying small ones is the **roll-up merger**. In a roll-up, a larger firm or a group of investors planning to quickly create a larger firm will buy up several smaller firms operating in the same market and combine them into an "instant big business." This may involve buying up firms in the same industry across a large geographic area. A firm wanting to take on Dunkin' Donuts could create a national or global doughnut store chain by acquiring thousands of mom-and-pop stores across America or the world.

A roll-up may also involve buying companies that have complementary resources and capabilities. Imagine combining a payday check-cashing firm with a money transfer company and a tax preparation/refund forwarding chain. This could create a single-stop solution for the financial services that many low-income individuals utilize.

A competitor might build a global donut challenger with a roll-up strategy.

Source: Polarpx/Shutterstock.com

In theory, acquisitions, like any economic transaction, work for both parties. However, the New Entrepreneurial Dynamic encourages you to recognize that economic theory is often not a reality when human beings are involved.

In the case of corporate acquisitions, the good news is that in the real world, a small business being acquired by a larger one most often benefits disproportionally. The acquirer allows inflated senses of value, expediency, and ego to affect the **valuation** of the firm they are planning to acquire. Large companies are run by human beings. If you are selling, the valuation of your small business will be done by individuals with real limitations. They have personal time constraints that limit their ability to make perfect decisions. Just like a consumer, businesspeople enjoy the process of acquisition. Buying things makes us feel good in the short term. Buying up several small businesses is something that a corporate executive can brag about at cocktail parties. It makes him or her feel "entrepreneurial" as well, and right now, entrepreneurship is "in," so take advantage of that feeling!

valuation

The process of determining the price for sale of a business.

The extra benefit the acquired company gets is called the **acquisition premium**, and on average, it is typically in the range of 20 to 50 percent. It's hard to know exactly what this amount is for small businesses, but it's very easy to track in large public firms whose stock sales are seen in public market movements. Bloomberg reports that the average acquisition premium observed in the publicly traded firms for 2015 was 28 percent,[3] a particularly low number in recent history.

acquisition premium

The amount by which the purchase price of a business exceeds the tangible value of that business.

If you have outside investors, you will find they are often inclined to pursue acquisition by a larger firm as an exit strategy. It's a clean and simple way for them to take their profits from your firm and move on to the next investment. This is something you should discuss with any potential investors before you accept their money, particularly if they are likely to acquire a controlling interest in your firm.

Selling to a Foreign Buyer

When a large firm considers entering a new geographic market, particularly one in which they lack expertise, acquiring a local company is often a preferred strategy. This is often the case in international expansions. A successful large business may try to acquire a similarly large foreign business in its target market to move into that market all at once. Imagine a big European retailer wanting to expand into the growing market in Latin America. Buying up existing national market chains in Mexico, Brazil, etc., might be the most expedient way to achieve this. However, buying up a major foreign company is not always a straightforward process. Most countries like keeping their **national champions**, strategic large firms that are associated with their country and help define their business culture, domestically owned. Even an effort to buy up retail stores may encounter opposition from the government. In many countries, such as China, most of the largest firms (including some retail chains) are state-owned enterprises(SOE), companies owned by the government. SOEs are usually not for sale.

national champions

Strategic large firms that are strongly associated with a country and often protected by that nation's government.

Airlines are often national champions. Emirates is owned by the government of Dubai.

Source: Bill Roque/Shutterstock.com

An alternative solution for a foreign buyer is to purchase a smaller firm and use that as a foothold to explore the new market. Surprisingly, your small business may be just what a large foreign buyer is looking for. In recent years, many Chinese companies looking to enter the valuable North American market have purchased small U.S., Mexican, and Canadian firms for this purpose.

A large international buyer might also be executing a roll-up merger in a particular country, buying up several small firms to create a substantial presence in a new market. Keep your eye out for these opportunities—they may only arrive once. Foreign buyers are notorious for paying higher acquisition premiums because of their lack of expertise in valuing assets in strange markets. Remember, if you don't sell out, your competitor across town very likely will, and you may find yourself facing a new, well-financed competitor.

Selling Your Business Model

Imagine that you've developed a brilliant and unique product or service and know there is demand for it in other areas, but you simply don't have the money or the time to expand geographically. It's frustrating not to be capturing those sales and worrisome that competitors might pop up in those areas to copy your idea and steal your opportunity. What can you do?

One way to quickly capture the potential demand in many geographic markets is to ask other people to make the investment, do the work for you, and send you profits. That's a crazy idea, right? Not really. Franchising is duplicating a proven business model for a fee. Franchises are a huge business. The U.S. Census Bureau reported that franchises accounted for $1.3 trillion in sales in 2010! This book has already addressed franchising as an opportunity for entrepreneurs lacking an original concept to get into business by buying into a chain like Subway, Hertz Rental Car, or Spain's Dia convenience stores.

Franchising is one way for successful entrepreneurs to harvest funds from their business model.

Source: Lux Blue/Shutterstock.com

Now consider the inverse opportunity offered by franchising. If you've developed a powerful, profit-generating business model, you could charge other potential entrepreneurs upfront fees and collect royalties from their work by allowing them to sell your product and use your business model and brand.

As with any business, a good place to start to explore franchising is to look at the information available from industry associations such as the International Franchise Association (IFA). Establishing a new franchising opportunity is not for the faint of heart. It's very complex and requires expert business and legal advice to do it right. In fact, you will probably need some investors to help you get it done. In the United States, the Small Business Administration (SBA) offers advice on franchising. Some propose, "All in all, you might be looking at $250,000 or more (in addition to the normal costs of running your business in the meantime) to create a sustainable franchise system."[4] However, that estimate is actually quite low—expect to spend $500,000 to $1 million to do it right.

You should also try to approach another successful franchisor for advice. Choose someone who retired successfully from the operation or whose business is not a direct competitor. You'd be surprised how eager many successful entrepreneurs are to help the younger versions of themselves get a leg up. You may even find they can't resist being part of the action, and they may want to work with you or maybe even invest some of their own winnings into expanding your idea.

Selling to Private Equity

private equity

Capital that is not noted on a public exchange.

leveraged buyout

An acquiring company uses a significant amount of borrowed money to purchase an existing company, often using the assets of the company to be purchased as collateral.

collateralize

A borrower pledges an asset as recourse to the lender in the event that the borrower defaults on the initial loan.

Another viable harvest strategy for an entrepreneur is selling ownership to a private equity group. **Private equity** (PE) investors are different from venture capitalists in that they invest in mature, fully operating companies rather than startups. They are generally interested in generating returns from real positive cash flow as well as building the market value of the company to where it might be sold for a significant profit. The amount of their investment may vary from loans that are convertible to equity to purchasing the entire firm outright. Often, they will use a **leveraged buyout** (LBO) model, in which they use the assets of the firm to **collateralize** loans for purchasing it.

Private equity firms usually seek a controlling interest in the company, which will enable them to implement strategic changes they believe will enhance its value. Sometimes they want to simply take over the whole thing. Other times they want to keep the original owners engaged in the business. Often, a well-run company's management will be asked to stay on. You, as the seller, could then continue working with your company in a meaningful way with a reduced risk and commitment, having sold a majority stake to the private equity (PE) firm.

In the past, private equity firms mostly focused on buying distressed, publicly traded firms. However, they are now increasingly seeking to purchase small and midsized companies where they believe a cash infusion, merger, or other strategic change would rapidly boost the value of the firm.

If your firm isn't big enough to be the primary target of a PE firm, it may be an appropriate acquisition for one of the firms they are turning around. Pay attention to the industry news and rumors in your market. If you see that your location, customer list, or another asset your firm controls would fit nicely with a larger firm being acquired by a PE firm, you might consider reaching out to the PE firm to see if they are interested in talking about what you have to offer.

Imagine you own a regional computer maintenance firm that has a solid contract for providing service to a large corporation in your area. You see a PE firm is buying up a larger firm that also services this corporation in many other parts of the world. That PE firm may find that spending a few million dollars to include the purchase of your little firm in the deal would be helpful and (from their viewpoint) inexpensive. They may even want to put you in charge of the larger firm if your organization is running more efficiently than your bigger competitor.

Bringing in a private equity investor may allow you to exit your firm or simply reduce your risk, get some cash out of your investment, and bring in a qualified team to help your company overcome immediate issues. Blackstone is one of the largest private equity firms in the world. A look at the companies in the Blackstone portfolio would shed some light on the typical qualifications PE investors seek.

Selling to Everyone

Occasionally a famous firm like Facebook or Alibaba makes a splash across the business press with a massive IPO that turns its founders into instant billionaires and makes entrepreneurs the world over salivate. It is important to realize that an IPO, a liquidity event that raises money by selling the firm's shares to the public, is extremely rare. In the United States, you may typically see 100 to 200 initial public offerings in a good year. Although IPOs vary with the strength of the stock market, there are never more than a few hundred. To put that in context, remember that there are nearly 28 million American businesses and the U.S. markets are open to foreign firms, such as Alibaba, as well. Basically, you're probably more likely to be struck by lightning than to take your firm public.

An IPO is not for everyone. Firms that go public sacrifice a lot of control. Their boards of directors are elected by thousands or millions of shareholders scattered around the world. Today's stock traders have sophisticated online trading tools and short attention spans. They drop in and out of stocks rapidly and are more concerned with tomorrow's stock price than the long-term success or goals of your firm. Financial news analysts are continually second-guessing every act of the firm, and many publicly traded companies find it difficult to continue to invest in ambitious research or bold market development. These difficulties and the rise of private equity investors have resulted in a general decline in IPO activity over the last few decades.

Executing an IPO is a complex strategic and legal operation that requires expert guidance. The public offering process requires listing with a public stock exchange such as the London, New York, or Shanghai stock exchanges. It also requires the filing of a lot of paperwork with extensive rules of governmental authorities; in the U.S., that authority is the Securities and Exchange Commission (SEC). The firm must also inform the investment community of the opportunity, often in a roadshow—a series of hosted events publicizing the stock offering. Long before you get to that point, you will have developed relationships with sophisticated angels, venture capitalists, or private equity investors. They will likely have the expertise to guide you through locating the financial, legal, and public relations experts required to execute an IPO. Recently, a new approach to public offerings has emerged that frees the startup from the burden of managing the IPO process. A **special acquisition company**, or SPAC, is created simply for the purpose of raising funds and completing an IPO. It is a **shell company**, a legal entity with no operations, and it has no defined market or business model. The sponsors or founders of the SPAC create a firm and offer stock for sale. They handle the SEC paperwork, conduct a roadshow, and list on an exchange. The only purpose of the SPAC is to go find an attractive target company, often a startup, to acquire. As a potential target, your company may reach out to SPACs to inquire as to their willingness to bring their capital to your firm in a merger. The newly formed entity is called the business combination, and it now has the expertise and business model of the startup with the capital of the SPAC and publicly traded stock listed on an exchange.

special acquisition company

A firm created simply for the purpose of raising funds and completing an IPO.

shell company

A legal entity with no operations and with no defined market or business model.

In 2019, Sir Richard Branson's space tourism startup, Virgin Galactic, used this mechanism to successfully raise funds from a SPAC called Social Capital Hedosophia Holdings Corp. The market initially valued the newly merged firm at $2.3 billion under the ticker symbol SPCE. During the COVID-19 crisis of the following year, the global airline industry fell on hard times, and Branson was able to support his Virgin Atlantic company through the sale of SPCE shares.

Virgin Galactic Holdings, Inc. (NYSE: SPCE) Goes Public

View in the online reader

Selling to Employees

While an IPO represents the ultimate transfer of control to outsiders, a firm owner can also raise money within the company by selling the firm to employees. Many retiring entrepreneurs prefer to see their firms transferred to those who care most about the company and who share the founder's vision for its future.

management buyout

A transaction in which the management team purchases the business that employs them.

In most cases, a firm's workers lack the cash to buy the owners out all at once. In a **management buyout** (MBO), the company is sold to its top managers. With the support of the owner, these critical employees can secure loans using the firm's physical assets as collateral. The benefit of this change of hands is that it provides a relatively smooth transition of power, with the entrepreneur receiving immediate liquidity.

Another strategy is an employee buyout done over time. The company owner may retire with a contract that requires the new employee-owners to forward a fixed amount or a percentage of firm profits each year. This can provide a business owner with a stream of income during retirement. Reducing the amount of income received in any one year may have tax advantages as well.

Another popular option is to slowly sell the business to the employees while the owner is still actively engaged in the firm. This may be done via the regular sale of shares or the issue of stock options to valuable employees as incentives. It may also have tax advantages for the firm. The U.S. Internal Revenue Service (IRS) has established the employee stock ownership plan (ESOP), a legal structure for a qualified, defined contribution trust operating for the benefit of the employees.

Employee-owned firms need not stay small, and many can be remarkably successful. In Great Britain, employee-owned Edinburgh Bicycle Co-operative has grown to five shops in Scotland and Northern England. The John Lewis Partnership is an employee-owned retail giant that operates department stores, supermarkets, and financial services companies across the UK. In the U.S., employee-owned Southwest Airlines is, at this writing, one of the most successful firms in a very competitive market.

Each of these employee ownership strategies requires expert planning and legal and accounting advice. Talk with your accountant and seek out experts in your area. If you have a friend or a colleague who has had a successful (or disastrous) employee buyout experience, get their advice as well.

Selling to the Family

Another common transfer of ownership of a small business is the transition from parents to their children. In some cases, the business is an inheritance that the parents pass on, but often the parents wish to retire and enjoy their "sunset years" with some income from the firm. In that case, the options for selling the business to the family are similar to those for selling it to employees.

Selling to family members can be especially rewarding, as well as problematic. Sometimes, your potential family buyers are already active in the firm, and sometimes they have been outsiders until the transition. If, for instance, your children are already managing the firm, the process is likely to be smooth. The employees have been working alongside these individuals and have already established relationships. Nobody is going to be displaced in this process, and the expectations of the transition were probably very clear.

nepotism

Favoritism given to relatives or close friends.

On the other hand, if a business owner hands control over to a child, niece, or another relative who has not been actively engaged in the development of the firm, the managers who built the business are likely to view this as **nepotism**. They may feel their years of hard work have gone unrewarded and become resentful. In this case, the key is to set expectations on all sides and avoid surprises.

While choosing a family member to continue the business is easy and ensures a certain level of loyalty, it introduces complications as well. If that person doesn't do well or the business doesn't do well under them, then stress will result. Is your niece truly passionate about your hardware store, or is she simply relieved to have a guaranteed job after college? If her dream job as an engineer suddenly comes up, will she bolt for that and leave your retirement in limbo?

In the end, the best person to run your business after you leave is probably the person who will generate the most value out of it. That rewards everyone, including your heirs.

Your family may be the best team to continue your business.

Source: © Shutterstock, Inc.

Valuation: What Is It Worth?

Once you have decided to sell your firm, the first question is usually, "What is it worth?" The answer to this question is very simple: "Your business is worth whatever you can get somebody to pay for it." The market will determine the value of what you have built. Your job is to get it in front of the right buyers and to *present it effectively for those buyers*. When you've identified a potential buyer for your business, the next task is to figure out *what your business is worth to the buyer*. You may have some formula from a magazine or a friend who talks about "four times revenue" or "seven times profit." Some industries have fairly standardized metrics around them because they are highly commoditized, meaning all the firms in the business operate about the same.

These market-based figures are interesting as a point of discussion, but outside of very commoditized businesses, they may be irrelevant to the buyer. Your target buyer may be willing to pay more than that or less than that, but the final price will be based on their own need for what your firm brings to their efforts. When Fred Ross sold Deckside Pools (see Chapter 4 Section 6), he valued the business at 5–7x EBIDTA based on the industry standards for pool service companies, but with some augmentation for the unique efficiencies he had created in his business model.

Imagine that you own a small boutique pizzeria in Central Hong Kong. Your amazing Asian-fusion pizza pies are a hit with the city's diverse international crowd. The atmosphere is hip and youthful. Students and young professionals line up around the block to get in every weekend evening. Cash flow is great, but your own creative itch is calling you to your next entrepreneurial adventure. You are thinking of moving on and selling the pizzeria while things are good. But what is it worth?

If you are selling the pizzeria to your manager, he would probably look at it as a means of support for his family. To him, your establishment represents a stream of profits over the twenty or so years he expects to operate it. He would likely offer you a percentage of that revenue, or you could agree on estimated annual returns and perform a net present value (NPV) calculation to determine a cash price. The NPV formula assumes some standard inflation or interest rate to determine what future income over time is worth today as compared to another, secure investment. You can find lessons on the NPV formula online as well as calculators to do the work for you.

You would also expect to be paid for any hard assets such as pizza ovens, freezers, and the like. Finally, as a seller, you are also likely to demand some extra value for the convenience of acquiring the business you've already built. After all, that's why he's buying your business rather than starting his own! This intangible value is known as **goodwill**, and it is the hardest item to value in a sale.

goodwill

An intangible asset that results from the acquisition of one company by another, including the value of a company's brand name, solid customer base, good customer relations, good employee relations, and any patents or proprietary technology.

book value

Valuation of a company's assets minus liabilities; essentially, the shareholder equity.

The bottom end of the valuation range might be determined by the **book value** of your firm. This is the value of all your assets minus your liabilities and is essentially equivalent to your shareholder equity. Theoretically, if you broke the business apart and sold everything and paid off the debts, this would be the cash left over. Doing this destroys any value from the business model itself or the goodwill, so you don't want to go there, but it is a starting point below which you should not go.

There may be some complications in the book value calculation, and these usually involve the market value of the assets. Often firms will have assets they value highly but that cannot actually be sold on any market for anywhere near the price they are on the books. The buyer might argue this point, but if they need those items to run the operation, and they cannot acquire them for less, their value to the buyer is what should set the value during negotiations. Alternatively, some firms have depreciated their assets far below market value for tax purposes. You may have equipment on your books that has been completely depreciated based on a schedule the U.S. Internal Revenue Service provides but is still completely functional and critical to your operation. In that case, you must discuss this disconnect between tax law and reality with the buyer during negotiations.

Establishing the book value as a bottom line lets you then add in the goodwill on top, negotiating each less tangible item one at a time. Your final price might be based on a formula such as this:

$$\textbf{Sales Price} = \textbf{Book Value} + \textbf{Brand Value} + \textbf{Customer Relationships} + \\ \textbf{Market Synergy with Buyer's Existing Product Line}$$

That last item, "market synergy with buyer's existing product line," might presume that with the addition of your technology, service, or accessory, the buyer will recognize increased sales, reduced costs, and higher profits from his normal operations. That's real value to the buyer, and some portion of this saving should be paid to you if you sell. Always think like the buyer when negotiating. What value will they get out of this, and how much of that new money will they pay you to keep the remainder?

Determining the value of a rapid growth startup during its growth phase is much trickier than valuing a Main Street business like a pizzeria. This is because the rapid growth startup's true potential is highly speculative until it matures. In this case, the NPV formula is useless because while the rapid growth firm is refining its technology or capturing market share, it is likely to be generating losses rather than profits. Estimating the potential market and subtracting the risk that the firm may fail to meet are important considerations here.

Once again, synergies with the buyer can provide substantial extra value. If your firm is developing the lightest weight, most powerful batteries in the world, then a firm that builds mobile consumer electronics would likely pay more because of the competitive advantage that exclusive access to your technology could bring to their existing business. Your batteries might allow them to capture additional market share and profits from their laptop or phone business. That could actually be far more profitable than selling your batteries on the market.

There is, however, a dark side to these value calculations. It may turn out that your firm has technology that another company would rather not see enter the market. Perhaps your batteries would make an electric car firm more competitive. An existing manufacturer of fuel-efficient diesel cars might simply want to keep them off the market. Occasionally firms really do buy up promising startups and simply shut them down or let them die from lack of support. Be sure you understand why a company really wants what you've created and, if they want to misuse or kill your dream, make sure the money is enough to satisfy your conscience (if that is even possible).

Key Takeaways

- Selling a business is the entrepreneurs' option.
- A business may be worth more to someone other than the entrepreneur.

- There are many different ways to sell your business.
- There are many different buyers for your business, including IPOs, larger firms, individuals, and existing stakeholders such as your employees.
- You may be able to capture value from your business model and keep running it by selling the concept to others as a franchise opportunity.
- Valuing the business is not a simple formula; it's a negotiation.

16.2 The Self-Sustaining Business

Learning Objectives

1. Recognize that exits are not required.
2. Understand the considerations for handing over a company to heirs.
3. Understand that some ownership transitions are unpredictable.

Building a company is often compared to raising a child. In much the same way, you hope that someday your company will reach the stage where it's really grown up and more or less independent. When your business advances to the point where it can function effectively under employee operation, without your constant supervision, the entrepreneurial life can be smooth sailing.

How do you know when you're there? Ask yourself these questions: Could you step away from your business right now without losing customers? Will your vendors continue to deliver quality inputs at a competitive price without you managing the relationships? Can your employees be trusted to do the right thing by all your stakeholders without your constant oversight? Is your management ready to handle an unexpected crisis?

If your answer to all those questions is "yes," then congratulations; you have yourself a self-sustaining business. If your answer to any of those questions is "no" or "not sure," then, unfortunately, you aren't quite there yet. Your business still *needs* you to be successful. But keep in mind that while believing that you are indispensable may boost your entrepreneurial ego, it can be a truly dangerous motivation. One of the worst managerial habits is creating an environment where *the manager is required.* A great business runs on its culture and processes and is independent of people and personalities. Such a business can be sold.

If your business runs itself, you can pursue what you love to do.

Source: © Shutterstock, Inc.

The Milking Strategy

milking

A strategy in which sustaining short-term revenues is prioritized over long-term growth or stability.

cash cow

A business generating a steady return of profits that far exceed the outlay of cash required to acquire or start it.

annuity

Sum contractually paid out annually.

If your business cannot be sold, another popular strategy for capturing its value is known as **milking**. Milking is the process of maximizing the extraction of profits from your firm. A firm undergoing milking is amusingly called a **cash cow**, and it can be a very good thing to own.

Since a cash cow business is returning profits to its investors, it is generally not investing in its own future. If you want to "exit" a cash cow, you still need to make sure it is self-sustaining. At that point, you can simply find a trustworthy individual to run day-to-day management while retaining ownership and enjoying a virtual **annuity**. Milking the cow is a great way for the business owner to maintain a stream of income while having the liberty to devote time toward other affairs, like another idea or business.

There is a very significant risk in the milking strategy. A firm that is not reinvesting in itself and lacks a strategic leader is vulnerable to disruption. If you are not paying attention to the competitive landscape, your relaxing retirement may come to an abrupt end when a competitor recognizes a vulnerability in your model and attacks it. One common strategy is to hire away your top employees. Employees are often loyal to a founding entrepreneur, but when that founder leaves them to pursue other interests, they may feel spurned and become less likely to stay with the firm.

Inheritance Strategies and Tax Considerations

Many business founders plan to leave their company to their family when they pass on. Sam Walton of Walmart famously pursued this plan, making his heirs some of the world's wealthiest people. Other founders plan to gift or sell the business to their kids. Most often, they will bring their children into the business and teach them the ropes while handing over more and more control until they retire.

Many important factors should be considered when working with family members, but the most crucial is whether your heirs really want to own and run your business. In many cases, they may prefer that you sell it and leave them cash or an income stream so that they can pursue their own dreams. If you determine that your kids (or whomever you've selected) are, in fact, passionate about your firm, you must then decide if they are capable of running it well. You will not be doing your children a favor by letting them take on a task they won't enjoy or be good at. Many firms have been run into the ground through mismanagement by the founder's children, leaving them and the firm's employees out of work.

You must have some plan for the ownership of your business after your death.

Source: © Shutterstock, Inc.

In most cases, a business can be passed on after death via a simple will. You can leave the assets of a sole proprietorship or partnership directly or leave the stock of a corporation. However, if the value of the estate makes it taxable in your area, a trust may be the best mechanism for tax purposes. As of 2020, inheritances of less than $11.58 million were excluded from federal inheritance taxes.

If you plan to gift your business or stock while you are alive, both parties may be subject to important tax considerations. It is important that you consult with your lawyer and your accountant well in advance to ensure that your business ends up in the hands you intend, not the hands of the government. Even if you are young and healthy, you should have a plan in place in case an unexpected tragedy strikes. Hopefully, it will never be needed, but you can rest better knowing you will not be leaving a mess behind for your business partners or family.

A final, extremely important point that any entrepreneur must consider is whether the heirs to the business can all get along. If you are part of a partnership or closely held corporation and your spouse or child is suddenly thrust into the picture, will your business partners and managers welcome their participation? It is not at all unusual for those who have built and have been running a business to resent the intrusion of "uninformed outsiders" into their realm. Likewise, many a husband or wife has presumed that their spouse's business partners have been taking advantage of that person's good nature, and they come into the situation with resentment. Everyone involved should be in sync with your plan. When you establish a will or trust, discuss the terms with each of them, and preferably all together, so there are no surprises.

Many startups are founded with stock buyback agreements in place (discussed in Chapter 6) that require the stock be returned to the firm when a partner exits. Similar agreements can cover death, and in this particular case, it may be a good strategy for the firm to secure **key person insurance** on those partners to fund the repurchase of their stock. In this scenario, if a partner dies, the firm receives a life insurance payout that is sufficient to purchase the stock back from the partner's heirs. The company continues with its management, and your spouse and children (or whomever) are rewarded for your work. It is critical that you regularly adjust the amount of the insurance payout to accurately reflect the value of the stock. Also, be aware that while life insurance (including key person insurance) is relatively inexpensive for healthy, young entrepreneurs, it can become very costly as you age.

key person insurance

A life insurance policy purchased by a business on an essential employee that names the business as the beneficiary.

Key Takeaways

- You may want to keep your business running and just milk the profits.
- If you plan to keep your business until the end, you will need to plan for your heirs.
- Don't assume your heirs want the business or would succeed.
- Plan ahead for unexpected ownership transitions.

16.3 The Sale

Learning Objectives

1. Understand the importance of due diligence during a sale or merger.
2. Recognize you can sell part of a business or exit over time.
3. Understand common payment structures in a business sale.
4. Understand that you should always be planning for a smooth exit.

Considering all these various exit strategies, which one should you plan for? Which one is perfect for your business today and in the future? Which one fits the needs of your family and your personal lifestyle goals? Which one will satisfy your investors?

Like the weather, you cannot predict the future of your business or life; you can only make forecasts based on what you know now. You honestly can't even know when you might want or need to exit, much less what the circumstances will be on that day. It is important that you understand the options and make plans for the most likely events. However, don't forget those plans and update them as circumstances change. The New Entrepreneurial Dynamic depends on constant, iterative adjustments to your strategies, and the exit strategy is no different. Recall our quote from General Dwight D. Eisenhower: "Plans are useless, but planning is indispensable."

Diligence

When you purchase produce at the grocery store, do you carefully inspect the fruits and vegetables before buying? Most people look carefully at the bananas and choose the ones without brown spots; they may smell the strength of the basil or cilantro; they may hold the watermelon to their ear and tap it—listening for just the right echo—or taste test a grape. Would you be any less careful if you were buying a business?

FIGURE 16.1 Dilbert Comic

Source: DILBERT © 1996 Scott Adams, Inc. Used By permission of ANDREWS MCMEEL SYNDICATION. All rights reserved.

due diligence

A detailed inspection of a business conducted by the buyer before closing a purchase deal.

Savvy individuals and firms that buy businesses will conduct a thorough review of their acquisition targets before completing a deal to ensure they are getting what they are paying for. This process, known as **due diligence**, usually includes a complete review of the financial accounts and a physical inspection of the facilities, inventory, and equipment. It may even include interviews with customers, vendors, and employees. In some cases, the buyers may check your personal credit ratings and conduct criminal background checks on the management team. If you are ever in the position of acquiring a business, you should be just as meticulous in your review.

Should you, the entrepreneur, conduct a review of the buyer? It's a good idea for several reasons. First, you are going to be working closely with the managers of this company during the transition process, and you'll want to make sure you can work with them. Secondly, you're likely to be owed money by the buyer, and you will want to be sure your buyer can afford what they say they will pay. Lastly, you're handing over your employees, customers, and vendors to these folks, and you will want to be sure that those important stakeholders in your business are treated well long after you are gone. In a merger or combination of two companies, each side should perform due diligence on the other for all these reasons.

The diligence process need not be a hostile undertaking and can, in fact, be valuable for everyone involved. It is a time for the two organizations and their people to get to know each other well and begin working together. Your warehouse workers will assist the buyer's team during the inventory, and your accounting staff will work closely with the buyers' team and managers. This can be a chance for them to establish credibility and good working relations.

However, there are times when company mergers include the elimination of "duplicate resources." A combined firm will not need two CFOs or two warehouse managers, and there may be a general reduction in headcount. In fact, this is one of the economic drivers that encourages small firms to combine into bigger ones; mergers create a new firm with higher revenues from combined operations and reduce operating costs as a percentage of revenues by eliminating redundant facilities, equipment, and staff. This is why small firms are often consumed in roll-ups.

Part Way In/Part Way Out

Sometimes an entrepreneur would like to take a significant portion of cash out to fund a more enjoyable lifestyle, deal with a life crisis, or pursue another opportunity but still remain engaged and invested in their business. If you can find the right investor, this is a perfectly reasonable way to go. You don't have to sell 100 percent of your equity, at least not at first. Most new owners actually value having the founder on board to guide the business through the transition, and often they'd just like to keep you running it. You can take some cash and also bring additional capital into the business to grow it. This transition can greatly reduce your stress by having both your own finances and those of your firm strengthened by the cash infusion. There can be issues with a lingering relationship with strangers. Can you think of how those would develop?

A gradual exit works particularly well with employee or family buyouts. Although conflicts can certainly arise, they are less likely because these stakeholders are usually very familiar with you and to you. Expectations are fairly clear on both sides; you've already worked out effective techniques for communications and negotiating disputes.

Sometimes an entrepreneur will choose to retain ownership over portions of the business or some of its assets while selling others. For instance, imagine you have a business that has grown over the years and has been able to successfully enter a number of different markets with its basic technology. You may want to keep one of the product lines that you've developed a passion for but never had the time to focus on. For instance, you could own a fiberglass tube fabricator that makes everything from antenna masts to knitting needles. Maybe you'd like to settle down and focus on fishing poles as a lifestyle business that would allow you to spend a great deal of time testing your equipment fly fishing in the Sierra Nevada mountains. Great, sell the company but write up a contract that gives you exclusive distribution rights in the fishing business. The new owner will make the tubes; you just finish off the rods and distribute them to outdoor activity resellers. You'll generate a little income, and you can declare those trips as product research to reduce your income taxes.

Often an entrepreneur may wish to unload the management and time-consuming operations of the business while retaining some valuable income-generating assets. This might include keeping the building you own and leasing it to your new owner. You might retain your patents or software copyrights and license those under an exclusive arrangement to the new owner. This is a great way to extract a stream of income from your business, and it may have tax advantages over getting a single large payment for your assets. Additionally, if your buyer mismanages the business, goes bankrupt, or just doesn't pay you what they owe you under the sales agreement, you have powerful leverage over them as well as an asset that can be sold, leased, or licensed to another party.

When you exit your business, you might retain the part you love.

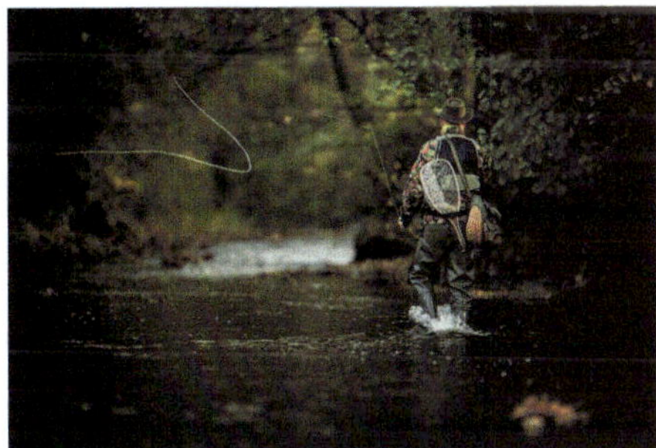

Source: © Shutterstock, Inc.

Payment Structures

It's unlikely that the buyer of your company is going to write you a check for the full amount and just send you on your way. If you sell your firm, you will most likely receive payments for it over several months or even over a few years. Can you think of reasons for that?

First, your buyer is surely a successful investor, and that is someone who has wisely kept their money productively engaged. They aren't likely to have a great deal of cash sitting in a checking account waiting for your deal. Second, although they will perform due diligence, paying for their purchase over time gives them an opportunity to be sure they are getting exactly what they were sold. Finally, either you or they may want to create an **earn-out**, a deal structure that ties the amount or timing of payments to the performance of the firm after the sale, and that usually requires you to hit certain financial or strategic milestones.

earn-out

A deal structure that ties payments to the performance of the firm after the sale.

contingent liabilities

Possible expensive obligations that may arise in the future from past actions. Lawsuits from employees, customers, or regulatory penalties from a violation of environmental laws are common examples.

asset purchase agreement

A contract for the purchase of select assets of a business that does not include everything in the firm and usually excludes any contingent liabilities.

successor liability

When the purchaser of a business is responsible for actions that occurred under the previous ownership.

It's also important to think about what the buyer is willing to pay a premium for in your business and what the buyer does not wish to acquire at all. There are certain assets your firm has built, such as customer accounts, intellectual property, and skilled employees, which will add a lot of value. There may be other things they don't care too much for. Significantly, what a buyer really doesn't want to acquire are any **contingent liabilities** that may pop up later. These are things such as lawsuits from previous customers, environmental clean-up problems at a facility, or unexpected charges from vendors. In a stock purchase agreement (SPA), the buying firm picks up everything in the company, good, bad, and ugly. As you can imagine, this is not always the first choice of the buyer, and a seller eager to make a deal doesn't want to reduce the purchase price to overcome the buyer's concerns with a few problem assets.

It is possible to separate the wheat from the chaff during the acquisition to the benefit of both parties. This is usually accomplished through a process known as an **asset purchase agreement** (APA). In an APA, the buyer picks and chooses what they want but does not actually legally acquire the company itself. The buyer may get the rights to the name, the facilities, the products, and the employees; the original corporation, LLC, or whatever remains is an independent, if hollowed-out entity owned by the original shareholders. This shell company usually changes its name so the acquiring firm can use that, and it keeps all the legal contracts and responsibilities for its previous actions. Since the shell company has virtually no cash or assets, it is not a particularly attractive target for predatory lawyers or aggressive regulators to pursue. Be sure to hire good lawyers to manage the APA; usually, the buyer will see to that because laws are not the same in all jurisdictions, and in some cases, the successor firm may find themselves exposed to **successor liability** when a claimant contends that a de facto merger actually occurred.

An APA may also be attractive because it can allow for the seller to keep specific assets they would like to retain. Perhaps you have a company truck that you also use to tow your boat on weekend fishing trips. That truck could stay with your shell company if the buyer doesn't require it.

Exit Strategy Starts at Day One

It's never too early to start preparing for an exit strategy. While this text has emphasized dynamically adapting to change rather than blindly following plans, your end goal can serve as your North Star, guiding you back to the true path on a journey that will surely have many detours. Decisions that you make early on will affect the options you have during an exit.

For example, the legal structure of your firm can impact your ability to participate in an IPO. In the U.S., all publicly traded firms are C Corporations. C Corps are responsible (technically) for paying corporate taxes, and they may have millions of investors. LLCs and LLPs distribute tax responsibility across their shareholders and may be limited in the number of participants they can have. Typically, when an LLC startup goes IPO, it will need to sell its assets to a C Corp, which will become the legal IPO entity. Most private investors prefer an LLC because they are likely to do their investing through their own LLC. An LLC can invest in another LLC easily but cannot technically be an owner in an S Corp.

The number and nature of your investors can be a big factor in the attractiveness to your buyers. Complex cap tables filled with lots of small investors, some of whom may not favor a sale, are less attractive to buyers who prefer a clean deal made with a very small number of owners. If you bring in friends or small investors, consider keeping them in a nonvoting shares category.

Remember our discussion of asset purchase agreements? As you grow your company, it is important to think about maximizing the attractiveness of your assets and minimizing liabilities and unattractive holdings. You may want to purchase a sweet four-wheel-drive truck as a delivery vehicle or decorate your office with stunning pieces of alternative art, but those are probably things your buyer is going to exclude from the APA. That's great if you want to collect those things, but if your goal is for you and your shareholders to cash out big, then you must reinvest your firm's earnings into the most purchasable assets as you grow.

Your Next Great Adventure

So you've sold your business and are sitting on a pile of cash or a comfortable stream of income. What now?

Most folks in this situation picture an "early retirement" to someplace in the world special to them. Picture a life of uninterrupted skiing, fishing, scuba diving, or whatever you like. Or maybe after all that work, you'd like to just grow old on a porch swing with your loved one, a stack of great novels, and a faithful golden retriever.

It turns out most entrepreneurs can't stand that sort of relaxing for long. . . . You'll likely find yourself at it again. With the real-world experience you've accumulated, you will surely do better than you did the first go around. You could be a great serial entrepreneur.

Remember that the New Entrepreneurial Dynamic doesn't require you to limit your horizons to business. You might also consider the freedom of financial independence that will allow you to achieve goals outside of business on which you could not otherwise afford to spend time. Many successful entrepreneurs become highly influential in arts, politics, or other domains. You could go back to school and get an advanced degree, write a book, make a documentary film, advocate for an important cause, or serve your government. I actually did all those things, and entrepreneurial success was what made that possible. Celebrate your success, and whatever your second act choice, aim for the stars!

Key Takeaways

- The entrepreneur and the buyer need to look carefully at any deal before it closes.
- Most sales happen over a period of time and may not involve the entire firm.
- You should be planning for your exit from the start.

16.4 Case Study: Selling Trojan Storage

When Brett Henry graduated from the University of Souther California's Marshall School of Business in May 2000, he wanted to be a commercial real estate developer. Not surprisingly, there weren't any offers for a fresh graduate to take over the construction of a major new project. The opportunity he found might not have looked promising, but he knew everyone has to start somewhere. Henry took a job working for $13/hour at a self-storage facility. He notes, "I had a better paying job offer elsewhere, but the firm that hired me had seasoned developers who promised me help on that path if I performed."

Some businesses are glamorous, and some aren't. Many young entrepreneurs find themselves drawn to technology, fashion, and entertainment markets because they find these fields fascinating and like the idea of being perceived as interesting themselves. Putting together apps that your friends all use, designing the clothes they wear, or working with media celebrities is, well, cool. On the other hand, outside of the peculiar reality show *Storage Wars*, it's hard to imagine what could be interesting about renting space to hoarders or folks in transition. Sometimes, however, the best place to be in business is a market nobody else wants to go.

The job was certainly not glamorous. "I was in a small run-down office working with generally hourly people, and it was nothing to brag about." Still, Brett was surprised how well things went for him. Rather than just putting in his time in the self-storage business, he was able to use his financial skills to quickly identify problems in the operations. In fact, he demonstrated to the owners that several of their managers were skimming profits. The owners fired the thieves and promoted Henry to director of property management. He was soon earning $200k a year and expanding operations.

While he was surprised at his success as a manager, he was even more surprised to discover that he saw a lot of opportunity in the self-storage industry. Henry comments, "It's an industry with a lot of opportunity, but one where most operations are small-time and very poorly run." He had already found a lot of ways to improve the financial performance of his facility for the owners, and he began to think about doing the same for a business of his own. Rather than moving into the glamorous but highly competitive markets of mall or office development, Henry decided to apply his skills and newly gained knowledge in the self-storage market. "Why compete head-to-head with the best and the brightest college graduates in an industry with intense rivalry, when you can instead enter a market filled by mom-and-pop operators and absentee owners using unreliable managers?"

In 2007 at age 29, Henry stepped out on his own within the storage industry. The new startup founder originally brought in his brother, Scott, and recruited John Koudsi, who was 35 and able to raise the backing required to get the new venture off the ground. John and Brett discovered they were a great team, and they became the core of the new firm, Trojan Storage.

The Trojan Storage founders looked forward to an exit from the start. Their goal was to reinvest almost all the firm's profits into new ventures and build up a number of valuable assets that could eventually be sold at a premium to a larger firm. The value-add for Trojan was to pick up self-storage units that were underperforming and apply professional financial management to these businesses. The result was nearly always a dramatic improvement in occupancy and rents, driving better profitability and cashflow. The Trojan team would usually bring in partners into the new LLC to fund these acquisitions for each specific facility. Refinancing was one way to extract cash from the facilities, but getting money out of banks was frustratingly time-consuming and distracting. Henry notes, "My job was to acquire facilities, not fill out SBA paperwork."

Henry had always presumed that this building process would take many years, "I thought we'd go fifteen or twenty years because that is the nature of real estate." However, by 2016 he was getting frustrated, "I'd look at the balance sheet and we'd have several million dollars, but it was difficult to get a loan." Scott had left, and Henry and John had about 60 percent of the equity in a company that a broker friend had suggested could be worth $200 million to $250 million.

Henry decided to test the waters and put Trojan on the market. "We listed with Nick Walker at CBRE and started to get noncompelling offers of $150 to $180 million." The eventual buyer came in at $165 million because they had a hard time believing Trojan's performance on their assets, which simply outpaced the industry. Henry and Koudsi were frustrated by this situation where they knew how much value the buyer was getting, but the buyer just couldn't see it. Henry explains, "The buyer was a $20B REIT (Real Estate Investment Trust) and very sophisticated, but I knew my industry and properties far better than they."

The solution turned out to be structuring the deal as a buyout. They agreed to take the $165 million and turned the firm over to the new owners in April 2017, while continuing to manage it for a few months under the scrutiny of the new buyers' accounting team. The results amazed everyone. "We were able to get occupancy up and get rent increases across the board at the same time. We took the last two months and annualized those results and divided it by the cap rate of 4.7." The Trojan Storage team hit the cash-out goal at $245 million. Even better, by arranging the sale as an asset purchase for a specific group of facilities, they were even able to continue in the self-storage business with their own brand. They still manage ten properties and are building up the business for another exit in the future.

Endnotes

1. Potter, S. B. (2020, January). U.S. IPOs raised more money in 2019. *Insight*.
2. Stanley, T. J., & Danko, W. D. (1996). *The millionaire next door: The surprising secrets of America's wealthy*. Longstreet Press.
3. https://www.bloomberg.com/news/articles/2015-11-23/shrinking-takeover-premiums-present-bearish-case-for-u-s-stocks
4. https://www.postbulletin.com/business/business/franchise-your-business-carefully-thoughtfully/article_7a2ba0f1-906f-58c1-bc0b-50c08dd969da.html

APPENDIX A

Final Thoughts

As I write these last words for the first edition of *A New Entrepreneurial Dynamic*, I'm overwhelmed with gratitude for the opportunity I've been given to share my insights and my passion for entrepreneurship with so many of you. Thank you for being my readers.

I hope you've been empowered by my text and inspired by your professors to go out and achieve something great in business. It doesn't matter whether that is in running a small business or in founding a unicorn startup. Your internal self-judgment will be the only measure of success that really counts. Be kind to your future self and all those you encounter.

I also wish you financial success in your endeavor. If you are fortunate enough to find extraordinary monetary success, I'd ask you to remember that you were lucky and that there are others who, for many reasons, have not succeeded. As Stan Lee reminded us in the first Spiderman comic, "With great power comes great responsibility." If you obtain wealth and power, it is incumbent upon you to do the right thing with it. That does not mean that you must give all your money away to some charitable cause. Becoming a philanthropist might be great, but reinvesting your hard-won capital into scaling an enterprise that provides good jobs and produces quality products that delight customers is a noble endeavor in its own right. If you spend your money enjoying yourself, that's fine too, but do it responsibly and with some dignity.

The number of chips you leave on the table when the game is over is the very least important measure of success. The money you didn't spend will be left for others to count and perhaps fight over. It is how you played the game, and if you enjoyed it, that should matter most to you.

I look forward to patronizing your new small business someday soon or perhaps reading about your climb to entrepreneurial stardom in the business press. *Ad astra*, dear readers.

Greg Autry, PhD

Lake Arrowhead, CA, December 2021

Index

abandoned cart
358

accountant
40, 141, 196, 228-233, 239, 393-397, 407-415, 424-426, 470, 474

accounts payable
387-388, 392, 402

accounts receivable
363-366, 380-393, 402-410, 450

accredited investors
198

accrual accounting
228, 380-384, 393

accuracy
8, 208, 259, 293-294, 344

acquisition
118, 167, 189, 199, 231, 308, 324, 388, 441, 464-471, 478

acquisition premium
465

ad copy
295

Adhocracy Culture
176

adulteration
257

advance
35, 41-45, 67-71, 100, 120, 149, 184, 205-207, 233, 287, 322, 328, 342-347, 393, 403, 410-413, 419, 432, 474

advertising
69-70, 75, 111, 119, 167, 179, 209, 221, 244, 251, 258-259, 266, 272-300, 304-311, 324, 342, 348, 404, 445

advertising campaign
275

affiliate marketing
332

agency
17, 23, 27, 198, 225, 242-243, 397, 447-449, 458

aging report
363, 380, 391-392

alpha test
146

amortization
381, 386-390, 406

anchor customer
403, 447

angel investor
18, 158, 191-192, 197-200, 207, 214, 227, 349, 439

angel investors
158, 191-192, 197-200, 207, 214, 349

animal spirits
429

annuity
474

archetype
18, 262, 420

ask
50, 71, 94, 116, 132-134, 140-144, 150, 178-185, 198, 208, 213, 226, 284-286, 290, 311-320, 324, 355, 382, 394, 407, 411, 457, 466, 473, 483

aspirational brand
280-281

aspirational good
85, 292

asset purchase agreement
478

assets
17, 126, 170, 184, 193-196, 204-210, 223-227, 324, 376, 381-383, 387-388, 399, 404-413, 424-426, 464-480

asynchronous communication
368-371

autocratic leadership
161

automated
29, 212, 243, 264, 309, 327, 353, 357, 438

B2B
119, 305-308, 314, 324-325, 345, 354, 382

B2C
119, 324

B-roll
283

b-team
181

backend
99, 168, 208

backlink
291

balance sheet
376, 380, 387-388, 480

bankruptcy
33, 142, 226, 235, 401-407, 411-416, 428

barriers to entry
24, 67-70, 74, 89, 98-99, 152-153, 251, 317-318, 423, 449

base salary
329

beachhead strategy
272, 278

benefit corporation (B Corp)
229

bespoke
419

best-in-class
376

beta test
144-148

black swan events
361

bond term
434

bond yield
434

book value
236, 388, 472

bookkeeper
393-394, 414, 457

bootstrap
149

bowling pin effect
272, 280

brand
21-26, 48-49, 66-69, 84-86, 107, 115-120, 126-130, 139, 152-154, 171, 181, 207, 231, 242, 247-275, 280-291, 295-300, 306-307, 311, 317, 348, 354, 358, 388, 420, 441, 452, 467, 471, 480

brand association
262-264, 281

brand coherence
264-266

brand definition
248-250, 264

brand management
264-266

brick-and-mortar
239, 347, 358-359

bucket list
36-37, 257

budget deficit
432

bureaucrats
367, 383, 414, 449

business culture
40, 66, 441, 465

business cycle
421, 428-436

business dashboard
341-342, 360

business development
99, 129, 135, 144, 305-308, 356, 464

business environment
48-50, 63, 156, 178, 245, 417-459

business model
17, 23-24, 37, 41, 48, 52-54, 60-61, 97-98, 113-115, 126-127, 144-148, 155-156, 176, 194, 200, 223, 238, 245, 254-255, 313, 342-343, 360-366, 402-403, 412, 466-473

business plan
11-12, 41-49, 54-57, 111, 135, 203, 343

Buyer Bargaining Power
90

buyer's remorse
305, 323

buyout
12, 131, 236-237, 408, 468-470, 480

capital
12, 18, 39, 46-52, 57-60, 67, 75, 89-92, 102, 112, 116, 122, 140, 148-149, 162, 174-177, 187-207, 211-216, 223, 240, 300, 331-334, 347-351, 356, 363-367, 374, 380-393, 404-412, 434, 439, 455, 461, 468-469, 477, 483

capital investment
18, 89-90, 116, 149, 192, 367, 386, 412

capital lease
408

cartel
91

cash accounting
382, 386, 393

cash conversion cycle
316

cash cow
474

cash flow
11, 149, 158, 173, 193, 233, 237, 360-366, 376, 380-383, 388-392, 401-415, 450, 464, 468-471

cash flow crisis
193, 402, 407, 412-414

cash flow statement
376, 389-390

certificate of deposit
51

certified public accountant
394

charged off
23

charlatan
304

chartered accountant
394

chasm
272, 277-278, 301

Clan Culture
176

click-bait
332

closely held firms
226, 411

closing
38, 52, 272, 305, 309-316, 324, 329-331, 476

cohesion
161-164, 176, 187, 335

cold calling
316-317

collateralize
410, 468

collateralized
210, 410

colocation
349

commercialize
22, 96, 115

commission
17, 198, 206, 238, 317, 329-330, 378, 392, 469

commodity
73, 115, 120, 248-251, 255, 288

competitive advantage
43, 61-99, 116, 120-128, 145, 152, 173, 207, 241, 267, 275, 328-331, 339, 346, 360, 366, 376, 396, 400, 421, 454, 464, 472

confirmation bias
462

consumer culture
441-445

contingency planning
45

contingent liabilities
478

continuous improvement process (CIP)
352

contraband
420

contract manufacturer
354-355

contractionary
432

controlling interest
197, 226, 381, 450, 468

conversion rate
259

conversions
188, 243, 282, 289, 295-298

core competency
113-115, 331

corporate bylaws
224, 427

corporate veil
225

corporation
13-16, 23, 27, 45-48, 95, 109-111, 124, 166, 182, 219-230, 236, 249, 300, 362, 411-413, 424-425, 451, 468, 474, 478

cost of goods sold
151, 361-363, 378-380, 402, 406

cost of goods sold (COGS)
151, 361, 378-380, 406

coup d'état
431

coworking space
240

crawler
291

creative destruction
104-108, 132

creditworthy
210

culture
12-13, 34, 40, 48, 52, 66, 72-74, 88, 113, 117, 121, 125-132, 174-190, 203, 220, 235-236, 250, 257, 269, 275, 295-298, 319, 361-366, 374, 441-446, 465, 473

customer acquisition cost
324

customer delight
106-107

customer discovery
50, 142-145, 233-234, 290, 304, 308

customer loyalty
90, 154-156, 323-324, 328, 342, 358

customer loyalty program
90, 342

customer relationship
304, 323-328, 358

customer relationship management (CRM)
304

customer validation
142-145

customs
56, 120, 180, 367, 441, 453

dashboard
132, 156, 341-343, 360, 364, 404, 409

data analytics
50

data collection
48, 342-343

DBA
222, 231, 424

de alio markets
74

de novo markets
74

death spiral
429

debt financing
208, 214, 412

debt load
413

decision-maker
93, 310, 319

deference
448-449

deflation
437

demand curve
76-86

demo
188, 317-321, 436

democratic leader
161, 183

depreciation
381, 386, 390-393, 406

developed nations
421, 431

developed world
29, 53-54, 180, 192-195, 252

developing countries
267, 431, 449

differentiation
69-72, 123, 145, 154

diminishing returns
272, 276

direct sales
30, 68, 279, 423

discriminatory pricing
75, 83-84

disposable income
267

disposition
408

disrupt
46-48, 64-66, 107, 155, 197, 207, 248, 255-256, 328, 352, 420

disruption
45-46, 50-52, 62-70, 104-110, 128-129, 140, 207, 216, 255, 474

disruption theory
108

distribution channel
45, 119, 280

distribution system
153, 266

diversity
116, 163, 174-181, 187, 216, 460

dividend
225

dog and pony show
321

domestic manufacturing
54, 356

down round
201

due diligence
23-24, 124, 128, 132, 170, 177, 182, 200, 207, 217, 286, 414, 475-477

duopoly
64, 331

early adopter
146, 153, 277-279

early adopters
146, 153, 277-278

earn-out
477

EBIT
380, 405-406

EBITDA
131-132, 406

economics of one unit
148-151

economies of scale
80, 137, 141, 147, 251, 260, 349-357, 361, 464

economy of scale
80, 137, 141, 147-150, 251, 260, 349-357, 361, 464

efficient market
78

elastic goods
79

electronic medical record (EMR)
231

elevator pitch
12, 286-287

emergency cash reserve
403

empirical evidence
46

encumber
209

enlightened self-interest
116

entitlements
433

entrenched competitors
43, 65

equity
75, 130-131, 169-173, 186-191, 196-198, 204-209, 214, 223, 235-236, 266, 282, 318, 349, 376, 387-388, 405, 409-412, 463, 468-472, 477-480

equity investment
204-205, 214

equity split
169-173, 236

evaluation
7-9, 133-157, 185-187, 309-311, 359

exclusive license
207

existential risk
220

existential threat
257

expansionary
432

expats
442

expenses
59, 149-151, 195, 212, 222, 348, 352, 366, 378-388, 393, 398-399, 414, 457

exploitation
102-104

exploration
28, 102-104, 121

exporting
54, 438, 452-456

factoring
410, 414, 450

factors of production
350, 431

fad
100, 109-110, 122, 128, 264-268

fair market value
408

fashion
21, 48, 55, 97, 104, 109, 150, 170, 242, 257, 264, 282, 294, 356, 418-421, 447, 453, 479

feasibility analysis
103, 133-157

fictitious name statement
222, 231, 424

financial feasibility
148-151, 194

financial ratio
404

finished product
119, 146, 350

first-mover advantage
11, 94-96, 153

fiscal policy
432

Five Forces model
87-88, 153-154

fixed cost
150

fixed costs
147-152, 156, 194, 241, 281, 329, 376-380, 402-409, 464

flanking maneuver
68

float
383

floating
383

floor planning
385

flooring
195, 313, 385, 394, 409, 413

focus group
142-144, 260-261

franchisee
126

franchising
22-24, 121, 125-127, 466-467

franchisor
23, 91, 126-127, 467

free cash flow
404

fulfillment services
357

funding round
200

fusion firms
22

future cash flow
464

game theory
64

gamification
184

gatekeeper
319

GDP components
430

generalist
163

gig economy
114, 221

globalism
454

globalization
24, 50, 54-55, 127, 241, 267-268, 367, 419, 442-446

goodwill
21, 193, 236, 248, 388, 471-472

granularity
280, 287

green tech
122

greenwashing
122

gross domestic product
430

gross profit
151, 255, 329, 380-381

gross profit margin
255

hang a shingle
102-103

harvest
461-481

Hierarchy Culture
176

honest broker
311

huckster
304

hyperinflation
431

hypothesis testing
48, 342

import
118-119, 180, 327, 367, 453

importer
420, 452

importing
120, 255, 437, 452, 456

in-kind
223

income statement
364, 376, 380-384

incubator
239, 255, 349

incumbent
45-48, 65, 74, 108-109, 113, 136, 140, 251, 255-256, 266, 318, 328, 423, 483

independent sales agent
332

industry culture
88

industry value chain
134, 139, 150

inelastic goods
79

infinitely scalable
276

inflation
51, 210, 421, 431-432, 455, 471

inflationary spiral
431

influencer
242, 280, 292, 298, 321

initial public offering (IPO)
12, 18, 227, 461

innovation
38, 46, 50-55, 66, 71-72, 104-118, 127, 162, 176, 184, 236, 298, 421, 454

innovation strategy
72

innovators
117, 144, 277

installment loan
385

insurance premium
237, 403

intangible asset
170, 387-388, 471

integrated marketing
307

intellectual property (IP)
173

intent
16, 66, 143, 235, 309, 329, 347, 367

interest
24, 51, 91, 116, 122, 164, 173, 185, 191, 196-197, 208-212, 223-231, 236, 258, 274, 285-290, 307-310, 316, 321-324, 353, 363, 380-385, 389, 405-413, 432-437, 446, 450-457, 464, 468-471

Internal Revenue Service (IRS)
225, 394, 470

inventory
19, 73, 135, 149-151, 194-196, 251, 313-316, 330-332, 342, 351, 357, 362-363, 380-387, 394, 398, 406-414, 424, 432, 452, 476

inventory financing
19, 385

inventory flooring
195, 385

inventory levels
342

inverted yield curve
435

invoice discounting
410

just-in-time (JIT)
351

key person insurance
237, 475

laissez-faire leadership
161

last mover advantage
107-111

leadership style
161-162, 176-178

leads
1, 56, 231, 244-245, 306-311, 315-318, 324, 329, 333, 427

leakage
263, 433

lean venture
174

lease
35, 93, 151, 195, 205-208, 239-240, 347-349, 387, 408-409, 464

leasehold improvements
240

legal form
222-230, 240

leverage
12, 21, 59, 90-92, 117, 262, 266-268, 279-282, 298, 314-317, 321, 356, 383, 405, 409, 451, 477

leveraged buyout
12, 468

liability
148, 219-230, 237-238, 352, 403, 478

liable
222-224, 480

licensing
24, 92, 100, 125-127, 266, 282

lien
224

lifestyle business
20, 262, 403, 463, 477

limited liability company (LLC)
227

line of credit
209-212, 403, 411

liquidated
204, 388, 406, 410

liquidating
204

liquidity event
463, 468

litigious
183

loan defaults
23

logistical complexities
78

logistical outsourcing
357

logistics
24, 69, 138, 171, 317, 336, 340, 357, 366-367

logo
60, 114-115, 119, 125, 248-252, 265-270, 281, 285, 299-300, 387

makers
27, 66, 99, 108, 211, 241, 274, 319, 329, 350-354

makerspace
353

management buyout
470

manufacturers' representative
331-332

marginal income
227

market
12, 23-24, 29-34, 43-58, 64-99, 104-120, 125-147, 152-158, 162, 167, 174-180, 185-188, 201-210, 217, 221-225, 231-244, 248-258, 263-266, 271-300, 304, 308, 316-321, 325, 331, 336, 342-344, 348, 354-358, 365-366, 370, 377, 382, 388, 397, 402, 408-410, 419-423, 427-432, 439-440, 445-448, 453, 462-472, 479-480

market capitalization
95-96

Market Culture
12, 176

market disruption
45, 64-65, 107

market equilibrium
77-78

market failure
429

market price
77-79, 388, 402

market quantity
77

market saturation
275

market share
43, 49, 65-66, 71, 88-89, 108, 136, 176, 185, 207, 344, 472

marketers
248-249, 260-262, 271-273, 283

marketing
11, 22-23, 50-52, 58-60, 69-72, 89-91, 109, 115, 119, 126-127, 131-145, 167-174, 179, 184-187, 205, 231-234, 242-260, 265, 271-310, 316-318, 324, 328-332, 358, 377-379, 402, 411, 454

marketing campaign
248, 265, 306, 379

marketing collateral
126, 286

mass marketing
248

mature industry
65

media kit
283

metrics
132, 184, 266, 289, 307, 336, 340-343, 404-406, 471

microeconomics
75, 87, 275, 463

micromanaging
370

milestones
329, 477

milking
474

mimetic isomorphism
420

minimum viable product (MVP)
142, 146

minor close
314

mission-critical component
115

monetary policy
432, 437-440

monetized
287

moonshot
53

multi-level marketing
22, 279, 318, 332

multitasking
370

myopic
49, 112, 162

Nash Equilibrium
64

national champions
465-466

national debt
432

negative working capital
363-366

nepotism
470

net present value
464, 471

net profit
150-151, 324, 376, 380, 386

net terms
195, 208, 213-214, 382-383, 404, 409, 428

net value
106

net worth
198, 387-388

nonprofit
16, 21, 38, 49, 230, 364

offshoring
29, 54, 354

oligopoly
64, 137

on message
257-258

onerous
54, 211, 382

open innovation
52, 113-118, 127

open market operations
432

operating agreement
224, 228, 236

operational effectiveness
71-72

operations
17, 21-24, 34, 45, 99-104, 127-138, 187, 194, 216, 222-225, 232, 236, 240-241, 258, 275, 300, 334, 339-384, 388-389, 393, 403-406, 411-413, 420-421, 425-428, 432, 469-472, 476-480

opportunity
11-12, 20-23, 32, 36, 45-48, 55, 70, 94-157, 177-179, 187-188, 195, 199-201, 206, 212-213, 231-232, 242-251, 255-258, 286, 300, 311, 316, 325-328, 336, 363-367, 420, 426, 431-434, 441-444, 449, 464-469, 473, 477-483

opportunity cost
32, 36, 151, 300, 316, 367, 434, 464

option
23, 40-43, 127, 134, 146, 151-153, 163, 183, 189, 193, 205, 216-219, 226-228, 240, 313, 321, 332-334, 343, 360, 371, 387, 398, 403, 408-410, 426, 449, 470-472

organic growth
19-22

organic search results
290

organizational chart
165

organizational culture
175-176, 187, 364-366

other people's money
27, 124, 147, 156, 201, 207, 455, 463

outflanked
68

overvaluation
266

owner equity
387-388

ownership stake
223

pain points
102-106, 112, 135, 183

parallel entrepreneur
27-28, 231

part count
351

part-time entrepreneurship
30

participative leader
162

partnership
99-100, 188, 213, 219-230, 236, 336, 383, 412, 427, 470, 474

partnership agreement
223-224, 236, 427

pay-to-play
289-292

pecuniary
116

perception management
248-249

performance analysis
341

performance-based pay plan
329-330

personal guarantee
208, 239, 412-413

pitch meeting
320

pivot
23, 43, 56-59, 134-135, 155, 176, 234-235

placement
115, 275, 290-291, 307

policies
147, 180, 184, 237, 359, 419-422, 431-432, 438-441, 454

post-money valuation
201

power relationship
448

pre-money valuation
201

pre-sales
233-234

pre-seed money
200

precision
11, 24, 46, 246, 293-294, 354

predatory plaintiffs
148

press release
283

price elasticity
79

private equity
191, 204, 468-469

product branding
248

production engineers
351

profit margin
119, 147-151, 255, 376, 424

profitable
20-21, 37, 49, 53, 66, 70, 87, 111, 119, 131, 141-142, 158, 189, 194, 208-212, 260, 275, 362, 372, 376-378, 394, 402-407, 414, 427, 434, 472

prohibition
153

promo code
295

proxy sales agent
318

purchase
68-71, 86, 102, 106, 114, 118, 125, 132, 146, 194, 210-213, 226, 233, 239-241, 252-255, 259, 266, 273-280, 289, 305-316, 323, 333-334, 347, 355-358, 363, 385, 393, 408-413, 419, 434, 450, 465-468, 475-480

pyramid scheme
332

qualified accountant
394

qualifying
215, 308-311, 316, 323-325, 451

quality fade
355

quota
184, 453

ready-to-wear
419

recession
51, 240, 364, 431, 435-437

referenceable
99, 213, 279, 324

referential
278

regulatory and tax climate
97

repossessed
209

request for bid
449

request for proposal
449

retained earnings
388

retainer
207, 244

revenue
16-20, 46-49, 79-83, 110, 116, 123-125, 130-131, 136, 146, 150-151, 157, 184-185, 208-210, 225-227, 237, 244-245, 255, 267-272, 278-282, 292, 326-332, 336, 343, 362-366, 376-388, 393-397, 402-406, 412-414, 426, 432, 447-448, 453, 463-464, 470-476

reverse engineer
355

revolving credit agreement
403, 407

rewards
51, 149, 162-163, 318, 329, 342, 362, 388, 412, 471

risk analysis
208

risk averse
51

risk tolerance
104

Rivalry with Competitors
88

roles
7, 48, 163-169, 174-176, 216, 308, 418, 422-423

roll-up merger
464-466

rule of law
449

saboteur
100, 319-321

sales agents
318, 331-332

sales art
306

sales cycle
100, 308, 316, 329

sales pipeline
306-307

sales process
99, 272, 304-316, 320-329, 333-335

sales volume
24, 342, 377

salesmanship
306

salesperson
168, 304-325, 329-334

satisficing
272-273, 344, 358

scale
11-20, 27, 80, 85, 118, 134-137, 141-142, 147-152, 156, 163, 168-171, 176, 251, 260, 275, 280, 318, 330, 344-361, 367, 395, 464

school of hard knocks
5, 377

search process
112

second-mover advantage
94

secular trend
436-437

secured debt
407

security deposit
194-195, 347

seed capital
102, 187, 191-196

seed round
200-203

selection process
210, 420

self-image
260

serendipity
111-113, 271, 370

serial entrepreneur
1, 27, 112, 479

Series A
200-203, 216

set asides
426, 450

severance package
102

shared workspace
240

shareholders
21, 34, 49, 96, 201-204, 225-232, 241, 252, 264, 376, 405, 411, 425, 468, 478-479

shell company
425, 469, 478

shifters
22

side agreements
236

signal
131, 154, 179, 205, 252, 259, 281

skunkworks
65-66

slack
104, 112, 132, 235, 368

Small Business Administration
17, 209, 230, 450, 467

smuggling
420, 453

snake oil
297

social entrepreneurship
21, 229

social networks
163

sole proprietorship
188, 222-226, 383, 474

solvent
401, 405

sound bites
283

spam
291, 316

special acquisition company
469

specialist
163, 168-169, 177, 181

spiff
330-332

spinoff
53, 191, 231-232

stakeholder theory
219, 229

stakeholders
11, 115, 229, 234, 246, 473-477

startup costs
24, 149

startup funding
191-196

state capitalism
417

state owned enterprise
31

state-owned enterprise (SOE)
90

STEM
52

step-up lease
348

stimulate
8, 432-435

strategic management
61, 400

strategy
18-20, 28, 43-48, 61-100, 107, 119-122, 135, 144-147, 153-154, 161, 176, 196, 231, 248, 256, 272-281, 287, 300, 304-307, 332, 340, 351, 364, 392-393, 402, 411, 415, 426, 464-470, 474-478

suboptimal choices
106, 364

successor liability
478

sunk cost fallacy
32, 36

supermajority
223

Supplier Bargaining Power
91

supply chain
54-55, 67, 118-121, 127, 135, 142, 344, 349-351, 360, 370, 424

supply chain management (SCM)
351

supply curve
76

survey
31, 50, 83, 135, 142-143, 148, 282, 290, 316, 359-360, 449

sustainable competitive advantage
71, 97, 116

swag
91, 285-286

switching cost
72, 90, 395

switching costs
72, 235, 255

SWOT Analysis
87, 92-93

synergy
231, 472

system integrator
333

tactics
47, 62-70, 97, 272-273, 286, 291, 307-309, 318, 340, 392

tagline
119, 262

tangible asset
210, 386

target customer
143, 150, 154, 258, 291, 316-317

tariff
132, 420, 453

tax deductible
209

tchotchkes
285

teamwork
34, 162, 213

technical ecosystem
333

technology adoption life cycle
272, 276-278

tenant
240, 347-348

tenant improvement allowance
348

tenant improvements
240, 348

terms
8, 17, 71, 90-91, 125, 180, 184, 188, 195, 208, 213-214, 221-224, 234-237, 289-290, 313, 349, 355, 382-383, 398, 404-414, 427-428, 434, 449, 475

the gig economy
114, 221

theory of the firm
221

third-party payer
145

Threat of New Entrants
89-92, 251

Threat of Substitute Products
89

three Fs
193-197

thresholds
341-343

top line
404

total quality management (TQM)
352

trade secrets
89, 116, 173, 355

trademark
125-126, 253, 263

trained accountant
394

transaction costs
221

transactional
162, 306

transactional leader
162

transformational leader
162

transit time
382

trend
24, 29, 48-50, 54-56, 64, 96-97, 118-122, 127, 229, 252, 256, 264, 282, 298, 328, 343-349, 357, 418, 428-432, 436-440, 446-447, 453, 460

true lease
408

trustee
406-407

turnkey
126, 333-334

turnkey solution
333-334

two-for-one sale
318

tyranny of success
108-109

unboxing
292, 335

underdog
89

unemployment rate
431, 460

unsecured debt
407

utility
106, 169, 275, 306

valuation
112, 142, 200-201, 216, 236, 251, 465, 471-472

value chain
68, 121, 134-140, 150-152

value-add
251, 350, 480

value-added reseller
333-334

Value-Added Tax (VAT)
424

variable costs
150-151, 194, 378-380

venture capital fund
201

venture capitalist
12, 18, 42, 46-49, 57-60, 107, 192, 200-207, 215-216, 461

vertical integration
68

vetting
134, 216

virtuous cycle
315

warm call
317-318

willingness to work
169, 183

working capital
363-366, 383, 409

yield curve
434-436